193

D0141655

WORLD HERITAGE SITES
(SEE BACK ENDPAPER FOR LISTING)

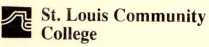

Masterworks of Man & Nature

PRESERVING OUR WORLD HERITAGE

HARPER – MACRAE
PUBLISHING PTY LTD

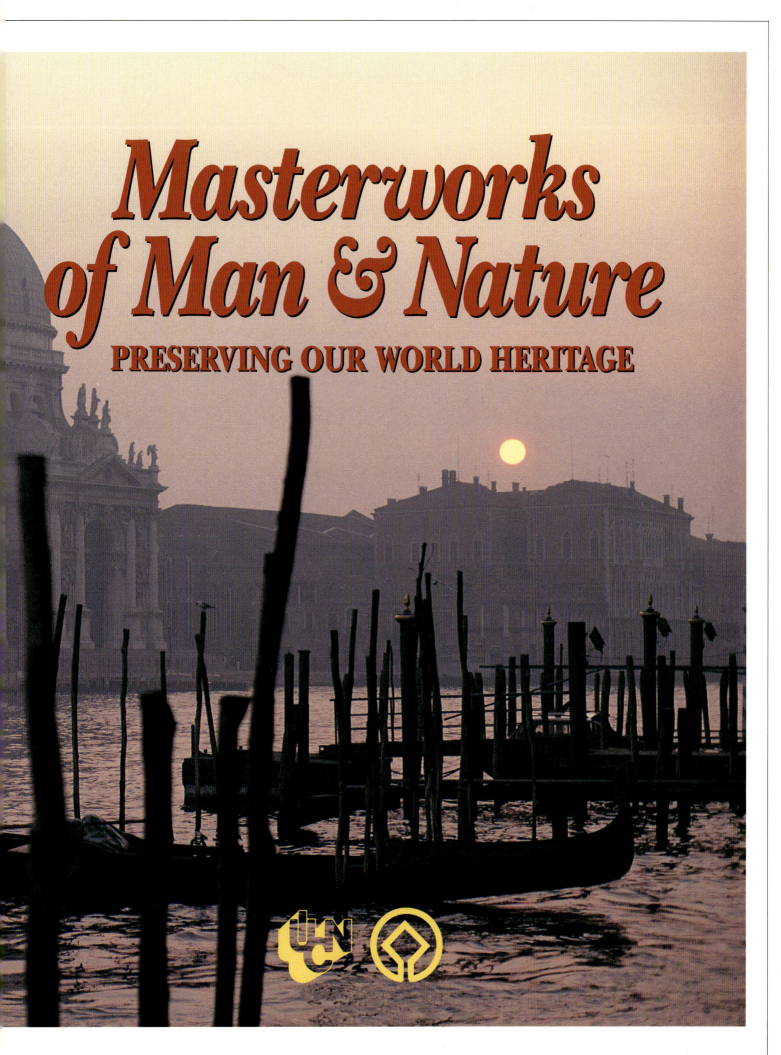

Masterworks
of Man & Nature

PRESERVING OUR WORLD HERITAGE

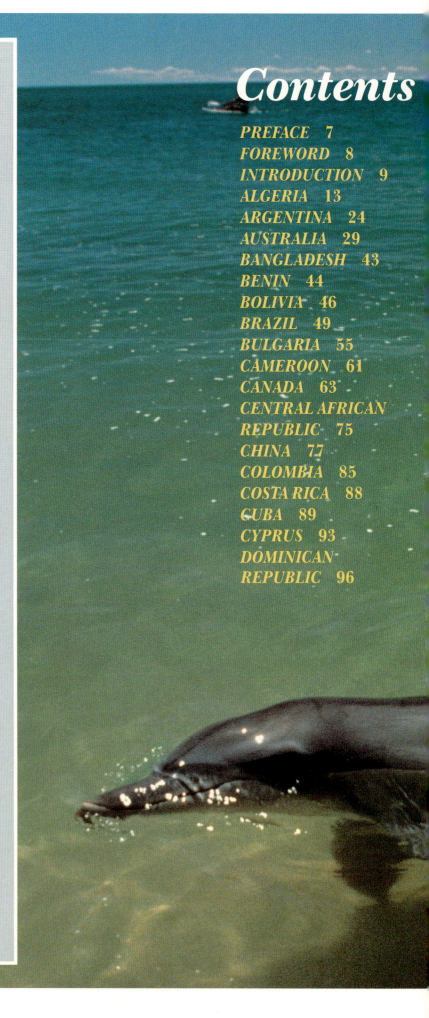

SPECIAL NOTES

JOINT WORLD HERITAGE LISTINGS

Of the 360 sites currently on the World Heritage List, four are sites listed jointly with neighbouring countries. These sites demonstrate the spirit of international co-operation which is so fundamental to the success of UNESCO's World Heritage Convention. These sites are:

ARGENTINA/BRAZIL:
Jesuit Missions of the Guarnis (page 27)
CANADA/USA:
Kluane and Wrangell-St. Elias Parks (page 72)
GUINEA/IVORY COAST (COTE D'IVOIRE):
Mount Nimba Reserves (page 200)
ZAMBIA/ZIMBABWE:
Victoria Falls (Mosi-Oa-Tunya) (page 416)

COUNTRY TITLES

For convenience, common country titles have been used throughout the text. See Appendix – State Parties to the World Heritage Convention (page 427) for formal titles.

The views expressed in this book are the writers' own, and not necessarily those of the Editors, Publisher, UNESCO's World Heritage Committee or the IUCN – World Conservation Union.

———

First published 1992 by
Harper-MacRae Publishing Pty. Limited. (ACN 003 376 583)
6-8 Patonga Drive, Patonga 2256 Australia.
Fax 61-2-43 79 1207
© Harper-MacRae Publishing Pty. Limited, 1992

Managing Editor: Mark Swadling

Design and Art Direction: Robin James

Paris Editor: Tim Baker

Writing: Mark Swadling and Tim Baker

Editorial Consultants: UNESCO: World Heritage Secretariat, IUCN – The World Conservation Union: Jeffrey McNeely, Chief Conservation Officer, Jim Thorsell, Senior Adviser Natural Heritage

Project Co-ordination: Robert Osborne, Kay Osborne, John Burke

Research: Tony Duffy, Kim Brelsford, George Shelvey, Keith Shelvey, Lydie Martin, Robert Mahoud, Kelvin McQueen

Flags: Tony Burton, Flag Society of Australia

Concept: Robert Osborne and Mark Swadling

Typesetting: Adtype Graphics Pty. Ltd.

National Library of Australia Cataloguing-in-Publication Data
Harper-MacRae Publishing Pty. Limited
Masterworks of Man & Nature: Preserving Our World Heritage
Includes Index
ISBN 0-646-05376-0

Printed in Australia by Globe Press Pty. Ltd.
for Harper-MacRae Publishing Pty. Limited

Page 1: Flower vendor, Quito, Equador.
Page 2/3: Gondolas at sunset in Venice – one of Italy's World Heritage sites.
Contents page: Shark Bay.

Contents

CONTRIBUTORS

PREFACE

I T IS NO CO-INCIDENCE THAT in 1972, when the World Heritage Convention was first adopted, it was also the centenary of the founding of the world's first national park at Yellowstone. In fact the establishment of this important convention was largely a direct result of an American initiative, one that was led by the distinguished American conservationist Mr. Russell Train, who refers in his essay on page 377 to the words he helped draft for President Nixon in 1971;

> Yellowstone is the first national park to have been created in the modern world, and the national park concept has represented a major contribution to world culture...It would be fitting by 1972 for the nations of the world to agree to the principle that there are certain areas of such unique worldwide value that they should be treated as part of the heritage of all mankind and accorded special recognition...

The next year the USA became the first state party to the World Heritage Convention and Yellowstone National Park was listed as the first World Heritage site. It is therefore appropriate that this book should begin by honouring that place. In the words of Mr. Gilbert Grosvenor, Chairman and President of the National Geographic Society (page 375);

> Visionary, idealistic, and democratic, preservation has often been called the best idea America ever had.

Yellowstone National Park, Wyoming, USA – the first site inscribed on the World Heritage List. Australian Picture Library.

FOREWORD

HERE IS A BOOK which leads us into a world of beauty in all its glorious diversity. This homage to the splendours of nature and to the genius of mankind presents beauty wrought by nature and beauty wrought by human hands. To read it is to travel through the high canopies of age-old forests, to alight upon the spires of great cathedrals, to wander the wide savannah or the mountain gorge alongside magnificent animals, and to drink in the poetry of ancient sites.

All of these wonders have been and are a source of inspiration for the whole of humanity. They recount the histories of civilisations that have enriched us all; they tell the story of the planet Earth. They *must* be preserved.

The adoption of the Convention concerning the protection of the World Cultural and Natural Heritage by the General Conference of UNESCO in 1972 was the earliest effective expression and first formal recognition of the urgent need to protect the heritage of humanity. In 1975, there were twenty state parties to the convention. Today there are 121.

This convention, innovative in many other ways, introduced for the first time a notion of a shared responsibility for the cultural and natural heritage. It was not the country in which the cultural or natural site was located which was alone responsible for its safeguarding, but the international community as a whole. In other words, the whole of humanity was to be involved in protecting our cultural and natural heritage.

In order to apply the principles of the 1972 convention, UNESCO set up a committee of 21 state parties to the convention. This is the World Heritage Committee, which, acting on proposals from all the state parties, is responsible for establishing the list of natural and cultural sites of exceptional and universal value. The 360 properties currently inscribed on the list represent the natural and spiritual treasures of 80 countries.

The committee meets once a year not only to extend and enrich the World Heritage List, but also to decide on financial and technical help to state parties for the preservation of the sites on their territory. The committee also guarantees the integrity and authenticity of any conservation or restoration work.

Sadly, the demands made on the committee increase in proportion with the increasing number of dangers which threaten our natural and cultural heritage. Turn away for a moment from these enchanting sites and consider their fragility. Time and the elements have already taken their toll on many, and to these natural dangers we must now add those of unconsidered industrial and urban development, pol-

Machu Picchu. Peru

lution and the growth of international tourism. Today, thousands of feet are marching where once time stood still.

UNESCO will fulfil to the utmost of its ability its role as the official 'curator' of the international heritage. But UNESCO cannot accomplish this task alone. It is essential that each and every one of us should be conscious of the threats posed to our natural and cultural sites and should contribute in every way possible to their preservation.

UNESCO is proud to be associated with 'Masterworks of Man and Nature'. It is my sincere hope that, in giving great pleasure to all its readers, it may also serve to increase awareness of the urgent need to save the thousand and one natural and cultural beauties of our planet which we hold in trust for future generations.

FEDERICO MAYOR
Director General, UNESCO

INTRODUCTION

WE LIVE IN A DIVERSE, beautiful and continually changing world. Over the past three thousand million years, the movement and collision of the continents has crumpled the earth and thrown up great ranges of mountains. The oscillations of climate have brought alternate glaciations and periods of warmth to vast tracts of land. These processes, which continue today, have provided a constantly shifting stage on which evolution has generated the wonderful assemblage of plants and animals we see around us.

Over the past three million years, and more especially within the last ten thousand, our own species has increasingly set its mark on nature. People have altered the world in order to cater more efficiently for their own needs. They have replaced forests by crop lands and pastures, domesticated some species of plant and animal and eliminated others, and, as an unwelcome but all-pervasive by-product of urban and industrial civilisations, have now polluted the planet on such a scale that the balance of the climate is in peril.

Wilderness and natural beauty have been in retreat before this onslaught. The retreat has accelerated within recent decades, and there is now no place on Earth that has wholly escaped the mark of humanity. Conservationists everywhere have become increasingly alarmed at these transformations and are concerned to save the best of the nature that remains to us.

There are a number of reasons why it is right to do this. First, the World Charter for Nature, adopted by the General Assembly of the United Nations in 1982, which asserts that species other than our own deserve respect regardless of their worth to us. Second, wild nature is our own life support system: green plants release the oxygen that makes the air breathable. Natural ecosystems recycle the elements essential for life, and control the flow of water from the hills to the sea. Third, we depend on nature for a vast range of products: food, fuel, fibre, medicines, and many other resources whose continual replenishment we take for granted. We have learned that we cannot just assume that nature will remain resilient in the face of human pressure. Conservation has become a global necessity, not just a minority concern.

UNESCO's World Heritage Convention was first discussed in the United States in 1965, and was given impetus at the 9th General Assembly of IUCN held in Lucerne, Switzerland, in 1966. It was proposed that there should be an international legal instrument under which the most outstanding samples of the world's natural and built heritage would be preserved, for the benefit of present and future generations. The criteria which have been

Keoladeo National Park. India

chosen to guide the selection of natural sites are themselves interesting. Under the convention, the aim is to safeguard outstanding areas that demonstrate the evolutionary stages in the history of the earth, include the most outstanding examples of scenic beauty, provide habitats for rare and endangered species, demonstrate evolution in action, and provide outstanding examples of harmonious relationships between humanity and the world of nature. IUCN, the World Conservation Union, is proud of its central role as independent assessor of natural sites proposed for listing under the convention, and believes that the long-term protection of these sites is of immense importance.

This book illustrates the wonderful places that have been listed under the convention, and the ways in which they meet these various criteria. But nominating a site under the convention is not just a matter of identifying somewhere outstanding, and putting it on a list. It is a positive political act by the governments concerned. It demonstrates that these governments recognise that the areas thus designated are not just important within their own frontiers, but are in a real sense a heritage shared with the whole world community. Designation confirms that the governments accept a responsibility to care for these areas, on behalf of all humanity, now and in the future.

Such actions are both timely and difficult. They are timely because we have come to realise that we live in a world where all people, and all nature are interdependent. Through the collective actions of people in all nations, the world climate is at risk and the ozone layer is being eroded. Pollution knows no frontiers. Nature can no longer defend itself from these threats: we have to change our life-styles and put conservation high up on the agenda if we want our descendants to live in a world that is diverse and beautiful. We have to change our behaviour out of self-interest if not altruism. Our nations share many environmental resources, such as great rivers and marine fisheries. Biological diversity is the foundation of all peoples' futures, even though individual governments are responsible for caring for those parts of it that are located within their territories. World trade, economics and communications link us and make us depend more on one another than ever before. We all have to work together to create a sustainable society — a society in which people live in enduring harmony within the natural world. It is therefore timely that the world has joined together in action to choose and protect its most outstanding natural sites and cultural heritage.

But it is difficult. The 5.3 billion people already living in the world are pressing heavily upon its fragile resources. In less than a century from now those resources may have to sustain between eight and twelve billion human individuals — if they can. The pressure on most areas of land and sea is becoming heavier, and safeguarding even the most outstanding natural areas designated under this convention requires a continuous effort of management, going far beyond the initial commitment of listing. We see around the world many sites, some designated under this convention and others worthy of such designation, that are in danger. We in IUCN regularly bring these problems to the attention of the World Heritage Committee, but their powers and resources, like those of many governments, are severely limited. Mining, forest destruction, over-fishing, pollution, urban encroachment, and the sheer pressure of the desperately poor are all eroding sites which the governments concerned, and the wider world community, would like to safeguard.

We shall only safeguard these masterworks of man and nature if there is genuine international co-operation, to help the governments that are custodians of these places to carry out the commitments they have entered into under the convention. Many lower-income countries lack the resources for monitoring and safeguarding the sites that they have named. Some lack even the capability to survey the sites that they know they would like to designate. Even in developed countries, with much more abundant resources, the apportionment of national budgets has very often placed less emphasis on protecting the environment than it should.

Nonetheless, this book shows how much has already been done. The achievements are extraordinary when you consider that the World Heritage Convention was run in 1990 on the tiny sum of US$2.5 million, with a relatively small full-time secretariat. There are immense gaps in coverage, and in monitoring the protection given to the sites on the list.

There is no World Heritage area designated in the whole of Antarctica, despite its immense scenic beauty and wonderful wildlife: largely because of

Kilimanjaro National Park. Tanzania

the disputed sovereignty there. Within Africa, there are no sites in Namibia, Botswana, Kenya or the Republic of South Africa, although they have many areas that would fully merit designation. No natural sites have been designated within the USSR. There are no natural sites in a broad swathe of northern South America, including much of the main basin of the Amazon. We have a long way to go before the World Heritage Convention lists the outstanding sites of our planet completely. We have yet longer to go before those sites are safeguarded for all time, as the convention intends that they should be.

The key to the future is in the commitment of human individuals. Those who read this book should not just treat it as a brochure for armchair travel. They should see it as a challenge. Only with their support, their commitment, their funding, their willingness to adopt life-styles that nature can sustain, their pressure on their governments and their demand for higher levels of international co-operation to safeguard their world's environment, can the objectives of the convention truly be fulfilled. We have a great deal more work to do, and I urge all those who buy or read this book to commit themselves to that end.

MARTIN W. HOLDGATE
Director General
IUCN — The World Conservation Union

World Heritage: an Important Concept

UNESCO *has been responsible for preserving all those sites where man first settled – in the Nile, Tigrus, Euphrates and Indus.*

GOUGH WHITLAM

THE ESTABLISHMENT OF the World Heritage List is not an academic exercise. It is an international undertaking of a juridical, technical and practical nature designed to mobilise active solidarity for the safeguard of the cultural and natural heritage.

This heritage is under constant threat from the effects of underdevelopment or ill-advised development. International co-operation is required to ensure the survival of vestiges of vanished cultures and of the riches of living cultures, to save living species from extinction, to make possible the sustained renewal of natural resources and to maintain the ecological balance. The implementation of the 1972 convention is in the forefront of this effort.

Making an inventory of properties of universal value is an exciting intellectual enterprise, but one which calls for a more restrictive definition of the notion of heritage, which is tending to become all-inclusive under the impact of scientific development and the expansion of the concepts of history and culture. It is true that everything belongs to history and that the whole of nature and all human artefacts leave traces worthy of interpretation. But the world is changing rapidly and if the truly essential traces of the heritage are not given special universal recognition, then even they may be swept away by the forces of change. If this happens, the notion of permanent value and its expression in specific sites and artefacts may be lost.

The properties chosen for inclusion on the World Heritage List are not the only ones that deserve to be safeguarded, however. On the contrary, properties privileged by inclusion are intended to serve as examples and to encourage the formulation of national or local policies for safeguarding the environment as a whole. The objectives of the convention are thus both ambitious and credible. It affords to every state party prestige, specific assistance and safeguards in the event of catastrophes against which no country can be forewarned, not even the most developed and the best equipped.

All countries possess an appreciable cultural and natural heritage. Many of the state parties to the convention have submitted dossiers to the World Heritage Committee and obtained the inscription on the list of numerous properties. But, it might be asked, why have they not all done so? It is not very logical for a state to ratify the convention (unless it attaches only a symbolic value to ratification), and then to take no further action. And why are there only 121 states parties to the convention? Why has the 1972 convention not won unanimous, universal support? Joint efforts by the states parties, UNESCO, and the International Council on Monuments and Sites (ICOMOS) to define fields of international co-operation (by areas of common culture, beliefs and architectural techniques, or by major communication and trade routes) are thwarted by the blank spaces which appear on the maps, like the gaps which indicated *terra incognita* in early atlases.

Admittedly there are also great disparities between states deriving from their size, population density, the age of their culture, the vicissitudes of their history or the care they have hitherto taken to conserve their cultural heritage. Likewise, the fact that cultural properties far outnumber natural properties on the list is not in itself significant. A cultural property may be a small or isolated building or even an archaeological vestige in the midst of a wilderness; a natural property may be an immense national park bigger than some states.

As the field of application of the convention is gradually defined, it is becoming clear that the means needed to accomplish its aims are far beyond the resources of the World Heritage Committee, which can only finance urgent work, expert studies, under-funded projects carried out over a long period, and the preventive work necessary to avoid the deterioration of properties and the costs that ensue, and to guarantee their authenticity.

The publication of information about the World Heritage in the media should help to encourage major safeguarding operations, but the rigour with which the list is established and the need to make it representative and fully credible will determine the success of media coverage. Finally, solidarity in aid of World Heritage properties calls for permanent monitoring of their condition, in order to guarantee that the convention is respected and that financial aid is put to good use. There should be no question of inscribing unworthy properties on the list. Fortunately this is not the case. But the extension and success of the World Heritage concept call for vigilance. Supra-national control should not be seen as an infringement of the sovereignty of states, since they have made their commitment freely after weighing up the advantages and constraints.

Any community can find in the convention support for the safeguard of its cultural identity which goes beyond material aid and may help to prevent that clandestine destruction of its heritage or to combat interests which have scant respect for it.

MICHEL PARENT, of France, was President of ICOMOS from 1981 to 1987. As a member of the committee which drafted the World Heritage Convention and later Chairman of the World Heritage Committee, he made a leading contribution to the birth and development of the World Heritage concept.

Reprinted from the *Unesco Courier*, August 1988

Common Heritage: A New Idea Takes Shape

THE 'CONVENTION CONCERNING the Protection of the World Cultural and Natural Heritage' or World Heritage Convention is a legal instrument through which states voluntarily commit themselves to protect monuments and sites within their territory that are recognised to be of such outstanding value that safeguarding them concerns humanity as a whole. States parties to the convention also undertake to respect the heritage of universal value located on the territory of other states and to make a financial contribution towards safeguarding this heritage in countries which lack the means to do so.

One hundred and twenty one states are already parties to the convention.

1960, a decisive year

In the 1960s, there was a danger that the monuments of Nubia would be permanently submerged beneath the waters of the Nile following the construction of the Aswan High Dam. The international community became aware that the disappearance of these monuments would be an irreparable loss, not only for Egypt and the Sudan, but for humanity as a whole. It was clear that the considerable resources required to save the monuments were beyond the means of the two countries concerned. The idea of common heritage – and of a common responsibility to safeguard it – took shape. On 8 March 1960, Mr René Maheu, the Director-General of UNESCO, launched an international appeal and some $30 million were eventually collected to save the Nubian monuments.

Around this time more and more voices were being raised in defence of the environment and for the protection of natural sites. This movement, which has grown constantly since then, has fostered an awareness of the need to respect the riches of nature which are indissociable from the past and future of humanity.

The World Heritage convention is a result of the meeting of these two trends. By affirming that the works of man and the works of nature belong to a single heritage, the convention was a profoundly original document when it was adopted by UNESCO's General Conference in 1972.

An inventory of the world heritage

The idea was to identify the cultural and natural properties within each country whose protection would be a matter of concern to the international community as a whole. The text of the convention describes these treasures as properties of *outstanding universal value* from the point of view of art or history, science or natural beauty.

States parties to the convention draw up an inventory of properties which they consider to fall within

these categories and then nominate them for inclusion on the World Heritage List. The World Heritage Committee, an intergovernmental committee comprising representatives of twenty-one states parties to the convention elected on a rota basis, studies these nominations in the light of detailed reports prepared by two non-governmental organisations, the International Council of Monuments and Sites (ICOMOS) and the International Union for Conservation of Nature and Natural Resources (IUCN). The number of dossiers studied each year is considerable, but only a handful of properties are inscribed on the World Heritage List.

The list currently comprises 360 properties located in 80 countries. It is an attempt to create a world inventory which will be as comprehensive, representative and coherent as possible.

The criteria for selection

The *cultural* monuments and sites chosen should:

- Constitute a unique achievement (the Fort and Shalamar Gardens, Pakistan; the Cha Kteau of Chambord, France);
- Have exercised considerable influence at a certain period (the historic centre of Florence, Italy);
- Provide evidence of a civilisation which has disappeared (the Royal Palaces of Abomey, Benin; Machu Picchu, Peru);
- Illustrate a significant historical period (Abu Mena, Egypt; the historic centre of Salvador de Bahia, Brazil);
- Constitute an outstanding example of a traditional way of life (the M'Zab Valley, Algeria; the village of Holloko, Hungary);
- Be associated with ideas or beliefs of universal significance (the sacred city of Kandy, Sri Lanka; Independence Hall, United States).

Natural heritage properties should:

- Illustrate a stage in the Earth's evolution (the Galapagos Islands, Ecuador);
- Represent ongoing geological processes (the Hawaii Volcanoes, United States; Los Glaciares, Argentina);
- Constitute remarkable natural formations of areas of exceptional natural beauty (Kilmanjaro National Park, United Republic of Tanzania; Cape Girolata and Scandola Nature Reserve in Corsica, France);
- Contain the natural habitats of endangered species (Garamba National Park, Zaire; Wood Buffalo National Park, Canada).

The properties inscribed on the list very often meet several of these criteria. Some of them are of outstanding cultural and natural value.

Hollókö. Hungary

The role of the convention

The convention only applies to properties inscribed on the World Heritage List, although the cultural and natural heritage at large is threatened.

Inscription on the list undeniably confers new prestige on a property, but at the same time it creates obligations for the state concerned, which must ensure that the property is protected and take responsibility for it vis-à-vis the international community. The World Heritage Committee, with the support of the media, may remind a state of its obligations if these are not being respected. Many positive results have been achieved by this kind of pressure, such as the cancellation of projects to construct dams, polluting factories, or over-intrusive tourist facilities.

The World Heritage Committee also acts directly on behalf of protected sites at the request of states parties to the convention. Through the World Heritage Fund (some $2.5 million a year), international co-operation can be organised, specialists and equipment can be provided, training and educational activities can be undertaken, and funds can be raised for major projects such as the restoration of monuments or the management of nature reserves. Such projects may be carried out as part of International Safeguarding Campaigns like that in which UNESCO is currently engaged for the old city of Sana'a in the Republic of Yemen.

Reprinted from the *Unesco Courier*, October 1990

ALGERIA

Algeria is Africa's second largest country after Sudan. Along with Morocco and Tunisia, it is one of the Maghreb or Barbary states – that area of northern Africa which was once inhabited mainly by the Berbers.

As with the rest of Maghreb, Algeria's original Berber inhabitants were influenced strongly by the Phoenicians from around the 9th century BC. After the Phoenicians were defeated in the Punic Wars by Rome (264 to 146 BC), the entire area became part of the Roman empire.

The Vandals came from Spain during the 5th century AD, defeated the Romans and ruled the area for a century. The Byzantine Roman empire then regained control until the latter half of the 7th century, when the Muslim Arabs invaded. After a painful war, Algeria achieved independence in 1962 from the French, who had dominated Algeria since 1830.

Today Berbers still comprise the largest ethnic grouping in Algeria, although there are three main languages – Arabic, French and Berber.

The rich legacy of Algeria's colourful past led to early ratification of the World Heritage Convention – in June 1974. Currently there are six sites listed; three of them Roman ruins – Djemila, Timgad and Tipasa. There is also a neolithic archaeological site at Tassili N'Ajjer, the remains of an 11th century town at Al Qal'a of Beni Hammad and the remains of five Berber villages at M'Zab Valley.

Al Qal'a of Beni Hammad

The Roman ruins of Tipasa

The rock art of Tassili N'Ajjer

FAMED FOR ITS thousands of prehistoric rock paintings and engravings, Tassili N'Ajjer is also one of the last bastions of the Tuareg Berber pastoralists. A 1,200 m (4,000 ft) high plateau shaded by cypress trees, some of which are over a thousand years old, it rises from the desert like a gigantic natural fortress. Its natural and archaeological wonders are spread over a vast area – the Tassili National Park covers more than 80,000 sq km (30,000 sq mi).

The first thing you notice about the high plateau is the extraordinary verticality of the landscape. Then, once you have got over your initial surprise, your attention is captured by the odd contours of the place. Curiously eroded sandstone blocks, vertiginous canyons and rock columns 20 to 30 metres (66 to 99 ft) high all bear witness to an eventful geological past. It is these remarkable rocks, some as massive as buildings, others as delicate as wax tapers, that give the region what one historian, F. Soleilhavoup, has described as 'the look of another planet, unique, mysterious, sometimes unnerving'.

Human activity, changes in climate and the wear and tear of time have all played a part in radically altering the heart of Africa. It is less than 4,000 years since the Sahara became a desert. The valleys, canyons and stacks worn away by erosion are the last vestiges of an earlier, humid time. The fossil record even indicates that, several hundred million years ago, the area formed part of the vast Silurian sea.

Then wind took over from water, shaping and polishing the rocks like a sculptor. What vegetation now survives the rigours of the desert climate does so thanks to the *gueltas* and *wadis*. Here the *tarout*, the ancient cypress unique to the Sahara, still adds a touch of green. Olive and myrtle, lavender and oleander, call to mind the softness of the Mediterranean climate. Along the Iherir and Edarène wadis, luxuriant reed-beds have survived. Other plants such as the date palm and the acacia play a primordial role in the Tassili ecosystem.

We are accustomed to think of the desert as a hostile, lifeless place, so the ways in which the surviving animal and plant species have adapted to it seem all the more marvellous. Most of the mammals, including the mouflon and the gazelles, have sand-coloured coats, the better to resist the heat and camouflage themselves in its vastness. In even the most arid areas rodents and reptiles survive. There are fish in the *gueltas*, which also serve as staging posts for birds migrating southwards towards black Africa.

The Tassili National Park is also one of the world's finest open-air museums of prehistory. The Neolithic civilization of the Sahara was closely linked to the prevailing geological and ecological conditions. Once

Tassili N'Ajjer Plateau

the desert started to advance, the people gradually lost much of their nomadic character.

The region's rock paintings illustrate the animals that were crucial to the survival of the inhabitants of Tassili at different periods in their history. It is possible to distinguish four separate eras via the prevailing fauna, though historians have not established a unanimously accepted chronology for them.

The first is that of the *bubal* or great buffalo, which is depicted in rock art from about 7000 to 4000 BC. Elephants, rhinoceroses and various savannah antelopes are all typical of this period. Oxen appear around 4000 BC. They are depicted without humps, and with horns that are short or splendidly lyre-like. After 1500 BC horses make their appearance, and finally, around 1500 AD, camels. About this time the first written characters in the Tuareg *tifinagh* script can also be observed.

There are three principal modes in Tassili's rock art. Size and symbolism are characteristic of the first, archaic manner. The animals are gigantic and are often represented in isolation; only magic seems to have been capable of coping with their terrible force. Simply drawn in the *bubal* style, they are depicted with an acute sense of observation. Along Wadi Djerat 4,000 separate figures have been itemized. One bestiary stretching over 120 sq m (1330 sq ft) features giraffes 8 m (27 ft) high: it is the largest complex of prehistoric engravings in the world.

The appearance of antelopes and mouflons marks the start of a second sub-period within the archaic style. The beasts are more often painted than engraved, and they are pursued by hunters with round heads. One can sense the presence of totem animals, masked men and ritual dances. As well as single figures, groups are depicted in frescoes whose splendours can be admired at Iharen or Séfar.

The second style, best typified at the Jabbaren site, is naturalistic. The images are smaller and more brightly coloured, reflecting a more sedentary lifestyle. Humankind is now in charge, dominating the surrounding animals.

The final mode is schematic or even abstract. The engravings are less finely executed, but the paintings are more elegant and skilful. There are wonderfully stylized horses, chariots and, later, dromedaries. The use of a wash technique allows for delicate portrayals such as the scene at Iharen in which a young antelope is shown being suckled by its mother.

Where are these works of rock art? Hardly any of them are to be found in the so-called 'forests of stone'. The strangest paintings are in the heart of the 'towns' of Tassili, such as Séfar and Jabbaren. F. Soleilhavoup has even suggested that there may have been a sanctuary where rituals were practised by Neolithic men in the archaic period.

The naturalistic works on the other hand, showing everyday scenes from the life of the shepherds and their flocks, are most often situated in isolated spots outside the towns, while the third, schematic style is best represented on standing stones in the *regs*, or stony deserts, where late works depicting camels point to the degeneration of rock art.

The wall paintings of Tassili provide glimpses of a whole society, its everyday life and the animals that were essential to it. The works indicate that a revolution took place in the region sometime in the Neolithic period, linked to the change from a hunter-gatherer lifestyle to one based on agriculture. Nevertheless, many mysteries still remain. Among them are:

The techniques used in rock art. The engravings generally seem to predate the paintings, yet at Tissoukai the existence of carved sketches suggests that the stone may have been engraved before the paintings were executed. Sculpture is rare in Tassili; the only examples are miniatures like the resting ruminant at Wadi Amazzar.

The lack of homogeneity within each style. The archaic manner, for instance, is very diverse. There is nothing to link the bull at Séfar with the masked figures also depicted there.

The secret world of magic and religion. What do the two-headed bulls at Wadi Djerat signify? What is the meaning of the magnificent spiral engraved on the great buffalo at the same site? Is it a symbol of the continuity of life? Or did it form part of a spell cast on the animal, as in hunting rites elsewhere?

Problems of dating. It was once thought that the Neolithic civilization of the Sahara was later than those of North Africa, Egypt and the Middle East. Now scholars tend to believe the opposite, maintaining that the Saharan culture was independent of and even earlier than the artistic flowering of Egypt. André Malraux considered the zoomorphic heads of Wadi Djerat to be 'prefigurations of Egyptian zoolatry'. If this is the case, Saharan representations of cattle with discs between their horns may be earlier than Egyptian images of the cow-goddess Hathor. As for the war-chariots of Tassili and Fezzan, their origins are still swathed in mystery.

The spectacle of this rock art, executed by generations of Tuareg and handed down almost intact to the present day, arouses strong emotions in the viewer. Despite their image as 'lords of the desert', warriors living in a hierarchical society, the Tuareg were in fact primarily herdsmen. According to one historian, J.D. Clark, they appeared less than 5,000 years ago, and led their flocks through the Sahara until the time when increasing desiccation drove them out.

Of all African people, it was the Tuareg, together with the Peul and the Masai, who remained most strongly committed to the pastoral life, which they refused to combine with arable farming. They also tamed and herded the biggest flocks. The sparse Tuareg population commuted seasonally between the desert regions of the Sahara and the high plateaux, the Hoggar and Tibesti as well as Tassili.

Pastoral skills were passed on from father to son. The herders learned how to find their bearings in the desert, how to read the stars and recognise plants.

Now a growing population and changing ways have created new pressures. Djanet, with between 5,000 and 6,000 inhabitants, Illizi and other centres have become the focus of a relatively sedentary lifestyle that the former nomads do not always handle well. Knowledge of skills is no longer being transmitted from generation to generation. And on top of these problems, the arrival of tourists has forced the Tuareg to come to terms with a radical change in their way of life.

The cliff walls themselves are at risk. Exposed to the desert winds and eroding particles of sand, they are showing signs of age. As the sandstone base starts to break up, rock crumbles, paintings lose their colour and engravings the sharpness of their line. The ageing of the rock is also leading to flaking, discolouration, encrustation, fissuring, blotching, and the growth of lichens. Other problems include oxydization and rainwater run-off on the walls themselves, and the damage caused by nests of flies.

Now, however, a new danger has been added to the wear and tear of time. The Sahara has become fashionable, and anarchic forms of tourism are developing, bringing in their wake a host of threats to Tassili's natural and cultural environment. Vandalism is one problem – some supposed lovers of the past do not scruple to break off pieces of rock as souvenirs. One person was arrested at Djanet airport with more than 800 archaeological specimens. Paintings and engravings are harshly treated. Photographers have been known to scratch or dampen the rock to bring out line or colour, or even to touch up the images. Sometimes graffiti are added as a joke.

The pristine desert is being polluted. Camps have no lavatories, rubbish is left behind, scant water resources are abused, *gueltas* are fouled. The natural pastures of Tassili, used for grazing since the Neolithic era, are today menaced by the gathering of fuel for cooking and by the comings and goings of vehicles off the recognized trails. It is hard to judge how much damage is being done by unauthorized hunting, but certainly there is a great demand for mouflon and gazelle, as well as for the flesh of some reptiles.

The idea is to preserve the heritage while also opening it up to visitors in a way that will not threaten its natural and cultural riches. For some years now, UNESCO has been working with the Algerian government and, locally, with the Tassili National Park authorities to promote acceptable forms of tourism. The accent is on stricter supervision of the park and on the training of guides.

Yet some local agencies seem completely unaware of the importance of Tassili's inheritance. Instead of protecting it, they drum up business by promising to take clients to off-limit sites and encouraging them to swim in the watercourses, and even to take away

Timgad – the Arch of Trajan

rock fragments as souvenirs. Sometimes they fail to bury the rubbish from their camps; and they permit long evenings round the camp-fire when it is vital to economize on firewood. These unscrupulous operators should not be allowed to cash in on the attraction of unspoiled sites, and clandestine archaeological excavations should be discouraged.

The preservation of the cultural heritage will require clearly thought-out conservation and security measures. All the rock art will need to be inventoried, and a guttering system will have to be installed to protect the works from rainwater run-off. Sand barriers will have to be constructed to ensure that visitors keep their distance.

Various ways of preserving the paintings and engravings are being tested. Since 1982 UNESCO has operated a solar-powered laboratory in the area and is working on samples from the worst-affected sites. The International Centre for Conservation (ICCROM) is experimenting with the application of silicone to preserve the paintings.

Another crucial problem is that of conserving Tassili's extraordinary natural environment. As part of a solution, tourists must be persuaded not to pollute the desert. Clear instructions must be given about the gathering of wood, and visitors must be made to understand that the maintenance of water resources is crucial to the ecosystem.

The Tuareg will need help to adjust to the new conditions. A pilot scheme that could serve as a model has already been set up at Ihérir, a magnificent site that has been at risk since it was opened up to visitors by the Djanet-Illisi road. The local people are being encouraged to develop their crafts, diversify their occupations, improve livestock raising, and above all to protect and develop the existing watercourses. Housing also affects the quality of life, and a special effort will have to be made to ensure that new buildings fit in with the local architecture and conform to the aesthetic imperatives of this region.

GLOSSARY
Bubal: great buffalo
Erg: a desert region of shifting sand
Gara: sandstone butte isolated by erosion
Guelta: a spring in rocky terrain
Méharée: a journey by camel
Reg: stony terrain
Tarout: the Duprez cypress, of which some 300 have survived, almost all a thousand years old
Tassili: plateau
Tifinagh: writing used by the Tuareg

CAROLINE HAARDT, French journalist, was a staff member of UNESCO's Division of Cultural Heritage from 1983 to 1987. She is currently preparing an exhibition as part of the UNESCO Silk Roads project on the *Croisière Jaune,* a motor rally from Beirut to Tibet held in 1931-1932.

Reprinted from the *Unesco Courier,* May 1991

TIMGAD

LOCATION   38km (23.6mi) southeast of Batna.

DESCRIPTION   The ruins of a Roman city featuring a theatre, a forum, a capitol southwest of the town, 2 temples, an imposing library, a basilica and 2 markets. Close to the markets is a large ornamental arch. The so called 'House of Sertius' was a private residence covering an area of 2,500sq m (27,750sq ft) and is a fine example of a house of the nobility of the time.

SIGNIFICANCE   The Roman colony of 'Thamugad' was founded in 100 AD under the reign of Trajan. It was originally fortified. The small town quickly expanded into a big city. During the 3rd century it became a centre of Christian activity. Destroyed during the 5th century, Timgad was rebuilt and enjoyed prosperity again as a Christian town, until disappearing from history in the 7th century with the coming of the Arabs. These ruins are quite intact, some having been restored, and include some interesting items such as numerous inscriptions and a series of standard measures.

TASSILI N'AJJER

LOCATION   Southeast of the Algerian desert, extending to the border with Libya, N 23° 26', E 05° 20'.

DESCRIPTION   Tassili N'Ajjer is an archaeological site 3,000sq km (1200sq mi) in area. It is triangular in shape and forms part of the scarcely populated Tassili Plateau. Much of the landscape is bare sandstone and vegetation is scarce. The altitude of the plateau rises to 1,800m (5,905ft) above sea level.

SIGNIFICANCE   This is a remarkable area of prehistoric remains with a fantastic gallery of Sharian neolithic paintings and rock engravings. The 'Elephant of Timenzouzin', dating back to 7000 BC, is one of the more spectacular examples of this ancient artwork.

AL QAL'A OF BENI HAMMAD

LOCATION   34km (21mi) southeast of M'sila, 7km (4mi) from the Hodna mountains.

DESCRIPTION   These are the ruins of an old fortified city. The city walls extend for 8km (5mi) and surround a multitude of palaces, government buildings and houses. An exceptionally large mosque stands in the centre of the town.

SIGNIFICANCE   This was the capital city of the Hammadite Empire during the 11th century AD. It was destroyed in 1152 by the Almohals. The mosque is of considerable architectural significance, it is the second largest in Algeria. Its minaret is almost 25m (82ft) high and is distinctive in being decorated on only one side.

A palm grove in the M'Zab Valley

groves of El Atteuf, Bou Noura, Beni Isguen, and Ghardaia; 3. the former sites of Arram n'tlasdit, Baba Hanni and Baba Saad; 4. 13 religious buildings outside the ksour; and 5. the natural site.

SIGNIFICANCE   Before the advent of Islam, this region was originally inhabited by nomadic Berber and Zanata tribes. The word 'M'zab' is thought to derive from the word for the first Berber Muslims – 'Beni Mesaab'. The first town, El Atteuf, was founded by Muslims in 1014 AD. The 5 Mozabite towns are striking for their architectural planning which reflects the religious, social and political organisation of the day. Typically, the mosque is built on a rocky knoll and forms the nucleus around which the town descends to the profane outer limits of its ramparts. The palm groves are situated outside the ksour; they provided an area for cultivation and relief from the intense summer heat. They are remarkable for their intricate water distribution systems which included

DJEMILA

LOCATION   50km (31mi) east of Setif, in the Babors mountains.

DESCRIPTION   The ruins of this ancient Roman town are exceptionally well preserved. The street plan is rectangular with a broad, colonnaded street running centrally from the northern gate through to the southern gate. The forum, capitol, basilica and market are all centrally located. Other important buildings include a family temple and a sanctuary to Saturn.

SIGNIFICANCE   This town was founded in the 1st century AD under the reign of Nerva. The sanctuary later became an important focus to the town as the deity, known as Saturn or Frugifer, was one of the great African gods whose importance was centred around the function of granting good crops for the year.

TIPASA

LOCATION   70km (43.5mi) west of Algiers, on the coast.

DESCRIPTION   Extensive Roman ruins are found on the western edge of the modern town of Tipasa. They include a 4,000 seat theatre, a forum, 2 temples, a necropolis, a basilica, the 'Villa of the Frescoes' and the 'Gate of Caesarea'. On the eastern side of the town are some Byzantine ruins which include houses, churches and cemeteries.

SIGNIFICANCE   Originally a Phoenician town, Tipasa was made a Roman military colony by Claudius. It was an early seat of Christianity, becoming a bishop's see in the 3rd century AD. After a period of Arab domination in the 5th century, the town declined. The Great Basilica here is the largest Christian monument in Algeria.

M'ZAB VALLEY

LOCATION   Laghouat Wilaya, 600km (373mi) south of Algiers, N 33° 00′ to 31° 15′, E 02° 30′ to 05° 00′.

DESCRIPTION   There are 5 main elements to this site: 1. the 5 ksour (plural of the Berber word ksar, meaning a fortified place), which are named: El Atteuf, Bou Noura, Melika, Beni Isguen and Ghardaia; 2. the palm

The beautifully preserved ruins of Djemila

ARGENTINA

A massive wedge-shaped country occupying most of the southern part of the South American continent, Argentina, at 2.74 million sq km (1.07 million sq mi), is the eighth largest country in the world.

The terrain and climate over such a vast area is naturally quite diverse. It varies from tropical in the north to subantarctic in the south. The climate is largely moderated by the proximity of two great oceans on either side, while the rugged Andes mountains form a towering border to the west and provide another enormous influence. The diversity of environments, from steamy rainforests to glacial peaks, has endowed the country with an impressive biodiversity.

This region was settled by Europeans early in the 16th century. At that time the entire area was inhabited by Indians of various tribes, speaking differing languages. Spanish explorations were frequent and hazardous – often suffering from the effects of a hostile Indian population and a harsh and isolated environment.

However, permanent settlements from neighbouring Spanish colonies continued to be established throughout the 16th century. The area was ruled by the Peruvian viceroyalty until the viceroyalty of La Plata was created in 1776. Thereafter, movement for national union grew steadily, culminating in a formal declaration of independence in 1816.

Argentina accepted the World Heritage Convention in August, 1978 and now has three sites listed. Two of these are found in the region of the Parana plateau to the northeast: Iguazu National Park and the Jesuit Missions of the Guaranis (listed in conjunction with similar sites in Brazil).

Iguazu is a sub-tropical region rich in wildlife and famous for its spectacular waterfalls notably the renowned Iguazu Falls. The Jesuit Missions are fascinating relics of a radical 17th century missionary plan for the region's Indian population. The accompanying article by Caroline Haardt outines the origins and development of these missions up to their abrupt abandonment in the late 18th century.

Argentina's third World Heritage listing is Los Glaciares National Park. Situated in the far south of the country and perched high up in the Andes, this rugged park represents a pristine glacial environment with significant populations of endemic flora and fauna.

The spectacular Iguazu Falls

The Jesuit Missions to the Guarani

IN THE SEVENTEENTH CENTURY the Jesuits organised a remarkable experiment in community living in the homeland of the Guarani Indians, on the borders of what are today Argentina, Brazil and Paraguay. The experiment, which was compared at the time to Thomas More's *Utopia*, to the design for a utopian commonwealth set forth by the Italian philosopher Tommaso Campanella in his book *The City of the Sun*, and even to Plato's *Republic*, lasted for over a century. It provoked admiration in some quarters and indignation in others, no one who knew anything about the matter was indifferent to it.

Attempts had been made to convert the Guarani to Christianity during the sixteenth century, when the area was being colonised by the Spaniards and the Portuguese. The Society of Jesus and other religious orders had sent itinerant missionaries into the Indian villages, where they preached the Gospel before hastily retreating back to the relative comfort of their colleges. These attempts to convert the Indians were a failure. Collective baptisms and other sacramental rites made no lasting change in their religious beliefs. Idolatry continued to be practised. The missions eventually led to disguised forms of slavery and encouraged abuses by European colonists and rich creoles who exploited the captive labour force.

The exploitation of the Indians, combined with the weakness of the religious orders, led to a crisis which Francisco de Toledo, the Spanish Viceroy of Peru, and the Jesuit fathers determined to resolve.

In 1602, the Jesuits began to replace the itinerant missions by founding villages in which the Indians could be concentrated and taught Christian doctrine in a stable environment. These villages became known as *reducciones* – reductions – since in them *ad ecclesiam et vitam civilem esse reducti* ('people were to be led to the church and to civic life'). The first of them were established by the Jesuits of the province of Paraguay.

It was no easy task to persuade the Indians, who were strongly attached to their homelands, to settle in the reductions. The Jesuits realised that they would have to create an environment in which Guarani tribes from different places could feel a sense of ethnic and cultural unity. They chose sites which could be easily defended, with forests, streams and land that could be farmed.

To the Indians, the missions offered a number of attractions – dwellings, trades and crafts, plenty of food (above all the beef they loved) and the beverage known as 'Jesuit tea', which was made from the maté plant and which also served as currency. Dances, theatre, music, processions and military manoeuvres were other blandishments that contributed to the success of the Jesuit missions.

Each reduction was self-governing, under the spiritual supervision of a priest. The Jesuit fathers maintained the powers of the traditional chiefs or caciques, and each village also had a *calbido* or council of notables. Agricultural produce and objects produced by craftsmen belonged to the community. Each family received the necessities of life. Any surplus went to widows, to the sick, to the church, or as taxes to the Spanish Crown.

Each reduction specialised in a particular activity, which was determined by the resources available to it. Some practised animal husbandry, others cultivated maté or cotton, or devoted themselves to carpentry or working in precious metals.

Right from the start, the Guarani missions provoked envy. They were violently attacked by *bandeirantes*, adventurers and gold prospectors from the São Paulo region of Brazil. The most severe attacks took place between 1628 and 1630, when groups of Indians were captured and taken into slavery. Eventually the incursions became so numerous that the Jesuits moved the reductions and established them between the Uruguay and Paraná rivers (in what is now Paraguay).

Furious to see the Indians slip out of their grasp, the Spanish colonists, and above all the *encomenderos* of Asunción, were also extremely hostile to the missionary villages. In the mid-seventeenth century, the Jesuits asked the King of Spain for permission to arm the reductions so that they could defend themselves against attack. Thus armed, they established thirty missions definitively: fifteen in Argentina, seven in Brazil, and eight in what is now Paraguay. They flourished, some comprised more than 6,000 Indians.

The experiment came to a sudden end in the second half of the eighteenth century, partly as a result of the new frontiers drawn by colonial treaties between Spain and Portugal, but above all because of the expulsion of the Jesuits from the Spanish and Portuguese dominions. The political and religious autonomy of the missions was seen as a threat to Spanish imperial power, and the Jesuits were replaced by lay administrators and priests belonging to other religious orders. The Indians were dispersed. The reductions were abandoned and fell into ruin.

CAROLINE HAARDT, French journalist, was a member of UNESCO's Division of Cultural Heritage from 1983 to 1987. She is currently preparing an exhibition as part of the UNESCO Silk Roads project on the *Croisiere Jaune*, a motor rally from Beirut to Tibet held in 1931-1932.

Reprinted from the *Unesco Courier*, January 1991

San Ignacio Mini – one of five Jesuit Missions in this joint listing with Brazil

IGUAZU NATIONAL PARK

LOCATION   Province of Missiones, (in the northeast of Argentina), S 25° 31′ to 25° 43′, E 54° 08′ to 54° 32′.

DESCRIPTION   This park consists of 49,200ha (121,578ac) of national park plus 6,300ha (15,568ac) of reserve. The vegetation is mainly subtropical rainforest. 2 main rivers, the Parana and the Iguazu, traverse the park, creating many spectacular waterfalls.

SIGNIFICANCE   Iguazu National Park was created in 1934 to protect the great diversity of unique wildlife and vegetation found here. Leopards, pumas, monkeys, caiman and yaguarete (a large native cat) are all found here, as well as a rich bird life, including the pato serrucho or saw duck, which is endangered.

JESUIT MISSIONS OF THE GUARANIS

LOCATION   Listed jointly with Argentina – in the Province of Missiones, and Brazil – Rio Grande do Sul State, around S 27° 00′, W 55° 00′.

DESCRIPTION   Here we have the remains of five settlements; San Ignacio Mini, Nuestra Señora de Santa Aná, Nuestra Señora de Loreto and Santa Maria la Mayor – all in Argentina, and São Miguel das Missôes in Brazil. These sites variously comprise, mainly in ruins, churches, residences, cemeteries, schools, workshops, Indian dwellings, vegetable gardens, prisons, town halls, colleges and chapels.

SIGNIFICANCE   The original settlements were founded by the Fathers of the Society of Jesus from 1609 to 1632 and were revolutionary in concept. To avoid the corruption and exploitation of the past, they were set up as self-governing communities where Indians lived under the spiritual and secular guidance of one or two priests. After heavy raids from bands of 'maloqueadores' and 'bandeirantes', particularly during the years 1628-30, the missions were all moved and resettled by the mid 17th century. 30 'pueblos' were then formed: 8 in Paraguay, 15 in Argentina and 7 in Brazil. These remains are the best preserved of those original 30.

LOS GLACIARES NATIONAL PARK

LOCATION   Southwest of Santa Cruz Province, S 49° 15′ to 50° 40′, W 72° 45′ to 73° 30′.

DESCRIPTION   The national park covers an area of 445,900ha (1.1 million ac). 154,100ha (380,796ac) of national reserve is also included in the listing. It is a mountainous area extending from Fitzroy in the north to Stokes in the south and includes numerous glaciers. The main ones are Moreno, Upsala, Ameghino and Fitzroy.

SIGNIFICANCE   Created in 1937, the national park is inhabited by pumas, coloured fox and llama, to name but a few of the varied fauna. There are also many fine bird species like the wild duck of Chile, the red ibis and the condor. Geologically, the park's landscape provides an important record of the effects of rapid glacial retreat.

Los Glaciares National Park – Moreno Glacier

Waratah in full bloom – Gibralter Range National Park

AUSTRALIA

Australia ratified the World Heritage Convention in August, 1974, the seventh country to do so. Since then the number of state parties to the convention has increased each year. There are currently 121 states participating.

There are presently 8 Australian properties on the World Heritage List. They are: the Great Barrier Reef, Kakadu, Willandra Lakes, the Lord Howe Island Group, the Tasmanian Wilderness, Uluru, the Wet Tropics of Queensland and the East Coast Temperate and Sub-Tropical Rainforest Parks.

The World Heritage Committee has adopted a set of 4 criteria for assessing nominations of natural properties. These are that the properties:

be outstanding examples representing the major stages of the Earth's evolutionary history;

be outstanding examples representing significant ongoing geological processes, biological evolution and man's interaction with the natural environment;

contain superlative natural phenomena, formations or features;

contain the most important and significant natural habitats where threatened species of outstanding universal value still survive.

Only 11 properties on the World Heritage List meet all 4 of these criteria and 3 of those are Australian – the Great Barrier Reef, the Wet Tropics and the Tasmanian Wilderness.

Australia also has 3 of only 13 sites that are listed for both natural and cultural criteria – Willandra Lakes, the Tasmanian Wilderness and Kakadu.

So it can be seen that Australia's contribution to the World Heritage List is indeed unique.

Another area where Australia has made an outstanding contribution is in implementing the World Heritage Convention Act, a legal mechanism that ensures the continued protection of Australia's posterity.

Australia deservedly stands in high esteem for the exceptional standards of management which apply to its sites. Such things as the establishment of the Great Barrier Reef Marine Park Authority, the extensive development of visitor information bureaus and the involvement of local people in park management, show that Australia not only recognises the advantages of World Heritage listing, but also accepts the responsibility that accompanies it.

'Pelodryadidae' – Mt. Lewis, Wet Tropics of Queensland

Australia and the World Heritage Convention

THE GENERAL CONFERENCE OF UNESCO adopted the World Heritage Convention in November 1972. In August 1974 Australia became the seventh state to lodge its ratification.

From the outset Australia took an active part in the operation of the convention. The convention is administered by the World Heritage Committee. Representatives of the World Conservation Union (IUCN), the International Centre for the Study of the Preservation and Restoration of 'Cultural Property (Rome Centre) (ICCROM) and the International Council of Monuments and Sites (ICOMOS) may attend the meetings of the committee in an advisory capacity. Australia became a member of these three bodies in 1973, 1975 and 1976 respectively.

The committee is elected during the UNESCO General Conference at the General Assembly of States Parties to the Convention. The first General Assembly took place during the 19th General Conference in November 1976. Australia was chosen to serve till the end of the 22nd session, which was due to be held in 1982 but was postponed till 1983. In 1983 Australia was elected for a further term, expiring at the end of the 25th session of the General Conference in 1989. By 1984 Australia had become a member of the governing bodies of IUCN, ICCROM and ICOMOS.

Eight Australian properties have been inscribed on the World Heritage List. They are predominately natural sites. Australians are indebted to IUCN for its advice and example in identifying and protecting them. The Australian nominations placed considerably strains on IUCN's resources, because they were the most distant from IUCN's headquarters and some of them were located along exceptionally complex coastlines.

Australia is one of the few states parties with a federal system of government. Responsibilities are shared by a central government, six State governments and two Territory governments. The central government has jurisdiction in matters of heritage and environment only if such matters fall within Australia's international obligations. Because two State governments and one Territory government initially opposed nominations by the Australian government, IUCN representatives had to be exceptionally diplomatic, dedicated and professional in ascertaining and certifying that the standards of the World Heritage Convention have been scrupulously observed. The committee has considered all the Australian properties to have outstanding universal value.

The committee itself was also confronted with Australia's federal frictions. In 1987 and 1988 a Territory and a State applied for permission to participate in the proceedings of the committee. The committee maintained the principle that member states are represented in international organisations by their national governments and that where member states have federal systems of government it is not possible for the constituent states, provinces, Lander, cantons and territories to participate. Representatives of the constituent units can watch proceedings as members of the public. Australians are grateful for the patience and skill which the members of the committee have brought to the discussion of Australian nominations.

In the middle of 1983 the Australian Parliament passed *The World Heritage Properties Conservation Act*. The supreme judicial body in Australia, the High Court, had to decide challenges by two States and a Territory to nominations by the Australian Government. At first the High Court rejected these challenges by a majority of four justices to three but later the Court rejected them unaminously. Early in 1988 the Chief Justice observed: 'Entry of a property in the World Heritage List, supported by the protection given by the Act, constitutes perhaps the strongest means of environment protection recognised by Australian law'.

Thus the Australian Government's fruitful membership of the World Heritage Committee and its successful submissions to the High Court of Australia throughout the 1980s have performed a remarkable educative process in relation to heritage and environment issues in the sixth largest country in the world. Further sites are now being harmoniously nominated.

In the middle of 1983 I was appointed the Australian permanent delegate to UNESCO. At that time no state party to the World Heritage Convention was geographically closer to Australia than India. It has to be recognised that states remote from the capitals of the UN system are often slow to participate in the international organisations in those capitals. Nevertheless, very largely as a result of the attention which the World Conservation Union and the World Heritage Committee have given to Australian nominations, the World Heritage Convention has attracted 13 more states parties in the Asia and Pacific region, Bangladesh (1983), New Zealand (1984), Philippines and China (1985), Maldives (1986), Laos, Thailand and Viet Nam (1987), ROK and Malaysia (1988), Indonesia (1989), Mongolia and Fiji (1990).

The convention now has 121 states parties. It is the only convention which requires a state party to make a financial contribution over and above the contribution which it must make to the organisation which draws up the convention. The United States remained a state party and the United Kingdom became a state party after they ceased to be

Uluru (Ayers Rock)

Great Barrier Reef – Double Island

Misty Queensland rainforest

member states of UNESCO; both continued to nominate sites for the World Heritage List and to seek election to the World Heritage Committee. The only conventions which have secured a greater number of ratifications and accessions are the four 1949 Red Cross Geneva Conventions with 164 members and the 1965 UN Racial Discrimination Convention with 129.

There are now 360 properties on the World Heritage List. Two Australian properties have been expanded. Kakadu National Park, inscribed in 1981, was extended to include Stage II in 1987. In the case of Western Tasmania Wilderness National Parks, inscribed in 1982, the committee in 1989 approved the site being extended by 78% in area and re-named 'Tasmanian Wilderness'.

Having chaired two sessions of the General Assembly and having served many times on the committee, I have had great opportunities to assess and admire the achievements of the states parties, the committee, the international public servants in UNESCO and the experts in the advisory bodies in identifying, preserving and presenting the world's cultural and natural heritage and transmitting it to future generations. The present generation has produced no finer landmark than the World Heritage Convention.

GOUGH WHITLAM, AC, QC, former Prime Minister of Australia (1972-1975), was Australian permanent delegate to UNESCO from 1983 to 1986 and member of the UNESCO Executive Board from 1985 to 1989. He was made a Member of Honour of the World Conservation Union in 1988.

Kakadu National Park

Cradle Mountain, part of the Tasmanian Wilderness

We Walked in Wilderness and Shone a Bright Light

IT WAS THE MORNING OF January 17th 1983, the last day of the 49th year of my life. The sweet rain which makes South West Tasmania what it is, a wonderland of Temperate Rain Forest had stopped. I looked out from my tent as a Wallaby bounded away through the wet undergrowth. It was time for me to go and get arrested and the reason why was all around me: Sassafras, Leatherwood and Myrtle steaming in the sun, a 360° panorama of untouched wilderness. A Pink-breasted Pigeon rose with me to meet the challenge of the day.

One hundred and sixty three days later – On Friday 1st July 1983, the High Court of Australia ruled that the Commonwealth Government had the power to stop the Gordon-below-Franklin dam. Within days the bulldozers and trucks were being dragged back to Strahan on barges that had only months earlier forced their way through our fragile lines of protest.

Thus reads the epilogue of the Franklin Blockade, written by the Blockaders and published by the Wilderness Society of Australia.

Thus ended an epic chapter in the story of World Heritage, for without the determination and dedication of the 2613 people who came to the town of Strahan in a remote corner of S.W. Tasmania, and the 1272 of us who were arrested during the Franklin River Blockade, the living heart of a critically important area of World Heritage would have been lost forever.

This is a brief timetable of the action which thrust the cause of World Heritage firmly into the arena of international politics.

16th June 1982 – Despite mounting public opposition in Tasmania, Australia and across the globe the Gordon River Hydro-Electric Power Development Bill was passed by the Tasmanian Government. The Hydro-Electric Commission (H.E.C.) could legally commence work to destroy Australia's last wild river.

26th July – at press conferences in Hobart and Melbourne, announcements were made by the Wilderness Society that the proposed dam site would be blockaded. Liaison with senior police officers commenced.

2nd September – large tracts of land were revoked from Wild Rivers National Park and were vested in the H.E.C.

16th September – Tasmanian Premier Gray threatened to secede from the Commonwealth if the Federal Government intervened to stop the work on the Gordon-below-Franklin dam.

13th November – Wilderness Society meeting agreed that a blockade on the dam site would begin on 14th December if the Federal Government refused to intervene and stop the dam. 15,000 people *walk for wilderness* in Melbourne.

24th November – in response to the Blockade plans the Tasmanian Government changed the Police Offences Act so that trespassing would be an arrestable offence.

4th December – in the Flinders by-election in the nearby State of Victoria, 40.04% of all the electorate wrote *NO DAMS* on their ballot papers.

8th December – despite its great track record in conservation the Government of Malcolm Fraser said it would not intervene with the dam.

14th December – South West Tasmania was given World Heritage Status as the Australian Democrats World Heritage Protection Bill was passed. As promised, the blockade swung into action – 53 people were arrested, 46 refused to accept bail conditions not to return to the H.E.C. land and were remanded in Risdon Gaol, Hobart.

16th December – Dr Bob Brown, spokesperson of the Tasmanian Wilderness Society was arrested and remanded in custody.

1st January 1983 – Bob Brown was voted Australian of the Year.

5th January – Bob Brown became a member of the Tasmanian State parliament.

12th January – rocks were hurled through the windows of the Wilderness Society's information centre in Strahan and their telephone and telex cables were cut, radio equipment was jammed, public telephones in Queenstown and Strahan were mysteriously out of order. The road to the main blockade camp was blocked by police cars and any protesters who attempted to pass were arrested. Eighty police escorted the first bulldozer into Strahan. Attempts to blockade failed as protesters were pulled from beneath the moving wheels of the low loader and were arrested.

13th January – the bulldozer left Strahan at dawn on a barge. At Butler Island at the entrance of the disputed area the boat broke through a blockade of duckies (tiny rubber boats) without slowing down and passed over a submerged diver in flagrant disregard of the Divers Flag. 54 people were arrested in the day's actions. Bob Brown was attacked in Strahan by Queenstown youths.

Prime Minister Fraser offered Tasmania $500 million to stop the scheme, Premier Gray declined the offer.

17th February – the thousandth arrest took place at one of the drill sites.

2nd March – the oldest blockader was arrested, she was 79.

5th March – a Federal Government committed to stopping the dam was elected to power.

Great Barrier Reef

Ringtail Possum – Daintree River, Queensland Wet Tropics

5th May – the World Heritage (Properties Conservation) Bill was passed in the House of Representatives.

18th May – in Hobart all charges of trespass were dropped.

I was just one of those people who walked in wilderness and so helped shine the light of Heritage across the world.

DAVID BELLAMY
Bedburn, 1991

The lagoon area, Lord Howe Island

EAST COAST TEMPERATE AND SUB-TROPICAL RAINFOREST PARKS

LOCATION   Eastern coastal regions of New South Wales, S 28° to 37°, E 150° to 154°.

DESCRIPTION   This listing is composed of 7 separate groups of rainforest sites scattered over a large area of the east coast; 1. Tweed Volcano Group; 2. Washpool/ Gibraltar Range Group; 3. Iluka Nature Reserve; 4. New England Group; 5. Hastings Group; 6. Barrington Tops National Park; 7. Mount Dromedary Flora Reserve.

SIGNIFICANCE   Rainforests are especially significant in a dry continent such as Australia, where they occupy a small but significant niche in the vegetation landscape. The great diversity of microclimates within rainforests sustains a large range of species. Over 350 trees and shrub species are found in these New South Wales rainforests, many of them endemic to these areas. The animal population is also extremely diverse, marsupials such as the mountain brushtail possum, reptiles like the southern angle-headed dragon, along with numerous species of frogs, fish and invertebrates. 37 species of bats have been recorded in New South Wales rainforests making them an extremely important habitat for these animals.

KAKADU NATIONAL PARK

LOCATION   S 13° 00', E 132° 30'.

DESCRIPTION   On the western fringe of the Arnhem Land plateau, Kakadu covers a massive area of over 6,000sq km (2,344sq mi). The landscape varies from the rugged sandstone of the plateau, down to the lowlands with its red soil and light tree cover and further on to the black-soiled flood plains, muddy tidal flats and mangrove estuaries.

SIGNIFICANCE   The strange and awesome beauty of this ancient land is striking. It is home to some of the most important Australian Aboriginal art, with its 'Mimi' and 'X-Ray' style cave paintings. Some of these date back 18,000 years, making them contemporary with the renowned Palaeolithic cave paintings of Europe. The flora and fauna are extremely rich in their diversity with over 41 species of mammals, 250 of birds, 75 of reptiles, 45 of fish and 10,000 of insects found in the area. More than a quarter of Australia's bird species are found here.

LORD HOWE ISLAND GROUP

LOCATION   Approximately 700km (435mi) northeast of Sydney, S 31° 30' to 31° 50', E 159° 00' to 159° 17'.

DESCRIPTION   This listing consists of Lord Howe Island, Ball's Pyramid, the Admiralty Islands and associated islets. All are the eroded remnants of a volcano.

They rise from a seafloor which is over 2,000m (6,562ft) deep. The area of the islands is around 1,540ha (3,713ac), Lord Howe itself is 1,455ha (3,508ac). All are owned by the New South Wales Government.

SIGNIFICANCE   Considered to be an outstanding example of an island group formed from volcanic activity, these islands are also spectacularly beautiful. They harbour a great diversity of rare and endemic species, both flora and fauna, and encapsulate a great diversity of landscapes. Another feature of significance is the reef, which is the most southern coral reef in the world.

GREAT BARRIER REEF

LOCATION   Off the east coast of the State of Queensland, S 24° 30' to 10° 41', E 142° 30' to 154° 00'.

DESCRIPTION   The Great Barrier Reef comprises approximately 2,000km (1,243mi) of broken coral reefs (around 2,500 separate reefs), covering an area of 348,700sq km (136,210sq mi). There are 71 coral islands, or cays scattered throughout its length. The coral is composed of calcium carbonate, being the remains of plant and animal material.

SIGNIFICANCE   The Great Barrier Reef is the world's largest and most complex expanse of living coral reefs. The area is of enormous scientific importance because of the great diversity in life forms. There are over 1,500 species of fish, 400 species of coral, 242 species of birds (109 of which have recorded breeding sites in the area), 6 species of turtles (including the green and loggerhead turtles which have crucial nesting sites within the reef area) along with many other animal groups. Also of importance are the wide range of algae and seagrasses found throughout the reef. The reef is of considerable historical significance to the Aboriginals and Torres Strait Islanders of the area. There are several important sites, notably on Lizard, Hinchinbrook, Stanley, Cliff and Clack Islands. Also of historical importance are the 30 odd ship wrecks dating from 1791.

ULURU NATIONAL PARK

LOCATION   Southwest corner of the Northern Territory, S 25° 20', E 131° 00'.

DESCRIPTION   This park is 132,566ha (319,617ac) of arid desert in the heart of Australia. It is owned by the Uluru-Katatjuta Aboriginal Land Trust and leased by the Director of National Parks and Wildlife for use as a national park. The huge monoliths found at Uluru (Ayers Rock) and Katatjuta (the Olgas) are remarkable geological features and stand in stark contrast to the surrounding flat sand plain environment.

SIGNIFICANCE   One of the most famous landmarks in Australia, Uluru is an awe inspiring sight. It is no sur-

Katatjuta (the Olgas)

prise that it has been a place of great mystical significance to the Aboriginals for tens of thousands of years. There are hundreds of painting sites around the base of 'the Rock' and a number of ancient rock engravings. 4 secret sacred sites are fenced off and protected by special legislation. Environmentally, the park is extremely important in protecting several unique desert ecosystems.

TASMANIAN WILDERNESS

LOCATION   Central and southwestern regions of Tasmania, E 145° 25′ to 146° 55′, S 41° 35′ to 43° 40′.

DESCRIPTION   This site is composed of numerous areas, including many islands, totalling a massive 1,374,000ha (3,312,714ac). There are a wide range of landscapes, geological features, vegetation and several important archaeological sites.

SIGNIFICANCE   In stark contrast to much of mainland Australia, the area covered by this listing is extremely rugged. There is much evidence of glacial activity which has created a myriad of high lakes (including the deepest lake in Australia, Lake St. Clair), steep gorges and fast running rivers. The unusual vegetation is a result both of the unique geological conditions and the cool wet climate. There are several ancient species, relics of bygone eras, like the Gondwanan conifers known only in this area. There are vast tracts of pristine rainforest as well as many unique examples of alpine vegetation, eucalypt forests, wet sclerophyll communities and many varieties of grassland. Notable amongst all this is the mountain ash, the world's tallest flowering plant, forming a towering 90m (295ft) canopy over the wet sclerophyll understorey. The area is also of great cultural significance, with some 37 cave sites showing human settlements up to 30,000 years old. One of the most valuable prehistoric sites in Australia is Kutikina Cave, one of the first Aboriginal sites where Ice Age occupation was recognised. Judd's Cavern is one of the largest river caves in Australia and is richly decorated with rock art dating from the Ice Age.

WET TROPICS OF QUEENSLAND

LOCATION   Northeastern coastal region of Queensland, S 15° 39′ to 19° 17′, E 144° 58′ to 146° 27′.

DESCRIPTION   Extending from just south of Cooktown to north of Townsville, there is around 7,000sq km (2,734sq mi) of tropical rainforest incorporated within the 9,200sq km (3,594sq mi) of this listing. This represents 90 percent of the total area of wet tropical rainforest in northeast Australia. The geographic range of this region is extremely diverse and subsequently the rainforests here are the most diverse in Australia. From the wet, mist covered and wind blown forests of the Bellenden Ker Range, down to the highly developed forests of the wet lowlands, the landscape is spectacular and harbours a rich array of rare and unusual plant species.

SIGNIFICANCE   This area contains the oldest continuously surviving rainforests on earth. Rainforests only cover 0.2 percent of the total area of Australia – this amounts to around 20,000sq km (8,000sq mi). Almost 30 percent of that total is incorporated in this listing. It is estimated that some 50 to 100 million years ago, the entire continent was covered with vegetation similar to that found in these forests today. Some of the more striking plants found in these forests include the beautiful and unusual fan palm; many different types of Proteaceae – at least 13 different types out of a world total of 36; over 90 species of orchids, many found in very limited areas; one of the largest cycads in the world, as well as one of the smallest, and the richest concentration of ferns to be found in Australia.

WILLANDRA LAKES REGION

LOCATION   Murray Basin, southwestern New South Wales, S 33° 00′, E 144° 00′.

DESCRIPTION   Around 6,000sq km (2,400sq mi) in area, this region incorporates a system of dry lakes which used to be fed from a tributary of the Lachlan River called Willandra Billabong Creek. There are several pastoral leases operating actively within the region, one of which was acquired by the New South Wales Government and is permanently reserved as Mungo National Park.

SIGNIFICANCE   This area has been the source of several important archaeological discoveries, including a 30,000 year old burial site, a 26,000 year old cremation site and 18,000 year old grinding stones. Further evidence points to human settlement up to 40,000 years old. Research here has determined that the earth's magnetic field was once at variance 120 degrees with today's field, so the area has importance for world studies of changes in earth magnetism. This is also a site of natural significance in that it is a pristine example of a semi-arid environment, unmodified by glacial or sea-level changes.

'Mungo's Lunette', Willandra Lakes

An Urgent Call to Replenish the Earth

ONE OF THE SCIENTISTS who discovered the relationship between chlorofluorocarbons and the depletion of the ozone layer is reported to have gone home one night and told his wife, 'The work is going well, but it looks like the end of the world'. There is extraordinary unanimity amongst ecologists as to the catastrophic effects of human activity on the life-support systems of the world. Their work is going well, but their predictions are dire. They see the world as a Titanic on a collision course. A cartoon summing up the tangled opinions of non-scientists on population growth, resource depletion, environmental deterioration and world poverty reads, 'Eventually we will run out of food to feed ourselves and air to breathe … this is something we must learn to live with!'.

There is something radically wrong with the way we are living on Earth today. The sort of society we are building with the aid of science and technology has built-in, self-destructive features.

That there are limits to the resources of the Earth and the capacity of the Earth to cope with pollution of its waters and atmosphere, has led to what is known as the 'imposibility theorem'. This states that the high rates of consumption and pollution of the rich nations would be impossible for all the peoples of the earth. This notion poses a problem of real justice. Can those who live in the rich world morally justify a way of life which would be impossible for the rest to enjoy?

The rich must live more simply so that the poor may simply live.

The ecological message is clear. Our basic task is to reduce as rapidly as possible the impact of humanity on the earth's life-support systems. That impact has three components: population, per capita consumption of resources (affluence), and the environmental damage caused by technologies used to support that affluence. It follows that to reduce this human impact we must reduce population, reduce consumption and change certain technologies such as eliminating chlorofluorocarbons.

The population problem is not primarily one of the poor world but of the rich world. It is not the crude number of people or population density that should concern us. It is the impact of people on the life-support systems and resources of the planet. The impact per person of the rich world is something like 60 times that of a person in the poor world. It is the rich world that is creating a lethal situation for the entire world. It is the rich who dump most of the carbondioxide and chlorofluorocarbons into the atmosphere. It is the rich who generate acid rain. And the rich are 'strip-mining' the seas of fish and pushing the world towards a major fisheries collapse. The agricultural technology of the rich is destroying soils, and draining supplies of underground water around the globe. And it is the rich who are wood-chipping forests to wrap around their electronic products.

It is not only the basis of human life that is being destroyed by our activities. We are annihilating at least one thousand species who share the planet with us each year. This is nothing less than a holocaust of nature. Total spiritual confusion prevails in the modern world about the relationship of humanity to nature in a technological culture. Churches and theologians, intimidated by secular culture, leave that task to others.

Our way of life is tied to an anthropocentric ethic that sees the non-human world as simply the stage on which the drama of human life is performed. All other creatures have no more than instrumental value to us. What is now urgently called for is a biocentric ethic that sees in all life some intrinsic value. Sentience or the capacity for feeling gives lives intrinsic value. This is true not only of us but of other living creatures.

A great achievement of the Enlightenment was to build a theory of human rights which made possible enormous advances towards social justice. A great achievement of our time could be to extend the concepts of compassion, rights and justice to all living creatures, in the practice of a biocentric ethic. Yet the advocacy of Western religious thought is most weak precisely here, where the ache of the world is most strong. The whole of creation cries out in agony for its liberation.

Every nation desperately needs to discover a vision of the future. Is all that matters increased GNP, reduced inflation and reduced overseas debt? Instead of measuring national health in terms of economic growth we could set our eyes on a more worthy goal. There is indeed such a goal that all could aspire to. It is for healthy (whole) people in a healthy environment with healthy relations to that environment, which includes the non-human creatures who share the earth with us.

Are we willing to pay the price of the redemption of that part of the earth we inhabit in terms of a revolution in values, in life styles, in economic and political goals and even in the nature of the science and technology we practise? The stage is set. Whether the play can be performed before the theatre burns down remains to be seen.

CHARLES BIRCH
Emeritus Professor, University of Sydney

Shait Gumbad Mosque at Bagerhat

BANGLADESH

Bangladesh was formed at the end of 1971 when the former province of East Pakistan seceded from the Pakistan Republic. This entire region has been known throughout antiquity as Bengal ('Bangladesh' means 'land of the Bengals').

Bengal's early history can be traced back to the 3rd century BC, when Asoka ruled the Maurya empire. The next millennium saw repeated invasions by various empires along with intermittent periods of anarchy, until the latter part of the 8th century AD, when the Palas came to power.

The Pala dynasty ruled for over three hundred years and are perhaps the most renowned of the region's rulers. This was an era of enlightenment and cultural advancement; the Palas were Buddhist and numerous monasteries and shrines were erected during their reign. One of these monasteries, Paharpur, survives today. It is one of two sites which are now on the World Heritage List after the Convention was accepted by Bangladesh in August 1983.

The second Bangladesh site is the mosque city at Bagerhat, a large ensemble of monuments from the 550 year period of Muslim rule. The Moguls, as the Muslim rulers were known, came at the turn of the 13th century and retained power until the conquest of the British in 1757.

RUINS OF THE BUDDHIST VIHARA AT PAHARPUR

LOCATION   Paharpur, northeast corner of Naogaon sub division, N 25° 02′, E 88° 59′.

DESCRIPTION   A very large brick monastery with outer walls, spreading over 9ha (22ac), now in ruins and partly underground. Over 60 stone sculptures are hidden underground, set into the base of the central shrine which rises to a height of about 20m (65.5ft).

SIGNIFICANCE   It is thought that this monastery, known as 'Somapura Mahavihara', dates from the end of the 8th century AD, when it was founded by Dharmapala, the second Pala monarch. Control of the monastery was wrested from the Palas roughly 100 years later by the Gurjara-Pratiharas. This lasted for another 100 years until the Palas gained control again. They ruled until the 12th century, when the Senas, who were Hindus, gained control. From this time, the monastery slowly declined until being abandoned. These ruins

The Vihara at Paharpur

were discovered and recognised as important at the beginning of the 19th century and were placed on the list of protected monuments roughly 100 years later.

THE HISTORIC MOSQUE CITY OF BAGERHAT

LOCATION   Immediately east of Bagerhat in the district of Khulna.

DESCRIPTION   There are more than 50 monuments scattered over an area of 6.5sq km (2.5sq mi). While there is a conservation program in place, at the moment most are in an advanced state of ruin and are overgrown with tropical vegetation. 8 mosques and 1 tomb complex have been clearly identified under this listing: 1. Shait-Gumbad Mosque; 2. Singar Mosque; 3. Bibi Begni's Mosque; 4. Chunakhola Mosque; 5. Khan Jahan's Tomb Complex; 6. Nine-Domed Mosque; 7. Reza-Koda Mosque; 8. Zindapir Mosque; 9. Ranvijoypur Mosque.

SIGNIFICANCE   Having been the city responsible for minting coins of the Independent Sultans of Bengal, these ruins bear witness to the accumulated wealth of Bagerhat. The Shait-Gumbad Mosque in particular reflects this past glory – it is the largest brick construction temple in Bangladesh, and one of the most impressive in the region.

One generation passeth away, and another generation cometh but the earth abideth forever. The sun also ariseth and the sun goeth down, and hasteth to his place where he arose. All the rivers run into the sea, yet the sea is not full; unto the place from whence the rivers come, thither they return again.

ECCLESIASTES

BENIN

With an area of 117,000 sq km (44,600 sq mi), Benin is, by African standards, a small country. However, the diversity of its population and cultures, as well as its vegetation, landscapes, fauna and flora, is enormous.

The people of Benin are members of several tribes, the dominant one being the Fon, who are also known as Abomey or Dahomey. These people founded the first kingdom in the area, according to tradition, in 1625 AD. Three kingdoms were eventually established, those of Abomey, Allada and Porto Nova.

These kingdoms were exceptionally powerful and wealthy, due mainly to the slave trade which was initiated by the Portugese in the 16th century and further consolidated by the British and French in the 17th and 18th centuries.

After defeating the Abomey at the end of the 19th century, France claimed the region as a protectorate. Independence from France was gained in 1960.

The Fon have a rich cultural heritage and a complex mythology, along with many advanced artistic and musical achievements. There is also a complex system of rituals and customs, many of which were described by Sir Richard Burton in his famous work 'A Mission to Gelele, King of Dahame'.

The sole World Heritage listing from Benin is the Royal Palaces of Abomey - a fascinating testament to this remarkable culture. Benin ratified the World Heritage Convention in June 1982.

ROYAL PALACES OF ABOMEY

LOCATION   Zou Province.

DESCRIPTION   The ruins of the 12 Royal Palaces of Abomey are to be found on this site which spreads over 40ha (96ac) right in the centre of the present day town of Abomey. There are 2 zones, both surrounded by partially preserved walls; the zone which contains Akaba Palace and another to the southeast which contains the balance of the palaces.

SIGNIFICANCE   The Kingdom of Abomey ruled for almost 300 years, from 1625 to 1900, with a succession of 12 kings. It was one of the most powerful kingdoms on the west coast of Africa with high levels of economic and military power and consequently, quite remarkable political stability. These ruins provide an important record of this once great kingdom.

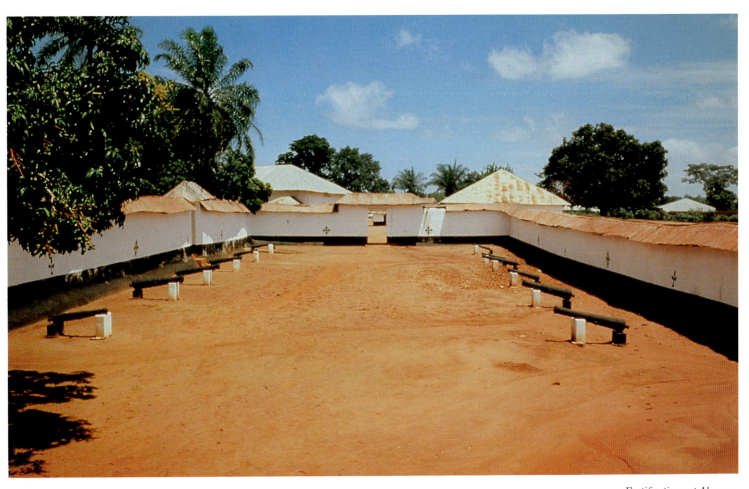

Fortifications at Abomey

Fon artwork on display

BOLIVIA

Bolivia is a land-locked republic of central South America. It is unusual in that the majority of its population inhabits the highest 30% of the country – a dry and barren treeless plateau which sits high up in the Andes.

This area was part of the great Inca empire which was conquered by the Spanish in the 16th century. Today Bolivia has, proportionally, the highest indigenous population on the continent – nearly 70% are pure blood Indians.

Soon after the Spanish conquest, the economic importance of mining came to the fore. Potosi was founded in 1545 after the discovery of immense silver deposits there. It grew into the largest and wealthiest city of the New World. Today Potosi is still a mining town; it is also one of Bolivia's two World Heritage sites.

The second site, which was inscribed on the World Heritage List only in 1991, is the Jesuit Missions of the Chiquitos. This site, along with those missions in Argentina and Brazil, preserves the unique attempt which was made by the Jesuits to establish self-supporting communities for the Indians who were otherwise severely exploited and abused. Bolivia ratified the World Heritage Convention in October 1976.

JESUIT MISSIONS OF THE CHIQUITOS

LOCATION   Department of Santa Cruz, S 16° 00' to 18° 00', W 60° 30' to 62° 40'.

DESCRIPTION   This broad listing includes the towns of San Javier, Concepción, Santa Ana, San Miguel, San Rafaél and San José. All towns are connected by roads and there are some railway connections as well. The average altitude of this area is around 500 metres (1,665ft). These towns are a development of Jesuit missions which were founded on the sites in the 17th and 18th centuries.

SIGNIFICANCE   These missions were founded after explorations by the Jesuits who founded the missions in Paraguay. San Javier was the first to be established in 1669, the others followed in the 18th century. Only indigenous peoples were allowed into these specially protected areas and so they enjoyed substantial political and religious independence. These missions present a unique testimony to the significant social and cultural advancements that were made here.

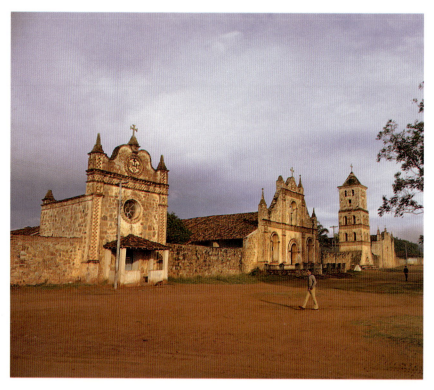

San José, Jesuit Missions of the Chiquitos

CITY OF POTOSI

LOCATION   In the Andes, S 19° 30', W 65° 30'.

DESCRIPTION   At 4,100m (13,451ft) above sea level, Potosi is one of the highest cities in the world. It stands in the shadow of the Cerro Rico (Silver Mountain). The modern town retains much of its colonial charm with the central square and numerous imposing buildings. One of the more important of these is La Casa Real de la Moneda, one of the largest public buildings in South America. The mining fields contain over 5,000 separate mines, 22 dams and over 130 crushing systems.

SIGNIFICANCE   According to legend, Potosi takes its name from 'Potojchi', meaning 'thunder' – a reference to rumblings inside the mountain. Silver was first discovered in 1542 and the city was founded soon after. The silver deposits here were massive: it soon became a common expression to say 'as rich as Potosi'. This enormous wealth generated a richness of architecture which is evident today in this magnificent city.

The aesthetic value of creation cannot be overlooked, our very contact with nature has a deep, restorative power. Contemplation of its magnificence impacts peace and serenity. A new ecological awareness is beginning to emerge, which, rather than being downplayed, ought to be encouraged to develop into concrete programs and initiatives.

POPE JOHN PAUL II

City of Potosi

Conservation in an Age of Confluence

UNPRECEDENTED CHANGES in the world's political landscape, begun in the late 1980s, have irreversibly altered the course of human history. Entire societies are changing direction, and millions of people have embarked on a promising path toward self-determination. For the first time since mid-century, the risk of nuclear war between the United States and the Soviet Union has diminished. As nations abandon the polarisation of the Cold War era, many leaders advocate new forms of common security based on economic integration and wise use of the environment.

The political and social events captured in daily headlines are signs of a deeper transformation, the consequences of which will affect all future generations. The extraordinary changes in human societies are flowing together with more ominous changes in the natural systems of the biosphere, altering both the character of the Earth and the palette of human possibilities.

This confluence of changes dictates a new agenda, and an integrated approach to the challenges of conservation and development. Conservation in the 1990s calls for approaches that blend economics and ecology, strategies as dynamic as the social, economic, and cultural settings in which natural ecosystems are entangled.

The urgency of conservation in this age of confluence rests on a simple observation: the forces rending the fabric of the planet itself are not as easily reversed as outmoded ideologies. None of the changes underway pose a more fundamental challenge than the biological diversity crisis – the accelerating loss of plant and animal species due to the global impact of human activities. Primary concern focuses on tropical rain forests in Africa, the Asia-Pacific region, and the neotropics, with their extraordinary share – two thirds or more – of all species on Earth. But the long shadow of mass extinction falls across every ecosystem, from Arctic tundra to intricate food webs in Antarctic seas.

Population growth continues on its troubling trajectory. Now at more than 5.3 billion, human numbers are expanding by 85 million each year, the largest annual increment ever. Demographers agree that the population will reach at least 10 billion before stabilising. Ninety-five percent of the next 5 billion will be added in developing countries – where poverty is deepest, soils are most difficult to work, economies are already burdened by debt, and the limits of social cohesion and ecological resilience are stretched by today's populations.

The world economy, in the midst of a transition to global integration that is not yet widely understood, is weighted with imbalances that threaten society's ability to cope with change. The external debt of developing countries – debt that has now grown far past US$1 trillion – stalls economic progress in the regions that need it most. Two major regions of the world, Africa and the neotropics, grew steadily poorer during the 1980s. More affluent regions, themselves burdened with troubling debts and financial imbalances, show little inclination to tackle the essential adjustments that new conditions demand.

The global atmosphere itself is being redesigned by human activities. As carbon dioxide and a range of synthetic gases released by power generation, deforestation, and commerce accumulate, the way Earth captures the sun's heat is affected. Droughts, floods, hurricanes of unusual intensity, and recent sweltering summers in the northern hemisphere have offered a mild foretaste of what scientists believe these global changes portend.

Conservation in this age of confluence faces enormous challenges. The conservation community must pioneer a new relationship between humanity and the Earth, one responsive to inevitable changes but seeking always to broaden economic and ecological possibilities.

Throughout most of its history, conservation has in effect been a 'museum' science, dedicated to defending undisturbed natural areas against external threats and pressures. The confluence of global changes demands a more strategic, experimental philosophy that seeks to integrate natural systems and human communities. Engagement with the forces of social and economic change has become essential.

The human relationship with the Earth's natural systems can and must be changed. The doubling of the human population and the transformation of the atmosphere are not abstractions, but realities of our time. At the threshold of a new millennium, we stand before a very different sort of world.

Most of the flow of ecological knowledge between industrial and developing countries has so far been one-way. Agriculture in the tropics, for instance, has been patterned on practices designed in Europe and North America. As a result, tropical ecosystems have been transformed by the misapplication of concepts developed for temperate zone conditions. In recent years, the misguided arrogance of this approach has become abundantly clear.

Is it possible that the reverse might be more fruitful? That approaches to conservation and regional development pioneered in the fragile ecosystems of the tropics might set an example of humility and attention to local conditions sufficient to restore balance to the relation between humanity and nature in the industrial societies of the

Salvador de Bahia

BRAZIL

Brazil accepted the World Heritage Convention in September 1977 and now has six sites inscribed on the World Heritage List. It is an enormous country, occupying almost half of the South American continent. The reason for its size is simply that, unlike the former Spanish colonies, the Portuguese colonies united into one country after independence.

This is a vibrant country, with large sprawling cities, extensive agricultural areas, numerous sizeable rivers, great expanses of white sandy beaches and the largest area of virgin rainforest in the world.

Portugal claimed Brazil, or 'Vera Cruz' (True Cross) as it was initially named, when it was sighted by Pedro Cabral on April 22, 1500. Colonial rule lasted some 300 years until Brazil gained independence early in the 19th century.

Of Brazil's six World Heritage sites, four relate to the country's colonial era – Olinda, Ouro Prêto and Salvador de Bahia are all old colonial towns, while the Sanctuary of Bom Jesus de Congonhas is an 18th century church with a remarkable rococo interior.

The two remaining sites include Brazil's largest National Park, Iguaçu – an enormous expanse of rainforest – and the modern capital city of Brasilia – a remarkable example of modern architectural planning.

temperate zone, indeed in the world as a whole?

CONSERVATION INTERNATIONAL is a Washington, D.C. based organisation created in 1987 to support local capacity to conserve threatened ecosystems and biological diversity worldwide. In 1990, CI launched 'The Rain Forest Imperative', a ten-year strategy to conserve the richest and most threatened forest ecosystems on Earth. This ambitious plan emphasises 15 rain forest 'hotspots' and three major tropical wilderness areas. CI works in biosphere reserves including La Amistad Biosphere Reserve in Costa Rica, the Beni Biosphere Reserve in Bolivia, and the Maya Biosphere Reserve in Guatemala.

Iguaçu Falls

Ouro Prêto, Brazil's City of Black Gold

THE PROBLEMS OF reconciling the traditional and the modern are raised in particularly acute form at Ouro Prêto, a historic city in Brazil's Minas Gerais state which is today surrounded by an industrial zone and lies on an important highway.

Ouro Prêto (Portuguese for 'Black Gold') grew out of a mining settlement which developed on the lower slope of the Serra do Ouro Prêto in the early eighteenth century when miners flocked into the region to prospect for gold. In 1711 it was given the status of a city and the name of Vila Rica. It is said that many houses used the entrances to mine shafts as their cellars.

In this rugged setting, narrow crooked streets and alleys were built along the mountain spur without any overall plan. The central square, today known as the Praça Tiradentes after a hero of Brazil's independence struggle, was not built until the mid eighteenth century. Around it stand the old colonial governor's palace, the town hall and the colonial penitentiary.

The houses of varying height, are strung haphazardly along steep, winding streets. Their picturesque beauty charms visitors and leads them from one surprise to another. The French specialist Michel Parent has described how, 'this straggling urban fabric reveals itself gradually to the eye, which slowly comes to dominate it, bringing together near and far, narrow streets set deep in the valley, a bell-tower atop a distant hill... It does not have the obvious advantage of a magnificent site, its beauty is at first hinted at, then becomes elusive, before finally yielding itself to the visitor'.

The mid-eighteenth century was the period of Ouro Prêto's greatest splendour, thanks to the abundance of gold which brought it wealth. The houses dating from that period were built in dressed stone. Decorated with a profusion of friezes and scrollwork, their architecture is more elaborate than the others. Many of these buildings are in Conde-Bobadela street and on the Praça Tiradentes, where the Casa dos Contos, the governor's palace, and the town hall are notable for the elegance and force of their late baroque style.

The religious architecture of Ouro Prêto is also remarkable for its originality, diversity and quality. Some of the buildings are among the most beautiful examples of baroque art in the world.

On either side of the spur of rock topped by the Praça Tiradentes are the Carmelite church of Our Lady and the church of St Francis of Assisi. The architect and sculptor of these two churches was Antonio Francisco Lisbôa, better known as 'O Aleijadinho' ('the little cripple'). The church of St Francis, which dates from 1764, was Aleijadinho's first project and his masterwork. It is remarkable for an ingenious combination of curves and ellipses, as well as the composition, of an astonishing expressive force, of the frontispiece carved in 'pedra-sabâo' (a kind of alabaster).

Problems of growth

Ouro Prêto was the seat of the military government and then the capital of Minas Gerais until the state administration was transferred to the new city of Belo Horizonte in 1897. As a result of this change in status and the exhaustion of its gold deposits, the city went into decline. If Ouro Prêto today still has a certain vitality, it is because of its position as a university city. When it was classified as a historic monument in 1938, it was living in the past. The city had virtually ceased to grow, and conservation activity was limited to religious and civic buildings.

In the 1950s, an aluminium plant was built at nearby Saramenha, and the highway between Saramenha and Bela Horizonte was metalled. Population growth and economic activity suddenly picked up again. Road traffic also sharply increased, largely because of the heavy trucks serving the Saramenha complex. This development threatened one of Brazil's finest jewels, and the institution responsible for its safeguard asked UNESCO to provide technical support for Ouro Prêto.

In 1966 international specialists carried out studies with a view to defining possible zones of development, reducing demographic growth and preserving the old city. Their proposals were taken up and worked out in greater detail by a team of Brazilian technicians acting under the auspices of the federal, provincial and municipal authorities. A number of measures were adopted, including the construction of a new road around the site and a bus station outside the historic centre so that buses and coaches do not need to park on or near the Praça Tiradentes. Trucks and other heavy-duty vehicles are not allowed in the city, where a new urbanisation zone is being created. Slopes subject to landslides are being consolidated. In 1979 a geological map was made of the whole urban area in order to indicate zones which can be built on without risk.

In December 1980, Ouro Prêto was included on UNESCO's World Heritage List.

AUGUSTO C. DA SILVA TELLES, Brazilian architect and historian, has been involved in the safeguarding of Ouro Prêto in his capacity as technical consultant to Brazil's Institute of the National Historical and Artistic Heritage. The author of many studies on Portuguese and Brazilian architecture, he was chairman of UNESCO's World Heritage Committee in 1988 and 1989.

Reprinted from the *Unesco Courier,* March 1991

Ouro Prêto

Salvador de Bahia

The National Cathedral, Brasilia

Olinda

BRASILIA

LOCATION   Territory of the Federal District, S 15° 30' to 16° 03', W 47° 25' to 48° 12'.

DESCRIPTION   Brasilia is a modern city of around 1 million people and sits up on the central plateau. Its numerous features include several important buildings such as the Alverado Palace, the Planalto Palace, the twin towered Congress Building and the National Cathedral. There are 3 important parks, the National Park of Brasilia, the Biological Reserve of Aguas Emendodas and the Botanical Gardens of Cabeja de Veado. Just outside the modern city are some old villages which also form an important part of this listing.

SIGNIFICANCE   The federal capital of Brazil is a new city with an old history. The search for a suitable site for a future capital was instigated in 1789 by an independence movement. When the Republic was founded 100 years later, the founding of a capital on the interior plateau was set down in the constitution. The site was finally chosen in 1956 and was the result of very careful deliberations. 1957 saw a national design competition which was won by Lucio Costa. The seat of government was moved there in 1960 and Oscar Niemeyer was commissioned to design the first major government buildings. Brasilia is now considered a masterpiece of modern architecture and art.

IGUAÇU NATIONAL PARK

LOCATION   In the southern state of Parana, S 25° 00' to 25° 45', W 53° 30' to W 54° 30'.

DESCRIPTION   The largest national park in the south of Brazil, Iguaçu has an area of 170,000ha (409,870ac). The vegetation is dominated by sub-tropical rainforest, typically with a 20 to 30m (65.6 to 98.4ft) high canopy.

SIGNIFICANCE   This national park represents one of the last extensive stands of rainforest left in the area. Many rare and endangered species of flora and fauna are sheltered here. The most spectacular site in the park is without doubt the Iguaçu Falls. From a 1,200m (3,937ft) width, they drop 72m (236ft) into a narrow chasm with high walls and turbulent rapids.

HISTORIC CENTRE OF SALVADOR de BAHIA

LOCATION   In the state of Bahia, northeast Brazil, S 12° 58', W 38° 30'.

DESCRIPTION   Salvador sits on the peninsula which separates its deep natural harbour, called All Saint's Bay, from the Atlantic Ocean. It is divided into 2 distinct sections, an upper town and a lower town. These 2 areas are connected by roads, a funicular railway and a series of elevators, the most famous of which is the Lacerda lift. The upper town houses most of the notable buildings, including the Palacio Rio Branio (the Governor's Palace) and the church and convent of Saint Francis.

SIGNIFICANCE   Officially known as São Salvador da Bahia de Todos os Santos, the city was founded in 1549 as the first capital of the Portugese colony. It prospered under a thriving sugar industry, suffering many attacks from pirates and also from the Dutch who controlled it briefly in 1624. After Brazilian independence the capital was transferred to Rio de Janeiro in 1763 and Salvador's decline began.

OURO PRETO

LOCATION   About 300km (186mi) north of Rio de Janeiro, S 20° 23', N 43° 30'.

DESCRIPTION   Originally a mining town, now a centre for tourism, Ouro Preto has been protected since 1933 when it was declared a National Monument. The shape of the town is irregular, due to the hilly nature of the surrounding landscape. Many of the buildings have elements of baroque and rococo architectural styles.

SIGNIFICANCE   Officially recognised as a small town in 1712, Vila Rica became the capital of the gold mining district called Minas Gerais. It was a very wealthy town and was heavily influenced by the religious brotherhoods. Consequently a large number of churches were built, all richly decorated with paintings, carvings and sculptures. In 1823 Vila Rica became the imperial town of Ouro Preto. Gold production had dwindled and the town became a centre for higher education. Since the 1930s, the town's well preserved colonial nature has proved a popular tourist attraction.

OLINDA (HISTORIC CENTRE)

LOCATION   In the north-east, around 11 km (7mi) north of Recife, N 08° 00', W 35° 00'.

DESCRIPTION   Although Olinda is now a modern town, the original layout of the town is almost entirely preserved. The original crossroads and open areas in front of the churches have become the squares of the modern town. There are 12 principal buildings to the historic centre, including 4 churches, a museum (the old gaol), a bishop's palace, a monastery, 4 convents with churches attached and a house.

SIGNIFICANCE   Olinda was founded in 1535 as a local administrative capital. It soon became a productive and wealthy town, due mainly to the local sugar industry. The Dutch invaded in 1630 and occupied it for a year before burning it to the ground and leaving. After Portugese rule was restored, Olinda developed slowly, never matching the growth of neighbouring Recife. It is this lack of development, along with the establishment of a Botanical Garden in 1811, which has allowed Olinda to retain its colonial charm and originality.

SANCTUARY OF BOM JESUS do CONGONHAS

LOCATION   In the village of Congonhas a few kilometres from Ouro Preto, S 20° 29′, W 43° 51′.

DESCRIPTION   This is a religious complex containing gardens with small chapels and the much larger Church of Bom Jesus de Matosinhos, built in 1757. The church is in rococo style with a monumental staircase entrance, decorated with 12 lifesize statues of the prophets. The smaller chapels of the complex house figures corresponding to the stations of the Cross.

SIGNIFICANCE   A superb example of a decorative rococo interior, the Church of Bom Jesus de Matosinhos is renowned for the 89 offerings covering the walls of 'The House of Miracles' which are of great artistic and anthropological value.

Interior detail, Bom Jesus do Congonhas

Nessebar

Rila Monastery

BULGARIA

The Republic of Bulgaria occupies the central part of the Balkan Peninsula, in the south-eastern corner of Europe. From west to east and from north to south, ancient routes traverse its territory.

At this crossroad of peoples and cultures the valleys are fertile, the mountains easy of access and the climate favorable. Every inch of this land bears the traces of millenia-long uninterrupted life.

Neolithic culture bloomed in the plains of today's Bulgaria. It is generally acknowledged that the highest achievements of European Chalcolith are manifested by the findings from the so called 'Golden Necropolis' near the city of Varna on the Bulgarian Black Sea coast.

In the Bronze Age the land of present Bulgaria was already populated by Thracians. Homer in his 'Iliad' described the ornamented armour of King Rezos and called it worthy of Gods and not for mortals. The Thracians left many golden and silver treasures of table and ritual vessels, jewels, ornaments for horses and chariots, ornaments on weapons, all amazing with their interesting themes and motives and the perfection of their workmanship. Stone and brick tombs with painted and sculpture decoration were constructed for the Thracian princes. Two of them – the Kazanlak Tomb and the Sveshtari Tomb are on the World Heritage List.

At the beginning of the Christian Era the Roman Empire held sway over the Thracian lands. A dense network of roads and well organized fortified towns, with beautiful architecture skirted by rich villas, covered this land. In many Bulgarian cities the monuments of ancient Roman urbanism exist side by side with contemporary architecture.

Christianity found favourable soil in Thracian lands quite early on. From the fourth to the sixth century AD they were covered with churches, some of which still stand to this day. During this period, under the pressure of new tribes and peoples, Europe threw off the domination of the Roman Empire.

In 681 AD, a time of great ethnic and political change in the heart of the Balkan Peninsula, Bulgaria was founded. It was one of the first States in the New Europe of the Middle Ages. Its people were composed of Protobulgarians who came to the plains of the lower Danube from the regions around the Sea of Azov, of southern Slavs and of native Thracians. As a result there emerged a vital

Fresco detail, Ivanovo

Ceiling fresco, Kazanlak Thracian tomb

nation which was able to withstand many trials throughout the ages.

In the year 864 Bulgaria accepted Christianity and shortly after that the Slavonic Alphabet, created by the Brothers St. Cyril and St. Methodius. Bulgarian letters also spread among other Slav peoples. It was a time of great cultural achievement; the tenth century is known as the golden age of Bulgarian culture. At that time Bulgaria had an outlet on three seas and was one of the biggest and strongest States of early Medieval Europe.

At the very beginning of its existence Bulgaria won recognition from her mighty neighbour Byzantium. This was commemorated by cutting a monumental rock relief of a Bulgarian Khan – the Madara Horseman, now protected by the World Heritage.

But the relations between Bulgaria and Byzantium remained complicated and unstable. Byzantium even interrupted Bulgaria's independent existence for a century and a half.

During the second Bulgarian Kingdom (1186 -1393) the arts underwent a new upsurge: The Boyana Church (1253) and the Ivanovo Rock-hewn Churches (XIII-XIV centuries) are today included on the list of the World Heritage because of the exceptional quality of their paintings. The Boyana murals reflect a new humanism which was to become a hallmark of the future European Renaissance.

In spite of the political rivalry, Medieval Bulgaria maintained constant cultural relations with Byzantium. The centuries old contacts with the Greek civilization are traceable in the old town of Nessebar, situated on the small rocky peninsula of Nessebar. It is also included in the World Heritage List and has its fortress, churches and old houses from different epochs which are all well preserved.

At the end of the 14th century Bulgaria was conquered by the Ottoman Turks. Its people lived through a difficult foreign rule which threatened its faith and nationhood, but the strong cultural traditions and the church helped to safeguard the national spirit. Especially important was the role of the monasteries. The biggest of them, the Rila Monastery, was founded during the 10th century in the Rila Mountains. It became a treasury of the Bulgarian Literary Heritage. Eminent Bulgarian builders, wood carvers and painters incarnated their art in its building.

After several heroic uprisings and the Russian-Turkish War of 1877-1878 Bulgaria got its independence. The Third Bulgarian Kingdom had to overcome the country's centuries-old backwardness. Yet, Bulgarian people advanced on the road of progress though its destiny was often plagued by the interests of the Great Powers.

Ever since the acquisition of independence, Bulgarian governments have cared for the country's cultural heritage. Today more than thirty thousand archaeological, ethnographical and historical monuments and many natural sites are protected by the State. Bulgaria accepted the World Heritage Convention in March 1974, and now nine of them are on the World Heritage List. Naturally, in a densely populated land there can be found only a few places untouched by human activity, but in the Pirin National Park there still exists endemic vegetation which does not exist elsewhere in Europe, and the Srebarna Natural Reserve is a sanctuary for rare local and migratory birds.

PROF. MAGDALINA STANCHEVA
Vice-President of the World Heritage Committee of UNESCO

Entrance porch, Rila Monastery

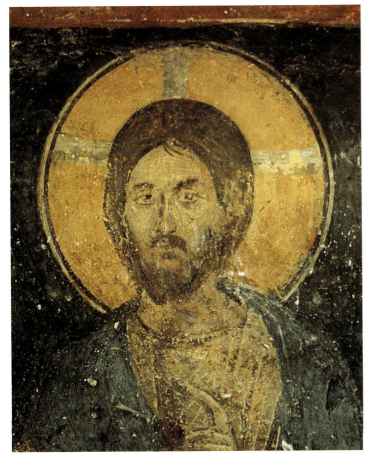

Fresco detail, Boyana Church

Female sculpture, Sveshtari Thracian tomb

〈57〉

Pelicans, Srebarna Nature Reserve

PIRIN NATIONAL PARK

LOCATION   Pirin Mountains, in the southwest corner of Bulgaria.

DESCRIPTION   Covering 27,400ha (66,061ac), this park was created in 1934 when 2,900ha (6,992ac) were set aside as a reserve. 60 percent of the park is coniferous forest and its altitude ranges from 1,000-2,915m (3,281-9,564ft) above sea level. Much of the landscape is glacially formed. There are around 70 glacial lakes scattered throughout the mountains.

SIGNIFICANCE   These beautiful and rugged mountains are a relic of the ancient glacial days of Europe. The unique landscape plays host to countless endemic species of flora and fauna.

SREBARNA NATURE RESERVE

LOCATION   16km (10mi) west of the town of Silistra, in the far north of Bulgaria, 1km (0.62mi) from the Romanian border.

DESCRIPTION   This reserve is 600ha (1,447ac) in area and is mainly comprised of a freshwater lake adjacent to the Danube River.

SIGNIFICANCE   The area is a very important breeding ground for 99 different species of birds, many of which are rare or endangered. The surrounding hills provide perfect sites for observing these birds and their activities without disturbing them.

THRACIAN TOMB OF KAZANLAK

LOCATION   The town of Kazanlak, in the Department of Stara Zagora, central Bulgaria.

DESCRIPTION   This tomb is situated at the southern slope of a burial mound and is composed of 3 chambers. The main part of the construction is the burial chamber, a brick construction in the shape of a beehive, 3.25 metres (11ft) in diameter, with a corridor.

SIGNIFICANCE   This tomb is important because it differs significantly from other tombs of a similar age. The main distinguishing features are the beehive shape of the burial chamber dome and the outstanding quality of the fresco artwork which decorates the walls in friezes. The most interesting fresco, the 'funeral banquet', alone deserves recognition as a landmark in the history of painting.

MADARA RIDER

LOCATION   Department of Shumen, eastern Bulgaria.

DESCRIPTION   This carving of a man on a horse is chiselled out of the solid rock of the Madara Plateau. A lion sits at the horse's feet and a dog follows behind. There are also Greek inscriptions carved in the rock.

SIGNIFICANCE   This sculpture is believed to represent the victory of a sovereign over his enemies. It dates from the 8th century, during the early years of the founding of the Bulgarian State. The inscriptions relate events that occurred between 705 AD and 831 AD. The detail and workmanship shown on this sculpture are remarkable.

NESSEBAR

LOCATION   On the Bulgarian coast of the Black Sea, 30km (18.6mi) north of Burgas, N 42° 07′, E 27° 39′.

DESCRIPTION   Situated on a 24ha (58ac) peninsula, the fortified City of Nessebar is connected by an isthmus to the mainland. The archaeological sites cover twice the area of the peninsula and are mostly under water.

SIGNIFICANCE   These ruins represent over 2,000 years of history. Perhaps the most interesting are the earliest – the remains of an acropolis, a temple and an agora from the Hellenistic period. There are several important churches dating from the 10th century up to the 14th century AD. Later remains of importance include some fine examples of wooden architecture from the period of the Bulgarian Resistance.

BOYANA CHURCH

LOCATION   The Boyana district of the City of Sofia.

DESCRIPTION   This church has 3 sections, the eastern church, the middle or Kaloyan Church and the western church. All differ in architectural style and were built in different eras, but still manage to form a harmonious whole.

SIGNIFICANCE   The eastern church is the oldest construction, dating back to the 10th century, it was part of the royal court at Boyana during medieval times. The Kaloyan Church can be more accurately dated by its frescoes which were completed in 1259, while the western church was built around 1845, the time of the Bulgarian national uprising. Over 900 years of Bulgarian history are represented in this remarkable building.

Lives of great men all remind us We can make our lives sublime, And, departing, leave behind us Footprints on the sands of time.

HENRY
WADSWORTH
LONGFELLOW

Madara Rider

RILA MONASTERY

LOCATION   Rila mountain, E 23° 06′, N 42° 07′.

DESCRIPTION   The main building is a rectangular fortress with 2 entrances. It comprises the monks' residences, 4 chapels, guestrooms, the kitchen, the 22m (72ft) high Khreljo Tower, the main church of the Dormition and the Orlitza Convent.

SIGNIFICANCE   The monastery was founded in the 10th century AD by followers of St. John of Rila. It is one of the more significant religious complexes in Europe. There are numerous works of art within its walls, including some superb 14th century frescoes, Byzantine paintings and intricate wood carvings. Perhaps the most important feature of this monastery is the crucial role it has played through the years in protecting and nurturing the Bulgarian culture, faith and language.

THRACIAN TOMB OF SVESHTARI

LOCATION   Razgrad District, northeastern Bulgaria.

DESCRIPTION   Only discovered in 1982, this tomb has 3 chambers and is constructed of stone blocks. It forms a mound some 80m (262ft) in diameter and almost 12m (39ft) high. The main burial chamber is particularly well preserved and is in the style of a dwelling with several interesting features, including 4 Doric columns, 10 sculptures of females which are attached to the wall and support the architraves, 2 stone beds for the deceased couple and a frieze on the wall which depicts the deceased.

SIGNIFICANCE   This tomb dates back to the 3rd century BC and is one of the best preserved of surviving Hellenistic tombs. It is a unique monument to Thracian culture and to Hellenistic art.

ROCK-HEWN CHURCHES OF IVANOVO

LOCATION   The village of Ivanovo, 16km (10mi) from Ruse, northeastern Bulgaria.

DESCRIPTION   Here we find a number of churches, monasteries, chapels and cells cut into the rock along the Rusenski River. There has been some serious damage inflicted to some of these monuments by rock slides. 5 of the churches are preserved in reasonably good order.

SIGNIFICANCE   These carved monuments date from the time of the second Bulgarian State, 1187 AD to 1396 AD. Their construction was initiated by Joachim, then a monk, but later to become Joachim I, the first Bulgarian Patriach when the Bulgarian Church was restored to independence in 1235. The 5 preserved churches are decorated with outstanding frescoes, especially in the church of 'Tsarkvata', where the frescoes are considered to be some of the finest surviving examples of Byzantine art.

5,000 Years of Town Planning

In coastal districts underwater research has brought to light the remains of the first sea-ports and relics of early navigation on the Black Sea, including a number of stone anchors used in the late Bronze Age about twelve hundred years before our era. On their outward journeys, the Thracian ships carried cargoes of sheet copper; the goods they brought back enabled the coastal cities to become the country's earliest centres of maritime trade.

So when Greek colonists settled on the Black Sea coast in the 6th century BC they found a string of flourishing Thracian cities. Before long they had imposed their own language, built theatres and introduced their own sculptors and potters; the towns in which they worked long continued to bear Greek names. The close relations the Greeks maintained with the Thracians were not only commercial. The two peoples exchanged customs and divinities and shared common festivals. Such cultural exchanges were often repeated down the centuries and have given Bulgaria its particular character.

But cultural interchange and the legacy of antiquity were not limited to the coastal cities. More than half the Bulgarian towns are at least five thousand years old. Cities like Sofia, Plovdiv, Varna, Nessebar and Stara Zagora are in themselves monuments to the history of town-planning, and in many cases it has been possible to explore their archaeological heritage deep down in the earth beneath the modern cities.

There is only one way into Nessebar and that is through the ancient gate in the ramparts. This small town on the Black Sea which still bears a Thracian name, Messembria, deserves more than any other somewhat misused title of '*living museum*'. It is built on a tiny peninsula linked to the coast by a narrow neck of land, and was one of the main Thracian ports. A Dorian colony was established there in the 6th century and grew rich through maritime trade and farming the fertile hinterland. Under Roman domination Nessebar remained prosperous and subsequently became one of the Byzantine empire's chief ports.

For centuries Bulgaria and Byzantium fought over this tiny strip of land surrounded by sea on all sides, and every time the peninsula changed hands it was endowed with new monuments. The Italian republics, especially Genoa, also asserted their influence at Nessebar, even after the Ottoman invasion. In spite of changing fortunes and the slow decline of its trade the city maintained its vitality with the passing centuries and its inhabitants have kept the customs and independent spirit of a seafaring people. Today this ancient city in the heart of Bulgaria's most

famous resort areas draws tens of thousands of tourists to its monuments and its picturesque site.

Among the masterpieces left here by three thousand years of civilisation, the most impressive are the churches. The dozen that remain represent almost every stage of Christianity in this area, from the oldest built in the 5th century to the most recent at the end of the last century. Most of them, however, date from the 13th and 14th centuries and these are also the most interesting, both for their style and for the originality of the building techniques used in their construction. Small blocks of tufa alternate with rows of bricks to form an unusual kind of decoration. Details such as cornices, arches and niches are embellished with inlaid ceramic circles and four-leaved clover, so that the facades of the buildings shine in the sun like so many pieces of multicoloured embroidery. These vivid patches of colour contrast with the plain facades of

1300 year old tree, Pirin National Park

the houses, whose wooden facing is weathered by sun and salt.

In Nessebar, as elsewhere in Bulgaria, modern life goes hand in hand both with distant antiquity and with the Middle Ages. Workmen digging the foundations of a youth centre some years ago discovered the altar of a church which has long since disappeared. It has been carefully preserved and incorporated into the new building where it is protected by a cement column and can be seen through a glass panel. In summer tourists attend concerts organised in the great 6th century basilica. But the most persevering visitors are the archaeologists, historians and restorers whose patient work continues season after season.

Prof. Magdalina Stancheva

Reprinted from the *Unesco Courier*, May 1981

CAMEROON

Cameroon is a long, wedge-shaped country on the west coast of Africa with an area of around 530,000 sq km (200,000sq mi).

The Portugese were the first European power to establish contacts in this region – during the 15th century. Colonisation did not begin though, until the 19th century, when the British signed a trade agreement with one of the dominant tribes. After a brief period of British rule, a German protectorate was formed in 1884. It lasted until their defeat in the First World War.

The modern country was formed in 1961 from a union of West Cameroon, which had been under English administration, and East Cameroon, which had been French.

The climate is mainly tropical, except in the highlands where temperatures are lower. The highest point, at 4,000m (13,000ft) is Cameroon Mountain, an active volcano. The western side of this peak is one of the rainiest regions in the world, with a yearly average of 10,160mm (400in).

The southern lowlands are covered by dense tropical rainforest with many massive trees such as mahoganies. Other typical vegetation includes orchids, palms, umbrella trees, ferns and huge tangles of rattans. Mangrove swamps are found on the coastline, while further north there is savanna woodland.

Cameroon ratified the World Heritage Convention in December 1982 and has one site inscribed on the World Heritage List, Dja Faunal Reserve. It is the south where the Dja River drains and is an area of relatively intact equatorial rainforest with a fascinating variety of fauna and flora.

DJA FAUNAL RESERVE

LOCATION   In the south of Cameroon, N 02° 50′ to 03° 40′, E 12° 25′ to 13° 54′.

DESCRIPTION   Covering an area of 526,000ha (1,300,000ac), this reserve is situated on a plateau which averages 600m (1,968ft) in altitude and is within the equatorial forest region of Cameroon.

SIGNIFICANCE   This area has never really been populated and subsequently it is a relatively pristine environment. It has very rich and diverse flora and fauna, including the forest elephant, buffalo, gorilla and 2 endemic species of both crocodile and tortoise.

Trees and Global Warming

THERE IS AMPLE evidence that the destruction of forests contributes to the build up of carbon dioxide released into the atmosphere – although to a lesser extent than the burning of fossil fuels.

If the greenhouse effect has been exacerbated by the destruction of forests, can the planting of new trees and letting them grow, along with preservation of remaining natural forests, alleviate the situation?

It seems that even extensive planting of forests can only slow down the change in global climate to a relatively small extent, and only temporarily, but every little bit helps and reforestation is now being taken seriously. Moreover, planting trees does no harm, and provides many benefits. In particular, reforestation in the form of agro-forestry not only slows soil erosion and protects water tables, but, in addition, supplies indigenous people with products which they can utilise for their own needs and also market: building poles, charcoal, firewood.

It is encouraging to find that villagers in some parts of Africa are beginning to understand the dangers of soil erosion and lack of water caused by indiscriminate slash and burn agriculture. Many small tree planting programmes are springing up throughout Tanzania, for example. These should be encouraged.

There are many ways in which the developed world, in an effort to slow down global warming, can assist economically poor countries to preserve their forests: debt swap for nature; developing forest tourism; carefully planning rural development programmes in surrounding villages. Agro-forestry is particularly important in this respect.

Timber companies should practise selective logging whenever possible, and industrial operations, such as oil exploration, should not only be conducted in such a way as to minimise environmental damage, but in conjunction with programmes designed to conserve the area as a whole.

Conserving the last of the great natural forests along with the planting and growing of trees, even though it only temporarily slows down the greenhouse effect, is, I believe, crucial. Even if we are ultimately doomed, we should strive to maintain tolerable living conditions for as long as possible for the sake of the next generation. Guarding and nurturing trees will help. It will improve the quality of life for thousands of people and their livestock, protect countless wild animals, and – at least for a while – save hundreds of animal and plant species from extinction.

DR JANE GOODALL
The Jane Goodall Institute (UK).

Kluane Lake

CANADA

Protecting natural and cultural heritage is important to Canadians. We recognise that our natural and cultural resources are irreplaceable possessions, and Canada has been an active participant in the World Heritage Convention and in two related agencies: the International Union for the Conservation of Natural Resources (IUCN) and the International Council on Monuments and Sites (ICOMOS).

Canada has played a significant role in World Heritage from the very beginning – from advising on early drafts of the World Heritage Convention in 1972, to providing chairpersons and technical advisers for evaluating both cultural and natural areas nominated to the World Heritage Committee meetings, either as members or observers.

Canada itself has ten World Heritage Sites, including six in the 'natural' category. These range from the towering walls of land-locked fjords on the east coast to fossilised remains and sculptured badlands on the prairies. From the Rocky Mountains in the west, with glaciers and a significant fossil site, to extensive salt plains, icefields and snow-capped mountains – including Canada's highest peak – to the north.

Four of Canada's ten World Heritage Sites fall into the 'cultural' category. These cover an abandoned Haida Indian village and totem poles; the best preserved bison jump on the continent; the cradle of French civilization in America; and the site of the oldest known European settlement of the New World.

Environment Canada's Parks Service in co-operation with other agencies, has the lead responsibility for protecting both natural and cultural areas in Canada, and for implementing the World Heritage program.

ROBERT DE COTRET
Minister for the Environment, Canada

To see the world in a grain of sand,
And heaven in a wild flower,
Hold infinity in the palm of your hand,
And eternity in an hour.
WILLIAM BLAKE

A Day in the Life...

A TYPICAL DAY in June for a World Heritage site Field Manager in Banff is never predictable. I started my day with the best intentions, monitoring the radio collared black bears which have Banff townsite within their home range. Not far from town we found 'Kootenay', an adult breeding male, feeding on an elk carcass left over from the winter. Decision time! Do we leave him alone to feed and move on, or do we post the area with bear warning signs to keep people away while he defends his meal?

Posting warnings involves bureaucracy and signatures and notifying a multitude of information outlets, so we'll take a chance and not post the area. Anyway, there are more bears to locate and document. There is also the data to input, and the weekly summary of bear activity to produce for the information outlets – to inform the public who may want to avoid bears as best they can.

But before we can finish monitoring the bears, there is a radio call that there is a carcass coming in. One of the Duty Wardens has just picked up a dead elk by the side of the road twenty kilometres west of town. Another night driver overdriving his headlights. These kills are an opportunity to document the general health of the ungulate population and full necropsies are best performed before they start to deteriorate. So it's off to the lab.

There are often surprises inside the carcasses which a Field Manager does not have the skills to identify, so someone mans a video camera while we cut away. This one has a badly infected liver, so we freeze it for later analysis, and keep cutting. A yearling animal, but looking quite thin, so the femur is saved for later marrow fat analysis. Keep cutting. Into the lungs, only a few worms, nothing to be concerned about. Glands OK, no signs of tuberculosis. This one's a wrap, but where to dispose of the remains? We don't want to remove biomass from the system, but where to dump it without causing a public safety problem? The public has access to the entire park.

Meanwhile another radio call to inform us that someone has just been attacked by a cow elk, apparently defending its newly born calf. Mixing people and wildlife is not always easy when the people and wildlife share common ground, especially in large numbers. One cannot risk immobilising an elk which has just given birth, and hope to successfully relocate her and her calf; so the only option is to close the area to human activity. By the time we get the Superintendent's approval to close, and then post the area and inform the information outlets, the day is shot.

We've forgotten about the meeting with the Vegetation Wardens concerning an important prescribed burn which will happen any day now,

Canadian Rocky Mountains Parks

weather permitting. Then there's the local press who always want to be kept informed about what is happening in their national parks. Time sheets have to be filled out, then there's the report on last year's goat census that we were going to get working on today...just hope that someone does not fall off a mountain and we have to back-up another mountain rescue.

There is so much happening in a popular World Heritage site that often we cannot even keep up with what our compatriots in the next office are doing. Life is never dull, and those of us lucky enough to work here would rarely consider trading our jobs for anything.

RICK KUNELIUS
Senior Wildlife Warden
Banff

Our Ancient Forests: Creating New Conflicts

THE HONOURABLE ROBERT DE COTRET opens this chapter noting Canada's commitment to World Heritage. It is a significant one, involving commitments by cities and provincial governments as well as the federal government. In Canada, World Heritage designations have been harmonious examples of federal provincial co-operation – rare phenomena during Canada's continuing debates over virgin forests, sovereignty and aboriginal land claims.

In contrast to the Canadian scene one cannot walk down the streets of Hobart, Sydney, Canberra, Cairns or Denham without hearing UNESCO praised or damned for what the World Heritage Convention is doing, to, or for, Australia's heritage.

Before the Tasmanian Wilderness Parks were added to the World Heritage List on December 14, 1982 some 1,272 protesters had been arrested. A major hydro-electric development (the Franklin River project) was stopped, and an unsuccessful 'peace offering' of A$500,000,000 failed to persuade the State Government of the World Heritage Values of Western Tasmania. Ultimately the 'World Heritage Conservation Act' was passed in Canberra. It withstood court challenges by State Government. Today, Australia remains as the only country in the world to have legislation of this nature. Leaving aside the political debate, it remains an incredible commitment by Australia to World Heritage. A Canadian politician once said, 'Conservation was a vote by the soul and not the pocket-book'. Australia has done both.

When one sees this Australian political commitment to World Heritage, one must ask about the underlying motivation. On one side, perhaps a struggle for political power, or perhaps a recognition that under the Australian constitution, wilderness was losing. Ancient forests were going 'down the tube'.

In Tasmania the fight against hydro-electric development was launched in the late 1960s and early 1970s with the damming of Lake Pedder. In the 1980s a second struggle became crystallised, the battle to save wilderness and the rain forests. It is this phenomenon which is still having a global impact. There is little doubt that the conservation world was ignited by the 1964 passage of the United States Wilderness Bill. The opportunity to focus interest on wilderness issues was seized and the non governmental community moved into a new era.

The growth of protected areas boomed throughout the 1970s and 1980s. Globally, land conserved reached almost 4%. At the same time, conservation biologists studying habitat fragmentation and the rates of species loss, brought new knowledge to park systems planning. Satellite photos began to demonstrate high losses of habitat, particularly in tropical forests. It is forecast that due to tropical deforestation the world may lose between 5 and 15% of its total species between 1990 and 2020.

In 1982, the World Park's Congress held in Bali, called for protection of 10% of the globe through a network of parks and reserves. This requires a doubling in the area dedicated to protection.

More frequent and alarming stories on the decimation of large mammals in Africa kept the public interest focused. The World Conservation Strategy of the 1980s summarised the data and stressed the continuing loss of species.

Increasing global population, increasing industrialisation and urbanisation, and increasing consumption further underline the continuing conservation crisis of the 1990s. A loss of habitat and species will continue.

Conservationists of the 1980s, sought new icons and found them in ancient, primitive, majestic old forests. Symbolically the battle to save the California Redwood, which has been ongoing since the 1930s, was launched on a global scale. Western Tasmania was one of the early manifestations of this new wave.

Similar action was taking place in New Zealand. The nomination of the extensive rain forests of the South-West Coast in 1986 spawned a conflict of significant scale between communities, foresters and conservationists.

Australia was not, however, to be left out. During the relatively calm World Heritage listing of the east coast temperate and sub-tropical forests of New South Wales in 1986, the arena shifted to Queensland. Here one of the most dramatic battles of the decade took place in the Daintree area. Again, the paddy wagons came, police dogs, chains and jails. It was not only a ground war, it was fought in the legislative halls of Brisbane, as well as the corridors of Canberra. It results in a World Heritage Site in 1988, but the full story can be better told by others. Suffice it to say, thousands of letters crossed the oceans and World Heritage received a new political profile in Australia and UNESCO.

Far across the Pacific, just off the coast of Vancouver Island, a small island called 'Meares' became the focus of another forestry controversy. Natives claimed the area as aboriginal lands of spiritual value. Conservationists joined to protect ancient cedar, hemlock and Douglas fir from the chain saw. Arrests, jail and court actions followed. Aboriginal land claims remain to be settled.

Five hundred kilometres to the north, in the Queen Charlotte Archipelago, the Haida Nation laid claim to Lyell Island. Ancient forests of cedar, spruce and hemlock were the focus of native spiritual values. Logs remained the focus of industry. Once again the jail doors opened. Court actions followed and a 'National Park Reserve', began to evolve. This was Canada's first truly national conservation battle of the decade. Petitions crossed the country. Parliament, with the agreement of British Columbia, took action and a National Park Reserve was created.

We need to travel a few years back in time to 1984 and a few thousand kilometres east to an area 250km north of Toronto for our next episode. Here a relatively innocuous logging road called the 'Red Squirrel Road', sparked the torch for the Temagami Wilderness society.

Again the issue is the logging of ancient forests, stands of white and red pine representing the last fragments of their past glory. Again, spiritual values of native peoples are involved. Again, the jail doors opened and protestors of logging were hauled away.

Today, similar sagas are being played out in the Carmanah Valley on Vancouver Island. In Oregon and Washington the spotted owl, which is listed on the U.S. endangered species list, has forced major cut-backs in logging grants. In Norway, small remnants of virgin forests are the focus of similar protests. The rest of Europe has been fairly well manicured; wild lands are no longer an issue.

A common thread runs through all of these geographic hot spots. They are scarce natural communities, they are increasing in value, the market is competitive and we don't know enough about ancient forests to protect them or to manage them effectively.

Old forests have clearly gained new values within the conservation community and in the public arena. There are a number of reasons for this but the root cause must lie in their increasing scarcity and in the increasing public knowledge about how these forests are used and abused.

Satellite photos and articles in weekly journals such as Times, the Economist and Newsweek, have raised public awareness. The National Geographic magazine has supplemented this with a scientific focus. The 'Eyes on the Earth' project, featured in the February 25, 1991 issue of Newsweek, places a truly global focus on the issue. The green of our terrestrial planet is wilting before our eyes.

Forest companies which have operated under the umbrella of sustainable use are unable to prove that their use is sustainable. 'In practical terms, no commercial logging of tropical moist forests has proven to be sustainable from the standpoint of the forest ecosystem'. In temperate forests 'the mother of all clear cuts' on north-western Vancouver Island, does little to enhance the foresters' image as the guardian of our heritage. A computer model of forest growth, shown to be realistic and accurate, projects that a forest of the north temperate zone of North America requires more than 400 years to reach a mature condition following a clear cut. Advertisements in national journals tell us that industry plants two trees for every tree it cuts. We are not told that the new planting equals eight ounces of 'biomass' while that removed is measured in hundreds of tons. The public is in desperate need of honesty in advertising.

Dr Dan Botkin, a biologist from the University of California, states that knowledge about nature is essential if we are to achieve a new harmony between ourselves and our environment. Sites required for baseline monitoring, and scientific research must be an integral part of the management of nature.

Dr Botkin goes on to say:

> We lack not only information about the state of nature, but also an adequate understanding of how ecological systems function, and we must continue to improve this understanding. Under the old perspective, such an understanding was not necessary in detail, because we believed that nature simply knew best and our understanding was irrelevant to management. We thought that we needed only an appreciation of nature, not an understanding of it. In the past, scientific research about nature was often regarded as an activity that interferred with recreation and conservation. The research that we did at Isle Royale was considered at times by the park's management to be a nuisance that interferred with the real function of the park, which was believed to be simply to provide recreation for visitors. Some conservation organisations have considered scientific research as inhumane and unnecessary. We no longer have the luxury to believe that we can live in harmony with the environment without knowledge and understanding of natural systems.

Much of the conflict in each of the areas touched upon in this essay lies in shifting social and economic values. These impose themselves on different sectors of society differentially. Yesterday's logger still needs work that he finds financially and psychologically satisfying. Today's timber barons must recognise shifting social values, the 'bull of the woods' is no longer an appropriate metaphor. 'Greenies' must also adopt a degree of pragmatism. Native people and 'environmentalists' see only fragments of ancient forests, and even these are under threat, they have a right to more than a 'hearing'.

Park managers need a profound increase in knowledge to manage protected areas in such a way that they help sustain society and the world's biological diversity in all of its rich variety. Foresters must change and recognise that there is more to the forest than logs and wood fibre.

Economists must now begin to build models which recognise that standing trees have economic value and that cut trees (logs) reduce a nation's 'natural capital', while at the same time they increase the gross domestic product. We desperately need new economic models and national

Woodman, spare that tree!
Touch not a single bough!
In youth it sheltered me,
And I'll protect it now.

GEORGE POPE MORRIS

Quebec

accounting systems which incorporate environmental components.

If we are to conserve our scarce and precious old forests, we must continue to pursue programs of public activism, build our scientific capability and enhance our means for reimbursing social and economic values to those who bear the heaviest burden – ordinary people who are caught in the 'battles of the titans'.

While we fight our social, political and economic battles, we should ensure the security of our ancient forests. They are symbols which represent the complex ecosystems that we must nurture if we are to preserve our global diversity.

HAROLD K EIDSVIK
Director, Canadian Parks Service

ANTHONY ISLAND

LOCATION   Just south of Queen Charlotte Islands, British Columbia, N 52° 06′, W 131° 12′.

DESCRIPTION   Owned by the British Columbian Provincial Government, this island is remote and unpopulated. Access is restricted. There are 7 sites of interest on the island; 2 cave sites, 4 shell midden sites and 1 village site.

SIGNIFICANCE   The most significant aspect of this island is the ruins of the village of Ninstints. It is the only remaining example of such an Indian village site. The ruins include the remains of 32 totem and mortuary poles, as well as 10 massive cedar long houses. Excavations of the shell midden sites have the potential to reveal over 2,000 years of Indian occupation.

NAHANNI NATIONAL PARK

LOCATION   Southwest corner of Northwest Territories, N 61° 04′ to 62° 00′, W 123° 36′ to 127° 23′.

DESCRIPTION   This enormous park covers 4,700sq km (1,880sq mi) of widely varying landscape. The area basically encapsulates the watershed of the Nahanni River. The upper reaches flow through tundra capped mountains, whereas the southern reaches flow through deeply forested valleys.

SIGNIFICANCE   Breathtakingly beautiful, this park has several important features. Virginia Falls are twice the height of Niagra, falling 90m (295ft); shortly after, the river wends its way tortuously through a narrow chasm appropriately named 'Hell's Gate'. There are 3 major canyons, several hot springs and an extensive system of caves. More than 40 species of mammals are found in the park including black bears, wolves, beavers, deer, grizzly bears, woodland caribou and moose.

Nahanni National Park

Gros Morne National Park

Dinosaur Provincial Park

Head-Smashed-in Buffalo Jump

HEAD-SMASHED-IN BUFFALO JUMP

LOCATION   Porcupine Hills, in the State of Alberta, N 49° 43′, W 113° 43′.

DESCRIPTION   This site is set on prime grazing land on the foothills bordering the Alberta plains and is privately owned. It consists of 3 parts; an 18m (60ft) high sandstone cliff, called 'the kill', over which Indians used to herd buffalo in order to kill them; the 'processing camp-site', an area 975m (3,247ft) long by 305m (1,016ft) wide situated below the cliff, where the buffalo were butchered; and finally an area above the cliff called the 'gathering basin', where the buffalo were gathered before being driven over the cliff.

SIGNIFICANCE   Dating back at least 5,700 years, this is the largest and oldest surviving example of a remarkably inventive and innovative harvesting process which allowed these early North American people to systematically kill buffalo in enormous numbers. Once killed, the animals were processed in every conceivable way: the meat was smoked and dried, bones were made into tools, skins and hair processed for clothing and bags amongst other things.

DINOSAUR PROVINCIAL PARK

LOCATION   Southeastern corner of Alberta.

DESCRIPTION   Almost 6,000ha (14,466ac) in area, this park has quite a variety of landscapes with extensive areas of badlands and a significant proportion of river bank habitats which are in a constant state of flux from the meanderings of the Red Deer River.

SIGNIFICANCE   The most important feature of the park lies in its fossil wealth. It has yielded some exceptionally well preserved dinosaur fossils from the Upper Cretaceous period. Specimens from 7 families of dinosaurs have been unearthed within the park's boundaries, including 60 separate species. Other features of significance within this park are its abundance of rare and endangered species, including the golden eagle and the prairie falcon. There are also several archaeological sites of significance to the history of North American Indian culture, including a Vision Quest Site, a Stone Effigy and Tipi Rings.

QUEBEC (HISTORIC AREA)

LOCATION   Within Quebec, capital of the Province of Quebec, N 47° 00′, W 71° 20′.

DESCRIPTION   The historic area covers 135ha (337ac) and corresponds exactly to the site covered by the old fortified town as it was in the mid 18th century. There are several distinct areas of importance: the Fortified Precinct with its ramparts, citadel and military buildings; the old urban centre of the Upper Town with over 700 buildings of historic importance; the Lower Town which is the oldest area and has several notable buildings and squares.

SIGNIFICANCE   Founded in 1608 by Samuel de Champlain, Quebec is Canada's oldest city. It has borne witness to a turbulent and often violent history. The fortified section was built in 1823-32 and is the only remaining walled town in North America. The vast number of well preserved historic buildings, streets and squares, many dating back to the 17th century, present an invaluable record of early North American history.

WOOD BUFFALO NATIONAL PARK

LOCATION   On the border of Alberta and Northwest Territories, N 58° to 60° 40′, W 111° to 115° 30′.

DESCRIPTION   This park is located entirely within Canada's boreal forest zone. It is 44,800sq km (17,500sq mi) in area and is situated on the eastern edge of the Interior Plains of North America. Other predominant landscapes include an extensive area of salt plains, an exceptionally large inland delta – the Peace Athabasca delta – and vast areas of grassland.

SIGNIFICANCE   Canada's largest national park and one of the largest national parks in the world, this area represents a pristine example of the boreal ecosystem; an ecosystem which is fascinating in that it is ruled by fire. On average, around 1 percent of the forest burns each year. This has created a unique environment which is dominated by trees like spruces, jack pines and the trembling aspen and is home to many interesting mammals, such as the beaver, moose, black bear, wolf, mink, snowshoe hare and lynx.

KLUANE AND WRANGELL-ST. ELIAS PARKS

LOCATION   Yukon Territory, Canada / Alaska, USA, N 60° 00′, W 141° 00′.

DESCRIPTION   This site is listed jointly with Canada and the United States of America as it's in the mountainous border country of Yukon and Alaska. The 4 mountain ranges of St. Elias, Kluane, Wrangell and Chugach dominate the landscape. Vegetation ranges over 4 main categories; coastal forest, montane forest, sub-alpine and alpine tundra.

SIGNIFICANCE   Here in the world's largest nature reserve we find the greatest concentration of mountain peaks over 4,500m (14,764ft) in North America. The tallest peak is Mt. Logan, at 5,950 m (19,521ft), the second tallest in North America. The landscape is glacial, with over 100 glaciers individually identified and a similar number remaining unnamed. Some of the world's largest glaciers are found here, the Malaspina Glacier probably the most famous. Snowfalls over 1.8m (6ft) are common and there are many enormous fields of

Every part of this earth is sacred to my people. Every shining pine needle, every sandy shore, every mist in the dark woods, every clearing and humming insect is holy in the memory and experience of my people. The sap which courses through the trees carries the memories of red man.

CHIEF SEATTLE

Anthony Island

Wood Buffalo National Park

L'Anse Aux Meadows National Historic Park

snow and ice. The central plateau contains the Bagley Icefield, the largest icefield in the world outside the polar regions. There is a rich array of wildlife, including many large mammals such as grizzly bears, dall's sheep, moose, black bears, foxes and wolves. Smaller mammals such as chipmunks, shrews and the arctic ground squirrel are also found. The bird life is abundant, notably the birds of prey like the golden eagle, bald eagle, gyr, peregrine falcon and an assortment of owls.

CANADIAN ROCKY MOUNTAINS PARKS

LOCATION   Rocky Mountains, border British Columbia/Alberta, N 50° 00′ to 54° 00′, W 115° 00′ to 119° 00′.

DESCRIPTION   This listing comprises 4 neighbouring national parks; Banff, Jasper, Yoho and Kootenay. The total area is 20,160sq km (8,000sq mi). Some of the more spectacular landscapes include the massive Columbian Icefield, the breathtakingly beautiful Maligne Lake and the deeply sculptured Maligne Canyon.

SIGNIFICANCE   This is one of the most famous national parks in the world. Accessibility allows over 9 million people each year to enjoy the outstanding beauty of this wild mountain environment, yet there are still enormous areas which remain untouched by man. 56 species of

mammals are to be found, including the nearly endangered grey wolf and bighorn sheep. 2 other important residents are the golden eagle and the bald-headed eagle. Burgess Shale, one of the most important fossil sites in the world, is also found within this park's boundaries.

L'ANSE AUX MEADOWS NATIONAL HISTORIC PARK

LOCATION   In the Provinces of Labrador and Newfoundland, southeast Canada, N 51° 40′, W 55° 30′.

DESCRIPTION   This site covers an area along the eastern shore of Epaves Bay and extends 200m (657ft) out to sea. It comprises the ruins of an 11th century Norse settlement. There are the remains of 8 buildings of sod and timber construction, 3 dwellings, 4 workshops and 1 Blacksmith's workshop. More than 2,400 items of archaeological interest have been uncovered here, including objects of iron, bronze, bone and wood.

SIGNIFICANCE   There is evidence of occupation at this site 5,000 years ago, but it was the Norse people from Iceland and Greenland who made the biggest impact on the site when they settled sometime in the 11th century and constructed the large sod and timber buildings whose remains we see today. This is the only Norse site

CENTRAL AFRICAN REPUBLIC

The Central African Republic is a land-locked country and, as its name implies, lies right in the centre of Africa. The equator lies not far to the south and so the climate is consistently hot and humid. Vegetation is mainly savanna.

The country's history dates back to prehistoric times, as evidenced by several archaeological sites which point to extensive settlements in the area before the rise of civilisation in ancient Egypt.

The 19th century saw tremendous damage inflicted upon the fabric of society by slave trading and forced labour. The country passed from French control when independence was granted in 1960.

The World Heritage Convention was ratified in December 1980 and there is presently one site inscribed on the list, that of Manovo—Gounda St Floria National Park. This large park lies to the north of the country and encompasses several differing landscapes and vegetation zones. It is an area extremely rich in biodiversity; many rare and endangered species find their homes here.

MANOVO-GOUNDA ST. FLORIS NATIONAL PARK

LOCATION   In the province of Bamingui – Bangoran, N 08° 05′ to 09° 50′, E 20° 28′ to 22° 22′.

DESCRIPTION   This park is located in the north of the country. Bounded by the Bongo Massif in the south, it mainly comprises the foothills of the Massif and the sandy plateau to its north. It covers an area of 17,400 sq km (6,960 sq mi) and may be divided into 3 vegetation zones: (i) a large grassy plain to the north, (ii) a savannah plain in the centre, (iii) the plateau of the Massif, with a marked escarpment which cuts the park's several rivers.

SIGNIFICANCE   The importance of this park rests with its wealth of flora and fauna. Over 1,200 species of flora have so far been identified, two of them new. The population of large mammals is particularly notable, with over 55 species, including the elephant, rhinoceros, hippopotamus and giraffe. There is also a healthy population of predators, including the panther and leopard. More than 320 species of birds have been identified, vultures, storks and ostriches among them. This wealth and diversity of species make this park an area vital to our world's heritage.

Manovo-Gounda St. Floris National Park

in North America and the earliest European settlement yet to be found in the New World. 400 years before Columbus, this was the site of the first meeting between Europeans, whose voyage had brought them via Greenland from Iceland, and inhabitants of the New World – the Beothuck Eskimos.

GROS MORNE NATIONAL PARK

LOCATION   West coast of the island of Newfoundland. Provinces of Newfoundland and Labrador, N 49° 20′ to 49° 55′, W 57° 25′ to 58° 10′.

DESCRIPTION   Geologically, this park lies at the top of the Appalachian Mountains and has 2 distinct physical components, a coastal plain and an alpine plateau. Bonne Bay, which runs into the Gulf of St. Lawrence, is included within the park's boundaries.

SIGNIFICANCE   The sheer drama of its magnificent landscapes is surely enough to justify this park's inclusion on the World Heritage List, yet there are several other important features. The park is of immense value to the study of the earth's geological history, particularly with regard to tectonic plate theory. There are also numerous valuable archaeological sites, revealing a rich history of occupation by, amongst others, Dorset Eskimos, Norse sailors and Basque whalers.

Conservation and Development: The New Symbiosis

WHAT DO A Masai herdsman in Tanzania's Ngorongoro Crater, a Sherpa trader in the Mt. Everest region of Nepal, and a campesino in Costa Rica's Talamanca Range region have in common? All are poor, all live in remote regions, all are seeking development, and all stand to benefit from the World Heritage Convention.

For example, in Ngorongoro Crater, which may be the most spectacular setting for large game animals in all of Africa, the World Heritage Fund has supported the preparation of a management plan which enables the Masai herdsmen to continue to graze their cattle in certain parts of the crater during certain times of the year. To compensate them for any losses incurred from restrictions necessary for the overall management of the site, they are provided with health-care centres, improved marketing facilities, and training in animal husbandry.

In Nepal's Sagarmatha National Park, the Sherpas have been incorporated into the management of the World Heritage site, providing lodging, goods, and services to tourists trekking to Mt. Everest. As part of this management, control over local forests has been returned to the local communities and major reforestation projects have been undertaken. World Heritage has helped open the area to the outside world, through improved trails and a small airport. The Sherpa communities within the World Heritage site are now among the most prosperous in all of Nepal.

In the Talamanca Range along Costa Rica's border with Panama, the Organization of American States has worked with local governments, other public institutions, indigenous peoples and private organizations to produce a strategy which seeks a balance among the conflicting forces of change in the region. Without proper management, these forces threaten both the quality of life of the rural people and the conservation objectives for which the World Heritage site was elected. With proper management, both the site and people can prosper.

Many development agencies are now giving high priority to rural development schemes which surround World Heritage properties, in the belief that the best way to conserve these sites is to improve the standard of living of the local people. World Heritage sites can thereby serve as a model for rural development which includes conserving nature as one of its foundations.

JEFFREY A. MCNEELY
Chief Conservation Officer IUCN

Imperial Palace of the Ming and Qing Dynasties

CHINA

China, a country with a venerable history of civilization, boasts many sites of outstanding natural beauty and historical significance that have been proclaimed by UNESCO as part of mankind's cultural heritage. Unique in the culture of the East, not only are they a crystalization of the ingenuity and wisdom of the Chinese nation, but among their number are several that mirror the ancient flow of culture between China and foreign countries.

China is proud of these natural and historical sites; it regards them as part of the world's cultural heritage. During the last four decades and more, the Chinese government has left no stone unturned in order to protect and preserve them, receiving much support and help from people of insight abroad in its effort to do so.

There are heritage sites of global importance scattered around the world. They are one of the friendly links between the world's people, and, on our common march toward a new era, I am sure they will play a major role in bringing the peoples of the world even closer together.

Finally, I would like to offer my warm congratulations on the publication of this book, *Masterpieces of Man and Nature*.

楊尚昆
一九九一年元月

YANG SHANGKUN
President, People's Republic of China

The Mausoleum of the first Qin Emperor

The Great Wall

UNLIKE CITY WALLS that are built to enclose and protect a small area, China's Great Wall stretches for more than 5000 kilometres (3100 miles) from east to west across the entire width of northern China. As the greatest construction project ever undertaken, not simply in China but in the entire world, the United Nations listed it in 1987 as one of the world's great heritage sites.

The first defensive walls to be built in China appeared in the State of Chu during the seventh century BC. At that time, China was divided into a number of states that were constantly at war with each other. The Chu walls are supposed to have stood at the juncture of present-day Hubei, Shaanxi and Henan provinces and had a total length of about 500 to 600 kilometres (310 to 370 miles). Chu's example was followed by the states of Qi, Qin, Han, Zhao, Wei, Yan and Zhongshan, each of which erected their own walls.

In 221 BC, Qin Shi Huang, the first emperor of the Qin Dynasty, unified China. To protect his empire from the harassment of northern nomadic tribes, he ordered that the walls built by Yan, Zhao and Qin be connected into one continuous wall fortified with watchtowers. Thus the first Great Wall was born, running at Gansu Province's Lintao in the west and ending in the Liaodong Peninsula in the east. During the following 1800 years, the Great Wall was repeatedly repaired and expanded by more than 20 central and local regimes including the Han, Northern Wei, Northern Qi, Northern Zhou, Sui, Liao, Jin, Yuan and Ming.

The overall length of the Great Wall has risen and fallen with the changing political and military situations of different periods of Chinese history. Some sections built at different times run parallel to each other and occasionally meet and cross. The Great Wall of the Qin, Han, Jin and Ming dynasties exceeded 5000 kilometres (3100 miles) in length, making it the longest in Chinese history. But the aggregate length of all the walls built down the centuries amounts to more than 50,000 kilometres (31,000 miles). Remains of all these sections can still be found in Liaoning, Jilin, Heilongjiang, Beijing, Tianjin, Hebei, Shanxi, Inner Mongolia, Shaanxi, Ningxia, Gansu, Xinjiang, Qinghai, Hubei and Shandong. In Inner Mongolia alone there exist the remains of 15,000 kilometres (9300 miles) of walls constructed over several dynasties.

The construction of the Great Wall was a mammoth task demanding tremendous toil and technical knowledge from countless military strategists and builders. Extending through loess plateaus and desert plains, rising to mountain crests and ridges and descending into river basins, it was largely constructed across terrain already almost invulnerable to outside attack.

The Great Wall

Peking Man Site at Zhoukoudian

A Cultural Heritage for All Mankind

The materials used in its construction were all secured locally. Some sections were built of rammed earth. Others were built of giant flagstones, bricks or tamarish twigs and reed mixed with rocks. The construction workers employed to build the wall were principally troops stationed along it, conscripted labourers and prisoners banished to the frontier. According to one inscribed stone tablet found on the wall, each length of the wall was divided up into smaller sections, each of which was in turn assigned to a group of builders.

During the Ming Dynasty, the Great Wall was divided into 9 sections guarded by 11 garrisons. A total of 1 million troops were stationed along the wall. Thousands of beacon towers stood along its length to serve as a means of communicating with Beijing by smoke during the day and with fire at night.

As a defensive work, the Great Wall played an important role in north China's political and economic development. It helped promote economic exchanges between northern and southern China in ancient times. Its western section, built during the Han Dynasty, also successfully guaranteed the safety of traffic along the Silk Road, China's trading link with the West 2000 years ago.

During the last few centuries, the Great Wall has had little military significance. However, as one of the world's architectural wonders, it deserves to be preserved in as original shape as possible. The Chinese government has designated it for state protection and restored sections at Shanhaiguan, Jiumenkou, Huangyaguan, Jinshanling, Mutianyu, Badaling and Jiayuguan to their former glory, opening them to tourists from China and abroad.

In 1986, China set up the China Great Wall Society and engaged a number of experts to conduct research into the Great Wall. Great efforts have been made to survey and preserve this gigantic monument, and much valuable support and aid has been received from UNESCO and many friends from abroad for China's work in ensuring the continued existence of one of the world's great historic constructions.

LUO ZHEWEN
Vice President of China Great Wall Society

CHINA HAS A LONG history of civilisation. Its capital, Beijing, is a world-famous historical-cultural city with roots stretching back more than 3,000 years. The city served the country's capital through the last five imperial dynasties. Built 570 years ago, the Forbidden City, and within the Forbidden City, the Imperial Palace, still stand intact at the heart of Beijing. As the largest and best-preserved palace-building complex in China, the Imperial Palace is the finest example of Chinese architecture. Its magnificent halls, designed to signify the absolute authority of the emperor, are grouped along a north-south axis running through the centre of Beijing. As the capital of the People's Republic, Beijing is now growing on a grander scale than ever before, but it still retains the Forbidden City as its core. The Imperial Palace has now been converted into a museum with a stunning collection of more than 1 million cultural relics and works of art.

In the search for the origins of Chinese culture, one naturally thinks of Peking Man. The first skull-cap belonging to Peking Man was discovered in 1929 on Dragon Bone Hill at Zhoukoudian, a famous site rich in archaeological and historical significance, on the south-western outskirts of Beijing. Peking Man or *Homo erectus pekinensis*, lived at Zhoukoudian 500,000 years ago during the lower palaeolithic era. During the middle and upper palaeolithic ages, Zhoukoudian was also the home of New Cave Man and Upper Cave Man, both examples of *Homo sapiens*, named after the two caves where their remains were discovered. Upper Cave Man continued to live at Zhoukoudian until some 10,000 years ago - the period from which the majority of chinese myths surrounding the origin of the Chinese people stem.

According to folklore, the Chinese people are descended from the mythical emperors Yan Di (the Divine Husbandman) and Huang Di (the Yellow Emperor). Tales associated with these two legendary figures, particularly with the Yellow Emperor, are legion. *The Records of the Historian*, written during the Western Han Dynasty (206 BC — 24 AD), claims that the first governor of the Beijing area, appointed during the early Zhou Dynasty more than 3,000 years ago, was a descendant of the Yellow Emperor. It is also said that Huangshan (Yellow) Mountain in east China's Anhui Province took its name from the Yellow Emperor. Today, Huangshan is celebrated for its magnificent mountain landscapes: spectacular rocky peaks, odd-shaped pines and seas of mist and clouds. The celebrated Ming Dynasty geographer Xu Xiake (1586-1641) wrote of the beauty of Huangshan

Mount Taishan

after climbing the lofty peak of Tiandu (Heavenly Capital): 'Mist followed me like shadow when I was labouring up towards the peak. The pines on its summit have crooked trunks with interwoven branches. The cypresses, with their branches as thick as one's arm spread horizontally above the surfaces of rocks, look like patches of moss. It is windy on the summit and mist and clouds drift from place to place. The green peaks below wrapped in clouds sometimes put in an appearance. The foothills, bright with sunlight, fascinate one's eyes'. The best scenic spots on Huangshan are scattered across an area of 150 square kilometres (58 square miles), or three-fifths of the total area occupied by the mountain.

The majestic Taishan Mountain on the North China Plain, an area of advanced culture in ancient times, is usually ranked the first of China's five holy mountains. In the *Book of Songs*, the first anthology of Chinese poetry, Taishan is described as 'Lofty and majestic, it is the pride of the State of Lu'. Confucious, China's greatest ancient thinker and a native of the State of Lu was so struck by Taishan's height that he said: 'Looking down from the summit, I found how small the surrounding world appeared as it lay below me'. In ancient times, emperors often made special trips to Taishan to worship and pray to heaven. They left behind them carved stone tablets, of which the most notable are the one inscribed with the Diamond Sutra and the one recording a visit to the mountain by the Tang Dynasty (618-907 AD) emperor, Xuanzong. With its natural beauty blended harmoniously with the cultural artefacts deposited on the mountain over the centuries, Taishan is now regarded as one of the world's most spectacular heritage sites.

The stone tablet erected on Taishan by Qin Shi Huang, the first emperor of the Qin Dynasty (221-206 BC), has long disappeared. However, large numbers of terra-cotta warriors and horses made and buried near his tomb in Shaanxi Province on his order have been discovered in recent years. To date, about 10,000 warriors and more than 4,000 horses have been unearthed, all arranged in military formations ready for battle. Qin Shi Huang also ordered that the defensive walls in north China be linked to form the massive construction now known as the Great Wall. The Great Wall was repeatedly repaired and expanded in the following centuries. In ancient times, it successfully protected the agriculturally advanced Yellow River Valley from harassment by northern nomadic tribes. It also safeguarded traffic along the Silk Road, the trading route that once linked China to the West and which perhaps did more than anything else to promote cultural and economic exchanges between Europe and the Orient.

Thanks to the protection of the Great Wall, grottoes, among them the Mogao Grottoes in Dunhuang, Gansu Province, appeared along the

Silk Road. Created over a period of about 1,000 years beginning in the fourth century, the Mogao grottoes are the finest and largest of their kind in China. They house a remarkable collection of 2,100 painted statues, 45,000sq m (500,000sq ft) of murals and tens of thousands of bas-reliefs. Since the founding of the People's Republic, restoration and conservation work has been carried out to restore the splendour of the grottoes. This has also helped promote worldwide research on the Dunhuang region.

China has a large number of cultural heritage sites; they are now part of the common wealth of mankind.

HOU RENZHI
Professor of Geography at Beijing University
Member of the Division of Earth Sciences under
the Chinese Academy of Sciences.

What dazzles, for the moment spends its spirit:
What's genuine, posterity shall inherit.

GOETHE, FAUST

THE GREAT WALL

LOCATION   Crosses many Provinces in northern and central areas, N 26° to 48°, E 74° to 72° 04'.

DESCRIPTION   Built over a period of more than 2,000 years, the Wall stretches out over more than 50,000km (31,000mi). It is in varying states of repair, much of it in ruins, the section built during the Ming Dynasty being in the best state of repair. Construction is generally of earth, stone and brick. The size varies, but it is typically 9m (30ft) high and several metres (yards) wide. Numerous towers were built along its length.

SIGNIFICANCE   The Great Wall is without doubt one of the greatest and most famous constructions of the ancient world. Construction began on several fronts sometime during the 7th century BC, when the great kingdoms of the day began erecting walls to protect themselves. During the period 221 BC to 206 BC, the Emperor Qin had created his Dynasty and began linking up some of the old walls and adding new sections in order to create one great wall. Throughout successive Dynasties that followed, the Wall was extended and repaired, most notably during the Ming Dynasty. The quality of work performed under Ming was quite astounding and consequently this 5,650km (3,511mi) section of the wall is remarkably well preserved and has been singled out for special protection. Taken as a whole, the Great Wall would have to be described as the greatest building project in human history.

Tang Dynasty pavilion at the Mogao Caves

PEKING MAN SITE AT ZHOUKOUDIAN

LOCATION   Municipality of Beijing, N 39° 44′, E 115° 55′.

DESCRIPTION   This has been the site of extensive archaeological excavations since 1921. It comprises countless fossils, tools and ornaments, including fossil remains of Peking Man and Upper Cave Man. There is also a cave which was used as a dwelling.

SIGNIFICANCE   The first complete skull of Peking Man, who lived 700,000 to 200,000 years ago, was found at this site. Since then, 6 other complete skulls have been found, along with numerous fragments of bones and teeth, tools, ornaments and evidence of the use of fire. The site of Upper Cave Man, who lived 18,000 to 11,000 years ago, is nearby. A cemetery was unearthed in a dwelling cave on the site yielding some important bone fragments, including 3 complete skullcaps.

THE MAUSOLEUM OF THE FIRST QIN EMPEROR

LOCATION   Lintong County, Shaanxi Province, N 34° 23′, E 109° 06′.

DESCRIPTION   The grounds of the mausoleum are very large, the length of the outer rectangular wall being 6.3km (3.9mi). The buildings are mostly in ruins but many life-size terracotta warriors and horses have been found in a good state of preservation.

SIGNIFICANCE   This mausoleum, easily the largest in Chinese history, was constructed for the first Emperor of the Qin Dynasty, Ying Zheng, in the period 246 BC to 208 BC. The most remarkable feature of this site is the contents of 3 large pits that were unearthed just outside the mausoleum grounds in 1974. The first pit contained over 3,000 life-sized terracotta warriors, horses and chariots, all lined up in perfect order, the second and third pits contained a lesser number of similarly life-sized soldiers. All of these figures are extremely lifelike and very well preserved.

MOUNT HUANGSHAN

LOCATION   Near the city of Huangshan, Anhui Province, N 30° 10′, E 118° 11′.

DESCRIPTION   The protected area itself is 154 sq kms (59sq mi) in area, with a peripheral buffer zone which covers 142 sq kms (54sq mi). The landscape is quite mountainous, with numerous peaks, the most famous of which is the Lotus-Flower Peak at 1,864 m (6,200ft) above sea level. Large, unusually shaped rocks abound, many of them resembling animals and mythical figures. The dominant vegetation is the Huangshan Pine – a species endemic to the area. The entire area forms the watershed of two major river systems – the Changjiang and the Qiantangjiang. There are 36 gorges, from which 36 fountainheads flow into 24 streams. Countless waterfalls, deep pools, ponds and springs are to be found, including the famous Huangshan Hot Spring.

SIGNIFICANCE   This area has been called a 'fairyland on earth'; it abounds with countless unique and wonderful sights. The 'four wonders of Mount Huangshan', namely, the pines, the rocks, the hot springs and the seas of cloud which encircle the peaks, form a harmonious whole; a breathtaking scenic wonder. The great mystical quality to this area's beauty has led to the development of an entire culture, the Huangshan culture. Endless paintings, poems, carvings and stories have been inspired by this, 'the first miraculous mountain on earth.'

MOGAO CAVES

LOCATION   At the eastern foot of Mt. Mingsha, Dunhuang County, Gansu Province, N 40° 08′, E 94° 49′.

DESCRIPTION   These caves are man made, having been dug into a 1.6km (1mi) portion of the cliff at the eastern foot of Mt. Mingsha. There are numerous caves, all varying in size. The largest is 40m (131ft) high and 900sq m (10,000sq ft) in area.

SIGNIFICANCE   The Mogao Caves hold the richest collection of Buddhist art in the world. They house more than 2,400 painted sculptures and over 45,000sq m (500,000sq ft) of richly coloured wall murals. It is believed that construction of the caves began around 366 AD when a Buddhist monk by the name of Yue Zhun started the first diggings. The period 581 AD to 1036 AD saw the greatest activity in construction when most of the larger caves were dug. By the 16th century they were largely deserted. The most important cave, the Cave of Scriptures, was discovered in 1900. It contains over 45,000 documents and relics from Buddhist, Taoist, Confucian, Manichaean and Parsiist scriptures as well as numerous works of art and important social documents.

MOUNT TAISHAN

LOCATION   Central Shandong Province, N 36° 11′ to 36° 31′, E 116° 50′ to 117° 06′.

DESCRIPTION   Mt. Taishan has 112 peaks, the main one being Jade Emperor's Peak. There are also 48 caves, 98 cliffs, 102 brooks and many pools, waterfalls and springs. In addition, there are many cultural elements to this site, with 22 temples, 97 ruins, 819 stone tablets and over 1,000 stone inscriptions.

SIGNIFICANCE   The cultural significance of this area complements perfectly the awesome and majestic beauty of its many forests, peaks, waterfalls, pools and

'Guest-Greeting Pine', Mount Huangshan

streams. This mountain rises spectacularly from the surrounding Shandong Plain and has been considered as a symbol of heaven for over 3,000 years. For around 2,000 of those years Mt. Taishan was the destination of the personal pilgrimages of the Emperors. Ceremonies were held on the summit and each time something new was left, so that now the mountain is a treasure trove of ancient religious artefacts and monuments.

IMPERIAL PALACE OF THE MING AND QING DYNASTIES

LOCATION   In the centre of Beijing, N 39° 30′, E 116° 00′.

DESCRIPTION   The Imperial Palace occupies 150,000sq m (1,665,000sq ft) and has over 9,000 rooms. The compound stretches out over 720,000sq m (7,992,000sq ft) and is surrounded by a wall 3km (1.86mi) long and 8m (26ft) high. There are 4 watchtowers standing at each corner of the wall and there is a 52m (170ft) wide moat surrounding it. Palace construction is of timber.

SIGNIFICANCE   Formerly called the Forbidden City, construction on this palace started in 1406AD and was completed in 1420. It is the largest complete complex of buildings preserved in China and one of the most significant preserved wooden structures in the world. The architectural style and planning employed is distinctive and impressive. A network of crosslinked primary and secondary enclosures presents an efficient use of space while emphasizing the importance of the 3 Great Halls where official functions and ceremonies were held.

COLOMBIA

Colombia accepted the World Heritage Convention in May, 1983 and presently has one site on the World Heritage List – the renowned fortified Spanish colonial town of Cartagena. This was one of South America's first Spanish cities, and certainly one of its most important in terms of trade between Spain and the New World colonies.

The Spanish influence has been strong ever since colonisation, and remains so to this day, even though Colombia has one of the most mixed populations in South America. The majority of people are triguenos – various mixtures of Indian, negro and white. In his essay that follows, Misael Borrero argues for the preservation of cultural heritage, not simply as an act of nostalgia, but as a necessary step for future cultural development.

This year marks the fifth centennial of what was once termed the 'discovery' of America. I say once, since now most would agree that rather than a discovery, it was more a clash of two cultures. Initially the two cultures collided harshly, but then, with time, this clash merged into the beginnings of the new American man; the inheritor of the Indian, Spanish and African races.

This was not only the 'New World', but also a part of the world where 'the sun never set'.

As is well known, just like Columbus and his hundred companions in the Caravels, the first Spaniards came to America with a 'return ticket'. They came seeking 'El Dorado'. The initial conquest of these lands was not the result of a co-ordinated effort by people with imperial hopes, but rather of many individuals acting individually against surprised locals who defended their land and their rights.

A Colombian journalist, Don Juan de Castellanos, once wrote: '...they (the indigenous Indian people) were men who fought for more than the saving of their lives – for the avenging of their deaths that they saw as certain'. The Spaniards felt this hostility from the Indians, as well as from the strange environment. So they were fierce and cruel in their actions, both with the venerable natives and with the natural habitat.

Later came the colonial times, peaceful and fertile. In these times the Spanish started to feel closer to the American land. They started to explore the huge reserves of natural resources that had been mostly overlooked due to the dominance of gold, the Conquistador's sole concern. A consequence of this exploration was the great botanical expedition of the New Reign of Granada. This was the beginning of the real common history between Spain and the American land. Its mentor was His Majesty Carlos III and the person to carry it out was the wise figure of Cadiz, José Celestino of Mutis.

This great enterprise constituted the real discovery of '...that land where the Creator had deposited an infinity of things of major admiration..', as Mutis described it. With this expedition, the first real inventory of floral resources was taken. It projected an integral vision of nature; a scientific orientation for its protection and use and, in a modern sense, designed an ecological treatment for the relationship between man and the tropical media surrounding him, a treatment which was naturally unknown up until then.

Colombia is still a young nation. It is the convergence of past and future. Only by conserving the richness of all that comprises its ambience; the artistic patrimony, the countless manifestations of cultures which have settled throughout its many chapters of history and the integrity of its racial variety; can this nation build its future.

In order to create its own destiny and not one borrowed from other nations, it is necessary to conserve the legacy of previous generations. To create and conserve its own features is the great compromise that will unify the national being.

MISAEL PASTRANA BORRERO
former President of Colombia

'A City with a Soul'

THE STRING OF tall luxury blocks stretched along torrid Caribbean beaches suggests a modern city meekly submissive to the demands of international tourism. This is only partially and superficially true. Not far away stand the steeply rising fortifications of old Cartagena, the city built on the lovely bay of the same name, on the Atlantic coast of Colombia, as a magnificent riposte to the attacks which this region, coveted by the enemies of imperial Spain, had to endure in the seventeenth century.

In the sixteenth century, Europeans were dazzled by the New World and longed to possess it. The seventeenth century, the age of pirates and privateers (the latter, unlike the former, obeyed the laws of the State which granted them 'letters of marque' authorising them to seize enemy ships and merchandise), saw the growth of strongholds whose ramparts and defences were vastly superior to those of medieval times.

Solid and massive fortresses were needed to withstand attack by heavy artillery and cannon. The Spanish forts in America met these specifications. Cartagena was one of the most typical of them and is, perhaps, the only one to have survived virtually intact.

Sir Francis Drake, the English sailor and privateer who fought the Spaniards in the Gulf of Mexico and ravaged the coasts of Chile and Peru, suffered a severe defeat at the hands of the terrorised but valiant citizens of Cartagena. The man who would

Cartagena

later take on the Invincible Armada attacked the city a second time, in 1586, when he granted it freedom in exchange for 100,000 ducats, 200 black slaves and the church bells. On account of this humiliation, the Council of the Indies in Madrid decided on the complete fortification of the city. For the Spanish empire, Cartagena, the prey of greedy pirates, was a vital point for the defence of its communications with the whole of South America, and especially with the viceroyalty of Peru, since it was through this warehouse and arsenal that all the treasures of the former Inca empire were sent to Spain.

Hence the exceptional geopolitical importance of Cartagena for the Spaniards and, or course, for their enemies. Hence too the strategic position of what was then called 'the key to the Indies of Peru'.

The walls of Cartagena, rebuilt and improved over two centuries, constitute a piece of military architecture that resisted repeated assaults by the Dutch, the English and the French. Treasures of colonial architecture are conserved within them. Traces of the original inhabitants, many of whom came from Andalusia, survive in the Mozarabic design of balconies, windows and patios, and in the language and traditions. Stone-lined pools and luxuriant gardens surround the inner thoroughfares of a still living city with moisture and magic.

Cartagena has not suffered from the excesses of progress. Thanks to its wise master plan and architects, a substantial part of the original layout has been preserved. It is still possible to relive the moments of the city's splendour. Saint Peter Claver (1580-1654), the Spanish missionary to the black slaves of America, still imbues the city with that heroic humanism that helped to mitigate the cruelties of the Inquisition (the place where its sombre ritual was performed has wisely been preserved almost intact). Convents, churches, public fountains, cobbled alleys, tiny circular plazas bring to the city an evocative charm. Even the vaults built here and there in the city walls have been preserved; they not only served as shelters for the inhabitants during attacks by the English and French but – ironically – were later used by the Creoles when they fought the Spaniards for independence, having previously served as prisons for these self-same heroes.

The forts of San Felipe de Barajas and San Fernando de Bocachica which defended the harbour are remarkable for their original and ingenious design. A group of fine mansions bears witness to the magnificence of a port that grew rich from the merchandise it redistributed throughout South America.

The city was a rallying point for people and ideas as well as for goods and ambitions. In Cartagena, a city with a soul, blacks, mulattoes, mestizos and whites lived – and still live – together. The crucible of a new world, it has been the scene of successive experiments in Latin American integration. The Andine Pact and the Cartagena Agreement are sufficient proof of this vocation. During the colonial period the city succeeded in integrating Catholic austerity with a passion for adventure; today it combines fidelity to the past with love of life. Cartagena's vitality greets the visitor at every step. Its present creativity gives the lie to those who simplistically identify conservation with stagnation. It is impossible to escape the bewitchment of the city's colonial atmosphere and fortress-like character, but its people are not drugged by the perfume of its past. On the contrary it stimulates them to face the challenges of today.

Cartagena de Indias is a city which has miraculously resisted the corrosion of time, the assaults of pirates and smugglers who also tried to sell its soul, and the indifference of the powers-that-be. But above all it has survived the more dangerous assaults of the worshippers of progress who, insensitive to the charm of the past, are always ready to demolish a colonial house and replace it with a pretentious concrete cube to show that the city is vigorously facing the future. Fortunately this wonderful city is also determined to preserve its past, and the intelligent expression of this determination is, perhaps, the best contribution Cartagena can make to the year 2000.

RENATA DURAN, Columbian lawyer and writer, is a member of her country's permanent delegation to UNESCO. She is the author of two volumes of poems, La Muñeca Pota (The Broken Doll) and, to be published shortly, Oculta Ceremonia (Secret Ceremony).

Reprinted from the *Unesco Courier,* April 1985

CARTAGENA

LOCATION   Carribean coast, Department of Bolivar, N 10° 25′, W 75° 32′.

DESCRIPTION   Included in this listing is the old fortified port town of Cartagena, the San Felipe Castle, the areas of Manga and El Cabrero and the Fort of San Fernando de Bocachica.

SIGNIFICANCE   Cartagena was founded in 1533 by Don Pedro de Heredia and quickly developed into a prosperous town. After suffering numerous attacks, a request was sent to the King of Spain, Felipe II, for assistance in constructing protective fortifications. After a period of time, a distinguished architect was dispatched in 1586 by the name of Bautista Antonelli. 30 years later the fortifications were complete and Cartagena was secure. There are numerous fine examples of colonial and republican architecture to be found within the walls.

COSTA RICA

Costa Rica is Central America's second smallest country (next to El Salvador), with a land area of 51,574 sq km (19,600 sq mi). After ratifying the World Heritage Convention in August 1977, it now has one inclusion on the World Heritage List, Talamanca Range-La Amistad Reserves.

The absolutely remarkable thing about Costa Rica's sole listing is that it covers over 10% of the country's total land area. This is a great testimony to Costa Rica's dedication and commitment, not just to the World Heritage Convention, but to the future of our Earth. This commitment is clearly exemplified in this essay by Rodrigo Carazo, one of Costa Rica's former Presidents and now a very highly respected international spokesman, particularly with respect to global environmental problems as they relate to developing countries.

Talamanca Range

Today, the world is debating the consumption – conservation alternative.

The developed countries have destroyed their natural resources and this is the price they have paid for what we commonly know as 'wealth'. The operation of industries continues to damage the little green remaining in the rich countries. The automotive park does the rest and pollution is aggravated by massive urban development.

The evils our planet is experiencing are worsening. Everyone is generally aware of the dangers represented by the depletion of the ozone layer and the greenhouse effect, just to mention two examples.

The wealthy nations continue their practices without stopping their substantial consumption of resources, exceeding greatly the world per capita average, while refusing to modify their habits and wastes.

Today's 'civilisation' has made a great majority believe that to be wealthy means to have money. There are relatively few people who believe that true wealth is represented by the Earth's green resources. Those resources are the ones capable of contributing towards the absorption of the CO_2 that contaminates the air, towards maintaining temperatures at their normal levels and towards feeding all living beings with oxygen.

The leaders and people of the poor countries ignore that they are the possessors of a real wealth (natural resources) which they are gratuitously supplying to the planet's inhabitants, including of course, the possessors of money (volatile wealth).

The poor countries also ignore that in the rich world an awareness is growing towards conservation which the developed countries themselves refuse to practice, instead directing the responsibility towards the poor world.

If we are not careful, we will be victims of this pressure and of the action of the powerful ones who desire to impose their will and policies upon our countries.

The developing nations must therefore devote special efforts to the conservation of resources. Foremost among those efforts should be directed towards forestry, devoting all of our land that is apt for such endeavour.

It is urgent that we publicise such practices and that we oppose and counteract the information that is discrediting us. It is also urgent that we request that it be known that our countries demand that the planet – which belongs to all of us – not be contaminated in the way it is being contaminated by the industrialised world.

It is urgent that we make known to the whole world that contributing towards the survival of the human race in the way our countries can do it, requires sacrifice and costs. It must be known that conserving a national park, protecting an area and creating a wildlife refuge, and in turn implementing laws to protect the natural resources, costs us a great deal of money.

The wealthy countries cannot be indifferent to these efforts if they want the human race to survive. They will have to contribute and pay for that conservation.

We must all contribute – by conservation of the

Puma on La Amistad Reserve

natural resources – towards the fate of the human race. The countries which have already destroyed their green resources must rebuild whatever they can, conserve whatever is left and pay in order to enable the nations who still have their natural resources, to conserve them.

A new attitude towards global justice is imperative.

RODRIGO CARAZO
Former President of Costa Rica

TALAMANCA RANGE AND LA AMISTAD RESERVES

LOCATION   The Provinces of San Jose, Cartago, Limon and Puntarenas, N 08° 44′ to 10° 02′, W 82° 43′ to 83° 44′.

DESCRIPTION   The area of this site is about 500,000ha (1,205,500ac) and comprises Chirripo National Park, Talamanca Range National Park, Hitoy-Cerere Biological Reserve, Barbilla Biological Reserve, Las Tablas Forest Protection Zone, and seven Indian reserves.

SIGNIFICANCE   This area has at least 13 species of mammals, 15 birds and 10 reptiles or amphibians that are not to be found anywhere else in the world. There are also many unique plant communities, such as high altitude bogs, pure stands of oaks and subalpine treeless plateaus. The Indian population on the reserves represents four tribes and numbers approximately 10,000. Traditional lifestyles have been remarkably well maintained.

CUBA

Cuba is the largest island in the Antilles, otherwise known as the West Indies. It is strategically located at the entrance of the Gulf of Mexico.

The population of Cuba is composed of peoples from Europe, Africa and Asia and of the Indians who inhabited the island at the time of its discovery by Columbus in 1492. It was one of Spain's first possessions in the new world and was the final Spanish colony in the Americas to gain independence.

Diego Vetazquez began the conquest of Cuba in 1511. By 1515 the Spanish had established several settlements including Havana which became the principal port and naval base.

Cuba suffered throughout the 17th century from Spain's wars with England, France and Holland and the island's economy was severely strained. The capture and looting of Havana in 1762 by the British marked a climax to the island's misfortunes.

From 1764 the island, again under Spanish control, began to flourish. Spain established commercial relations with the US and new trade channels were opened. The 19th century saw a desire for independence due to Spain's repressive measures. Revolts increased and by 1868 the island was plunged into a bloody civil war that ended in 1878. The armistice was short lived and war again broke out with Spain in 1895. This was followed by US military occupation from 1899 to 1902. The first Cuban Congress met on May 5, 1902.

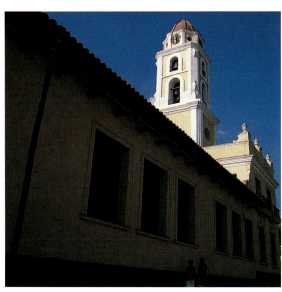

Trinidad

View of Havana from la Cabaña Fort

Cuba ratified the World Heritage Convention in March 1981 and currently has two sites inscribed on the World Heritage List. Both of these sites, Old Havana and Trinidad, are classic Spanish colonial settlements and relate directly to this island's turbulent colonial past.

OLD HAVANA AND ITS FORTIFICATIONS

LOCATION   Havana, northern coast facing Gulf of Mexico, N 23° 08', W 82° 21'.

DESCRIPTION   The historic centre of the capital city of Cuba covers an area of 142.5ha (343.5ac). It is bounded by the lines of the old walls, which are now Monserrate and Egido Streets, and the Bay of Havana. The centre of this old area is Plaza de Armas. On its eastern side stands the old palace of the Spanish governors, probably the most notable building. Other buildings include the Castillo de Principe, the National Library and the well preserved fort, La Fuerza. Morro Castle and La Punta are the landmark fortresses which guard the harbour. Behind these sits La Cabana, Havana's largest fort.

SIGNIFICANCE   Havana was the last of the original colonial towns in Cuba to be founded. Its growth was rapid, due mainly to its excellent strategic situation, facing the Gulf of Mexico. In 1550 the Governor moved from Santiago to make Havana the main town in the country. By 1740 it had become the naval station for the Spanish Fleet and was one of the wealthiest ports in the Americas.

TRINIDAD AND THE VALLEY DE LOS INGENIOS

LOCATION   Province of Sancti Spiritus, N 21° 48' W 79° 59'.

DESCRIPTION   The historic area of the city of Trinidad covers 37ha (89ac). A further 40 hectares (100 ac) has some historic buildings mixed in with more modern architecture. There are a total of 1,207 buildings in the historic centre; 279 from the 17th century, 729 from the 19th century and 199 from the 20th century which have been built in the traditional style. The Valley de los Ingenios (Valley of the Sugar Mills) has 58 industrial buildings of historical significance.

SIGNIFICANCE   One of the original 7 cities of Cuba founded by Diego Velasquez, Trinidad was initially on the coast, but was moved inland after suffering repeated pirate attacks. Sugar production became significant during the 18th century and the city grew into Cuba's fifth largest. This prosperity continued until the second half of the 19th century when the slave market, on which it depended, declined and the war against Spain took its economic toll. The subsequent rapid economic decline was probably the major factor in Trinidad's colonial architecture having been so well preserved.

Paphos

CYPRUS

Cyprus is a small island in the Eastern Mediterranean and one of the smallest states in the world community. In matters of cultural heritage, however, the island is one of the richest, having entered the cultural scene of the old world already at the end of the 9th millennium B.C. Numerous vestiges of the island's past, ranging from the prehistoric period (end of the Palaeolithic) down to the most recent past (folk architecture) are scattered all over its territory, illustrating most vividly the various phases of its life.

The Government of the Republic of Cyprus, mainly through the Department of Antiquities, makes every effort to safeguard the cultural heritage of the people of Cyprus, being very conscious that this is part of the world's heritage. UNESCO, recognising the importance of the cultural property of Cyprus, has included two archaeological areas (the monuments of the Paphos area and nine Byzantine painted churches in the Troodos area) in the World Heritage List, thus emphasising the importance of this heritage for the whole of mankind. Since 1974, that part of the Cypriot heritage in the area of foreign occupation has suffered severe damage and is in constant danger.

I take this opportunity to appeal to the world community to do all they can in order to save the cultural heritage of Cyprus for the benefit of all mankind.

MR GEORGE VASSILIOU
The President of the Republic of Cyprus

Panayia Phorviotissa, Troodos Region

Our Cultural Heritage in Cyprus

THE SMALL ISLAND of Cyprus in the eastern Mediterranean had already entered the field of culture at the end of the 9th millennium BC and has for some ten millennia been a cradle of culture and art. The geographical position of Cyprus in the cross-roads of the great civilisations of the Aegean and the Near East naturally affected the development of its artistic creation. This does not mean that Cypriot art does not have a strong physiognomy of its own, echoing the various phases of its long and eventful past. Numerous monuments are scattered throughout the island, ranging from the neolithic huts of Khirokitia and Kalavassos to the Byzantine churches of the mountains of Troodos and the medieval castles of the Kyrenia mountains.

Religion has always played an important part in the lives of the Cypriots. The notion of fertility was at the centre of prehistoric cults, and in historical times this developed into the worship of Aphrodite, the goddess of love and beauty of the Greek pantheon. Mythical tradition places her birth in Cyprus. Homer, in the Odyssey, refers to her as the Cyprian goddess, who has a temple and a fragrant altar in Paphos, in the western part of the island. She rose from the foams of the sea near the picturesque Paphian coast and has graced the whole region since.

The mild climate and beautiful natural environment of Paphos constitute a perfect setting for its numerous monuments, bathed in light and surrounded by colour. UNESCO included them in the World Heritage List in 1980.

The remains of the sanctuary of Aphrodite at old Paphos evoke Homeric epic and recall the strong impact which the cult of the great goddess exercised for more than one thousand years on the political and cultural developments of this region.

Some ten miles to the north-west of old Paphos are the remains of new Paphos. These include a spacious palace and various villas of the Roman period, adorned with colourful mosaic floors depicting scenes from Greek mythology. They illustrate most eloquently the splendours of imperial Rome and some of them also herald a new era, the coming of Christianity.

Early Christian basilicas in new Paphos, monumental rock-cut tombs of the Hellenistic period, Byzantine wall paintings at Yeroskipou (between old Paphos and new Paphos) blend harmoniously and illustrate vividly human piety.

What makes the archaeological remains of Paphos unique, apart from their monumental artistic beauty, is their harmonious blending with the natural environment. The sea, the clear skies, the picturesque hillocks with a rich variety of colourful vegetation, all form an attractive cadre.

The inclusion of these monuments in the World Heritage List of UNESCO presents extra incentive and in fact an obligation for the Cypriot Government, not only to preserve the monuments themselves but also to present them within their natural environment. In this region which is experiencing a rapid development of tourism, there are not many places in the world which are better suited than Paphos to the development of 'cultural tourism'. Intensive archaeological excavations in the Paphos area during the last twenty-five years or so by Cypriot and foreign archaeologists as well as the restoration of monuments and excavated remains by the Department of Antiquities have placed Paphos prominently on the archaeological map of the Mediterranean. This place should be maintained at all costs, for the benefit of scholarship and for the enjoyment of visitors, both local and foreign.

In 1986, nine painted Byzantine churches of the Troodos mountain region were included in the World Heritage List. Scattered on the mountains among pine trees and bushes, they are an eloquent witness to man's search for the divine.

Cyprus has a rich Byzantine heritage. After recovering from the damage caused by the Arab invaders during the 7th century AD, the island entered an era of cultural and artistic development with its re-incorporation into the Byzantine Empire in 965 AD. The wall-paintings of the Comnenian period (early 12th century) which adorn some of the churches of the Troodos region are masterpieces of Byzantine art, following very closely the artistic styles of Constantinople. The churches of Asinou and Ayios Nicolaos 'of the roof' are but a few examples.

The political conditions in Cyprus during the 14th and 15th centuries and the foreign domination of Cyprus are reflected in the styles of wall-paintings, sometimes seen in the repainting of the same older churches, as is the case of Asinou. The influence of Constantinople continued to be manifest, but indirectly, through portable icons.

The nine painted churches of the Troodos region offer the opportunity for each visitor to 'discover' the refreshing beauty of Byzantine art and to join the Byzantine Cypriots who created them in the worship of God. The serenity of the mountain region and the unspoiled natural environment create the proper atmosphere for artistic enjoyment and contemplation.

The conservation of these churches and their wall-paintings have been one of the main tasks of the Cyprus Department of Antiquities. Their inclusion in the World Heritage List is a justified reward for these efforts but also a tribute to their artistic merit.

Art in Cyprus, whether prehistoric, Classical or Byzantine, is of universal importance and the

Fresco detail, Archangelos Michael at Pedhoulos, Troodos Region

inclusion of the monuments of the Paphos and the Troodos regions in the World Heritage List is a deserving homage. It is also a heavy responsibility for the Cypriot authorities who must prove worthy of the trust which UNESCO has placed in them, as guardians of this important cultural heritage of mankind.

VASSOS KARAGEORGHIS
Former Director of the Department of Antiquities of Cyprus (1963–1989)

PAPHOS

LOCATION   Paphos district, southeastern coastline, N 34° 39′ to 34° 46′, E 32° 24′ to 32° 37′.

DESCRIPTION   The World Heritage area of Paphos comprises 3 sites; the coastline that is the legendary birthplace of Aphrodite; Aphrodite's sanctuary at Kouklia village; Aphrodite's sacred city at Kato Paphos town.

SIGNIFICANCE   All 3 places were of tremendous significance in the ancient world. Aphrodite, the Greek Goddess of Love, was born, according to Homeric legend, when she emerged from the foaming sea at the very spot cited in this listing. The Sanctuary of Aphrodite at Kouklia was mentioned by Homer and other ancient authors and is considered to be the most important of the many that were built in the ancient world. The sacred city has many impressive buildings, including the ruins of a theatre, a gymnasium, an odeon, baths, a necropolis, catacombs and early Christian basilicas.

PAINTED CHURCHES IN THE TROODOS REGION

LOCATION   Troodos Region, N 34° 58′ to 35°, E 32° 49′ to 33° 02′.

DESCRIPTION   This listing comprises 9 churches: 1. Ayios Nikolaostis Steyis at Kakopetria; 2. Ayios Ionnis Lambadhistis Monastery at Kalopanayiotis; 3. Panayia Phorviotissa at Nikitari; 4. Panayia tou Arakou at Lagoudhera; 5. Panayia at Moutoullas; 6. Archangelos Michael at Pedhoulas; 7. Timios Stavros at Pelendria; 8. Panayia Podhithou at Galata; 9. Stavros Ayiasmati at Platanistasa.

SIGNIFICANCE   All 9 churches are in a good state of preservation, but their styles and dates of construction vary. The earliest was built in the 11th century. The paintings represent different styles of art, including that of the 13th century crusaders, 12th century Constantinople, 15th century Middle East, Italian Renaissance and a style influenced by medieval manuscripts.

DOMINICAN REPUBLIC

A small country of only 48,360 sq km (18,658 sq mi), much of the Dominican Republic is given over to the production of sugar. Its capital city, Santo Domingo, is the oldest permanent city founded by Europeans in the New World.

Three years after Christopher Columbus founded Isabella, the first Spanish settlement in the Americas, his brother Bartholomew moved the settlement to the mouth of the Ozama River and renamed it Santo Domingo. It was from here that independence was proclaimed in 1844 after a period of turmoil which saw Spain, France and the Dominican Republic's neighbour, Haiti, all laying claim to the country.

For many years Santo Domingo was the centre of Spanish colonial government in America. It is the seat of both the oldest archbishopric and the oldest university in the western hemisphere. Consequently it developed an exceptionally rich architectural and cultural heritage, much of which has been retained to this day.

The Dominican Republic ratified the World Heritage Convention in February 1985 and had its capital city inscribed on the World Heritage List in 1991.

THE COLONIAL CITY OF SANTO DOMINGO

LOCATION   The Colonial town of Santo Domingo lies to the south of Santo Domingo de Guzman and the capital of the Dominican Republic, W 69° 55′, N 18° 29′. The archeological site of La Isabela is found in the province of Puerto Piata in the north of the island, W 71°05′, N 19° 56′. La Concepcion de la Vega lies in the province of La Vega, N 70° 28′, W 19° 20′.

DESCRIPTION   Santo Domingo with its 16th century style monuments, squares, and majestic cathedral, evokes the atmosphere of the exploration and expansion of the New World. As well as a living testament to Spanish colonialism, the city also provides the visitor with an image of Dominican pride and history. The major monuments include: the Santo Domingo cathedral, the 15th century royal residences, numerous churches, the Alcazar de Colon, Plaza Mayor, convents, monasteries, the first ramparts and important early government buildings. The small town of *La Isabela* was the first urban centre in the New World. The European style of architecture in the town contrasts with the tropical landscape.

Santo Domingo

Using both imported and local resources, the churches, major houses and government edifices (town hall) were built proudly for the first community of the New World. *La Conceptcion de la Vega* was actually founded by Christopher Columbus. Established as a military settlement, the town developed into an important urban centre. Its churches, public monuments and archeological sites make it the most important town on the islands of Santo Domingo.

SIGNIFICANCE   The colonial past of Santo Domingo, La Isabela and Concepcion de la Vega traces the earliest movements of Spanish exploration and expansion. The image of peninsular Spain transported to a new and exotic location can be found in the layout of the towns. The meticulous detail used for the construction of the monuments and combination of local and Spanish materials (ceramics) make Santo Domingo a 15th and 16th century jewel. The archaeological relics of Concepcion de la Vega preserve the beginnings of Latin American exploration. The cathedral of Santo Domingo is a symbol of the colony's progression and La Isabela shows the changes in town planning from a 15th century fortress to an urban and cultural centre.

ECUADOR

Fur seals, Galapagos Islands

Ecuador is located in South America's tropical region along the Pacific coastline, with an area of 270,667 sq kms (104,044 sq mi). It is bisected east to west by the equator, and north to south by the Andes mountain range. These two geographical factors are essential to the ecological division of Ecuador's territory into four main natural regions: the coast (24.67% of the country's total land area), the inter-Andean region or highlands (23.93%), the Amazon region (48.45%) and the archipelago of the Galapagos Islands (2.96%).

The Ecuadorian economy has been affected in general, throughout the eighties, by similar problems to those of other Latin American countries: stagnation of the gross domestic product in real terms; decapitalisation of the agricultural sector leading to a widening of the gap between the city and the countryside, resulting in increased rural poverty; decreased national revenues and lost buying power of wages; unemployment, which has doubled in the last five years, to 13% of the economically active population (1988); inflation rates generally higher than 50% per year; reduced domestic-market supply of food products; and stagnation of the industrial sector. All these phenomena are intimately related to the foreign debt (some 12 billion dollars), which imposes severe obligations on the country and limits its possibilities for development. It can accurately be said that the structural conditions of the crisis are fundamentally derived from the current international economic order, and that no policy for conservation of natural resources and improvement of the human environment in Ecuador can succeed in the long term if such conditions are not changed, because poverty and this economic crisis prevent sustainable development.

From the demographic standpoint, Ecuador has grown rapidly, although this growth seems to have begun to decline during the last two decades. The annual population growth rate for 1950-62 was 2.89%; for 1962-74, 3.19%; for 1974-1982, 2.69%; and for 1982-1990, 2.27%. This has brought the nation's population to a total by the year-end 1990 of 9,622,608, with an average population density of 35.55 inhabitants per square kilometre (92.5/sq mi). In addition to this rapid growth and high density, access to resources – particularly land – is asymmetrically distributed. This has led considerable sectors of the rural population to actively pressure natural woodlands, which in turn has generated a process of settlement on tropical soils that is aggressively destroying the rain forest.

Ecuador has been especially favoured by biological diversity. Although it is a small country, it has an enormous wealth of flora; it may have more species of plants per unit of area than any other country in South America. This high diversity is due to the tropical rain forests lying on both sides of the Andes, and to the species differentiation associated with the northern part of this mountain range.

The region of Ecuador's western mountain slopes had, up until several decades ago, some 8 to 10 thousand plant species, of which some 40 to 60% were endemic. Considering that similar regions have from 10 to 30 animal species per plant species, we might estimate that this zone must have had about 200 thousand species, of which about 50 thousand have been eliminated during the last 25 years. (CMMAD, 1987.)

Western Ecuador's primary forests, together with those of Madagascar and the Atlantic coast of Brazil, are currently top priority for a number of specialists, within the group of critical areas in the world, due to their biotic wealth and high risk status. Under 10% of the original vegetation remains in each of these areas, or is expected to remain by the end of the century, and recent or expected extinctions may total 6200 species of plants and at least 124 thousand species of animals. It is estimated that one species of flora will be wiped out every three days, and five animal species, at the current destruction rate (Ibid.).

Ecuador's three World Heritage listings include two crucially important natural listings – Galapagos Islands and Sangay National Parks. Both of these areas have been blessed with a mega-biodiversity of species and an exceptionally high level of endemism.

The third listing is at present Ecuador's sole cultural contribution to the World Heritage List – the capital city of Quito.

Ecuador accepted the World Heritage Convention in June 1975. This country's incredible wealth of natural and cultural riches will no doubt see more listings forthcoming in the not too distant future.

GONZALO OVIEDO CARRILLO
Nature Foundation
Ecuador

GALAPAGOS ISLANDS

LOCATION   Between 800-1,100km (497-684mi) west of Ecuador's coast, around 0° 00′, W 90° 00′.

DESCRIPTION   This group of 19 islands is scattered over roughly 60,000 sq km (24,000sq mi) of equatorial Pacific Ocean. Approximately half of the group's total land mass is covered by the main island, Isabela. The islands are composed largely of lava and are dotted with numerous volcanoes, mostly extinct. The climate is remarkably unequatorial in character – coastal rainfall is low and air temperature is rarely over 30°C (86°F). This is due mainly to the cold waters which are carried by a current from the south.

SIGNIFICANCE   Perhaps most famous for their namesake, the Galapagos Tortoise, these islands are home to many other unusual animals. These tortoises are considered to be one of the longest living animals on earth and can weigh up to 240kg (529lb). Other unusual animals include the large spiny Iguanas, a four-eyed fish and several unique species of birds. The high number of unusual animals found here inspired many of Charles Darwin's theories on natural selection after he visited these shores in 1835.

QUITO

LOCATION   W 78° 29′, S 00° 12′.

DESCRIPTION   Quito sits at an altitude of 2,818m (9,384ft), on the lower slopes of the Pichincha volcano. The central square is bounded by a cathedral, the palaces of the President and Archbishop and the town hall. The town is intersected by 2 steep ravines which are spanned by old masonry bridges. Numerous church spires, squares, balconied houses, fountains, secluded gardens and iron gates distinguish this quaint old town.

SIGNIFICANCE   This ancient site now hosts a sprawling modern city, but the tranquil charm of the old town

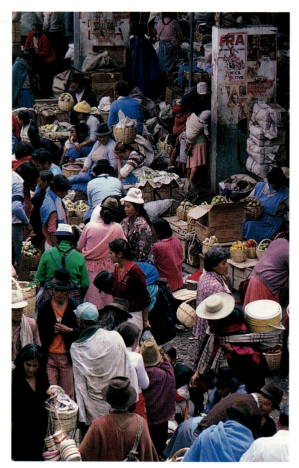
Central markets, Quito

centre still endures. Its history is thought to begin with the Quitus, a large federation of Indian tribes. Between 1000 AD and the late 15th century it was occupied by the people known as Caras. The Incas controlled the town from 1487 until 1534 when the Spanish gained control. The old town as it now stands is in the classic Spanish plan and style. It is very well preserved and, combined with the spectacular mountainous backdrop, offers one of the most sublime settings imaginable.

SANGAY NATIONAL PARK

LOCATION   Central Ecuador, Provinces of Morana Satiago, Chimborazo and Tungurahua, S 01° 28′ to 02° 15′, W 78° 04′ to 78° 31′.

DESCRIPTION   2,700 sq km (1,080sq mi) of largely inaccessible terrain which ranges from high altitude treeless plateaus, to lowland subtropical rainforest. The altitude ranges between 1,000m (3,280ft) and 5,000m (16,404ft).

SIGNIFICANCE   The natural beauty of this park is as spectacular as the contrast between its landscapes; the dense subtropical forests sitting beneath snow covered peaks, with 2 active volcanoes not far away. The high altitude forests that reach up to 4,000m (13,123ft) are distinctive of this area's proximity to the equator. A wide range of animals are supported in these environments, including the spectacled bear, the woolly mountain tapir, the jaguar, and the condor.

Sangay National Park

Biodiversity: the Wealth of Our World

THE PLANET Earth is blessed with a great diversity of genes, species, habitats, cultures, and ecosystems. This biodiversity is the result of hundreds of millions of years of history, including drifting continents, changes in sea level, ice ages, volcanoes, and evolution.

More recent times have seen our species emerge as a dominant force in ecosystems throughout the world, with numerous local cultures earning a living from locally available resources. People have domesticated plants and animals, and are exerting increasing control over the landscape. The spread of major crops has changed the face of the Earth. Wheat from the Middle East, maize and potatoes from the Americas, rubber from Brazil, rice from tropical Asia, palm oil from Africa, and a small handful of others have replaced far more diverse systems, and have produced more for people. Combined with improved medical care, improved communications, fossil fuel energy, and greatly expanded industrial production, the growth in agricultural productivity has enabled the human population to increase to well over 5 billion. Our share of the planet's natural wealth has therefore expanded considerably. According to one estimate, almost 40 per cent of our planet's net primary terrestrial photosynthetic productivity is now directly consumed, diverted, or wasted as a result of human activities, a startling indication of how powerful our ecological influence has been.

Many people would say that major habitat changes and losses of biodiversity are the inevitable price we must pay for progress, as humans become an ever more dominant species on Earth. But in the late 20th century, many people are beginning to worry that we may be squandering the natural wealth which supports our way of life, and that resources which once were renewable are now being exhausted. Some scientists predict that, if present trends continue, up to 25 per cent of the world's species will be lost in the next several decades, accompanied by an equally alarming degradation of habitats and ecosystems. Even worse, indications are that present trends in the loss of species and habitats are in fact accelerating. If projections on the growth of human populations and economic activities prove to be accurate, the loss of diversity could be so great as to undermine prospects for even the sustainable use of natural systems at present levels of production. What can be done to stem the loss?

The World Heritage Convention provides one of the most effective bastions against the onslaughts of human greed. It protects areas like Manu National Park in Peru, which by itself contains more species of plants and birds than all of North America; Serengeti National Park in Tanzania, the last place in the tropics where huge migrations of wildebeests and zebras can still be seen; Salonga National Park in Zaire, with its vast expanses of tropical forests; and the Great Barrier Reef in Australia, where marine ecosystems in all their diversity continue to evolve.

World Heritage sites are also a symbolic expression of the way things ought to be: where governments make a statement about their commitment to conserve places with outstanding biodiversity. When the government of Cameroon adds a diverse tropical forest like Dja to the World Heritage List, it is making a political statement: its contribution to the world is biodiversity, not just logs to be shipped to market. Such statements are increasingly important in a time when most habitats are being over-exploited. World Heritage helps governments demonstrate that maintaining the productivity of natural ecosystems is one of their highest priorities, along with national defence, health, and education.

But there is no room for complacency. The World Heritage network still has large gaps, leaving much of the world's biodiversity still unprotected. The Amazon, Mexico, southern Africa, Indochina, and many marine habitats are still poorly represented. Even so, World Heritage provides one of the best available mechanisms to mobilize greater support for conserving areas containing outstanding examples of our planet's biological wealth.

JEFFREY A MCNEELY
Chief Convservation Officer IUCN

Entrance to crypt, Abu Mena

EGYPT

Egypt is one of the greatest names of antiquity. More than 6,000 years of history may be traced within this famous land.

The numerous dynasties that ruled Egypt for the 4,500 years leading up to Cleopatra's suicide in 30 BC, included many foreign conquerors – the Hyksos, Libyans, Assyrians, Persians and Macedonians all had their influence, and in turn felt the tremendous influence of the depth of Egyptian culture and learning upon their own civilisations.

There were three great periods of consolidated Egyptian rule: the Old Kingdom (2613-2181 BC); the Middle Kingdom (2050-1786 BC); and the New Kingdom (1567-1085 BC).

After Cleopatra's death, the Romans ruled Egypt for almost 700 years, until the coming of the Arabs in 642 AD.

The introduction of Islam to Egypt heralded the dawn of a new cultural and academic resurgence, especially in Cairo which became one of the greatest centres of Islamic culture and learning in the world.

As with so many countries in this region, Egypt fell to the Ottoman Turks in the early 16th century. The next 400 years of Egyptian rule was a tangled web of foreign intervention – by the Turks, English and French, until independence was finally gained in the early 20th century.

Egypt ratified the World Heritage Convention in February 1974, the second country to do so. Currently there are five Egyptian listings, including three ancient sites – Memphis, Thebes and the Nubian ensemble and one site from the days of Roman occupation – the ruins at Abu Mena. The fifth site is Islamic Cairo; the old part of the town which dates from the days of the Arab conquest when Cairo was at the height of its Islamic glory.

Glance at the sun. See the moon and stars. Gaze at the beauty of earth's greenings. Now, think. What delight God gives to us with all these things...All nature is at our disposal. We are to work with it. For without it we cannot survive.

HILDEGARD OF BINGEN

Abu Simbel

Workers' village, Thebes

Safeguarding the Splendour of the Pyramids

FEW GROUPS OF great monuments blend so well with their natural surroundings as the pyramids of Giza. At night beneath a canopy of stars, or in the blinding light of the desert in daytime, the pyramids rise, impressive and alone in a world of rock and sand. Those who built this royal necropolis long ago clearly intended it to be a haven of peace, isolation and silence.

The tranquility of the archaeological site is today threatened by a rash of uncontrolled building development, and the plateau is being taken over by tourist coaches and amenities. Some promoters have even envisaged making golf courses and artificial lakes for pleasure boats. In short, there is a risk that one of the wonders of the world may lose its splendour owing to the anarchic growth of tourism.

To prevent this from happening and to restore serenity to the plateau, the Egyptian Minister of Culture, Farouk Hosny, has decided to take a number of measures.

- Access to the plateau, today open to all, will be strictly controlled, as is the case with almost all historic monuments elsewhere in the world;
- The modern buildings which have been constructed near the site over the years, contrary to the advice of architects, will be demolished. Also scheduled for demolition is the structure which houses the famous royal boat of pharaoh Khufu and which disfigures one side of the Great Pyramid near which it was excavated. The boat will of course not be removed until all necessary technical precautions have been taken to prevent damage to this fragile masterpiece;
- The tarmac roads, whose colour clashes with that of the site, will be replaced by roads made of solidified sand;
- Motor traffic, a source of noise and pollution which damages the stone of the monuments, will be prohibited. Archaeologists and service staff will use electric vehicles;
- Unsupervised animals such as dogs and goats which harm the monuments and discourage visitors will be prohibited;
- Bridle paths will be designed to provide spectacular views for visitors on camel and horse-back. They will also make it easier to keep the site free of litter;
- Also in the interests of tourists and visitors, the area set aside beneath the Sphinx for *son et lumiére* (sound and light) shows will be extended. This area will be lowered so as to improve the view of the Sphinx and the pyramids from the eastern access road to the plateau;
- As is the case with other historic monuments, revenue from visitors will contribute to the conservation of the irreplaceable heritage left by the ancient Egyptians;
- The existing buffer zone will be defined more clearly and improved both aesthetically and functionally, so as to provide a better view of the monuments and to respect the dignity of the site. The cafeteria to the east of the pyramids will disappear.

It is clearly necessary that the plateau of Giza should be fenced off to channel the movement of visitors – at least in the part which is accessible to everyone. Inconspicuous light fencing would be quite suitable for this.

Anyone who has ever marvelled at the mysterious silhouette of the Sphinx and the majestic mass of the pyramids as they suddenly come into view from behind a sand dune will appreciate the importance of safeguarding their timeless splendour.

GERARD BOLLA, Swiss jurist and economist, is a former Assistant Director-General of UNESCO. From 1971 to 1981 he was in charge of UNESCO's programme for the conservation of the cultural heritage, and was notably responsible for archaeological safeguard and rescue operations at Philae (Egypt), Venice, Borobudur and Carthage. He has served as chairman of an international advisory committee of experts on the development projects for the plateau of the pyramids.

Reprinted from the *Unesco Courier*, April 1991.

Sphinx, Memphis

The pyramids of Giza

UNESCO and the Conservation of Old Cairo

T HE INCLUSION of the old city of Cairo in the World Heritage List by the World Heritage Convention, in 1979, underlined the international cultural significance of historic Cairo. But with over six hundred listed buildings in an expanding city whose population is expected to rise from twelve million to between sixteen and twenty million by the year 2000 the problems of preservation are enormous.

In February 1980, in response to a request from the Egyptian Government, UNESCO undertook to send a mission to prepare a report on a conservation strategy for the old city of Cairo. The members of this mission made a number of visits during the period February to August 1980.

The team concentrated its attention on a study area of some three and a half square kilometres (1.3 square miles) containing 450 listed buildings. They found that the resources available for the maintenance of these historic monuments were totally inadequate to the magnitude of the problem. The area's narrow medieval streets are choked with traffic, new and unsuitable industrial and business activities are driving out the traditional craftsmen and small tradesmen, and building fabric is deteriorating due to general decay, inadequate maintenance and the ravages of a rising groundwater table.

The team's report proposed two levels of priority action for the study area. The first of these covers the study area as a whole and suggests a general programme of housing improvement, limitation of the size, speed and number of vehicles allowed into the area and improvement of road maintenance, street cleaning and rubbish collection.

At the second level of action the report proposes a five-year emergency programme for six priority zones containing clusters of monuments. Within each zone urgent action is required to deal with the restoration of monuments, to control the design and construction of new buildings, to rehabilitate and improve existing sites and buildings, to introduce new compatible functions for monuments and to improve and contribute to the social facilities of the neighbourhood.

The six clusters of monuments have been selected to form potential conservation and rehabilitation zones and are spaced out at almost equal distances between the northern gates and the Ibn Tulun Mosque, each focussing on a single street. Each group is thus tightly integrated, yet they are spaced out in such a way that their upgrading will have the maximum impact on the whole of the central area of the old city.

Cairo – Al Rifai and Sultan Hassan Mosque minarets at sunset

The six priority zones, or monument clusters, which form the second level of this emergency restoration program, are listed and described below:

Zone One, centred on Sharia (street) al Muizz li-Din Allah, covers the heart of Fatimid Cairo and is the site of the former Fatimid palaces which were replaced by other major buildings during the Ayyubid and Mamluk periods. Historically the zone demonstrates the development of the typical Cairene madrasa-mosque with attached mausoleum of the founder. Major public buildings and commercial structures prevail, with shopfronts often obstructing the view of important monuments. Due to the vicinity of Khan al Khalili and the Sharia al-Azhar, this zone is the most frequented tourist area and, with its unique architectural heritage, represents a showcase of Islamic Cairo.

Zone Two, centred on Sharia al-Gamaliya, represents one of the finest and most homogeneous street scenes of the old city. It includes the *wakallas* (buildings facing on to courtyards and consisting of shops on the ground floor with living quarters above) and *sabilkuttabs* (buildings with a single ground floor room in which is installed a public fountain, with a balcony room above where young children are taught to chant the Koran) on the north-south spine of Fatimid Cairo, leading from Bab (gate) al-Nasr to the shrine of Hussein. The street is also a sub-centre for the adjacent housing districts which are accessible through the many lanes branching off from the spine.

Zone Three, centred on the Ghouriya, contains the buildings of the Mamluk Sultan al-Ghoury and a series of traditional *suqs* (markets). These originally extended from the Sharia Muski southwards as far as the Mu'ayyad complex (Zone Four) and were cut by the Sharia al-Azhar. To the east, close to the Sharia Hammam al-Masbaja is a vegetable market which acts as a local focus for the surrounding area. Further east, the al-Azhar Mosque, which is adjacent to this zone, is both a major tourist attraction and an important religious centre.

Zone Four is centred on Bab Zuweila, the southern gate of the Fatimid city, linking the walled city with its southern extensions. Immediately south of the gate, the spine features a unique sequence in the old city, from the small open space outside the gate to the covered Street of the Tent-Makers. Due to industrial activities nearby this zone suffers from the impact of heavy vehicular traffic and contains many dilapidated and abandoned plots. Yet it remains a vital centre of life for the southern part of the Fatimid city.

Zone Five stretches along the Sharia Ba al-Wazir, a section of the street running from Bab Zuweila to the citadel which is itself a ramification of the main north-south spine of Islamic Cairo. This street has kept much more of its traditional character and activities than the main spine south of Bab Zuweila. With several Mamluk mosques and mausoleums projecting diagonally into the street space and with some fine specimens of traditional housing structures surviving, the area offers an important potential for rehabilitation. This zone includes a number of modern housing blocks and a large irregular open space behind the Blue Mosque which is used as a youth centre. Traffic is less of a problem than in other zones, although large buses operating on this spine often cause congestion.

Zone Six contains a fine sequence of Mamluk and Ottoman monuments on the road leading from the Ibn Tulun Mosque to the Citadel. The zone is crossed by the main north-south spine leading from Bab Zuweila to the cemetery of Saida Nafisa and offers possibilities of future extension. More than any other zone it has suffered from the impact of change and redevelopment, due to the fact that Saliba Road is today a major traffic artery.

THIS TEXT is based on *The Conservation of the Old City of Cairo*, the technical report on the UNESCO mission to Cairo.

Reprinted from the *Unesco Courier*, March 1985

ABU MENA

LOCATION   Mariut Desert, District of Burg al-Arab, N 30° 51′, E 29° 40′.

DESCRIPTION   An archaeological site 1sq km (0.4sq mi) in area, it comprises 2 churches, a baptistery, several public buildings, baths and workshops.

SIGNIFICANCE   Abu Mena was an early centre of pilgrimage for Christians as it was the burial place for Saint Menas, an Egyptian serving in the Roman army who was martyred for his faith. During the 5th and 6th centuries AD its importance increased. It was heavily patronised by several Byzantine emperors and bishops from Alexandria. Its importance declined after the advent of Islam, until being abandoned during the 9th century.

ANCIENT THEBES AND ITS NECROPOLIS

LOCATION   At the town of Luxor, N 25° 43′, E 32° 37′.

DESCRIPTION   The ancient town of Thebes is situated underneath the modern town of Luxor on the east bank of the Nile River. There are 2 massive neighbouring temple complexes, Karnak and Luxor, while on the west bank is the necropolis, with its many pharaonic mortuary temples, including the spectacular, multi-terraced temple of Hatshepsut. The Necropolis also contains the famous tomb complexes known as 'The Valley of the Kings and The Valley of the Queens'. Dozens of other funerary monuments include the Tomb-Chapels of the Nobles and the Workmen's tombs.

SIGNIFICANCE   Thebes has a rich and important history. It was founded almost 5,000 years ago and became the capital of a united Egypt at around 2000 BC. It was ruled by the Hyksos for a while until Egypt was liberated and became the centre of a vast empire, stretching from North Sudan up to the Euphrates. During the 19th Dynasty, Thebes lost its role as capital, but not as the first city in the empire; later when it started to decline, it still remained an important religious centre. It was an important city for the Greeks – Homer called it 'the city of the one hundred gates' – and a popular tourist destination for the Romans.

ISLAMIC CAIRO

LOCATION   Cairo, N 30° 06′, E 31° 26′.

DESCRIPTION   The historic part of Cairo is on the east bank of the Nile, surrounded by the modern city. It contains many notable buildings and monuments, including a large necropolis, several important mosques, Coptic churches, a citadel and extensive remnants of the city's fortifications, including the impressive 11th century city gates.

SIGNIFICANCE   Cairo became an Islamic city after the Muslim conquest of 641 AD. Its importance in the Islamic world grew steadily, reaching its zenith after the fall of Baghdad in 1261, when it was the capital of a vast empire which embraced the Sudan, Northern Mesopotamia, Palestine, Syria and the Hejaz, which included the 2 Holy cities of Mecca and Medina. The historic centre retains a remarkable degree of originality, a testimony, not just to its commercial importance but to the high regard in which Cairo has always been held in the Islamic world.

MEMPHIS AND ITS NECROPOLIS WITH THE PYRAMID FIELDS

LOCATION   Giza Governorate, N 29° 45′ to 30° 00′, E 31° 10′ to 31° 15′.

DESCRIPTION   There are 2 main elements to this site: 1. the ruins of the town of Memphis which is partly excavated and includes part of a temple, an embalming place, an alabaster sphinx and a statue of Ramesses II; 2. the royal tombs, or pyramids, of which there are 6 groups, probably the most well known being those of Cheops, Chephren and Mycerinus, all found at Giza.

SIGNIFICANCE   When the kingdoms of Upper and Lower Egypt were united at around 3000 BC, Memphis was created as the centre of the new State's administration. Remnants of this original Pharaonic civilization still exist in the ruins of the stone tombs, or mastabas, at the Archaic Pharaonic Cemetery at Saqqara where the 'Step Pyramid' is located. One of the 'Seven Wonders of

Always something new out of Africa.
PLINY THE ELDER

the World', the pyramids are famous for their enormous scale and simple beauty. We of the modern world can only gaze in awe and wonder at these remarkable feats of ancient engineering.

NUBIAN MONUMENTS FROM ABU SIMBEL TO PHILAE

LOCATION   Aswan Governorate, N 22° 46′ to 24° 05′, E 31° 37′ to 32° 54′.

DESCRIPTION   There are 5 groups of temples which were restored and re-erected in the most spectacular architectural rescues ever undertaken, when UNESCO mounted a successful operation to save them from being flooded by the waters of the newly created Lake Nassar, thus preserving this priceless ensemble: 1. the 2 rock temples of Ramesses II at Abu Simbel; 2. the temples of Amada and Derr at Amada; 3. the temples of Wadies Sebua, Dakka and Maharaqqa at Wadi Sebua; 4. the temple of Kalabsha and the rock temple of Beit et Wali, both near the High Dam; 5. the temple complex of Philae, which has been moved to the island of Agilkia. The second element to this listing comprises a group of monuments at Aswan, including the remains of stone quarries, tombs, a monastery and an Islamic cemetery.

SIGNIFICANCE   A border town built on the Nile between Egypt and Nubia, Aswan was important as a centre for political and military control, finances and trade. The Nubian temples testify to the richness of Egyptian architecture and art. The temples of Ramesses II in particular are of outstanding value with their unique architectural features and timeless beauty. The largest temple has a 38m (125ft) facade with a sanctuary cut 63m (207ft) into the rock. Before being moved in 1968, this was positioned so that at sunrise on the 2 days of the yearly equinoxes, the statues inside the sanctuary were illuminated by the rays of the morning sun.

ETHIOPIA

Ethiopia has been inhabited for several million years, as testified by the World Heritage listed prehistoric sites of the Omo and Awash Lower Valleys.

'Aithiopes', or 'burned faces' are first mentioned by Homer who described them as the furthest of mankind, the inhabitants of a land where the sun sets. In those ancient days, 'Aethiopia' was a general term for that part of the world beyond Egypt.

The first kingdom in this land was founded by immigrants from southern Arabia sometime around the 5th century BC and was known as the kingdom of Aksum. The ruins of ancient Aksum are another of Ethiopia's present day World Heritage sites.

Located in the region of the Horn of Africa and with an area of nearly 1,222,000 sq km (472,000 sq mi), the climate varies with the terrain: the high plateaus enjoying temperate weather with a good rainfall, the lowlands arid and prone to drought.

Ethiopia ratified the World Heritage Convention in July 1977 and now has seven sites inscribed on the list. Apart from the three sites mentioned above, there is one other ancient site, that of Tiya. Also on the list are two more recent monumental sites – those of Lalibela where there are eleven churches carved out of rock – and in the Gondar region, an ensemble of significant religious buildings. Ethiopia also has one natural listing – Simien National Park, an extremely rugged area with numerous endemic species of fauna.

Omo Lower Valley

Simien National Park

Appeal For Our World Heritage

EPICENTRED IN THE EPIC of our daily presence
And in each brave generation's life
This collective imagery of our monumental
    memory,
Our World Heritage, our one symbolic banner
For our one family of the humankind,
From our yesterdays to our tomorrows
Rising above all the ominous clouds
Bridging all our global and prejudicial distances,
Gloriously glows in us the great miracles
Our ancestors achieved for our human harmony.
That's why we must keep on protecting it, please
With all our resources and with our lives.
By its very invaluable presence in time
Our World Heritage challenges each brave new
    generation
Relentlessly towards a higher human perfection.
It protects our indomitable spirit from
    corruptibility
And annihilates the moral midgets that crawl
To deform the boundless humanity in us.
Our World Heritage is itself the eternal witness
The eternal code and the eternal reminder
That the humankind is still the supreme architect
In whose masterful creative gifts
We must entrust this greater wonder
Our World Heritage, our one symbolic banner
For our one family of the humankind.
That's why we must keep on protecting it, please
With all our resources and with our lives.

TSEGAYE GABRE-MEDHIN
Ethiopian Poet Laureate

Biet Ghiorgis at Lalibela

AKSUM

LOCATION   Northern Ethiopia, in the Tigre region, N 14° 09', E 34° 42'.

DESCRIPTION   This archaeological site consists of palace ruins, over 100 stelae (carved stone monoliths) and various other stone remains, such as thrones and walls.

SIGNIFICANCE   These ruins date back to the 1st century AD and were built by the powerful Aksumites. Testimony to their power was the size of their stelae, the tallest being a massive 33m (110ft) in height. Another important feature of this site are the ruins of St. Mary of Zion, thought to be the earliest Christian church built in Ethiopia, probably around 340 AD.

FASIL GHEBBI AND GONDAR MONUMENTS

LOCATION   Gondar Region, N 12° 34', E 37° 36'.

DESCRIPTION   There are numerous monuments and buildings in this listing. Some of the more important are: the monastery and church of Socinios, the palace of Guzara, the monastery and church of Debre Berhan Selassie and the bath of Fassilides.

SIGNIFICANCE   All of these buildings and monuments are considered to be of the same architectural style – that of the 'Gondar' period. This period is normally dated from the beginning of the 15th century through to the beginning of the 19th century. It is a style that is thought to have been created when Jesuit Priests brought the technique of lime burning from India. The Socinios monastery and church is believed to be the earliest construction. It is thought to have been designed and built by Pedro Paez, a Jesuit under King Socinios.

LALIBELA ROCK-HEWN CHURCHES

LOCATION   Wollo region of the Lasta District, N 12° 02', E 38° 49'.

DESCRIPTION   There are 11 churches in 2 groups of 5, with one, Biet Ghiorgis, isolated from the others. The others are, in the first group: Biet Modhani Alem, Biet Mariam, Biet Denagel, Biet Golgotha Mikael, Biet Mascal, and in the second group: Biet Amanuel, Biet Cheddus Morcoreos, Biet Abba Libanos, Biet Gabriel Raphael and Biet Lehem.

SIGNIFICANCE   These churches are all carved and chiselled out of solid rock, an amazing testimony to the faith and dedication of those involved in their construction. More astonishing still, there is an extensive system of trenches, passageways and drainage tunnels lying under each church. These buildings are laid out according to a secret religious pattern based on the topography of Palestine or of a new Jerusalem, with each church thought to represent a stage in the life of Christ.

The tallest of the stelae at Aksum

A village in the Awash Valley

AWASH LOWER VALLEY

LOCATION   Eastern Ethiopia, in the region of Harrar.

DESCRIPTION   This prehistoric archaeological site has been under study since 1973, when excavations were commenced by an international team of experts.

SIGNIFICANCE   The site has uncovered a wealth of exceptionally well preserved fossils. Dating back 4 million years, the remains include one of the most complete hominid skeletons ever found. Remains of animals such as elephants, rhinoceros and monkeys have also been found.

OMO LOWER VALLEY

LOCATION   Southern Ethiopia, in the Gemo Gofa region. N 04° 48', E 35° 58'.

DESCRIPTION   This prehistoric site is protected by the Administration of Antiquities and is very well preserved. The deposits of humanoid fossils uncovered here have been particularly rich, with numerous teeth, jaw bones and other bones. Many stone objects and tools have also been unearthed.

SIGNIFICANCE   The evidence from some of the stone objects on this site points to one of the oldest known campsites of prehistoric humanoids in existence. There is also evidence which further suggests some of the most ancient technical activity (use of tools). These factors, along with the wealth of humanoid fossils make this site crucial to a better understanding of our ancestors.

SIMIEN NATIONAL PARK

LOCATION   100km (62mi) from the town of Gondar, N 13° 11', E 38° 04'.

DESCRIPTION   This park covers 165sq km (66sq mi) and is part of the Simien mountain massif. These mountains are volcanic in origin and extremely rugged and rocky. Numerous cliffs and precipices are a feature of the landscape, some with a sheer drop of 1,500m (4,921ft) or more.

SIGNIFICANCE   This difficult terrain provides the perfect environment for numerous animals, in particular 3 that are endangered. The walia ibex and the Simien fox are totally unique to the area and this park was created specifically to protect their remnant populations. The gelada baboon is also endemic.

TIYA

LOCATION   In the Soddo region, south of Addis Ababa, 38km (23.6mi) south of Awash.

DESCRIPTION   There are 36 monuments found within this site. 32 of these are 'stelae', sculptured monoliths with unique carvings and a distinctive funerary character. These vary between 1-5m (3-17ft) in height.

SIGNIFICANCE   This is one of the most important of some 160 sites that have been discovered in the Soddo region. The stelae provide valuable and scarce information about ancient Ethiopian civilisation.

Ruined palace at Gondar

FRANCE

The wonders of the ancient world numbered only seven. Things are no longer so simple. Our planet, having been totally chartered and mapped, contains an evergrowing number of buildings and sites listed under World Heritage, which reflects a concern for preserving our cultural roots.

In France, the notion of heritage is quite ancient, dating back to Italian influences of antiquity. Nowadays, laws protect and maintain not only artistic treasures but also urban zones, factories of social significance and machines. In fact, the idea of preservation follows and embraces the great changes due to wars, revolutions and agrarian reform.

Our commitment to historical monuments stems from the Revolution and from the Romantic period. Within days of the First World War, we were lamenting the destruction of the Arras squares and discovering the importance of civil architecture. The Second World War brought with it the obliteration of the old quarters of Rouen, Tours and Le Havre. As a result, laws have been drafted to protect areas of historical importance. Profound economic changes of the sixties were as destructive as both wars, resulting in the transformation of much of the countryside into desert and the neglect of numerous small towns, in particular the industrial areas of the north and east of France.

Consequently, a greater interest in both monuments and urban structures developed. This interest in our heritage has entered our consciousness and made a large impact. It goes beyond creating cultural ghettos which only become isolated and artificial. Indeed we need to preserve old estates and incorporate them into a contemporary world, creating catalysts for our future's evolution.

If all the elements of heritage preservation benefit a nation, they should also benefit society at a universal level.

The World Heritage List represents more than an honour list for a particular country. Rather, it shoud be an anthology contrasting the exceptional and the marvellous, to be used as a reference for all humanity.

Lascaux, Carnac and Mont Saint-Michel are fine examples of the exceptional, while Chartres, Vezelay or Versailles represent the marvellous. The perfect expression of the spiritual life-blood of a society can only be assured if the authenticity of a site is undeniably preserved. Is it not true that the *aura* of a particular place is linked to the emotional impact of

One of the carved stelae at Tiya

Church of St. Savin-sur-Gartempe

having our consciousness raised? Can we separate Cologne Cathedral from Goethe, Notre Dame from Victor Hugo, the Colosseum from Chateaubriand and Chartres from Peguy? Isn't this the value of World Heritage work?

La Douce France should also figure on a World Heritage list. Yet where does the cultural begin and the natural end? Auvers-Sur-Oise, Saint Victoire Mountain and the sunflowers around Arles should be kept for the world to cherish.

One of the major duties of World Heritage is to place the preservation of what belongs to everyone in the hands of those who are dedicated to this monumental task. The Parthenon, the Dogon Statues and the Temple of Angor are all living testimony to this feat. Yet, the idea of international scientific co-operation along the lines of a *Doctors Without Borders* (a French based, international aid organisation – Ed.) concept would be a strong show of heritage unity. I believe that France would play a major role in this area.

André Malraux dedicated many prophetic pages to the imaginary museum of mankind. It is vital that mankind strives to preserve the works which constitute our own, real heritage.

Jack Lang

MR JACK LANG
Minister for Culture, France
Translated by Nick Baker

Saving a Sanctuary of Prehistoric Art

THE PREHISTORIC painted cave of Lascaux is situated near the little town of Montignac in the Périgord region of south-west France. The whole area is rich in prehistoric sites, but it is in the limestone cliffs which run beside the winding course of the Vézère river that the ancient rock shelters and caves are most abundant.

The Lascaux cave was discovered on 12 September 1940 by four children from Montignac while they were playing among the pines and chestnut trees on a steep slope above the river a kilometre or two outside the town.

The opening of the cave, barely 80cm square, was half hidden beneath a layer of dead leaves. It plunged vertically into the hillside, ending in a pile of debris and rubble.

In the next few weeks, the undergrowth surrounding the entrance was cleared, and an enormous pit several dozen metres wide was dug in front of the hole. The excavations provided virtually direct access to the grotto which, because of the animals depicted on its ceiling and walls, was to become known as the Hall of Bulls.

Access to the cave had probably never been easy. After the last of the cave artists had left, rocks falling from the roof gradually piled up and sealed off the grotto for thousands of years. Air currents and water infiltrating through the debris caused little damage, except possibly during the period at the end of the Ice Age, when geologists believe that the calcite hollows known as *gours* were formed. The calcification of the surface of the cone of rubble, the formation of stalactites, and the infiltration of sand and clay washed down by glacial meltwater must have consolidated the barrier at the entrance. Studies would later show the importance of this barrier in preserving the frescoes on the walls of the cave. The roof of the limestone vault, between six and eight metres (6.6 to 8.8 yards) thick, was covered by a layer of impermeable clay. As a result, the paintings, including the 'unicorn' situated less than ten metres from the original passageway, remained in a perfect state of preservation.

The listing of the site as a historic monument on 27 December 1940 enabled the French authorities to intervene on what was a piece of private property, and the owner was wisely persuaded to erect a wooden door at the entrance to the cave. However, this was mainly to prevent uncontrolled access by the public, not to preserve the grotto's 'microclimate', the significance of which was still unsuspected.

Major operations at Lascaux did not begin until World War II was over, and it was not until 14 July, 1948 that, with a stone staircase, a bronze door,

Fontainebleau

Neptune's Fountain, Place Stanislas

Sculptured stone portal, Chartres Cathedral

an entrance hall and a paved pathway through the grotto which had been equipped with protective barriers and lighting, Lascaux was opened to the public.

The scenes portrayed in colour on the brilliant white calcite crust are a supremely beautiful and impressive display of Palaeolithic art, with their remarkably skilful use of the relief of the cave walls to depict animals caught in mid-movement, and their highly individual mixture of perspectives and profiles. The conservation of the frescoes called for scrupulous care and constant supervision.

In July 1955, the curator noticed that during peak visiting periods condensation coloured by pigments from the frescoes was dripping from the walls and ceiling. Scientific investigation established that this was caused by the carbon dioxide exhaled by the visitors.

In 1958, an air conditioning system was installed. The air in the cave was sucked through a filter to remove dust, decarbonated, and cooled to a constant temperature of 14°C/57°F, while the humidity was kept close to dew point (95-98 percent). This elec-

tronically regulated system was hooked up to a turnstile which recorded the number of visitors entering the cave.

It proved so successful in eliminating condensation and purifying the atmosphere that the owner was authorised to keep it running at full power at the height of the summer tourist season, when on some days over a thousand visitors filed through the grotto.

In September 1960, the curator noticed a green spot, so tiny as to be scarcely perceptible, on the ceiling of the cave. Despite the application of a treatment recommended by the Pasteur Institute, tests the following year showed that more spots had appeared. And so, in March 1963, the Minister of Cultural Affairs, André Malraux, appointed a special committee of scientists from a wide range of disciplines to investigate the problem and propose solutions. It took over ten years of dedicated efforts and close collaboration between scientists from over a score of laboratories before the frescoes were finally saved.

The closure of the cave, on 20 April 1963, was no

solution to the problem. The colonies of microscopic plant organisms which were the source of the danger continued to spread, and within a few months had increased from three to 720. Laboratory tests revealed the presence of many species of algae, as well as growths of ferns, mosses and fungi. Shock treatment was clearly required to eliminate these sources of pollution.

After making sure that the paintings would not be harmed, the scientists rid the cave of bacteria in the air by spraying the cave with antibiotics. The algae on the walls, which had by now spread out in to 1,350 colonies, were gradually destroyed by spraying with solutions of formalin, in concentrations of 1:10 on the cave floor, 1:20 on the bare rock, and 1:200 on the paintings. After two years of treatment, the micro-organisms had been totally wiped out, but in order to prevent further contamination, visits were limited in number and duration, and the intensity of the lighting was considerably reduced. Regular analysis of the bacteria and the algae in the atmosphere and on the floor of the cave, and inspections of the walls and ceiling have made it possible to limit precautionary measures against new outbreaks to a minimum.

Scarcely had the biological attack been repulsed, however, than a new threat to the paintings materialised. The right-hand wall of a smaller cave which is decorated with stags, began to disappear under a fine crust of calcite crystals. The same thing began to happen, to a lesser extent, to the unicorn in the main grotto.

After examining the formation of the calcite crystals by means of microphotography, the scientists undertook a comprehensive examination of the entire structure and the climate of the cave, using various other ultra-modern hydrological and geological techniques. The outline of the cave, and its relation to the surface of the hillside, were plotted in detail. The soil was analysed and, by means of a vertical photogrammetric survey carried out every 5 mm, contour lines were established for all the painted areas.

The pigmentation of the paintings was examined in depth and content, and the temperature of the soil was studied by infra-red radiometry. At the same time, the temperature at various points on the cave walls was measured to within 1/100th of a degree, and the volume of the enclosed space was accurately determined (1778m³/63,000 ft³). Aerodynamic studies were carried out to detect the existence of microclimates through data provided by electronic equipment which recorded in minute detail the temperature, humidity, carbon dioxide content and barometric pressure.

The processing of all the data obtained over several years led the scientific committee to decide on a course of action designed to preserve as far as possible the 'natural' climate of the cave, and more particularly to prevent changes in temperature,

Roman arena, Arles

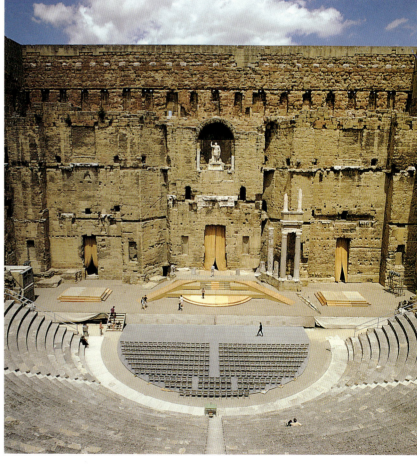

Roman Theatre at Orange

Arc-et-Senans (Royal Saltworks)

Cistercian Abbey of Fontenay

Chambord (Chateau and Estate)

Interior of the Basilica at Vézelay

Mont St. Michel

humidity and carbon dioxide content.

Air entering the cave is now chilled; excess carbon dioxide of natural origin is tapped at its source (the so-called 'Wizard's Well') and pumped out of the cave. Partitioning of the cave into several compartments also helps to stabilise the temperature (at 13°C/55°F), humidity (at 98 percent), and carbon dioxide content (at 1 percent). No more than five visitors, who must be bona fide scientists, may enter the cave on any one day. The cave is completely sealed on two days each week.

Eighteen years after the cave was closed to the public, the wall paintings of Lascaux have been saved from what had seemed to be certain destruction.

MAGDALEINE HOURS
Reprinted from the *Unesco Courier*, March 1981

PONT du GARD

LOCATION   Languedoc-Roussillon, N 43° 56', E 04° 32'.

DESCRIPTION   A sandstone bridge, just under 49m (161ft) high, the Pont du Gard is constructed with 3 levels of arches. The first level has 6 arches, the second level 11 and the top level 35. The largest of the arches, under which the river flows, is almost 25m (82ft) wide.

SIGNIFICANCE   Remarkably large for this style of construction, this bridge formed part of a 50km (31mi) long aqueduct which was built around 20 BC to supply water to the town of Nimes. The harmony of the design, the amazing state of preservation and the sheer vastness of this aqueduct bridge provides a superb monument to the daring of Roman engineering.

MONT ST. MICHEL

LOCATION   On the borders of lower Normandy and Brittany.

DESCRIPTION   This monastery is perched on a small granite outcrop 80m (263ft) high, linked to the mainland by a 19th century causeway. On the islet there is a fortified gothic abbey and a small village with one street – Grande Rue. There is a church crowning the mount with a large spire which rises 152m (500ft) above the surrounding sea.

SIGNIFICANCE   The monastery was founded in 96 AD by 12 Benedictine monks, as a sanctuary dedicated to St. Michel. The early Romanesque church of Notre-Dame-Sous-Terre dates from that period. It was an important pilgrimage centre for many kings. The monastic community had a great sphere of spiritual and artistic influence as demonstrated by the numerous beautifully illuminated manuscripts found here. Mont-Saint Michel is one of the most dramatic sites in Europe, particularly when the famous tides course into the bay.

VÉZELAY (BASILICA AND HILL)

LOCATION   In Burgundy, about 150km (93mi) west of Dijon.

DESCRIPTION   Known in France as the 'Eternal Hill', the fortified village of Vézelay, perched on a hill above the Burgundy countryside, is dominated by the magnificent abbey church of la Madeleine, built mainly in the Romanesque style. The interior is striking for its simplicity and the exceptional quality of its capitals.

SIGNIFICANCE   The abbey was first founded around 875 AD. After a short decline in the 11th century, it prospered due to the rumour that the body of Marie Madeleine was buried in the church. The nave dates from that period, around 1140 AD. The 3 door portal was carved between 1125-1130 and is a remarkable example of early Romanesque art. In 1146, the Second Crusade was preached here by Saint Bernard, and in 1217 the first Franciscan building in France was established on this site.

AMIENS CATHEDRAL

LOCATION   In the town of Amiens, province of Picardy, Department of Somme.

DESCRIPTION   The cathedral is 133m (435ft) long and 65m (213ft) wide. It is built on 3 levels, reaching a height of 42m (138ft) with large arcades covering half of the interior. On the western side are 2 large towers, a rose window, and a magnificent array of stone sculptures, including a 13th century Christ and a scene of the Last Judgement. The enormous interior is striking for the purity of its lines and the carved wood choir stalls.

SIGNIFICANCE   Built on the site of a Romanesque church of 1220 AD, the cathedral is the largest in France. The imposing structure with its tri-level construction is acknowledged as the finest example of a Chartrian Grand Basilica. The vast collection of statues is remarkable for its diversity and quality.

ARC-ET-SENANS (ROYAL SALTWORKS)

LOCATION   Franche-Comté, N 47° 03′, E 05° 04′.

DESCRIPTION   The saltworks complex consists of the director's villa at the centre, with the factory buildings arranged in a semi-circle around it. There are 2 large workshops either side of the villa, where the salty brine was processed in massive vats. The raw material was pumped some distance to this complex through a system of wooden piping.

SIGNIFICANCE   In 1776 these saltworks were built according to a grand scheme designed by master 18th century architect, Claude-Nicolas Ledoux, that would have seen an entire city built around them. Unfortunately they never operated entirely successfully and changed hands quite a few times. The current owners, the District of Doubs, bought the Works in 1927 and soon after launched a campaign to restore them. Today it houses an information centre concerned with future trends and is open to the public.

CHAMBORD (CHATEAU AND ESTATE)

LOCATION   In the Loire Valley, N 47° 37′, E 01° 32′.

DESCRIPTION   The estate of Chambord is entirely owned by the State. It is situated on the Cosson River and occupies an area of over 5,000ha (12,055ac). A 32km (20mi) wall with 6 gates surrounds the entire estate. The chateau dominates the site. It is rectangular in plan, the sides being 770m (2,526ft) by 156m (512ft). 4 large cylindrical towers sit at each corner of the building.

Cape Porto

SIGNIFICANCE   Originally built as a hunting lodge, the chateau was completely rebuilt by Francis I and Henry II. It subsequently passed through many royal and noble hands, including Stanislaw I, Louis XV and Napoleon. It was purchased by the State in 1932. Today the chateau is considered to be one of the true marvels of Renaissance architecture. Particularly famous are the roof, a forest of elaborate chimneys and ornate lanterns, and the spiral staircases which wind around each other without touching.

STRASBOURG – GRAND ILE

LOCATION   Strasbourg, Alsace, N 48° 33′, E 07° 40′.

DESCRIPTION   The protected sector of the city is an island in the middle of the town. The river Ill surrounds it, forming channels around the district known as 'petite France'. This old quarter is very striking with its numerous timbered houses along the channels. Several covered bridges cross the waterways. The most remarkable building is the famous Gothic cathedral built in red sandstone over a period of 8 centuries, (11th to 19th), on Place Kleber. The facades are richly decorated with carvings and statues and the church is enhanced by a beautiful 142m (466ft) high spire.

SIGNIFICANCE   This island is the site of the original town, which was a Celtic settlement. After the Romans captured it, the town passed to the Franks who gave it its

Pont du Gard

Strasbourg – bridge and Notre Dame Cathedral

present name in the 5th century AD. 7 centuries of German domination began in 842 AD when the 'Strasbourg oaths' were taken between Charles the Bald and Louis the German. This town's fame lies in its rich and often bloody history resulting from its strategic importance, its striking architectural heritage and its crucial role as a centre for artistic and intellectual endeavours, especially through the renowned University of Strasbourg.

ARLES (ROMAN AND ROMANESQUE MONUMENTS)

LOCATION   Arles, Provence, N 43° 41′, E 04° 38′.

DESCRIPTION   The historic section of the township of Arles contains 8 buildings or monuments from Roman times or later that are of importance: 1. the arena – a very early amphitheatre; 2. the ancient theatre; 3. an underground gallery called the Crypto-Porticus; 4. the thermae of Constantine – old heated baths; 5. miscellaneous ruins that include stonework from the protective

wall of an old fortress; 6. a necropolis called the Alyscamps; 7. the church of St. Trophime; 8. Montmajour abbey.

SIGNIFICANCE   Some of the earlier buildings, such as the ancient theatre, date from the reign of Augustus, around the end of the 1st century BC. At this time Arles was a thriving shipyard and enjoyed substantial material prosperity. By around 400 AD Arles had become the second city of the Roman Empire and an important religious centre. Later buildings, like the church of St. Trophime, are typical of Romanesque architecture.

CHARTRES CATHEDRAL

LOCATION   Chartres, 100km (62mi) southwest of Paris.

DESCRIPTION   This massive Gothic cathedral is 130m (427ft) long, 45m (148ft) across and 36m (118ft) high. The highest spire is the Clocher Neuf, at 113m (371ft),

Amiens Cathedral

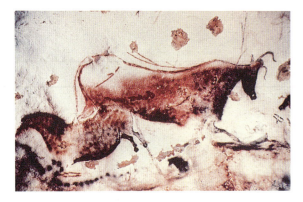

Interior detail, Vézère Valley

while the Clocher Vieux is 105m (344ft) above the ground. There are 7 side chapels and the entire structure is supported by numerous methods of internal and external buttressing.

SIGNIFICANCE   The Cathedral of Notre Dame in Chartres was founded in the 11th century AD by Bishop Fulbert on the site of an older church. It was destroyed by fire in 1194 and the cathedral that stands today was built in the mid 13th century. This cathedral is considered to be one of the outstanding examples of high Gothic architecture. Its 13th century stained glass, the statuary of the portals and the Renaissance choir screens are all unique. The view of the irregular spires against the horizon is one of the most famous sights in France.

VERSAILLES (PALACE AND PARK)

LOCATION   Versailles, west of Paris.

DESCRIPTION   The palace grounds are 100ha (241ac) in area with magnificently landscaped gardens created between 1661 and 1668 by Le Notre. The palace itself consists of 3 sections in the form of 2 flanking wings and an extended open rectangle, the interior of which forms 2 courtyards, the Cour de Marbre and the larger Cour Royale. The interior is notable for its reception hall and 'Galerie des Glaces'.

SIGNIFICANCE   Originally built in 1624 as a hunting lodge for Louis XIII, the palace was enlarged around 1682 for Louis XIV and became his seat of government. One of its more remarkable features is the 'Galerie des Glaces', a magnificent hall 76m (250ft) long and 10m (33ft) wide which is illuminated by 17 large windows on one side and enhanced by 17 panels of 400 mirrors on the opposite wall. This palace is associated with 2 monumental events; the French Revolution and the signing of the peace treaty in 1919.

CISTERCIAN ABBEY OF FONTENAY

LOCATION   In the Cote d'Or department, Burgundy, E 04° 24', N 47° 39'.

DESCRIPTION   The Abbey of Fontenay is situated at the bottom of the valley of the Egraves. It is a self contained complex of 2 buildings. The first is a lodge and

chapel for visitors, while the second, a monastic complex, comprises a church, refectory and cellars. There is also an infirmary built upon the banks of the river along with a blacksmiths' works.

SIGNIFICANCE   Founded in 1188, Fontenay quickly developed into one of the most prosperous of the Cistercian monasteries. It became a royal abbey and had as many as 300 monks in the 14th century. Its position as one of the foremost religious centres in France continued until its decline during the Hundred Year's War.

DECORATED CAVES OF THE VÉZÈRE

LOCATION   Near the town of Les Eyzies, in Dordogne, N 45° 00', E 01° 00'.

DESCRIPTION   There are 16 sites within this extensive prehistoric listing which follows the course of the Vézère river. Near the town of Les Eyzies, there are 4 grottoes, 3 rock shelters and 6 sites of fossil deposits. Scattered at various places nearby are 3 other grottoes.

SIGNIFICANCE   These sites date way back into prehistory and show signs of continuous occupation for up to 100,000 years. This extraordinary length of occupation has left an exceptionally rich legacy of ancient artwork, artefacts and fossils. It was here that the first remains of Cro-Magnon Man were found. Such a wealth of information has emanated from these sites that the area is considered by many to be the single most important prehistoric site yet uncovered.

CHURCH OF ST. SAVIN-SUR-GARTEMPE

LOCATION   In the Poitou region, department of Vienne.

DESCRIPTION   The main body of the church is 70m (230ft) long and is complemented by 5 chapels. It is crowned by a 94m (310ft) lanced tower. 10 columns decorated with animals and demons correspond to the chapels which are arranged in a semi-circle around the centre. 2 old rectangular crypts are found under the altar and one of the chapels. Most of the monastic buildings have disappeared except a building east of the church.

SIGNIFICANCE   A monastery was first founded on this site in 811 AD by Charlemagne. Construction of the abbey commenced around 200 years later. It suffered a tortuous history, being destroyed several times, until the Benedictine monks of St. Maur rebuilt it in 1640. There are several exceptional murals within this complex, notably those dating back to the 11th century which depict scenes from Genesis and Exodus.

FONTAINEBLEAU (PALACE AND PARK)

LOCATION   In the Ile de France area, department of Seine-et-Jarne, N 48° 24', E 02° 42'.

Hall of Mirrors, Palace of Versailles

DESCRIPTION   This large and rambling palace has a very complex plan due to its long history of extensions and renovations. Some of its more notable features include the massive main entrance, 115m (378ft) by 112m (368ft), known as the Cour des Adieux, and the horseshoe shaped staircase which leads to the first floor apartments. To the east of the palace, there is an 84ha (210.5ac) area of parkland.

SIGNIFICANCE   Fontainebleau is rich in royal history. Originally built as the royal hunting lodge in 1137 under St. Louis, Phillipe IV was born here in 1268. After being abandoned in the 15th century, Francois I gave it new prosperity by making it his residence. It was further extended between 1594 and 1609 by Henri IV. Napoleon chose the palace as his first imperial residence and restored it extensively.

CAPE GIROLATA, CAPE PORTO AND SCANDOLA RESERVE

LOCATION   Mid west coast of Corsica.

DESCRIPTION   This area covers 12,000ha (30,000ac) of natural land and seascape. It includes the wild scrubby country of the d'Elbo Peninsular and the Isle of Gargalo, the Gulf of Girolata and the Gulf of Porto. There are also some Roman and Genoese ruins to be found within this area.

SIGNIFICANCE   The waters are rich in marine life, particularly pelagic species of fish. Several species of flora are endemic to this rugged and unusual coastline. The ruins are also of some significance, especially the remains of a Genoese fortification system.

ORANGE (ROMAN THEATRE AND TRIUMPHAL ARCH)

LOCATION   Orange, Provence, N 44° 08′, E 04° 48′.

DESCRIPTION   Standing to the north of the town of Orange is the Triumphal Arch comprising 3 archways, the outer pair smaller in size. Nearby is the large Roman theatre built under Augustus having a southern facade 103m (338ft) long with a 38m (125ft) high wall. The mighty statue of the Emperor Augustus is in a central niche with the lower 5 rows of the 10,000 seat auditorium having been restored.

SIGNIFICANCE   The arch commemorates the founding of the colony of Arausio (Orange) and numerous land and naval battles. Its decorations and military trophies are extremely well preserved giving detailed records of several campaigns. The immense scale of the southern facade, which is virtually complete, makes this theatre unique in the world of Roman architecture.

PLACE STANISLAS, PLACE DE LA CARRIÈRE AND PLACE D'ALLIANCE IN NANCY

LOCATION   Nancy, Lorraine.

DESCRIPTION   Apart from the 3 squares, there are many buildings, monuments, statues, fountains and facades, including: Hotel de Ville, a vast palace, Arc de Triumphe, a main arch with 2 lower flanking arches, Café de Foy, a former medical college and Palais de l'Intendance, now a military residence.

SIGNIFICANCE   In 1751, Stanislaw, the father-in-law of Louis XV, conceived the plan to link the old town and the new town by means of a 500m (1,640ft) long vista which would be formed by creating these 3 squares. The result was a magnificent blend of classical and baroque architecture which today stands as a testimony to 18th century urban planning.

Versailles (Palace and Park)

GERMANY

Anybody who has followed politics in Europe knows that, as from the 3rd October, 1990, the 'German question' has been resolved: Germany has been re-united!

For more than forty years people and nature were physically separated by the 'Iron Curtain'. Politically, there were two German states in existence. That is why the German Federal Republic had already entered into the agreement to protect the world's natural and cultural heritage on 23rd August, 1976, while it took the German Democratic Republic until 12th December, 1988, to join.

During the period of separation after the Second World War, the United Nations has been of special significance to Germany: through their programs and agreements they brought both German states into early negotiations through bonds of common responsibilities. In future we will remember this with gratitude.

The Second World War had grave consequences for Germany's common cultural heritage. The enormous damage done to the cathedral and monastery at Hildersheim and to the castle in Potsdam has only in very recent times been able to be partially repaired.

At the same time, our monuments throughout the country are threatened by new dangers. Extensive air pollution is causing worrying damage to old and new materials alike. It is becoming increasingly necessary to reorganise, conserve and restore monuments which have existed for hundreds of years.

To assist in this work, the Ministry of the Environment, through the Environment Department, maintains a co-ordination and advisory branch concerned with environmental damage to monuments. Through exchange of information, this branch encourages co-operation in the protection of monuments.

The fundamental contribution to environmental policy concentrates on reorganisation, conservation and restoration. As a result of careful environmental policy – utilising protective measures for soil, air and water as well as climate – extensive damage from emissions will be avoided. Only in this way is it possible to permanently protect cultural and natural values.

That is why I would like to see, within the framework of both the World Heritage Convention and the relevant EEC conventions, clear political emphasis

Aachen Cathedral

Speyer Cathedral

'Tis not what man Does that exalts him, but what man Would do!

ROBERT BROWNING

placed on the fight against pollution which crosses international boundaries.

I greet the publication of this book with great enthusiasm. It pictures the unique heritage of our common natural and cultural past, and in so doing leads us to the realisation of the importance of both national effort and international co-operation.

It especially pleases me that nine of Germany's cultural monuments have fulfilled the requirements for acceptance and so have been included on the World Heritage List. I see however, that we, despite our multi-faceted and beautiful countryside, have not as yet nominated any natural sites for World Heritage inclusion. In this I see a great and rewarding challenge for the future.

PROFESSOR DR. KLAUS TOPFER
Federal Minister for the Environment, Conservation and Reactor Safety

Interior, Würzburg Residence

Glenika Palace, Potsdam

Augustusburg Castle

Interior, Falkenlust Castle

AACHEN CATHEDRAL

LOCATION   The town Aachen, around 100km (62mi) west of Bonn, N 56° 00′, E 06° 00′.

DESCRIPTION   The central structure of this building is the original palace cathedral. This is in the Carolingian style, it is octagonal in shape and is crowned by a large dome or cupola. An important feature is the bronze cast main portal, known as 'Wolf's Doors'. Several substantial extentions have been made over the centuries including the present day town hall and the choir hall, which are both in the Gothic style. Also an addition, the Hungarian chapel to the southwest contains a rich collection of art.

SIGNIFICANCE   This cathedral was built under Charlemagne's direction during the period 790 to 800 AD by his master builder, Odo. It was the first church of Charlemagne's 'Empire' and its construction was considered by his contemporaries to be a 'miracle'. The illustrious Emperor was buried here and it continued after his death to serve as the place of coronation for more than 30 succeeding German kings and emperors. The cathedral possesses numerous sacred relics which are brought out for public display once every 7 years.

BRÜHL (AUGUSTUSBURG AND FALKENLUST CASTLES)

LOCATION   Between Cologne and Bonn, in North Rhine-Westphalia Land,

DESCRIPTION   Augustusburg has 3 brick-built wings with 2 adjoining hot houses for oranges. The facade is composed of a series of embrasures and pilasters with ornately decorated sculptures. There are a number of large rooms, including that of the Prince Elector of Cologne, called the Yellow Room. The castle is set in gardens with many symmetrical flower beds leading to an ornamental lake. The main alley is lined with lime trees, leading to Falkenlust. Falkenlust is a 2 storey, rough-rendered brick building in the country style. There are 2 adjoining exhibition rooms. Set in a small park, it was used as a base for Prince Elector, Clemens August to practice his favourite sport, falconry.

SIGNIFICANCE   Construction of Augustusburg commenced in 1725. It remained the residence of the Prince Elector until 1794. For the next 21 years it was the property of France until it became the official residence of the Prussian Royal Family, and afterwards of the German Kaisers. It has been a museum since 1918. Falkenlust was built from 1729 on, and was conceived as a large country residence. It was constructed to allow the Prince Elector, Clemens August, to practise his favourite sport of falconry. It has been a government museum since 1960. The two buildings which originally housed the Prince Elector's falcons are now used for exhibitions. Both castles are considered to be exquisite examples of rococo architecture.

St. Michael's Chruch at Hildesheim

The Roman baths at Trier

PILGRIMAGE CHURCH OF WIES

LOCATION   In Steingaden, Upper Bavaria, N 47° 40′, E 10° 50′.

DESCRIPTION   Situated in a large expanse of meadow, this harmonious rococo style church is roughly oval in shape. The interior is rich and colourful, with countless ceiling and wall paintings, highly ornamental stucco work and many statues. The steeply walled altar dominates the room and the focus is on the ornate pulpit.

SIGNIFICANCE   The church is a famous centre of pilgrimage. It was built upon the spot where a local woman is said to have found a wooden figure of Christ crying. After hearing about this miracle, several famous artists gave their services in the construction of the church. These works, which include pieces by Albrecht, Bergmuller and Mages, make this church very important in the world of European art.

TRIER (HISTORIC MONUMENTS)

LOCATION   Province of Rhineland-Palatinate, N 49° 45′, E 06° 47′.

DESCRIPTION   This beautiful old town abounds with historical monuments. Of the numerous Roman buildings, the most impressive include the amphitheatre, which seated 30,000 people; the remarkable Porta Nigra, a massive fortified gate, 30m (98ft) high; the ornately decorated Barbara baths; and the 9 piered Moselle bridge. Later monuments include the Romanesque Trier cathedral, an early Gothic church named the Church of Our Lady and the old town hall.

SIGNIFICANCE   Trier is the oldest town in Germany. It was founded in 15 BC by the Romans and soon became known as 'Roma secunda'. The collection of Roman monuments is certainly without parallel in Germany and is barely rivalled elsewhere. The later monuments are also of significance; the Church of Our Lady is thought to be the oldest Gothic church in Germany.

PALACES AND PARKS OF POTSDAM AND BERLIN

LOCATION   Potsdam County and Berlin, N 52° 24′, E 13° 02′.

DESCRIPTION   Here we have a large ensemble of palaces and parks from the 18th and 19th centuries. The centrepiece is Sans-Souci Palace. This is a three-winged masonry building of one storey, with a central courtyard bounded by a colonnaded porch. There are extensive grounds adjacent, including a large terraced vineyard, several large guest residences, a Chinese tea house and numerous objects of garden architecture. Numerous other palaces, churches, guest houses and gardens are to be found in the immediate vicinity of these central palace grounds.

SIGNIFICANCE   These buildings and gardens were designed and constructed by the best available architects, craftsmen, builders and artists of the day. They represent the zenith of the 18th and 19th century north German rococo styles. The preservation of this entire ensemble in such original condition, plus the retention of this rich collection of artwork in its original setting, presents a unique and invaluable record of the artistic, architectural and social history of those times.

LÜBECK (HANSEATIC CITY)

LOCATION   Schleswig-Holstein, N 53° 51′, E 10° 43′.

DESCRIPTION   The centre of this old Hanseatic seaport is dominated by its 7 church towers. St. Mary's is the most famous of these Gothic churches. Of the remaining buildings, the town hall, which dates from the Middle Ages is the most well known. One of the distinctive features of the town is its rows of well preserved houses, all adorned with ornate facades.

SIGNIFICANCE   The historic centre of this fine old city represents the best preserved example of a typical medieval northern European townscape. Particular importance is given to St. Mary's Cathedral, one of the finest examples of early Gothic architecture in Europe, and to the town hall which is famous for its staircase and its intricate wood carvings.

SPEYER CATHEDRAL

LOCATION   Speyer, Rhineland-Palatinate, N 49° 20′, E 08° 25′.

DESCRIPTION   This is a large cruciform sandstone basilica with 3 main chambers (naves). Its design is distinguished by the considerable incorporation of arches (vaulting). There are several other important features, including 2 octagonal towers, a series of large, round-arched windows and extensive gabling of the ceilings. The interior walls are decorated with spectacular frescoes.

SIGNIFICANCE   This church has had a colourful and chequered history. Construction of the original cathedral began under Emperor Konrad II in 1030 AD and continued until 1061 when it was consecrated by Henry III. In 1082 Henry IV commenced reinforcing the structure and constructing towers and an apse. The entire structure was gutted by fire in 1689 when the French soldiers of Louis XIV attacked during the Palatine War of Succession. Restoration and extentions proceeded during 1772-1784, but damage was again inflicted by French hands in 1794. Further restoration and the addition of some beautiful frescoes were completed between 1846-1858. Most recently, extensive renovations were completed in 1968 and the cathedral now stands as a superb example of an early Romanesque basilica with equally impressive Gothic additions.

Interior, Pilgrimage Church of Wies

Lübeck Museum

ST. MARY'S CATHEDRAL AND ST. MICHAEL'S CHURCH AT HILDESHEIM

LOCATION   Hildesheim, Lower Saxony, N 52° 15′, E 09° 48′.

DESCRIPTION   St. Mary's is in the centre of the town of Hildesheim, while St. Michael's is found on a hill-top a little to the north-west of the centre. St. Michael's is architecturally the more interesting, being exceptionally broad and built in ashlar masonry. It has 4 slender towers with 3 apses projecting from the eastern end. The flat ceiling is supported by typical Saxon column-piers with arcade arches alternating in red and white stone. This ceiling is of wood and has a representation of the 'Tree of Jesus' painted on it.

SIGNIFICANCE   St. Michael's was founded by Bishop Bernward who, later canonized, is buried there. The painted ceiling is of great beauty and is a unique example of 12th century art. The gold cross and candelabras to be found in St. Mary's are of exceptional quality. These examples of the famed Hildesheim metalwork were executed by St. Bernward.

WÜRZBURG RESIDENCE

LOCATION   District of Lower Franconia in the State of Bavaria, E 09° 56′, N 49° 47′.

DESCRIPTION   Surrounded by extensive gardens, the central building, the Corps-de-Logis, is decorated with sandstone statues in a severe classical baroque style. The state rooms have lavish decor culminating in the imperial hall with its triple flight staircase. There is a development throughout the residence from the early 18th century decorative style to the mature rococo outside. The court gardens are skilfully laid out to take advantage of the area which is limited by the bastions of the city fortifications.

SIGNIFICANCE   The residence, and especially the imperial hall, are amongst the greatest examples of European baroque architecture. The ceiling paintings in the hall are regarded as the high point of that art in Europe, while the Prince-Bishop's Court Church has great decorative works from painter Rudolph Byss, stuccoist Antonio Bassi and sculptor Wolfgang van der Auvers.

GHANA

Formed in 1960 by a merger between the Gold Coast and part of Togoland, Ghana is a small west African country with a long and rich history of occupation. As far back as the 13th century, there were a number of kingdoms flourishing, mainly under the influence of the trans-Saharan trading routes.

The most famous and powerful of the kingdoms that arose was that of the Ashante. The centre of their kingdom, Kumasi, was highly organised, with an infrastructure equal to most Western cities of the day. The ruler, known as the Ashantehene, operated from here, using a network of highly educated Islamic traders. A complex political and cultural network was developed from the basic unit of the village. A clan of village elders elected a chief who represented them in the larger regional unit of the state. In turn, each state would elect a chief and would also provide one clan for the royal lineage. Behind this structure was a deeply rooted belief in the everpresent spirits of ancestors who directly influenced political decisions.

Thirteen Ashanti villages form one of two listings under the World Heritage Convention, which Ghana ratified in July 1975.

The other listing, that of the forts and castles of Ghana, preserves a number of important monuments from this country's colonial times, when the Portuguese vied with the British, Dutch and Danish for the right to trade gold and run slaves to the plantations of North America.

Shrine of an Ashante spirit medium

ASHANTE TRADITIONAL BUILDINGS

LOCATION   In the Ashante Region, N 06° 30′ to 07° 30′, W 03° 30′ to 00° 00′.

DESCRIPTION   This listing comprises 13 villages all similar in plan. Each village consists of an open-air rectangular court surrounded by 4 rectangular covered buildings. The thatched-roof houses are built with mud-brick and the walls are decorated with traditional paintings related to popular culture.

SIGNIFICANCE   These traditional buildings of the Ashante people were constructed at the beginning of this century. Originally used as residences for the chiefs, they are now used as sanctuaries and mausoleums. Their architecture is distinctive and unusual in its use of sloping thatched roofs. They now serve as a living museum of a valuable and threatened culture.

FORTS AND CASTLES OF GHANA

LOCATION   In the provinces of Volta, Greater Accra, Central and Western Regions between the towns of Keta and Beyin, E 02° 36′ to 01° 02′, N 04° 58′ to 05° 09′.

DESCRIPTION   There are numerous forts and castles in varying states of disrepair up and down the coast of Ghana. Many have been renovated and converted for such uses as guesthouses, nurses residences, prisons, lighthouses and museums.

SIGNIFICANCE   These fortifications date from Portuguese times through to the 19th century. Many were originally forts of the numerous trading companies which plied the 'Gold Coast'. This trade, which began in gold, eventually turned to slaving in the 18th century. The forts are a record of the shifting balance of trading power throughout those turbulent times.

Elmina Castle, one of many forts and castles on the coast of Ghana

GREECE

Greece ratified the World Heritage Convention in July 1981. There are presently twelve Greek sites on the World Heritage List, a number that will no doubt grow steadily as the enormous depth of Greek heritage unfolds and is placed in the world's hands; to be preserved for all time.

The following essay from Elliniki Etairia (Hellenic Society for the Protection of the Environment and Cultural Heritage) discusses this Greek heritage and its importance as 'our only ticket for survival'.

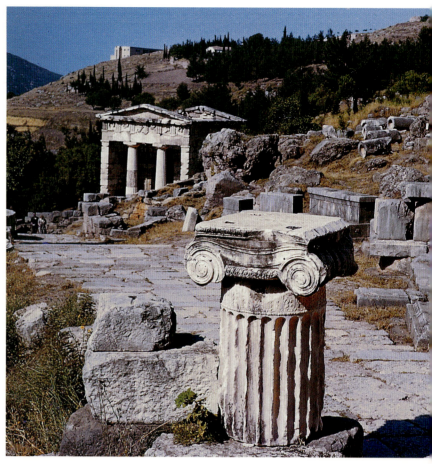

Olympia

In few civilisations could one trace and document an unbreakable cultural continuity throughout 5000 years based on the same language, similar traditions and ideals, the same striking peculiarities and characteristics which indicate the connection of culture with the environment. The Greek cultural heritage is such a case. Indeed the Greek culture is closely and inseparably connected with nature. Its principle to obtain harmony with nature is also reflected in the prevailing human scale and dimensions. All the monuments in Greece, from the prehistoric period to classical antiquity, the Helenistic period, the Byzantine middle ages, the Paleologian Renaissance, the pre-revolutionary period and the neoclassical revival of the 19th century, are in perfect harmony with the landscape, the natural environment and the light.

The assignment of the residence of ancient gods, nymphs and mythological heroes of antiquity with monuments of nature, such as springs and mountains (the most famous of which, Olympus and Parnassos were declared in 1938 as the first Greek national parks), confirms the close original connections between nature, religion, society and art in Greece; between nature and Greek culture.

Present day society and the coming one of the 21st century, will not achieve sustainable development unless its ethical foundations are strengthened. 'Ethos' according to its original meaning is not morality, although connected with it. It is the way of living: a harmonious way of living connected to the adopted aesthetic social behaviour, shared values and structures. To this extent the cultural heritage of Greece, perhaps the heritage most shared internationally, if properly understood and interpreted in all its phases and dimensions, could provide again a new source of inspiration and paradigm.

From the simplicity and abstraction of the cycladic marble idols of the Aegean, where the material is totally transfigured to a living symbol; to the magnificent art treasures and monuments of Minoan Knossos and Phaestos in Crete and in Thera; the Mycenian maturity in Mycenae and Tyrinth; the Geometric vases and the Archaic Kouroi; one could follow the wonderful evolution of human civilisation to the peak of the classical period.

During this peak, free, abstract, deep philosophical thinking coexisted with a fertile plastic and poetical creation, and social developments, mainly in the city of Athens, gave birth to the democratic processes. All monuments and pieces of art of that period, with the Parthenon and the Acropolis of Athens as its colophon, emit a 'natural' beauty full of truth and harmony. This explains of course their influence on the following generations and their use as prototypes during the Hellenistic and Roman period, the Renaissance and all the 'revivals' since.

Greece and the entire Mediterranean are full of such monuments of Greek antiquity which are undoubtedly universal, belonging not only to the Greeks but to mankind, and therefore should be included in the World Heritage List. Monuments and sites such as those at Delphi, Sounion, Aphea in Aegina, Vravron, Vassae, Lindos, Elefsis, Corinth, Epidaurus, Olympia, Phillipoi, Vergina, Dion, Pella, Ancient Thera, Dodoni, Kos, Delos and a very long list of others, give an idea not only of the wealth, but

also of the efforts and the resources needed for their protection. Many of these are suffering serious deterioration due to negligence, pollution, and a series of pressures deriving from lack of efficient preservation and sustainable development policies.

The detrimental effects of inefficient protection of the Greek architectural heritage is even more obvious in Byzantine and modern monuments. For long periods the ancient antiquities were regarded as the only worthy cultural heritage of the country. Only in relatively recent decades have even major Byzantine and 'modern' monuments, such as Mystras, the cluster of Byzantine monasteries and churches of Athos, those of Meteora, of St. John in Patmos, of Daphni, of Arta and numerous others, been considered and valued. Among the latter are also important Venetian castles and Ottoman buildings as well as 16th, 17th and 18th century bridges, and entire settlements many of which are inhabited today.

The Elliniki Etairia (Hellenic Society for the Protection of the Environment and the Cultural Heritage), since its establishment in 1972 has tried to raise the awareness of citizens and of local and national authorities of the need for active protection of the heritage of this country. Major restoration work has been carried out by the society in the Byzantine monasteries of Nea Moni in Chios Island and of Osios Loukas. Apart from the restoration work in both these monuments, two small museums have been created.

The restoration of our own headquarters, which will also house an information centre for the protection of the cultural and natural heritage for the public in Athens, it is hoped will contribute to the change of mentality of modern Athenians, particularly young ones who seem to have lost their connection and appreciation for their city and whatever has survived in it. This is probably due to the destruction of the balance between the city and the surrounding natural environment, due to a series of complex historical and socio-economic reasons and the lack of coherent policies in the design and the development of the town.

Cities of the past were part of the environment and even many of them which have suffered undesirable changes and damages, still hold a wealth of cultural treasures. They constitute a major asset for the future. Most of them were meant to be places which people could take pride in, places with identity, able to give substance, inspiration and definition to the lives of their citizens.

Protection, conservation and care of these cities and towns could prompt a review of our determination to search for a better future and for a redefinition of the purposes of our cities of tomorrow. One thing is certain: the earlier dream of a city entirely independent of nature, sustained by the machine, and based on the production of agriculture and industry placed somewhere else, as far as possible from the city, is rapidly becoming a nightmare.

Elliniki Etairia's interests extend also to the natural environment. Greece has an extremely wide range of environments with a vast variety of natural conditions including high mountainous areas as well as sub-tropical ones. There are also many lakes and streams and more than 1500 small and large islands with rocky or sandy coasts, dunes, caves, bushes and woods. Due to this diversity of micro-environments, the country supports one of the richest floras and faunas in Europe. More than six thousand species of higher plants are found, most of the rare and endangered big mammals of Europe (the Begoar goat/Agrimi, brown bear, Monk seal, otter, wolf, deer, wild cats, etc.), and large numbers of the most endangered and rare species of aquatic birds (pelicans, cormorants, egrettas, etc.) and raptors. Greece is also the richest European country in reptiles (Caretta caretta, etc.), and most probably in fishes and marine organisms.

During the last decades, much pressure has been exerted on the wildlife of the country and its natural heritage, mainly as a result of the impact of poorly designed and uncoordinated development schemes. Many pressures from touristic development, urbanization, industrialization, agriculture, collection and overgrazing, intensive fishing, illegal hunting as well as forest fires, pose significant threats.

There are many specially protected areas, such as the island reserve of Northern Sporades, a coastal zone in the island of Zakynthos, the Gorge of Samaria in Crete, Olympus and Parnassus mountains, Vikos-Aoos and Prespa. In the National park of Prespa alone, in which Elliniki Etairia has run a biological station since 1974, there are more than 40 species of mammals, 11 of amphibians, more than 20 of reptiles and 15 species of fresh water fish. Its flora includes more than 1300 species of higher plants.

In order to safeguard the future for our children and their grandchildren, policies for the protection of the landmarks of our natural and cultural heritage should be drafted with a horizon clearly broader than the usual five year one, worked out by a consensus of governments and politicians. These policies, in order to be implemented, should be properly regarded as the backbone of all efforts of international cooperation and should be supported by mechanisms of adequate funding, and effective intervention for prevention or restoration of damage.

After all, the protection of our natural and cultural heritage should be considered as more than a duty to our fathers, a right of our children and a pleasure for ourselves. It is the only ticket for survival.

PROFESSOR M SCOULLOS
Elliniki Etairia

How Athens' Acropolis can be Preserved

This article was written 14 years ago, it is as relevant today as it was then. It gives an important insight into the tremendous amount of work which is required to preserve our world's heritage.

THE 40 YEARS which have elapsed between the end of World War II and the present day constitute a very short period of time in comparison with the age of Athens, but one which has been of great significance for the development and appearance of the city.

As far as the Acropolis itself is concerned, these four decades have passed without any major changes (the large-scale works of restoration undertaken by Nicolas Balanos were completed by 1933), but they have quietly and relentlessly created a series of new problems that confront us today.

These problems, moreover, are so serious that there are those who are now talking of the destruction of the Acropolis, or at least of serious and irreparable deterioration of its masterpieces of classical architecture and sculpture.

The problems are in fact directly related to the rapid and uncontrolled change in the environment surrounding the monuments. The last 40 years have seen enormous economic, demographic and social changes in Athens, converting it from a small peaceful city, full of reminders of its historical past and well-proportioned neo-classical buildings, into a great capital.

In addition to 2 million inhabitants, it has acquired important industries, tall apartment blocks, international ports and airports, together with an increasing amount of environmental disturbance and pollution. Each day increases the alienation of the urban landscape from the natural terrain, the landmarks of classical topography, and the remnants of the buildings of antiquity. The famous crystal-clear atmosphere of Attica is covered with a pall of fumes; while a flood of tourists inundates the city, and the Acropolis in particular.

The Greek Archaeological Service has always worked, on a limited scale, to preserve the temples of the Acropolis, but it was only about 10 years ago that specialists became fully aware of the new conditions and problems.

In June 1968, an article in the *Unesco Courier* by George Dontas, the Director responsible for the Acropolis, brought the disquiet felt by Greek archaeologists to the attention of a wider public. UNESCO sent two scientific missions to Athens; a group of three specialists in 1969, and a photogrammetry team from the French National Geographic Institute in the spring of 1971.

The real work of studying and solving the problems of the Acropolis, however, only began in February 1975, with the formation of a committee and a working group of specialists, archaeologists and technical experts, and with a generous allocation of funds for the whole operation.

From the outset there has been lively public interest in the fate of the monuments on the Acropolis. The Greeks today look on these buildings as the most precious part of the architectural heritage, while people the world over consider them as the finest expression of the classical spirit of the ancient world.

Both the Greek Government and the authorities responsible for the Acropolis, aware of this general interest and of the responsibility of the scientific community towards the monuments, began to take action in earnest two years ago. At the international level, they appealed for funds to finance the rescue work, while at the national level they organised a thorough-going study of the dangers threatening the monuments, in order to eradicate their causes. Here, too, international help was sought, and UNESCO sent another team of experts in October 1975.

The problems involved in preserving the Acropolis and its monuments must be exhaustively studied before even the smallest stone is moved from its place. Furthermore, any action must respect three basic principles: the external appearance of the monuments should be changed as little as possible; the internationally recognised provisions of the Charter of Venice should be fully observed; and whatever steps are taken should not be irreversible.

The Acropolis rock as a whole was investigated first by geologists and engineers. After exhaustive research, they were able to allay earlier fears that it was unstable or was being eroded by underground water.

They also showed that both the natural bedrock and the foundations of the monuments, with the exception of the Pinakothek (the north wing of the Propylaea) and the base of the statue of Agrippa, are in a good state of preservation.

Investigation of the stability of the super-structure of the monuments is now in progress. All these buildings were constructed of blocks of white Pentelic marble, so perfectly hewn and fitted together than no mortar was needed to bind them. Each building is therefore first examined as a whole, to detect fatigue as a result of earthquakes and wind pressure, and secondly in detail, to establish the extent to which its various components (columns, capitals and beams) are capable of supporting a wide range of stresses.

The overall examination of the monuments includes an experimental study of the phenomena affecting the Parthenon, using the modern tech-

The Parthenon at the Acropolis, Athens

nique of photoelasticity: a 1:100 scale model made of epoxy resin is subjected to stresses proportionate to those affecting the monument itself.

Detailed investigation includes examination of the cracks and internal hollows in the marble caused by earlier fires and explosions, by means of such modern techniques as ultrasonic measurements and gammagraphy.

Both these techniques make it possible to measure the strength of the structure without taking samples of the building material itself. The first involves measuring the speed at which ultrasonic waves travel through the marble, and has already been used on the elements supporting the coffered ceiling of the west part of the Parthenon.

Gammagraphy, which is being applied to marble for the first time, involves taking photographs with gamma rays from a cobalt source. These rays are capable of penetrating the marble architectural structure and producing a film similar to an X-ray. These photographs reveal any cracks and internal fissures in the marble, and thus allow a diagnosis of the causes of its weakness to be made.

The most serious cause for concern about the monuments on the Acropolis is not, however, connected with their general stability, but with the cracks which have been and which are still being caused by the oxidation of the iron inside the marble structures.

The ancient Greeks used small iron bolts and clamps in their architecture, but made them almost rustproof by coating them with lead. Nicolas

Balanos failed to take similar precautions with the steel elements used in his extensive restoration between 1896 and 1933, possibly because he overestimated the properties of steel. Thus, almost all the buildings on the Acropolis had bolts inserted into them to join broken pieces, while steel girders were used, as in the porch of the Caryatids on the Erechtheum, to reinforce architraves and ancient beams.

All these metal parts rust because of the humidity of Athens and its proximity to the sea. Rusting not only lowers their resistance, but also causes the metal to swell and crack the marble into which it is embedded. A large number of fissures exist already, and in some places there is an immediate danger of collapse.

Thorough investigation has demonstrated that the only solution to this exceptionally serious problem is to remove all the steel elements and replace them with bolts of titanium, a metal that will not rust under any natural conditions.

Where the plans left by Balanos provide inadequate information concerning the position of the steel elements embedded in the marble, they can be located by means of gammagraphy.

The steel bolts and beams cannot be replaced without dismantling and reassembling all those parts of the monuments on the Acropolis which have been restored in the 19th and 20th centuries. A programme as extensive as this, which must conform with the principles noted above, requires many years' work, exceptional organisation, and most important of all, exhaustive preliminary study.

In addition to the compilation of all available information from bibliographies, archives and earlier reports on the buildings of the Acropolis, minute documentation of these buildings began two years ago, including the preparation of photographs and detailed drawings of their present form. In the case of the Erechtheum, this task is approaching completion and detailed proposals of the measures needed for the building have almost been finalised.

In producing measured architectural drawings of the temples on the Acropolis, the technique of photogrammetry has been used on a limited scale. More traditional methods have been preferred which permit a diagnosis of the state of decay of each piece of marble, at the same time as the measurements are taken.

Another cause for alarm is the deterioration of the marble surfaces and especially the sculpture of almost all the monuments of the Acropolis. The surface of the Pentelic marble, a building material of splendid appearance and great strength, is becoming corroded and is disintegrating.

The main cause of the trouble is the sulphur dioxide contained in industrial fumes and in smoke from central heating systems. The smallest degree of humidity is enough to let this sulphur dioxide attack the marble surfaces, turning them into gypsum. This plaster-like substance either dissolves in the rain and is washed away or else retains the soot and dust of the city to form an ugly crust that subsequently cracks.

If one adds to this the continuous natural decay of the marble over a period of 24 centuries as a result of rain, hail, wind and above all frost, it may easily be appreciated why the Athenian masterpieces have for the past few years been facing an unprecedented danger.

The problem is obviously particularly acute in the case of the sculptures: the Caryatids of the Erechtheum, and the frieze and pedimental statues that are still on the Parthenon.

To remedy these ills, some temporary measures have been proposed in addition to a longterm clampdown on pollution. The Parthenon frieze and the Caryatids are already protected from rain and frost by relatively unobtrusive temporary wooden shelters, and the two statues from the west pediment have been replaced by copies and temporarily housed in the Acropolis Museum.

One proposal under consideration is that the Caryatids be completely enclosed in a transparent air-conditioned box, until the unavoidable task begins of dismantling the south portico of the Erechtheum in order to replace the steel reinforcements in its beams.

It has also been proposed (though the final decision has not been taken) to transfer the Caryatids to air-conditioned rooms in the Museum, so that they may be restored to their proper position as soon as environmental conditions permit. The copies which would take their place are already being cast. Finally, the possibility of protecting the marble by treating it locally remains under consideration; in this connexion the Second International Symposium on the deterioration of building stones was held in Athens in September 1976.

However, the requirement that any operation performed on the ancient structures should not be irreversible has ruled out the use of almost all the materials currently employed in building for the purposes of on-the-spot protection.

The Greek Government is actively seeking a radical solution to the problem of the polluted atmosphere of Athens. A zone has been defined around the Acropolis within which it is forbidden to burn oil, which is rich in sulphur, in the central heating systems of apartment blocks.

Meanwhile, a study has been made of the technical and economic problems involved in replacing oil on a wider scale by some other source of energy, such as diesel, gas or electricity. The high cost of this operation, which involves 5 million cubic metres of dwelling space, and the length of time required to implement the change, are now being examined by the city authorities.

Street scene in Rhodes

the monuments and on the rock itself, that is, on the surfaces that were visible during antiquity. Ancient carvings, cavities to hold the bases of statues or the foundations of buildings, and the layout of the ancient pathways - all features of great interest - are in danger of disappearing.

The attempt to solve this problem began with a careful analysis of the present situation. Detailed topographical plans were prepared on a scale 1:100, and photographs were taken of the surface of the rock from a small balloon. An inventory of the scattered pieces of masonry is planned, as well as a methodical system of indexing them before they are moved, so that they may easily be recognised and classified before they are put in their final place.

A study has also been made of the possibility of covering a large area of the rock with soil, so as to create easy access to the monuments, as well as an esplanade to the east of the Erechtheum.

Also being considered is the feasibility of moving the pieces of masonry and arranging them in such a way as to make the archaeology of the Acropolis more readily comprehensible and to facilitate future research. A new ramp leading to the Propylaea, similar to that of ancient times, has also been proposed.

Finally, a decision has been taken to build a large new Acropolis Museum nearby, with modern facilities, to exhibit all the finds from the Acropolis, some of which are at present hidden away in storerooms. An architectural competition has been announced for the plans of this new museum.

As far as the urban landscape of Athens and its relation to the Acropolis are concerned, some improvements can be made. A number of town-planning provisions have been put into effect: tall buildings can no longer be put up close to the Acropolis and the neighbouring archaeological sites. Measures have also been proposed for the preservation of Plaka, the old quarter that clusters around the lower northern slopes of the rock. Finally, expropriations of property have made it possible to reopen the Peripatos, a pathway for pedestrians that encircled the Acropolis in antiquity.

The Acropolis and its monuments have passed through difficult times before, during the course of their long history, and have survived to the present day with their ageless beauty, as a unique testimony to a great age in the history of Western civilisation. In the attempt to hand on this cultural heritage intact to future generations, no effort can be considered too great.

CHARALAMBOS BOURAS, former architect of the Greek Archaeological Service, has published many articles and books on ancient and medieval Greek monuments.

Reprinted from the *Unesco Courier* October 1977.

The feeling of space on the Acropolis has changed considerably since antiquity. This is due in great measure to the archaeological excavations of the 19th century (mainly after 1885), which exposed the bedrock at almost every point. These excavations uncovered the foundations of the buildings which had not been visible during the classical period, and made it difficult to walk on the surface of the rock.

The general disorder is increased by the hundreds of large and small pieces of stonework from buildings of different periods, which occupy a large area of space and obstruct the visitor's passage.

Finally, irreparable damage is caused by the feet of the visitors themselves. The destruction has reached alarming proportions both on the floors of

Hossios Lucas Monastery

Interior of Hossios Lucas

Temple of Apollo Epicurius at Bassae

DELOS

LOCATION   The island of Delos is part of the Cyclades group in the central Aegean, N 22° 56′, N 37° 33′.

DESCRIPTION   This listing comprises the entire island of Delos, which is a protected archaeological zone. It is only 5kms (3mi) long and 1,300m (4,330ft) wide, but contains a fabulous collection of ancient monuments, sites and associated articles. There are three harbours which were all used in ancient times, an ancient town, a sacred precinct which was dedicated to Apollo and which includes several temples, many residences and an agora.

SIGNIFICANCE   According to Homer, Delos was the birthplace of Apollo, who, next to his father Zeus, was the most feared of the ancient Greek gods. Hence the island was from early times a sacred place and an important religious sanctuary. The other factor that has contributed to the fame of this island is its location. Occupying

such a central position, it was inevitable that Delos would develop into a major trading centre. These two factors combined to make this tiny island one of the most important destinations in Greek antiquity. The enormous wealth of information available from the numerous archaeological sites on Delos provide an invaluable record of a great and varied history that spans almost 3,000 years.

DELPHI

LOCATION   In Boetia, Central Greece, E 22° 30′, N 38° 29′.

DESCRIPTION   The site of Delphi is situated at the foot of the southern slope of Mt. Parnassos between the Phaedriades. It includes: 1. the Sanctuary of Athena Pronaia (5th century BC) with its temple and famous tholos (rotunda 4th century BC); 2. the ruins of the gymnasium, with baths, palaestra and chystos (covered colonnade); 3. the Sanctuary of Pythian Apollo, with the Sacred Way and its treasuries, the Temple of Apollo, the theatre (4th century BC); 4. the Castalian Fountain, in which the Pythia purified herself; 5. the stadium, situated in the highest part; 6. the ancient city and its 2 necropolises, spread between the 2 sanctuaries.

SIGNIFICANCE   Delphi was considered to be the centre of the ancient Greek world. Mythology tells the story of how Zeus released 2 eagles, one from the east and one from the west. They met at Delphi and the spot was marked by a stone in the temple. The Oracle of Apollo at Delphi was one of the most famous in the ancient world and became one of the more prestigious pilgrimage centres of the times. Destroyed in 373 BC by an earthquake, it was later rebuilt and restored by the Roman Emperor Hadrian. Modern excavations commenced on the site in 1892 and have since revealed a wealth of invaluable information.

EPIDAURUS

LOCATION   Nafplia Province, N 37° 30′, E 23° 07′.

DESCRIPTION   The Sanctuary of Apollon Malaetas and Asklepeion was the cultural centre of the ancient city-state of Epidaurus. The sanctuary was a medical centre dedicated to healing and convalescence. There is also an extremely well-preserved theatre; the ruins of richly decorated temples, dormitories, hotels and banquet halls.

SIGNIFICANCE   Regarded as the starting point of healing-practices in ancient Greece, the sanctuary was renowned throughout the classical world. The theatre was famous for its stunning acoustics and in many ways this site is considered to have been of primary importance in the development of modern civilisation. The tholos here is one of the finest buildings to have survived from classical times.

Meteora

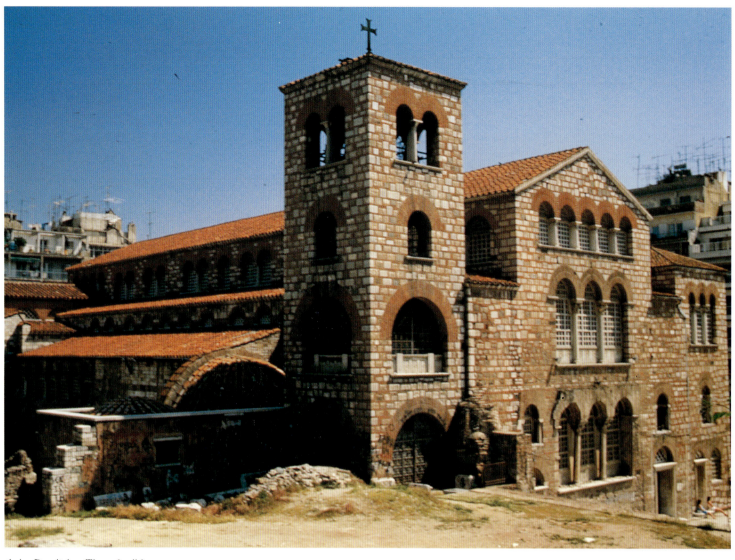

Agios Demitrios, Thessaloniki

MYSTRAS

LOCATION   In the province of Laconia, on the Peloponnese, west of Sparta, E 22° 21′, N 37° 04′.

DESCRIPTION   These ruins are of a medieval town built on a 621m (2,050ft) high hill at the foot of Mount Taiyetos. The upper town consists of the Frankish fortified castle at the summit, the Palaces of the Despots, Seigneurial residences, several monasteries and the Church of St. Sophia. All are surrounded by a wall which has 2 gates. The lower town is surrounded by a second wall and is centred around the 13th century Cathedral of St. Demitrios. There is also a monastery and the 14th century Church of Pantanassa.

SIGNIFICANCE   Mystras was fortified by the Franks in 1249 and became the site of a Byzantine military government between 1262 and 1348 AD. It was the capital of the Despots of Morea from 1348 and 1460 AD. The city was conquered by the Turks in 1460 and the Venetians in 1687. It was a flourishing trading centre thanks to its silk worm industry and was populated until 1830. King Otto built the new town of Sparta, sparking the decline of Mystras. Fine examples of Byzantine architecture and wall paintings have been preserved amongst the ruins.

METEORA

LOCATION   District of Thessaly, N 39° 43′, E 21° 38′.

DESCRIPTION   This is a group of 7 monasteries, all perched high up on some very unusual rock formations. These formations jut straight out of the surrounding Thessalian plain, the highest soaring up to 400m (1,312ft). The names of the monasteries are: Saint Nikolas Anapafsas, Roussanou, Transfiguration of the Saviour, Varlaam, Holy Trinity, Saint Stephen and The Ascension of Jesus Christ. All of the monasteries are rich in artwork, with numerous paintings, frescoes, sculptures and relics, many of great importance.

SIGNIFICANCE   'Meteora' in the Greek language means literally 'suspended in the air'. The description could not be better, especially when viewing these spectacular monasteries on a misty morning; they float in the air just as they have floated down through the ages. It is thought that the first hermits started settling on these rocks around 1000 AD. The monastic community was not established until the 14th century. The construction was a feat of wonder, considered a miracle of the Byzantine world. At its peak, around the beginning of

Tholos of the Temple of Athena at Delphi

Mount Athos

Ancient ruins stand guard on Delos

Mystras

the 16th century, the community boasted 24 monasteries. The next 100 years saw a steady decline under Turkish rule until only 8 monasteries remained at the beginning of the 17th century. The 7 monasteries standing today are living testament to those wondrous days of the Byzantine age.

MONASTERIES OF DAPHNI, HOSSIOS LUCAS AND NEA MONI CHIOU

LOCATION   *Daphni:* N 38° 01', E 23° 38'. *Chiou:* Island of Chios, N 38° 00', E 26° 00'. *Lucas:* Beotia, N 38° 24', E 22° 45'.

DESCRIPTION   This listing comprises three Byzantine monasteries. All are similar in design, basically consisting of an octagonal church with a full width porch across the front and a domed roof. Mosaics and paintings decorate the interior walls.

SIGNIFICANCE   These monasteries are the best preserved of their type and represent the zenith of Byzantine civilization and culture. The mosaics and wall paintings are invaluable records of Byzantine art.

MOUNT ATHOS

LOCATION   On the peninsula of Athos, in the province of Macedonia.

DESCRIPTION   This fortified medieval monastic city comprises 20 monasteries, 12 skites (small retreats), 700 cells and numerous caves spread over an area of 360sq km (144mi). The area is wooded and mountainous and is accessible only by boat. Karyes, a small village, is the capital of this Theocratic Republic and contains the oldest basilican church on the Mount, the Protaton, built in the 10th century AD.

SIGNIFICANCE   Monastic life started in the 10th century AD when the first monastery was built in 963. Of the 40 monasteries built over the centuries, only 20 have survived. They date from the 13th century to the 19th century. Mount Athos is a veritable museum of treasures. The Library of Vatopedi has over 13,000 manuscripts and is probably the richest manuscript library in the world. There are over 100,000sq m (1,111,000sq ft) of murals and frescoes and countless icons, mosaics, sculptures and paintings.

ARCHAEOLOGICAL SITE OF OLYMPIA

LOCATION   On the Peloponnese in the Province of Elis, between the confluence of the Alpheics and Kladeos Rivers, N 37° 40', E 21° 36'.

DESCRIPTION   The Panhellenic Sanctuary of Olympia was famous throughout the ancient world. Site of the quadrennial Olympic Games, it has the ruins of the ancient stadium, training buildings for the athletes and hotels for the visitors. There is also the Bouleuterion where the Olympic Senate met, various temples and monuments to games victors and patrons. The temple which held the world famous Statue of Zeus from sculptor Pheidias was also here. Earlier tomb remains etc., are to be found along the river banks.

SIGNIFICANCE   The Olympic Games were the greatest celebration in antiquity. Their fame was such that even wars were halted to allow athletes to compete. For over 1,000 years the Olympic ideal inspired the youth of Greece and its colonies to feats of athletic and artistic prowess. These ruins and the ideals of the original Games inspired the modern Olympics.

RHODES (MEDIEVAL CITY)

LOCATION   One of the Dodecanese group of islands, N 36° 22', E 25° 56'.

DESCRIPTION   A fortified medieval city, its outer walls are very well preserved. Inside can be found the Collachium, the fortified castle of the Knights, as well as the Palace of the Grand Masters and several inns or residences. There is also the hospital of the Knights and the remains of a 3rd century BC temple to Aphrodite.

SIGNIFICANCE   Founded in 408 BC, Rhodes was a prestigious city in the 3rd and 4th centuries BC, and became part of the Eastern Empire in 395 AD. Independent in the 13th century, it was conquered in 1309 by the Knights of St. John of Jerusalem who first took refuge on the island in 1306. They were defeated by the Turks in 1523. Today the old city is remarkably intact and so provides a valuable record of the civilisations that founded it and subsequently controlled and enriched it.

TEMPLE OF APOLLO EPICURIUS AT BASSAE

LOCATION   On the Peloponnese in the limits of 3 departments; Messenia, Arcadia and Elis.

DESCRIPTION   The temple is a colonnaded rectangle with a gabled roof. Externally, a classic temple in Doric style, it is 39.87m (131ft) by 16.13m (53ft) and is constructed of light grey limestone. A number of features are of marble. A magnificent Ionic frieze in 23 slabs depicts both the battle of the Centaurs and the Amazons. The temple stands isolated on a natural plateau on Mount Kotilion and is in a fine state of preservation.

SIGNIFICANCE   Of tremendous natural beauty in the harsh and lonely mountains of the Peloponnese, the temple's 'rediscovery' in 1765 by French archaeologist Joachim Blocher caused a sensation in Europe. The frieze went to the British Museum, and many scholars flocked to study the well preserved temple.

THE ACROPOLIS, ATHENS

LOCATION   Centre of Athens, N 37° 58′, E 23° 43′.

DESCRIPTION   This famous complex consists of 4 main buildings: 1. the Parthenon – a pitched roof building of brick construction, surrounded by a colonnaded verandah; 2. the Propylaea – the gate house to the Acropolis complex, it is constructed of marble and shows both Ionic and Doric styles; 3 the Erechtheion – an Ionic style building with projecting porticoes and sculptured figures used instead of columns; 4. the Temple of Athena Nike — a perfect miniature square temple.

SIGNIFICANCE   'Acropolis', meaning 'city at the top' was the name used by the ancient Greeks for citadels built on elevated sites. The one at Athens is by far the most famous. It shows every phase of Greek architecture right up to the fall of Athens. The Parthenon is the best known of all Greek temples and is considered the apogee of Hellenistic architecture. Extensive renovations have been going on for many years.

THESSALONIKI (PALEOCHRISTIAN AND BYZANTINE MONUMENTS)

LOCATION   Macedonia, N 40° 40′, E 23° 00′.

DESCRIPTION   There are 4 main elements: 1. the old city walls, 4km (2.5mi) long, 10m (33ft) high, over 2m (7ft) thick with 46 towers; 2. the Byzantine bath which dates from the 13th century; 3. Church of St. Catherine, built around 1320, a Byzantine church which was converted to a mosque in 1430; 4. Church of St. Panteleimon, built in the late 13th century.

SIGNIFICANCE   A fascinating and diverse collection of remains, all in good repair, which preserve the varied and often turbulent history of this important city.

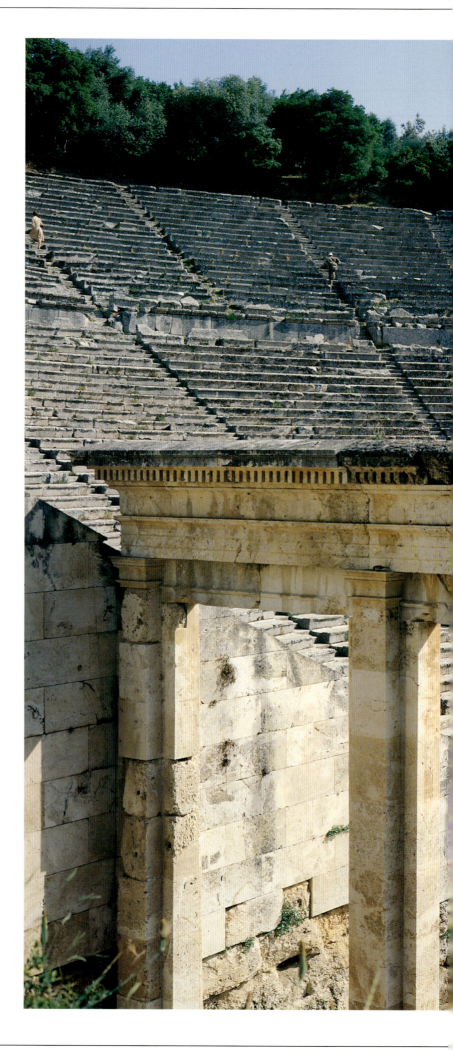

The theatre at Epiduarus

GUATEMALA

Guatemala lies at the top of Central America, with Mexico to the north, the Pacific Ocean to the west, El Salvador to the south, and both Belize and the Caribbean Sea to the east.

This is a region with a fascinating and ancient history. The roots of the Mayan Indian civilisation which flourished here can be traced back to around 2,000 BC.

The Mayans were not centralised like the Aztecs and Incas, they were more an agglomeration of independent city states. Despite this however, they managed to develop an extremely advanced civilisation which included a multitude of arts, hieroglyphic writing, a sophisticated spiritual and ceremonial culture and one particularly outstanding phenomenon – an extremely accurate system of measuring calendar time.

The Indians were conquered by the Spanish in the early 16th century and Guatemala remained, with the exception of a brief period of Mexican rule, part of the Spanish possessions until independence in the early 19th century.

The World Heritage Convention was ratified in January 1979. Of Guatamala's three World Heritage listings, two are important Mayan archaeological sites – Tikal and Quirigua – while the third is the old part of Guatemala City which became the capital after the original capital, Antigua, was devastated by an earthquake in 1773.

Quirigua

Antigua Guatemala

A Time of Crisis

EXCEPT TO the well educated European, African or Asian, the Central American countries were very little known outside the Western Hemisphere until relatively recent times. Today the names El Salvador, Guatemala and Nicaragua are known all over the world, thanks, sadly, to the low level warfare that has been waged over the last ten years.

But even in these troubled nations there is a growing awareness of the need to protect our environment. In many, the conservation of nature is taking place under the concept of 'protected areas'. As a sign of the vision that strives for peace, whenever two countries (or three) share a border covered by forest, the establishment of international parks is being proposed, carrying with it the hope that through sharing a territory and caring for the well-being of the natural world that it encompasses, we may learn to work and live together.

In terms of our natural heritage, we are living in the most critical of times. Never before have the effects of the war we have been waging against nature been so obvious. We live in times of ozone depletion, contamination and extinction. We also live in the age of computer communications. We can't plead ignorance anymore.

Chinese wisdom teaches that times of crises are really times of opportunity, change and growth. Maybe these crises will provide the momentum needed to help us get together on common grounds that make us all equal human beings. We are all creatures of planet Earth, with a shared need to save our wonderful, threatened and only home.

What are we willing to do to save the living world of planet Earth that we are annihilating today? There has never been a more important time in the history of humanity than the present to make peace with our environment. It means making peace with one's origin. It means making peace with God. There is a part of His divinity in each of the creatures. Every time we deny a species the right to exist, we lose some of this divine presence. We are trading the sacredness of life for the glow of development and technology, as sadly and ignorantly as our forefathers traded their land and valuables for the mirrors and trinkets that fascinated them for a short while. We don't seem to understand what the destruction of our natural heritage means, or we would shudder...

Perhaps it is time to call upon our elders and urge them to use all their wisdom and creative capacity to work together to save our Earth. If only we could believe this now, it would not be too late to achieve success. For if we continue this destruction our time will surely, one of these days, run out.

MAGALI REY ROSA
Defensores de la Naturaleza, Guatemala

ANTIGUA GUATEMALA

LOCATION   24km (15mi) from Guatemala City, N 14° 36′, W 90° 40′.

DESCRIPTION   Set at the base of towering volcanoes, Antigua is a mixture of Spanish colonial ruins and modern hotels. The old area covers almost 5ha (12ac). Most buildings are in ruins but the original town plan is very clear. Plaza Mayor sits in the very centre and is bounded on the north by a zone of local government buildings, to the east by the Episcopal Palace and Church of San Jose, to the south by colonial government buildings and to the west by the 'Baker's Portico'.

SIGNIFICANCE   Antigua Guatemala (Old Guatemala) was the capital city from 1527 until 1773, when an earthquake demolished it. Now a noted museum of Spanish colonial architecture, a few buildings are still in use and some have been restored. The town plan is considered to be a perfect example of a Renaissance style grid.

QUIRIGUA

LOCATION   In the department of Izabel.

DESCRIPTION   This was an ancient Mayan capital of the late classical period (600-900 AD) and has many monuments and hieroglyphic carvings, not yet fully deciphered, of great importance. The 13 monumental carved stelae to be found on the site measure up to 10.5m (35ft) in height.

SIGNIFICANCE   The hieroglyphic inscriptions, slowly being deciphered contain historical records of social, political and economic events which are adding enormously to a deeper understanding of the Mayan civilisation. The aesthetic values of the society are reflected in the supreme quality of the carvings found in Quirigua. They represent one of the highest achievements of ancient Mesoamerican culture.

TIKAL NATIONAL PARK

LOCATION   Dept. of El Peten, N 17° 13′, W 89° 38′.

DESCRIPTION   An ancient city of Mayan origin covering 576sq km (230sq mi) there are over 3,000 pre-Hispanic buildings found here. They include palaces, temples, ceremonial platforms, residences, ball-courts, terraces, squares and roads. Tombs and mausoleums with treasures and offerings as well as several large subterranean storage areas have also been found. More than 10,000 artefacts are stored in the site museums.

SIGNIFICANCE   Tikal is one of the most important archaeological sites in the world, displaying the full extent of Mayan achievement. The site was occupied from 600 BC to 900 AD covering a number of different epochs, during which time the Mayan culture developed and refined its architecture, arts and crafts.

Great Jaguar Stairway, Tikal

Sans-Souci Palace

The Citadel

A Time to Live

BUILT IN THE EARLY 19th century by Henri Christophe (1767-1820), who in 1811 proclaimed himself sovereign ruler of the kingdom of Haiti, the imposing palace of Sans Souci is one of the earliest symbols of Haitian independence. The palace, surrounded by gardens which covered 8 hectares (19 acres) at the height of their splendour, was pillaged after Christophe's death, and later seriously damaged in an earthquake. In 1973, Haiti launched an emergency programme to halt the deterioration threatening Sans Souci and other parts of its cultural heritage and to create a national historic park. Today UNESCO is co-operating with the Haitian Government on a project, financed by the United Nations Development Programme, to preserve Sans Souci, the Citadel Laferriere, which was built to protect Haiti against attack by colonial forces, and Les Ramiers, a fortification above the citadel.

Reprinted from the *Unesco Courier*, September 1985.

HAITI

Haiti, a densely populated, rural based nation, occupies the western third of Hispaniola, an island it shares with the Dominican Republic (qv).

Columbus landed on the north western tip of the island in December 1492 and named it Espanola (anglicised to Hispaniola). Spanish colonisation followed, but mainly on the eastern two thirds. Subsequently French explorers occupied the western third which led to French possession of the territory in 1697. They named it Saint-Domingue.

Following the French-Revolution at the end of the 18th century, the push for independence from France grew. After one abortive uprising, independence was finally proclaimed in 1804 and the territory was renamed with the indigenous Indian 'Haiti'. Haiti's sole World Heritage listing relates to the early years of independence. The Citadel and Palace of Sans Souci were erected by the first rulers of the newly independent nation. Haiti ratified the World Heritage Convention in January 1980.

CITADEL, SANS-SOUCI AND RAMIERS HISTORIC PARK

LOCATION   Dept. du Nord, N 19° 34′, W 72° 14′.

DESCRIPTION   Covering 25sq km (10sq mi) at an altitude of up to 875m (2,871ft) the Park contains 3 important complexes. The Palais de Sans Souci includes the royal residence, council of state, mint, library, chapel, barracks, prison, arsenal and stables. Many parts are now in ruin but under repair. The king's palace is largely derelict. The citadel is a massive stone fortress, on top of the peak Laferrière. It is protected by 4 flanking towers, the main tower, the Tour de l'Eperon being the most famous feature of the fortress. The battery contains hundreds of cannons and a huge powder magazine. Ramiers is a small plateau upon which are the ruins of a number of residential buildings.

SIGNIFICANCE   These monuments all date back to the beginning of the 19th century when Haiti proclaimed its independence from France. The citadel and the buildings at Ramiers were founded under the first Haitian emperor – Jacques I. The Palais de Sans Souci was constructed under Christophe, or King Henry I. After Christophe's suicide in 1820, all these monuments were looted and left abandoned. These ruins are a record of those turbulent early days of independence.

HOLY SEE

The magnificent colonnade at St. Peter's Square

The term 'Vatican' has two meanings: an autonomous state created by the Lateran Treaty of 1929 or a juridical expression of an international body supervising the life of the Catholic Church and known in international law by the title 'Holy See'. Accordingly, this article is divided in two parts:

i) The Vatican City State;

ii) The Holy See.

i) The Vatican City State

The entire state of Vatican City, with its extraterritorial buildings has been included, along with other member states, as part of the world patrimony.

The supervision of the historic and artistic heritage of the Vatican City State has been assigned to the Pontifical Commission for the Conservation of the Historic and Artistic Monuments of Vatican City State. This commission was founded in 1923 by Pius XI in order to supervise the maintenance of all buildings pertaining to the city state proper, first and foremost the Basilica of St. Peter along with the museums and the Pontifical galleries established by Clement XIV and Pius VI.

The mere size and richness of these artistic collections of inestimable value, has made them known worldwide. They include the Vatican Picture Gallery; the Museum of Egyptian Artefacts; the Etruscan Museum; the Lateran Museum (with statues, low-reliefs, and mosaics from Roman times) along with the adjoining Christian Museum (with sculptures, sarcophagi, archaeological finds); the world famous Sistine Chapel; the Raphael Stanze and Logge; the Chapel of Beato Angelico; the Tapestry Rooms; the Map Gallery instituted under the Pontificate of Gregory XIII; the collection of Modern Religious Art inaugurated by Paul VI in 1973; and the Museum of History.

ii) The Holy See

The Holy See is made up of those offices which assist the Pontiff in his role as Universal Pastor of the Catholic Church. Since the Catholic Church extends its activity throughout the world, the jurisdiction of these offices extends to all those nations of the world where there are Catholic faithful gathered in diocesan communities.

From the start of its pastoral mission, the Catholic Church has availed itself of the visual arts as a privileged means of turning man's attention towards the contemplation of God. The Church has depended on the language of art as an instrument capable of handing down the legal texts and the cultural acquisitions concerning its history to future generations. But in certain periods of history the Catholic Church has also salvaged and protected the artistic, historic, philosophical and literary heritage of mankind.

The supervision and promotion of the various activities carried out for the conservation of the cultural heritage in the dioceses of the world has been assigned to the Pontifical Commission for the Conservation of the Artistic and Historic Patrimony of the Church.

The commission was established by Pope John Paul II on June 28, 1988, and has launched numerous initiatives worldwide:

1) A survey of the artistic and historic heritage of the Catholic Church in the nations of the world. This heritage includes not only those artistic treasures on view in single collections or in Church buildings, but also those archive and library collections, historical documents which attest to the development and growth of the local Church community.

2) Based on the documentation received from the general survey, the commission is planning to establish an information network, placed at the service of each Church community. The possibility of exchanging information will serve to encourage and guide those younger Church communities in developing countries which are just beginning or are thinking of starting their own local policy of conservation and preservation of their cultural heritage.

3) In order to ensure adequate placement and protection of the artistic and historic patrimony in each diocesan territory, the commission has underlined the need to establish an up-to-date catalogue and inventory of the collections with the aid of photographic material and computerised technology, and adequate storage facilities. These measures also ensure the safeguarding of the collections from the dangers of professional theft, a growing concern among European community member states as the 1992 deadline for the opening of the internal frontiers quickly approaches.

4) An adequate inventory procedure also involves the appropriate training of professional staff

St. Peter's Square, Vatican City

which can discern and evaluate the collections. For this purpose, the commission has just recently launched a one year training program at the Pontifical Gregorian University in Rome beginning this fall 1991. The program offers university level instruction in art history, art and liturgy, archive science, restoration, library science and museum management.

As the commission enters into its full operative phase, a number of projects have been lined up for the immediate future concerning the relationship between art and faith, the training of future clergymen on their responsibility in the area of the cultural heritage, the relationship between ecclesiastical commissions and the artist, and the role of art critics.

In meeting the important challenges ahead, the commission intends to carry out its activities with total dedication in order to join those worldwide efforts which favour a new consciousness of the fundamental value of cultural traditions as a contribution to mankind and its future generations.

HIS LORDSHIP MOST REVEREND FRANCESCO MARCHISANO, *Secretary, Pontifical Commission for the Conservation of the Artistic and Historic Patrimony of the Church, Holy See*

THE VATICAN CITY

LOCATION   Within the City of Rome, E 12° 39′, N 41° 53′.

DESCRIPTION   The territory of the Vatican City covers an area of 44ha (106ac). St. Peter's Basilica, built on the foundations of Constantine's Basilica, has a dome which is 132m (430ft) high and dominates the Vatican skyline. St. Peter's Square which is 320m (1,050ft) long and 240m (800ft) wide has a large colonnade which is supported by 240 columns and is adorned with 140 statues. Other important buildings include the Pope's palace, a complex of buildings dating mainly from the 15th and 16th centuries, the Sistine Chapel which was built in 1473 and is the Pope's personal chapel, 11 museums, famous for their antiquities, collections, sculptures and paintings. There are also 3 'extraterritorial' churches included as part of the Vatican's inventory: San Giovanni in Laterano (the actual Cathedral of Rome); Santa Maria Maggiore; San Paolo Fuori.

SIGNIFICANCE   The Vatican City State was established by the Lateran Treaty, signed between the Holy See and Italy in 1929. It is the centre of the Roman Catholic Church, and a place of pilgrimage. St. Peter's Basilica is the biggest funeral building in the world with the tombs of more than 240 Popes. The painting on the ceiling of the Sistine Chapel by Michelangelo, entitled 'Creation of the World', along with the fresco 'The Last Judgement' on the wall above the altar are the most famous of a multitude of art treasures held within the Vatican.

The Power of an Idea

AS WE APPROACH the end of the millennium, it often becomes too easy for us to grow despondent about the fate of the world. It is said that the planet is in grave danger, that we threaten to destroy the air we breathe and the water we drink. The future is predicted to be an ongoing battle against threats – or submission to them.

We are indeed endangered, and our planet's survival is in question. But we needn't be discouraged. A vast change is in the air, thanks to the power of an idea, an idea that is gaining converts every day.

The idea is simple: people are connected to the world, to the ground, the air, the water and to the creatures who share that space. This is not a new idea. But for the technological world, it is an idea whose time has come. Traditional societies have lived this idea for time immemorial – to exist in harmony with the earth is enshrined in their being.

Audubon too has lived this idea for the better part of a century. Sanctuaries for nature, birds, and youth education are part of our heritage. We have learned that nature often cannot fend for itself in today's world. Humans must therefore be stewards

Cocobila village, Rio Platano Biosphere Reserve

HONDURAS

Honduras is an extremely mountainous country right in the middle of Central America. It has a wide frontage on the Caribbean Sea as well as a narrow Pacific Ocean coastline. Much of the landscape is spectacular, with vast stands of forest covering endless rugged ridges and valleys. The climate is continually hot and humid with high rainfall. On the eastern coastline there are numerous mangroves, lagoons and palm forests.

Apart from its magnificent natural heritage, Honduras has a rich cultural heritage, steeped, as with Guatemala and Belize, in the ancient Mayan civilisations. The Spanish came, with Columbus, in 1502 and the country was named after the deep waters off the north coast – 'honduras' means 'depths' in Spanish.

Recognising the value of its unique heritage, Honduras ratified the World Heritage Convention in June 1979 and now has two sites inscribed on the World Heritage List – the Mayan ruins at Copan and the Biosphere Reserve at Platano.

The Copan ruins were discovered in 1839 amongst thick jungle. They are spread over a large area and are built on two levels. The stone carving found here is considered to be some of the best Mayan art extant.

The Biosphere Reserve at Platano covers the Platano River basin and includes a great diversity of flora and fauna, including extensive stretches of virgin rainforest.

RIO PLATANO BIOSPHERE RESERVE

LOCATION   Northeast Honduras, N 15° 57′, W 84° 35′.

DESCRIPTION   This reserve is comprised mainly of the hydrographical basin of the Platano river which drains an area approximately 1,300sq km (520sq mi). The broad leaved forests contain the greatest concentration of fauna within Honduras. The park is often hilly or mountainous, up to 1,326m (4,350ft) above sea level. Only 10 percent of the park is plains, which stretch 22km (13.7mi) from the sea. Within the total area are 5 distinct ecosystems: 1. Estuaries and mangrove swamps; 2. lacustrine; 3. savanna; 4. gallery forest; and 5. degraded secondary forest.

SIGNIFICANCE   There is an abundance of virgin rainforest within this area and the remainder is largely undis-

of nature. We must recognise our interdependence with other life.

Audubon is part of the movement to personalise the world – to get away from systems, dogma, and theories, and back to people helping people helping nature. Audubon expresses this spirit, of the love of nature as nature, and a respect for nature and what it gives us.

It is a spirit that lets us see each other as equals, yet value those differences which make us members of distinct cultures. It is a spirit that leads us to cherish our history and build for our future. Living that spirit, we join with partners of other cultures across the world to address locally and globally many issues: population and overconsumption; degradation of soils, freshwater, and oceans; climate change; and habitat protection.

The spirit has many names, but always the same directive: to value and preserve the past, while fighting to ensure a future for all of us – and nature. Many cultures in the world revere their ancestors for giving them the natural world in a perfect form, with the changing of the seasons and the blessings of the harvest. Will our children's children so honour us as their cherished heritage?

MARK BONTA, *Audubon, Washington, USA*

An overgrown temple at Copan

turbed by man. An amazing diversity of flora and fauna inhabit the region including many endemic species. The indigenous people of this area, the Payas, are believed to descend from the Mayans.

MAYA RUINS OF COPAN

LOCATION   Copan, western Honduras, N 10° 50', W 89° 10'.

DESCRIPTION   These ruins cover 25ha (60ac) and are divided into a main group and several secondary groups. The main group has an 'acropolis' and 5 plazas. The acropolis is a complex of pyramids, temples and terraces. One of the main features of this site is that the nearby river has changed course, cut into the acropolis and exposed floor after floor of the various ruins over which the existing acropolis was built. There are also several ball-game courts and some highly developed structures for astronomical studies.

SIGNIFICANCE   The sudden emergence of the classical Mayan period (300-900 AD) is seen in Copan in the numerous plaza/mound arrangements. It is in the new styles of ceramics, the stelae altar complex and ball-game courts that the Copan ruins allow for a full appreciation of just how advanced this civilisation was.

HUNGARY

Out of Hungary's numerous architectural treasures, two have so far been chosen to be placed 'in the world's hands'. The World Heritage Convention was accepted in July, 1985, and now the heart of the capital city, Budapest, is accompanied on the World Heritage List by the pristine rural village of Hollókö.

Budapest has one of the longest histories of any European city. Traces of settlements have been uncovered which date back to the Neolithic Age. Around 70 BC, the Eraviscans settled in the region. These people were of Celtic origin, but had adapted the Illyrian culture. The Romans appeared in 9 BC and built the town of Aquincum right next to the site of present day Budapest.

After the collapse of the Roman empire, this strategic site on the Danube was controlled by a people known as the Magyars. Along with them were other Germanic and Slavic settlers who formed villages on both sides of the river; one on the left bank called Pest, and two on the right bank, one the forerunner of Buda an another on the old Roman site called Obuda. This area prospered and developed up until 1241 when the Mongols invaded. Six years later, they had gone and King Bela IV had begun to build his residence on Castle Hill. The Royal Palace and adjoining settlements were all surrounded by walls. By the turn of the 14th century, Buda had become recognised as the capital city.

Buda's prosperity continued to grow up until 1541 when the Turks invaded. The next 150 years of Turkish rule saw Buda decay and Pest fall into ruin. The Austrians defeated the Turks, but at great cost to the Gothic and Renaissance architecture of the towns. Much rebuilding was completed during the 18th century, mainly in the baroque style.

Buda and Pest were united in 1872 into a large city of almost three quarters of a million people. More rebuilding followed, usually with an eye to the preservation of the towns' great historical value. Much damage was inflicted upon Budapest during the Second World War, but after 1945, reconstruction was rapid. Despite all that has gone before, the old part of Budapest stands today as a very well preserved inclusion on the World Heritage List.

The second Hungarian World Heritage inclusion, Hollókö, is the only complete village found on the World Heritage List.

Hollókö

Buda Castle on the Danube

A Village in the Hills

THE ROAD WOUND its way through wooden hills or between copses, with now and then a glimpse of a few sleepy cows. I was driving in northern Hungary, looking for a village. Tucked away at the end of a road, it rarely appears on maps and the signposts along the road are somewhat erratic. At each fork I hesitated: left or right?

Yet Hollókö is no ordinary place. Since 1987 it has been the only village in the world inscribed on UNESCO's World Heritage List. Situated in the Cserhát mountains, some hundred kilometres northwest of Budapest, it is still a backwater as far as large-scale tourism is concerned.

Suddenly, through the foliage of the trees lining the road, I caught sight of a green sign and on it, in white lettering, there at long last was the name of the village. A few hundred metres further on, at the crest of a slope, I came across the first houses and was beset by doubt. These were sturdy modern buildings, surrounded by gardens, of the kind which has been springing up in the Hungarian countryside over the past few years. Could Hollókö be a tourist trap, with a pile of stones passed off as a historic ruin?

Before long I came across a sign bearing the World Heritage emblem. Then, all at once, the look of the place changed. The real village sprang into view. As though in a fairy tale, cottages as white as wedding gowns, each with a wooden balcony, appeared along the main street. This street of uneven cobblestones is named after Sándor Petöfi, the great Hungarian revolutionary poet who died in 1849. With rare exceptions, cars are not permitted here.

Unlike other Hungarian villages, which are centred on a church, this ancient village in the Cserhát mountains leads to a tiny and charming whitewashed chapel dating from the fifteenth century. With its pointed, slate-covered steeple, it is the last vestige of the Middle Ages. Inside, there is no baroque ornamentation, just plain whitewashed walls and a wooden ceiling. To the right of the entrance hangs a crucifix by Ferenc Kelemen, a local sculptor. On feast days, old villagers still attend mass in traditional costume.

No more than a hundred people live in the old village. Dressed in typical Hungarian peasant fashion, black trousers or gaily coloured skirts, they go about their business, some bearing pitchforks, others carrying baskets of vegetables. On the nearby hills are a few vines, vegetable gardens, fields of maize and sunflowers. Sheep graze in the meadows. The farmland is divided into small plots. I did not see a tractor. The bucolic landscape adds to the charm of the village.

The neat rows of immaculate houses, facades embellished with finely carved wooden balustrades, surmounted by tiled roofs with tiny square windows set in them, are built in a uniform style characteristic of the architecture of northern Hungary. Their patches of garden, filled with summer flowers, are enclosed by low fences. Often, above the front door, there hangs a horseshoe, a garland of red paprikas, a cob of maize or a holy picture.

The village museum, situated in an old house converted for the purpose, is a perfect reconstruction of a traditional interior. The front door leads straight into the main living room, furnished with a dining table and benches decked out in embroidered covers. The kitchen is at the back and to the left is the bedroom in which parents and children all slept. A pair of boots is suspended from the ceiling to stop mice from nesting in them during the night. An adjoining room houses the loom on which the women embroidered tablecloths, head-dresses and cushions. To the right of the living room is a more spacious room, reserved for the grandparents, where farm implements, firewood and provisions for the harsh winter months are stacked up in a corner. Porcelain or pewter plates, generally hanging from the walls, gaily coloured blankets, red and green cushions, and hand-decorated earthenware vases brighten the place up.

All the houses in Hollókö date from the beginning of the century. Unfortunately, nothing remains from earlier periods. The wooden houses have been reduced to ashes in successive fires. Mongol hordes laid waste this area in the mid-thirteenth century, and in the sixteenth the village was sacked by Turkish troops, who left a garrison of sixty men in a fortress which towers over the neighbourhood. The ruins, accessible by a steep path, are in such a state of disrepair that they have been closed to visitors for the past seventeen years. But the fortress, which is indissociable from the history of Hollókö, is now being restored and will soon regain its former splendour.

'Now that we are part of the UNESCO heritage,' a village woman told me, 'we are no longer anxious about our future'. The entire village is the focus of attention from both local and regional authorities. Since last year it has even had its own post office, and it also boasts a grocery store, a primary school, an old people's home and three small café-restaurants, which are open until late in the evening.

To lovers of the past, the local tourist office rents out at a modest price a few charming cottages equipped with modern amenities. The number of these dwellings is limited so as not to alter the life of the village. In the summer season, romantics can hold weddings and country dances here, for which the village women will deck themselves out in all their finery.

'I was born to make people happy,' says Ferenc Kelemen. Born at Hollókö in 1927, he has worked with wood since his childhood and carves allegorical figures, birds, forest animals and groups of young peasant girls. There are piles of sculptures in the pretty little cottage where he lives.

Ferenc Kelemen is a voluble man who likes to repeat without any false modesty that he 'has no regrets about having been born with talent'. His fame has long ago travelled beyond the wooden fences of his native village.

ÉDOUARD BAILBY, French journalist and former correspondent with the Paris weekly magazine *L'Express,* served for a number of years as press officer with UNESCO's Office of Public Information.

Reprinted from the *Unesco Courier* September 1990

BUDAPEST (BANKS OF THE DANUBE WITH THE DISTRICT OF BUDA CASTLE)

LOCATION   Budapest.

DESCRIPTION   The city of Budapest is divided by the Danube. On the flat left bank is Pest, with the Parliament House as its most striking feature. On the right bank rises Buda, with its medieval fortifications on Castle Hill, its massive baroque royal palaces, the Neo-Roman fishermen's bastion, the staircase leading to the river, Matthias church, famous for its coloured tiles on the roof and the Gothic tower of Mary Magdelena. In the centre of the old quarter of the castle is St. Trinity Square with the Coronation Church distinguished by its graceful spire. There are also numerous medieval houses with 18th century facades.

SIGNIFICANCE   The fortress of Buda was built by King Bella IV in the second half of the 13th century to protect the city from the Tartars invasions. 150 years of Turkish occupation left the castle in ruins. Buda was extensively restored in the 19th and 20th centuries. One of the features of the castle quarter of Buda are all the Gothic niches at the entrances to the houses.

HOLLÓKÖ

LOCATION   Northeastern part of Hungary, 100km (62mi) from Budapest in the Paloc region.

DESCRIPTION   This listing includes 141ha (340ac) of vales, pastures and forests. The village of Hollókö is nestled on the slope of a hill. The ruins of a fortified castle sit on the top of the hill. The historical centre of the town includes 126 houses and a small Roman Catholic church.

SIGNIFICANCE   One of the most authentic reminders of traditional Paloc rural architecture, Hollókö is a complete and lasting testimony to a now vanished rural European lifestyle. The adjoining essay by Edouard Bailby gives a fascinating insight into this fairytale town.

Ajanta Caves

INDIA

Without a doubt one of the most extraordinary nations on earth, India is a land of gigantic proportions: the world's largest democracy, the second largest population, the seventh largest country with a size of 3,275,555 sq km (1,264,555 sq mi), with one of the world's highest peaks, K2 (28,250 ft - 8,611m) thrusting out of the Himalayan range it shares with Tibet, Nepal and Bhutan.

Indian pre-history is usually thought to begin with the Harappans around 5,000 years ago. Traditionally associated with the Indus valley, they were highly organized. They practised urban planning and cultivated crops.

The Arayans, a nomadic people, invaded in extraordinary numbers sometime around 1,200 BC, bringing with them their language, Sanskrit. They penetrated to the south of the land, gradually intermingling with the indigenous peoples.

Various states emerged over the centuries until India came under the influence of a significant foreign power, Persia, in the 5th century BC. It was Alexander the Great's conflict with Persia which brought his army to India. Resentment at this European invasion allowed Chandra Gupta to forge enough popular support to drive out Alexander's troops. He proclaimed himself Emperor, beginning

Ellora Caves

Monolithic carvings at Mahabalipuram

the Mauryas dynasty, which established a centrally controlled government over almost all of the subcontinent. The Dynasty endured for 150 years, including the enlightened reign of one of antiquity's greatest rulers, Asoka, (274-237 BC) who devoted himself to spreading the Buddhist doctrine of non-violence to living things.

It was not until the 4th to the 7th centuries AD and the Guptas Dynasty that India again came under a centrally controlled government. This period is often thought of as the classic period in Indian culture when the arts and literature flourished and great advances were made in the sciences and education.

Over the next twelve hundred years there were three significant foreign presences in India: the coming of Islam, which first appeared in the 8th century; the establishment of the Mogul Empire from the 16th to the early 18th century, which sought to integrate Hindus into the Muslim administration but which collapsed in the face of regionalism; and the British influence which first manifested itself with the British victory over Mogul forces in 1757 at the

battle of Plassey. One hundred years later there were widespread demonstrations against British rule which were eventually put down by the British with terrible ferocity.

While British rule brought a return to a centralized administration, it couldn't reconcile itself with Indian nationalist aspirations. After the bloody massacre at Amritsar in 1919, Gandhi emerged as an effective leader who, by instigating boycotts of British goods and advocating non-violent opposition to British intransigence, created what became a mass movement for independence.

On August 15th, 1947, India divided into two states: India and Pakistan.

Today Hindi is the official language, although English often functions as the same. The main religion is Hinduism, but Islam, Sikhism, Jainism and Zoroastrianism are all also important. Its diversity of cultures and traditions is reflected in its 19 World Heritage sites, more than any other country, which shows its commitment not just to the World Heritage, which it ratified in November 1977, but to its own rich history.

Agra Fort

The Abode of Gods

THE CONSERVATION of nature and natural resources has gained a quintessential relevance in recent years on national and international levels. The protection and conservation of natural, historical and cultural heritage is the biggest poser today before the world. Some of the rarest species of flora and fauna are on the brink of extinction. The witch hunt for luxury and comfort has added to the gravity of the situation. So much so that the environment and so-called development have become diametrically opposed.

Within India, national heritage sites like the Ajanta and Ellora Caves or other such important places can be protected by strict regulation and administrative laws, but the conservation of environmentally important zones is not possible without the will of the masses.

There are umpteen examples, like Keoladeo National Park, where rules exist but are being neglected due to public ignorance and non-participation by the local people. In the Himalaya, the beautiful pastures like the 'Manpai Bugyal', (meadow) Nanda Devi National Park, Rudranath and Mad Maheshwar are flourishing only due to the belief in myths and mysteries about the place by the local populace.

The Himalaya has always been revered and worshipped. The great Indian poet Kalidas described Himalaya in these words:

> In the north is situated the king of mountains, Himalaya which extends from eastern coast to west and forms the axis of the world.

The 2400 km (1500 mi) expanse of the Himalaya is the abode of many sky touching peaks, beautiful valleys and lush green pastures. Nanda Devi group of mountains constitutes one of the prominent ranges of Himalaya. The area of national park (now a biosphere reserve) is in the form of an arch.

Nanda Devi National Park is situated in the northern region of Chamoli District in Garhwal Himalaya.

The crystal clear waters in the river channels and glacial lakes reflect the grandeur and scenic beauty of the surrounding snow clad peaks. The undulating pastures stretching over miles are laden with numerous beautiful Himalayan flowers. The reverence for these Himalayan uplands and its rich flora was a traditional conservation measure enshrined by the myths and beliefs of the local people. Violation of this tradition by humans was believed to earn the wrath of gods by way of being kidnapped or possessed by evil spirits.

In 1974, an order was passed to fell a large number of trees in Dasholi block no. 7 near Reni Village which is on the periphery of the Nanda Devi Sanctuary. This move was resisted by the local people in

Siberian cranes, Keoladeo National Park

Indian one-horned rhinoceros, Kaziranga National Park

Manas Wildlife Sanctuary

March 1974 and this was called the Chipko Movement. Chipko Movement brought a halt to deforestation not only in this area but also in the entire Rishi ganga and Alakanada valleys. Later the Uttar Pradesh Government formed a high level committee with Dr Virendra Kumar as the chairman. This committee confirmed the vulnerability of the region and gave scientific credibility to the Chipko Movement. This region was thus saved from deforestation. The women of this area came forward as leaders of this movement and clung to the trees contesting that the jungle was their mother and they would not allow it to be chopped by the timber contractors or State Forest Corporation.

The Rishi ganga Valley including the Nanda Devi region is a place of worship for the local people. Most of the mountain peaks are named after gods and goddesses. Nanda Devi is believed to be the presiding deity of this region and is revered as a part of every home. The Nanda Devi basin is called 'Dev sthanam' or the abode of gods. Every year people from the interior of Garhwal and Kumaon gather at a particular place to worship the goddess Nanda. The venue chosen is at the elevation of 900 m (3000 ft) and is located at such a site from where the Nanda Devi peak is clearly visible. This festival is called Nandashtami and its date falls between 15th August and 15th September every year. This is the time when the lush Himalayan meadows are blooming with a myriad of flowers and

human beings bow to the grandeur and beauty of nature. The newly harvested fruits and flowers are offered to the goddess. The rarest flowers like *Brahm kamal* are brought in limited number from the higher reaches and offered to the goddess with prayers. These wild flowers are never plucked by hand; if it becomes necessary to pluck them for medicinal purposes, they are plucked by the mouth, symbolising that the person plucking them is an animal and is ignorant. The people used to go in this area barefoot. They were prohibited to call out loudly or to wear red and gaudy clothes in this region. This could be related to the sensitivity of this area, many wild animals found here are easily scared and disturbed by the faintest sound. Such precautions, therefore, were very essential. Killing the animals and eating meat was prohibited here from mid-January to mid-February and July to August because this is the period of conception and gestation for the animals. All such beliefs acted as conservation rules in this area and the region remained conserved until the middle of this century.

The inhabitants of this area have a natural right to these forests, pastures and meadows which were legalised by the State. The cultivation rights were so distributed that there was no place for conflict. Extreme care was taken in dividing the land for cultivation purposes and for the pastures. A very good example of this awareness were two small parks in Rudranath mountains which were very carefully maintained by the local people. These parks, though, were of small size, yet their maintenance through traditional belief system of the local inhabitants was highly conservation oriented. Unfortunately, when the state administration took over these parks and the forest authorities opened them for grazing, they were destroyed in no time. The same can be said about poachers hunting the wild animals. There are many examples when local villagers have helped the state authorities to arrest these poachers.

We believe that merely enacting laws and using force cannot prove successful in conservation. The local people should be taken into confidence and their traditional beliefs and myths should be re-evaluated scientifically and included in present conservation measures. It is extremely important to understand the role of socio-cultural practices of the inhabitants in consonance with their environment. These practices should be carefully studied and understood and a practical plan be formulated on this basis. The youth and the women of the area should be organised in groups and entrusted with the responsibility of conservation and management of these heritage sites. The villagers who are adversely affected by the conservation plan should be given alternatives which acknowledge that people of this region have played a vital role in conserving nature. It is due to their efforts there now exists a balance between the plant and animal population in this region. If there is any problem it is because of external influences and the difficulty in preventing trespassing.

The reverence and faith of the people in the Himalaya as a symbol of their cultural heritage and an integral part of Indian tradition should be respected and added to the World Conservation Strategy. The local inhabitants and their belief in the sacredness of nature should be made part and parcel of the conservation programme.

CHANDI PRASAD BHATT, *Chipko Movement*
(Translated from Hindi by Rachna Pandit)

ELEPHANTA CAVES

LOCATION   Elephanta Island, eastern side of Bombay Harbour, E 72° 56′, N 18° 57′.

DESCRIPTION   7 man made caves are found on this island. The most notable, the Main or Great Cave, is 39m (128ft) from front to back. There are many sculptures and carvings inside the caves.

SIGNIFICANCE   Originally called Gharapuri, the name became Elephanta after a massive stone sculpture of an elephant was found by the Portuguese standing at the southern end of the island. The Great Cave is the last important monument to stone sculpture in western India. All the caves are dedicated to Siva, one of the supreme Hindu gods.

AJANTA CAVES

LOCATION   In the Maharashtra State, Aurangabad district, N 20° 32′, E 75° 45′.

DESCRIPTION   These two complexes of Buddhist cave temples have both been dug in the side of a steep cliff and are connected by a pathway. The ruins of an old staircase cut into the rock lead up from the Waghora River which flows below. 30 structures were built in the caves, 5 are Chaithyagriha (sanctuaries) and the rest are Sangharama (monasteries).

SIGNIFICANCE   These caves were carved in 2 distinct periods. The first period was between 2nd century BC and 2nd century AD, the second from 5th century AD to 7th century AD. The sanctuaries and monasteries are remarkable for their attention to detail and for the countless engravings, sculptures and paintings they contain.

BRIHADISVARA TEMPLE, THANJAVUR

LOCATION   Thanjavur District, Tamil Nadu, E 79° 05′, N 10° 45′.

DESCRIPTION   Comprising the principal temple, which is located in the centre of a large open courtyard surrounded by a number of smaller shrines, the whole complex has been enclosed by inner double storeyed walls. This is then enclosed by another set of outer walls. The inner and outer complex is again enclosed by a vast brick fortification with a moat, occupying an area of 14.75ha (35.5ac).

SIGNIFICANCE   Built by the Emperor Raja Raja who ruled between 985 to 1012 AD, this represents the highest form of temple architecture in southern India. It is laid out on a massive scale and is embellished with many important paintings and sculptures.

BUDDHIST MONUMENTS AT SANCHI

LOCATION   Madhya Pradesh, E 77° 45′, N 23° 29′.

DESCRIPTION   These monuments consist of several 'stupas' (domed Buddhist shrines), monolithic pillars and temples. They are all situated on a small hill, around 91m (300ft) high, just outside the village of Sanchi.

SIGNIFICANCE   The first monuments were erected during the reign of Asaka, between 272 to 237 BC. Construction continued over the years up until the 12th century AD. The later monuments show a distinctive Hindu influence in style.

ELLORA CAVES

LOCATION   Near the village of Verul Khulatabad Taluka, State of Maharashtra, N 20° 01′, E 75° 11′.

DESCRIPTION   There is a total of 34 caves in three groups, each group the work of a different religious sect: (1) the Buddhist group has 12 caves, including an immense and ornate sanctuary with a magnificent statue of Buddha and a stupa. The remaining caves are monasteries; (2) the Brahman group has 17 caves and includes an elaborate two storey cavern with remarkable wall reliefs, as well as a massive temple 82m (270 ft) long, by 46m (142 ft) wide by 32m (106 ft) high; (3) the last group of five was built by the Jainists and includes some of the most remarkable frescoes to be found in India.

SIGNIFICANCE   These magnificent caves represent one of the most impressive collections of religious architecture and artwork in India. The Buddhist caves are the oldest, dating back to the period between the 5th and 7th centuries, the Brahman caves were excavated between the 7th and the 10th centuries, while the Jainist caves go back to the period from the 10th to 13th centuries.

The Sun Temple at Konarak

Taj Mahal

Pilgrim, Fatehpur Sikri

Hampi

Khajuraho

SUNDARBANS NATIONAL PARK

LOCATION   West Bengal, E 88° 30′ to 89° 10′, N 21° 30′ to 22° 15′.

DESCRIPTION   This national park covers 1,330sq km (532sq mi) and lies within the deltaic mangrove ecosystem of the Sundarbans on coastal West Bengal.

SIGNIFICANCE   This pristine wilderness is breathtakingly beautiful and is home to many endangered species of fauna. The most important of these is the tiger – the colony here numbers around 250 and is the largest in India.

TAJ MAHAL

LOCATION   Just outside Agra, N 27° 10′, E 78° 02′.

DESCRIPTION   This mausoleum stands on a marble plinth, roughly 100m (330ft) on each side and 7m (22ft) high. It is square in plan with chamfered corners and a large arch on each side. A massive double dome sits on top of a pinnacle that reaches almost 80m (260ft) above the ground. 4 minarets stand at each corner of the plinth. The building was decoratively and skilfully completed with colourful, individual flower-petal motifs cut from marble and inlaid in the interior and exterior.

SIGNIFICANCE   Construction began in 1632 upon the decree of Mogul Emperor Shah Jahan in memory of his wife. According to inscriptions, it was built by a Turk to the design of an architect from Lahore. 'Taj Mahal' is a corruption of 'Mumtaz-i-Mahal' which means 'chosen one of the palace'. The building itself was completed by 1643, using 20,000 workers each day. The entire complex took another 11 years to complete. The Taj Mahal is without dispute one of the most beautiful and impressive buildings in the world today.

GOA (CHURCHES AND CONVENTS)

LOCATION   Goa, E 73° 50′, N 15° 33′.

DESCRIPTION   There are 7 churches at Goa, all the product of different religious orders. All are similar in plan, so far as the various components like the belfry, altars, choir and sacristy are concerned. The Church of St. Cajetan is modelled on the original design of St. Peter's Church in Rome. The Church of Bom Jesus with its facade, decorated with Ionic, Doric and Corinthian pilasters, shows the application of the classical order. All churches were built of locally available red shale and coated with lime to protect them from weathering.

SIGNIFICANCE   Many of these churches built between the 15th and 17th centuries were inspired by Roman churches which had a touch of the Renaissance with baroque interiors. The result in Goa was an interesting blend of styles with numerous unique features.

AGRA FORT

LOCATION   In the Agra district, N 27° 10′, E 78° 02′.

DESCRIPTION   Situated on the west bank of the Yamuna River, this fort is surrounded by 20m (66ft) high sandstone walls that are 2.5km (1.5mi) in circumference. Within the walls are several important buildings, including the Pearl Mosque built by Shah Jahan during 1648 to 1655 and the Jahangiri Mahal built around 1570 by Emperor Akbar.

SIGNIFICANCE   The Fort was constructed during the period 1564 to 1575 under the reign of the Emperor Akbar. Some of the buildings within were constructed later under the reign of Shah Jahan (1637 to 1655). Many of these buildings have great architectural significance, with the blending of Mogul and Hindu styles and the use of marble and other stone to spectacular effect.

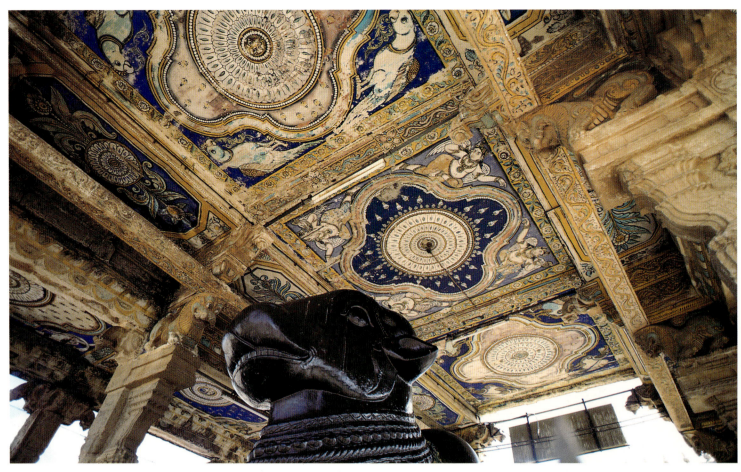

Brihadisvara Temple, Thanjavur

Sundarbans National Park

Group of Monuments at Pattadakal

Sanchi

GROUP OF MONUMENTS AT PATTADAKAL

LOCATION   Badami Taluk, E 76° 00′, N 16° 00′.

DESCRIPTION   The oldest temple here is a massive structure but very simple in design. There is no ante-chamber and the pillars are plain. Visupaksha is the largest and most important Sravida style temple of the Chalukyan period.

SIGNIFICANCE   Pattadakal was not only popular for Chalukyan architectural activities but also a holy place for royal coronations. Temples constructed here mark developmental stages and the culmination of the Chalukyan style of architecture.

HAMPI MONUMENTS

LOCATION   Karnataka, E 76° 30′, N 15° 02′.

DESCRIPTION   There are several temple complexes, all products of different times and different kings. The temples contain shrines with ornate carvings and fine bas-reliefs. There is a fortified citadel, which encloses many non-religious buildings, like the queen's bath, the king's palace enclosure, the Lotus Mahal, the mint, the Sandanayakb enclosure, a water pavilion and the elephant's stable.

SIGNIFICANCE   Construction of the temples and citadel took place between 1377 and 1576 AD. This was the time of the reign of the Vijayanagar Dynasty who were great defenders of the Hindu faith and its rich culture. The result was a unique art and architecture that attained new heights of splendour.

MAHABALIPURAM

LOCATION   Tamil Nadu State, E 80° 10′, N 12° 35′.

DESCRIPTION   There are 4 features to this listing: the monoliths carved out of solid granite rock, caves cut into the hills used as temples, bas-reliefs or sculptured scenes carved into rock faces and the structural temples.

SIGNIFICANCE   These monuments date from the period 630-800 AD and were built under the patronage of the great Pallava rulers. Many of them contain valuable inscriptions and carvings, revealing a wealth of information about these grand civilisations.

KEOLADEO NATIONAL PARK

LOCATION   Rajasthan, E 77° 20′, N 27° 11′.

DESCRIPTION   The Keoladeo National Park is part of the Indo-Gangetic Plain. It is fresh water swampland and is flooded during the monsoon. For most of the year, the effective wetland is only 10sq km (4sq mi), the rest of the area remaining dry. The alternate wet and dry seasons

Goa

help maintain the ecology of the freshwater swamp – ideal for waterfowl and wading birds.

SIGNIFICANCE   The park is outstanding for its numerous and diverse bird life. There are 353 different bird species so far identified. There are also many lizard, snake and fish species.

KHAJURAHO MONUMENTS

LOCATION   Madhya Prabesh, E 79° 56′, N 24° 51′.

DESCRIPTION   This listing comprises 3 groups of temples. All have an entrance porch, vestibule and sanctuary. They are erected on a lofty platform terrace with a high basement-storey which supports the walls of the temple with balconied windows. The roof consists of a series of graded peaks resembling a mountain range. The temples also contain erotic sculptures which reveal the aesthetic as well as the sexual charms of the body.

SIGNIFICANCE   These grand and powerful temples were constructed between the 9th and 12th centuries. They are outstanding examples of Hindu temple architecture.

MANAS WILDLIFE SANCTUARY

LOCATION   Assam, E 90° 45′ to 91° 15′, N 26° 35′ to 26° 50′.

DESCRIPTION   360sq km (144sq mi) in area, this park is situated on the outermost hills of the Bhutan Himalayas. There are many alluvial terraces and ancient water courses. Deep layers of boulders and sandy soil are characteristic of the region.

SIGNIFICANCE   It is possible that attempts at human habitation were made in ancient days, but this area has been largely untouched by man. It has been managed as a wildlife sanctuary since 1928. There are some 19 endangered species of fauna in the area, including the golden langur, hispid hare and the pygmy hog.

KAZIRANGA NATIONAL PARK

LOCATION   Assam, E 93° 05′ to 93° 40′, N 26° 30′ to 26° 45′.

DESCRIPTION   This park comprises 430sq km (172sq mi) in the alluvial flood plain of the Brahmaputra River. There is no evidence of human habitation for the last few centuries. It is managed as a wildlife sanctuary.

SIGNIFICANCE   The emphasis on managing this park is to provide optimum conditions for the continued existence of the great Indian one horned rhinoceros. The greatest concentration of this rare animal is found within this park's boundaries – the population is currently around 1,000. There are around 14 other endangered species of fauna found within this park.

Elephanta Caves

The abode of the gods, Nanda Devi National Park

NANDA DEVI NATIONAL PARK

LOCATION   Garhwal region of Uttar Pradesh, E 79° 44′ to 80° 02′, N 30° 16′ to 30° 32′.

DESCRIPTION   Situated in the central Himalayas, the entire 630sq km (156sq mi) of this park is part of an enormous glacial basin which, with the exception of Rishi Gorge, is all over 3,500m (11,483ft) in altitude. The peak of Nanda Devi, which is on the southern rim of the park, is India's second highest mountain at 7,816m (26,000ft).

SIGNIFICANCE   Wild and largely inaccessible, this area's history is almost totally devoid of human interference. Strong winds (except in the gorge which is very sheltered), daily drizzle and regular heavy snowfall have created a unique climate and hence a distinctive flora and fauna. Notable amongst the fauna are the musk deer, leopard, Himalayan black bear and the snow partridge. Flora ranges from grasslands in the higher areas to forests of birch and conifers in the gorge.

FATEHPUR SIKRI

LOCATION   Uttar Pradesh, E 77° 40′, N 27° 05′.

DESCRIPTION   The ancient city site is 9.5km (5.9mi) in circumference and is surrounded on 3 sides by a high wall about 6km (3.7mi) long. There are 9 gates and an artificial lake on the northwest side. The city, originally rectangular in plan with a grid pattern of roads and lanes intersecting at right angles, contained a well defined administrative block, royal palaces and the Jami Mosque at the centre.

SIGNIFICANCE   This famous deserted city with its impressive red sandstone buildings represents the most spectacular building activities of the rule of Akbar. The Jami Mosque is not only the largest and the most impressive of the whole group of the city monuments, but one of the largest and finest mosques in India.

THE SUN TEMPLE AT KONARAK

LOCATION   Puri district of Orissa, E 86° 06′, N 19° 54′.

DESCRIPTION   Now in ruins, this temple was originally designed in the form of the chariot of the Sun God. It had a tower almost 60m (200ft) high and a massive porch covered with many carvings and sculptures of lions, elephants, human figures and floral decorations.

SIGNIFICANCE   Constructed during the 13th century, this temple was dedicated to the Sun God. It has been described as 'the most richly ornamented building in the whole world'.

The Commonwealth and World Heritage

ONE OF THE GREAT tragedies of modern life has been the progressive estrangement of people from nature and from their cultural roots in the feverish quest for advancement defined in purely material terms. Tremendous damage has been inflicted on our physical environment, in some cases irreversibly so, since the first Industrial Revolution over two hundred years ago. The world is only now coming to grips with some of the global problems this has caused – ozone depletion, global warming, the loss of bio-diversity and marine pollution. In the name of progress, many natural landscapes, of little value in narrow economic terms, but of great beauty and wider significance, have been destroyed in countless parts of the world. So too have many irreplaceable monuments representing ancient cultures and traditions. In many past civilisations, people lived in greater harmony with nature. The natural environment in which they lived and respected played a crucial role in forming their distinct cultural identities. In all but a few parts of the world, this is no longer true today. Humankind has paid a high price for economic development, in both environmental and cultural terms.

The ethic of 'sustainable development', to which almost everyone subscribes today, requires the present generation to use the world's environmental resources in ways which do not jeopardise the ability of future generations to meet their own needs. I would suggest that this principle has another important dimension. It also means that development should preserve, not destroy, those assets of nature and of our cultural heritage which future generations would wish to enjoy and cherish. The world needs to make development sustainable, both environmentally and culturally. UNESCO's 1972 Convention to Protect the World's Cultural and Natural Heritage is vital for ensuring this.

The Commonwealth, which spans all the major continents, represents more than a quarter of the world's people, some of its member countries were cradles of the world's most ancient civilisations. It is culturally diverse, representing many races, religions, languages and traditions. It is also diverse in ecological terms.

It is therefore not surprising that the Commonwealth is the custodian of a significant part of the world's natural and cultural heritage, ranging from the Great Barrier Reef in Australia and Serengeti Park in Tanzania, to the Tower of London, the ancient ruins of Mohenjodaro in Pakistan, the sacred cities of Anuradhapura and Kandy in Sri Lanka, and the Taj Mahal in India. The beauty and splendour of these and many other natural and cultural treasures in the Commonwealth, which are on the World Heritage List, are vividly portrayed in this book.

A significant responsibility for safeguarding the world's heritage therefore lies with Commonwealth governments. Many are deeply involved in the activities which have flowed from the 1972 convention. Several have developed considerable expertise and knowledge in protecting nature reserves and valuable ancient cultural and architectural monuments. That expertise has been placed at the disposal of other Commonwealth countries and other members of the international community. I believe this is an area where there is much potential for furthering functional co-operation, and not only within the Commonwealth.

The preservation and protection of the physical environment is also an important duty for the Commonwealth. In 1989, at their meeting in Malaysia, Commonwealth leaders made a pact with the future by adopting the Langkawi declaration on the Environment. In that declaration they unanimously agreed on the crucial environmental problems which threaten that future, and made a joint commitment to tackle these problems through a programme of collective and national action. The environment is not a new subject on the Commonwealth's agenda. But the declaration recognised that environmental concerns must receive a higher priority in the Commonwealth's work. It signalled a deepening Commonwealth involvement in international efforts to resolve global environmental problems, and in helping member countries to deal with problems at national levels.

The world's rich biological resources constitute a vital part of our natural heritage. There is much international concern today about the need to protect and use those resources wisely, particularly in the world's greatest biological treasure-house – the Amazonian forests. The Commonwealth has recently embarked on a challenging enterprise in this area. At the 1989 Commonwealth summit, President Hoyte of Guyana offered almost a million acres of his country's virgin rainforest for a project, under the Commonwealth's auspices, to develop and demonstrate methods of conserving biological diversity and tropical forestry while achieving sustainable development.

As an international venture, the Programme for Sustainable Tropical Forestry to which his offer led, has great promise as an experiment to show how it is possible to make use of the rainforests' abundant riches while preserving for posterity the environmental capital they embody. It will also address the urgent global need for greater forest conservation in order to preserve our rich but declining biological

Darius under a parasol, Persepolis

diversity. A wilderness preserve will be established in two-fifths of the project area to maintain the rainforest in its pristine purity. This will enable continued natural evolution of biological diversity. It will also provide opportunities for scientists and scholars from all over the world to study nature in action and to fathom the richness of the evolutionary biological processes in a virgin rainforest. Potentially, there is much that other countries can learn from a programme of this nature. The Commonwealth Secretariat and the Government of Guyana are now co-ordinating an international collaborative effort, under Commonwealth auspices, to implement the programme.

This is but one example of the ways in which the Commonwealth will continue to address the needs of development while protecting the natural and cultural heritage of humankind. I am confident that the Commonwealth will make an increasingly significant contribution to the world's efforts to conserve and bequeath its rich heritage to future generations.

CHIEF EMEKA ANYAOKU
Commonwealth Secretary-General

IRAN

Iran is a large Middle Eastern nation of 1,646,050 sq km (635,932 sq mi). It shares its borders with Afghanistan to the east, the USSR to the north and Turkey and Iraq to the west. It possesses coastline along the Caspian Sea in the north and the Persian Gulf and Gulf of Oman in the south. Its main geographical feature is a central plateau bordered by mountains and ridges and an extensive area of southern lowlands. The climate is dry and the heat can be fierce, although this is tempered in the highlands. At an altitude of 1,200m (4,000ft) the capital, Teheran, is spared the sweltering summers experienced in the southern lowlands.

Two large tribes are believed to have entered Iran from the north: the Medians, around 900 BC and the Persians, around 700 BC. The Medians sacked Ninevah in 612 BC but they were defeated by the Persian leader Cyrus the Great in 549 BC. He went on to defeat Babylonia in 539 BC, and established the Achaemenid Empire, which at its height reached into India to the east and menaced Greece to the west. Its doctrine of military discipline combined with the vision of an extensive empire ruled by a centralized power is believed to have inspired the Romans.

Alexander conquered the Persians, introducing Hellenistic influences before a period of anarchy set in, with the country breaking into various tribal monarchies. Centralized rule returned in the 3rd century AD with the emergence of the Sassanian Empire, which spread the Zoroatrian religion and created a rigid, hierarchical society. They were defeated by the Arabs in 637 AD at the battle of Qadisya. Thereafter Iran became part of a Caliphate from 661 to 1258. During this period it was regarded as a relatively unimportant region, and so was able to retain many of its national characteristics, including its own language. Most importantly, its dedication to Shiite Islam helped preserve its sense of national identity and mission.

Beginning in 1501 a Shiite revolutionary movement arose which unified the country and brought it into direct conflict with the Sunni Ottomans. Its opposition to the Turks made it an ally with the European powers and strong trading links were developed. In the second half of the 18th century there was again a period of regional warfare, followed by the establishment of the Kajan dynasty in 1795 which endured until 1925 when, led by Shiite clergymen, the popular discontent with corruption and the

Persepolis

Esfahan (Meidam Emam)

Head of a priest, Tchogha Zanbil

extent of foreign influence in the country's affairs finally brought it down.

An army officer turned rebel became shah, or king, in 1925, and immediately adopted anti-clerical policies. Caught between the two warring factions, he was forced by the Allies to step down in 1941 in favour of his son, Muhammed Reza Pahlavi, who ruled as shah until 1979 when he was forced to flee. On April 1st 1979 Ayatollah Khomeini proclaimed the Islamic Republic of Iran.

Iran accepted the World Heritage Convention in February 1975 and presently has three sites on the World Heritage List: Persepolis, Esfahan and Tchoga Zambil.

ESFAHAN (MEIDAM EMAM)

LOCATION   Within the city of Esfahan, central Iran, N 32° 31', E 51° 39'.

DESCRIPTION   This listing comprises a plaza, 500m (1,640ft) by 160m (525ft), which is surrounded by a 2 storey facade. The ground floor forms a covered bazaar. There are 2 mosques, a palace and a large decorated portico within the precincts of the square.

SIGNIFICANCE   During the winter of 1597-1598 Shah Abbas I, the Safavid, moved his capital from Qazvin to Esfahan. The plaza was built in 1612. This, and the construction of the mosques, palace and portico, so embellished the city that it became known as 'Nesfe Jahan' or 'Half of the World'. The plaza itself was named 'Naqsh e Jahan' or 'Image of the World'.

PERSEPOLIS

LOCATION   Fars, E 52° 54', N 29° 56'.

DESCRIPTION   The Persepolis complex comprises a terrace built of huge stone blocks. On this terrace several palaces and buildings have been erected. There are 14 main buildings, essentially built of mudbrick. There are some sections of fortified wall remaining around the terraces. Near the site are 3 rock graves attributed to Artaxerxes II and III, and Darius III, all great Archaemenian Kings.

SIGNIFICANCE   When Darius III ordered a new city to be built, he envisioned it to be a spiritual centre of the Empire. The work started around 518 BC, continuing under various rulers until 428 BC. The site, essentially used for great festivals of the Iranian New Year, was destroyed by the Greeks of Alexander in 330 BC when it was burnt to the ground. Some inscriptions authored by Darius, a follower of Zarathustra – the founder of the ancient Iranian religion – still survive. One of them reads: 'I wish to think of justice as long as I can.'

TCHOGHA ZANBIL

LOCATION   Khuzestan, E 48° 32', N 32° 01'.

DESCRIPTION   This complex is composed of 3 concentric mudbrick walls inside which are arranged palaces and temples, with a 'ziggurat' (a pyramidal tower) occupying the central location. The various temples and palaces are all connected by paths paved with bricks.

SIGNIFICANCE   This site was founded in the middle of the 13th century BC by King Untash Napirisha. The complex was, at that stage, foreseen as the new religious centre of the Elamite empire, but it was never finished and was abandoned after the death of the king. The site was destroyed by the Assyrians in 640 BC. The ziggurat is the largest of its type conserved today.

*And I have felt
A presence that
disturbs me with
the joy
Of elevated
thoughts: a sense
sublime
Of something far
more deeply
interfused,
Whose dwelling is
the light of setting
suns,
And the round
ocean and the
living air,
And the blue sky,
and in the mind of
man.*

**WILLIAM
WORDSWORTH**

Creating Values: a Path to Action

IT IS QUITE SIMPLE to drop a glass onto the floor. Sometimes the glass does not break. Sometimes the glass shatters into a thousand pieces. When the glass has shattered you can never put the pieces together again to give the beauty and usefulness of the glass.

If the dropped glass has not broken then you have been lucky and the preservation of the glass has not been due to your care or good sense.

Hundreds of species of living creatures have disappeared for good. Others are still surviving, many of them with difficulty. That there are survivors has not been due to the general good sense of humanity but to luck and, more recently, to the determined efforts of a few who treasure the survival of all living creatures.

There is an awful lack of symmetry between destruction and creation. Destruction is so very easy that it hardly requires an effort. Carelessness is enough. But once something has gone then it cannot be brought back.

If there were no birds left in the world would we miss them? Probably not. If there was very much less vegetation in the world would we miss the vegetation? Probably not. The human being is marvellous at adaptation. People who live in cities all their lives do not consciously miss the sights, sounds and smells of the countryside. People who have never seen wild animals in their natural habitat do not miss seeing them and are content to watch wildlife documentaries. If all animals became extinct we would still be able to watch the wildlife films provided we converted them to digital form so that we could make endless perfect copies.

On the other hand would you like to be able to go somewhere to see live dinosaurs and pterodactyls and mastodons? We can only see bleached bones in museums and reconstructions of these creatures. We could do nothing about the disappearance of such creatures but conscious destruction and careless neglect can so easily give the dinosaur destiny to many creatures alive today.

We do not miss beauty and we would not miss the beauty of living things in all their variety and personality. But when beauty is present then we can appreciate it. Because you do not miss having a wonderful meal or meeting a wonderful person does not mean that you do not really appreciate both those things. No one's life is full of wonderful meals and wonderful people but there is always that possibility. If you knew that you were never going to have a wonderful meal and never going to meet a wonderful person you would survive and even get used to the idea. But you would still be missing a great deal – missing the possibility of excitement and pleasure.

There is probably no sadder caricature of man's careless selfishness than the destruction of the rhinoceros. There is the belief that the upsticking horn of the rhinoceros is of value in curing male impotence and increasing virility. There is probably a good basis for this belief in as much as belief in a remedy can act in a psychosomatic fashion to cure the problem. So these rare creatures are killed by poachers for the sake of their small horns. The rest of the carcass is left to rot in the sun. The poachers get paid handsomely for their efforts. In an afternoon a poacher may earn more than in a year of hard toil. The middle-men get paid for their involvement. The ultimate retailer makes a good profit and the purchaser of the remedy is buying hope, possibly some psychological effectiveness and the feeling that he has done all that is possible – and at great expense. But none of the parties know or care too much about the survival of the rhinoceros. That is the business of the rhinoceros.

This may be an extreme case but it does illustrate how different people acting quite logically and sensibly and with no direct intention to cause harm can actually do immense harm. In the case of the rhinoceros each of the parties is locked into a belief, a culture and a market structure. Like players in a play each person acts out the role without ever thinking what the whole play is about and whether it should be performed. Each player considers that such large questions are someone else's business. But who is someone else?

That man is able to appreciate beauty makes it automatically part of man's destiny that there should be a responsibility for preservation of that beauty. In the end such preservation must have a priority that over-rides almost every other priority. Yet there is no obvious personal gain in giving priority to this preservation of beauty.

In many countries there is the joke about the man who jumps off the top of a tall building. As he flashes past the third floor window he is heard to mutter 'so far so good'. Each little part of a journey may seem harmless but then, when the destination is reached, it is suddenly too late to realise the direction that has been followed.

It seems sensible to seek a few votes at the moment and to give priority to industrial development over rural preservation – after all the dignity of man requires that he has an opportunity to work for a living. Overall this makes sense but because it also makes sense at every moment means that such an argument can be applied insidiously to achieve considerable destruction of man's natural heritage.

Unfortunately man's thinking is very poorly equipped with ways of handling the dilemma between development and destruction. As usual there is an either/or conflict with each side claiming

Hatra

that it is right and blaming the other side for selfishness, foolishness or both.

Is there a way out of this dilemma? There is a way out and it is already beginning to be used. The unknown aspect is whether the solution will be adopted widely enough and quickly enough to prevent irreversible destruction.

The solution lies in a gradual shift of values so that preservation of man's heritage becomes a real value. At this point there will be more votes to be gained by following such values than by opposing them. This is already beginning to happen in the USA with environmental issues which are now seen as vote catchers.

What can an individual do? The simplest and the most effective thing is to take up the values of caring for the environment and those heritage treasures. This does not mean a blanket condemnation of any change at all. Such blanket condemnation actually weakens the values because it is unrealistic and makes all environmental values seem unrealistic. If an individual takes the values on board then these values spread to groups and become the cultural values. There may be a need for additional effort to spread the values to those who are slow to pick them up. Value changes can spread like an epidemic, slow at first but picking up speed.

When values change, then thinking changes and action choices change.

DR. EDWARD DE BONO, originator of the term 'lateral thinking', has been a prolific author, having published more than twenty five books.

IRAQ

The modern state of Iraq was formed after the First World War out of the three Turkish Provinces of Basra, Baghdad and Mosul. It roughly corresponds to the area that was known in ancient times as Mesopotamia – 'the land between the rivers'; the rivers, of course, being the Tigris and the Euphrates. It was these fertile valleys, along with those of the Nile and the Indus, which were the great cradles of human civilisation. The Sumerians of southern Mesopotamia were responsible, during the third millennium BC, for the development of the first cities and for the invention of writing.

Present day Iraq is a country of some fourteen million people. The capital city, Bagdad, was founded in the 8th century AD. Until the outbreak of the Gulf War, it was a thriving, modern metropolis, the commercial, industrial and spiritual centre of a country with an extraordinary history.

It is clear that Iraq's credentials for participating in the World Heritage Convention are very impressive indeed. In fact, Iraq was one of the first countries to ratify the Convention, signing in March 1974. At present Hatra is the only site listed, but there are many more sites which will no doubt prove more than worthy of World Heritage recognition in the future.

HATRA

LOCATION   110km (68m) southwest of Mosul, N 35° 34′, E 42° 42′.

DESCRIPTION   This ancient, fortified city lies in ruins. It occupies an area of about 320ha (772ac). There is an outer clay wall surrounding the town which is surrounded by a 20m (66ft) wide moat. Access is gained by 4 large gates. There are numerous temples and other buildings inside the walls, with attention focused on a large main temple which stands in the centre.

SIGNIFICANCE   From around the 3rd century BC until the 3rd century AD, Hatra was the religious and commercial centre for a large area situated between the Tigris and Euphrates Rivers, known as 'Arabaya'. During the 2nd century AD the town became the capital of the first Arabic Royal Dynasty and was the home to the god Shamash. Left in ruins after the great war between the Sassanians and the Romans during the 3rd century AD, Hatra never recovered. Excavations were instigated by the Iraqi Director of Antiquities in 1951.

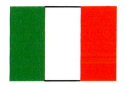

ITALY

This extraordinary country of 301,262 sq km (139,087 sq mi) which thrusts deep into the Mediterranean is dominated in the north by the Alps and the Dolomites while the Appennines range follows the southern course of the country. The central regions of Umbria and Tuscany are famous for their beauty, characterized by rolling hills and stately cypresses. The south and Sicily possess a relatively dry climate and dazzling sunlight. The countryside around the Abruzzi is rugged and relatively wild.

Italy boasts some of the most magnificent sites under the auspices of the World Heritage Convention, which it ratified in June 1978, including the historic hearts of three large urban centres: Rome, Florence and Venice.

According to tradition, Rome was founded by Romulus in 753 BC. Extraordinary administrators, engineers and architects, with a flair for commerce and military adventurism, the Romans lacked the artistic grace of the Greeks but possessed ambition and a powerful belief in their own glorious destiny.

By 100 BC the Romans had established control of Southern Italy and Sicily, defeated Hannibal and destroyed Carthage, and seized control of Greece and Spain. At its height, the Empire embraced the whole of the Mediterranean world. Civil war and persistent barbarian assaults pushed it into a decline which was dramatically demonstrated when the capital of the Empire was moved to Constantinople in the 4th century AD by Constantine.

Although the Empire itself was failing, Rome had

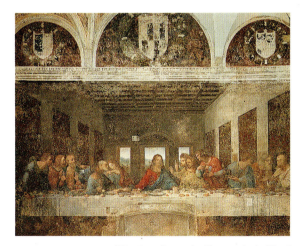

Venice

'The Last Supper' of Leonardo da Vinci

Rock Drawings at Valcamonica

become the centre of the Christian faith by the 2nd century AD and managed to retain this role even though the Pope's authority was without significant temporal power until Pope Leo III initiated strategic alliances and gifts of land from the French kings Pepin le Bref and Charlemagne (qv), to establish the Papal States which the Popes ruled for 1,000 years.

Over the next 700 years Florence and Venice emerged as the strongest of the independent city states.

Venice used her strategic trading location to forge an impressive empire and accrue great wealth. It played an important part in the Crusades and defeated the Turks in 1416 and again in 1571 at the battle of Lepanto. Today the stagnating, lustrous beauty of its lagoon invests Venice with a haunted romanticism which is impossible to resist.

The Florentines rose to prominence as bankers, introducing the first bills of exchange, and their rulers, most famous of whom were the Medicis, used their enormous wealth to enrich their city with magnificent works of art, crowned by the dome of the Cathedral, a geometric design of profound purity and grace.

Austrian domination engendered a wave of nationalism which eventually lead to Italian unification in 1870 with Victor Emmanuel as king. The Pope was forced to give up his extensive holdings and retreated to the Vatican where he remained a virtual prisoner until Pius XI signed the Lateran Treaties with Mussolini in 1929. After dictatorship and defeat in World War II, Italy finally became a republic in 1946.

The four sites at San Gimignano, Pisa, Valcamonica and Santa Maria delle Grazie comprise the balance of Italy's seven World Heritage listings. Significantly, all listings are primarily of a cultural nature – hardly surprising for a country which, on Italian Government estimates, holds almost half of the world's total artistic treasures.

Brunelleschi – the Renaissance Florentine

WITH THE COMING of the Renaissance in the early 15th century, Italian art underwent a fundamental change. The development of a new humanist outlook created a cultural climate which favoured the blending of the arts and the sciences and in the city of Florence liberated the creative genius of exceptional men such as the painter Masaccio, the sculptor Donatello and the architect Filippo Brunelleschi.

Brunelleschi was born in Florence in 1377. The son of a prosperous notary who occupied an important position in the Florentine Republic, he trained initially as a goldsmith and sculptor, being admitted to the Goldsmiths' Guild at the age of 21. Small in stature, he was a witty and highly cultivated man. We know how effective he could be in answering back his critics from one of his poems in which he lashes out at a denigrator of his greatest masterpiece, the dome of Florence cathedral.

At this period of Italian history, the communes – towns and cities ruled by free, self-governing institutions – were yielding one after the other to the power of new overlords, the *signorie*. Florence, however, a city of powerful businessmen and merchants, succeeded in preserving its constitution and its right to self-government, as well as freedom of expression for its humanists and scholars. Its rulers were men of letters whose influence stemmed less from their rank than from the esteem in which they were held by the people. This was the age of Florence's great 'humanist chancellors', men such as Coluccio Salutati, Leonardo Bruni and Possio Bracciolini, whose names have passed into the history of Italian literature.

Brunelleschi's first biographer, the mathematician Antonio Manetti, reports that his subject was deeply interested in science, and particularly in optics (then closely related to medicine and physics). Thanks to his studies in this field, he formulated revolutionary principles of perspective and applied these laws to a new concept of architectural space. Another biographer, Giorgio Vasari, refers to Brunelleschi's close relations with mathematicians and physicists.

In 1401, at the age of 24, Brunelleschi entered the famous competition for the bronze relief decoration of the second door of the Baptistery in Florence. His trial piece won the competition jointly with that of Lorenzo Ghiberti. The two artists were invited to share the commission, but Brunelleschi refused to collaborate with his rival and Ghiberti did the door. From then on he turned increasingly to architecture, where far greater successes awaited him.

Florence from Piazza Michelangelo

In the early years of the 15th century, Brunelleschi is thought to have visited Rome to study the ancient monuments. According to Vasari, he was accompanied by his friend Donatello the sculptor, and the two men spent so much time measuring the ruins of temples and palaces that the Romans thought they were searching for hidden treasure.

Brunelleschi's interest in the relics of classical art reflected much more than a mere concern with style. He was aiming to create new modes of harmony and beauty, as well as investigating building techniques. The result was that he invented an entirely new architectural language which was far from being a slavish imitation of classical models.

It was not until 1418, by which time he was 41, that Brunelleschi began to reveal the full scope of his creative genius. In that year he built a chapel (which has not survived) for the church of San Jacopo Sopramo in Florence. According to Manetti he was trying to prove that the system of vaulting by interlocking or 'herringbone' courses of masonry, which he had perfected, could be used to construct a dome without the use of a temporary wooden supporting framework.

This ingenious new technique of alternating horizontal and vertical rows of bricks in a herringbone pattern was to be a characteristic feature of all Brunelleschi's domes, both large and small. In his search for perfection the architect closely supervised the fitting together of the brickwork and every other detail of the construction work: each brick in the cathedral dome was manufactured according to his precise measurements and specifications.

In 1418, Brunelleschi also drew up a project for the reconstruction of the ancient Romanesque church of San Lorenzo. Taking into account the ground-plan of the ancient edifice, he devised a new church with a nave and two side-aisles, each flanked by small chapels. Even the lateral views, from the nave towards each chapel off the aisles, were conceived in conformity with the rules of perspective.

Later in the same year, he began work on the Old Sacristy of San Lorenzo, intended to become the family chapel of the Medicis. The building, a remarkable example of purity of form, consists of a cubic hall above which rises a circular melon dome.

In the following year, 1419, Brunelleschi began to produce projects for the Ospedale degli Innocenti, Florence's founding hospital, whose harmoniously proportioned facade is still admired today. The Ospedale, which would serve as a model for later generations of hospital builders, marks the birth of a new and authentically modern type of building created along functional lines by an architect who was also conscious of the imperatives and problems of urban planning.

In August 1420, work began on the dome of Santa Maria del Fiore, the cathedral of Florence, a mammoth undertaking in which Brunelleschi was to be involved through the second half of his life.

The dome, which rises over 80 metres (267 feet) above ground level, is without parallel in the history of architecture. Its construction posed innumerable problems of design and building technique, to which Brunelleschi, as great an engineer as he was an architect, devised some astonishing solutions.

The eight master-architects who had preceded him in directing the work had left the octagonal drum on which the dome was to rest open to the sky. It stood there like a vast crater, and no one knew how to cover it. In 1417, the project was thrown open to public competition, and engineers and architects submitted a number of designs incorporating a variety of different approaches. Brunelleschi's solution to the problem was novel and attractive, but it alarmed the organisers of the competition. He proposed to build the dome without using the traditional wooden supporting framework. The technique was revolutionary but feasible.

When construction work began, it was directed by Brunelleschi, Lorenzo Ghiberti and Battista d'Antonio. By 1426, however, Brunelleschi was virtually in complete control. Among the many admirers of the dome was the great architect and theoretician Leon Battista Alberti (1404-1472), who praised it as 'a structure so great, rising above the skies, large enough to shelter all the people of Tuscany in its shadow'.

The dome, some 40 metres (132 feet) in diameter, consists of an outer and an inner shell, separated by a gap through which access is given to the top. The thickness of the inner shell is just over 2 metres (7 feet) and that of the outer shell 0.75 metres (2.5 feet), while the gap between them is over 1 metre (3 feet, 4 inches) wide.

The red and green clay tiles which cover the outer surface of the dome, together with the white marble ribbing, create a matchless interplay of colours against the blue Florentine sky.

Brunelleschi's solution to the problem of the dome expresses the humanist ideals of the great architect and embodies a new vision of the relationship between art and mankind. The future development of Florence was dominated by his monumental work, and through its association with this new conception of art the city became identified for all time with the rise of humanism.

Many other designs have been attributed to Brunelleschi, including work on the Pitti Palace and fortifications in Pisa and Vicopisano. The basilica of Santo Spirito, planned in 1436 and begun in 1444, show that his boldness in manipulating architectural forms in no way diminished as he grew older.

The work of Filippo Brunelleschi marks a turning point in the history of architecture. In future, plans would be drawn accurately and methodically, and checked against the laws of perspective. Buildings

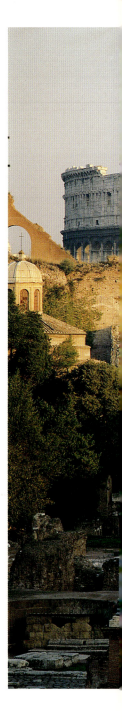

View of Rome's Colosseum

would be carefully sited in their urban surroundings.

Brunelleschi died in 1466. He is buried in Florence cathedral, in the shadow of the great dome which represents one of the greatest triumphs of man's creative genius.

FRANCESCO GURRIERI, Italian architect, art critic and historian of architecture, is assistant superintendent of Monuments in Florence. A specialist on Tuscan architecture, he lectures on architectural restoration techniques at Florence University and has collaborated with the International Council of Monuments and Sites (ICOMOS).

Reprinted from the *Unesco Courier*, January 1978, originally entitled Brunelleschi – The Florentine who launched Renaissance Architecture.

FLORENCE (HISTORIC CENTRE)

LOCATION   Florence, Tuscany, E 11° 15′, N 43° 46′.

DESCRIPTION   Overlooked by the graceful dome of its cathedral, Florence lies in a natural setting which rivals the architectural beauty of the town renowned as the birthplace of the Renaissance. Originally a Roman town, it was not until the 13th century that it rose to real prominence, with the building of religious and civic monuments reflecting its new position of economic, cultural and political power. After the period of Ducal Florence, few important changes were made to the squares and public buildings, and the artistic activity of the whole region became concentrated within the city itself.

SIGNIFICANCE   Florence was a Roman colony conquered in the 1st century BC and laid out as a garrison town. The town flourished under Hadrian until the 4th century AD. It was during the rise of the Medici family (1418-34) that new scientific and artistic visions came into prominence. The court of the Medicis became the centre of the Renaissance and this was expressed through brilliant new architecture and an intense concentration of artistic activity within the city.

ROME (HISTORIC CENTRE)

LOCATION   Central Rome, E 12° 29′, N 41° 54′.

DESCRIPTION   This is an extensive listing that includes countless buildings, arches, aqueducts, statues, archaeological sites and other monuments. The remains of the old town wall, built by Emperor Hadrian, define the limits of this site. Some of the well known features are the Roman Forum, the Colosseum, Hadrian's Temple, the Pantheon and the various Roman baths.

SIGNIFICANCE   Capital of the ancient Roman republic and of the entire Roman Empire, Rome has a longer record of continuous political and religious importance than any other city. The historic centre is home to the finest urban antiquarian ensemble in the world. It has been the centre of the Christian church for many centuries and is an important destination for pilgrims. The extensive remains of the old city continue to provide invaluable clues to the understanding of the greatest of all the ancient empires.

SAN GIMIGNANO (HISTORIC CENTRE)

LOCATION   40km (24mi) northwest of Siena, Tuscany, N 43° 28′ to E 11° 24′.

DESCRIPTION   San Gimignano is a remarkably well preserved medieval town. The centre is protected by ramparts that extend for 2,177m (7,250ft) and incorporate five cylindrical towers. There are five gateways, two facing north, two facing south and one facing east. There is also an outer rampart, much of it in ruins. The circuit between the ramparts holds the town's famous towers, which were built by the families of nobility of the day. 14 of these towers remain standing of the 72 originally built. There are also numerous civil buildings, a cathedral, many palaces and several town squares.

SIGNIFICANCE   This town is a living museum of regional medieval architecture and planning. Each of the Sienese, Pisan and Florentine styles are represented in very well preserved and original forms. Several notable frescoes are housed in the buildings of this town, including works by Benozzo Gozzoli on the life of Saint Augustine and by Lippo Memmi on the Madonna.

VENICE AND ITS LAGOON

LOCATION   On the Adriatic coast, N 45° 26′, E 12° 33′.

DESCRIPTION   Occupying one of the most remarkable sites in the world, the city of Venice is situated in the estuaries of the rivers Brenta and Sile. It is exposed to the tides of the Adriatic and is annually threatened by floods. The centre of the 'sinking city' is well defined by the Piazza San Marco with the Basilica of St. Mark, the Palazzo ducale (Palace of the doges) and the Procuratie – 2 parallel buildings on the sides of the palace. The main avenue is the Grand Canal adorned with innumerable Renaissance palaces and crossed by the world famous Rialto Bridge. The Gallery dell' Academia as well as the campanile (bell tower) are some of the other notable landmarks. The lagoon of Venice is composed of several islands, each with an historical centre. The main ones are Venice itself, Chioggia, Murano, Burano, and Torcello.

SIGNIFICANCE   Venice has a long and colourful history. From its humble beginnings as a fishing community, through its fiercely fought independence and growth into a major trading power throughout the rule of the Byzantium Empire; thence on to its rapid expansion after claiming the spoils from the 4th Crusade; through the bitterly fought Genoese Wars, on to decline through the Turkish Wars and the final blow to the Empire, struck by Napoleon in 1797. The legacy of such a rich history lies in the wealth of architectural and artistic heritage which is now being preserved 'en masse'.

PISA (PIAZZA DEL DUOMO)

LOCATION   In the north of Tuscany, N 43° 42′ to E 10° 25′.

DESCRIPTION   Piazza del Duomo includes the complex of the Cathedral of Santa Maria Assunta, which is in the Latin cruciform pattern, a large baptistery with an octagonal front and the famous campanile, or the 'Leaning Tower is famous worldwide as the symbol of the town. Construction of this belltower began in 1173 and

was not completed until two centuries later. It stands 60m (200ft) tall and is inclined 5m (17) from the perpendicular. This inclination began almost as soon as work started and has shown no signs of diminishing, prompting many studies aimed at stabilisation.

SIGNIFICANCE   The remaining buildings in the Piazza del Duomo bear witness to the former supremacy of the maritime republic which centred around Pisa. The Leaning Tower is famous worldwide as the symbol of the town. Construction of this belltower began in 1173 and was not completed until two centuries later. It stands 60m (200ft) tall and is inclined 5m (17ft) from the perpendicular. This inclination began almost as soon as work started and has shown no signs of diminishing, prompting many studies aimed at stabilisation.

ROCK DRAWINGS OF VALCAMONICA

LOCATION   Lombardy region, E 10° 10′ to 10° 20′, N 45° 30′ to 46° 30′.

DESCRIPTION   There are more than 130,000 individual carvings to be found on approximately 2,400 different rock surfaces in this area. The area itself stretches over 70sq km (28sq mi), is lightly timbered, and includes many fields of long grass and shrubs.

SIGNIFICANCE   These carvings were created over an 8,000 year period, beginning in the Camunian era. Due to the overgrown nature of the local vegetation, these carvings remained unstudied until 1929. It was not until 1956 that serious research commenced on the site. Studies over the following 8 years brought the tremendous significance of these finds to light. Valcamonica is now considered to be the most important complex of prehistoric art in the world.

SANTA MARIA DELLE GRAZIE WITH 'THE LAST SUPPER' OF LEONARDO DA VINCI

LOCATION   Milan, Lombardy, E 09° 12′, N 45° 28′.

DESCRIPTION   The Church of Santa Maria delle Grazie was built in the second half of the 15th century. The magnificent Renaissance architecture is overshadowed by Leonardo da Vinci's 'Last Supper' painted on the end wall of the refectory. The work is rectangular in shape – 8.85m (29ft) long and 4.97m (16.3ft) high.

SIGNIFICANCE   The complex of Santa Maria delle Grazie represents a milestone in the history of Italian architecture. Built originally by the famous architect Solari, the gallery was added by the great architect Bramante before he left for his period of activity in Rome. A masterpiece of perspective and compassion, 'The Last Supper' is considered a pivotal painting in the development of western art. It is currently undergoing restoration.

A thing of beauty is a joy for ever. Its loveliness increases; it will never pass into nothingness; but still will keep A bower quiet for us, and a sleep Full of sweet dreams, and health, and quiet breathing.

JOHN KEATS

The Leaning Tower of Pisa

San Gimignano (Historic Centre)

Natural Sites Under Threat: a Global Problem

CIVIL WAR, poaching, illicit gold mining and expanding tourism are threatening some of the natural sites listed under the World Heritage Convention. Unless these can be brought under control the survival of many endangered plant and animal species and their habitats will remain at risk.

Over the past 30 years WWF, The World Wide Fund for Nature, has spent over 11 million Swiss francs in protecting and managing some of these World Heritage sites. They range from the Great Barrier Reef in Australia and the Galapagos Islands in Equador to the Serengeti National Park in Tanzania and the Manas Tiger Reserve in India. Although these include widely differing environments, each fulfils one or more of the World Heritage criteria. Every natural site must be of outstanding biological importance or contain the natural habitats of endangered plants and animals.

Every year the list gets longer as more sites are selected from those put forward by the 119 countries which are signatories to the Convention. So far 79 Natural sites have been listed. The World Conservation Union (IUCN) advises the World Heritage Committee on this selection process and closely monitors sites once they are on the list. Jim Thorsell, IUCN's Senior Advisor on Natural Heritage, has said: 'Inclusion on the list means access to better funding and focuses attention on the protected area'.

Dam building schemes, logging and ski developments have all been prevented by strong opposition from an informed public, he added. When a site is seriously endangered it may be added to the World Heritage in Danger List which provides for special emergency measures. 'Its like a red flag to the international community', he explained. 'Because there is a monitoring system in place, once an area is inscribed on the list it becomes open to greater scrutiny. The public can bring moral and other pressure to bear and in many cases these interventions have been effective.'

There is also a provision to remove listed sites which no longer fulfil the required criteria but surprisingly this has not yet happened. Only one site, Garamba National Park in Zaire, is currently on the danger list. It was added after heavy poaching reduced the white rhino population from 1,300 to 15. Since then the management of the park has been strengthened, the budget quadrupled and the rhino population is up to 26. Now IUCN is recommending that Garamba should be taken off the danger list.

The Manas Tiger Reserve in India's northeastern state of Assam was designated a World Heritage Site in 1986. Subsequently, the Indian Government halted a scheme to build a massive hydro-electric and flood control project on the Manas River which would have affected the core of the tiger reserve. Manas contains more endangered species than any other in the subcontinent – possibly throughout the whole of Asia. Its vegetation varies from tropical semi-evergreen through moist and dry deciduous forests to alluvial grasslands. It is home to more than 300 species of birds – including the endangered Bengal florican – and its range of threatened species includes 22 endangered mammals listed under the Indian Wildlife Protection Act. In 1971 two of these, the pygmy hog and the hispid hare, were rediscovered in Manas – ten years after both were thought to have become extinct.

Manas was one of the first reserves created under India's Project Tiger in 1973 with US$1 million support from WWF and more than US$16 million from the Indian Government. It has important populations of wild buffalo and one-horned rhinos and forms part of an elephant corridor along the foot of the Himalayas.

Now the reserve is critically threatened after becoming a refuge for armed groups fighting for a separate homeland. For the second year running, IUCN is to recommend that Manas should be added to the World Heritage in Danger List. Over the past two years, terrorists have carried out acts of sabotage, arson and murder within the reserve. More than a dozen wildlife guards were killed when the fighting first broke out and the sanctuary staff had to be evacuated. The anarchy that inevitably ensued opened the door to professional poachers, timber smugglers and local villagers who now use the reserve for grazing and gathering fuelwood and fodder.

Although the civil strife is still continuing, WWF is planning to launch a new project along the southern edge of the park in a bid to ease the pressure from local villagers. The idea is to provide them with alternative sources of fuel and construction material for housing together with suitable grazing land for their livestock. Other development schemes include education, health care and income generation. It is also hoped that the villagers, mainly poor farmers and their families, can be involved in the management of the park. The project, which will be carried out by WWF India, is expected to cost almost 30,000 Swiss francs over the first year.

Elsewhere in Asia, WWF has launched an ambitious programme to co-ordinate international assistance for the protection of Huay Kha Khaeng and the adjoining forest complex of Thung Yai Yaresuan in Thailand – jointly nominated as a World Heritage site (to be considered in 1991). These two wildlife sanctuaries form part of the largest and most diverse forest in Indo-China and provide a wide range of habitat for wildlife. The rich mosaic of forest cover extends from moist and hilly evergreen, through mixed and dry deciduous to bamboo, secondary forest and scrub. Within it range many rare and endangered species; tapir, gaur, banteng, the clouded leopard, the white-winged wood duck, green peacock and Fea's muntjak.

Yet both these wildlife sanctuaries are threatened. Road construction, illegal logging, forest fires and poaching are all major problems. International attention was focussed on Huay Kha Khaeng late last year when the head of the sanctuary, outstanding conservationist Seub Nakhasathien, committed suicide in despair of the continuing degradation of the area. Only two years earlier he had headed a successful campaign to block a dam building scheme which would have severely disrupted the wildlife sanctuary.

The aim of the new programme, which is being carried out jointly by WWF and the Thai Royal Forest Department, is to address some of the major problems. An overall umbrella agreement was signed with the RFD in 1990 and the programme is expected to cost more than 2.3 million Swiss francs over five years. High priority will be given to establishing model village systems in the buffer zones to demonstrate how living standards can be improved by sustainable use of forest resources and the development of cash crops. A land-use plan will also be mapped out for the buffer zone – to establish land-use patterns and rights in land that borders protected forest areas.

WWF will also help the Royal Forestry Department in the recruitment and training of wildlife managers, guards and biologists to protect the two sanctuaries. A research centre is to be established at Khao Nang Rum to co-ordinate field research and provide technical training in nature protection and wildlife management. The centre, which will serve the whole southwestern region, is being funded by WWF–US for the first five years. There are also plans to set up an education centre for visitors in the Thung Yai Naresuan wildlife sanctuary. It is hoped that improved scientific knowledge and public awareness will help promote the conservation of these outstanding wildlife sanctuaries.

The Tai National Park in the Ivory Coast was founded in 1972 after consultations between WWF, IUCN and the Government. This single largest tract of undisturbed tropical rainforest in West Africa contains almost all of the 54 large mammals known to occur in Guinea rainforest, including five threatened species. Within its 3,300 square kilometre area (1270 square miles) live the pygmy hippopotamus, the African golden cat, water chevrotain, pangolins and an exceptional variety of duikers. Birds include the white-breasted guineafowl, western wattled cuckoo-shrike, yellow-throated olive greenbul and Nimba flycatcher. Tai

became a World Heritage site in 1982. Two years later it was on the IUCN's list of the world's most threatened protected areas. Today it is reeling from the combined onslaught of poaching, logging, illegal gold mining and farming. Poaching is on the increase – due, possibly to an influx of refugees fleeing the fighting in Liberia. IUCN's Directory of Afrotropical Protected Areas catalogues the disaster: 'In 1977, there were said to be many elephants, conspicuous even in the buffer zone. Now only a few remain, probably due to a combination of disturbance and poaching'.

Timber companies operate along the fringes of the park. Once the trees have been felled, slash and burn farming for cocoa and coffee is established – encroaching into the buffer zone. In 1988 the Government gave farmers a three-year ultimatum to quit the buffer zone but some large-scale farmers have warned they will dispute this.

Since 1988 WWF has been involved in carrying out aerial and ground surveys of the core and buffer areas of the park with the aim of clearly demarcating boundaries. WWF is also helping co-ordinate park management and advising on anti-poaching methods. An education programme is being developed for the people who live along the edges of the park. During the current financial year WWF is planning to spend more than quarter of a million Swiss francs on protecting the Tai National Park.

The Galapagos Islands in Equador was one of the first four natural sites to receive World Heritage status. Over the past 30 years WWF has spent more than 3 million Swiss francs supporting the island park and the prestigious Charles Darwin Research Station based there. Galapagos is famous for its unique species of flora and fauna. The giant tortoise, marine and land iguanas and large numbers of reptiles and birds can be found there. There is also a wide variety of plants and invertebrates.

Early surveys in the park revealed that many indigenous species – endemic snakes, the dark-rumped petrel, the land iguana and giant tortoise – were steadily being exterminated by the presence of exotic (introduced) species such as pigs, goats and rats which damaged the environment. These were removed and breeding programmes introduced for giant tortoises and land iguanas. Other activities have included training of national park personnel and education courses for local people. Since 1989, WWF has provided money through a local debt swap which is managed by the Charles Darwin Foundation. When fire broke out on the largest island, Isabela, in 1985, ravaging up to 400 square kilometres (154 square miles) of wilderness, WWF and IUCN headed efforts to help the area recover. Emergency action to relocate dozens of giant tortoises was successful. Only two suffered minor burns to the feet. But some indigenous species, such as the slow-growing soapberry tree, could

Great Blue Herron, Galapagos Islands

take up to 50 years to recover.

Now Galapagos is facing new problems. In 1990 fishermen from Japan, Taiwan and Korea caught some 40,000 sharks in the protected waters around the islands – using local sea lions as bait. Thousands of mutilated carcasses were later washed up on shore – missing only their fins, which were destined for shark fin soup. The slaughter was halted after an international campaign headed by Fundacion Natura, in Equador. But the effectiveness of the ban is doubtful. The waters surrounding the islands have not yet been designated as part of the World Heritage site.

Tourism is also becoming a problem. The park management plan stipulates a maximum of 25,000 tourists a year, but that number has now doubled.

The Ecuadorean Government has licenced another 32 tourist agencies from Guayaquil to operate boats in the park, in addition to the 66 permits already given to local islanders. The new permits have been strongly contested as the increase in tourism will put additional pressure on the park.

World Heritage status may be an honour but it is clearly no guarantee of the future sanctity of a natural site. Constant vigilance will always be needed. As Jim Thorsell says: 'The monitoring of the condition of natural World Heritage properties is now as important a procedure as nominating new sites to the list'.

SHEILA DAVEY
WWF International

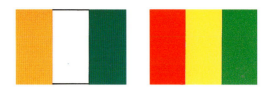

THE IVORY COAST AND GUINEA

Both Guinea and the Ivory Coast are countries of steamy equatorial forests, heavily indented coast-lines, alluvial coastal plains, deeply cut mountain ranges and low lying savannas.

French is the main language in both countries, a legacy of French colonial rule which ended in 1958 for Guinea and two years later for the Ivory Coast.

Another legacy of colonialism, in common with many other countries around the world, is the permanent damage that was inflicted upon the environment during the rush to exploit natural resources. Logging and agricultural intrusion in particular caused much damage to these once pristine equatorial African environments.

The World Heritage Convention was ratified by Guinea in March 1979 and by the Ivory Coast in January 1981. Now there are three environmentally important areas which are permanently protected through their inclusion on the World Heritage List: Mount Nimba Reserve, which is on the border of the two countries and so is jointly listed, protects a now unique equatorial African sub-montane ecosystem. Tai and Comoe National Parks, the two sites within the Ivory Coast, are each also unique, protecting countless species of endemic flora and fauna.

MOUNT NIMBA RESERVES

LOCATION   This is a joint listing between Guinea and Ivory Coast. The reserves are situated on the southern extremities of these countries, bordering with Liberia. N 07° 14' to 07° 44', W 08° 20' to 10° 40'.

DESCRIPTION   The reserves cover a total area of over 22,000ha (52,800ac). The terrain is mountainous and heavily forested. The highest peak is Mount Richard-Molard, at 1752m (5830ft) above sea level. Climatically, the area is classified as montane/sub-equatorial, differentiating it from the surrounding tropical plateau. The higher slopes are characterised by subalpine meadows.

SIGNIFICANCE   This beautiful and isolated environment is largely untouched by man. It protects a large number of endemic species, including 7 species of bats, 10 mammal species of the genus 'crocidura' and numerous beetles. Amongst the unique plants are some fascinating variations of lichen, fungi and mosses.

Villagers near Mount Nimba Reserve

COMOE NATIONAL PARK

LOCATION   Northeast Ivory Coast, N 08° 05' to 09° 06', W 03° 01' to 04° 04'.

DESCRIPTION   Mainly a plateau, Comoe covers an area of 1,150,000ha (2,770,000ac). The altitude is generally between 250-300m (820-984ft), although some rocky outcrops rise to 650m (2,133ft). The Comoe River flows through the park, its banks covered with forests.

SIGNIFICANCE   This park is rich in animal life, with 11 species of apes, 17 species of different hoofed mammals, 3 different crocodiles, 4 out of the 6 storks found in West Africa and 5 out of the 6 species of vultures. The great diversity of landscapes and vegetations give this park an ecological prominence in West Africa.

TAI NATIONAL PARK

LOCATION   Southwest Ivory Coast, N 06° 07' to 05° 15', W 07° 25' to 07° 54'.

DESCRIPTION   This park covers 330,000ha (792,000ac) of dense tropical rainforest. There is also a peripheral buffer zone of a further 156,000ha (374,400ac) which was created in 1977 to protect the national park proper.

SIGNIFICANCE   This park represents the last surviving remnant of an ancient block of dense tropical forest which once covered much of West Africa. The national park was created in 1972 to preserve this last remaining forest, and to protect its extremely rich population of endemic flora and fauna.

Village near Comoe National Park

Comoe National Park

JERUSALEM

Of enormous importance to the world's three great monotheistic faiths, the history of Jerusalem goes back to the Old Stone Age. By 1400 BC, 'Urusalim' (meaning either 'the foundation of the [God] Shalem' or else derived from Sumerian, meaning 'city of peace') had developed into an important fortress under the Egyptians, controlling the surrounding desert, and protecting important trading routes.

It was conquered by King David in 1000 BC who made it the capital of the unified tribes and took the Ark of the covenant there, thus establishing it as an important religious centre. Under King Solomon, the city developed into an important trading centre. In 597 BC and 586 BC, King Nebuchadnezzar II of Babylon sacked the city, the second time destroying the Temple of Solomon.

After a period of Persian domination the city fell under the control of the Egyptian Macedonian dynasty, the Ptolemies, and then the Seleucids from Syria. The Hasmonaean dynasty re-established Jerusalem as a leading centre for Jews from 164 to 64 BC, when Pompey entered the city.

Perhaps the most famous period was during the reign of Herod the Great. He gained power in 37 BC and proceeded to make profound changes architecturally, culturally and politically. Turning to Rome for assistance, he set about turning Jerusalem into a 'city of marble'. Jesus Christ lived under Herod's rule and was crucified in Jerusalem four years after Herod's death.

After his crucifixion, the Romans destroyed much of the Jewish built city. Following the Jewish war of Freedom in 132 AD, the Jews were defeated and Jerusalem was completely levelled. A new city was built, named Aelia Capitolina, and many temples were erected to Roman gods.

Two centuries of 'darkness' followed: then, in 326 AD, Constantine ordered the sites of Christ's crucifixion and burial to be recovered. One of them, the Church of the Holy Sepulchre, was built on the site where today a more recent church of the same name is found.

This church, along with many others, was destroyed in 614 AD when Chosroes II of Persia captured the city. The Romans recaptured Jerusalem in 629 but were ousted eight years later by Omar. Islamic rule continued for the next 462 years until the Crusaders entered to reclaim the Holy City. It was reconquered by the Muslims yet again 88 years

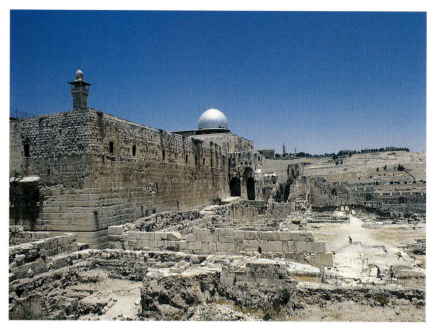

Excavations at Jerusalem

later under Saladin, and remained mostly under Islamic control until 1917, when it was captured by Lord Allenby.

Jerusalem then became the capital of the British mandated territory of Palestine. After the Second World War, the city was divided: the 'old city' passed into the hands of Jordan, while the 'new city' became part of the newly created state of Israel.

During the Six Day War of 1967, Israel occupied the old city. It has remained under Israeli control ever since.

Jerusalem was nominated for inclusion on the World Heritage List by Jordan in 1981.

JERUSALEM (OLD CITY AND ITS WALLS)

LOCATION   Central eastern Israel, on the Jordanian border, N 31° 47', E 35° 13'.

DESCRIPTION   220 monuments are listed within the old city. The most important area is Haram, where the Mount of the Temple is situated. This is a large quadrangle which has been used by the 3 great religions of Christianity, Islam and Judaism. Other important monuments are the Dome of the Rock, the Church of the Holy Sepulchre and the Wailing Wall.

SIGNIFICANCE   Jerusalem is unique in being a Holy City for 3 major religions. It has had a great and varied history which dates back to the Stone Age. The most famous period is without doubt during the lifetime of Jesus Christ. Numerous places in the city are traditionally connected with Jesus, the most notable being the Church of the Holy Sepulchre, reputed to have been built on the site of the Crucifixion. Via Dolorosa is considered to be the route on which he bore his cross and the Grotto of Gesthemane is thought to be the cave where he was when he was betrayed by Judas. Mohammed also visited Jerusalem, the Dome of the Rock being the place where it is said his night journey to Heaven began.

Worshipper at the Wailing Wall, Jerusalem

Renewing the Whole Creation: a Task to Share

FOR CHRISTIANS, or people of the Book, our understanding of creation has often been tied to individualism and personal salvation. The created order has been seen merely as the stage upon which the drama of humankind's salvation has been acted out. Partly for this reason, we now find ourselves in a new and precarious situation, one that we share with others.

As the race for development sputters to an inconclusive end and the vista of an ever improving lifestyle dissolves before our eyes, we are all beginning to understand the damage we have done to the Earth and the injustice we have wrought among its people. For those who believe in creation, this causes particular pain:

> God sits weeping,
> The beautiful creation tapestry
> She wove with such joy
> is mutilated, torn into shreds
> reduced to rags
> its beauty fragmented by force. (M. Rienstra)

How can we pray to God in the midst of this global, ecological crisis? With the psalmist, we would rather ask, 'How shall we sing the Lord's song in a foreign land?' (Ps. 137:4, RSV). But is the landscape really so foreign? Do we not see in the world that is dying around us the results of all our acquisitiveness? The path of development has run into the quicksands of limited resources and endless competition. Where should we look for the road ahead?

If we are prepared to wait by the side of the road and listen, we may hear other voices singing a new song. Often the voices of scientists and people of primal cultures, these voices are singing a song of the interconnectedness of the whole of life. 'The events and discoveries of recent years have forced upon us the knowledge that all creation coinheres, that the web of life in which all is connected is a reality', write Cashmore and Puls ('Clearing the Way', Cashmore and Puls, WCC 1990, p20).

> This we know. The earth does not belong to man (sic); man belongs to the earth. This we know. All things are connected like the blood which unites one family. All things are connected. (Chief Seattle, 1854).

All things are connected. Is this the Lord's song that we hear? We Christians have been slow to remember that all of life is one and indivisible. It is the scientists and people of primal cultures who have been reteaching the world this central mystery of our interdependence. Nevertheless, it is deeply embedded in our faith, in the Bible and in the writings of many mystics. And it is cause for rejoicing.

Francis of Assisi saw the world very clearly as one. He himself was a most orthodox believer, yet he called the whole of creation to worship God. In his life – and this is well documented – he called a sheep, waterfowl, birds, a cricket and a wolf to pray to the Lord. St Bonaventure, Francis' biographer and one of his successors as head of the Order, wrote that Francis really did expect animals to pray in their own fashion.

To modern ears this all sounds a little peculiar. Yet Adam and Noah also seem to have communicated God's purposes to animals or shared God's plans with them. Jesus cursed a fig tree because it would not bear fruit as its creator intended. At the very least, these incidents add up to the mystical idea that creation is somehow all of a piece: unified and indivisible.

All this background is gathered up into the note of praise sounded by the Church's celebration of the Eucharist, or the Mass, or the Lord's Supper (or whatever we choose to name Jesus' sacrament of bread and wine). In the Great Prayer of Thanksgiving, which is the centre of the Eucharist, we are called to praise God 'with the faithful of every time and place, joining with choirs of angels AND THE WHOLE CREATION'.

If we take this call to praise seriously, every time we celebrate the Eucharist, we are affirming that the whole of life, and all creation, is woven together. The universe is one. All is inter-related and bound together. All things are connected. Month by month, or week by week, as we celebrate the Eucharist in all the congregations of the Church, we join not only the whole inhabited Earth, but the whole creation in a cosmic hymn of praise.

When we celebrate the Eucharist, we each celebrate much more than our individual relationship with Christ. When we celebrate the Eucharist, we each celebrate much more than our personal salvation. When we celebrate the Eucharist, we celebrate together 'what the world is to become: an offering and hymn of praise to the Creator, a universal communion in the body of Christ, a kingdom of justice, love and peace in the Holy Spirit'.

This moves us far beyond the heresy of individualism, towards a community in solidarity with the Earth, its people and the whole of creation. In the face of the global ecological crisis, the Eucharist then becomes a celebration of hope. More than this, it becomes a call to all people who are struggling for life to join together their own celebrations of hope in an offering and hymn of praise to the Creator.

The Seventh Assembly of the World Council of Churches was held recently in Canberra, Australia. At one point, the Assembly was addressed by Dr Chung Hyun-Kyung, professor of systematic theology at Ewha Woman's University in Seoul, Korea.

Dome of the Rock, Jerusalem

doing that. They obliged. She then knelt and invoked the spirits of people and other living things who had died an unjust death. People like Steve Biko and Mahatma Ghandi, other living things like the Amazon rainforest.

'In my tradition,' she said, 'people who were killed or died unjustly became the wandering spirits, the *han*-ridden spirits. The living people's responsibility is to listen to the voices of the *han*-ridden spirits and to share in their work of making the wrong right'.

'These *han*-ridden spirits in our people's history have been agents through whom the Holy Spirit has spoken her compassion and wisdom for life. Without hearing the cries of these spirits we cannot hear the voice of the Holy Spirit,' she said.

Chung's presentation drew charges of syncretism and paganism from representatives of some of the older, European churches. In particular, the Orthodox churches. In reply, Chung alleged an anti-feminist, anti-Asian bias on the part of the western churches. 'Our understanding today comes from ourselves, from our own language and culture,' she said. She also said, 'Asian tradition is like my mother, Christian tradition is like my father'.

The cultural heritage of humankind is neither a neutral nor an optional part of life. Our culture is essential to understanding ourselves and, often, an obstacle to understanding others. However, the fact that Christian faith is being understood and interpreted from within the whole variety of human culture is a sign of hope for humankind. Bridges can be built. A common understanding of the threats to life can be articulated. In the face of racism, militarism, economic injustice and ecological destruction, the struggle for life can become a global struggle.

As we who celebrate the Eucharist identify ourselves with people around the world who are struggling for life, so the Eucharist becomes for us a celebration of hope that is grounded in the realities of life for the whole inhabited Earth.

Through this process we begin to know in our hearts what our Eucharistic faith has always told us to be true: that, even in the midst of the present global ecological crisis, the world is not without hope. Thomas Merton puts it this way:

No despair of ours can alter the reality of things, or stain the joy of the cosmic dance which is always there. Indeed, we are in the midst of it, and it is in the midst of us, for it beats in our very blood, whether we want it to or not.

Her presentation began with two Aboriginal Australians on centre stage, one playing the didgeridoo, the other slowly dancing. From the back of the theatre came the shock sound of an Asian gong. Two lines of young Korean Australians – and Dr Chung – then progressed through the audience to the stage. There the two cultures mingled their dance and their music.

This was the introduction to Dr Chung's presentation on the theme of the Assembly, 'Come, Holy Spirit: Renew the Whole Creation'. Surprise followed surprise.

'For many Asian and Pacific people,' said Dr Chung, 'taking off our shoes is the first act of humbling ourselves to encounter the spirit of God'. She invited those gathered at the Assembly to join her in

REVEREND PAUL SWADLING, former Resource Development Secretary for the Australian Council of Churches, he was the Local Media Relations Co-ordinator for the World Council of Churches' Seventh Assembly. He is presently attached to St. Margaret's Uniting Church in Canberra, Australia.

The Earth One Country, Mankind its Citizens

'BLESSED IS THE SPOT, and the house, and the place, and the city, and the heart, and the mountain, and the refuge, and the cave, and the valley, and the land, and the sea, and the island, and the meadow where mention of God hath been made, and His praise glorified.' – Bahá'u'lláh.

This simple yet eloquent verse paints a vivid picture of the importance of place in the relationship between humanity, culture, nature, and the divine. It reminds us that places, both man-made and natural – cities, mountains houses, and valleys – have value beyond their physical purpose. It suggests the sacredness of those places and sites in the world around us – whether divinely created or built by man.

The purpose of this book, to laud, appreciate and protect those masterpieces of man and nature that comprise our world heritage, carries with it an understanding that there are places that have a distinctive capacity to take individuals beyond themselves: to awaken, to inspire, and to help them understand their place in society, in nature and before the divine.

The natural sites that comprise our world heritage represent some of the most grand, the most beautiful, and the most inspiring places in the natural world. These sites mirror the divine and serve to remind us of our insignificance. They are holy, in the truest sense of the word.

More than 100 years ago, Bahá'u'lláh, the Prophet-Founder of the Bahá'í Faith wrote: 'Nature in its essence is the embodiment of (God's) Name, the Maker, the Creator...Nature is God's Will and is its expression in and through the contingent world'.

Bahá'í's understand that nature is to be respected and protected as part of a divine trust for which humanity is answerable. Many of the World Heritage sites, despite their qualities of majesty and grandeur, are also among the most delicate sites on Earth. In this sense, they serve also to remind us of the fragile nature of the global ecological system. And they are surely a special part of this divine trust.

The human sites and cultural monuments that comprise our world heritage represent a rich cultural mosaic that is a celebration of the myriad peoples on this planet. They reflect the summits of human creation and genius. They are a record of our social and cultural diversity, written in boldface type across the surface of the planet. Many such sites also record, in the art and architecture of pious devotion and towering majesty, the record of humanity's search for a closer relationship with the Creator.

The recognition that such diverse places, both man-made and natural, are part of our common world heritage implies a profound new reality: that we exist today in a world society. That specific sites and places, deemed to be of high value to one culture or one nation, should be valued by all, carries with it an implicit recognition of the oneness of humanity. That humanity has begun to take tentative steps to protect and preserve these sites further demonstrates the growing recognition of humanity's fundamental oneness.

The oneness of humanity is a theme that best reflects the spirit of our age. Recognition and acceptance of this idea determines the rate at which human civilisation will advance.

The world, it has been said, has become a global village. The World Heritage sites can be likened to those features of terrain, architecture, and culture that define and bring cohesiveness to a village. A village is defined by its location in relation to a nearby river, valley, or mountain. It is defined by the nature and the culture of the people who live there. In the global village, those features of natural and man-made beauty that represent our common heritage likewise help to define who and what humanity is, giving substance to our collective identity, and locating our place in the universe.

Human society has reached a new stage of maturity. The forces of change in the world today reflect part of an organic process of social evolution leading ultimately and irresistibly to the unification of the human race into a single social order whose boundaries are those of the planet. 'The Earth is one country, and mankind its citizens' wrote Bahá'u'lláh.

In the next stage of this evolution, a world federal system, guided by universally agreed upon and enforceable laws, will inevitably emerge, allowing nation states to manage co-operatively the resources – including the treasury of World Heritage sites – that sustain our increasingly interdependent and diverse world.

Supported by a consciousness of world citizenship, this system will ultimately address the problems of economic relations and the sustainable use of natural resources from a global perspective, providing for the needs of all peoples. It will of necessity avoid the evils of excessive centralisation, respecting the rich diversity of cultures and climates and engaging communities in making the decisions that affect their lives.

Such a new civilisation will also mean a broad transformation in the relationships between individuals. An individual's worth to society will no longer be defined by material wealth or status; rather, service to humanity as a whole, instead of to any particular nationality or group, will be the watchwords. Personal trustworthiness and compassion will be

Petra

among the foundations for such a new order, as will humility before others, before nature, and before God.

Bahá'í teachings, which are in essential harmony with the spiritual truths that underlie every major world religion, emphasise this understanding of humanity's nobility and the importance of building an ever-advancing and self-sustaining civilisation. Bahá'í teachings also stress the fundamental connections that tie humanity to the natural world, and the concomitant need to respect and protect it.

The masterpieces of man and nature compose part of the treasury on which humanity will of necessity draw to advance its unity. As a record of human attainment and a living testimony to the beauty and grandeur of the natural world, these places comprise a powerful force for the binding together of humanity. The preservation and protection of these sites are a responsibility for all.

THE BAHÁ'Í INTERNATIONAL COMMUNITY, an international non-governmental organisation that represents and encompasses the millions of members of the Bahá'í Faith who live in more than 150 countries around the world.

JORDAN

Jordan's World Heritage sites of Petra and Quseir Amra are dramatic, often awe inspiring examples of the engineering and aesthetic skills developed by the inhabitants of this land. Both are enduring testaments to a sophisticated urbanism which developed and matured in our Arab region on the strength of powerful trans-national cultural interaction with other great civilisations around the Mediterranean basin.

Petra, the older of the two listings, emerged by the 3rd century BC as the capital of the kingdom of the Nabateans – a formerly nomadic Arab people from northern Arabia who, from their heartland in southern Jordan, controlled a pivotal junction along the spice and incense routes for nearly half a millennium. Secured by a double ring of natural fortifications comprising mountains and desert expanses, Petra developed as a spectacularly beautiful city of mostly rock-cut tombs, theatres, temples, funerary banqueting halls, water works and religious high places. To wander through Petra is to step back 2,000 years in time, to a world defined by powerful architectural, aesthetic and religious impulses from the civilisations of ancient Arabia, Egypt, Greece, Rome, the Old Testament kingdoms, and early Christianity. Over 800 individual monuments and structures have survived to this day, largely intact within a natural landscape of chocolate, salmon and cinnamon-coloured cliffs and dales – always enchanting visitors from the four corners of the earth with their stunning example of harmony between the glory of God and hand of man. There are only a few very special places in the world which people spend the first part of their lifetime hoping to visit – and, once visited, the rest of their lifetime hoping to return to. Petra is one of them.

Quseir Amra represents a more recent stage in Jordan's history. This 8th century bathing complex provides a fascinating glimpse into our country's diverse cultural heritage; a heritage which conveys a powerful sense of a successful urban tradition through the ages.

It was a message of a human culture which endured and matured because it responded to human needs and lived according to principles which are still relevant to us in modern Jordan.

The most important of those principles was that of human interchange – of free movement, commercial trade, political contacts, technological synthesis and cultural interaction amongst different cultures and

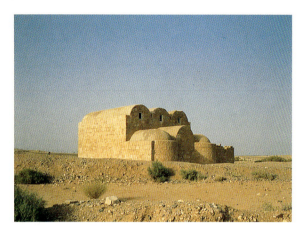

Quseir Amra

nations. The results of such interaction are easily visible at Quseir Amra and Petra in architecture, art, technology, ceramics, political organisation and economic activity. Both of these ancient cities prospered for centuries because they were pivotal junctions along international trade routes, linking cultures and people from China and Indonesia in the East to the British Isles and North Africa in the West.

Though Quseir Amra and Petra are physically located in the land of Jordan, we view them as part of the cultural patrimony and aesthetic legacy of all humankind. They constantly remind us that in order to achieve our aspirations for peace, dignity and coexistence among all people today and in the future, we should honour the timeless lesson of the past: that genuine and lasting peace emanates most consistently from constructive interaction among peoples and nations who enjoy stability, liberty and justice. This is the deeper, moral human lesson which we perceive behind the impressive physical monuments of the World Heritage List. It is the legacy of our land, the hope of our children, and the patrimony of all humankind which it is our privilege to preserve in trust for the entire world.

HER MAJESTY QUEEN NOOR OF JORDAN

PETRA

LOCATION   District of Ma'an, Jordan, E 35° 26', N 30° 19'.

DESCRIPTION   The site of the ancient city of Petra is one of the most striking on Earth. Its haunting natural setting of hills and canyons was transformed by early inhabitants into something absolutely unique: a city carved out of stone. The area is the centre of intense activity with excavations and restorations being continually carried out. The many buildings and monuments include; a theatre, a temple adorned with winged lions, baths, a neolithic village and several frescoes.

SIGNIFICANCE   Petra has a rich and fascinating history. Settlement dates back to 10,000 BC and throughout the Iron Age (8th century to 6th century BC) it was an important centre. During the Greek and Roman periods

Petra

it became a major point on the eastern caravan trade route. The seat of a bishop during Byzantine times, Petra was levelled by an earthquake in 363 AD. Recovering slightly, its importance again rose during the Crusades until it was finally abandoned. It was rediscovered in 1812 by European explorer Burkhardt.

QUSEIR AMRA

LOCATION   Approximately 85km (53mi) east of Amman, E 36° 34', N 31° 47'.

DESCRIPTION   This complex of baths has 3 distinct sections; the auditorium, which is 8.5 by 7.5m (28 by 25ft); the pump house and the baths themselves, which are in 3 rooms.

SIGNIFICANCE   Dating from the rule of the caliph Al-Walid I at the beginning of the 8th century AD, this is one of the oldest remaining Islamic baths. The interior decorations are of particular interest, with numerous frescoes covering the walls and the representation of a zodiac on the hemispheric ceiling of the auditorium – the first of its kind.

LEBANON

Lebanon lies at the eastern end of the Mediterranean sea, between Syria, to the north, and Israel to the south. The modern incarnation of this ancient state was determined after the fall of the Ottoman empire when the entire region (known as 'The Levant') was placed under French and British control.

The coast of Lebanon was important throughout antiquity as a gateway for trade to and from Asia, Egypt and Arabia. Several notable seaports were established, including two of Lebanon's World Heritage sites – Byblos and Tyr. Both of these famous seafaring towns were established in the third millennium BC by the Phoenicians and retained their importance up until the time of the Crusades.

The Assyrians, Babylonians, Greeks, Egyptians, Romans, Arabs and Turks also had a significant impact upon the area. Today there are numerous remains of these past civilisations, notably Anjar and Baalbek – Lebanon's remaining two World Heritage sites.

Presently a country in great turmoil, it is perhaps ironic that the forces tearing Lebanon apart today are the same forces which have left it with such a rich cultural heritage. Our hope is that Lebanon will survive intact and be able to nominate further sites for inclusion within the World Heritage Convention which it ratified in February 1983. For all of us, this link with the past is one of our few hopes for the future.

ANJAR

LOCATION   In the Bequaa province, N 34° 00′, E 36° 00′.

DESCRIPTION   These ruins of an 8th century city consist of a massive rectangular fortification with 4 large buildings, each having a gate protected by towers. Diagonally opposed gates were connected by 20m (66ft) wide roads. These roads cut the town from east to west and south to north, dividing it in 4 blocks. Today most of the eastern part of the town has been excavated and reconstructed. There are 2 palaces, a mosque, some baths, arcades and shops along the main street.

SIGNIFICANCE   Prior to the excavation at Anjar, all of the major periods of Arab history, with the exception of the Omayyad, had been found in Lebanon. With the

Anjar

discovery of these Omayyad ruins, that missing link has been uncovered and now points the way to a fuller understanding of the rich and colourful Arabic history of this region.

BAALBEK

LOCATION   N 34° 00′, E 36° 12′.

DESCRIPTION   These ruins of the ancient town are centred around the so called acropolis which incorporates the Temple of Jupiter and the Temple of Bacchus. Jupiter is the larger of the 2 with a massive stairway and entrance to a hexagonal courtyard which then leads to the main court where 2 huge altars once stood. Bacchus is smaller but much better preserved. Other ruins include the city walls, 2 temples, a mosque, Roman mosaics and Arab fortifications.

SIGNIFICANCE   In ancient times known as Heliopolis, which is Greek for 'city of the sun', the modern name may be connected with the ancient Canaanite god 'Baal'. The Temple of Jupiter took 200 years to complete and was an important religious centre, with its own oracle. The Temple of Bacchus was erected around 150 AD. Both temples were dedicated to the 'Heliopolitan triad' – Hadal, the Syrian God of Thunder, equivalent to Jupiter; Atorgatis, the Syrian Goddess of Nature, equivalent to Venus and a youthful god who was a protector of the crops, equivalent to Hermes. These ruins are an important relic of the so called 'pagan' cults of the time.

Byblos

Baalbek

BYBLOS

LOCATION   Approximately 40km (25mi) north of Beirut, N 34° 08', E 35° 38'.

DESCRIPTION   The ruins of this ancient Phoenician city include the perimeter walls with their 2 gates, the Temple of Baalat-Gebal (the goddess of the city), an L-shaped temple, the Temple of the Gbelisks and the royal tombs. There are also some later ruins dating from Roman times, including 2 temples, a theatre, baths and a colonnade.

SIGNIFICANCE   Reputed to be the oldest continuously inhabited town in the world, Byblos was the major seaport of the east Mediterranean during the 3rd millennium BC. By far the most important trade was in selling cedar to Egypt, where it was used for shipbuilding and oil extracted for embalming. It is believed that the Phoenician alphabet was created here, the oldest known example is found on the sarcophagus of King Ahiram (1200 BC). Many large buildings were erected under the Romans. The decline of the city came soon after the departure of the Crusaders.

TYR

LOCATION   On the South Coast, N 33° 16', E 35° 12'.

DESCRIPTION   The archaeological site of Tyr includes the Temple of Melkart (Heracles) built in 2750 BC and some very important Roman ruins including an arch, aqueduct, baths, theatre and the Great Necropolis, containing hundreds of sculptured stones and amarble sarcophagus. One of the largest Roman hippodromes ever found has been excavated here.

SIGNIFICANCE   Founded in 2750 BC, Tyr later became an important Phoenician seaport. Originally an island city, Tyr's defences were impenetrable and rebuffed many assaults from Assyrians and Babylonians. Passing under Roman influence, Herod the Great built a temple there in 68 BC. During these times, Tyr was famous for its purple silk. A famous visitor was St. Paul, who spent a week there on his way to Jerusalem. Falling into the hands of Muslims in the 7th century, it was reconquered by Christians once more with the victories of the Crusaders in the 12th century. The city was destroyed by Muslims in 1291.

Tyr

Climate Change – World Heritage Can Help

THERE IS WIDESPREAD concern that the world is warming and the sea is rising. Since the late 19th century, the world's mean temperature has increased by about 0.5°C and the average sea level has risen by 10-15 cm (0.4-0.6 in). Five of the warmest years on record occurred in the 1980s. Concentrations in the atmosphere of greenhouse gases (those chemicals that decrease the loss of heat from the earth's surface) are also rising, so it is likely (but not completely proven) that global warming and sea level rises are due to this increase.

Chemicals called chlorofluorocarbons (CFCs) have been widely used in refrigeration systems and in aerosol sprays. Burning of coal, oil and gas and industrial use of CFCs are the biggest sources of greenhouse gases. This is closely followed by deforestation and agricultural activities such as land clearance, rice paddy cultivation, livestock production, burning of vegetation and use of nitrogenous fertilizers.

Even assuming effective control over CFCs, as provided for by an international agreement, the scientific consensus is that increasing concentrations of greenhouse gases will raise global mean temperature an additional 1-2°C by the year 2030. The world would then be warmer than at any time in the past 120,000 years. It would not stop there. Due to the slow absorption of heat by the oceans, the global mean temperature would continue to rise to 1.5-3°C higher than today's, even if greenhouse gas concentrations stabilized.

Of more concern than the extent of this change is its speed. Global temperature changes of 1-2°C have generally occurred over 1000 to 10,000 year periods. At the rates foreseen in the near future, such changes would take only 40 years. The consequences could also be unusually sudden. Among them, shifts of climate and ecological regions, altered precipitation patterns, and increases in the frequency and intensity of extreme climatic events, such as crippling droughts and violent tropical cyclones.

The sea level could conceivably rise 10-20 cm (0.4-0.8 in) by 2030, increasing the vulnerability of coastal areas to flooding from storm surges. Since storm surges are also expected to be more frequent, this adds to the danger for low-lying coastal areas with large populations and inadequate sea defences, such as the Bay of Bengal. Salt water intrusions into surface and ground water systems could also increase, damaging agriculture and water supply.

The ozone layer is a gaseous layer which encompasses the earth at about 10-45 kilometres (6-28 miles) altitude. It is important because it shields the Earth from ultraviolet rays. These reduce the productivity of marine phytoplankton and the yields of sensitive crops, and can suppress the human immune system causing snow blindness, eye damage, severe sunburn and even skin cancer. The ozone layer is being depleted by CFCs, nitrous oxide, and other gases. Since 1979, there has been a 5% decline in the mean ozone concentration over Antarctica, and a 4% reduction in the ozone layer worldwide.

Acid rain kills trees and aquatic life (20% of Sweden's lakes are now fishless or about to become so), pollutes water, acidifies vulnerable soils, and damages buildings and materials because of acid deposits. Ancient historic sites like the Parthenon in Athens have decayed more in the last 50 years than in the previous 2000. Photochemical oxidants harm crops and natural vegetation (depressing crop yield in the USA by an estimated 5-10%, a loss of $1-2 billion a year), and are the main ingredients of urban smog, damaging human health. The combination of acid rain and other chemicals is believed to be the chief agent in the decline of forests in Europe and North America. The sulphur dioxide and nitrogen oxides in acid rain mainly come from the burning of fossil fuels.

The World Heritage Convention could make a contribution to tackling the global climate issue. According to this convention they should be sites possessing outstanding natural qualities and managed according to the highest international standards. As such they could provide a network of areas in which ecosystem processes suffer little disturbance from man's influence and therefore serve as locations for research and monitoring of global climatic change. Because of their high public profile, they could also be used as a focus for public education to highlight the global change issue and help to communicate the urgent need for action by governments and the public at large.

DANNY ELDER
IUCN

The world grows smaller and smaller, more and more interdependent – today more than ever before life must be characterised by a sense of Universal Responsibility, not only nation to nation and human to human, but also human to other forms of life.

HIS HOLINESS THE DALAI LAMA

LIBYA

Libya was, in ancient times, understood to be that part of northern Africa which was west of Egypt. Not until 1934, when the Italian colony was formalised, did Libya cease to be a geographical expression and become a country with well defined borders.

This area has been variously conquered and settled from ancient times by the Phoenicians, Greeks, Romans, Berbers, Arabs and Turks.

After almost 400 years of Turkish rule, Libya was taken by Italy in 1911, then placed in United Nations' trusteeship from the end of the Second World War until 1951, when it became an independent nation.

Today, Libya is a wealthy republic with a strong Islamic culture and a profound respect for its ancient past. Libya ratified the World Heritage Convention in October 1978.

Evidence of these influential past civilisations can be viewed in the numerous ruined cities along the coast, including three of Libya's five World Heritage sites – Cyrene, Leptis Magna and Sabratha. Ghadames, another site, is positioned inland next to an oasis and is considered to represent the traditional architectural style of 'ancient Libya'.

The fifth site, at Tadrart Acacos, provides evi-

Roman ruins, Leptis Magna

Rock art, Tadrart Acacus

Amphitheatre, Sabratha

dence of a much older history. The rock paintings in this area date back 8,000 years into African prehistory.

CYRENE

LOCATION   District of Gebel Akhdar, E 21° 51′, N 32° 40′.

DESCRIPTION   This site is the remains of an ancient city and several large cemeteries which surrounded it. Its most important features are; the Sanctuary of Apollo, the acropolis, the Greek agora and Roman forum. There are also various remains which have been excavated along Valley Street. To the northeast of the town is another excavation zone with the remains of a large temple to Zeus.

SIGNIFICANCE   The city was founded in 630 BC by Greeks from Santorini who were in search of a reliable water supply. It was an important city of northeast Libya for the next 1,200 years, until the arrival of the Arabs, after which it declined and then fell into ruin. The Great Temple of Zeus is the largest Greek temple in North Africa.

GHADAMÈS

LOCATION   Al Hamadah Al Hamra, E 09° 30′, N 30° 08′.

DESCRIPTION   This city is unique in both its style and planning. It forms small irregular blocks in the southwest part of an oasis of palm trees and is protected by a system of walls and towers. The outer walls of the houses themselves form the surrounding wall with gates and a guard chamber on every gate. The surrounding wall has bastions which frequently project 6m (20ft) outwards and vary in thickness. The houses all have 3 levels and are linked by terraces.

SIGNIFICANCE   Ghadamès (ancient Cydamae), once referred to by the Arabs as 'the pearl of the desert', is situated on the 3 main lines of communication between the interior and the coast and played a key role in trans-Saharan trade. The architecture is considered to be the original ancient Libyan style, with massive walls and covered passageways. A special feature is the walled terraces that link the houses, allowing women freedom of movement without contravening the cultural tradition of separation of the sexes.

Ruins of the Forum at Cyrene

Ghadamès

LEPTIS MAGNA

LOCATION   District of Khoms, E 14° 18, N 32° 38'.

DESCRIPTION   There are traces of a Phoenician-Punic city, but the main component to this site is the collection of Roman ruins dating from the 1st century AD. Here we have remains from 3 periods including a theatre, 2 forums, an amphitheatre, a complex of thermal baths, several arches and 2 churches.

SIGNIFICANCE   During the whole of the 1st millennium BC Tripolitania was profoundly influenced by the Phoenicians and their successors the Carthagenians. Leptis Magna was a major market of the period. It was one of the largest olive oil producers, producing 1,067,000 litres (250,000 gal) for Julius Caesar. The town was finally conquered around 698 AD, deserted by the inhabitants and left to the engulfing sands.

ROCK-ART SITES OF TADRART ACACUS

LOCATION   Southwest region, east of Ghat, N 24° 30' to 27° 00', E 09° 00' to 11° 00'.

DESCRIPTION   This site covers an extensive area of the Tadrart Acacus mountain range. Scattered throughout the valleys of these mountains are the remains of

many prehistoric communities. Most importantly, the artwork of these ancient peoples has been well preserved. Some 300 frescoes and thousands of rock paintings have been preserved at different sites such as Matkendush, Galghien and Tilizzagham.

SIGNIFICANCE   These paintings date back over 8,000 years and are unique in providing a continuous artistic record over a period of almost 6,000 years. Both the development of artistic styles and the evolution of subject matter provide a comprehensive record of cultural changes over this long period of time.

SABRATHA

LOCATION   District of Zawia, E 12° 29', N 32° 48'.

DESCRIPTION   There are several Roman and Byzantine monuments, including a forum, Temple of Antoninus Pius, Temple of Serapis, Temple of Isis, an amphitheatre and a theatre. Some Phoenician-Punic remains have also been uncovered including a Punic mausoleum.

SIGNIFICANCE   The Roman and Byzantine monuments of Sabratha constitute landmarks of classical architecture in Africa. The Phoenician-Punic ruins are crucial to the understanding of the early history of the area.

The Global Climate: Part of Our Heritage

IN THE WORLD TODAY, there is increasing awareness that the very nature of quality of life does not depend only on the satisfaction of material needs. There is also a need to ensure the quality of the environment, among other things.

Environment, certainly, can take on a variety of meanings. It can encompass the physical environment in which man thrives – the atmosphere, the land, the seas, oceans and other water bodies. It can also take on a social character, as well as a cultural one. In this context, the various cultures and cultural heritage are part of the environment which needs to be preserved.

It is noteworthy that there is now a strong movement to preserve our heritage, through the World Heritage Convention, under the auspices of our sister organisation UNESCO.

In past decades, it has been established that there is a serious threat to historical sites caused by physical deterioration associated with weathering, that is, the combined effects of weather elements such as wind, precipitation, humidity, and in many cases, air pollution.

The rapid increase in the use of fossil fuel in this century has led to continuously high levels of sulphur dioxide and carbonaceous particles. Chemical processes in the atmosphere have caused the formation of sulphates and increased the acidity of precipitation, resulting in the acceleration of the damaging process.

Structures consisting of sandstone, limestone and marble are thought to be particularly at risk. Examples of damage are reported to have occurred at the Parthenon in Athens, at historic buildings in Venice and London and at various locations in France and Germany. Others at risk include frescoes, stained glass, metal constructions, as well as books and documents in archives, especially in a number of developing countries. Studies are being undertaken to gain a better understanding of the processes involved, primarily focusing on exposure-effects relationships for combinations of agents and material.

It is heartening to note that there is now increasing consciousness of the need to reduce emissions. Such reduction also results in a likely slow-down of damage to important cultural structures.

Nevertheless, another serious threat is looming on the horizon, that of possible climate change and its concomitant effects. Changes in the chemical composition of the atmosphere, temperature, sea level, rainfall rates, humidity, and radiation might pose new threats in the next century.

The nature and impact of the likely change in the climate were considered in the First Assessment Report of the Intergovernmental Panel on Climate Change (IPCC), established by WMO and UNEP.

The most reliable estimates of the global mean temperature rise to date are 0.3 to 0.6°C over the last hundred years, with the six warmest years on record being in the 1980s. WMO observing networks have been the source of much of the data used to analyse this temperature trend.

The *rate* of change in global mean temperature predicted by the IPCC with a 'business as usual' scenario in emissions of greenhouse gases, is characterised as being greater than at any time in the last 10,000 years. Using the best models available, the IPCC scientists predict a global mean temperature by 2025 of about 1°C above 1990 levels. By the end of the next century, the average temperature will increase by 3°C above present values. With these projections, the Earth will be warmer by the middle of the next century than at any time in the past 150,000 years.

The rise in sea level, which has been 1-2 cm (0.4-0.8 in) per decade over the past century, will accelerate to 3-10 cm (1.2-4 in) per decade with a predicted rise by the end of the next century of 65cm (26 in). These changes would profoundly alter the world as we know it, affecting the physical and biological setting for all human activities, as well as the preservation of cultural sites.

In line with the increased consciousness relating to the climate change issue, the United Nations General Assembly adopted Resolution 45.212 (Protection of Global Climate for Present and Future Generations of Mankind) on 21 December 1990. This resolution sets forth the arrangements for negotiations of a global convention on climate change. As the World Heritage Convention seeks to promote co-operation among nations to protect worldwide heritage which is of such universal value that its conservation is a concern to all people, the Framework Convention on Climate Change that is being evolved will also pave the way for international co-operation to protect another world resource – our global climate.

Indeed, through the protection of the planetary atmosphere which is a basic component of the climate system, we should also see some benefits accruing to the preservation of World Heritage sites. I take this occasion to call on the national agencies responsible for the protection of the World Heritage listed sites to also involve the national Meteorological and Hydrological Services in their efforts. I believe they can contribute their experience and know-how in this important endeavour.

WMO, for its part, is ready to assist. Preservation of our natural and cultural heritage is a noble goal, and we are proud to be associated with it.

PROFESSOR G.O.P. OBASI
Secretary General, World Meteorological Organisation

MADAGASCAR

Madagascar, positioned about 400 kilometres (250 miles) off the eastern coast of Africa, is one of the world's larger islands. It covers about 600,000 square kilometres (228,000 square miles) and sits almost entirely within the tropics.

This island is distinguished from mainland Africa in both its human and animal populations. The Malagasy people are thought to descend from Indian, Indonesian, Malay and African migrants who probably started arriving around the 6th century AD.

The animal life is unique not only in that it includes a host of endemic species, but also in that it excludes numerous species which are found on the African mainland such as the elephant, lion, antelope or any apes.

In the words of Edouard Bailby:

> The primitive plant and animal life of Madagascar is of great scientific interest and should be strictly protected if only because Madagascar has been separated from the continent of Africa for tens of millions of years and its ecosystems are unique.

The Tsingy de Bemaraha Integral Nature Reserve, which is Madagascar's sole World Heritage listing (the Convention was ratified by Madagascar in July 1983) goes some way towards achieving that goal.

Many of the island's rare and endangered species are protected within this reserve, including seven species of lemurs. This is an animal which is of particular interest in Madagascar as the island provides the world's only remaining natural habitat for these rare little mammals.

Fish Drying, Lake Malawi

TSINGY DE BEMARAHA STRICT NATURE RESERVE

LOCATION   Located almost in the centre of the island of Madagascar, S 18° 17′ to 19° 06′, E 44° 36′ to 44° 58′.

DESCRIPTION   This immense reserve sits on the western plateau of Madagascar. It is rich in flora and fauna including some rare and endangered species. Lush vegetation is typical of the reserve which also includes large savanas. Many gorges and the rugged nature of the reserve offer spectacular views. Within the Manambolo gorges, ancient tombs reputedly housing the remains of the Island's first inhabitants (the 'Vazimbas') can be found.

SIGNIFICANCE   The reserve provides a sanctuary for several endangered species, including the island's famous lemurs. The geological formations of the ranges form impressive walls and gorges. In particular, the erosion of the lime-stone cliffs make them visually spectacular. The combination of cliffs, gorges and grottoes make the reserve unique, especially from a geological point of view. The dry arid forests provide an abundance of plant life including six species of Vangidae which are native to Madagascar. The reserve also is the home to a large number of endemic land birds, including the giant Coua and Madagascan Owl.

Lemurs, Tsingy de Bemaraha Strict Nature Reserve

MALAWI

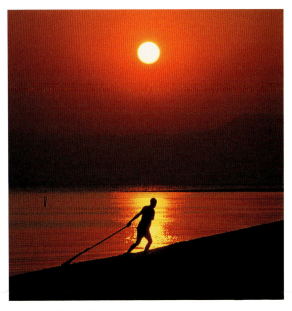

Sunset on Lake Malawi

Malawi is one of southern Africa's smallest countries at 128,000 square kilometres (49,000 square miles) in area. It is dominated by Lake Malawi which runs the length of the country, north to south, and covers 20% of its total area. The Lake is Malawi's sole World Heritage listing after ratifying the Convention in January 1982. The following article, from the Department of Parks and Wildlife, gives a tremendous insight into the value of this magnificent lacustrine park.

Darting swiftly through their crystal clear aquatic environment, the fishes of Lake Malawi form an underwater rainbow of colour more than 570kms (350mi) long. These brilliantly coloured fish constitute one of the biological wonders of the world.

Over 100 years ago scientists recognised that the rock dwelling fish, or mbuna, of Lake Malawi were both beautiful and incredibly diverse. Since the 1940's intensive scientific research has established that the fish in the lake are unique. They display a range of adaptions and speciation which makes them as significant to the study of evolution as Darwin's finches.

Evolving from one ancestral cichlid in a relatively short evolutionary time span, more species of fish dwell in Lake Malawi than any lake in the world. Scientific work is ongoing to classify and identify the many different groups. Of the possible 1000 species, 98% are endemic.

Because of their sedentary habits, most of these mbuna rarely travel more than a few metres during their lives, and will not leave the rocks to cross even small sandy areas. The resultant isolation of communities has led to species endemic not only to the lake but to certain restricted areas within the lake itself.

As with the Galapagos finches, the primary adaptation is in the feeding mechanism. Most mbuna feed on aufwuchs, the algae layer growing on the rocks. Because of individual adaptations, however, each species uses this food source in a different manner. Some feed parallel to the rock and mow the aufwuchs, others attack the algae from a 90 degree angle, nipping it with specialised teeth, while a few suck loose particles from the rocks. This type of resource partitioning allows large numbers of fishes to live within a small area.

Other feeding adaptations include one species coloured to resemble rotted flesh, which springs to life and devours unsuspecting passers-by. Another predator hangs motionless, head downward in the underwater grasses. Its camouflage stripe conceals it from passing fish until it darts at them from the weeds.

Animal behavioralists have long studied Lake Malawi's cichlids for their variety of unusual characteristics. One of the most interesting adaptations involves reproductive behaviour. Almost all Lake Malawi cichlids are mouth brooders. Eggs and developing fry are carried in the mother's mouth until the juveniles are able to fend for themselves. When they are mature, she opens her mouth and spits them out. A few species remain with their young and continue to protect them. When a predator approaches, the mother opens her mouth and the young swim back inside to safety. Another specialised feeding mechanism has evolved in conjunction with this. One predator rams the head of a brooding female to disgorge the eggs, which are then eaten. Because of the scenic beauty of the area and its fascinating underwater wildlife, a significant tourist trade has developed around the cichlids and the lake in which they live.

Born of the African Rift Valley millenniums ago, Lake Malawi is the eleventh largest and fourth deepest lake in the world. Used for centuries as transportation, water supply, and an abundant food source, the lake is a valuable resource. Because it is surrounded by non-industrial countries, it is one of the most unpolluted great lakes in the world. The sparkling waters are virtually pristine.

As in most natural communities coexisting with the activities of a developing world, the lake is faced with environmental threats. The possibility of future industrial pollution, uncontrolled oil exploration, siltation resulting from deforestation of surrounding lands, introduction of exotic species, overdevelopment, and unregulated fishing are among the most serious.

It is against this backdrop – subsistence use of the lake, scientific study of the fish, tourism, and potential environmental damage – that Lake Malawi National Park was established in 1980. Created primarily to protect and interpret the aquatic communities of the lake, it is the first freshwater, underwater national park in the world. Declared a World Heritage Site in 1984, the park is a microcosm of the biological diversity of Lake Malawi. Problems facing the park are representative of those facing the lake as a whole.

When the park was created the Government of Malawi stipulated that populations existing within the newly drawn park boundaries not be relocated. Most of these are fishing communities, including the largest traditional fishing village in Malawi.

To protect the rock dwelling cichlids, fishing has been prohibited within 100m (330ft) of the park shoreline. This minimally impacts traditional fishing waters as food fish are pelagic, or open water fish. Conflicts do arise, however, when fishermen inadvertently net the mbuna.

Another source of conflict, the cutting of live trees, was banned within the park boundaries. Due to increasing population pressures, however, deforestation is a significant problem. In the first years of the park's existence, these problems were dealt with primarily through enforcement.

In 1988 WWF U.S. initiated a conservation, education, and development program in Lake Malawi National Park. As the project evolved, it became clear that a major focus should be the integration of local communities with the resource. The World Heritage Convention has recognised that cultural and natural resources cannot exist without each other.

Over $200,000 has been allocated by WWF to develop an environmental education complex in the park. An interpretive centre, office and conference facilities, accommodation for educational and scientific groups, display aquariums, and support staff housing have been developed.

The aquariums are stocked with colourful mbuna, underwater videos, and interpretive displays are presented in the centre. Through programs or a self-guided tour of the facility, school classes, professional organisations, and visitors, both national and international, are exposed to the importance of the lake and its underwater wildlife. Special exhibits address the importance of fishing restrictions. A tree nursery established in conjunction with the project grows and distributes free seedlings and information on the care of individual and community woodlots, thereby reducing encroachments on park lands.

Economically, local populations have benefited from the project. Approximately 35% of the allocated funds have gone directly to area residents in the form of wages, artisan contracts, and purchase of construction materials. This money directly supports some 15% of local populations. In addition, fish sellers, woodcarvers, produce sellers, local guides,

restaurants and rest houses, all catering to the tourist trade, realise significant important economic returns from the park.

The education effort, coupled with the economic benefits, has resulted in greater community support of the park, and local residents are starting to actively support policies to safeguard their vital tourism income.

Successes experienced at Lake Malawi National Park cannot be construed as protecting the lake as a whole. International boundaries will require enlightened legislation and multinational co-operation in the coming years. Careful utilisation of the lake's resources and responsible development policies will be crucial. That the Government of Malawi is cognisant of the importance of its role in natural resource conservation is reflected both in governmental policies and in the establishment and management of the nation's national park, game reserve, and forest reserve systems.

One thing is certain. The grass roots approach at Lake Malawi National Park is working. Walking through the villages at night, one hears songs entitled 'What is an Aquarium' or 'A Trip to the Islands'. On any given day local residents, both children and adults, visit the interpretation centre to learn more about the history and fish of the lake or just to enjoy their park. With continuing programs in education, conservation, and development planned by the Department of National Parks and Wildlife, the outlook for the future of Lake Malawi National Park and its inhabitants, both human and aquatic, is optimistic. The cultural and the natural are coming together to form the whole.

SCOTT GRENFELL AND LYN ROBINSON
Edited by Matthew Matemba,
Malawi Department of Parks and Wildlife

LAKE MALAWI NATIONAL PARK

LOCATION   Central and southern regions, E 34° 53', S 14° 02'.

DESCRIPTION   The park is an area of great natural beauty with rugged precipitous slopes falling directly to the lake shore. Within its boundaries are 3 areas of mainland, Cape Maclean peninsular and 12 islands. There is an early missionary site in the area, as well as several prehistoric archaeological sites.

SIGNIFICANCE   This is the only lacustrine national park in Africa. Human occupation has been long established and dates back to Stone Age times. There are several Iron Age sites. Early missionaries established a mission in 1873, but it was later abandoned due to the prevalence of malaria. The lake waters are exceptionally clear and hundreds of fish species inhabit it, including many that are endemic to the area.

Timbuktu

MALI

Mali covers an area that was an important part of the trans-Saharan trading routes in ancient times when the Phoenicians ruled in the north.

After several invasions this trade declined and it was not until the coming of the Muslims in the 6th century AD that it was revived.

In fact the area now occupied by Mali became one of the most important trading centres in the Islamic world. The towns of Timbuktu and Djenne, both now inscribed on the World Heritage List, became famous as wealthy academic, cultural and religious centres.

Mali emerged as a separate kingdom during the 13th century and enjoyed several centuries of stability and prosperity, cementing its reputation in the Islamic world.

During the 15th century, the Malian empire was overthrown by the Songhay – a people who survive in Mali to this day. They ruled for around 150 years until an invasion from Morocco precipitated their fall.

The end of the 19th century saw Mali fall under French colonial rule. This lasted until 1960 when Mali became independent, initially in a federation with Senegal.

Mali accepted the World Heritage Convention in April 1977. Apart from the two famous Islamic trading towns of Timbuktu and Djenne, Mali has a third World Heritage listing, the Cliff of Bandiagara. This region is home to a people known as the Dogons, a race who have changed little since ancient times and who have been the subject of countless anthropological studies.

For thousands of years the earth has been generous to us. But now there is drought in Africa and this is not just due to the lack of rain. It is a question of destructive activity. Because governments wanted the foreign exchange, forests were cut down and not replaced. To get fuel, people destroy the trees that are left. This process causes the deserts to grow. The integrity of creation is destroyed for economic reasons.

FATHER JOHN MUTISO MBINDA

The Dogon, Mali's People of the Cliffs

WITHIN THE LOOP of the Niger River in Mali, between the town of Mopti and the Burkina Faso border, there is a place where steep cliffs at the edge of an arid plateau dominate a sandy plain. Over 500 m (1665 ft) high in places, the escarpment is fissured with deep ravines, where rain caught in the cracks of the grey rock supports the growth of dense and varied vegetation. This is the Land of the Dogon, whose natural features alone would justify exceptional measures of protection.

Against the rock face and on the scree slope below, the Dogon have built villages which are remakable for their architecture and for the profoundly original culture of those who live in them, described by the French ethnologist Marcel Griaule as a 'relic of a lost Africa'. In 1989, an area of some 400,000 ha (960,000 ac) along the Bandiagara cliffs, including almost 250 traditional villages, was placed on UNESCO's World Heritage List as a site of outstanding natural and cultural importance.

The Dogon, who today number about 300,000 are of Malinke (Mandingo) stock. Their ancestors are thought to have fled from the Keita empire in the fifteenth century and found refuge at the Bandiagara cliffs, where they displaced another people, the Tellem, who left behind abundant evidence of their own cultural traditions in tombs set in caves in the rock face.

Most of these caves can only be reached with the aid of ropes and crampons. Some have been explored in the past decade, and have revealed interesting evidence of the highly developed techniques, especially for weaving, which had been employed by the Tellem since the Iron Age.

On the cliffs themselves, aspects of Dogon ritual and cosmogony are illustrated by cryptic signs and paintings, the best-known of which adorn the famous 'Shelter of Masks', at the village of Songo (fifteen kilometres from Bandiagara) which forms part of the World Heritage site.

The Pale Fox, Bringer of Anarchy

According to Dogon cosmogony, from the union of the supreme deity Amma and his creation, the Earth, issued a being known as the Pale Fox. Unique and imperfect, the Fox introduced the principle of disorder into creation. It is associated with human weakness and the anarchy inherent in the universe. Amma also created Nommo, a hermaphroditic creature who represents celestial harmony and is linked symbolically to water and to fecundity. Then Amma modelled a human couple from clay. They gave birth to the eight ancestors of the Dogon, whom Nommo taught to speak.

Every aspect of Dogon domestic, social and eco-

nomic life is linked to this cosmogony. Villages are designed in the image of the cosmos. Built on rock in order to preserve scarce arable land, they are laid out on a north-south axis in the form of a prone human body, supposedly that of Nommo, the great ancestor. The head is represented by the *togu na* (literally, 'big shelter'), a meeting-place reserved for men. This open-sided structure is always the first to be built in a new village. It consists of a platform on which stand several rows of rough-hewn timber pillars that support a roof of branches topped by a thick mat of millet straw. The number of pillars has significance. Decisions taken in the *togu na* are solemn and irrevocable.

In each settlement there is also a large family dwelling, or *ginna*, which is reserved for the spiritual leader. Corresponding to Nommo's breast, this building has a raised living area reached by a ladder carved from a tree trunk. The windowless facade is decorated with eighty niches, representing the eight original ancestors and their descendants. The two doors are often carved with rows of male and female figures which, like the niches, symbolise earlier generations.

Ordinary homes, which are smaller and are generally made of mud-brick, are grouped around the *ginna*. They are built to a rectangular design, with flat-roofed rooms opening onto an inner court-yard. They are flanked by granaries with distinctive conical thatched roofs. These structures are used for storing millet, seeds, rice, dried onions and various other foodstuffs. Their narrow entrances are protected by wooden doors, which are often carved and secured by ornate locks.

Many of the granaries are circular, like the houses at the edge of the village where menstruating women are sequestered. The forge, and the homes of members of various artisan castes – blacksmiths, wood and leather workers and griots – are also on the outskirts. Those who farm the land are the aristocrats of this patriarchal, agrarian society.

Almost all the villages, and certainly the oldest ones, possess one or more shrines, whose walls are decorated with totems or chessboard patterns. The most venerated of these shrines, which are square chambers in the rock containing altars, are protected by the *hogon*, a spiritual leader who serves several villages and who formerly dispensed justice and presided over the council of elders that directed public affairs. Today he still conducts major religious ceremonies and transmits to posterity the people's myths and beliefs.

A century and a half ago the influence of Islam began to reach the land of the Dogon from the neighbouring Tukulor and Fulani (Peul) peoples, nomadic pastoralists of the plain, and many of the villages now

Dogon village

have mosques. Whether modest or imposing, the mosque is often built next to the *togu na,* which even among the Islamicised Dogon has kept the role of men's house and council chamber.

Statues and masks: a rich artistic heritage
Among the many different arts mastered by the Dogon, the most sacred is weaving, held to be the first art bestowed on humanity, at the same time as speech. In fact the Dogon have a single word for the two concepts, both of which are considered to have a question-and-answer structure. Griaule sees the act of weaving as a metaphor for culture itself: the warp represents uncultivated land; the weft, life-giving human activity.

But the aesthetic talents of the Dogon are probably best illustrated by their sculpture, whose primary purpose is ritualistic. Roughly carved or highly elaborate figures represent ancestors or mythical heroes. They are usually made by the village blacksmith, who also carves the wooden doors and shutters, while his wife is responsible for making pottery for ceremonial use.

Masks, associated with the spirits of the dead, are used only in funeral rites or to mark the end of a period of mourning, which may be celebrated either by public dances and ceremonies or by secret gatherings for initiates. The masks form part of a costume made of fabric or plant fibres, complete with trimmings and accessories. They may be fashioned from wood, bark or braided fibres decorated with cowrie shells and painted designs, or topped with high crests like the *kanaga* mask, whose upper portion is shaped like a cross of Lorraine. Its two branches represent the demiurge Amma gesturing towards his creations, Earth and sky.

CAROLINE HAARDT, French journalist, was a staff member of UNESCO's Division of Cultural Heritage from 1983 to 1987. She is currently preparing an exhibition as part of the UNESCO Silk Roads project on the *Croisière Jaune,* a motor rally from Beirut to Tibet held in 1931–1932.

Reprinted from the *Unesco Courier,* May 1991.

West Africa's oldest metropolis

THE RESULTS OF archaeological excavations carried out in 1977 and 1981 on an ancient site near the city of Jenné (Djenné), in Mali, have contradicted previous assumptions about the history of west Africa by pushing back the date of the emergence of this city which became one of the region's most prosperous trading centres, by almost a thousand years.

The archaeological site of Jenné-jeno ('ancient Jenné' in the local Songhay language) lies three kilometres south of the modern city of Jenné, on a floodplain of the inland Niger Delta rich in fish, cereals (especially rice and millet), and livestock.

Food has for centuries been produced in abundance in the hinterland, supplying the population of Timbuktu further north, to which Jenné is linked by 500 kilometres (300 miles) of navigable riverway. The gold trade route originating in the forested region of West Africa passed through the two cities and then crossed the Sahara to north Africa.

Until the excavations, directed by two American archaeologists, husband-and-wife Roderick J. McIntosh and Susan Keech McIntosh, it was generally accepted that Jenné had developed simultaneously with Timbuktu (founded around 1100) in the mid-thirteenth century as an artefact of the trans-Saharan trade which brought urbanism to west Africa.

However, excavations carried out on the main site, a 33 hectare (80 acre) artificial mound formed of ruins of buildings and the debris of human occupation, and an extensive reconnaissance of sites in a surrounding area of 1,100 square kilometres (400 square miles), have revealed that a settlement already existed at Jenné-jeno as early as the third century BC and was inhabited by a population which made iron and practised trade. By 800 AD Jenné-jeno had become a prosperous cosmopolitan centre with a population of some 10,000 people.

In the course of the centuries the city's trade expanded and diversified. Jenné-jeno imported from far away, stone, iron ore, copper from the Sahara and, around 600—800 AD, gold. In return for these goods, the rich city had various products and foodstuffs to barter, notably rice (African rice, *Oryza glaberrima*, was cultivated at Jenné-jeno as early as the first century AD), fish and fish oil.

The key to the city's success was a combination of food production and craftsmanship. By the year 50 AD the settlement extended over 12 hectares (30 acres). In 300 AD it had expanded to some 25 hectares (60 acres), and around 750 AD it covered 33 hectares (79 acres) and was girded by a stone wall some 2 kilometres (1.2 miles) long, 3.6 metres

Present day Djenné

(12 feet) wide and 4 metres (13 feet) or more high.

At the height of its development, between 750 and 1150, it is thought that Jenné-jeno and its nearby satellite villages may have had almost 20,000 inhabitants, and that the density of settlement in its hinterland may have been ten times higher than today.

The city's decline is thought to have begun around 1200. The fact that it was abandoned around 1400 for the site of present-day Jenné may perhaps be explained by the desire of a new Muslim trading élite to change their capital.

The discoveries at Jenné-jeno, along with others such as the eighth-century 'bronzes' from Igbo-Ukwu in Nigeria open up major new historical perspectives. It is now known that long-distance trade and urbanism existed in west Africa in the first millennium AD. It is also established that Jenné-jeno played a central role in the creation of the great trade-routes between the Sahara and the Niger Bend and was not, as was previously believed, a later off-shoot of the trans-Saharan salt and gold trade. The early urban settlements of the inland Niger Delta are thus seen to rank among the world's great known civilisations.

Reprinted from *Unesco Courier*, May 1984

OLD TOWNS OF DJENNÉ

LOCATION   In the Mopti province, N 13° 54′, W 04° 25′.

DESCRIPTION   This site consists of the existing town of Djenng and the ruins of the ancient town. The modern town of Djenng was founded on several 'Toggere' (mounds) surrounded by a 7-gated rampart. The historic centre spreads around the market place which is dominated by the mosque. There are many traditional buildings, mainly in ruins, and more than 50 two-level houses. The 'Nana Wangera', a sacred well erected in the residence of the heir prince, is a magnificent piece of art. The royal palaces northeast of the town were the residences of the Songhay Emperors. The tomb of Tepama is one of the oldest monuments of the city. The archaeological site of the ancient city lies 3km (1.9mi) southeast of the modern town in the flood plain of Barii. It is composed of 6 'Toggere', spread 5km (3.1mi) around the town. Most of them are entirely covered by ceramic pieces.

SIGNIFICANCE   Djenné was a very important African trading place and a centre of Koranic studies. According to legend it was founded by the Nonos in 10th century A.D. who sacrificed a young girl, Tepama, to gain the favours of the gods and bring prosperity to the city. In 1240 the Emperor Koikombero, converted to Islam and turned his palace into a mosque. The city became part of the Mali Empire in 1325 and was conquered by Sonni Ali Ber in 1468. Its importance continued to grow after the 1591 Moroccan invasion when several new buildings were erected. It was not until 1870 and the Penth invasion with the subsequent closure of most mosques, that the city's decline began. However Djenne's earlier preeminence is clearly evident in these surviving buildings.

TIMBUKTU

LOCATION   Northern region, N 16° 45′, W 03° 04′.

DESCRIPTION   Lying on the southern fringe of the Sahara Desert, Timbuktu is surrounded by sand dunes. The ruins of the ancient town sit to the west and to the north of the modern town. There are 3 mosques of significance – the Great Mosque, the Mosque of Sawkore and the Mosque of Sidi Yahia.

SIGNIFICANCE   Described as 'the meeting point of the camel and the canoe', Timbuktu's importance developed from its strategic proximity to the Niger River and the 'Sahelian Tracks' – a series of ancient tracks across the desert. The town possesses several notable Arabic texts – including the 'Tarik es-Sudan', an important 17th century historical treatise on the Sudan. It has been an intellectual and teaching centre for Islam for many centuries and has been a principal meeting point for the various Saharan and Sudanese races.

CLIFF OF BANDIAGARA
(LAND OF THE DOGONS)

LOCATION   Region of Mopti, N 14° 00′ to 14° 45′, W 03° 00′ to 03° 50′.

DESCRIPTION   The arid, rocky plateau land of the Bandiagara escarpment in eastern Mali is the remote homeland of the Dogon, the unique and renowned people of this area. They live primarily on the escarpment which extends about 200km (124mi) from Bandiagara to Docientza. The listing covers 400,000ha (964,400ac) and represents the authentic secular culture of the Dogon, its houses, granaries, altars, sanctuaries and garden complexes.

SIGNIFICANCE   The Dogons are well known for their sophisticated religious and cultural systems. Their entire demeanour reflects the Dogon concept of creation. In their dress, their colourful and distinctive face masks, their unique mud brick houses and their behaviour, the metaphysical world is ever present. Sirius, the dog star, plays an important part in their religion and some of their traditional beliefs have been traced back to the ancient Egyptians. It is unfortunate that a lot of insensitive tourism is ruining the area and affecting the culture – exemplified by many tourists' blatant disregard for the Dogon belief that cameras steal the soul.

Valletta

MALTA

There are five Maltese islands, Malta, Gozo, Comino, Cominotto, and Filfla, the latter two being uninhabited rocks. These islands are situated between Europe and Africa and have a fascinating history of occupation dating back to prehistoric times. Malta is perhaps most famous for being the final home of the Order of the Knights of St. John. Michael Ellul, in the following article, presents a brief study of the capital of the Knights and of Malta – Valletta. After accepting the World Heritage Convention in November 1978, Malta now has three sites listed, Valletta, the Ggantija Temples and the Hal Saflieni Hypogeum.

The Order of the Knights of St John of Jerusalem owes its origin to a small band of pious Amalfitan merchants who, towards the middle of the eleventh century, opened a hospital and a hospice in Jerusalem for the succour of Christian pilgrims visiting the Holy Places. In 1099, after the capture of the Holy City by the First Crusade, the members of the small fraternity organised themselves into a Nursing Brotherhood, and were recognised as a Religious Order by Pope Paschal II in 1113. In 1187, the Knights of St John, as they came to be called, were driven out of Jerusalem by the Emperor Saladin, and subsequently settled in Acre, a town on the eastern coast of the Mediterranean. In 1291 they withdrew to Cyprus, and thence to the island of Rhodes where, after a gallant resistance, were again driven out by the dreaded Suleiman the Magnificent in 1522.

After eight years of peregrinations all over the Italian peninsula, the knights were offered the islands of Malta and Gozo by Charles V in 1530 as their new home. The offer was accepted with great reluctance, mainly because the island was practically devoid of the defences which would be necessary to ward off an expected Turkish attack.

The knights settled in a small township called Il Borgo at the back of Fort St Angelo, a small dilapidated defence post with ancient crumbling walls. The next few years saw the re-building of St Angelo, and the construction of a small fort at the tip of a peninsula jutting out of the mainland between the islands's two main deep-water harbours, and another fort in the inner reaches of the harbour. Then came the Great Siege of 1565, when the might of the Turkish Empire was unleashed against the meagre defences of Malta. Fighting went on all through the summer, and the siege was finally lifted in September when the Turkish generals withdrew defeated. The battle was won, but the fortifications were reduced to a heap of rubble, the countryside sacked, villages burned and razed to the ground, the population starved and impoverished.

The dust of the battle had hardly settled when Grand Master Jean de La Valette, the head of the Order and hero of the siege, decided to build a new city on the bare land between the harbours. It would be a walled city impregnable against attack, its walls bristling with cannon, and a citadel which would provide shelter and safety to all the island's inhabitants in the eventuality of a future siege. Above all, it would be a city worthy of its proud builders, a fitting habitation for the flower of Europe's aristocracy and for a chivalrous military and hospitaller Order now basking in the glory of freshly-won laurels.

But after the siege, the coffers of the Order were empty, and La Valette turned to the princes of Europe for assistance. Recognising the importance of Malta as Christendom's bulwark in the south of Europe, Pope Pius IV, Charles IX of France, Philip II of Spain and the Order's priories in Europe provided money, munitions, arms and men. The Pope sent one of his best military architects and engineers Capitan Francesco Laparelli da Cortona, who at the time was assisting Michelangelo on St Peter's dome in Rome, to design and supervise the construction of Malta's new capital city. On March 28, 1566, its first stone was laid with unprecedented pomp and circumstance amidst the joy of the knights and of the population. A new city was born and christened Valletta in honour of its founder. Initial work was concentrated on the fortified walls, and in a relatively short time, during which all the male population, slaves and men brought over from nearby Sicily, toiled day and night, the fortifications were completed. Laparelli was assisted throughout the initial planning and works by the eminent Maltese architect and engineer Girolamo Cassar, who was later charged with the sole direction of the works after Laparelli's departure. Laparelli and Cassar together designed a precise, ordered mass of ditches, bastions, curtains, ravelins, counterguards and cavaliers, rising one above the other in tiers of solid massive masonry, the like of which had rarely been seen before or since. On the seaward side the formidable walls rise sheer from the water's edge along both arms of the promontory, and meet in a dramatic climax in the stupendous re-built Fort of St Elmo.

The town-planning aspect of Valletta engaged Laparelli's attention as much as the fortifications themselves. His original plan was for one main wide street running from the city entrance to the top of the peninsula, with the other longitudinal and cross-streets 'in a sweet serpentine way'. But at the last moment, he changed his plan, and the grid-iron system, rigid and almost symmetrical, was finally adopted. Brilliant use was made of the natural contours of the land, and Elizabeth Schermerhorn writing in her *Malta of the Knights* says, 'the palaces and houses rise terraced tier upon tier which break the uniformity of the flat roofs and facades, and present a varied and interesting sky-line ... Girolamo Cassar was a real artist, the interpreter of the new spirit of the Order of St John in stone, and he gave homogeneity without monotony to the small, closely-built city, where a less restrained taste might have left us monstrosities'.

By 1571, many buildings in the new city were completed, and the Order transferred its seat from the *Borgo*, now re-named Vittoriosa, to Valletta. In a few years, the seven Auberges or Inns of the various Langues, the Conventual Church, the Holy Infirmary, the Magisterial Palace, numerous churches, convents, palaces for the knights and modest dwellings for the inhabitants rose from the rocky bareness to make Valletta one of the finest cities of sixteenth century Europe. Building and re-building in Valletta continued throughout the following two centuries, but Malta's capital retained its character to a remarkable degree despite the difference in styles and changes in taste. An English traveller, John Gadsby, writing in 1850, had this to say about Valletta, 'The view of Malta, on entering the Grand Harbour, is exceedingly imposing ...The creeks full of shipping with the little towns that are formed on each side of them; the lofty houses, all of stone, rising one above the other, row after row; the public promenades...the elegant naval hospital and other large stone buildings...the many church towers; all, as it were, catching the eye at the same moment, and present a scene not to be passed for grandeur, and to see it, as I on several occasions did on a lovely moonlit night, creates a sensation not easily to be got rid of. It is truly sublime'.

To the modern traveller who flies into Malta, the view of Valletta from the air is certainly no less imposing. The limestone buildings, bathed in the Maltese sun, cast their square shadows in chiaroscuro on the narrow streets. The palaces, the churches and the houses are hugged by the all-encircling walls, their honey-coloured stonework magnificently set off by the deep blue-green of the sea on three sides of the Valletta headland.

Valletta is a city difficult to describe, but how very easy to fall in love with! Sir Walter Scott called it 'The splendid city which seems like a dream'; Disraeli, 'A splendid city, something between Venice and Cadiz', and, again, 'Valletta equals in its noble architecture, even if it does not excel, any capital in Europe...fair Valletta, with its streets of palaces, its picturesque forts and magnificent churches'.

For almost four and a half centuries Valletta has

Ggantija Temples

been the administrative, commercial and cultural hub of life in Malta, and, besides, an important residential centre. Time, neglect and the ravages of war have all taken their toll especially during World War II, when Valletta, along with the other harbour towns, was cruelly savaged by continuous aerial bombing for more than two years. Post-war reconstruction was long and painful, but the capital's architectural character and its unique atmosphere were generally preserved.

Valletta, like all old European towns and cities, is, nevertheless, facing major conservation and environmental problems. Its buildings, all constructed in the soft and porous local limestone, suffer from the effects of the island's sub-tropical climatic conditions, the salt-laden winds which blow from the sea with regularity for most of the year, and the considerable variation in temperature between day and night. Restoration of building facades is a painstakingly slow process and extremely costly. Ministries, government departments and public offices are mainly housed in large historic buildings, and this fact prompts the government to provide considerable funds for their regular maintenance. But previous years of neglect have necessitated the wholesale restoration of their external stonework. One must remember, that in spite of Malta's ancient history and civilisation, it is young as a nation, having obtained its first self-government as a colony in 1921, which was short-lived, and again in 1947, and complete independence only twenty-five years ago. Employment, social services, full educational facilities at all levels and citizens' health were the government's most pressing priorities, and the national

heritage could not be accorded the attention it deserved.

Valletta is a walled-city and horizontal development is therefore not possible, but frequent demands are made by developers for additional floors to existing buildings, mainly office and commercial apartments, which are either refused or strictly controlled by the planning authorities for the integral preservation of the city's skyline. Design of shop fronts is also subject to strict regulations: the exposure of the original stone facade is enforced, and the use of modern materials, such as steel, large glass areas and aluminium is officially discouraged or reduced to minimum requirements.

Circulation of traffic in the narrow, and in many cases, steep streets of Valletta is a perennial problem, further compounded by the almost impossible parking situation. Malta has the highest rate of private cars per head of population in Europe, and office workers and shoppers use their cars to Valletta every day in preference to public transport, although it is cheap and frequent and reaches all parts of the island. Parking lots are restricted to a few open squares which thus have their architectural value down-graded as a result.

These and other aspects of Valletta's threatened future have created an encouraging public awareness and concern for the city's continuing life. The Maltese government, itself conscious of Valletta's precious history and its importance in Malta's cultural life, has responded generously and a medium-term and long-term rehabilitation programme was initiated a few years ago and will, hopefully, continue until Valletta achieves again its former glory, and the Maltese, especially the citizens of Valletta, are satisfied that their much-loved city will endure for many years to come.

MICHAEL ELLUL
Adviser to the Prime Minister of Malta

HAL SAFLIENI HYPOGEUM

LOCATION   Near the centre of the town of Paola, Island of Malta, E 14° 30′, N 35° 52′.

DESCRIPTION   The Hal Saflieni Hypogeum is an underground monument consisting of several series of manmade chambers and passages on 3 main levels, the deepest of which descends to 10.6m (34.5ft) below ground level. These days the hypogeum is accessible from a modern spiral staircase. Its uppermost level may have been of natural origin, a cave or caves used for cult purposes, but the lower levels were hewn out and shaped as megalithic architectural features with great precision and sophistication.

SIGNIFICANCE   The hypogeum is unique among the prehistoric temples of the Maltese Cooper Age (c. 3500-2200 BC) in that it was excavated below ground

Hal Saflieni Hypogeum

level. The monument, when discovered in 1902, was found to contain the jumbled remains of some 7,000 individuals taken as evidence that in prehistoric times it had been converted from a place of worship to an ossuary.

VALLETTA

LOCATION   Valletta (capital city), island of Malta, E 14° 30′, N 35° 54′.

DESCRIPTION   There are around 320 buildings in Valletta considered to be of architectural or historical significance. There is an old city wall which encloses an area of about 55ha (133ac). Some of the more notable monuments are: the Grandmaster's Palace; several 'auberges' – headquarters for the different divisions of the Knights; the National Library and also Manoel Theatre.

SIGNIFICANCE   Valletta was established by the Order of St. John, the first foundation stone being laid by Grandmaster Jean de La Valette in 1566. The architectural style developed over the years, blending the Roman baroque style with indigenous forms to create a distinctive new style. Physically and aesthetically, the capital is still very much a city of the Knights, its outward appearance having changed little since the Order of St. John left in 1798.

GGANTIJA TEMPLES

LOCATION   Island of Gozo, E 14° 15′, N 36° 02′.

DESCRIPTION   The prehistoric monument of Ggantija consists of a complex of 2 separate temples enclosed within a continuously curving outside wall and a common facade. There is an open space in front of the monument which was the original terrace. It is supported by a retaining wall of huge blocks.

SIGNIFICANCE   These prehistoric temples are some of the oldest free standing stone monuments in existence. The earliest construction dates back to 3000 BC.

MAURITANIA

An Islamic republic, Mauritania is covered largely by the Sahara desert. It is a landscape of rocky outcrops, sand dunes and rugged mountains 1,030,700 sq km (398,000 sq mi) in area. Activity centres around the Senegal River, the coast and several oases. Neolithic remains have been discovered in the north of the country.

It was from Mauritania that the Berber Almoravids rose to conquer Morocco, establishing desert caravan trade routes between the two countries. By the 15th century the Arabs controlled the region, which had become a central part of the thriving trade route from western Africa to the Maghreb; a trade that was centred around gold, salt and slaves.

France took control of the area in the 19th century and ruled until 1960 when Mauritania gained independence. French and Arabic are now the main languages.

Mauritania ratified the World Heritage Convention in 1981 and presently has one site listed – 'Banc d'Arguin' National Park, an area crucial to the survival of the numerous migratory water birds which flock there each year.

Banc d'Arguin National Park

Mediterranean monk seals, Banc d'Arguin National Park

Our Invaluable Wetlands

This article, from Ducks Unlimited Canada, demonstrates the importance of the world's wetlands and how a group of dedicated and determined people have succeeded in protecting water birds and their natural habitats.

The article appears alongside Mauritania's World Heritage listings, in recognition of the crucial role played by the National Park of 'Banc d'Arguin' in protecting literally millions of the world's water birds as they play out their timeless annual migratory cycle.

OUR HERITAGE, in the broadest sense, is the biosphere. That vital combination of natural systems that nurtured our evolution, sustains our lives, and will continue to do so unless, as seems likely, we destroy it. Mass extinctions are replete in the geological record. Man may be unique as the only species to engineer his own!

Too often 'heritage' is synonymous with remnant. This is especially true of natural heritages, particularly wildlife species and natural landscapes. Sudden realization of impending extinction or obliteration brings frantic and costly action to preserve the remnant. Foresight, unfortunately, is seldom characteristic of expanding agriculture in new lands, of which the exploitation of the prairies and wetlands of North America is a prime example. Though not as dramatic as the on-going ravage of the rainforests, over the last 100 years it has been almost as ruthless. And while the ramifications may not be global, the local effects are just being realized.

The last North American glaciation, which receded only some 10,000 years ago, determined the land forms of the three northern praire states of the United States, Minnesota and North and South Dakota, and the Canadian prairie provinces, Manitoba, Saskatchewan and Alberta. The great post glacial lakes soon drained, becoming flat open plain. Elsewhere, the uneven deposition of glacial drift left undulating topography with shallow lakes and marshes, and abundant small ponds in hummocky old glacial moraines.

The aboriginal people, wandering hunters and gatherers, and relatively few in number, saw the land as common heritage and developed a culture with an intimate mystical relationship to land and wildlife. There was little evidence of their presence.

But the horde of settlers, lured by the promise of free land, which poured on to the prairies from eastern Canada and the United States, Europe and Great Britain in the late 19th century, had no such land ethic. The prairies, where a man could plow all day with no trees to clear, were soon converted to cereal crops in the more humid areas, and fenced for grazing in arid areas further west.

The glacial legacy of millions of wetlands was not spared. Larger marshes were easily drained, either by speculators for selling to land hungry farmers, or by governments to appease local pressure for more land or flood control. Many of these drainage programs failed because the land was unsuitable for agriculture, but only in a few instances have the marshes been restored.

Smaller wetlands in cultivated fields were relatively safe until large machinery made cultivation up to and through them possible. That technology gave farmers the efficiency of straight open fields, but destroyed the wetland and marsh edge ecosystems which once produced the great masses of migratory waterfowl. Up to 1988, 71 per cent of the prairie wetlands in Canada had been drained and 75 per cent of those in the northern plain states of the United States. No data are available for those hundreds of thousands of small wetlands whose biological potential has been destroyed by intensive cultivation. These once fertile wetlands remain only as spring puddles in cultivated fields.

In the short term, wetlands drainage and intensive cultivation seems to make agriculture economic sense. Only in the last decade has it been realized that the obvious short term economic benefits have long term and perhaps prohibitive costs. In 1984, a Senate Committee of the Canadian Government reported that, due to intensive and inappropriate agriculture procedures, Canada was facing the most serious agricultural crises in its history and unless action was taken, would lose a major portion of its agriculture capability. This report also stimulated investigations of the role of wetlands in agricultural conservation programs.

But while soil erosion by wind and water and salinization are obvious to a farmer, the detrimental effects of his wetland drainage are not, since they may occur far removed from his operation. Ironically, though, he may unknowingly be suffering the results of similar unwise drainage elsewhere!

Locally he can see that wetland edges trap snow and store run off water, but he is unaware that wetlands also recharge ground water; affect water levels in local or distant wells, and play an important role in moderating local climates by providing surface water for evaporation, transpiration and precipitation. By storing water, wetlands retain precipitation where it falls, reducing downstream flooding and erosion. When drained into public ditches there seems little realization that flood problems may be created downstream. Ironically, water drained from marginal agriculture land often floods better land farther down the watershed!

Wetlands are pleasing aesthetically, giving a varied landscape and habitat for wetland wildlife. But aesthetics usually have little weight in farm economic decisions. What is pleasing to the farmer is open, unencumbered expanses where big machinery can be used most efficiently. For him this is aesthetic!

Many environmentalists however, who deplore the loss of natural landscapes and the wildlife associated with them, are urbanites, whose environmental aspirations involve no personal economic sacrifice. Wetlands, and wildlife living on them, may be of passing interest to the landowner but they are usually seen as a liability since they provide no visible economic benefits to him.

The problem then becomes one of how the aspirations of urban environmentalists to preserve natural landscapes and wildlife, can be translated into rural action. This can only be done by organization and money. There must be economic rewards to landowners to preserve their wetlands either from governments or private organizations. And the reward must exceed, or at least equal, what he preceives as the agricultural benefit of drainage or other utilization.

Ducks Unlimited, Inc. was a pioneer in this area. Formed by United States duck hunters in 1937, near the end of the great prairie drought of the 1930s when waterfowl populations fell to their lowest level in history, the organization sought to increase waterfowl numbers by developing and improving breeding habitats in prairie Canada, where at least 70 per cent of the continental waterfowl were known to be produced. This was unique in that money from American waterfowlers by direct solicitation, banquets, and other fund-raising activities, was sent to a foreign country (Canada) to be spent by a Canadian affiliate, Ducks Unlimited (Canada) to achieve the objectives of the American organization. In this process, no land was purchased or leased. Free flood easements were obtained from landowners for the benefits either aesthetic or economic, which would accure to them. Thus waterfowlers, perhaps thousands of miles away, paid for the product from a distant landowner's wetland, a relationship that neither likely conceptualized, but one that is fundamental to wildlife and environmental preservation.

The Ducks Unlimited plan has been highly successful. An annual budget in 1938 of $100,000 has increased to $55 million in 1991. Over these 53 years, $400 million has been spent in wetlands development for waterfowl production. These developments also provide habitat for many other wetland species.

Until the mid 1960s, in response to the drought experience of the 1930s, water storage and management was emphasized. But with increasing biological input it was more fully realized that waterfowl were a product of complex wetland ecosystems where food, nesting cover, freedom from disturbance, were as important components as water. Cooperative programs with farmers and agricultural organizations to improve these conditions were initiated. This involved leasing and purchasing land, a radical departure from former policy, and programs to illustrate the benefits of minimum tillage in soil conservation and the advantage of rotational grazing. Both of which contribute significantly to waterfowl nesting success.

To date, Ducks Unlimited has secured 17 million acres (7.08 million ha) of waterfowl habitat of which 2.3 million has been developed. Of the 5,200 projects developed, eleven have been given the status of Heritage Marshes as wetlands of international importance under the 1975 Ramsar agreement.

These are real achievements but perhaps the greatest role of Ducks Unlimited has been as a catalyst. In the beginning it established a value for waterfowl. Landowners and even governments were surprised that money could be privately raised and spent to produce wild ducks!

Ducks Unlimited is now playing a major role in developing and financing the North American Waterfowl Management Plan, a cooperative program of public and private organizations, which will spend 1.5 billion dollars on waterfowl habitat between 1986 and the year 2000. Through joint programs with agriculture, uplands as well as wetlands will be involved, improving land use on a wide scale as well as benefiting waterfowl.

Ducks Unlimited is no longer just a water-fowlers' organization. Many supporters have no desire to hunt ducks but see in Duck Unlimited, which now extends continent wide with independent organizations in New Zealand and Australia, the answer to a nostalgia to preserve and restore examples of the beauty, diversity, history and wildlife, of our pristine landscapes.

WILLIAM G. LEITCH
Ducks Unlimited, Canada

'BANC D'ARGUIN' NATIONAL PARK

LOCATION   155km (95mi) north of Nouakchott, N 20° 34', W 16° 32'.

DESCRIPTION   This is an extensive aquatic parkland on the northwest African coast. The waters are extremely shallow here, even 25km (15.5mi) from the shore the depth is only several metres. Islands of sand are scattered throughout, providing ideal conditions for a multitude of water birds such as sandpiper, black terns, flamingoes, pelicans, spoonbills, herons, and cormorants. Fish are also abundant in these waters.

SIGNIFICANCE   This national park is known around the world by bird watchers as an important crossroad for the multitudes of aquatic birds that migrate between the northern countries and Africa. The bird life is nothing short of astounding, with over 2 million broad-billed sandpiper having been recorded within the park during one winter. The park provides a safe haven for these various bird species and is crucial to their survival.

MEXICO

Wherever you wish to take the southern geographical limit of the North American continent, one thing is certain: it lies within the bounds of Mexico.

In so many ways, this country is one of the most interesting on Earth. Its people, some 80 million of them, consist largely of 'mestizos' – people of mixed Spanish and Indian blood. Unlike the Indian population of their powerful northern neighbour, the Mexican Indians survived in substantial numbers.

The landscape reflects Mexico's position as a land of transition. The northern third of the country is covered by the Meseta Central – a massive plain which rises up to 2,580m (8,600ft) at its southern edge. This plateau is flanked on both eastern and western sides by mountain ranges. The southern rim is crossed by spectacular volcanic peaks. The highest peak in Mexico is found here – Pico de Orizaba at 5,600m (18,600ft).

This immense diversity in landscapes and the subsequent variation in climates, explains the remarkable biodiversity of this land, from the desert adapted flora and fauna of the north, to the luxuriant tropical species of the Caribbean coast.

Along with Guatemala, Belize, El Salvador and part of Honduras, much of Mexico falls within that area which archaeologists consider to have constituted a cultural unit in pre-Columbian times. This area is termed 'Mesoamerica'.

Like the Indus, Nile, Tigris and Euphrates valley, this area is considered one of the cradles of civilisation. Traces of civilisation dating back to 3,000 BC have been found. The Olmec, Tottec, Aztec and Mayan cultures all thrived at various times in different parts of what is now Mexico.

Of Mexico's eight World Heritage sites, seven include archaeological zones which relate to past Indian cultures. Of these, five are some of the most famous and significant ruins in the world – Teotihuacan, Oaxaca, Palenque, Xochimilco and Chichén-Itzá. Puebla/Cholula and Guanajuato are both Spanish colonial sites, the former also including a massive Indian pyramid.

The eighth site is predominantly a natural listing – Sian Ka'an Reserve is a wonderland of tropical forests, mangroves, swamps and deciduous forests which also contains some important archaeological sites.

Mexico accepted the World Heritage Convention in February 1984.

Sian Ka'an, the Land Where the Sky Begins

SIAN KA'AN IS Mayan for 'birth of the sky', where the turquoise waters of the Caribbean meet the azure of the tropical sky; where the centuries-old ruins of the Mayan civilisation remain in counterpoint to the high-rise hotels and white-sand beaches of Cancun; where paved roads end and the barrier reefs, jaguar, tapir and thousands upon thousands of birds still thrive: this is the Biosphere Reserve of Sian Ka'an.

One-third tropical forest, one-third wetlands and one-third coastal and marine environments, Sian Ka'an is a 542,000 ha (1.3 million ac) reserve in which environmental conservation and sustainable development go hand in hand. Eighty percent of the land area is part of the core zones which are being preserved in their natural state. The remainder comprise buffer zones where appropriate, low-impact development will support local inhabitants.

Sian Ka'an lies on a huge limestone flat on the Caribbean coast of Mexico's Yucatan Peninsula, in the state of Quintana Roo. In the reserve, terrestrial and marine environments merge and the landscape includes coral reefs, beaches, dunes, mangrove forests, marshes, wet savannas, lagoons and large tracts of lowland tropical forests. The highest elevation is less than 18m (60 ft) above sea level.

Sian Ka'an's barrier reef forms part of the second longest such reef in the world. Its great, shallow bays are important spiny lobster nurseries. In these bays scattered keys provide nesting sites for thousands of water birds such as the roseate spoonbill, woodstork, magnificent frigatebird and boat-billed heron. The rare jabiru stork nests in the reserve and the beaches are nesting grounds for four species of endangered sea turtles.

The reserve also serves as habitat for wild cats such as jaguar, margay, jaguarundi and cougar. Two species of crocodiles, howler and spider monkeys, tapir and west Indian manatee are among other species; as well as forest birds such as the ocellated turkey and great curassow.

Plant diversity is high with approximately 1200 species found in the reserve. Hardwood hummocks, called 'petenes' occur like islands among the wetlands, some of them with sinkholes – huge natural wells more than 45m (150 ft) in diameter – at their centres.

The human population of the area is about 35,000, primarily of Mayan stock; with fewer than one thousand people, mostly fishermen actually inhabiting the buffer zones of the reserve. The management plan for the reserve includes scientific research and field projects focused on developing and promoting sustainable use of natural resources that will support the residents' livelihood.

The Sian Ka'an Biosphere Reserve was established by Presidential Decree on January 20, 1986. It is integrated in the International Network of Biosphere Reserves and in 1987 was included in the UNESCO list of World Heritage sites.

The management of the reserve is based on a partnership between the Federal, State and Municipal Governments, who integrate a committee that delegates everyday operations to the reserve's director.

Various experiments to integrate the local population in the reserve's decision-making process have taken place and are still in progress. A local research center carries out basic research in Sian Ka'an. Amigos de Sian Ka'an, a private Mexican conservation organisation, channels national and international support into the reserve and executes applied research projects for sustainable development, community outreach and public information projects to support and promote the conservation and wise use of the Sian Ka'an Biosphere Reserve.

Mexico's conservation efforts have to be made compatible with its growing social needs. Biosphere reserves are the arena where a new relationship between man and nature should become a reality. We don't perceive conservation as prohibiting use, but rather as wise use of our natural resources.

The success of this reserve depends on several factors. First, the people of Quintana Roo, and indeed of all Mexico, must come to value the benefits of reserves such as Sian Ka'an as an economic, cultural, and ecological resource. Second, the agencies charged with daily management of the reserve must acquire the resources to conduct such activities as gathering baseline biological information and implementing a management plan. Third, the various institutions with roles to play in research, management, development and regulations must cooperate and work together.

Fourth, the people living in and around the reserve must have clear economic incentives and technical know-how to preserve the natural resource base upon which their livelihood depends. Finally, the hotel and resort industry developing along the coast must be managed as it approaches the reserve so that its impact can be controlled.

Fortunately, Sian Ka'an is not so imminently threatened that any one of these challenges is insurmountable. Thus, the reserve is blessed with a somewhat unique resource: time to establish a working model of a Mexican Biosphere Reserve that can show the way for other similar reserves throughout the region.

JUAN E. BEZAURY CREEL
Executive Director and Secretary,
Amigos de Sian Ka'an

Chichén-Itza

El Templo Mayor

On the night of 21 February 1978, workers of the Light and Power Company were digging on the corner of Guatemala and Argentina Streets in the centre of Mexico City. After breaking the thick concrete surface and penetrating about 2m (7ft) down, they encountered a hard stone which put a stop to further progress. On removing the clay adhering to it they found that the stone was covered with a series of reliefs and decided to suspend operations until the next day. A telephone call to the Office of Salvage Archaeology of the National Institute of Anthropology and History led to the dispatch of a team of archaeologists to identify the find. On 23 February it was established that on part of the stone was a piece of sculpture showing a face in profile with adornments on the head.

Salvage operations continued until the 27th under the supervision of the archaeologists. An enormous monolith, 3.25m (11ft) in diameter, was uncovered. Its upper surface bore a sculptured representation of a decapitated, naked woman, whose arms and legs were separated from the torso. Clearly this was Coyolxauhqui, a lunar deity and sister of Huitzilopochtli, the Aztec god of war who, according to legend, killed his sister in single combat on the hill of Coatepec.

This discovery marked the start of the Great Temple Project. From the outset it was planned in three principal phases. This enabled us to apply the theory and methods that would give us a clearer picture of the chief temple of the Aztecs or Mexicas, who settled on the little islands in the lake of Texcoco around 1325 AD and later became subject to the lordship of Azcapotzalco, before achieving independence around 1428. They then became an expansionist community and conquered large areas of central America, until in 1521 they succumbed to the dominion of the Spaniards who under Hernán Cortés conquered Mexico during the sixteen century and destroyed the Aztec city of Tenochtitlán, and with it the city's Great Temple – *el Templo Mayor*.

The project was carried out in three phases. The first phase consisted in assembling all available information about the Great Temple, both from historical sources and from reports of previous archaeological investigations, either on the site or on nearby sites. On the basis of this information, a general plan covering both theoretical and practical aspects was drawn up.

The second phase consisted of the excavations proper, which were begun on 20 March 1978 and completed in November 1982. Suitable techniques were employed to ensure adequate control of the excavation process, the area being divided up into 2m (7ft) square grids. The site was also divided

The Cathedral in Zocalo Square, Mexico City

into three sections, each supervised by an archaeologist and his assistants. Support units included a team of restorers with a field laboratory, as well as biologists, chemists, geologists and other specialists from the Department of Prehistory. There were also photographic laboratories, a design section and a section for the excavated material.

The third phase comprises the study and analysis of the material covered in the preceding phase. After four years' continuous work, the first two phases have been completed, and we are now engaged on the third phase which will take longer.

We shall now summarise the results of nearly five years of excavations and of the investigations currently being carried out.

Architecture – Until a few years ago the chief sources of information about the Great Temple were the accounts of sixteenth-century chroniclers. Now, thanks to archaeology, we have the temple before our eyes, and we can see that in fact the chroniclers' descriptions correspond very closely to what they saw or to what the indigenous people told them. Thanks to archaeology we have also been able to learn about very early periods in the temple's history, of which even the last generations of Mexicas know nothing.

The main facade faced west. The temple stood on a vast platform, with a base of four elements, including two stairways leading up to two sanctuaries – one on the south side dedicated to the tutelary war god Huitzilopochtli, and another on the north side to Tlaloc, the god of water, rain and fertility.

For various reasons the temple was repeatedly enlarged. For instance, the city of Tenochtitlán suffered from flooding, which made it necessary to raise the level of its buildings, as well as from structural faults due to the instability of the terrain. Again we know from historical sources that certain rulers ordered a new temple to be raised on top of the existing one, so that different construction Epochs are superimposed upon each other. We now know that the temple was enlarged on all four sides at least seven times. There were also four enlargements of the main facade.

We shall now briefly describe each of these construction Epochs, except for Epoch I, which was located inside Epoch II and was in a state of such deterioration that it would be pointless to describe it. The Roman figures indicate total enlargements on all four sides and, if followed by a letter, enlargements of the main facade only.

Epoch II – This structure is notable for the fact that its upper part is remarkably complete. We can see remains of the two stone sanctuaries with some of the stucco (mixture of sand and lime) which covered them. Facing the entrance to the sanctuary of Huitzilopochtli is the sacrificial stone. On the top step, in line with this stone, is a head with a glyph, or carved pictograph, of two rabbits above it, corresponding to the year 1390.

Inside the sanctuary a platform runs from north to south, in the middle of which there is a small altar on which an image of the deity must have been placed. On the Tlaloc (north) side there is a *chacmool* – a polychrome stone sculpture of the divine messenger responsible for carrying the offering into the sanctuary. The pillars at the entrance to the sanctuary are still decorated with mural paintings of black and white circles (perhaps depicting the god's eyes) on blue and red bands. Below these are alternating vertical black and white bands. Inside can be seen the platform on which the image of the god must have stood. This Epoch is mostly earlier than 1428, the year when the Mexicas became independent of Azcapotzalco.

Epoch III – To this Epoch belong well-made stairways, and the facings of the steps of the base are still upright. Eight sculptures of standard-bearers were found in recumbent positions on the steps of the stairway on the Huizilopochtli side. These figures may have adorned the edifice, but when a new construction Epoch was begun they were collected and ceremonially placed on the stairway where they were discovered. On the back wall of the platform, on the Huitzilopochtli side, is carved the glyph '4 Reed' , which corresponds to the year 1431.

Epoch IV – This Epoch, with its additions, is one of the richest in decorative elements. The main platform was decorated on all four sides with braziers and serpent heads. The braziers on Tlaloc side are adorned with the face of the god, while those on the Huitzilopochtli side bear a knot, a symbol of the warrior deity. Various offerings were found below the braziers and serpents.

Epoch IVb is an addition to the main (west) facade which was very rich in decorative elements. It consists of the vast platform on which the Great Temple stands. This platform had a continuous perron, at both ends of which enormous serpents with undulating bodies and huge heads were unearthed, still bearing some of the paint which originally covered them. The stairs leading to the platform are interrupted only by a small altar flanked by two frogs standing on the stone flags of which the altar is constructed. This altar is in line with the middle of the stairs that once led to the upper part of the temple dedicated to Tlaloc.

On the Huitzilopochtli side, opposite the stairs leading to the sanctuary of this god, a 2m (7ft) wide stone block decorated with serpents forms part of the top of the platform. The base formed by the remains of the two stairways which led to the upper part includes four serpent heads, one at each end and two in the middle, marking the junction of the two halves of the temple. In the middle of the platform, on the Huitzilopochtli side, is the place where the monumental stone sculpture of the god's sister, Coyolxauhqui, was found.

Chronologically, we believe the Epoch IV corre-sponds broadly to the reign of the Aztec ruler Moctezuma I, because the glyph '1 rabbit', equivalent to the year 1454, is carved on the back part of the platform on the Huitzilopochtli side. Coyolxauhqui and the serpents may have been added during the reign of Axayacatl. Another glyph on the south side of the edifice, with the symbol '3 house', corresponds to 1469, the year in which Axayacatl's reign began.

Epoch V – All that has been discovered of this period is the stuccoed main platform and part of the stone floor of the ceremonial precinct.

Epoch VI – This is the last Epoch but one. Its vestiges consist of part of the main platform. A wall of the main west facade is decorated with three serpent heads.

Epoch VII – This is the last Epoch of the Great Temple and the one the Spaniards saw. All that remains of it are part of the slab floor of the ceremonial precinct, some traces of the temple site, and part of the platform on the north side.

Offerings – During nearly five years of excavations, some 7,000 objects – the remains of almost a hundred offerings – were unearthed. These offerings were found in three distinct places – in stone cists whose sides and bottoms bore trades of stucco, inside movable stone boxes with stone lids, and actually in the fill of stone and earth covering a construction Epoch.

It may be said that, as a general rule, the manner in which objects were placed in the offerings was not haphazard but premeditated, conforming to some kind of symbolism which has still to be interpreted. In other words these objects and their positions correspond to a language. Thus in some offerings certain objects occupy the lower position, while others are always found higher up. We also noticed that the objects were placed facing in a certain direction. Both the offerings on the west (main facade) side as well as those at the back of the temple faced the spot where the sun sets, whereas those found in the middle of the edifice, in its northern and southern facades, were facing north and south respectively.

Offerings 7 and 61, located towards the middle of the edifice on the south side and on the north side, respectively, contained the same arrangement of objects – at the base, seashells facing north to south; above them, crocodiles; and at the top, seated deities which we thought to be representations of Xiuhtecutli, an ancient fire-god, centre of the universe and of the hearth. To the right of these gods was a coral, and to the left an earthenware vase bearing an effigy of the god Tlaloc. Perhaps this arrangement means that the shells represent the sea, the crocodiles the earthly level, and Xiuhtecutli and Tlaloc the heavenly level. The same arrangement is found in offerings 11 and 17, the first located in the main facade between the two serpent heads marking the junction of the temples of Tlaloc and

Guanajuato

Huitzilopochtli, and the second at the back where the two edifices are joined.

Some of the objects unearthed were of purely Mexica origin; others came from tributary areas. The former include sculptures of seated ancients wearing only the 'maxtatl' of loincloth and a headdress with two protuberances. They are thought to represent Xiuhtecutli. Others are effigies of the god Tlaloc sculpted in 'tezontle' (volcanic stone) and in other kinds of stone. There are also representation of coiled serpents, serpent heads and rattlesnakes carved in obsidian, stone braziers with knots, and, of course, the magnificent representations of seashells which are real works of art although, like the Coyolxauhqui and serpent heads adorning the temple facade, they did not figure among the offerings.

Interesting objects from the tributary areas figure in greater numbers among the offerings from Epoch IV onwards (around 1454) when the Mexicas were in full expansion. They include a large quantity of masks and figures in the Mezcala style (from what is now the State of Guerrero), of various types and sizes, alabaster pieces from the Peubla region representing deer heads, arrows and seated deities. There are two magnificent orange ceramic funerary urns from the Gulf Coast. Inside them were the remains of burnt bones, necklaces, and other objects. The great variety of seashells, fishbones, sawfish bills and corals come from the coasts. So do the crocodiles and jaguars, which may have come from Veracruz or Tabasco.

Another group of objects can definitely be attributed to societies very much earlier than the Mexica. Such are the Teotihuacan masks, which can be dated around the year 400 AD, and an Olmec mask. Petrographic analysis has shown that the latter originated in the area now occupied by the States of Puebla, Oaxaca and Guerrero. It is believed to be the oldest object discovered (800 BC).

We can say that most of the objects represent Tlaloc or symbols associated with him, including such objects associated with the sea as canoes and fishes. But there are also objects associated with Heuitzilopochtli, a god who is only represented symbolically, in the form of braziers with a knot, skulls, 'tecpatl' sacrificial knives with eyes and teeth of conch shell and, generally, objects from tributary areas, the spoils of military conquest. All this confirms our thesis of the existence of an agricultural and warrior people who depended for their sustenance on both agriculture and tribute.

EDUARDO MATOS MOCTEZUMA is general director of the Centro de Investigaciones y Estudios Superiores en Antropologia Social at *Tlalpán*. Before beginning the excavation of the Great Temple in Mexico City he had done extensive field work on the pre-Columbian sites of Mexico.

Reprinted from the *Unesco Courier*, July 1985

〈241〉

CHICHÉN-ITZÀ

LOCATION   Yucatan, W 88° 35′, N 20° 40′.

DESCRIPTION   This major archaeological site of 300ha
(740ac) is rich in monuments and includes a stellar
observatory and the Pyramid of Quetzalcoatt. Surrounding this are terraces where the major monumental
complexes were built; the Great Ball Court, the Skull
Wall, Jaguar Temple, House of Eagles, Temple of Warriors, the Group of the Thousand Columns, the market,
the ball courts and the Tomb of the High Priest.

SIGNIFICANCE   The site is most significant in historical
terms because it illustrates 2 major periods in pre-
Hispanic civilisations in Mesoamerica. The settlement
probably developed around 415-455 AD, but a second
settlement of migrating Toltec warriors in the 10th century was even more important. Many monuments exhibit a blending of Mayan and Toltec styles in
architecture. This architecture became known as Maya-
Yucatec.

PALENQUE

LOCATION   Northern part of the State of Chiapas,
N 17° 28′, W 92° 01′ (approximately).

DESCRIPTION   This listing includes 1,772ha (4,250ac)
of national park which is characterised by tropical rainforest. Within the park's boundaries, and set in a valley,
sits the deserted city of Palenque, which is in ruins and
overgrown by tropical vegetation. Only a small portion of
the city's original 81sq km (32sq mi) site has been excavated. The main buildings are a group of temples and a
palace complex. Numerous buildings lie on terraced platforms up the side of the mountain.

SIGNIFICANCE   These vast ruins which are as yet only
partially investigated will no doubt hold many keys to a
fuller understanding of ancient Mesoamerica. Many
hieroglyphics are to be found inscribed on stone, particularly in the Temple of Inscriptions. The park is particularly beautiful with many spectacular waterfalls. The tall
rainforest provides an ideal habitat for several
endangered species of flora and fauna.

SIAN KA'AN

LOCATION   In the state of Guintana Roo on the Yacutan
Peninsula, N 14° 05′ to 20° 06′, W 87° 30′ to 88° 00′.

DESCRIPTION   The reserve of Sian Ka'an is defined by
the Caribbean Sea on the east, swamps in the southwest
and the towns of Felipe Carrillo Puerto and Otton P.
Blanco in the south. It covers an area of 528,000ha
(1,270,000ac) with 150,000ha (361,650ac) of tropical
forests, swamps, mangrove forests and semi deciduous
forests. The reserve includes 100km (62mi) of coastal
dunes, 90 percent of which are covered by coconut palms

Palenque

and the 110km (68mi) Barrier Reef of Sian Ka'an. In the
upper part the only water is found in 35 wells, caused by
the depression of the karst. There are 70 organically rich
lagoons that have formed in cavities. They are very shallow and have a diameter of 100m (328ft) or more. There
are 23 registered archaeological zones.

SIGNIFICANCE   The archaeological sites are of some
note, especially Tulum, which is unusual in that it is
positioned on the coast. It is also particularly well preserved. The park is of great importance in preserving
many unique ecosystems. The 'petemes' are of particular interest – they are islands of forest found on upraised
land amongst the swamp, often with a large well in the
centre. It is thought that up to 1,500 different species of
flora are to be found here and the mammal population is
particularly rich, with jaguars, monkeys, pumas and
tapirs all in abundance.

TEOTIHUACAN

LOCATION   45km (30mi) northeast of Mexico City,
N 19° 41′, W 98° 50′.

DESCRIPTION   The site of these ruins lies in the Great
Valley of Anfhuac. The town was built on open ground
and had no walls. Several large palaces and pyramidal
temples, known as the citadel complex, form the nucleus
of the town. A wide street, the 'Avenue of the Dead' runs
to the south of the citadel and is lined with numerous
structures adorned with rich murals. An extensive
underground drainage system was built and all streets
and plazas were paved.

SIGNIFICANCE   Founded between 300-250 BC, this
town, now in ruins, is archetypal of the second major
epoch of ancient Mexico. From its beginnings, until its
inexplicably violent destruction some time between the

Oaxaca

8th and 10th centuries AD, this town experienced one continuous and fruitful occupation. The period 450 to 600 AD, when the rich mural art was created, was probably Teotihuacan's zenith.

MEXICO CITY (HISTORIC CENTRE AND XOCHIMILCO)

LOCATION   On the southern fringe of the Mesa Central, N 19° 25′, W 99° 08′.

DESCRIPTION   The historic centre is based around Zocalo Square (Constitution Square). The remains of an Aztec temple have been uncovered here. Almost on top of these ruins sits an imposing cathedral, the Church of La Asuncíon de María Santísima. There are several other important buildings, including the National Palace and the Municipal Palace. Xochimilco lies south of the modern city. It is the site of original Aztec settlements. Known as the 'floating gardens', it is now a water park, with a large lake that has numerous islets and channels. Many ruins are found here.

SIGNIFICANCE   Mexico City or Tenochtitlan was founded around 1300 AD by the Aztecs. According to legend, the Aztecs located their promised land by following an eagle which landed on a cactus growing on a swampy island in Lake Texcoco. By the time of the Spanish invasion, the Aztecs had built up a considerable and far reaching power base. The town was rebuilt by the Spanish in 1521 as Mexico City and has since enjoyed a colourful and turbulent history. It is now the most populous city in the world.

OAXACA AND MONTE ALBAN

LOCATION   In the state of Oaxaca, N 17° 03′ to 17° 43′, W 96° 43′ to 96° 45′.

DESCRIPTION   The town of Oaxaca lies 4km (2.5mi) from the pre-Columbian site of Monte Alban, in a mountain valley at an altitude of 1,550m (5,160ft). The zone of historical monuments covers an area of 5 sq km (3sq mi) and holds 1,200 classified buildings, 242 of which are of primary importance. Monte Alban is a mountainous site and is separated from the city by a river. The site covers an area of 40sq km (16sq mi) with more than 100 tombs scattered at an altitude of 2,000m (6,600ft). Cuilapan, at the foot of Monte Alban, is an important complex of convents and basilicas.

SIGNIFICANCE   These excavations are one of the most extensive in all of Mesoamerica and have revealed an exceptionally long occupation dating from the 6th century BC up until the Spanish conquest. Initially the settlement was a residential as well as a ceremonial centre. In later years it became an important burial place. There is evidence that the early civilisation had systems of writing, numbers and a calendar – possibly the oldest in Mesoamerica.

Monte Alban

Sian Ka'an Barrier Reef

Temple of the Sun, Teotihuacan

PUEBLA (HISTORIC CENTRE) – CHOLULA

LOCATION   Capital of the state of Puebla, N 19° 02′, W 98° 15′.

DESCRIPTION   Puebla is a Spanish colonial city built in an area of fertile valleys. It is rich in religious and civil buildings from the 16th century. The cathedral on the hill of San Juan dominates the city. 18km (11mi) west of Puebla is the town of Cholula. It is remarkable for its gigantic pyramid in the centre of the modern town on top of which the Spanish built a chapel. The town counts numerous colonial civil and religious buildings as well, including the immense complex of the Franciscan convent of San Gabriel and its royal chapel.

SIGNIFICANCE   Puebla was founded in 1531, on a site reputedly chosen because of a dream had by Fray Julian Garcgs, of 2 angels walking along a beautiful plain flanked by 2 volcanoes. The architecture of the town is typically Spanish and comparable to Spain's famous fortified city of Toledo. One of the first permanent theatres in the Americas was established here – Teatra Principal.

Cholula is famed for its multitude of domed churches – by legend it was reputed to have a church for every day of the year. The pyramid in this town is remarkable for its sheer size – 54m (177ft) high and covering 18ha (43ac) at the base.

GUANAJUATO

LOCATION   Guanajuato State, Mexico, W 101° 15′, N 21° 01′.

DESCRIPTION   The town sprawls through a winding valley at an altitude of just over 2,000m (6,500ft). There are 4 fortifications which were erected for defence purposes. It is a picturesque town with distinctive architecture, including several 'subterranean' streets, many plazas, hospitals, churches and palaces.

SIGNIFICANCE   Spaniards settled in this area in 1529. They discovered silver deposits 19 years later. The township grew to its zenith in the 19th century when it was the world's most important silver mining area.

Aït-Ben-Haddou

MOROCCO

Morocco is the western most of the three Maghreb states of northern Africa (see Algeria and Tunisia). The history of its occupation dates back to Paleolithic times. Its indigenous people, the Berbers, are thought to have first arrived in the area around the time of the New Stone Age.

These people, who today still form the majority of Morocco's population, have a long and rich history along with a complex and diverse culture. A fiercely independent people, they are mentioned as the merchants who controlled the trans-Saharan trade in gold, ivory and salt, first doing business with the Phoenicians around the 9th century BC.

The coming of the Arabs in 682 AD, accompanied with Islam, changed the nature of society permanently. One of the Prophet Mohammed's fugitive descendants, Idris The Elder, united the Berbers into a kingdom which was to become known as the Moorish empire. His son, Idris II, founded Fez. In the 11th century, the Almoravide dynasty took control, their principal legacy being the founding of Marrakesh.

After a series of tribal revolts, this dynasty too was overthrown and replaced by the Almohads. This era was in many ways the zenith of Moroccan cultural development. At this time the empire embraced much of northern Africa and Spain. During the 16th century, neither Spain nor Turkey could gain control of Morocco where yet another successful dynasty was established – the Saadids: Morocco's present ruler, King Hassan, is descended from this dynasty.

Morocco ratified the World Heritage Convention in October 1975 and now has three sites on the list. Ait-Ben-Haddou is an ancient village site, while the Medinas of Fez and Marrakesh are both legacies of Morocco's glorious days of the Moorish empire.

AÏT-BEN-HADDOU

LOCATION   In the province of Uuarzazate, sub-Saharan region.

DESCRIPTION   This collection of monuments at Ait-Ben-Haddou represents an ancient village site. There are 6 main kasbahs or fortified residential buildings, plus a structure which is situated up on the hill overlooking the village. All of these buildings are constructed of bricks made from pounded earth.

SIGNIFICANCE   The unique geometric arrangement of the bricks at oblique angles and in zig zag patterns is distinctive of buildings in this region. These ruins at Ait-Ben-Haddou are the earliest surviving examples of this architectural style.

THE MEDINA OF FEZ

LOCATION   Approximately 160km (99.4mi) inland from the the Atlantic Coast, N 34° 06', W 04° 38'.

DESCRIPTION   This is a fortified medieval city spanning 10 centuries of history through military, religious and civil buildings. It is situated in a deep valley. There are 2 main zones, Andalusian and Qarawiyin, which are separated by the river Fez.

SIGNIFICANCE   Founded in 809 AD by Idriss II, the great Moorish king, the original settlement was divided into 2 zones – the Andalusian which was settled by Arab refugees from Spain and the Qarawiyin, settled by Arabs from Tunisia. The Qarawiyin zone houses the University Mosque, El Qarawiyin, the largest in Morocco. Its roof is supported by 366 pillars of stone. Fez flourished under the Merinid Dynasty and was the most important intellectual and religious centre in Morocco. With the expulsion of the Moors from Spain, refugees flocked to Fez bringing with them knowledge of the arts, sciences and manufacturing, thus encouraging students to utilize its extensive libraries. The colleges of Fez and Jadid, built in the 13th century to house foreign students are the purest examples of Spanish-Moorish art in Morocco.

THE MEDINA OF MARRAKESH

LOCATION   In a plain surrounded by the high Atlas Mountains, N 31° 36', W 08° 00'.

DESCRIPTION   The city is surrounded by high walls with 8 gates. The mosque of Koutoubia with its magnificent 7m (23ft) high minaret dominates the town. The Kasbah (citadel) includes many splendid palaces, a Great Mosque, a large market, the gates of Bag Agnoou and Bab Rob, and the ruins of the Al Badi Palace. Marrakesh is a city of gardens and famous for its palm groves dating back to the Almoravid Empire.

SIGNIFICANCE   Marrakesh was founded in 1062 AD by Yussef ibn Tashfin, ruler of the Almoravid Dynasty from 1062-1147 AD. He was responsible for introducing the irrigation canals which still supply the city's gardens with water. The city was destroyed by the Almohads in 1147. It was rebuilt and became the capital of the empire until its collapse in 1262. It was restored to its position as capital after the defeat of the Meriniclo by the Saadians in 1520. Marrakesh was restored to some of its former Moroccan brilliance in the arts by Monlay Hassan in 1873. The numerous monuments and buildings that now stand are important records of the major dynasties which shaped this great city.

Koutoubia Mosque, Marrakesh

The fortified Medieval city of Fez

Marrakesh

NEPAL

Nepal, one of the most scenic countries on earth, stretches across a third of the Himalayan chain. From this rectangular area of 147,181 sq km (56,516 sq mi) rise 1,300 peaks and pinnacles, twenty of which exceed 6,000 m (19,800 ft). Highest of all is mighty Sagarmartha (Mt Everest), rising 8,848 m (29,460 ft). This majestic peak is located within a 1,200 sq km (500 sq mi) park, known as Sagarmartha National Park. After Nepal accepted the World Heritage Convention in June 1978, this park became one of the country's three World Heritage sites.

The key word to describe every aspect of Nepal's natural and cultural heritage is diversity. From the alpine peaks of the Himalaya, the waters of three major river systems cascade down through countless deep valleys and gorges containing varied micro-climates and ecosystems, and sheltering an immense biological wealth of flora and fauna. The people form an ethnic mosaic whose diverse languages and traditions have survived for millenniums.

The highest Himalayan regions are covered with an Arctic tundra resembling the Tibetan Plateau. The slopes lower down, (4,800 to 3,000 m/16,000 to 9,990 ft) are forested with magnificent stands of fir, spruce, juniper, hemlock, birch, elm, maple and rhododendron. Temperate forests of chir pine, blue pine, oak and rhododendron cover the mid-mountains. Sal forests and grasslands dominate the plains of the Terai.

Nepal's unique position between two of the world's major geographic regions, the Paleoarctic Zone in the north, and the Oriental/Indo-Malayan Zone in the south, makes it a biological meeting place of an unusually high number of species. At least 100 mammals, 850 bird species and 120 fish species have been recorded. Musk deer, Himalayan thar, serow, blue sheep and snow leopards inhabit the high mountains. Large mammals – tigers, leopards, elephants, and wild water buffalo roam the lower landscape.

Nepal was first settled by migrants from both north and south, Tibeto-Burmans and Indo-Aryans. The earliest civilisations are recorded from about 800 BC to 300 AD, a succession of Kirat dynasties whose rich legacy of language and culture still endures.

Modern Nepal dates to the Shah dynasty whose first monarch, King Prithvi Narayan Shah, unified the many small principalities into a vast country that extended from Kashmir to Sikkim. An 1816 treaty with India trimmed the country to its present size. In 1846, the Shahs were replaced with an autocratic Rana regime that ended with the advent of constitutional monarchy in 1951. Four decades later, in 1991, Nepal's one-party panchayat system was replaced by an elected democratic government, under the constitutional reign of King Birendra Bir Bikram Shah Dev.

Historically, the political, economic and cultural life of Nepal converged in the Kathmandu Valley, where a wealth of artistic and architectural masterpieces have been preserved through the centuries. For this reason, Kathmandu has been named a World Heritage site.

The remaining World Heritage site is that of Chitwan National Park. Situated on the outer Himalaya, this park was established by King Mahendra in 1962 as a rhinoceros reserve and was in fact Nepal's first national park. It is now famous for its large mammals, including the extremely rare one-horned rhinoceros and the Bengal tiger.

Much of Nepal's rich artistic and natural heritage has been preserved into the 20th Century by the geographic isolation of the Himalaya, as well as the political isolation which was imposed by its leaders until 1951.

However, this unique heritage is now threatened in many ways: the pressure placed on natural resources by population growth; the decay of important architectural monuments and the exodus of valuable artworks from the country.

The major challenge facing Nepal today is to achieve a balance between old and new, preserving the best of the past while moving forward into the future. New technologies can be the key to meeting this challenge if they are used as a positive force to preserve the country's vast wealth of natural and cultural resources. The people of Nepal are grateful for the concern of organisations such as the World Heritage Committee, and their help in meeting this challenge.

MR B N UPRETI
Director General
Department of National Parks and Wildlife, Nepal

And up on the hillside it's quiet Where the shepherd is tending his sheep And over the mountains and the valleys The countryside is so green Standing on the highest hill with a sense of wonder You can see everything is made in God Head back down the roadside and give thanks for it all.

VAN MORRISON

Darbar Square, Kathmandu

One-horned rhinoceros, Chitwan National Park

CHITWAN NATIONAL PARK

LOCATION   Chitwan District, E 84° 20', N 27° 30'.

DESCRIPTION   The 932sq km (373sq mi) of this park are located in the 'Lowland Terai'. This comprises several river valleys and part of the Siwilak Range of the outer Himalayas. The climate of the park is its dominating feature, with dramatic monsoonal flooding regularly changing the landscape. The forest, grasslands and changing rivers make Chitwan one of the most attractive parts of Nepal's lowlands.

SIGNIFICANCE   The park is of prime significance in providing habitats for rare, threatened and endangered species. Its most outstanding feature is its fauna, with some 35 species of large mammals and over 350 bird species reported, one of the highest concentrations of bird species in the world. Some rare species of mammal include the one-horned rhinoceros and the Bengal tiger.

KATHMANDU VALLEY

LOCATION   Central Nepal, N 27° to 42°, E 85° 18'.

DESCRIPTION   The Kathmandu Valley, high in the Himalayan foothills, measures 25 by 19km (15.5 by 12mi). Within the valley there are 7 monument zones and over 130 monuments, comprising 61 temples, palaces, public squares, stupas and sacred sites.

SIGNIFICANCE   Throughout history, this small valley has been the political and cultural heart of Nepal. Religious art and architecture, both Buddhist and Hindu, document successive and competing political dynasties of the region. Monuments represent legendary and political history and are sites of veneration by both of the above religious groups. These include pilgrimage centres, shrines, bathing sites, rest houses and open gardens. Many decorations and bas-reliefs on temples can be dated back to the 6th century BC. The Hanuman Dhoku Palace is the current residence of H.M. King Birendra, the 10th ruler of the Shah Dynasty.

SAGARMATHA NATIONAL PARK

LOCATION   Solu – Khumbu district, E 86° 28' to 87° 07', N 27° 45' to 28° 07'.

DESCRIPTION   This park covers 1,244sq km (500sq mi) of dramatic mountain ranges, glaciers and deep valleys. The lowest point in the park is 2,845m (9,334ft) above sea level, the highest Sagarmatha itself, more commonly known as Mount Everest, which reaches 8,848m (29,029ft) above sea level.

SIGNIFICANCE   There are 7 peaks over 7,000m (22,966ft) high which form a 20km (12.4mi) long barrier. Crowning this massive block is the highest point on the earth's surface – Sagarmatha. As well as being an area of intense geological interest, this park contains an extremely distinctive array of flora and fauna, including juniper, fir and beech forests, several varieties of rhododendron, the musk deer, the snow leopard, the Himalayan black bear and the lesser panda. For the Sherpas, who live within the park, this area is of deep spiritual significance.

Kathmandu Valley

A Declaration on Environmental Ethics

PEACE AND SURVIVAL of life on Earth as we know it are threatened by human activities which lack a commitment to humanitarian values.

Destruction of nature and natural resources results from ignorance, greed and lack of respect for the Earth's living things.

This lack of respect extends even to Earth's human descendants, the future generations who will inherit a vastly degraded planet if world peace does not become a reality, and destruction of the natural environment continues at the present rate.

Our ancestors viewed the Earth as rich and bountiful, which it is. Many people in the past also saw nature as inexhaustibly sustainable, which we now know is the case only if we care for it.

It is not difficult to forgive destruction in the past which resulted from ignorance. Today however, we have access to more information, and it is essential that we re-examine ethically what we have inherited, what we are responsible for, and what we will pass on to coming generations.

Clearly this is a pivotal generation. Global communication is possible, yet confrontations more often than meaningful dialogues for peace take place.

Our marvels of science and technology are matched if not outweighed by many current tragedies, including human starvation in some parts of the world, and extinction of other life forms.

Exploration of outer space takes place at the same time as the Earth's own oceans, seas, and fresh water areas grow increasingly polluted, and their life forms are still largely unknown or misunderstood.

Many of the Earth's habitats, animals, plants, insects, and even micro-organisms that we know are rare may not be known at all by future generations. We have the capability and the responsibility. We must act before it is too late.

THIS MESSAGE, FROM HIS HOLINESS TENZIN GYATSO, *Fourteenth Dalai Lama of Tibet, is reprinted with the kind permission of Buddhist Perception of Nature.*

Most of the world's human population have yet to realise that conservation is an essential element of human progress in economics, development, sustainable yields of food, in short the very life support systems of our planet.
SIR PETER SCOTT

NEW ZEALAND

'The islands of New Zealand are a remarkable biological storehouse, with so much of the biota having an ancestry on the supercontinent of Gondwanaland 200 to 150 million years ago.'

Les Molloy,
The Ancient Islands (1982).

'The biotas of New Zealand and Madagascar are the closest we shall ever come to observing the products of continental evolution in island-like isolation, unless we discover higher life on another planet.'

Jared Diamond,
New Zealand as an Archipelago (1990).

The contribution of New Zealand to the world's heritage can be summed up most simply in the word 'isolation'. They are probably the largest group of islands to have long remained isolated from continental land masses, in their case for the last 80 million years. Consequently, this cargo of southern plants and animals followed a distinctive evolutionary path in the absence of more advanced life forms, particularly the mammals (both carnivores and herbivores) which proliferated in the southern continents of Australia, Africa and South America.

New Zealand is a natural history paradox in that its ancient biota survived in one of the most dynamic and mobile sectors of the globe, the south-western terminus of the 'Pacific Ring of Fire'. For here the Pacific and Indian-Australian plates are continually grinding past, or over, each other – pushing up the great wall of the Southern Alps, plunging into the depths of Kermadec Trench, and giving rise to the continuous volcanic activity of the rift known as the Taupo Volcanic Zone.

This theme of isolation extended, surprisingly, to isolation from human habitation until a mere 1200 years ago with the arrival from the Pacific of the Polynesian seafarers known as the Maori. Their Aotearoa was the last major temperate land which had to adjust to the impact of human settlers.

To date, New Zealand has two World Heritage sites – Te Wa'hipounamu (South-west New Zealand) and Tongariro – which are very different in physical character. Yet, each reflects the ancient/youthful paradox and each is of great spiritual significance to the *tangata whenua*, the Maori 'people of the land'.

Te Wāhipounamu (Southwest New Zealand)

Tongariro National Park

Te Wāhipounamu (South-west New Zealand)

'Te Wāhipounamu' is an old Maori word meaning 'The Place of the Greenstone', reflecting the importance of this huge wilderness to the early Ngai Tahu people as a source of the beautiful hard green nephrite, *pounamu*. This stone was prized for tools, weapons and ornaments, bestowing prestige and wealth within a neolithic society.

The south-west of the South Island of New Zealand is a vast uninhabited wilderness of forests, fiords, glaciers and coastal wetlands; at 2.6 million hectares (6.5 million acres) it covers 10% of the area of New Zealand and is one of the world's larger natural heritage sites. Many of its outstanding landscapes are international tourist features – Mt Cook and the Southern Alps; Milford Sound, Mitre Peak and the Sutherland Falls in Fiordland; Lakes Te Anau and Manapouri; and the Franz Josef, Fox and Tasman Glaciers.

Three national parks – Fiordland, Westland and Mt Cook – make up 50% of the area and were designated World Heritage sites in 1986. In many quarters, however, they were considered to be only key parts of the great South-West heritage site concept; the eventual goal was the designation of the most complete Gondwanaland heritage site. This became a possibility in 1989 with two far-reaching decisions by the New Zealand government: to foreclose logging and strictly protect the 300,000 ha (750,000 acres) of South Westland rainforest as conservation land, and to incorporate the ecologically-important (but mineral-rich) Red Mountain area into Mt Aspiring National Park. The coastal lagoons and lowland rainforests of South Westland, and the mountainous wilderness of Mt Aspiring National Park, were the final key pieces to the South-West concept which was accepted as a World Heritage site in December, 1990.

Te Wāhipounamu was accepted as World Heritage value on all four natural property criteria:

- It illustrates major stages in the Earth's evolutionary history with the upthrust of the 3000m (10,000ft) high Southern Alps and over 200km (124mi) of the Alpine Fault dramatically marking the plate boundary; with its Gondwanaland plant and animal heritage, especially the great podocarp forests of rimu and kahikatea trees, considered to most closely approximate the great swamp forests of the Mesozoic; and the ubiquitous imprint of Pleistocene glaciation.

- It has outstanding examples of ongoing ecological processes (such as changes to modern day glaciers, plant succession on surfaces exposed by glacial retreat) and biological evolution (such as the high degree of endemism – 93% – in the extensive alpine flora, and its rapid evolutionary development through hybridism).

- Areas of exceptional natural beauty have already been listed. Furthermore, tourism has not been allowed to detrimentally affect the overwhelming naturalness and wilderness character of the area.

- The area is the habitat of a number of rare and endangered species, including birds such as the takahe, brown kiwi and kakapo.

Overall, Te Wāhipounamu is a natural heritage of great contrasts and surprises: it is one of the wettest and windiest areas on the globe yet there is a pronounced 'rainshadow' in the montane basins of the east; near the Franz Josef and Fox Glaciers luxuriant tree ferns grow close by glacial ice; the red (ultramafic) rock of the Red Mountain area starkly contrasts with the silver beech forest on the adjacent schist rock of the Olivine Range; glaciers (like that on Mt Pembroke in Milford Sound) exist only 5km (3mi) from the sea; the remarkable silver beech (*Nothofagus menzesii*), a tree that can dominate the forest at both sea level and the timber line 100m (333ft) above on the steep walls of the fiords; whereas most parrots are associated with warm climates and tropical forests, the kea inhabits the alpine region, delighting visitors with its cheeky amusing antics; the enigmatic 'beech gap' – the absence of beech forest from 200km (124mi) of the forested lowlands of the West Coast; the contrast between the gentle slope of the flights of uplifted marine terraces in the Waitutu sector of Fiordland compared with the sheer rock walls of the fiords; and the enigma of the greatest variety of plants growing in the harshest climatic area – the alpine zone.

Tongariro National Park

Ko Tongariro te maunga
Ko Taupo to moana
Ko Tuwharetoa te iwi
Ko Te Heu Heu te tangata

Tongariro is the mountain
Taupo is the sea
Tuwharetoa are the people
Te Heu Heu is the man

[Proverb of Ngati Tuwharetoa people]

Tongariro National Park lies in the centre of the North Island. Its 80,000ha (200,000 acres) encompasses the three main volcanic cones – Ruapehu (at 2800m (9300ft), the highest point in the North Island), Tongariro and Ngauruhoe – and three smaller outlying volcanoes, Pihanga, Kakaramea and Tihia, to the north-east. The volcanoes of the park dominate the landscape, rising abruptly from the southern shores of Lake Taupo, the huge caldera left by the Taupo eruption of around 1800 years ago – possibly the most powerful volcanic eruption ever documented. The enormous Taupo eruption ejected over 60 times the volume of tephras compared with the well-documented 1980 Mt St Helens eruption; its effect was so global that its atmospheric influence was noted in Chinese and Roman writings of that time and Taupo ash has been found in ice deposits in Antarctica.

Tongariro National Park is a joint natural/cultural heritage site. The natural significance of the park lies in the unique features of the two outstanding andesitic stratovolcanoes – Mt Ruapehu and the Tongariro/Ngauruhoe complex. Along with the island volcano of White Island 50km (31 mi) off-shore in the Bay of Plenty, these two are the most continuously active stratovolcanoes in the world.

The international cultural importance of Tongariro National Park is that it was the first national park to be freely gifted to a nation by the indigenous owners, in this case the Ngati Tuwharetoa tribe who trace their ancestry back to a famous ancestor, Ngatoro-i-rangi, the tohunga (scientist/priest) who arrived on the Te Arawa canoe when it made its landfall at Maketu estuary in the Bay of Plenty. It was his descendant, Te Heu Heu (Horonuku) who gifted the summits of Tongariro, Ngauruhoe and Ruapehu to the New Zealand Government in September 1887 to protect these sacred mountains from exploitation. This was the nucleus of New Zealand's first national park – only the fourth national park in the world.

To the Tuwaharetoa people the volcanoes have deep spiritual significance. They look upon the mountains as ancestors and symbols of the authority of nature. This relationship is commemorated in tribal songs and sayings, like the proverb quoted in introducing this site. Furthermore, Tongariro mountain is synonymous with the security and strength of the Maori people in the present-day Arawa and Ngati Tuwharetoa tribes who trace their ancestry back to the great Te Arawa canoe:

The death of a high chief is likened to the tip of a mountain having broken off the stern anchor of the Arawa Canoe. Te Rangi Haruru or Toka Turua is firmly fixed on Tongariro with the prow anchor, 'Toka Parore', firmly fixed at Maketu giving rise to the saying 'Mai Maketu Ki Tongariro', inferring thereby its unshakeable stability. All these are paid tributes to the mountains.

K.P. Mariu, Tuwharetoa Elder

Dr. L.F. Molloy

TE WĀHIPOUNAMU (SOUTHWEST NEW ZEALAND)

LOCATION   Southland, Otago, Westland and Canterbury districts of the South Island, E 166 00′ to 170 00′, S 43 00′ to 46 35′.

DESCRIPTION   This massive park covers around 2.6 million ha (6.2 million ac). It is an amalgamation of the previous sites of Fiordland and Mt. Cook/Westland National Parks, as well as incorporating Mt. Aspiring National Park and a large area of former State forest. The landscape varies tremendously; it includes the deeply indented, glacially cut mountains of Fiordland, more than 450km (280mi) of largely isolated coastland, 28 of New Zealand's 29 mountain peaks over 3,000m (9,842ft), 3 of the most spectacular glaciers to be found anywhere – Franz Josef, Fox and Tasman, sand dunes and rocky estuaries. The vegetation includes evergreen temperate rainforest, alpine tussock grasslands, herbfields, fellfields, wetlands and bogs. Fauna comprises mainly birds and invertebrates, many of which are endemic.

SIGNIFICANCE   Southwest New Zealand covers almost 10 percent of the total land mass of New Zealand and it is the 10 percent of the country which is least modified by human influences. The area demonstrates the world's finest remaining examples of Gondwana flora and fauna in their natural habitats. Distinctive flora, such as the extensive forests of southern beech and podocarps, are all a reflection of this ancient Gondwana origin and New Zealand's 80 million year isolation. The fauna is likewise distinctive. Most notable are 2 species of kiwis, the kea – the world's only alpine parrot, its forest relative, the kaka and the rail or takahe – a rare and endangered flightless bird which is now confined to a limited area of Fiordland.

TONGARIRO NATIONAL PARK

LOCATION   Tongariro and Wanganui regions, North Island, S 38° 58′ to 39° 25′, E 175° 22′ to 175° 48′.

DESCRIPTION   Covering 795 sq km (300sq mi), this park is situated on the central volcanic plateau of the North Island. The altitude ranges from 500m (1,665ft) to 2,797m (9,314ft) at Mount Tongariro – the highest peak in the North Island. Both glacial and volcanic landscapes are to be found, and the vegetation includes tussock/grassland and forests of hardwood and beech. There are three ski fields within the park, although the area affected by tourism covers only 2% of the total area.

SIGNIFICANCE   This area is linked with the arrival of the first Maoris from the Pacific. The name 'Tongariro' is derived from 'Tonga', meaning 'fire', and 'riro', meaning 'carried away'. These sacred mountain tops were given to the New Zealand Government in 1887 and formed the nucleus of New Zealand's first national park. This extensive natural area also has strong ecological significance. There is a long history of volcanism in the area, which is still active today. This has produced a diverse range of ecosystems and highly scenic landscapes which are invaluable from both scientific and aesthetic viewpoints.

The Southwest New Zealand area is the 10 per cent of the country least modified by human influences and, because of this, it best demonstrates the world's remaining examples of Gondwana biota in their natural habitats.

A. F. MARK

UNESCO's Valuable, but Fragile Creation

THE IDEA OF A CONVENTION which would protect on a global level the natural and cultural heritage of the planet has excited and inspired many who have an interest in stopping the madness of the all-pervasive unsustainable development ethic. The Convention Concerning the Protection of the World Cultural and Natural Heritage, to give the World Heritage Convention its full name, was adopted by the General Conference of UNESCO in November 1972. The euphoria of the 'Stockholm Conference' – the United Nations Conference on the Human Environment, held in June that year – was still fresh in the minds of the public and negotiators alike. In that respect, 1972 can be seen as the year in which the world 'discovered' the need to protect the environment, and began to develop practical measures to achieve that.

As a tool to protect natural ecosystems from human depredation, however, the convention has had little direct influence because ultimate control over the ecosystems still remains with the state on whose territory they lie. In practice, effective protection of ecosystems needs to be provided at a national or regional level. Further, the convention does not in itself prohibit any kind of activities. However, it does play an important role in assisting states which have World Heritage sites on their territories, but which lack finance or technical expertise, to manage these sites in a way which will ensure their integrity is maintained. It also provides an important symbolic protection for these sites.

The convention has been very successful, in that 337 properties, including sites of both natural and cultural values, have been inscribed on the World Heritage List up to December 1990. Many of these sites represent extremely important ecosystems which have benefited from the recognition afforded by the convention.

There had been some severe political difficulties, however. In 1981, Jordan nominated the Old City of Jerusalem and its Walls for World heritage designation. Israel had occupied a substantial area of Jordanian territory, including East Jerusalem, in the Six Day War of 1967. Almost immediately afterwards the city was integrated into Israel. In July 1980 Israel passed legislation which declared that Jerusalem should forever be the undivided capital of Israel. Jordan's 'mistake' was to nominate territory that was not under its effective control, and which Israel considered to be an integral part of the Israeli state.

The ensuing debate nearly paralysed the organisation, which had to conduct an 'extraordinary session' to resolve the issue. A majority of the World Heritage Committee, the decision making body, voted in favour of listing the site, but a number of states abstained. The United States was alone in opposing the nomination. Israel was not a party to the convention, and so was ineligible for membership of the committee, and unable to take part in the decision.

The idea of nominating the entire continent of Antarctica for listing has also been canvassed, but has never been formally put to the committee. Many environmentalists feel that such a listing would give an important symbolic protection to the continent. The idea was also raised during the discussions on the Antarctic Minerals Convention (CRAMRA) by the Soviet Union, as an option in the event of the failure of those talks. However, the idea was not taken seriously by other states.

The difficulties which would need to be surmounted to achieve an Antarctic nomination are an illustration of the political weakness of the convention. A party to the Antarctic treaty would be unlikely to rock the boat by unilaterally making a nomination, as extreme diplomatic pressure would be brought to bear against any such state on the grounds that it would severely undermine the 'accommodation' with respect to Antarctic sovereignty that the Antarctic treaty itself provides. However, few states outside the Antarctic treaty have enough knowledge of the Antarctic to put forward a serious nomination and management plan for the continent.

Further, an Antarctic nomination would, like that of the Old City of Jerusalem, severely test the convention. Seven countries claim territory in Antarctica, and five of these territorial claims, those of the United Kingdom, France, Australia, New Zealand and Norway, are mutually recognised. However, the other claims, those of Argentina and Chile, overlap, not only with each other but also with the United Kingdom claim. The 39-member Antarctic treaty itself has political difficulties justifying its stewardship of the Antarctic in forums such as the United Nations, where there is a substantial segment of opinion that the Antarctic should form part of the common heritage of mankind.

Once sites are listed on the World Heritage List, there are no guarantees that their futures are secure, however, since the effective control of sites can become a political issue at a national level. One of the most controversial examples of this type involved south-west Tasmania. After a large wilderness area was approved as a World Heritage site, the State of Tasmania proposed to build a dam in the Franklin River which would have resulted in the flooding of a considerable part of the site. It required a considerable public outcry, campaigning by non-government organisations and a court battle to ensure the future of the site. The site was further enhanced by the approval of a substantial

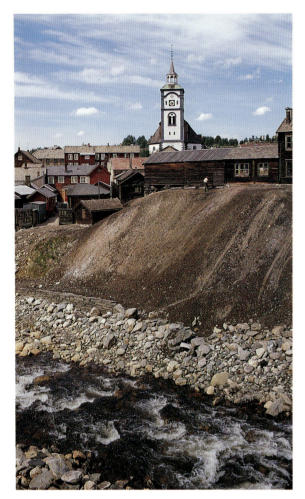

Røros

extension by the World Heritage Committee in 1989.

Finance for the convention is also a problem. The committee relies for a large part on the contributions of the parties to the convention to fund the operation of the convention. Contributions cannot always be relied on, even from wealthy states. For example, the United States Congress removed all funding for the World Heritage Convention from the National Park Service budget in 1981. Under heavy lobbying pressure from non-governmental organisations, the funding was restored in 1985. However, control of the budget was then given to the State Department, the foreign affairs arm of the Administration. This gives the potential, at least, for the United States position on the convention to be politicised in a way which was unlikely under the National Park Service.

In sum, the World Heritage Convention is an enormously valuable, but fragile creation. Its success is dependent not only on financial resources being made available but also on the goodwill of states toward each other. Most of all, however, its success is dependent on a commitment by individual states to take the first step towards protecting their own heritage.

ROGER WILSON
Director,
Treaties and Conventions Division
Greenpeace International

NORWAY

Norway, as the name of the country indicates, is situated where the roads of European culture meet in the north. It is a long, narrow and mountainous country reaching well into the Arctic circle. Its sea coast measures 2,650km (1640mi), but the actual coastline measures over 21,000km (13,000mi) when the fjords and islands are included. Inland, the country is dominated by steep mountains, isolated valleys, barren mountain plateaux, forests and glaciers. These special geographical conditions have also played a part in the selection of the four Norwegian monuments on UNESCO's World Heritage List, which cover the cultural history of the country from prehistoric times through the Middle Ages and onto the eighteenth century.

The most northerly monument is the great area of rock carvings at Alta, lying at 70°N. Discovered in 1973, more than 3,000 carvings have now been recorded singly or in groups over an area of 30,000 sq m (36,000 sq yd), including reindeer, moose, bears, birds, human figures and boats. The carvings are grouped into four phases: 4200-3600 BC, 3600-2600 BC, 2600-1700 BC, and 1700-500 BC, on the basis of stylistic changes and their altitude, which reflects the changing height of the shore line due to the post-glacial land rise. An important feature is the evidence for social organisation, shown in the scenes of reindeer hunting, with animals being driven towards fenced areas.

The area is partly in state ownership, and partly private. The Ministry of Environment is in the process of purchasing the whole area of 460,000 sq m (550,000 sq yd) and converting it to an open-air museum.

The medieval stave-church at Urnes is situated on an inner arm of Sognefjord, Norway's longest fjord, standing proudly on a headland jutting out into the fjord. Surrounded by high mountains, the community at Urnes would not have been as isolated in the Middle Ages when communication was mainly by water, as it was later on.

Norwegian stave-churches have their origins in the early wooden architecture of Europe, but represent a particular structural development. The corner posts, or 'staves', stand on sole plates and are joined together at the top by wall plates to form a rigid framework. A similar construction of lower height runs around three or four sides of the central structure, and there is also often a low external pentice. The external walls are formed

The waterfront at Bryggen

by vertical boards slotted into grooves in the top and bottom beams.

Of the 29 medieval stave-churches which have survived in Norway, Urnes is thought to be the earliest. The present building dates from the second half of the twelfth century. Re-used material, including wall-planks and a doorway with intricately carved decoration, indicates that an earlier stave-church stood at the same place a century before. Archaeological excavations have confirmed this. The chancel was extended around 1600 and in 1709 the roof turret was altered.

Bryggen – the wharf – in Bergen lies on the eastern shore of the bay which forms the harbour and comprises a dense group of wooden buildings in long parallel rows running up from the waterfront. The oldest surviving buildings date from the early eighteenth century, but the history of Bryggen can be traced back to the time of the sagas. Extensive archaeological excavations have shown that the site was built up in the eleventh century, which agrees with the alleged foundation of the city by King Olav Kyrre in 1070. Bryggen was totally destroyed by fire on several occasions during the Middle Ages and after each fire the built-up area was extended further out into the bay. However, the main structure of Bryggen was always maintained with the buildings erected gable to gable in double rows with a central passage.

Until about 1300 Bryggen was owned mainly by members of the Norwegian nobility, who controlled the overseas trade. After this hegemony had been taken over by the Hanse in the late Middle Ages, German merchants who spent the winter in Bergen began first to rent and later to buy premises, so that Bryggen eventually became a Hanseatic colony with almost extra-territorial rights. The German Office, or Comptoir, at Bryggen outlived the Hanseatic League. It existed officially until 1754, when it was succeeded by Det Norske Kontor (The Norwegian Office), which was founded by merchants of German extraction and survived until 1898.

A great fire in 1955 destroyed a third of the standing buildings and this led to the most extensive urban archaeological investigation in Norway. Remains of medieval buildings found during excavation are incorporated into a modern museum on the site, which also houses all the finds from the excavations.

The copper mining town of Røros lies in central Norway, 160km (100mi) south-east of Trondheim. Copper ore was discovered by chance in 1644 and Europe's most northerly mining town soon grew up on the forested highland plateau, 600m (1980ft) above sea level. In 1678-79 it was destroyed by fire and the present town dates from the 1680s with timber buildings occupying square plots along two parallel main streets. The upper end of the town is dominated by the church and the vast slag heaps from the smelting works. The copper mining and smelting

'German Wharf' at Bryggen

industry finally ceased in 1977, but the smelting works have recently been restored as a museum and some of the mines are also open to the public.

The typical Røros citizen was a unique combination of farmer and miner. This is reflected in the development of the properties with a dwelling house facing the street and with stables, byres and other outbuildings appropriate to a farm, grouped around a courtyard behind. Until the mid-18th century the dwelling house was a simple one-storey log building, but most now have two storeys and are clad in weatherboarding. Pastureland near the town was kept for hay-growing in the summer and the cattle were put out to pasture further away. There are still meadows close to the town.

These first four Norwegian monuments on the World Heritage List span 6,000 years in time and represent widely differing aspects of our cultural history. It is natural for us now to consider our unique geographical situation and to ask ourselves whether the Norwegian fjord landscape with apparently unapproachable farms and settlements clinging to sheer mountainsides is not worthy of a place on the World Heritage list.

STEPHAN TSCHUDI-MADSEN
Director of Historic Monuments and Sites, Norway
Former President of ICOMOS Council

Our Only Heaven

BLUE IS our only heaven
Green is our only earth
Our only future is dark
And now is for making our mark.

We know all we need and more
Of the folly of bygone days:
They chopped down forests with axes
And topsoil was washed off and blew away:
All for a short-lived profit
Leaving the scars
To which we are heirs.

We know all we need and more
About using more dangerous tools
But our folly matches theirs.
We don't want to know that gains
Can be losses in future years,
That prosperity can cause pains
And success can poison our heirs.

We don't want to see
That piling more riches on riches
Impoverishes the earth.
We don't want to hear
The future weeping
Through riot and mirth.

Borrowing, buying and selling
In markets run by thieves
We are robbing ourselves and humanity's home:
No sponsors pay to see
A lake, a peak, a tree.

But ever-approaching desert sand
Will force us to understand
That time is short, time is short.
Every night marks the death of a day
And the trial begins tomorrow.

All of us are guilty
No one can go free
What will our legacy be?

Blue is our only heaven
Green is our only earth.
Our only future is dark
And now is for making our mark!

Sidsel Morck

SIDSEL MORCK
Translated by Peter Bilton
This poem was originally written for a Norwegian TV
documentary on the Brundtland Commission.

Urnes Stave Church

BRYGGEN

LOCATION   City of Bergen, E 05° 19', N 60° 23'.

DESCRIPTION   The Bryggen area is found on the eastern shore of the old harbour of Bergen. The 58 remaining buildings represent only about a quarter of the original settlement. Most of them are 3 storeyed timber houses which stand in slightly curved parallel rows, perpendicular to the harbour shore.

SIGNIFICANCE   Archaeological evidence dates this site back to the 12th century. It is extremely likely, however, that it dates back further to the foundation of Bergen, thought to be in 1070 by King Olar Kyrre. Fires destroyed many buildings in 1198, 1248, 1476 and 1702. Each time the buildings were reconstructed, they increased in size a little but retained their traditional features.

ROCK DRAWINGS OF ALTA

LOCATION   Alta Municipality, E 23° 12', N 69° 55'.

DESCRIPTION   These rock drawings and carvings are located in 5 areas. The carvings, most of which are 20 to 40cm (8 to 16in) across, are of reindeer and moose, humans, other animals, birds, boats, pattern lines and dots. There are more than 3,000 carvings, and 15 red-brown paintings between 2,700-2,400 years old.

SIGNIFICANCE   The oldest carvings date back to 6,000 years. Along with the paintings, they provide a crucial key to the understanding of ancient rock art. Excavations to prehistoric settlements adjacent to the sites have uncovered tools and materials which would have been used for the carvings and paintings.

A Viking ship and reindeer at Alta

RØROS

LOCATION   Municipality of Røros, E 11° 23′, N 62° 35′.

DESCRIPTION   This heavily populated town comprises 3 major streets and several interesting narrow side streets which cross the river over numerous bridges. The buildings resemble compact farmhouses and are constructed to face the street. Some 80 buildings are protected by law.

SIGNIFICANCE   Mining and smelting activity commenced in Røros in 1644 and continued uninterrupted for 333 years until 1977. The community evolved slowly and many of the early 17th century buildings have survived remarkably well. Residential and commercial structures from the 18th, 19th and early 20th centuries are also in an excellent state of preservation, presenting a representative cross section of changing architectural styles throughout the centuries.

URNES STAVE CHURCH

LOCATION   Municipality of Luster, E 07° 02′, N 61° 18′.

DESCRIPTION   An entirely wooden structure, much of the timber within the church is intricately carved. The portal, shaped like a keyhole contains a carved decoration of interlaced fighting animals. The walls are covered with paintings, scrolls, architectural motifs and carved apostles all dating back to 1601.

SIGNIFICANCE   Urnes Staves Church was built in the second half of the 12th century and is the oldest and best preserved of Norway's 30 surviving stave churches. Much of the timber used to construct it came from a structure about 100 years older. Some of this reused material is adorned with exceptionally fine wood carving, giving rise to the term 'Urnes style'.

OMAN

Oman lies on the south-eastern corner of the Arabian peninsular. It is a hot and dry country, the landscape ancient and extremely rocky, mountainous and rugged. The highest point is Jabal Akhdar, at 3,060 metres (10,200 ft) above sea level. There are many fertile valleys to be found in between the steps of the remnant mountain block. The *wadis* are a unique feature of the landscape; they are deeply gouged channels which remain dry most of the year and provide routes into the largely inaccessible interior.

The people of Oman are mainly of Arabian and Negro lineage. Arabic is the official language and Islam the official religion. Muscat is the capital and the main harbour. This city was in Portuguese hands for 150 years from the beginning of the 16th century until the coming of Ahmed ibn Sa'id, a descendant of the powerful Yemenite imams.

The history of this region dates back to the 3rd millennium BC, as is witnessed by the World Heritage site of Bat, Al-Khutm and Al-ayn. Oman accepted the World Heritage Convention in October 1981 and has one other site on the list, that of Bahla Fort. This old fortified complex was once the country's capital.

BAT, AL-KHUTM AND AL-AYN (ARCHAEOLOGICAL SITES)

LOCATION   In the proximity of the village of Bat, 30km (18.5mi) from Ibri, E 56° 30′, N 23° 14′.

DESCRIPTION   There are three separate archaeological zones within this listing: (1) Just to the north of Bat, there are the remains of a settlement and of a necropolis. The settlement is comprised of five stone towers and a series of rectangular houses. The necropolis is in two parts; (i) a series of stone tombs scattered along a rocky slope, and; (ii) a much more densely concentrated collection of 'bee hive' style stone tombs. (2) The tower of Al-Khutm, 2 km (1.2 mi) west of Bat. (3) Another group of 'bee hive' tombs at Al-Ayn, 21 km (13 mi) south east of Bat.

SIGNIFICANCE   These sites date back to the 3rd millennium BC when the area was an important source of stone and copper for Mesopotamia. Some of the tombs in particular, are remarkably well preserved and excavations in this area have proved to be crucial to the understanding of the early history of the Arabian peninsula.

Bahla Fort

BAHLA FORT

LOCATION   Sultanate of Oman,

DESCRIPTION   Bahla Fort has a fortified wall, about 12km (7.5mi) long, which encloses the various quarters of the town, as well as most of its cultivated land. In the centre lies a large fortified compound, containing a castle with towers which rise 50m (164ft) above the surrounding plain. Most of the compound is constructed of clay and straw.

SIGNIFICANCE   Bahla Fort at various times in the past was the capital of the country. Parts of the vast castle date from pre-Islamic times and were probably originally Persian in construction. The surrounding walls and the large cultivated areas they enclose, are reminiscent of Sumerian cities like the city of Gilgamesh in Iraq. Ibidism, which is strangely confined to Oman and north west Africa, has its deepest roots here.

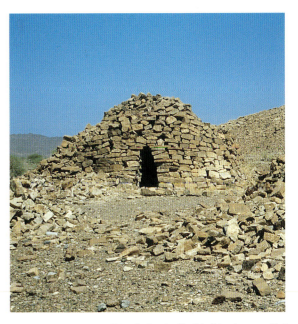

The distinctive 'beehive' tombs near Bat

Sustainable Development and the Role of World Heritage

SUSTAINABLE DEVELOPMENT is one of the buzz-words of the late 20th century, coined to express concern that past forms of development may not have been sustainable, and may have been leading instead to long-term depletion of the resources that people require to survive. But people still need the resources, and development is the top priority for many governments. What to do?

Governments recognize that as demands for development expand, the renewable and locally available biological resources and the knowledge of how to use these resources sustainably, will be more important than ever. Some governments are hoping that World Heritage will provide them a mechanism for utilizing this information now and in the future.

One of the foundations of World Heritage is that natural resources need to be conserved to enable humanity to adapt to our changing environment, both physically and psychologically. The amount of biodiversity that will be available to adapt to changes in human population, global chemistry, climate, and so forth is ultimately a question of values, which puts it into the political arena. Ecologists and other scientists working in World Heritage sites need to present their findings in a form which will help politicians and the general public make wise decisions. They should then be ready to provide the technologies that will be required to implement the political decisions that are taken.

Many of the issues that require new policies do not await new scientific discovery. Nor do they stand apart from the larger set of problems that

The Great Bath, Moenjodaro

need urgent attention during the coming decade if society is to avoid large-scale problems in health, nutrition, sanitation, security and peace. While conservation is thus one element of a larger package, it helps to ensure the continued availability of biodiversity; the fundamental resource base upon which human life and the ecological functioning of the biosphere depend. Conserving biodiversity is not a North or a South problem: it relates to everyone's backyard. The environment reaches across both land and sea. It is both a local and a global challenge.

As concerns about sustainability and loss of biodiversity are increasingly voiced, both by governments and the mass media, World Heritage is seen increasingly as an important part of a vigorous global response to these issues.

Organizations around the world, both governmental and non-governmental, are increasingly aware of the threats posed by unsustainable forms of development leading to loss of biodiversity. Governments are passing new legislation, establishing new protected areas, and making greater investments in managing natural resources. Scientists are discovering new ways of utilizing biodiversity for human benefit. Non-government organizations are raising public awareness, and relating conservation to a broad range of public concerns. Community groups are actively conserving traditional seed varieties, planting indigenous trees, defending their rights to manage traditional common-property resources and seeking ways to make their voices heard in the halls of government. The combined influence of public support, scientific evidence and government programmes is now demonstrating that real change is possible. The concept of living in balance with renewable resources is gaining acceptance in all parts of the world. The challenge of the 1990s is to convert the image of World Heritage into a practical reality.

JEFFREY A. McNEELY
Chief Conservation Officer IUCN

PAKISTAN

Pakistan is the inheritor of a unique cultural phenomenon taking its initiation in the Paleolithic Age some two million years ago. Evidence of cultural activities has been found in the Potowar Plateau in the shape of crude stone implements which prehistoric man used for hunting animals. The evidence of the initial stage of organised social living in the seventh millennium BC based on an agricultural economy, was first found at Mehrgarh in the Kacchi Plains of Baluchistan Province.

Pakistan was the homeland of the Bronze Age civilisation generally referred to as the Indus by the archaeologists. It extended for well over a thousand years (between 2750 and 1750 BC). Harappa in Punjab and Moenjodaro in Singh were the biggest and most spectacular centres of this civilisation.

There is a gap in our knowledge between the fall of the Indus civilisation and the advent of the historic period which has been partially filled by the discovery of the 'Gandhara Grave Culture' in the northern areas of Pakistan.

The dawn of history in ancient Pakistan begins with the Achaemenian period. The Macedonian invasion led by Alexander the Great in 325 BC is, likewise, a significant event which served as a catalyst in the process of cultural fusion of the East and West in ancient Pakistan. The impetus given to Buddhists by the Mauryan Emperor, Asoka, and the artistic impulses emanating later on, led to the fruition of Gandhara Art under the patronage of the Kushans and their successors up to the fourth century AD.

The decline of the Greco-Buddhist culture in ancient Pakistan resulted in the revival of Brahmanism, although Buddhism continued in a much weaker form.

The first impulses of Islam were actually felt in the north-western regions of this sub-continent almost immediately after its stabilisation in the Arabian peninsula. However, its real impact was witnessed a little later when the sea-port of Debul was attacked and reduced by an energetic young Arab General, Muhammad ibn Al-Qasim at the close of the first century Hijra (711-12 AD).

The next wave in Islamic culture came from Central Asia through the military excursions of the Ghaznavids and Ghuris in the 10th and the early decades of the 11th century AD. A new and distinct style of architecture was introduced and perpetuated through the buildings of this period.

The vast cemetery at Thatta

The sixteenth century saw yet another power at the socio-political scene of the sub-continent. In 1526 Zaheeruddin Mohammad Babar from Farghana defeated the Lodi troops at Panipat and established the Mughal Empire. These Emperors introduced a much refined socio-cultural pattern mainly based and influenced by Iranian cultural traditions. During this period a large number of important monuments were built.

For the preservation and maintenance of our glorious cultural heritage a Department of Archaeology was set up immediately after the establishment of Pakistan. We have as many as 375 archaeological sites and historical monuments protected by the Government of Pakistan under an Act of Parliament. Out of these, the five most outstanding sites are inscribed on UNESCO's World Heritage List.

OMAR KHAN AFRIDI
Secretary, Ministry of Culture & Tourism

Star of the Punjab

I SAW LAHORE, star of the Punjab, at night, and took its soul unawares. The birds were roosting in the shadow of the banyan trees. The pellucid notes of a sitar were heard, and suddenly a flute joined in.

According to the books, and to hearsay, Lahore is the most beautiful city in Pakistan. The Indus makes the plain of the Punjab gleam with its tributaries, which from earliest Antiquity have brought life and cultural riches with them. Here at this fertile crossroads Lahore was born and grew, to become a key administrative, religious and business centre.

Lahore lies on a secondary track of the Silk Road, and is watered by the River Ravi. It assumed its importance in the eleventh century, when it became the capital of the sultans of Rhazni. After a long period of turmoil, destruction and short-lived rulers it became in the sixteenth and seventeenth centuries one of the great cities of Mogul India.

Babur, founder of the Mogul empire, made it a star of the first order: under the Mogul dynasty Lahore was adorned with buildings that now form a splendid legacy.

I walked to the moonlit red sandstone Fort. Founded, according to legend, by Prince Loth, son of Rama, it was rebuilt in the sixteenth century by Babur's descendant Akbar and embellished by his son Jahangir and his grandson Shah Jahan. The twenty or so buildings contained within its ramparts afford an excellent picture of the development of Mogul art over nearly two centuries. Audience chambers and mosques, princely apartments, royal baths and pavilions are disposed around gardens, terraces and ornamental ponds.

I dreamed a while in the Naulakha, a small marble pavilion encrusted with semi-precious stones in floral and geometrical designs. I left the Fort by the Elephant Passage (Hathi Paer); and as I stood in front of the mosaics on the enclosure wall my imagination for a moment conjured up the festivities and pleasures of the court, the elephant and camel contests, and the polo games. Nowadays, in the dry moat, men in dazzlingly white cotton scythe the grass, as though to obliterate the passage of time.

I saw the sun rise over Lahore, and the rosy droplets in the dawn, when the faithful come home from prayers. I saw the sun light up the Shalimar Gardens – the famous 'Garden of Love' laid out by Shah Jahan himself in 1642. He had a canal dug to bring water from the Ravi, to replenish the ponds and irrigate the orchards and beds of roses, cyclamen and iris.

The royal family would have come out on to the three terraces, with their slender marble and sandstone pavilions set amid the delights of the trees, and the music of the birds and fountains, in search of coolness and to be entertained with dances and concerts. At nocturnal festivities the light of camphor-scented candles would have given the cypresses, pomegranate trees and waterfalls mysterious shapes.

The following lines, carved in the stone beside a fountain, were once wrung from the sorrowing heart of Princess Zebun-Nisa, daughter of the emperor Aurangzeb:

'O waterfall, for love of whom shed'st thou thy tears?

Whom mournest thou? In whose memory hast thou furrowed thy brow?'

I saw Lahore unfolding to the light, its women clad in tulip and mango coloured fabrics. The men sweltered in the heat. In the Shahdara Gardens I walked to Jahangir's tomb, erected by his son Shah Jahan, who also built the Taj Mahal at Agra, in India. An avenue of venerable banyans and huge fig trees leads to the marble and sandstone mausoleum. On the enclosure wall a plethora of white marble ornament representing bowls of fruit, flowers and ewers is arranged in elegant mosaics.

To reach the heart of the monument I followed a passage decorated entirely with frescoes from wall to ceiling, and found myself in another world. The wind sighed through the cloisters of the cenotaph. All white marble, it bears sacred inscriptions in black marble – the ninety-nine attributes of the name of Allah. Around the plinth run floral mouldings in semi-precious stones – lapis lazuli, amethyst, agate and turquoise – mined in the Karakorum Mountains. How gentle death seems, by the side of this tomb!

I heard the five calls to prayer ring out over Lahore. At the mosque of Wazir Khan, in the heart of the old city, I admired the brilliance of the paradise flowers in the splendid ceramic mosaics of this shrine built in the reign of Shah Jahan. At the Badshahi mosque with its daring marble domes, built likewise in the seventeenth century by Aurangzeb, the sun flooded the huge square courtyard in which 60,000 worshippers can pray at once. Its four minarets climb high into the sky like soaring birds.

I saw the burial-place of guru Arjan, fifth prophet of the Sikhs, and the Samadhi, tomb of the illustrious ruler Ranjit Singh – magnificent relics, with their fluted golden domes, of the period (1764-1849) when Lahore was the capital of the Sikh kingdom.

I saw Lahore in the middle of the day, when men surrender to sleep and a nightingale sings in the shade. I saw the peacocks displaying in the English parks, and breathed the heady scent of the frangipani trees. During the century of British rule (1849-1947), a university, cathedral and other public buildings were built in the composite style known as Mogul Gothic, and parks and broad tree-lined

Lahore Fort

avenues were laid out. The first curator of the fine Lahore Museum, which contains *inter alia* a splendid collection of Mogul paintings, was Rudyard Kipling's father, John Lockwood Kipling.

I left Lahore at the time of day when people weave garlands of roses, zinnias and marigolds for the dead. Just before daybreak I betook myself to the poet's tomb, cooled my hands and forehead at a nearby fountain, and murmured to myself these lines by Mohammad Iqbal:

'I would not let my heart become attached to this garden'
I went my way, free of all ties.'

CHANTAL LYARD, French Sinologist, poet and essayist, is a member of UNESCO's cultural heritage division where she is concerned with the implementation of the World Heritage Convention.

Reprinted from the *Unesco Courier,* December 1990

Threatened Centre of an Ancient Civilisation

AN INCOMPARABLE MONUMENT to a great civilisation that flourished in the Indus Valley some 5,000 years ago, the vast ruins of the city of Moenjodaro are located in the Sind Province of present-day Pakistan, some 400kms (260mi) north of Karachi. Sometimes referred to as 'the Manhattan of the Bronze Age' because of its extraordinarily modern, scientifically-planned layout, Moenjodaro, even at the height of its splendour, has always been at risk from flooding by the Indus. Preserved for centuries beneath a protective layer of soil, the excavated city (the excavations began in 1922) now faces two additional threats: a rising water table and corrosion by salts. Since the 1960s UNESCO has been collaborating with the Government of Pakistan in preserving this outstanding site. With the aid of Pakistani experts, UNESCO has established a master plan for the work of preservation, launched an international fund-raising campaign and included Moenjodaro on its World Heritage List.

Moenjodaro, a metropolis of the five-thousand-year-old Indus Valley civilisation in Pakistan, presents the earliest example of town-planning and a setting for the future. Even in the limited area laid bare by the archaeologist's spade, it is like walking through a fossilised embryo of Manhattan. In the lower city, we find the crisscross grid-iron system of street layout, a broad boulevard over 9m (30ft) wide, running north to south and crossed at right angles by somewhat smaller east-west streets. The blocks of residential houses between are served by narrow lanes.

The prime considerations in planning the houses were safety and comfort. Avoiding the risk of heavy traffic on the main streets, the doors of the houses usually opened on to the side-lanes. Interior courtyards provided light and air, and windows were screened with grilles of terra-cotta or alabaster. The thickness of the walls of the houses in Moenjodaro proves the existence of at least two-storey-high structures. Most houses had stairways that led either to the second storey or to the roof, often used in Pakistan and elsewhere in the East as a cool sleeping place in summer. Besides other basic amenities, many houses also had wells for water supply which were lined with brickwork and had protective revetments at their head to prevent accidents to children and domestic animals.

The grid layout and residential architecture are not the only indications of the perception and care that went into the planning of Moenjodaro. Never before, and not until Greek and Roman times, was so much attention paid to sanitation and civic facilities. The water-discharge sluices from the houses first collected refuse in small cesspits lined with bricks at the base of the walls, from which the dirty water was led through conduits to the main drains which ran along the streets below pavement level and were covered with sturdy bricks. This drainage system was connected to the larger sewerage outlets, also covered at the top, which finally led the dirty water outside the populated area.

A few hundred metres to the west of this densely built part of the city, excavations have revealed some most conspicuous monuments located on an artificial hill some seven to fourteen metres (23 to 47ft high). The Great Bath, a highly complex brick structure, symbolises a triumph of engineering at that time. The pool, 11.9 metres (40ft) long, 7 metres (23ft) wide and 1.9 metres (6ft) deep, was made watertight by an inner facing of bricks set on edge in gypsum mortar which was laid over a layer of asphalt 2.5 cm (1 inch) thick trowelled on to double brick walls. The floor sloped to an outlet that led in turn to a corbelled arched drain. This corbelled arch was one of the earliest achievements of architectural engineering, spanning an opening without using wooden beams. (The possibilities of spanning wider openings were extended later on by the discovery of the keystone, and in our times developed still further with the use of reinforced concrete.)

A second architectural feature is the podium of the Great Granary situated on the western flank of the mound. The podium, made of solid brick square-shaped platforms separated by a gridiron of straight and narrow passages, is thought to have been covered by a floor of wooden boards, and probably the superstructure was also made of wood. It has been suggested that it served as a State Treasury to which bullock carts brought sacks of grain from farmers, since in those days coins had not yet been minted. A quantity of charred grains of wheat collected from the excavations puts the nature of the building beyond any doubt. A third important building in this area is the Pillared Hall. It has twenty pillars and encloses a small courtyard, and probably served as the centre of administration.

The people respected the rule of law which helped them to develop an egalitarian society on such a vast scale about 5,000 years ago, an achievement unparalleled in the history of mankind. By inference, therefore, the Indus Valley possessed an efficient mechanism of control, communication and transportation and an administrative framework free of such grandiose structures as forts, palaces or great temples serving as centres of authoritarian rule. It was here in those ancient times that a concept of some kind of Government of the people, for the people was envolved, laying the seed of democratic rule.

Of course the proof of this inference lies in the results of further research into the socio-cultural pattern of the Indus Valley civilisation and particularly the deciphering of its enigmatic script which appears on seals and sealings discovered in the Indus Valley. The epigraphists and linguistic experts of the world have made many attempts to decipher this script in the last sixty years. An account of their efforts would make a long tale of trials and errors.

The net gain of their researches so far has been recognition of nearly 350 different pictographs and the fact that the script was written from right to left. But in the absence of long texts even the use of computer technology has not yielded any positive results and one can only hope for a day when a bilingual inscription will be discovered making it possible to unravel the mysteries of the Harappan culture in the same way as the Rosetta Stone did in Egypt and the Behistun inscription in Iran.

A further insight into the skill of the people is provided by a wide range of utilitarian, recreational, artistic and cult objects made of baked clay, stone, metals, ivory, conch shell, faience and other substances. A whole range of pottery types, most wheel-turned, presents a multitude of forms, sizes and decorative features. Amongst the innumerable terracotta toys, miniature bullock carts with solid wheels are particularly striking. Such carts are being used even today around Moenjodaro. Here we also find the beginnings of a chess-board designed on brick tiles, with gamesmen made of agate or ivory.

Who were the founders of this far-reaching, long-vanished civilisation? Scholars believe that the people of the Indus came down into the valley from the foothills of the mountains to the west. Of the early Harappan sites, recent discoveries at Mehrgarth in Baluchistan, southeast of the Sulaiman and Kirthar ranges, show an unbroken sequence of cultural evolution from the sixth millennium BC to the mature Harappan culture.

As to the end of this highly developed civilisation around 1500 BC, several theories have been put forward by archaeologists. Some of them attribute it to the Aryan invaders who swept over the Indus Valley about that time, others consider it due to a tectonic shift in the coastline of the Arabian Sea affecting the entire ecological system of the Valley. However, further research is needed to shed light on the sudden demise of this great civilisation.

The ancient remains of Moenjodaro are now on the World Heritage List as a monument of universal interest and UNESCO has launched an international campaign for their preservation. When excavations started at the site in 1922, the structural remains were in excellent condition. Soon after they were afflicted by the plague of waterlogging and the leprosy of salinity. These two diseases, combined with the menace of erosion by the River Indus, posed a grim threat to the very existence of Moenjodaro. This problem required not only finances which were beyond the resources of the Government of Pakistan, but also technical know-how of a multidisciplinary nature.

At the request of the Government of Pakistan, the General Conference of UNESCO adopted a resolution at its seventeenth session, authorising an international campaign for the preservation of Moenjodaro. In January 1974, the Director-General of UNESCO launched an appeal for international solidarity, stating that, 'By the generous provision of money, equipment and services, governments, public and private individuals will not merely be helping to save a precious record of man's past, they will also be demonstrating and strengthening that intellectual and moral solidarity on which true peace must be founded'.

Since then, over US$4 million have been received in the UNESCO Trust Fund from member states and private sources. The Government of Pakistan, from its own resources, has already invested about US$6 million for the execution of the masterplan, which includes schemes for groundwater control, conservation of structural remains and the training of the River Indus, at a total estimated cost of US$19 million.

The first phase of the groundwater control scheme, which envisaged fourteen tubewells, collector and disposal drains, and a pump house, has already been completed. Work on the conservation of structural remains has also advanced considerably. The amount required for the implementation of the river training scheme, about US$9 million, has yet to be collected and work on this project has not yet begun. The Director-General of UNESCO has, therefore, addressed a second appeal to the international community urging that, 'This challenge is commensurate with the responsibility we all bear for our common history, to which Moenjodaro is a moving testimony we cannot and must not allow to disappear'.

SYED A. NAQVI, internationally known archaeologist and museologist, was head of the national Museum of Pakistan, and then General Director of Pakistan's Department of Archaeology and Museums. He has excavated at many Pakistani sites including Moenjodaro, Taxila and Mansura. In July 1973 he joined UNESCO's Division of Cultural Heritage, which he has headed since January 1982. He has been directly responsible for the successful campaigns for Nubia and Borobudur, as well as supervising all UNESCO's activities for the preservation of the cultural heritage. Among his studies on archaeology and ancient art are The Muslim Art (1966), Gandhara Art (1967) and 1,400 Years of Quranic Calligraphy (1973).

Reprinted from the *Unesco Courier*, July 1985

God Almighty first planted a garden; and, indeed, it is the purest of human pleasures.

FRANCIS BACON

Buddhist stupa, Taxila

Takht-i-Bahi Buddhist Ruins

LAHORE (FORT AND SHALAMAR GARDENS)

LOCATION   Lahore, N 31° 34', E 74° 20'.

DESCRIPTION   The fort is situated in the northwest corner of the city and is approximately 450m (1,476ft) by 360m (1,181ft) around the base. It is constructed from baked bricks and encloses 21 monuments including the Shish Mahal (Mirror Palace). The gardens are formed in 3 descending terraces and are surrounded by a high perimeter wall. They cover an area of 16ha (38ac) and contain more than 400 cascades and fountains.

SIGNIFICANCE   Lahore Fort is the only monument in Pakistan which represents a complete history of Mughal (Mogul) architecture. Not much is known of its early history, legend attributes its foundation to the mythical Loh, son of the heroic Rama. The earliest recorded reference to the fort is 1021 AD. 'Shalamar' means 'the abode of joy', the perfect name for these magnificent gardens. They were created in 1642 as a haven of peace and relaxation for the emperor while staying in Lahore. Together these 2 grand monuments represent the zenith of Mughal architecture.

THATTA

LOCATION   100km (62mi) southeast of Karachi, E 67° 09', N 24° 07'.

DESCRIPTION   There are 2 groups of monuments at this site. On the hill, there is an enormous cemetery with hundreds of tombs and gravestones. In the valley below lie the ruins of the old town. There are numerous buildings, the most notable being the Jamia Mosque.

SIGNIFICANCE   This area is one of the richest sources of historical information on the Indus region. The vast cemetery contains the final resting places of princes, scholars and saints of the Sammah Dynasty (14th to 16th centuries, AD), as well as Argun rulers and Tarkhan rulers (16th century). It was also a seat of the Mughal (Mogul) governors until the early 18th century. The Jamia Mosque in the old city area contains splendid brickwork covered with richly coloured tiles.

TAXILA

LOCATION   Punjab, E 72° 50', N 33° 40'.

DESCRIPTION   This is an archaeological site with various ruins including a cave site from the Mesolithic period, a large number of Buddhist monasteries, several medieval mosques and 4 settlement sites.

SIGNIFICANCE   Taxila is the oldest living city in the Indus region, lying on the historic routes from Central Asia to the Gangetic Plain and from Sinkiang in China to the Arabian Sea. Taxila became a meeting ground for cultures east and west. The romantic ruins are associ-

ated with the great historic names of Alexander the Great, the Maurian Emperor Asoka, Bactrian Greek rulers, the Kushana Emperors and the destructive Huns. It also had commercial and cultural contact with the Roman Empire.

TAKHT-I-BAHI BUDDHIST RUINS

LOCATION   Northwest frontier Province, E 71° 08', N 34° 04'.

DESCRIPTION   Located on a rocky hill, this Buddhist monastic complex comprises a court of stupas surrounded by tall niches around the courtyard to enshrine Buddhist statues. Scattered over the hill are residential cells, courtyards, assembly halls, meditation cells and other buildings attached to the monastery. The remains of an ancient town called Sahr-i-Bahlol are found on an elongated, 9m (30ft) high mound, with intermittent stretches of defensive walls.

SIGNIFICANCE   Both the city and the monastic complex date back to at least the 1st century AD. Apparently surviving the period of the Huns, this Buddhist com-

Lower battery, Portobello

munity continued until the 7th century AD. These remains have preserved the character of Buddhist monastic life in those early days.

MOENJODARO

LOCATION   Sind, E 67° 09', N 27° 03'.

DESCRIPTION   This archaeological site of approximately 41ha (100ac) is only one-third excavated. There are 2 parts; a high artificial mound rising to about 12m (40ft) on the west, and a low much broader city area on the east. Structures include the Great Bath, the Great Granary, the College Square, the Pillared Hall and the Square Towers. Private and public houses, industrial shops and commercial buildings, all built in brick masonry, are lined along the straight streets, which are intersected at right angles by smaller side streets.

SIGNIFICANCE   This site dates back to 2350 BC. The remarkable level of sophistication in the town planning and the drainage system in particular, are unique to such a Bronze Age community. These ruins reveal the workings of the Indus civilization at its zenith.

PANAMA

Famous for its canal, Panama is the southern most country in Central America, its boundary with Colombia marking the division between Central America and the South American continent.

This is a hot and humid land of tropical jungle, coastal mangroves and palm forests, rolling hills and rugged mountains. This thick and oppressive habitat, which was the bane of the early Spanish explorers, provides many unique ecosystems, important to the survival of numerous species of flora and fauna.

In recognition of the crucial importance of these tropical habitats, Panama, after ratifying the World Heritage Convention in March 1978, now has two vital areas included on the World Heritage List – La Amistad and Darien National Parks. Together these parks cover almost 800,000 ha (333,000 ac) of mainly tropical habitat, roughly 10% of Panama's total land mass.

The third World Heritage listing is the remains of the old town of Porto Bello, once the largest and richest commercial port in the New World.

LA AMISTAD NATIONAL PARK

LOCATION   In the province of Bocas del Toro and Chiriqui and located in the Talamanca ranges, W 82° 56', E 82° 25'.

DESCRIPTION   This park covers more than 221,000 ha (530,000 ac) and stretches to both the Caribbean and Pacific oceans. There are mountainous areas, tropical rain forests, four major rivers, rapids and two major volcanic sites. The lush vegetation and varying weather conditions account for the abundance of plant and animal life including several endangered species.

SIGNIFICANCE   The reserve is ecologically one of the richest and most diverse in Central America. The fauna includes a variety of mammals, reptiles, amphibians, insects and bird-life. Of the 850 birds listed in Panama, 550-600 are found in the reserve, most of which live high up on the ranges. The area is also a sanctuary for 40 endangered species of birds including the beautiful quetzal. The region is also of vital importance due to the volcanic basins which feed the various rivers within the park. Historically, the reserve was home to various indigenous people, most of whom have been displaced since colonisation.

Park patroller's cabin, La Amistad National Park

PORTOBELLO AND SAN LORENZO FORTIFICATIONS

LOCATION   On the Caribbean coast, N 09° 20', W 80° 00'.

DESCRIPTION   This listing is a series of ruined forts, walls and associated buildings in 2 zones. Portobello is now a small town, but the ruins of the original town and fortifications remain. They include the Castle of San Felipe de Sotomayor which stands at the harbour entrance, the Fortress of Santiago and Fort Farngse. The ruins at San Lorenzo are strictly of a military nature, with barracks, artillery stores, gun batteries and a moat.

SIGNIFICANCE   Columbus named the site Porto Bello, meaning 'beautiful harbour', in 1502. The city was established 95 years later as an important shipping point for the exchange of goods between South America and Spain. At one stage the busiest and wealthiest city in the New World, Porto Bello was a target for many raiders, including Sir Francis Drake, who is buried there. San Lorenzo was the centre of military activity in the area.

DARIEN NATIONAL PARK

LOCATION   Darien Province, N 07° 12' to 08° 31', W 77° 09' to 78° 26'.

DESCRIPTION   Covering almost 575,000ha (1,380,000ac), this park borders Colombia. It is populated and agriculture is practised within its boundaries. The landscape and vegetation varies from low lying mangrove forests, through tropical rainforest, up to the large and remote primary forests of the highlands which reach up to a maximum altitude 3,500m (11,483ft). Numerous rivers and streams cut through the park. Around 20,000 people live within its boundaries.

SIGNIFICANCE   The variety of vegetation within this park represents one of the most diverse ecosystems in tropical America. Much of the topography is rugged and inaccessible, so many plant species are yet to be identified. Fauna diversity is likewise rich and several species are threatened including the jaguar, tigrillo and the red monkey.

Rainforest Riches — Our Vanishing Heritage

RAINFORESTS ARE the most diverse terrestrial ecosystem in the world. They cover a mere six per cent of the world's land surface, yet shelter at least half of the world's species. Approximately 155,000 of the world's quarter million plant species are housed in tropical forests and tropical forest regions, providing the habitat for ninety per cent of all primates. Many more vertebrate species are located in tropical forests than in temperate forests. An astonishing example of this is found in the Manu National Park in Peru, one of the World Heritage forests, which contains nearly 1,000 species of birds, the same number as the entire United States.

Worldwide, of the 29 million sq km (11 million sq mi) of closed forests, 32 per cent are boreal (subarctic), 26 per cent are temperate (found in both hemispheres) and 42 per cent are tropical. There are 1.7 billion ha (4.08 billion acres) of rainforests located in a tropical belt around the equator (principally between the tropics of Cancer and Capricorn). Rainforests occur where the annual rainfall exceeds 2,000 mm (or 80 inches) and is spread evenly throughout the year. Tropical forests comprise a variety of forest types including montane, lowland, cloud forests and flooded forests.

Existing forest cover is variable: while forests in the Amazon and Zaire remain relatively intact, those in South East Asia, Central America and Western Africa are fragmented and altered. Countries like Brazil, Zaire and Indonesia, which are still densely forested, possess over fifty per cent of the world's closed canopy tropical moist forests.

Known as a reservoir of genetic material, rainforests are capable of providing a wide range of forest produce which can be sustainably extracted. Forest products (such as nuts, berries, game, fish, honey, resins, oils, rattans, flowers, waxes, dyes, skins, fibres, fodder, fruit, etc.) sustain forest dwellers and have potential for wider markets. The wealth of rainforests has historically extended to medical products including tranquillizers, heart regulatory medication, and leukemia immunization. Though only less than 1 per cent have been chemically screened, over 1,400 plant species are believed to possess anti-cancer properties.

Services provided by forests, such as the regeneration of soils, hydrological balance, protection downstream from floods, sedimentation and erosion, are invaluable. Tropical forests also play a crucial role in regulating the atmosphere and local climate. Trees act as a major store of carbon, which serves to moderate local climates and act as a 'stabiliser', by providing milder, more moist and less variable conditions than non-forested land. Forests are also of recreational and spiritual value.

Among the forest sites under the World Heritage Convention, those found in Africa are the following: Dja Faunal Reserve, Cameroon; Mt Nimba Reserve, Guinea and Cdte d'Ivoire; Kahuzi-Biéga National Park, Zaire; and Salonga National Park, Zaire. In Australasia, two sites are found in Australia: the East Coast Temperate and the Sub-tropical Forests and the Wet Tropics of Queensland, and one in India, the Sundarbans National Park. South and Central America boast several sites, including: Rio Platano Biosphere Reserve, Honduras; Talamanca Range and La Amistad Reserves, Costa Rica/Panama; Darien National Park, Panama; Iguazu/Iguacu National Park, Brazil and Argentina; Manu National Park, Peru and Rio Abiseo National Park, Peru.

Rainforests are vanishing before some species are even discovered. It is difficult to estimate the rates of deforestation as statistics are based on different definitions of forest cover, disturbance and clearance. However, it is generally accepted that the present rate of forest loss is almost 2 per cent annually. Tropical forests are diminishing at a rate as high as 18 million ha (43 million ac) a year.

Loss of forests stems from many factors, among these are conversion of land for agricultural purposes, ranching, transmigration, plantations, shifting cultivation, timber exploitation, and demands for fuel. All are contributing to the rapid loss of tropical forest cover.

JILL BLOCKHUS
IUCN
Tropical Forests Programe Assistant

Darien National Park

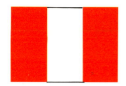

PERU

Historically one of the most fascinating of the South American nations, and the third largest at 1,285,215 sq km (496,222 sq mi), Peru is divided geographically into 3 regions: the Pacific coast, the Andes, and the eastern forest area known as the Montaña or Selva.

The coastal desert which follows roughly 2,250 km (1,350 mi) of coastline is surprisingly cool and extremely dry, with rain sometimes not falling for years. When it does, it is invariably excessive, resulting in severe flooding. Although this area amounts to just over 10 percent of the country's area, nearly half the population live in the coastal region, which is completely covered by clouds from June to October. Agricultural production is only possible through irrigation and fishing is a vital industry.

The Andes or sierra region comprises towering peaks, a huge plateau and many valleys and gorges and occupies a quarter of Peru's terrain, with an average altitude of 3,000m (10,000ft) (the highest peak, Mt Huascaran, is 6,768m (22,540ft)). It is here that the source of the Amazon lies, and there is a surprising amount of agricultural activity in the valleys and along the plateau.

The Montaña, while occupying nearly two thirds of the country, accounts for only 5% of the population. This dense forest region receives heavy rainfalls from October to April and is largely inaccessible.

Very little is known about the earliest civilisations which inhabited Peru at least 4,000 years ago, but remains including primitive statuettes have been found at Aspero. A number of civilisations pre-date the famous Incas, among them being the Chavhn culture which built burial mounds and which flourished from around 800 BC to 200 BC. The remains of this civilisation are now protected by its World Heritage listing. The Mochica culture appeared sometime around 300-200 BC and during its 800 years constructed impressive adobe pyramids in the Moche Valley.

The Chimó were another ancient civilisation and their capital city, Chan Chan, is also protected by World Heritage listing.

It was the Incas though, who created, from around the 9th century AD until the arrival of the Spaniards in 1532, an empire which embraced all of Peru and Bolivia, as well as large tracts of Argentina, Chile and Ecuador. The Incas organised communal agri-

Cuzco (Old City)

cultural activities, laid out roads, introduced an official language – Quechua – and built centralised food storage areas to safeguard against famine. They established a rigidly tiered society with the family as the basic unit, ruled over by the Sapa Inca – the supreme chief, who was considered to be an incarnation of the Sun God.

Many would consider the main attraction in Peru today to be the World Heritage listed Machu Picchu – 'the lost city of the Incas'. Cuzco, the ancient Incan capital, is also on the list.

Peru ratified the World Heritage Convention in February 1982 and now has eight sites listed. Apart from the four ancient sites mentioned, there are three national parks – Huascaran, Rio Abiseo and Manu and one Spanish colonial listing – the Convent Ensemble at Lima.

Machu Picchu (Historic Sanctuary)

A Jewel of Latin American Baroque Art

WHEN THE ARTS of Latin America are discussed outside the continent, the first thing that springs to mind, for both specialists and the general public, is the exceptional pre-Columbian legacy. Colonial art, both sacred and profane, was long considered a provincial outgrowth of the manneristic and baroque art of the Old World, and attitudes towards it have been very slow in changing. Yet this period produced important works in architecture, sculpture, painting and gold and silver work, of which the Convent of San Francisco de Lima is one of the most outstanding examples.

In 1535, the Emperor Charles V ordered the conquistador Francisco Pizarro to earmark two sites in the urban plan of Lima then under preparation, to be used by the Franciscans to erect their church and convent. Situated right in the centre of Lima on the banks of the River Rimac, these lots (with later additions) formed the largest area ever to have been occupied by a convent in the New World: one eighth of the area of the colonial city which had 14,000 inhabitants at the beginning of the seventeenth century. On 4 February 1656, an earthquake destroyed a major part of the church and convent. The Portuguese architect Constantino de Vasconcellos, who lived in Lima, was entrusted with the task of rebuilding the complex, generally known as the Convent of San Francisco, which now comprises the churches of San Francisco, La Soledad and El Milagro, with their cloisters, patios and outbuildings.

The problem facing Vasconcellos was how to erect a monumental church able to withstand earthquakes. His solution was twofold. On the one hand, he built a barrel vault resting on solid pillars, a technique which allowed for the construction of tall and resistant structures. On the other hand, the building materials he used were wood and a mixture that the conquistadors had borrowed from the Indians: *quincha*, a conglomerate of rushes, mud and plaster. Both light and relatively elastic, *quincha* is considered to be an earthquake-resistant material, and was later to be used for a whole series of buildings along the coast of Peru, for which San Francisco was the model. Thanks to these building methods, the complex has survived the earthquakes of three centuries.

While the profuse ornamentation of the Convent of San Francisco is clearly inspired by European art, in the Spanish *mudejar*, manneristic and baroque styles, the materials are an original response to local conditions. With the exception of the 'altar-piece-portal' and the lateral portal, both of stone, the whole church, including the towers, some 35 metres (117ft) in height, are made of *quincha*. This makes the whole complex look like a giant clay sculpture.

The most talented artists of the day – goldsmiths, silversmiths, sculptors, painters and wood carvers – contributed to the ornamentation. A factory was even set up to produce painted and glazed tiles *(azulejos)* to decorate the outbuildings. San Francisco thus became a sort of college of arts and crafts. After the death of Vasconcellos, his disciple, Manuel de Escobar, from Lima, completed the work in 1672. It is to him we owe the beautiful lateral portal.

As in the case of most baroque churches in Spanish America and in contrast to European and Brazilian baroque, the architectural groundplan of San Francisco is very simple: three 7-span aisles, a transept and a presbytery. Decorative exuberance spills over the facades, altarpieces, domes and towers. Wealth of form makes up for modesty of materials: the church is literally covered in relief decoration.

The two bossed towers flank a stone 'altarpiece-portal'. It dates from 1664 and is the work of Vasconcellos. Damian Bayon, an Argentine historian, describes it as 'stone chiaroscuro proliferation', a lavish but harmonious mass of sculptures, niches, frontispieces, windows and pilasters.

These 'altarpiece-portals', typical of Latin American churches, date back to sixteenth century Spain. The altarpiece is brought forward to the church portal, bringing religion to the street. This was considered essential by the conquistadors, who saw Christianity as a great unifying bond between populations of different origins.

San Francisco was the church attended by the Viceroy of Peru and his Court, and for this reason it received many donations and legacies, generated by the rich Peruvian gold and silver mines. The convent thus accumulated a vast treasure, part of which disappeared in the nineteenth century during the wars of independence. Nevertheless it can boast today some outstanding works of art.

Besides the fifteen canvases of the *Apostolado* (one of only three in the world) painted by the Spanish artist Francisco de Zurbarán and his workshop, there are thirty-nine canvases in the main cloister, painted between 1670 and 1672 by four local artists (Francisco Escobar, Fernando de Noriega, Andrés de Liébana and Diego de Aguilera), representing the life of the founder of the Order; a triptych by Anelino Medoro and a *St. Bonaventura* by the same artist; eleven seventeenth century Flemish canvases of the school of Rubens; a *Coronation of the Virgin* by Juan Solórzano, a native of Cuzco, and many other paintings of the same school. An exceptional ensemble of Sevillian *azulejos* adorns the main cloister, not to mention all the carvings, furniture, and delicately wrought silver and gold ware. The library deserves special mention. It con-

Inca ruins at Cuzco

tains numerous manuscripts and more than 25,000 printed volumes, including fifteenth century incunabula and many sixteenth century first editions.

Earthquakes (especially that of 1974), the ravages of time, constant humidity, but also human negligence, have gravely damaged the convent. In 1941, the Government of Peru declared it a national monument and began urgent restoration work. Since 1978, UNESCO, in collaboration with the United Nations Development Programme (UNDP), has contributed some 300,000 dollars towards technical assistance, training of restoration experts and equipment.

Some of the consolidation work to be carried out is particularly urgent, but Peru is experiencing a difficult economic situation and cannot meet all the costs involved. To raise the 3 million dollars that are needed, it is essential that the international community rally to the country's aid, as the Director-General of UNESCO explained in his appeal launched from Lima on 2 April 1987. It is to be hoped that the response will be generous, as it has been in favour of other major universal works of art which bear witness to past cultures, such as the Borobudur monument or the Nubian temples. The loss of what was the most beautiful ornament of the 'city of the kings', today a living testimony to the history of South America, would be irreparable.

CHRISTINA BARBIN, of Argentina, has worked for several years as an editor in UNESCO's Office of Public Information. She has published a number of articles on cultural themes in the information bulletins of different countries, and is the author of a monograph (1986) on the Colombian painter Omar Rayo.

Reprinted from the *Unesco Courier,* March 1988

CUZCO (OLD CITY)

LOCATION   Department of Cuzco, S 13° 31', W 72° 00'.

DESCRIPTION   The present day departmental capital, Cuzco is a blend of ancient, old and new. Inca ruins include the baths, a throne, Kenco Amphitheatre and the famous Fortress of Sacsahuamín. Spanish colonial architecture predominates, the most imposing building being the cathedral which is built on top of the Inca Place of Huiracocha. There are several other churches and convents.

SIGNIFICANCE   Cuzco was the capital of the Inca empire and, as such, ruled over a vast area. It dates from the 11th century and remained the centre of Inca civilisation until 1534, when Francisco Pizarro claimed it for the Spanish King. At this time, the total Inca population is thought to have exceeded 10 million people. The combination of Inca ruins and Spanish colonial architecture is typical of the Spanish colonisers' arrogance in those days, when entire cultures at their peak were wantonly destroyed.

MACHU PICCHU (HISTORIC SANCTUARY)

LOCATION   In the southeastern mountains about 100km (62mi) northwest of Cuzco City, S 13° 07', W 72° 35'.

DESCRIPTION   An historic sanctuary 32,000ha (77,000ac) in area surrounds the ruins of Machu Picchu. The topography is extremely mountainous and the vegetation lush. Some 200 buildings are found on the archaeological site which exists on 2 levels. The upper and lower towns are separated by a large esplanade.

SIGNIFICANCE   Known as the 'Lost city of the Incas', Machu Picchu has been shrouded in mystery since its discovery by Hiram Bingham in 1911. It is believed to have been built in the 15th century, at the zenith of Inca civilisation.

MANU NATIONAL PARK

LOCATION   Provinces of Manu and Paucartambo, S 11° 11' to 12° 18', W 71° 10' to 72° 22'.

DESCRIPTION   Manu National Park is part of a larger area known as Manu Biosphere Reserve – a total of just over 1.5 million ha (3.6 million ac) in area, it also includes a reserve zone and a cultural zone. The national park incorporates the entire Manu River Basin and part of the Rio Alto Madre de Dios Basin. Altitude ranges from 360-4,000m (1,200-13,300ft). The landscape varies from alluvial plain to rugged, forest covered mountains.

SIGNIFICANCE   Much of the park is rugged and largely inaccessible. Consequently, there are rich and diverse

Manu National Park

populations of flora and fauna. Some animals however, such as the river wolf, are threatened with extinction. Twelve other mammals are endangered. It is thought that up to 10 percent of the flora species within the park are as yet unknown to science. There are several indigenous Indian populations within the park, people such as the Machiguengas and the Kogajakoris who have had little contact with civilisation.

CHAN CHAN (ARCHAEOLOGICAL AREA)

LOCATION   Trujillo Province, northeast coast, S 08° 05′, W 79° 04′.

DESCRIPTION   The central area of the ruins of this ancient city covers 6sq km (2.4sq mi). Construction is of mud brick and most buildings are well preserved – mainly due to the dry climate of this coastal area. Ten large palaces sit in the heart of the city, sur rounded by 14m (46ft) high walls. Nearby is a burial platform with a principal tomb, surrounded by lesser tombs. Four residential quarters surround the centre. The outlying areas were devoted to agriculture.

Huascarán National Park

Chan Chan

SIGNIFICANCE   This was the capital of a very advanced and powerful civilisation known as the Chimu. The ruins are in excellent condition and reveal in marvellous detail the culture and day to day life of this ancient race. The Chimu preceeded the Incas, who later became their main rivals, conquering the Chimu in 1465-70 AD.

RIO ABISEO NATIONAL PARK

LOCATION   Province of Mariscal Cáceres, S 07° 24', W 77° 02'.

DESCRIPTION   This park comprises a rugged area of mountainous forest which can be divided into five broad life zones: (i) sub-alpine rain plains; (ii) mountainous rainforest, (iii) lower mountainous rainforest, (iv) pre-mountainous rainforest and (v) humid rainforest. The altitude ranges up to 4,100m (13,650ft) above sea level. As well as its countless natural assets, the park contains numerous important archaeological sites.

SIGNIFICANCE   There is a very high level of endemism amongst the fauna and flora species of this park. More than nine bird species have been identified as endemic, with a further five which have limited distribution. The yellow-tailed woolly monkey was pre viously thought to be extinct and is only found in this area. The diversity of flora species is nothing short of amazing with over 1,000 identified in the highest, northwestern section of the park alone. The area's cultural significance is measured by the more than 36 archaeological sites identified since 1985, altogether spanning 8,000 years of Peruvian history and pre-history.

HUASCARÁN NATIONAL PARK

LOCATION   In the department of Ancash and incorporating the provinces of Recuay, Carhaus, Huaráz, Yungay, W 77° 49', S 10° 40'.

DESCRIPTION   The Blanca Cordillera is the highest tropical snow region in the world. There are several beautiful valleys and dramatic slopes, offering breath-taking views of enormous glaciers. The snow-covered mountains offer a variety of grades for mountain climbing. Over 120 glacial lagoons are found in the ranges as well as three important springs. There are also mountain rainforests containing over 120 plant species and 100 animal species. Pre-Inca ruins can also be found, the most important being those in Pueblo Viejo (Recuay), Aija (Chuchunpunta) Huaráz (Wilcawahin) and Yungay (Cueva del Cruitarnero, Ranrahirca, Ayra).

SIGNIFICANCE   Huascarán National Park affords a natural environment for an abundance of wildlife and flora. In addition to offering the greatest concentration of mountain climbing routes in Latin America, it was once the home to diverse tribes including the Huaras and the Huaylas people. Although the ruins have been ransacked for their treasures, they still offer an important link to pre-Incan cultures.

CHAVIN (ARCHAEOLOGICAL SITE)

LOCATION   Northern highlands, Huari Province, S 09° 33′, W 77° 09′.

DESCRIPTION   These ruins are of an ancient ceremonial site. The main building is immense and pyramidal in shape. Construction is characterised by superb masonry and is in 3 storeys with stairs, ramps, ventilation shafts and a multi-storey drainage system. There are several other, smaller, pyramidal structures, all similar in layout and construction.

SIGNIFICANCE   These ruins reflect one of the earliest known Andean cultures with any level of sophistication. They date back before 800 BC, when extensions were made to the site. It is believed that Chavin was the centre of a religious cult, in which the jaguar is believed to have played an important role.

CONVENT ENSEMBLE OF SAN FRANCISCO DE LIMA

LOCATION   City of Lima, Lima Province, S 12° 12′, W 77° 00′.

DESCRIPTION   Located in the centre of the city, the monastic complex is composed of numerous buildings, mainly dating from the 17th century. They include the Churches of La Soledad, El Milagro and San Francisco and several cloisters. There are several important works of art, including 15 paintings of apostles attributed to the famous artist Zurbaran.

SIGNIFICANCE   Construction of this Franciscan convent began in 1535. It was relocated to the present site in 1546, but was demolished in 1656 and rebuilt over a period of 16 years. This introduced a new wave of mudejar influence to the architectural styles of the day. The large portal, which was finished in 1674, introduced the late baroque style of facade to this area. The impressive art collection is substantial and of great significance to the history of art in South America.

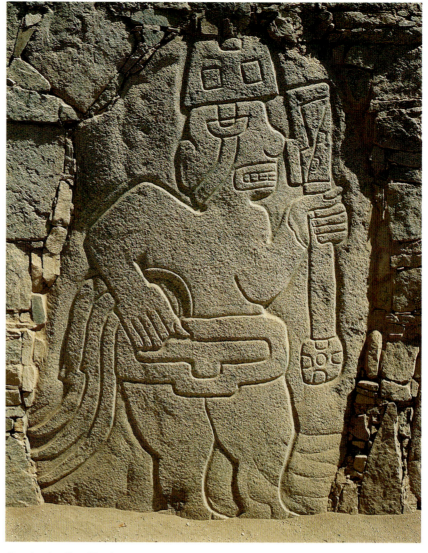

Carving detail at Chavin

Convent Ensemble of San Francisco de Lima

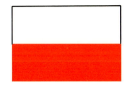

POLAND

Inside Wieliczka Salt Mine

European bison, Bialowieza National Park

In 1786 Father Franciszek Zubowski inaugurated the first Polish attempt at describing relics of the past. He postulated 'to make those monuments universally known and permanent'. Just how apt this thought was became apparent only ten years later, when the Polish state ceased to exist for 150 years due to a partition conducted by the three powers – Russia, Prussia and Austria.

It was possible to survive this period, to retain language, culture and national identity only thanks to the living memory of the past, whose testimony took on the form of material and spiritual relics.

When the Second World War put an end to the two decades of the independent Polish state, and the country became the victim of another partition, this task was just as important for twentieth–century Poland. In the subsequent 45 years attempts were made to exploit tradition selectively, and to treat it instrumentally and ideologically. These endeavours failed owing to the fact that the protection of the national legacy enjoyed constant civic support, and unified the population regardless of the divergent political views.

It was obvious that Poland would take part in an international convention concerning the protection of cultural and natural heritage, and in the formulation of criteria for the establishment of a world list. The latter constitutes a symbol of the accomplishments of particular nations, and at the same time, of a community of humanist tradition with universal values.

These components of cultural and natural heritage included from the very beginning five sites from Poland. Of course, there are many countries in Europe whose ancient and outstanding works of art and civilisation as well as natural phenomena far exceed those of Poland. The explanation is quite simple. This list of our global legacy is not a competition for the most outstanding works, but a collection of relics of special symbolic and social significance.

The five Polish contributions comprise two towns whose rank for world culture is quite different. The first is Cracow, the former capital of the country, an urban configuration that harmoniously expanded from the Middle Ages on, and which plays, as it did some 800 years ago, the role of a centre.

Historical and symbolic merits of particular prominence belong to the Royal Castle – the Wawel –

and the cathedral, which is the necropolis of the Polish monarchs, political leaders and poets. Cracow is also the site of the oldest university in Central Europe, whose students included Nicholas Copernicus. Fragments of medieval fortifications and, within their range, architectonic complexes and buildings – churches, monasteries, municipal buildings and houses which represent styles and artworks from the tenth to the twentieth century, are exceptionally well preserved.

Finally, symbolic mounds honouring legendary heroes and historical figures – Tadeusz Kósciuszko and Józef Pilsudski – towers on the outskirts of the town. This is a unique place for the Poles but also of great interest for foreigners – one of the seven holy stones of the religion of the East is located on the Wawel hill.

The Heritage List also mentions the old town in Warsaw, the oldest part of the present–day capital of Poland. Despite its undoubtable beauty, it is not exceptional for its size, antiquity or architectural merits when compared to many other European towns. The old town was placed on the list due to the unprecedented scale of resistance shown by the Polish nation against an attempt to remove the city from the pages of history.

In accordance with Nazi plans, the old town was to have been destroyed and built anew. In 1944, in

Replica of Liberty Bell, Warsaw Historic Centre

the course of the armed uprising against the occupying army, it was ruined. As a symbol of national identity, the old town became the site of a unique reconstruction performed in the period 1949-1954. It is precisely the outcome of that reconstruction – the result of many years of amazing work conducted by the whole population – which is now protected and included in the World Heritage List.

The third site listed is Auschwitz–Birkenau, the largest of the Nazi death camps, where vast numbers of Jews, Gypsies, Poles, Russians, French and other innocent people were exterminated. Part of mankind's darker history, Auschwitz is a symbol of the downfall of humanity, and a tragic piece of our heritage which must never be forgotten.

The fourth Polish contribution is the salt mine in Wieliczka near Cracow. Here, salt has been excavated from as far back as the Stone Age, and the mine was exploited from the thirteenth century up to this day. The multi–storied technical structure below the surface is filled with machines from centuries past, kilometres of corridors in salt, works of art and chapels dating from the seventeenth to the eighteenth century as well as natural salt formations of exceptional originality.

The fifth Polish item is the Bialowieza Forest in north–eastern Poland. This is the only extant fragment of natural woodlands which in the Middle Ages covered sizeable parts of Europe. The forest encompasses an area of 4,747 hectares (11,870 acres) undisturbed by man's activity, a fragment of a complex some 1,250 square kilometres (480 square miles) in area, and contains an enclave with numerous species of fauna, including the last European bison living in the wilderness.

It seems worthwhile to mention two other items which may one day be nominated for placement on the World Heritage List. These are Zamość, an ideal town established in the sixteenth century by a private founder and retained in an uncontaminated urban form, and Jasna Gira, a monastery in Częstochowa, which houses the picture of the Black Madonna, a religious and national sanctuary which differs from others of its type by the fact that it combines both religious and national elements.

The sites which represent Poland on the World Heritage List reveal extremely varying elements. They reflect local, national, European and global values as well as cultural and natural features but, at the same time, remain unique. This list of world heritage constitutes a continuation and extension of the same idea which influenced Father Zubowski – a concept shared by the humanists and thinkers of the whole world.

TADEUSZ ZIELNIEWICZ
General Conservator of Historical Monuments, Poland

Wawel Castle, Cracow

Cracow Historic Centre

The entrance to Auschwitz Concentration Camp

WIELICZKA SALT MINE

LOCATION   About 13km (8mi) southeast of Cracow, N 50° 00', E 20° 05'.

DESCRIPTION   The mining works are underneath the town of Wieliczka. There are 9 levels of descent and the depth is 327m (1,073ft) at the lowest point. There are 16 extraction ponds inside the mine. The east-west axis is 5km (3mi) long and it is 1km (0.62mi) along the north-south axis. There is a museum with an historical exhibition attached to the mine.

SIGNIFICANCE   The richest salt mines in Poland, these works are also one of the oldest operational salt mines in Europe. Salt was being extracted here as early as the 11th century. It was opened as a royal mine in the 13th century. The most remarkable feature of the mine is the multitude of carvings found underground – throughout the long history of the mine, many 'mining artists' have left their unique stamp. There are various statues, and many altars, chapels and pulpits all painstakingly carved out of the rock salt.

WARSAW HISTORIC CENTRE

LOCATION   Warsaw, capital city, E 21° 00', N 52° 15'.

DESCRIPTION   Situated mainly on the left bank of the Vistula River, most of the buildings of Warsaw are reproductions constructed after the bombings of World War II. The old city was focused on the Royal Castle (Zamek), but this was not rebuilt after being destroyed. One of the main areas of interest is the market place as well as the 14th century Gothic Cathedral of St. John – faithfully reconstructed. Cracow Boulevard, which is lined with palaces and churches, dates to the 15th century and is most imposing.

SIGNIFICANCE   Founded as a city at the beginning of the 13th century, Warsaw originally had protective walls, towers and gates. Around 150 years later it became capital of the Duchy of Mazovia and then in 1596 King Sigismund III ordained it as the capital. Numerous palaces, churches, residences and new town walls were built. An extremely turbulent and violent history culminated in 1944 when the retreating Germans methodically destroyed this grand old city. The massive and detailed reconstruction that followed is one of the amazing building feats of this century.

BIALOWIEZA NATIONAL PARK

LOCATION   N 52° 43' to 52° 48', E 23° 48' to 23° 56'.

DESCRIPTION   The park covers 5,069ha (12,221ac) and is divided into a very large, strictly protected, nature reserve, (4,747ha/11,445ac), with adjoining areas for bison and wild forest horse management (272ha/656ac). There is also a botanical park (50ha/121ac). The entire complex is situated on the watershed of the Baltic and Black Seas.

SIGNIFICANCE   This area has been carefully managed for over 60 years and so its unique lowland woods have been well preserved. More than 50 species of mammals are found in these forests and the bird life is particularly rich, with over 200 species to be found, around 90 of them breeding here. The European bison and the tarpan wild horse, in particular, are flourishing here.

CRACOW HISTORIC CENTRE

LOCATION   Southern Poland, N 50° 03', W 20° 00'.

DESCRIPTION   The old city lies at the centre of Cracow. Originally surrounded by walls and a moat, only two towers and two gates remain. Market Square (Ryneb) forms the nucleus of the town, three parallel streets running from each of its four sides. Draper's Hall (Sukiennice) and the Church of the Virgin Mary dominate the square. Wawel Hill holds ruins of the oldest buildings. Traces of two cathedrals, preceding the existing one, have been found. The Royal Castle dominates the hill. There is a multitude of other historic buildings including no less than 58 old churches.

SIGNIFICANCE   Cracow is the early capital of Poland and, like the rest of the country, has had an extremely turbulent history. No Polish city has more historical monuments than this one. Items like the silver coffin, which holds the alleged relics of Poland's patron saint, St. Stanislaw, are invaluable relics of this country's history. Its University is the second oldest in Europe and its library contains more than 1 million books.

AUSCHWITZ CONCENTRATION CAMP

LOCATION   N 50° 04', E 19° 21'.

DESCRIPTION   The camps of Auschwitz and Birkenau cover areas of 20ha (48ac) and 171ha (412ac) respectively. Auschwitz has 41 stone buildings, 8 wooden barracks and 8 watchtowers. Birkenau counts 47 stone buildings, 22 wooden barracks and 27 watchtowers. Within the camps are the remains of gas chambers and 4 crematoria. The camps are surrounded by a total length of 15km (9.3mi) of barbed wire.

SIGNIFICANCE   These camps were the scene of the largest scale mass murder in the history of humanity. 4 million people of mixed race and religion were killed here between June 1940 and 27th January 1945 – the date of the liberation by the Soviet armies. A national museum, the camps have been declared a monument to the martyrdom of the Polish people and to the people of 29 other nations.

PORTUGAL

Portugal ratified the World Heritage Convention in September 1980 and now has six sites on the World Heritage List. Each of these sites is inscribed on the list for its cultural characteristics, a reflection of Portugal's exciting and influential history.

Nonetheless, Portugal is also a country of great natural beauty and significance. So the challenge that lies ahead is for Portugal to place a site of natural significance on the World Heritage List.

Our natural environment is being eroded away. The many pressures on it are gradually destroying our natural habitats and biotopes. This is no less the case in Portugal.

Portugal is a unique place in Europe, climatically and geologically. It is both in the Atlantic and the Mediterranean climatic zones. Rainfall varies from 2,800 mm (110in) per year on the North Atlantic Coast to 300 mm (12in) per year in the interior of the Algarve. This is in spite of the fact that the country is only about 600km (370mi) long and 170km (105mi) wide. Consequently, there are many plants and ani-

Tower of Belém

Monastery of Hieronymites

Angra do Heroismo (Azores)

mals endemic to Portugal which cannot be found elsewhere. There are also geological formations unique to Portugal, such as the Serra Arrabida and the Ria Formosa in the Algarve.

With these climatic conditions, Portugal suffers from the extra pressure exerted by mass tourism on its delicate coastal heritage areas, the home of many important biotopes. Hotels and tourist facilities have been built on these areas. One village can swell from the native population of 2,000 people to 40,000 people in the peak holiday month of August. This exerts pressure on the infrastructure and services to the detriment of the natural environment.

This situation is a common one throughout the whole world. Three things need to be done; some untouched areas must be set aside as sanctuaries for wildlife and plants, and people must be prohibited from entering these areas; a network of national parks should be established at the same time, which would safeguard the natural environment and also provide recreation areas where people can learn how to treat nature with respect and of course, to have fun! Finally, comprehensive land use plans must be established to prevent destruction of the fragile natural environment.

None of these ideas is new, but short term private profit almost always has won over the defence of our common values and heritage of those living or yet to be born. Public awareness and information are important in the fight to save our habitat. I hope that the readers of this book will be inspired by its contents to fight long and hard.

CARLOS PIMENTA
Portuguese Member of the European Parliament

MONASTERY OF HIERONYMITES AND TOWER OF BELÉM

LOCATION   In Belém, a suburb of Lisbon, N 38° 41′, W 09° 12′.

DESCRIPTION   The Monastery of Santa Maria of Belém of the order of St. Jeromimo consists of a church and a cloister, both built of limestone. The church is remarkable for its southern and western portals, which are extensively decorated with statues. There are two commemorative tombs dedicated to Vasco da Gama, the explorer, and Camoes, the famous poet, to be found in the church. The hexagonal tower of Belém is built from limestone on a basalt foundation. Designed as a defensive tower, it has sentry boxes and a bastion that overlooks the Tagus River. There are extensive external decorations, including maritime and religious motifs. Entrance is gained by crossing a drawbridge.

Sunset over Roman ruins, Evora

SIGNIFICANCE   These 16th century buildings are some of the few remaining examples of Manoellian architecture – a style that is named after King Manoel I. It is also one of the few structures to survive the devastating earthquake that struck Lisbon in 1775.

MONASTERY OF SANTA MARIA DE ALCOBAÇA

LOCATION   On the northern part of Province Estremadusa, N 39° 33', W 08° 58'.

DESCRIPTION   This is a 12th century Cistercian monastery dedicated to St. Bernard and is situated in a marshy plain where the 2 rivers Alcoa and Baça meet. The interior of the church is massive but simple in design, with the chapel of St. Bernard standing opposite the Royal Pantheon. The imposing 221m (725ft) façade is composed of 3 parts; the north aisle, the church and the south aisle. The façade was modified in 1702, conserving only 7 portals in the Gothic style. The Cloister of Dinis also known as the Cloister of Silence, the dormitory, the refectory, the chapter house and the Hall of the Kings which is richly decorated, are the other main buildings.

SIGNIFICANCE   The monastery was founded in 1153 by King Afonso Henriques after his victorious conquest over the Moorish town of Santarem. This was the golden age of the Cistercians, or White Monks as they were known. This monastery is well preserved and is one of the most significant monuments of medieval Cistercian architecture in Europe.

EVORA (HISTORIC CENTRE)

LOCATION   In the province of Alentejo, N 38° 00', W 08° 00'.

DESCRIPTION   The modern day capital of Alentejo Province, Evora is an old fortified town. It is protected by walls, towers and 2 forts. There is a richly decorated Romanesque cathedral which has been restored in the Gothic style. The Church of São Francisco is in the distinctive Manoellian style. There are several Roman ruins, including the Temple of Diana.

SIGNIFICANCE   Originally known as Ebora, the town's origins predate 80 BC when it was an important Roman military station. A bishopric in the 5th century AD, it was conquered by Moors around 712 AD and held by them for around 450 years. The Spanish ruled from 1663 to 1665. The town's long history of religious and political importance has left a rich heritage of architectural and artistic treasures, many of which are stored in the numerous museums.

Convent of Christ in Tomar

Statue of King João, Monastery at Batalha

ANGRA DO HEROISMO (AZORES)

LOCATION   The main town on the island of Terceira, part of the Azores group, N 38° 38′, W 27° 12′.

DESCRIPTION   Angra is an old fortified port town. There are 2 imposing fortresses to defend the natural twin harbour. Religious buildings abound – São João Baptista do Castelo, San Francisco Convent, Colegio Church and São Gonçalo Convent are the most notable.

SIGNIFICANCE   These volcanic isles were discovered at the beginning of the 15th century by Diogo de Silves, a pilot of the Portuguese king. Settlement began around 1432. They were the scene of many a battle, especially between the English and the Spanish. The fortifications at Angra are a vestige of those turbulent times.

CONVENT OF CHRIST IN TOMAR

LOCATION   In the province of Ribatejo, 143km (89mi) northeast of Lisbon, N 39° 36′, W 08° 25′.

DESCRIPTION   This complex was founded when the small Oratory of the Templars was erected at the end of the 12th century. It has a Roman-Byzantine interior. Several cloisters were later added, including the main cloister and the hastately cloister. The window of the sacristy and the portal of the nave are both fine examples of the decorative art to be found within this convent.

SIGNIFICANCE   The origin of the complex dates from the mid 12th century when several members of the Knights Templar Order settled here. In 1320 this became known as the Order of Christ. The main cloister was built by Diego de Torralva in 1557. It is a fine example of Portuguese High Renaissance architecture and shows a marked Italian influence.

MONASTERY OF BATALHA

LOCATION   In the province of Estremaøura, south of the town of Leiria, N 39° 39′, W 08° 49′.

DESCRIPTION   This monastic complex includes a royal cloister, built in Gothic and Manoellian styles by Alfonso Domingues as a place of prayer and meditation. The pantheon of King João I and his Queen, along with the Unfinished Chapels are the other notable buildings. The monumental portal, which is 15m (49ft) high and 7.5m (24.5ft) wide, was built by King Manoel.

SIGNIFICANCE   King João I built this complex in gratitude to his loyal subjects who fought fiercely for their independence against the Castillians in the Battle of Aljubarrota on the 15th August 1385. The Unfinished Chapels were started in 1433 by King Duarte but were left after his death in 1438. The portal was erected in 1509. The complex is well preserved and presents a broad segment of Portuguese architectural history.

Monastery of Santa Maria de Alcobaça

The OECD and Sustainable Development

THIRTY YEARS AGO, the founders of the Organisation for Economic Co-operation and Development (OECD) agreed that its principal purpose should be to 'promote policies to achieve the highest sustainable economic growth and a rising living standard in member countries'.

With the year 2000 now looming large on the horizon, the OECD joins other international bodies and governments in conceding that the type of economic growth that has characterized this century does not meet the test of 'sustainability'. It fails on two counts: the stresses that economic growth is placing on the Earth's life-support systems are not sustainable on *ecological* grounds; and the unequal distribution of the growth among, and within, the nations of the world is not sustainable on *political* and *social* grounds.

This perspective embraces and reinforces the central message of the World Commission on Environment and Development in its April 1987 landmark report (*Our Common Future*) which called upon the international community to pursue a new type of growth, one based on the concept of 'sustainable development'. Sustainable development, as advanced by the commission, requires a revolution in the manner in which institutions and individuals perceive and treat environmental values; a new human ethic to guide the sharing of the benefits of development within and among succeeding generations; and a revised philosophy of economic growth that values the *quality* of growth as much as its absolute quantity.

To state that the world community is today confronted with an array of daunting environmental challenges is to confess the obvious. Examples abound of the continuing degradation of air and water quality, and the loss of irreplaceable natural resources, at local, national and regional levels. In addition, we now face threats of stratospheric ozone depletion and climate warming, portents that mankind's quest for economic growth and prosperity may indeed be over-taxing planet Earth's capacity.

These environmental problems have been widely publicized and debated. However, at the risk of surprising those who see only one side of the picture – or of offending others who might feel that any suggestion of progress might dampen enthusiasm for the war to protect the environment – let me suggest that there is beginning to be some very good news.

First of all, we have the sustainable development concept itself. There has been a groundswell of international support for this concept since the World Commission's report four years ago. Clearly, a forward-looking, growth-oriented world development model was a welcome replacement for its gloomy 'limits to growth' antecedent of the 1970s.

While some continue to express scepticism that progress can be made in the absence of a commonly-agreed operational definition of sustainability, there is, in my view, an emerging consensus on the critical measures that must be taken to achieve it. These include:

- controlling population growth rates;
- accelerating economic development in developing countries;
- promoting technological change toward 'clean, green' growth;
- pricing resources to reflect relative scarcities and to integrate environmental 'externalities';
- placing unique and vulnerable ecosystems, and world heritage, under sound management;
- reforming institutions to ensure the complementarity of environment and development policies;
- upgrading the quality and stock of factors contributing to well-being (e.g., skilled labour, education);
- modifying production and consumption patterns to maintain the stock of scarce resources and to advance equity goals.

We are also beginning to reap the benefits of two decades of investment in environmental education, training and research and development.

This is showing up in many ways. In the 24 countries of the OECD, for example, environmentally-sensitive consumers are expressing their concerns and preferences in the marketplace. The better college graduates are opting for positions in firms which have good environmental records. Industry is beginning to discover that sound environmental management makes good economic sense. The science and technology community is providing a rapidly expanding capacity for the detection, assessment and monitoring of environmental risks.

One of the major emerging success stories concerns technology innovation, a prerequisite for sustainable development. Industry has been making major breakthroughs in decreasing the emission of pollutants while reducing the inputs of raw materials and energy.

Institutional changes are also being made to promote better integration of economic growth and environmental policies. Governments are preparing national plans and strategies for sustainable development, requiring departments to be more accountable for the environmental consequences of their actions, and establishing procedures to monitor and measure performance.

Also, a 'new economics' is starting to evolve; one that takes better account of environmental costs and benefits when calculating the wealth of a nation or the proper price of a commodity. Efforts are under-

Niokolo-Koba National Park

way to design new economic instruments (e.g., charges, taxes, tradeable permits) that can achieve greater effectiveness and efficiency in environmental management, and to re-design regulatory approaches to provide clearer guidance and better stimuli to industry and individuals.

Clearly, we have a long way to go: in promoting sound environmental policies within market-based, democratic societies; in stimulating a new technological revolution; in re-structuring our institutions; in developing and introducing a new economics; and in creating the conditions for improved ethical action and patterns of behavior. But, times are changing, and success stories are beginning to emerge. The challenge is to maintain and build on the momentum, and especially to carry the benefits to the hundreds of millions of people who are still untouched by the process of positive change.

MR BILL LONG *OECD, Paris*
(The opinions expressed here are the writer's and not necessarily those of the OECD)

The Green movement doesn't want to take everything, but what we do want is to stop needlessly destroying, particularly when we still don't know what it contains — and when there are alternatives.
PETER GARRETT

SENEGAL

In Senegal, everything revolves around a river. Whether called Senegal, Saloum or Cassamance, the Fouta-Djalon River remains the focal point of the country.

Senegal benefits from an ideal climate, a grand variety of fauna and flora, and a strong sense of hospitality and openness to people from all around the world.

Perhaps the highlights of any visit to our country are the World Heritage sites. Senegal ratified the World Heritage Convention in February 1976 and now has three sites on the list.

Goree Island is just south of the capital, Dakar, at Cape Vert. This small, rocky island holds a remarkable collection of fortifications dating from the 17th century and is an invaluable testament to the terrible years of the brutal slave trade.

Eastern Senegal boasts the Niokolo-Koba National Park and the fascinating Bassari country. This national park covers just over 4% of Senegal's total land area. It is the largest such park in West Africa and boasts a thriving population of wild elephants.

The third World Heritage site is Djoudj National Park, an immense aquatic wonderland, teeming with thousands of water birds and other wetland fauna, such as the crocodile.

There are, of course, many other areas of interest within Senegal, and no doubt many possibilities for future World Heritage listings. In the meantime, welcome to Senegal!

MR. JACQUES BAUDIN
Minister for Tourism and the Environment
Senegal

NIOKOLO-KOBA NATIONAL PARK

LOCATION Eastern Senegal and upper Casamance regions, N 13° 00', W 12° 00' (approximate mid-point).

DESCRIPTION This is an extremely large park, covering 850,000ha (2,040,000ac). Agriculture and grazing are strictly prohibited throughout the area. Much of the country is grassland and the climate is harsh.

SIGNIFICANCE This is the largest protected area in West Africa. A rare feature of the park is the sizeable elephant population (around 400) that sustains itself

Gorée Island

without difficulty. Something like 100,000 large mammals live here and the indigenous predator populations of lions, leopards and wild dogs are developing naturally.

DJOUDJ BIRD SANCTUARY

LOCATION   In the delta area of the river Senegal, 60 km (37mi) from St. Louis. N 16° 30', W 16° 10'.

DESCRIPTION   This park covers more than 18,000ha (43,200ac) and a quarter of it is covered by lake. Three rivers cross this area which is largely swampland. Water birds travel here in the thousands, migrating each year from Europe and East Africa. Numerous animals have been reintroduced, most importantly the crocodile, which is now thriving.

SIGNIFICANCE   This bird sanctuary is the only natural environment for the thousands of water birds that migrate annually 2,000km (1,200mi) across the Sahara Desert. It has the largest concentration of herons in west Africa and many other species such as the white pelican, great egret, African spoonbill and cormorant find nesting areas within its boundaries. The large, fast running bird, the big bustard, is found only in this park.

GORÉE ISLAND

LOCATION   Islet south of Dakar, W 17° 24', N 14° 00'.

DESCRIPTION   Gorée lies at the entrance to the large harbour that is naturally formed by the peninsula of Cape Vert. It is quite small, roughly 540 by 200m (1,800 by 660ft), and is mostly barren and rocky. Most of the island is taken up by the town which was established as a military and trading post. There is a complex of fortifications, a gun battery at the north end, several forts, and a large water reservoir in the south. There are ruins of a former residential area with a mosque.

SIGNIFICANCE   The history of Gorée is closely connected with the slave trade. Until the abolition of slavery in the French colonies in 1875, the island was a 'warehouse', with more than 10 slave holdings. Slaves were stored here awaiting shipment to the Americas. First occupied by the Dutch in the early 17th century, it was held by the English for one year in 1663, returning to the Dutch, then to the French in 1677. The English managed to wrest control once more, before the island finally fell into French hands for the last time.

The first rule of intelligent thinking is to save all the parts.

ALDO LEOPOLD

Djoudji Bird Sanctuary

SEYCHELLES

Seychelles is an archipelago of islands and islets in the Indian Ocean, some 1,500 kilometres (930mi) off the African east coast and about 3,000 kilometres (1860mi) from India. There are around 90 islands in total, 38 of them formed from granite, the balance from coral.

This country is a true unspoilt tropical paradise with crystal clear seas and palm-fringed, white sandy beaches. When first sighted by the Portuguese at the beginning of the 16th century, these islands were uninhabited. The first visitors were the British in 1609. It was another 159 years before a permanent settlement was made – by the French, who gave the name Seychelles, after Louis XV's Treasurer.

Today, these islands are inhabited by many ethnic groups, including descendants of the original Mauritian and Creole settlers, Africans, Indians, Chinese, French and English.

Seychelles accepted the World Heritage Convention in April 1980 and now has two sites on the World Heritage List. The Vallee de Mai Nature Reserve is on one of the main islands, Praslin, and comprises a remnant pocket of tropical palm forest, vegetation that was once distinctive of this island that used to be called the 'Isle of Palms'.

The other site is world renowned for its famous inhabitant, the giant tortoise. In this natural environment on Aldabra Atoll, the tortoise is at the top of the food chain; so its population here is the world's largest.

ALDABRA ATOLL

LOCATION   640km (398mi) off the African east coast, E 46° 25', S 09° 25'.

DESCRIPTION   Aldabra is a classic coral atoll which has been uplifted above the sea. The atoll consists of 4 main islands of coral limestone, separated by narrow passages and enclosing a large shallow lagoon. The elevation of the atoll rarely exceeds 3m (10ft) above sea level. It contains many diverse habitats, from coral reefs to mangroves.

SIGNIFICANCE   Due to its isolation the atoll has become a refuge for species that have become extinct elsewhere. The unpolluted and undisturbed environment make Aldabra of outstanding universal value to conservation

Vallée de Mai Nature Reserve

and science. This is probably the sole terrestrial environment where a reptile is the dominant herbivore: the giant tortoise (geochelone gigantea) population of 152,000 is the largest in the world and without doubt the atoll's most outstanding feature.

VALLÉE DE MAI NATURE RESERVE

LOCATION Praslin Island, E 55° 44′, S 04° 19′.

DESCRIPTION The Valley de Mai is an 18ha (43ac) nature reserve. Acquired by the government some years ago, it forms the nucleus of the Praslin National Park. The vegetation is lush rainforest with a predominance of palm trees.

SIGNIFICANCE Most of Praslin Island, once known as the 'Isle of Palms', has been burnt and cultivated, but this small pocket of palm forest in the valley has been preserved close to its original, primeval state. The most notable feature of the park is the famous double coconut which bears the largest seed in the plant kingdom; it can weigh up to 20kg (44lb).

The habitats of the tropics are the main repository of Earth's natural diversity – nearly two thirds of all species live there.

ALVARO UMAN

Aldabra Atoll

The Oceans: Our Lifeblood Threatened

THE PREDOMINANT physical feature of our planet is the oceans. They cover two-thirds of its surface. They play a key part in the chemistry of the atmosphere, hydrological cycle and in determining climate and weather conditions.

Life in the oceans is dominated by physical factors such as waves, tides, currents, salinity, temperature, pressure and light intensity. These contribute to determining the makeup of the biological communities which in turn have an effect on the composition and chemistry of the oceans.

The vastness of the oceans has led people to believe that they cannot be harmed. This is not so. Before this century the notion was largely correct because fewer people were exploiting the resources of the sea and they were limited by the very simple technologies at their disposal. During this century, however, the number of people exploiting ocean resources has increased dramatically and extensive developments have been made in ocean technologies. Not only have older, simpler methods been improved, totally new techniques have also been discovered which make new uses possible. These include radar and sonar that have contributed to safer navigation and easier detection of fish; man-made stuctures on the continental shelf which make possible the routine exploration and exploitation of petroleum far from land; freezer-factory trawlers capable of spending long periods at sea not only catching fish but processing them on board to a market ready state; and design and material improvements in shipbuilding.

These technological advances have led to dramatic increases in our capability and effort to harvest fish stocks, but we have probably approached the limit. During the 1980s the world marine fish catch increased steadily, reaching 84 million tonnes a year in 1988. Many fisheries scientists consider the limit of fisheries production to be around 100 million tonnes per year. With the possible exception of deep ocean squid and Antarctic krill, new resources will not be readily available to exploit. At present the technology to exploit squid is limited and many believe krill could not sustain extended heavy fishing pressure. If these assumptions are valid then by the year 2000 it is estimated that the demand for fish and shellfish would exceed supply by around 20 million tonnes. This would raise world market prices and increase the pressure for governments to sell marine products to derive development income. Such a situation could become critical for many tropical developing countries that derive between 40 and 100% of their animal protein from fisheries.

The interface between the land and sea, the coastal zone, consists of continental shelves and coastal plains. This area is not simply a transition area but has special characteristics of its own. It is a band of highly diverse ecosystems and habitats that are among the most biologically productive on earth. These include extensive inter-tidal mudflats, rocky shores, sandy beaches, mangroves, saltmarshes, estuaries and other wetlands, seagrass and seaweed beds, and coral reefs. These are vital for coastal protection and provide food and shelter for a great variety of organisms, including the fishes, crustaceans and molluscs that account for more than two-thirds of the world fisheries production.

The coastal zone is also home to much of the world's population who depend on its resources and largely determine the state of its health. The world population – now at 5 billion – is expected to grow to nearly 10 billion, double its present size, by the year 2050. It has been estimated that sixty per cent of the world's population already live within 60kms (40mi) of coastal waters, including two-thirds of the cities with populations of 2.5 million or more which are located on the coast or are near tidal estuaries. Despite the importance of maintaining the high productivity of coastal ecosystems, the coastal zone is manipulated through land-fill and coastal engineering projects for human settlements and industrial development. For the most part this discharged waste ends up in coastal waters. Seventy per cent of reported fish kills in some industrialized nations are a result of dumping sludge waste, or arise from urban, industrial and agricultural run-off.

Intensive efforts to address the situation of deteriorating ocean and coastal resources during the last two decades have been undertaken as the loss of resources has become more apparent and acute. Most notable have been the development of a number of action plans and international treaties such as the Baltic Convention, the Oslo-Paris Convention for the North Sea and the Barcelona Convention for the Mediterranean. There are a least ten other such regional agreements (including one for the South Pacific) which are in the process of being adopted and implemented as well as the Law of the Sea Treaty under which 'States have the obligation to protect and preserve the marine environment'. Such agreements help to commit countries to expand their efforts toward coastal and ocean resource management. This is a vital step but much more is needed.

Effective marine conservation, and the recognition of the need for it, lags far behind terrestrial conservation. It is interesting to note that only sixteen out of ninety three natural World Heritage sites are marine. In part this is because of the tradition of treating ocean resources as common property – available for anyone with the capability of

Cáceres

exploiting them – but also it is that often what we do to degrade the marine environment is not obvious to us. Instead it is 'out of sight, out of mind'. More needs to be done to change these attitudes. This would be aided by increased effort to identify the real threats to the marine and coastal environment, to communicate information about those threats to the public and to governments in a clear and understandable way, and to strengthen worldwide understanding through better education and training programmes. The World Heritage Convention provides one framework for accomplishing these tasks by identifying which coastal and marine areas are of universal value and by ensuring that these sites are managed to the highest international standards.

DANNY ELDER
IUCN

SPAIN

Occupying more than three quarters of the Iberian Peninsula, (581,000 sq km – 194,930 sq mi) Spain is dominated by the Central Meseta, an enormous plateau in the centre of the country. The plateau is ringed by many important cordilleras, or mountain chains, including the Picos de Europa, the Sierra de Gredos and the Sierra Nevada, a natural formation which has been likened to fortifications encircling a citadel.

Although the northern Atlantic regions of the Basque Country, Cantabria, Austurias, and Galicia have an abundance of rain, the climate elsewhere tends to be dry and often harsh, and the country has endured many devastating droughts, particularly in the south. Yet there is a certain quality to the Spanish countryside which is to be found nowhere else in Europe: the rich ochre colours of the earth, the silver green of the great olive trees and the confident luminosity of its blue skies imbue the landscape with a rugged assuredness.

The peninsula was settled by Celts, Iberians, Phoenicians, Greeks and Romans. In the 5th century AD it was invaded by the barbarians, among them the Vandals and the Visigoths, and this was

El Greco's house, Toledo

followed in 711 by the Moorish occupation, a time of outstanding artistic achievement which lasted until the 'Reconquest' in 1492. In the same year, Isabel and Ferdinand expelled the Jews and instituted the Inquisition which became a notorious instrument of terror. Spain's extraordinary naval exploits during their reign and that of Carlos I's were tempered by the consequences of colonization: whole indigenous populations wiped out by militarism and the introduction of European diseases.

During the reign of the first Habsburg king, Carlos I (Charles V) 1516-1556, Spain reached its zenith as a world power, yet under his heirs Spain suffered significant losses of territory in the 30 Years War, the War of Devolution, and the War of the Spanish Succession, and went into decline. During the 18th and 19th centuries, Spain was an agricultural nation dominated by its landed aristocracy and a Bourbon Monarchy which alternated between despotism and enfeebled rule. The twentieth century brought enormous change to Spain. The first thirty years were ones of turmoil, challenge and hope, reflected in the extraordinary work of artists such as Picasso, Miro, Gris and Dali (who left an incalculable impression on the history of modern art). But the physical and emotional devastation of a vicious civil war left nearly a million dead and the country exhausted and isolated.

After 36 years of dictatorship under Franco, a new constitution was promulgated in 1978 and today Spain is a flourishing, energetic democracy. Spain has been able to retain its distinctive national and regional identities, and this, together with its art and architectural treasures and extensive coastline has made it the country with the highest number of tourists in the world. It now has more tourists than citizens (38 million vs 40 million visitors a year). Unfortunately, its once magnificent coasts have suffered extensive degradation. Spain's greatest challenge now is to halt further high rise development along the ravaged Mediterranean shoreline and to prevent the same fate from befalling its relatively untouched northern coast.

Spain accepted the World Heritage Convention in May 1982 and presently has sixteeen sites on the World Heritage List. Remarkably, all but one of these are cultural sites – Garanjonay National Park in the Canary Islands is the sole natural listing.

The fifteen cultural listings represent various phases of Spain's exciting and influential development. From the invaluable collection of prehistoric art at Altamira Cave, to the Roman ruins at Salamanca, Caceres, Segovia and Toledo; through the multitude of sites which have special significance to Christendom and Islam, to the architectural treasures of the medieval Spanish kingdoms: this vast and varied ensemble of treasures now form an invaluable part of the world's heritage.

The Alhambra and the Generalife in Granada

Altamira Cave

The Romanesque cathedral at Santiago de Compostela

The aqueduct of Segovia

TOLEDO (HISTORIC TOWN)

LOCATION   Region of Castille la Nueva, 70km (43mi) southwest of Madrid, N 39° 51′, W 00° 20′.

DESCRIPTION   Surrounded on all sides except the north by the River Tagus, Toledo sits on a rugged outcrop of granite 720m (2,400ft) above sea level. A pair of Moorish bridges span the river, and numerous gateways allow entrance to the old town. The alcázar, a massive stone structure with 4 corner towers, sits on the highest point and dominates the setting. A large cathedral with Gothic, Renaissance and baroque features has an impressive spire which towers over the streets below. Numerous other churches, a Franciscan convent, several synagogues, Arabic baths and many significant residential mansions are also found in this magnificent town.

SIGNIFICANCE   Toledo was conquered in 193 BC by the Romans and became a major regional centre. Its history is strongly rooted in Catholicism, and it was one of the important early Christian centres until the Moorish invasion. Prospering under Moorish rule, it became an important trading centre, especially in textiles. The large Jewish community thrived and the city's culture developed into a unique blend of Arab and Hebrew. When the Catholics recaptured the city in 1085, it was made Spain's capital and remained so for almost 500 turbulent years which saw, amongst other events, the infamous massacre of the Jews in 1392. Today, the old city is very well preserved and so remains an important relic of the vibrant history of this region.

SALAMANCA (OLD CITY)

LOCATION   In the region of Castille la Vieja, N 40° 58′, W 05° 40′.

DESCRIPTION   The city of Salamanca is situated on the northern bank of the Tormes River and is entered by crossing a Roman bridge. Within the walls are the old quarter of the cathedral and the baroque square of Plaza Mayor. The city has 2 cathedrals which are joined; the old 12th century cathedral and the newer 17th century cathedral. The facade of the old university is in the Spanish Renaissance style called plateresque. There are numerous convents, churches and mansions.

SIGNIFICANCE   Conquered by Hannibal in 222 BC, Salamanca not long after became an important Roman station. Gothic and Moorish control was followed by Alphonso VI at around 1100 AD. Soon after, the town's university gained much acclaim and prosperity endured until the 16th century. The university is still renowned and is the oldest on the Iberian Peninsula. The Plaza Mayor is one of the finest squares in Europe. It could hold 20,000 people – notably for bullfights – and is surrounded by Corinthian columns surmounted by a series of 90 arches. As one of the more important cities during the Renaissance, Salamanca holds an invaluable heritage.

Casa Milá in Barcelona

Mosque of Córdoba

The Alcazar at Toledo

Casa de las Conchas, Salamanca

Burgos Cathedral

THE ESCORIAL

LOCATION   55km (34mi) north of Madrid, W 04° 10',
N 40° 35'.

DESCRIPTION   This complex is of considerable size and
is composed of 5 distinct areas; 'the College for the Sons
of Noblemen', the seminary, the monastery, the palace
and the church. The monastery, which is perfectly symmetrical, stands at the centre of the complex which was
built between 1563-1584.

SIGNIFICANCE   The ground plan of the monastery was
based, according to scholars of the period, on that of the
Temple of Jerusalem. This vast architectural ensemble is
remarkable for its austerity and simplicity. The 4 solid
towers which stand at the 4 corners of the monastery and
the large dome are distinctly Spanish, but the slate-tiled
roofs, virtually the first in Spain, are distinctly central
European.

THE ALHAMBRA AND THE
GENERALIFE IN GRANADA

LOCATION   Granada, Andalucia, W 03° 33', W 37°
10'.

DESCRIPTION   This magnificent complex of fortified
palaces, the jewel of the final period of Moorish domination of Spain, was built on one of Granada's three hills.
The quality and intricacy of the stucco work is unsur-
passed. Ceramic tiles are used with verve and imagination. Amongst the many beautiful gardens and courtyards is the celebrated Court of Lions.

SIGNIFICANCE   The Alhambra and its extension, the
Generalife, are the single most important pieces of
architectural heritage from the Nasrides – the last of the
Spanish Muslim dynasties. Nasrid art represents the
zenith of Muslim art in the Iberian Peninsula.

TERUEL
(MUDEJAR ARCHITECTURE)

LOCATION   Teruel, Aragon, N 40° 20', W 01° 06'.

DESCRIPTION   This is a group of 4 towers in the centre
of the old town, all built at the back of churches bearing
the same name. They are; St. Peter, St. Salvador, St.
Martin and the cathedral.

SIGNIFICANCE   These towers are the most important
and best preserved examples of Mudejar architecture in
Spain. This style was developed in Spain during the
Middle Ages directly after the Christian re-conquest of
Moorish-held territories, when Muslims were working
under the supervision of Christians. It reached its
apotheosis in the delicate brick and tile work that can be
seen at Teruel.

Teruel

SANTIAGO DE COMPOSTELA

LOCATION   In the region of Galicia, northwest Spain, N 42° 52', W 08° 32'.

DESCRIPTION   Santiago has many buildings of historical and architectural significance, particularly its religious buildings. The main ones include the Romanesque cruciform cathedral with its Portico de la Gloria – a magnificent Gothic piece of art, the Palace Gelmirez, the Monastery of St. Martin Pinario, the Royal Hospital and the Place Rajoy.

SIGNIFICANCE   This town has a long and important history in Christendom. After the Moorish conquests of Spain, the northwest was the only area left unaffected. So the beginnings of the assault to reconquer Spain for Christianity began in Santiago. This created tremendous enthusiasm for the religion which was further inflamed with the reputed discovery of the remains of Saint James. A church was built over the spot and it rapidly gained acclaim as a pilgrimage destination. As a result, the town now has one of the richest legacies of Christian art and architecture to be found on the Iberian Peninsula.

GARAJONAY NATIONAL PARK

LOCATION   Island of Gomera, Canary Islands, N 28° 05' to 28° 12', W 17° 10' to 17° 18'.

DESCRIPTION   Situated right in the centre of the island, Garajonay has an area of 3,984ha (9,605ac), just over 10 percent of the island's total. Its highest point is 1,492m (4,895ft) above sea level and vegetation is largely subtropical rainforest.

SIGNIFICANCE   The majestic forests of this mountainous island park are remnants of the subtropical vegetation which once flourished in southern Europe until sudden climatic changes led to their disappearance. The flora is particularly rich here, with over 450 different species, 34 of them endemic to the region and 8 endemic to the park.

OLD TOWN OF ÁVILA AND ITS EXTRA MUROS CHURCHES

LOCATION   Ávila 100km (62mi) northwest of Madrid. W 01° 00', N 40° 39'.

DESCRIPTION   The old town of Ávila is wholly enclosed by some 2.5km (1.5mi) of massive stone walls which are on average 12m (39ft) high and 3m (10ft) thick. These walls incorporate 82 forts and 9 fortified gates. The historic centre is characterised by narrow streets and small squares with low houses. There are several palaces and mansions and numerous religious buildings, the most significant are: the Cathedral of Salvador, the Church of Santo Tomé and the Convent of Saint Teresa. Outside the walls are 4 important 12th century Romanesque churches: San Vicente, San Pedro, San Andrés and San Segundo.

SIGNIFICANCE   This superb example of a medieval fortified town was built during the 12th century after Spain was reconquered from the Moors. Prior to that, it was the site of several ancient Roman, Celtic and Arab settlements. Its strong religious character stems largely from its being the birthplace of St. Teresa. Several notable works of art are kept in the town, particularly the paintings of Pedro de Berruguete and the work of goldsmith Juan de Arfe y Villafane.

OLD TOWN OF SEGOVIA AND ITS AQUEDUCT

LOCATION   Segovia, Castilla la Vieja, around 80km (50mi) northwest of Madrid, N 40° 57', W 04° 26'.

DESCRIPTION   The old part of Segovia is placed high up on a narrow ridge and is encircled by stone walls. Plaza Mayor forms the centre of the town and the main cathedral sits on one side of it. 'El Puente' is the Roman aqueduct which crosses the Plaza del Azoguejo. It is constructed of dark granite without the use of mortar and its highest point is 27m (90ft) above the ground. Consisting of 2 levels of arches, it is still in use. Numerous Romanesque churches are found within the walls, including those of San Lorenzo, Vera Cruz and San Esteban. The fortified castle, or alcázar, of the Castilian Kings is one of the best known monuments.

SIGNIFICANCE   A place of some importance in Roman times, Segovia was founded around 700 BC. The first major upheaval was at the beginning of the 8th century AD when the Moors conquered the town. Almost 300 years later it was recaptured by Alfonso VI. Its position was then consolidated and the town grew and prospered, eventually becoming a major industrial centre of the Middle Ages. The old town's state of preservation is excellent and the town now presents a storehouse of architectural wealth, particularly Romanesque and Gothic. The aqueduct is of particular significance, being easily the best preserved of its type.

Interior of the Alcazar at Sevilla

Garajonay National Park

The Escorial

PARQUE AND PALACIO GÜELL AND CASA MILÁ IN BARCELONA

LOCATION   City of Barcelona, Cataluva, E 05° 50', N 44° 00'.

DESCRIPTION   Güell Park, which was originally proposed as a revolutionary residential centre by Catalan architect Antonio Gaudi, was left unfinished after Gaudi was tragically struck by a trolley. It is now enjoyed as a public park. Palacio Güell was designed and built on the commission of Eugenio Güell, a Catalan philanthropist, as his main residence. Casa Milá stands on a plot of 1,600sq m (18,000sq ft) and is privately owned.

SIGNIFICANCE   These 3 artistic architectural monuments celebrate the achievements of Antonio Gaudi Cornet (1852-1926), a brilliant architect of Catalian modernism. These 3 structures illuminate Gaudi's interest in medieval and Gothic tradition. Much of his work includes innovative and daring sculptural forms, and he is considered to have been one of the great architects of his time.

SEVILLA (CATHEDRAL, ALCÁZAR AND ARCHIVO DE INDIAS)

LOCATION   In the region of Andalucia, southern Spain, E 05° 05', N 37° 25'.

DESCRIPTION   An inland city on the left bank of the Guadalquivir River, the old part of Seville is a maze of small streets and squares, although the district of the alcázar and the cathedral is more spacious. The alcázar is a fortified Moorish palace with 10 sides and is of brick construction. The Cathedral of Santa Maria de la Sede is mainly in the Gothic style and is of immense proportions – 90m (300ft) wide and 30m (100ft) high. Casa Lonja is a superb Renaissance building and houses the Archivo de Indias – a collection of documents, books, manuscripts, maps and plans all relating to Spain's administration of its empire in the Americas.

SIGNIFICANCE   The Cathedral was erected to commemorate the reconquest of Spain by Christianity – it is the second largest in area of all Gothic churches and the largest in Europe. The alcázar, begun in 1181 AD, is a superb example of Moorish architecture. The Archivo de Indias is the definitive documentation of the Spanish Empire in the New World and, as such, is of absolutely crucial historical importance.

ALTAMIRA CAVE

LOCATION   Region of Vispieres in Cantabria Province, N 43° 22', W 00° 25'.

DESCRIPTION   Situated at the summit of a limestone cliff, this cave is almost 300m (1000ft) in length and of varying width. There are numerous galleries branching off from the main chamber. Most of the paintings are found inside the 'Great Hall', 18 by 9m (60 by 30ft) wide. Its ceiling is covered with paintings of bisons in bright shades of red, violet and black. There are also hand prints and outlines as well as some paintings of horses, boars and human figures. Other chambers have paintings of deer, cattle, goats, antelope and symbols. The total number of paintings is around 150.

SIGNIFICANCE   First discovered in 1868, the paintings in this cave were not recognised for their true value until some 40 years later. They are now considered one of the most valuable collections of prehistoric art in the world. It has been coined the 'Sistine Chapel of Quaternary art'.

BURGOS CATHEDRAL

LOCATION   Burgos, 240km (150mi) north of Madrid, W 03° 40', N 42° 23'.

DESCRIPTION   This massive limestone cathedral dominates the entire town of Burgos. Its cruciform design is somewhat hidden by the wealth of additions that have been made since its initial construction. There are 15 chapels, a 14th century cloister and an archiepiscopal palace, joined to and surrounding the original structure. The western facade holds the 3 central doorways and is flanked by 2 lofty towers. It is also crowned by a dome, another late addition. The interior features a famous curiosity: a crucifix covered with buffalo hide to resemble human skin.

SIGNIFICANCE   Founded in 1221, this magnificent example of a floral Gothic cathedral was not completed until 1567. The bones of that most celebrated of medieval Spanish captains, 'El Cid' have rested here since 1919.

CÁCERES (OLD TOWN)

LOCATION   300km (186mi) west-southwest of Madrid, N 39° 28', W 06° 22'.

DESCRIPTION   The old part of Cáceres sits above the modern town and is protected by stone walls that are 1.2km (0.75mi) in length. There are 3 gates and originally there were 30 towers; now only several remain. The dominant feature is the tower of the Gothic church of San Mateo. There is a former Jesuit college and monastery which is now a hospital, as well as the Churches of Santa Maria and San Francisco Javier.

SIGNIFICANCE   Cáceres is of Roman origin and it is thought it occupies the site of the ancient Roman town Norba Caesarina. It enjoyed considerable prosperity in the Middle Ages, mainly due to its proximity to the coast and the consequent trade with the New World of the Americas. Today, it is a fine example of an early fortified town with its extremely well preserved fortifications which are half Roman and half Arabic.

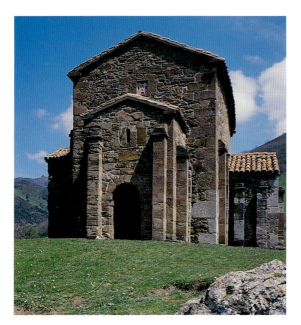

Santa Cristina de Lina, Asturias

CHURCHES OF THE KINGDOM OF THE ASTURIAS

LOCATION Asturias Region, N 43° 09' to 43° 22', W 02° 11' to 02° 33'.

DESCRIPTION There are 3 churches here: Santa Maria del Naranco, San Miguel de Lillo and Santa Cristina de Lena. The first 2 are situated on Naranco Hill which is a specially protected area.

SIGNIFICANCE Asturias was formerly an independent Christian kingdom founded after the Muslim invasion of Spain. These churches are representative of the later stages of this kingdom. They are the first Asturian churches not built according to the 'Visigothic' style. Pillars instead of columns, round-headed arches, wider aisles and a larger sense of space are distinctive of this innovative style.

MOSQUE OF CÓRDOBA

LOCATION Córdoba, W 04° 35', N 37° 50'.

DESCRIPTION The mosque, including successive additions to the original building, occupies a rectangular site 180 by 130m (600 by 430ft). It is surrounded by a massive wall which is strengthened by square towers. Each tower has several doors which give access to the building. There is a courtyard on the northern side with orange trees which is surrounded by a high wall with archways on 3 sides. The interior is dark and low-ceilinged, with forests of pillars and superb red and white arches.

SIGNIFICANCE Probably modelled on the mosque in Damascus, this one nonetheless is more advanced architecturally. The series of double arches which supports the roof was a brilliant innovation for its time. Apart from being a major centre of architectural experimentation and innovation, this mosque is also a storehouse for some fabulous artistic treasures.

Political Courage for the Environment

IN 1750, KING FERDINAND VI of Spain bought some arable land and olive groves close to Madrid and decided to plant them with green oak acorns, so that a suitable hunting ground would, in time, develop. Considering the fact that a self-respecting green oak takes between 100 and 150 years to reach a decent size, the king's decision can be seen as a curious example of an early – and laudable – environmental decision. As a result, Madrid is now the only European capital that has at its very gates 10,000 hectares (24,000 ac) of practically natural forest where some of the rarest birds in Europe thrive.

Nowadays, environmental problems – and the right environmental decisions – are never so simple. Politicians and decision-makers in general are usually well aware of the importance and well-founded nature of the environmental arguments placed

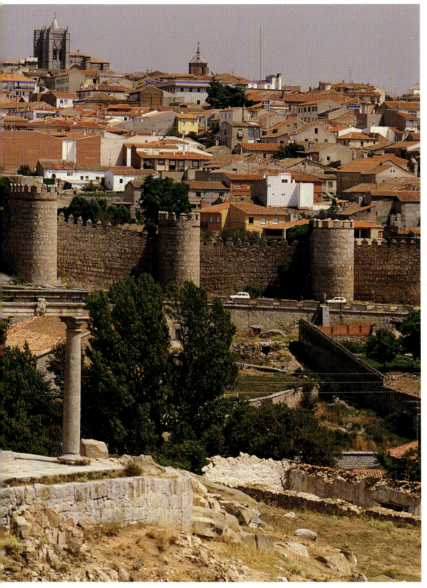
Old Town of Avila

before them, yet they sometimes hesitate to take a firm stand on environmental issues or postpone decisions.

One of the reasons may be that, more often than not, environmentally correct decisions are not very rewarding in political terms. They may require quite a lot of investment, which has to be diverted from other more electorally rewarding infrastructures such as hospitals, roads or schools. Furthermore some good environmental decisions – such as reducing air and water pollution, for instance – are long-term tasks which invariably stretch beyond the periods for which politicians are elected, so few tangible results can be presented at campaigns, thus reducing their attraction.

Even if environmental groups do at times support politicians, some decisions may create conflicts with other interest groups. Take for instance the establishment of a national park for the preservation of the wildlife it contains. Whereas such an idea may satisfy city-dwellers and potential visitors, it can be a very difficult concept to sell to farmers living within the park boundary, to hunters who will find their activi-

ties restricted by new regulations or to land developers planning holiday resorts.

The situation is particularly complicated when an environmental problem has an international dimension, such as the control of cross-border pollution causing acid rain, the prevention of climatic change by reduction of carbon dioxide emissions or the conservation of the ozone layer. For all such problems, the short term interest of different countries diverge and the measures needed to solve them may require a profound transformation of their industrial and development policies.

Thus it seems that in environmental issues it is easy to agree on the real dimension of the problem but very difficult to agree on the necessary remedies and even more difficult to make the sacrifices that are required. Yet environmental problems only become more critical with time, and thus it is courage, a great deal of courage, which is needed to make the right choices now. Take as an example – an example *not* to follow – what has happened in the Central and Eastern European countries which have recently experienced political change. Forty years of absence of democracy has bequeathed a disastrous economic situation but an even worse ecological heritage of air and water pollution, forests devastated by acid rain and land contaminated by hazardous industrial waste. The clean-up may last longer than the forty years it took to pollute. And it will cost billions in any currency.

But it is not just in Eastern Europe that mistakes have been made. Even the most advanced countries have often neglected the impact that industrial development and intensive farming have on the natural environment. The relatively high number of extinct or severely endangered species in Europe speaks for itself.

A particularly unfortunate aspect of environmental decision-making is that there is never a second chance. When considering, for instance, different alternatives for routing a motorway, we can perhaps choose the most economic alternative at high cost to the environment. But we should be conscious that no matter how great the resources, it will never be possible to recreate the heathland that was destroyed in the process.

I feel it is important that decision-makers understand their responsibility and that they play their role as the vanguard of environmental improvement, by the wisdom of their decisions and by the courage needed to take them. They are well placed to understand the challenge of working for a better world. After all, in 100 or 150 years time there will still be people around to remember that we planted acorns on bare ground. At least, in the 23 democratic states which make up the Council of Europe we think so, and it is my task as Secretary General to promote the appropriate policies.

CATHERINE LALUMIERE
Secretary General of the Council of Europe

SRI LANKA

Sri Lanka is an island state, approximately half the size of England, situated in the Indian Ocean just off the south eastern corner of India. There are several ethnic groups to be found in this country, but two predominate; the Singhalese and the Tamils.

The Singhalese came to the island from India in 550 BC and found in residence a people called the Vedda who were nomadic hunters and food gatherers. They brought with them agriculture and iron, and so easily dominated the land. Buddhism came to Ceylon, as Sri Lanka used to be known, in the 3rd century BC, also from India.

Anuradhapura became the centre of religious and cultural activity. It is now one of six Sri Lankan World Heritage sites on the list after the convention was accepted in June 1980.

Two other important ancient Buddhist sites are Polonnaruwa and Sigiriya, both also on the World Heritage List. Of the remaining three sites, one is the Sacred City of Kandy. Situated in the central mountains, Kandy was established in the 14th century and remained a Singhalese and Buddhist bastion, even through the turbulent years of Portuguese colonialism.

Galle is another of the sites; this is a well preserved 16th century, mainly Portuguese, fortified colonial city. The remaining site is Sri Lanka's sole natural listing and represents the last surviving pocket of pristine rainforest on the island.

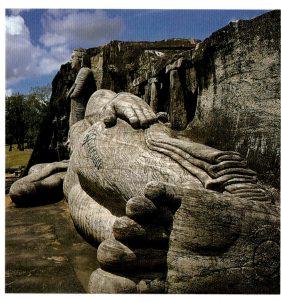

Monolithic sculptures at Polonnaruwa

The temple complex of the Tooth Relic, Kandy

Sinharaja Forest

TWO MAJOR ecological zones have been identified in Sri Lanka. The wet zone receiving an annual rainfall of 3000-5100mm (118-200ins) is confined to the hilly central and south western parts of the country and comprises about 23% of the island. The balance is a relatively flat dry zone receiving under 1500mm (59ins) of rain. Over the last two centuries much of the wet zone has been subject to high population pressures as well as demand for land for the cultivation of tea, rubber and coconut, leaving a mere 9% of the area under forests.

Amongst the few irregularly distributed tropical lowland rain forests in this region, is a substantially undisturbed and very special forest area of more than 11,000 ha (26,400acs) known as Sinharaja, meaning 'Lion King' in the Sinhala language. The tall canopy of this picturesque forest supports spiralling woody climbers and many epiphytes, including orchids. Ferns, epiphyllous mosses and liverworts are also present. Tall spiny canes find their way to the top canopy in search of light. The streams flowing in the forest and on the valley bottoms carry crystal clear water over well worn rock formations, stones and rounded pebbles. The parent material of the soil in these forests is highly weathered and leached, as a result, the soils are poor in nutrients. However, this tropical lowland rain forest is productive and supports a large biomass per unit area. The nutrients are mostly contained in the biomass and not in the soil.

The flora of Sri Lanka includes about 3365 species of angiosperms. Species richness and endemism in Sri Lanka are centred in the primary tropical lowland rain forests of the Sinharaja type which harbour 495 of the 830 species of endemic plants found in the island. In some families, eg dipterocarpaceae, endemism is greater than 90%. Similarly, a high level of endemism is found among the lower plants such as ferns.

Recent studies of the fauna of Sinharaja have revealed that endemism is highest for birds (95%). Other groups with decreasing levels of endemism are: mammals (57%), amphibia (53%), butterflies (51%), tetrapod reptiles (39%), fish (19%) and snakes (18%).

The birds, while feeding, have been observed to move in mixed flocks of up to 40 species. These flocks are regularly found in the company of other animals such as giant squirrel, jungle squirrel, the purple-faced leaf monkey and the mouse deer. Plant and animal interaction relating to pollination, seed dispersal and germination is considered high.

Human Interactions:

In comparison with other forests of Sri Lanka, human activities within Sinharaja forest have been

Sinharaja Forest Reserve

minimal. An aerial photo study in 1957 showed that 15% of the Sinharaja forest Reserve had been subjected to slash and burn cultivation along the fringes with even a few instances of open pit gem mining within the forest. More recently several places along the fringes have also been cultivated with more permanent economic crops such as tea. Continued cultivation along the fringes in this manner over a long period has led to the establishment of twenty four small settlements around the periphery with a population of about 5000. Two of these settlements are completely within the forest. About 8% of households in these peripheral settlements are totally dependent on the resources of the forest, others to a lesser degree. Extraction of firewood and smallwood, production of 'Jaggery' (a form of brown sugar from the phloem sap tapped from the Caryota palm), cutting of cane, collection of medicinal plants and harvesting of wild cardamon (Elletaria ensal) are the main resources from the forest. Socio-economic studies are being carried out to collect more information on settlements within the forest.

Development of Legal and Conservation Status

The future conservation of Sinharaja is based on strategies derived from modern concepts of protected natural area management. However, the original legal status of Sinharaja permitted the felling of trees on a selective basis and in keeping with this status, a section of the Sinharaja Forest was selectively logged in the early 1970s. It resulted in a public outcry and protests by Sri Lankan and foreign scientists against the exploitation of a beautiful and undisturbed lowland rain forest. By the mid 1970s the importance of Sinharaja as a conservation area was highlighted as a result of pioneer scientific work by national scientists. The status of Sinharaja was re-examined and

Sigiriya

in 1978 Sinharaja was included in the international network of biosphere reserves established and maintained as a part of UNESCO's Man and the Biosphere (MAB) program.

Based on studies by local scientists, the IUCN and the Ministry of Lands and Land Development of the Government of Sri Lanka formulated a project proposal for the conservation and development of Sinharaja with funding from the governments of Norway (NORAD) and Sri Lanka. About the same time, Sinharaja Reserve, together with a north-eastern extension including the Thangamalai plains, was declared Sri Lanka's first National Wilderness Heritage Area. In December 1988, the Sinharaja biosphere reserve was inscribed as Sri Lanka's first natural site under UNESCO's World Heritage Convention thereby giving recognition to its outstanding universal value.

Management of Sinharaja

In formulating plans for the management of Sinharaja, one of the problems as regards conservation is the dependence of fringe settlements on a variety of resources available within the forest and the surrounding areas. Future plans have to recognise the needs of the local people as having high priority. Long term solutions have to be found to ensure that the villagers in the course of time will minimise their demands on the forest.

An approach to conservation and management of these areas is being planned to indentify a central core area of the forest with no human activity whatsoever, and a buffer zone divided into inner and outer areas. As an extreme measure, relocating some families by providing incentives such as land or alternative employment, mainly to young people, is also being contemplated.

Buffer zone development is mostly confined to the outer buffer zone where private home gardens are located. Direct and indirect benefits to the settlers are planned by increasing awareness amongst local communities of forest conservation, improving agricultural methods such as soil conservation, introducing economic crops and encouraging better health standards. In addition, State sponsored buffer zone activities, such as establishment and maintenance of fast growing timber and fuel species and raising forest plantations with economic possibilities on denuded buffer zone lands are being carried out. The ultimate aim is to develop small-scale industries in the buffer zone which will have significant and sustainable employment and income generating value to the people living in marginal forest communities. While this work is in progress, national and international scientists are continuing studies to learn more about the unique bio-diversity of this forest.

M S RANATUNGA
IUCN Country Representative, Colombo, Sri Lanka

Galle

ANURADHAPURA (SACRED CITY)

LOCATION   North central province, E 80° 22' to 80° 27', N 08° 19' to 08° 23'.

DESCRIPTION   The site of the ancient capital city consists of the palace, the Temple of the Sacred Tooth, 13 monasteries, 5 great water reservoirs and associated settlements, 4 ancient gates, a rampart and a moat. The city was designed and built in 4 residential sections, divided according to profession or social status.

SIGNIFICANCE   The sacred city is thought to date back to 500 BC, becoming the capital in the 3rd century BC. It played a key role in the development of Buddhist culture, later becoming one of the most important centres of the faith. The stupas of dagobas (a specific type of Buddhist building) of Anuradhapura are particularly well known, especially the Ruaneli dagoba which is on the scale of the Egyptian pyramids and was conceived as an enormous model of the universe. It contains the largest collection of Buddhist relics on the island.

GALLE

LOCATION   City of Galle, Southern Province, E 80° 25', N 06° 00'.

DESCRIPTION   This old fortified city is extremely well preserved and is still occupied. It sits on 40ha (96ac) and originally had a moat surrounding its walls which has since been filled in. 3 gates are in existence today, one is disused and one was added by the British in 1873.

SIGNIFICANCE   The site was established by the Portuguese in 1543 but the fortifications were not built until 1663 when the Dutch conquered the city. This is by far the best preserved fortified city in south and southeast Asia. It has great historical value in preserving some architectural features of each of three major colonial powers – Portuguese, Dutch and British.

POLONNARUWA (ANCIENT CITY)

LOCATION   North central Province, N 07° 52' to 07° 59', E 80° 56' to 81° 02'.

DESCRIPTION   The ruins of this city are most famous for the collection of shrines that are found in The Great Quadrangle. A 7 storeyed brick pyramid, named the Sat Mahal Pasala, the Hata-da-ge, a rectangular masonry structure and the Wata-da-ge, a circular stone shrine are particularly notable.

SIGNIFICANCE   Polonnaruwa was established as the capital not long after the fall of Anuradhapura at the end of the 10th century AD. The greatest building activity was seen between 1059 and 1207 AD when the 3 great Polonnaruwa sovereigns reigned – Vijayabahu I, Parakramabahu I and Nissanka Malla. The fine legacy

Anuradhapura

left by this civilisation includes many superb bronze sculptures of religious figures as well as a grand and daring architectural style.

SACRED CITY OF KANDY

LOCATION   Central province, E 80° 38′, N 07° 17′.

DESCRIPTION   Lying in a valley 488m (1,600ft) above sea level, this old city is surrounded by mountains. Among the many important buildings found here are the temple complex of the Tooth Relic, the massive timber Audience Hall, the large monastery complex of Malwatte Vihara and the Palace of King Sri Wikrama.

SIGNIFICANCE   Established in the 14th century by King Vikramabahu, it later became the island's capital and remained so until 1815. The most important feature of the city is the temple which houses the Tooth Relic of Lord Buddha. Venerated by millions of Buddhists around the world, this temple complex is a treasure house of Kandyan arts.

SIGIRIYA (ANCIENT CITY)

LOCATION   Matale District, N 07° 55′ to 07° 58′, E 80° 44′ to 80° 47′.

DESCRIPTION   This complex of city ruins is based on a rock approximately 180m (591ft) high. A palace with surrounding buildings sits on the summit. Numerous pathways, some tunnelled through rock, lead down to the plain below where there is a large complex of water gardens to the west and a wall on the east. An inner and an outer moat surround the site which also includes two monasteries and a residential area.

SIGNIFICANCE   Sigiriya, meaning 'lion', takes its name from the staircase to the summit which is built in the form of a lion. Created by Prince Kassapa in the 4th century BC, it was intended to be an inaccessible stronghold for his treasures. After having his father killed, Kassapa ruled as king for 18 years and for this period Sigiriya was the capital. During this time a monastery was founded. After being defeated in battle by his brother, Kassapa killed himself and his brother handed Sigiriya over to the priests.

SINHARAJA FOREST RESERVE

LOCATION   Sabaragamuwa and southern provinces, E 80° 21′ to 80° 34′, N 06° 21′ to 06° 26′.

DESCRIPTION   Situated in the low wetlands of the southwest, this reserve covers an area of some 8,800ha (21,000ac). The terrain is mostly rolling hills with the highest peak at 1,150m (3,800ft). Rainfall is moderately high and the vegetation is typically tropical rainforest.

SIGNIFICANCE   This is the only surviving area of relatively undisturbed rainforest in Sri Lanka. Almost 70 percent of the flora in the reserve is endemic to the area. It is a crucially important habitat for Sri Lanka's endemic bird species – all of them spend at least some time in this reserve.

Statue commemorating the founding of Berne

SWITZERLAND

Switzerland ratified the World Heritage Convention in September 1975 and soon had three sites inscribed on the World Heritage List. Each of these sites reflects something of the intricate history of this small central European country, which is actually a confederation of 22 *cantons*.

This confederation has its origins in the 'Everlasting league for the purpose of self-defence against all who should attack or trouble them...' which was formed in 1291. Small pieces of the imperial empires of Germany, France and Italy joined together for the purpose of common defence, largely against the Hapsburgs. By the beginning of the 15th century, this alliance had, for all practical purposes, gained its independence, although it was not formalised until 1648.

Of Switzerland's three World Heritage listings, two are important Catholic monuments. Both the Benedictine Convent of Mustair and the Convent of Saint Gall are 8th century monastic complexes with significant architectural and artistic features.

The third listing is the old part of Switzerland's capital city, Berne. This beautiful old medieval town sits in a spectacular alpine setting and possesses many extremely well preserved monuments and buildings.

Berne (Old City)

Convent of St. Gall

BENEDICTINE CONVENT OF MÜSTAIR

LOCATION   In the Canton of les Grisons, N 48° 00′, E 11° 00′.

DESCRIPTION   This Benedictine convent sits at the foot of the pass of Ofen. It has a Carolingian church, a Gothic bishop's residence, the Tower of the Abbess von Planta, a museum with a 17th century chamber and a cloister. There are numerous Carolingian frescoes in the church as well as 11th century mural decorations in the chapel of the bishop's residence.

SIGNIFICANCE   Built around 780 AD, with its fortress-like design and multiple chapels, this convent exemplifies the Carolingian style (named after the Emperor Charlemagne) of architecture. The frescoes and murals inside depicting Biblical scenes are world renowned.

CONVENT OF ST. GALL

LOCATION   The city of St. Gall, Canton of St. Gall, N 47° 24′, E 09° 24′.

DESCRIPTION   The convent is surrounded by walls and is situated amongst several medieval buildings in the quarter of the town known as Gallusplatz. It is a complex of mixed architectural styles, originally Gothic in conception, it has been added to several times. The library is in the baroque style, while other additions display traits of Renaissance and Carolingian styles.

SIGNIFICANCE   Saint Gall was an Irish hermit who lived amongst others in a collection of cells in the forest that covered this area between 612 and 640 AD. A Benedictine convent, or monastery, was built on the site in the 8th century which became an important European centre of education. About 954 AD a wall was built around the monastery and so began the building of a town. After a period of decline, the monastery was dissolved in 1805 and the buildings were used by the Catholic church as an administrative centre. Its library is one of the most renowned in Europe and now houses an important collection of manuscripts, books and documents.

Benedictine Convent of Müstair

BERNE (OLD CITY)

LOCATION   The capital of Switzerland, Canton of Berne, N 46° 57′, E 07° 25′.

DESCRIPTION   The picturesque old town of Berne is connected to the modern town by several bridges over the Aare River. The ancient castle of Nydegg guards the eastern end of the town while the Gothic cathedral dominates the centre. Remains of original outlying fortifications have been converted to promenades and the wide streets are used as markets. Other important buildings include the parliament, university, library and the 2 remaining towers of the original walls – the Prison Tower and the Clock Tower.

SIGNIFICANCE   This beautiful old town with its breathtaking alpine scenery preserves its medieval appearance better than any other in Switzerland. A relatively late entry into the Swiss Federation in 1353, Berne soon took the lead and in 1848 became the capital. Its importance in Swiss history is reflected in the many fine buildings and monuments which are found there. One of the fascinating features of the town is the old bear pit which was built in 1513 and still has bears to this day. The heraldic symbol of the town is the bear, the animal from which the town is said to have taken its name.

A New Partnership in the Making

SOME PEOPLE MAY be surprised to see the pyramids of Egypt and the national park of the Galapagos Islands incorporated within a single framework and inscribed on a single list. What can ancient monuments have in common with a group of rocky islands thronged with iguanas and tortoises? – except, perhaps, the equal ingenuity with which travel agencies arrange organised tours to each of these sites. But are the travel agents' efforts not proof that our contemporaries, when they have the opportunity, are attracted both by cultural masterpieces and by the wonders of nature?

What then is meant by this 'common heritage of mankind'?

In addition to books, music, craft and artistry, the collections of paintings and sculptures in the world's museums, the cultural heritage comprises much 'immovable' property such as monuments and groups of historic buildings. It is this 'immovable' property with which the World Heritage Convention is concerned.

As for the natural heritage, it consists first of all of the plant and animal species whose conservation is of vital importance for human survival. These species are today protected as such by various (still extremely inadequate) conventions which deal notably with international trade in or hunting of them. But the natural heritage also includes unique sites, landscapes of exceptional beauty or of great value from the point of view of science or conservation, which can neither be replaced nor reproduced. It is this 'immovable' natural heritage which is covered by the World Heritage Convention, although certain threatened plant and animal species are automatically protected when their habitat is chosen for inclusion on the World Heritage List.

But although the protection of cultural property and the protection of natural property may be parallel activities, they raise very different problems. In most countries the two functions are entrusted to separate administrative structures, and architects who, for example, are concerned with the preservation of historic buildings have little to do with the biologists who administer national parks. So the question of why nature and culture should not be brought together within a single international convention might well be countered by the point that they have been separated, and even treated as rivals, for far too long.

At the beginning of his long emergence, man was able to make only a very slight impact on his physical and biological environment. He was, in a sense, 'within' nature. But as soon as he mastered fire he became the agent of important modifications, deliberate or accidental, in the natural world. By the end of the Palaeolithic age, when he still lived from hunting and gathering, he was already making an imprint on the natural environment in which he was pursuing his ascent. It is precisely this imprint, the result of his capacity for invention, that makes man what he is. What had yet to be called culture was already at odds with nature.

In Neolithic times, with the appearance of agriculture and the domestication of animals, the imprint would become deeper and the range of transformations would grow. Some 6,000 years ago, when man enters history, the discord between culture and nature was already etched on the face of the earth in those places where forests had been burned and where certain types of plants had been favoured to the exclusion of others.

But this was merely the modest beginning of a long process. The domination of the human species over every aspect of its environment would grow with its mastery of increasingly powerful tools, with its hunger for new objects, with the development of new needs, and with the multiplication of its members.

The material progress of techniques and societies took place essentially at the expense of nature and natural resources. And many philosophies and beliefs glorify his successful struggle of man 'against' nature.

A tragic misunderstanding arose and persisted down the centuries: mankind's mastery of his own 'animal nature' became confused with his wanton domination of the world around him. The warning of Francis Bacon, who announced at the dawn of the scientific revolution that 'Nature, to be commanded, must be obeyed', was ignored. The pre-eminence of mind over matter, which is the honour and the essence of man, was wrongly identified with a superiority that culture, especially in its technological forms, was considered to have over nature, thus confusing the moral order with the material order.

And so we reach the industrial revolution when the tempo quickens and matters come to a head. Industrial man has begotten prodigious technical achievements; he has gone some way to solving the problems of hunger and sickness. But at the same time his numbers grow to excess, he consumes relentlessly, he perfects lethal weaponry. His progress towards self-mastery is thus open to doubt.

Meanwhile, he has taken his conquest of nature so far that it is threatened with extinction. For nature, the reckoning is too heavy: massive deforestation; the erosion and degradation of soils; the disappearance of animal and plant species; water, air, land and marine pollution of many kinds; proliferating slums and shantytowns; expanding concrete and asphalt; dwindling open spaces...

And yet the message is not hard to grasp. Will modern men realise in time that if they snap the

The old city gates of Aleppo

umbilical cord which attaches them to the natural world then they are bound inexorably to destroy themselves? Will they turn to the healthiest sources of their different cultures and learn at long last how to live 'with' nature?

It would be possible to cite many examples of the benefits man has skilfully reaped from the resources of the biosphere without endangering the mechanisms which give birth to these resources: the harmonious landscapes shaped by human toil, for instance, or the natural sites used for cultural purposes.

It is highly significant that the convention already covers some of these privileged places where nature and culture meet: Ohrid and its lake in Yugoslavia, Tikal and its forest in Guatemala, Mont Saint-Michel and its bay in France. Let us hope that soon these sites will be joined by others of a similar kinds, such as the tree-girdled temples of Angkor or the ruins of Machu Picchu in their grandiose Andean setting (since listed–Ed.).

And so the association of nature and culture in the World Heritage Convention has first and foremost the value of a symbol – a symbol of the new alliance which must now be cemented between these two poles of human development, which only exists when they are combined.

MICHEL BATISSE, French engineer and physicist, is internationally known for his work on the environment and natural resources. Currently a consultant with UNESCO and the United Nations Environment Program, he has headed the Blue Plan Regional Activity Centre for the Mediterranean at Sophia Antipolis, France, since it was created in 1985.

Reprinted from the *Unesco Courier,* August 1980

SYRIA

Syria bears a proud and ancient history. Its situation at the convergence of Africa, Asia and Europe has caused it to be strongly influenced by many great civilisations – the Hittites, Egyptians, Babylonians, Persians, Greeks, Romans, Arabs and Ottoman Turks all held sway at some time in Syria's history. Both tools dating from the Paleolithic period and pottery remains from around 5,000 BC have been unearthed.

For three hundred years Syria was an Ottoman province. It was Napoleon Bonaparte who sought to end Turkish rule when he invaded in 1799. Although he failed to gain control, it was the beginning of the French influence which had such important consequences for the whole region.

The states of Syria and Lebanon were both created from the French mandated territory. After a period of union with Egypt, the Syrian Arab Republic was formed in 1961.

Present day Syria is a republic with a strong cultural identity reflected in its early acceptance of the World Heritage Convention in August 1975. Currently there are four sites listed.

The theatre at Bosra

Palmyra (Archaeological Site)

Ebla and Ancient Syria

THE RECENT DISCOVERY in Syria, not far from Aleppo, of the 4,000-year-old royal archives of the kingdom of Ebla is an event that could revolutionise historical studies of the ancient Near East. The remains of Ebla were brought to light by the Italian Archaeological Mission of the University of Rome.

It will require several decades to evaluate the full significance of the finds made in this Mesopotamian metropolis of Antiquity. This is because the texts inscribed on the clay tablets unearthed by the Italian archaeologists concern many sectors of the social and cultural life of the Near East during a period of great splendour (2300-2000 BC) about which only tenuous and fragmentary evidence has so far been available.

The value of the Ebla discovery extends far beyond the horizons of northern Syria and opens a window on the world of the Near East as a whole in ancient times.

Urban civilisation began to develop during the later centuries of the fourth millennium BC in southern Mesopotamia where the number of cities progressively increased. Uruk, on the left bank of the Euphrates, was one remarkable example.

But the way in which this urban civilisation spread through the Near East during the 3rd millennium BC is still shrouded in mystery, and particularly so in the region of Syria.

The evidence for the sequence of cultures comes from secondary sources such as archaeological remains unearthed around Antakya in Turkey or at Hamma in northern Syria.

Written records, in Mesopotamian, Sumerian and Akkadian texts are limited to the mention of a few cities conquered by the great kings of the dynasty of Akkad (2340-2220 BC), or tributaries of the kings of the third dynasty of Ur (circa 2120-2000 BC).

In the absence of any detailed archaeological or written evidence, historians have believed that the great Mesopotamian urban culture of the third millennium BC, located in the region of the lower Euphrates and the Tigris, had provided a model from which all the forms of urban culture in the Near East were derived.

Research by the Italian Archaeological Mission of Rome University, begun in Syria in 1964, aimed to throw some light on the origins and the development of Syrian urban culture in relation to the Mesopotamian world.

The Italian Mission, under my direction, therefore planned a systematic archaeological excavation of Tell Mardikh, a large man-made mound lying about 60kms (40mi) south of Aleppo in northern Syria. The mound was thought to cover the vestiges of an important urban centre. Permission to excavate was granted by the Syrian Arab Republic's Department of Antiquities, which gave the Italian mission constant support and close collaboration.

Excavations carried out between 1964 and 1972 on the uppermost part of the mound and at its centre revealed the existence of a major city. This metropolis is believed to have flourished between 2000 and 1700 to 1600 BC, during the period of the Amorite dynasty in Mesopotamia, to which the great king Hammurabi of Babylon belonged.

Extending over 56 hectares (138 acres) and dominated by the acropolis built at the summit of the site, the city was protected by strong ramparts raised on earth platforms 60 metres (65.6 yards) thick.

Along the line of the ramparts were four monumental gates each defended by jutting fortifications and flanked by wide bastions topped by towers. Each gateway had two or three adjoining entrances spanned by an arch and supported by piers covered with plaques of limestone and of basalt.

From these gateways radiated the streets which divided the lower city into quarters where the private dwellings were built. Around the acropolis (whose slopes must have been terraced) stood the administrative and religious buildings.

Each temple was dedicated to a different divinity and in most cases consisted of a single central hall whose massive towering walls dominated the city's single storey dwellings made of sun-dried brick.

On the acropolis stood the royal palace. It was unearthed in a badly damaged state, owing to repeated sackings over the centuries and to the fact that its stones, perfectly squared and smoothed, had been used for the construction of later buildings.

Near to the palace stood the Great Temple which, unlike the smaller temples, had a series of rooms: a long chamber ending in a deep niche for the worship of the god, a small ante-chamber and an open frontal vestibule at the opposite end, approached by a short staircase.

A decisive discovery made during the 1968 excavations finally revealed the name of the city as Ebla. A statue found in one of the temples bore an Akkadian cuneiform inscription on its torso with the name of a prince, Ibbit-Lim, son of a king, Igrish-Khep, who proclaimed himself lord of Ebla. The statue dated from about 2000 BC.

Ebla had been mentioned in earlier Sumerian and Akkadian inscriptions of the 3rd millennium BC as a powerful city that submitted to the great Sargon of Akkad around 2340-2300 BC and subsequently fell into the hands of this monarch's grandson, Naram-Sin of Akkad, between 2250 and 2225 BC. Later the city regained its independence and between 2120 and 2000 BC rose again to major importance.

After 2000 BC few texts mentioned Ebla, although according to one text there was a king of Ebla around 1700 BC. After 1600 BC the city had probably become a heap of ruins. This is what it must have seemed around 1500 BC to the great Pharaoh Thutmoses III, who recorded on a monument at Karnak that Ebla was one of the places through which the Egyptian army passed on its victorious march to the Euphrates.

After this Ebla became a forgotten city. The Italian excavations revealed, however, that during the 9th and 8th centuries BC, a small Aramaic fortification stood on the acropolis of Ebla. One or two centuries later, in the Achaemenid period, there was a modest village there.

Then even these traces of settlement disappeared from Tell Mardikh. The mound was completely abandoned and its surface became ploughed land. Only for a short while — perhaps just one season — was the acropolis used as a military camp site, possibly in the campaigns that devastated the region during the Crusades.

The picture of Ebla, as reconstituted by the excavations of the Italian Mission, makes a major contribution to the history of ancient Syria. Ebla is seen to have been a leading political centre of northern Syria

between 2000 BC and 1850 to 1700 BC. After the later date the city must have become a vassal of Aleppo, one of the leading states at the time of Hammurabi of Babylon.

The Italian archaeologists estimate that at its most flourishing period Ebla had between 20,000 and 30,000 inhabitants (an extremely large population for that time).

Ebla remained a vassal of Aleppo until about 1600 BC, when it must certainly have fallen to the Hittite invaders who under Khattushili I and Mushili I overcame first Aleppo and then Babylon.

Our discovery of Ebla as it was at its zenith, and in particular the discovery of artistic and architectural features of the period between 2000 BC and 1700 BC, give an entirely new historical valuation to Syria, greater than the one usually accepted in historiography.

Syria, a land with an ethnically diverse population, often subjected to outside domination and varied cultural influences, had hitherto seemed to be a meeting ground for other peoples rather than the centre of an autonomous cultural development.

The systematic exploration of Ebla as it existed from 2000 to 1600 BC during the Amorite dynasties has produced evidence to refute the traditional interpretation. For the period of the Amorite dynasties, or more correctly the paleo-Syrian period, saw the formation of a specifically Syrian culture, with an urban organisation, architecture and artistic vision of striking originality.

Moreover, the most fruitful aspects of this paleo-Syrian culture are to be found in other centres of Norther Syria even as late as the first millennium BC. They testify very clearly to the continuity of the tradition, showing that the originality of Ebla was no mere transitory process.

However, the very originality of the paleo-Syrian culture shown at Tell Mardikh raised the problem of the historical roots of this culture, and it was on this question that the Italian Archaeological Museum focussed its research from 1973.

Its studies were concentrated on the remains of Ebla dating from the third millennium BC to find evidence of the city destroyed by Sargon and by Naram-Sin of Akkad. Ebla was mentioned by Gudea, governor of the Sumerian city of Lagash, as a source of timber, and documents of the great kings of the third dynasty of Ur describe Ebla as a centre producing highly prized textiles.

So in 1973 our mission began the systematic exploration of the western slope of Tell Mardikh, hoping to discover traces of an important settlement dating from the third millennium BC.

After three years of excavation, we have brought to light part of the royal palace whose period of greatest splendour must have been between 2400 and 2250 BC. Archaeological and epigraphic evidence indicate that this was indeed the palace destroyed by Naram-Sin of Akkad in 2225 BC.

The section of the palace now unearthed has proved to be a striking monumental achievement of proto-Syrian architecture. So far the only part explored is the monumental audience court surrounded by porticoes with tall wooden columns.

On one side of the court lay a raised podium where the king sat during official audiences. On another was a great doorway giving access to the palace. Of the palace itself only two rooms have so far been excavated, plus a great ceremonial staircase with four ramps. The steps were decorated with jewelled encrustations now lost. Apart from this a few smaller spaces have been cleared, including some used as small storerooms.

With walls sometimes reaching 2.80 metres (9 feet) thick, the structure has a very impressive appearance. This and the refinement of certain building details express an original architectural concept, some of whose characteristics were handed down and later influenced the Aramaic palaces of northern Syria of the first millennium BC.

But the most astounding find at Ebla is undoubtedly that of the palace archives, inscribed with cuneiform writings on clay tablets. The tablets were arranged in two small closed rooms, in corners of the court of audience. The smaller room contained a collection of about 1,000 clay tablets or fragments of tablets. In the bigger room we discovered about 15,000 tablets or fragments of tablets.

These two sets of archives escaped destruction by Naram-Sin's soldiers because they were not considered of any value. The smaller collection (about 1,000 tablets) was strewn in heaps between the ruins of the collapsed ceiling and of the masonry.

In the larger collection, the thousands of tablets must have been stored on wooden shelves running along the walls and held by vertical wooden poles fixed to the floor. The tablets were found piled up still more or less in order on the floor where they have fallen when the shelving burned.

The cuneiform tablets are written in Sumerian and in the Eblaite tongue, a Semitic language that shows strong resemblances – though it is older by more than a thousand years – to the Semitic languages of the 'Canaanite' group of the first millennium B.C., and especially to Phoenician.

Professor Giovanni Pettinato, the epigraphist of the Italian Mission and professor of Assyriology of the University of Rome, has studied the Eblaite tongue in the Tell Mardikh texts. He had already succeeded in identifying a Semitic language, which he defined as 'Paleo-Canaanite', by studying the few tables already discovered in one of the rooms of the palace in 1974 before the great collection of archives was brought to light.

An examination of the huge mass of texts discovered in the palace in September and October 1975 has fully confirmed his interpretation. The Eblaite texts of the royal archives of Ebla thus represent extraordinarily rich documentation that will advance the deciphering of the texts and the reconstruction of this language, along with the study of Semitic languages in general.

The majority of the Eblan texts are bookkeeping statements concerning an international trade in textiles and metals. Ebla was famous for both these items of merchandise in the Mesopotamian world of that time. The palace itself kept the files on what we would call registers of consignments.

An interesting detail is that the texts mention, among the various qualities of cloth, some which were 'lined with gold'. These must have been high quality textiles which even today are known as 'damask' (from the Syrian city of Damascus where they were first produced).

The tablets provide detailed information on trade in the Near East in the third millennium BC and also much data on the historical geography of that period. They name many cities to which goods were sent. They show that this trade had very wide horizons, because it extended from the Mediterranean coast to the east of Mesopotamia, and from Anatolia to Palestine.

The archives also contain many texts made up of lists of Sumerian words and phrases, and of bilingual vocabularies with indications of the Sumerian pronunciation.

In addition to giving linguistic information of the greatest importance, the tablets also provide valuable information on the organisation of education at that time. They show that all instruction was strictly controlled by the state, (as in Mesopotamia during the same period) and was designed to train students to become state administrators. The archives contain school exercise written by students whose names appear in later official documents as leading civil servants.

The archives also contain administrative, legal and diplomatic documents. Some deal with budgetary aspects of the administration and throw light on the internal organisation of the state, at the 'ministerial level', on the organisation and government of the provinces and on the financial structures of the state, including the collection of taxes.

There are also facts on the population of Ebla, on administrative and juridical problems, such as questions of inheritance or the dividing up of booty. Diplomatic documents include three international treaties, one of them being a pact between Ebla and Assur, of particular interest because of the complexity of its clauses and the political relationships it reveals.

A certain number of literary texts are of exceptional value. One seems to be an Eblaite version of a passage from the Mesopotamian saga of Gilgamesh, the great Assyrian hero who according to legend was king of Uruk.

Other literary texts include myths, hymns, and

exorcist spells and are most probably translations into the Eblaite tongue of Sumerian works whose originals have previously reached us only in relatively late Mesopotamian versions, written down about 1800 B.C. when Sumerian was no longer a spoken language.

From this rich harvest, one more example can well illustrate the revolutionary character of the discoveries. The texts tell us about a complete dynasty of at least five kings of Ebla who appear to be contemporaries of the kings of Akkad, from Sargon to Naram-Sin.

This Eblan dynasty, of which written tradition had lost the record, appears to have dominated the Near East from Northern Mesopotamia to the Mediterranean, and to have been inspired by a universalist ideology.

It is now almost certain that in order to express the Eblaite language in writing, the royal chancery of Ebla successfully undertook the complex adaptation of the cuneiform syllabic script (invented in Mesopotamia to write Sumerian).

With the findings of Ebla, Syria has rediscovered one of the most brilliant pages of its long history, and thus takes its place alongside Mesopotamia and Egypt in the early progress of mankind towards civilisation.

PAOLO MATTHIAE
Reprinted from the *Unesco Courier*, February 1977

ALEPPO (OLD CITY)

LOCATION   Far northwest, N 36° 14′, E 37° 10′.

DESCRIPTION   A large city and administrative centre, Aleppo sits on limestone hills 360m (1,181ft) above sea level. The old part of the city has many notable features including covered bazaars that are built of stone, an imposing citadel and many mosques. Ruins include the original city walls and gates.

SIGNIFICANCE   The Arabic name is Haleb or halpa which is said to derive from the Semetic word for milk – it is believed that Abraham grazed his cows here. The various ruins and old buildings are an invaluable record of this city's rich and important history.

PALMYRA (ARCHAEOLOGICAL SITE)

LOCATION   Province of Homs, 240km (150mi) northeast of Damascus, N 34° 36′, E 38° 15′.

DESCRIPTION   The ruins of this city cover about 50ha (121ac) and reveal the town plan of the ancient city. Along the principal street there is a double portico which is heavily ornamented. The agora, the senate house and the theatre lie to the south. Within the ruins lies a vast

complex called Diocletian's Camp, as well as the chief Palmyrene sanctuary.

SIGNIFICANCE   Lying in an oasis of the Syrian desert 390m (1,300ft) above sea level, Tadmor, as Palmyra was known in Arabic, was in ancient times the intersecting point of 2 great trading routes. Reference to the town was made as far back as the 12th century BC. The original caravan stopover point gradually developed into a large city and an important centre for worship to the sun god as witnessed by the ruins of the Great Temple of the Sun.

DAMASCUS (OLD CITY)

LOCATION   In the southwest, N 37° 05′, E 40° 05′.

DESCRIPTION   Positioned on the rivers of Barada and A'waj, the old part of Damascus is partially walled and lies on the southern side of the Barada River. It contains the Great Mosque which was built within the walls of a 1st century temple, a Roman citadel, several souks (markets) and khaus (trading inns) and the Azam Palace. There are three distinct 'quarters' to the town – the Meidan, settled by tribesmen, the Christian and the Druse.

SIGNIFICANCE   Legend has it that 'Dimasqa' was founded by Uz, son of Aram and was already a city by the time of Abraham. It is also known as 'Al Fayha' – 'the fragrant' – from its many scented gardens. The history of this famed city has been turbulent and dynamic, passing through the hands of ancient Egypt, Assyria, Persia, Alexander the Great, Egypt, Nabataea, Rome, Arabia, Rome and finally Arabia again in 635 AD. With such a fabulous history, the antiquities of Damascus will remain forever invaluable to the heritage of man.

BOSRA (ANCIENT CITY)

LOCATION   Department of Deraa, 100km (62mi) south of Damascus, N 32° 36′, E 36° 40′.

DESCRIPTION   Situated in the fertile valley of the Nukru River the ruins of ancient Bosra sit on a bed of volcanic rock at an altitude of 850m (1,600ft) above sea level. The remains include the walls and gates, a wide avenue with colonnades, a theatre, baths, markets and in the oldest quarter, named Vabateau, a monumental gate which leads to the Palace of Trajan, a cathedral and several mosques.

SIGNIFICANCE   Originally the city of the Arabian people known as Nabateans, Bosra was conquered by the Romans and made capital of their Province of Arabia by Emperor Trajan in 106 AD. After becoming a Roman colony, the city fell to the Arabs in 636 AD. The Crusaders held it but briefly in the 12th century. Only a matter of years later a series of earthquakes devastated the city and it never recovered from the subsequent decline.

The energies of our system will decay, the glory of the sun will be dimmed, and the earth, tideless and inert, will no longer tolerate the race which has for a moment disturbed its solitude. Man will go down into the pit, and all his thoughts will perish.

ARTHUR JAMES BALFOUR

Damascus

Damascus

TANZANIA

Tanzania ratified the World Heritage Convention in August 1977 and since then has contributed some of the most famous and significant natural sites to the World Heritage List.

Selous Game Reserve is one of the oldest in Africa; 50,000 sq km (20,000sq mi) of totally natural grassed and wooded habitats. Kilimanjaro is Africa's highest peak and one of its great scenic wonders. Serengeti National Park, easily the most renowned wildlife park on earth, and the adjoining Ngorongoro Conservation Area, with its famous crater, together make up almost 100,000 sq km (40,000sq mi) of uninhabited savanna which is absolutely teeming with wildlife.

Put together, all four of Tanzania's World Heritage listings account for around 15% of the country's total land mass; a remarkable testament to this country's commitment to the World Heritage Convention and to wildlife preservation in general.

The fifth listing includes two sites, both medieval Arabic towns, on the islands of Kilwa Kisiwani and Songo Mnara.

Ngorongoro Conservation Area

Ngorongoro Crater

Profiting from Wildlife Conservation

RUVUMA VILLAGE WILDLIFE Management Programme (RVWMP) is part of the Selous Conservation Programme (SCP) which is a joint venture between the Governments of Tanzania and Germany.

The prime objective of the programme is to conserve, manage and utilise wildlife resources inside the Selous Game Reserve (SGR) and the entire ecological system on the basis of sustainable yield. While the SGR covers an area of approximately 50,000 sq kms (19,000 sq mi) of south eastern Tanzania, the entire ecosystem incorporates a much larger area of over 80,000 sq kms (31,000 sq mi), including land in Morogoro, Ruvuma, Lindi and coastal regions. The effective range for certain wildlife species includes the entire ecosystem. In other words under natural conditions, wild animals do not recognise man-made boundaries. As with the animals, it is also accepted in principle that no ecosystem is devoid of human interaction, because people form part of, and influence, the ecosystem and the Selous is not an exception.

It has been observed that the villagers living around the SGR derive many of their means of subsistence from wildlife, ie animals, fish, fruits, vegetables, firewood, mushroom, honey, medicine. A close look at the Wildlife Conservation Act of 1974 however, emphasises excluding, rather than integrating, villagers around SGR, with conservation denying the villagers the right to benefit directly from these resources. Far removed from these expectations of villagers abiding with the law; human-exclusion conservation policy is not working due to the vast size of the protected areas and increased demand for land.

As a result of management ineffectiveness, villagers poach both inside and outside the reserve. Consequently key wildlife species have recently been threatened or exposed to the dangers of extinction. Typical on the list of affected species due to poaching are the African elephant, *Lexodanta africana* and the black rhinoceros, *Dioeros birconis*. These two species registered a decline of about 70% and 98% respectively between 1976 and 1989. This drastic decline in species population numbers called for action to research and design a pragmatic approach to conservation through community involvement, enabling them to profit from wildlife in order to sustain resource conservation.

Background

The RVWMP started in 1989. Five villages in the Songea District were selected to serve as pilot areas. The pilot area incorporated the villages of Kitanda, Nambecha, Likuyu Sekamaganga, Mehomoro and Kilimasera. All these selected villages share borders with SGR in the north and boast a human population of approximately 12,000 indigenous villagers and 13,000 refugees from Mozambique.

The land between the reserve and the pilot villages form important habitats for the elephant sable antelope – *Hippatrogus niger,* cape buffalo – *Syncerus caffer,* livingstone eland – *aurotragus petersonianus livingstonii* and many other typical *Brachystegia* woodland species.

The vegetation cover is characterised by mosaics of habitat types ranging from dense evergreen riverine along the valleys; flood grass areas; seasonal and permanently marshy and swampy areas. The extensive woodland grassland habitats are dominated by tree species of the genus *Brachystegia* with *B. bohemii,* popularly called muyombo, being the most dominant. Species of commercial interest include *Adina Microcephala* and *Pterocarpus spp.* These two species are found in localised places which are inaccessible. Otherwise over exploitation is responsible for their rarity.

In addition to being an important catchment area for major tributaries which join and form Rufiji river, natural ponds which were once rich in aquatic life are found. Recently however, illegal application of pesticides has depleted the endemic aquatic species. The degree of depletion is not possible to assess, because limnological studies have not been carried out in the area.

Source of meat

As mentioned before, the villagers do not keep cattle, therefore wildlife forms an important source of meat. But again, the inhibition of wildlife law as stated earlier, coupled with low income status, together generate constraints for the villagers to acquire legal firearms and buy a hunting licences. This situation precludes villagers from access to legal game meat, a resource whose survival is the result of their traditional ways. Otherwise had the villagers opted for agriculture, there would be no wildlife left. Despite their traditional role in saving what remains of the past, the making of conservation laws did not take into account the positive role of the traditional people and instead they were ignored and treated as aliens in their ancestral land. In such a situation commonsense dictates that villagers had only two options; either starve and perish due to lack of protein or violate the law to get the needed meat.

Sustainable Utilisation

'Poaching for the pot', then, was sustainable in the sense that only appropriate tools were available and used to hunt. For instance, muzzle loaders and

Selous Game Reserve. Flood area of the Rufiji River

spears could enable the traditional hunter to kill just enough game for himself and the community. Another feature responsible in ascertaining resource sustainability is the traditional preservation and conservation of wildlife habitats inherently practised by rural communities. This arises from their respect for the bush which is the mother source of life. This unique quality of life is lacking in modern development, which views natural environs as hostile, requiring to be tamed.

In the eyes of the rural communities the causes of wildlife destruction are the well-to-do people. The villagers, they argue, did not introduce machine guns to the poaching industry. The affluent people did. Their motives were to generate wealth as quickly as possible by 'mining' wildlife resources.

The era of wildlife mining in Tanzania and in particular Ruvuma region, dates back to the early 1980s. However, large scale elephant poaching and unsustainable utilisation of other wildlife species was first reported in 1984.

Some villagers bordering SGR grew into infamous centres for the nefarious trade in ivory, with villagers assuming the role of primary producers of illegal ivory, while buyers came from different parts of the country and abroad. Whether it is accepted or not, ivory poaching and smuggling was an important source of income for different levels of people.

During the era of commercial poaching, relations between rural communities and wildlife employees in the field were cool and hostile, often resulting in overt clashes. Occasionally such hostilities ended in loss of life from either party. A critical review of the overall situation indicated a struggle which neither party could win as long as wild animals remained in the SGR and environs. The poachers, being heavily armed and backed by influential people were accepted by villagers as being the winning side at least while the game was still available in the wild, but eventually they would have been losers once the animals were gone.

The main assumption now is that if villagers benefit directly from wildlife resources, they will support conservation efforts and therefore minimise destruction of the natural environment, thus sustaining wildlife.

This implies that positive results can only come about if the villagers' economic situation improves. It is a fact which must be accepted that hungry people do not have time to think of conservation, particularly when they compare the high standards of living enjoyed by residents in urban centres.

This concept was also sold to the villagers by educating them to the advantages of communal wildlife conservation and sustained yield resource utilisation. Recognising their knowledge of adaptive conservation, the villagers were given a mandate to prepare wildlife plans to show how wildlife could be conserved and utilised.

Direct dialogue and public discussions with villagers finally opened up communications between the Project Leader on behalf of the Wildlife Department and the rural communities concerned. Previous hostilities have now been minimised.

Villagers have willingly established wildlife committees and selected some members to serve as village scouts, whose responsibilities include the supervision of sustainable conservation and utilisation of natural resources. Village scouts carry out routine patrols, sometimes jointly with Game Wardens and Game Scouts.

Poaching has been completely eliminated in Mohomoro and Kilimasera village areas. In general, villagers in all pilot areas have stopped poaching. The only poaching is done by core poachers, normally from villages not involved in the programme. Occasionally they land up in the hands of the village scouts.

Reduction in poaching is apparently resulting in an increased population of big game including elephants. Crop damage is being reported frequently and as positive gesture reflecting the wildlife authority's commitment to delegate responsibilities,

Kilimanjaro National Park

Serengeti National Park

the villagers are fully involved in choosing suitable methods of protecting human life and minimising crop damage.

Based on the results of two years of operation, the programme plans to design and implement programmes in three major areas. They are, conservation education to the peasant farmers; sustainable utilisation programmes to benefit the concerned rural communities; and research on traditional values of wildlife.

If the rural communities have been instrumental in preserving these natural habitats, a phenomenon which is the secret to wildlife species survival, then it is their natural right to benefit directly from wildlife within the legal framework. In short, the success of the programme will depend on how fast the government effects changes that will finally give rural communities the right to profit directly from wildlife resources.

IRENEUS F NDUNGURU
Regional Game Officer and Project Leader
Songea, Tanzania

NGORONGORO CONSERVATION AREA

LOCATION   East of the Serengeti National Park in the Arusha region, E 35° 30′, S 03° 15′.

DESCRIPTION   This area is 80,944sq km (32,400sq mi) of largely savanna grassland. There are several notable geological features, including 2 huge volcanic craters or calderas, a large volcanically formed lake – Lake Empakaai and Olduvai Gorge.

SIGNIFICANCE   Along with neighbouring Serengeti National Park, Ngorongo forms a huge interdependent ecosystem, containing the largest concentration of wildlife on earth. These huge resources are managed in such a way that the tribal hunters living nearby may benefit without causing any deterioration in the quality of the environment. At Olduvai Gorge, under the leadership of Dr. Louis Leakey and Mrs. Mary Leakey, archaeological excavations have unearthed the remains of the oldest known ancestors of man.

SELOUS GAME RESERVE

LOCATION   Coast Morogoro, Lindi, Mtwara and Ruvuma Regions, S 07° 17′ to 10° 15′, E 36° 04′ to 38° 46′.

DESCRIPTION   With 50,000sq km (20,000sq mi), moderate rainfall and temperatures in a yearly range of 13°-41°C (56°-106°F), this park has a variety of vegetation zones from dense thickets to open wooded grasslands. However 2 broad divisions, east and west, may be discerned. In the east where grasslands exist, cheetah and giraffe may be found, while in the west the Miombo

Bush sunset – Serengeti National Park

woodlands have some elephants and hartebeest but are generally devoid of plains animals.

SIGNIFICANCE   One of the oldest game reserves in Africa, first gazetted in 1905 at just 2,500sq km (1,554 sq mi), it has been constantly expanded while the local population has been evacuated to allow the animals full reign. This lack of hunting pressure has helped maintain the area in a natural condition, allowing the animals to wander, free of further human interference.

SERENGETI NATIONAL PARK

LOCATION   In Mara, Arusha and Shinyanga Provinces, 130km (81mi) west-northwest of Arusha, S 01° 15′ to 03° 20′, E 34° 00′ to 35° 15′.

DESCRIPTION   Serengeti National Park is 1,476,300ha (3,559,359ac) of largely uninhabited savannas. The area is famous for its vast plains upon which huge herds of animals roam, followed by numerous packs of attendant predators. Water is not in abundance, so the presence of permanent waterholes in the west leads to massive annual herd migrations.

SIGNIFICANCE   This is easily the most widely renowned wildlife park on earth. It is the archetypal safari park with immense herds of gazelles, giraffes, wildebeests, topi, warthogs, elephants, hippos and black rhinos. Lions, cheetah and leopards also roam these plains in great numbers. The movement of some herds can be in lines up to 10km (6.2mi) long and presents one of the most awe inspiring wildlife spectacles imaginable.

KILIMANJARO NATIONAL PARK

LOCATION   Kilimanjaro Region in the north, on the border with Kenya, S 02° 50′ to 03° 20′, E 37° 00′ to 37° 43′.

DESCRIPTION   Mt. Kilimanjaro is of volcanic origin and is 5,895m (19,347ft) high. It is encircled by native deciduous forest rising to 2,740m (8,989ft) above sealevel. This mountain, much photographed, has the classic pointed shape and is perpetually snow-topped and often shrouded in cloud. In the plains surrounding it are herds of wildlife and upon its slopes are found monkeys, bush pigs, tree hyrix and numerous small mammals. Leopards and rhinoceros are often to be seen. Facilities for visitors and climbers are well developed with numerous well-kept huts on the mountains.

SIGNIFICANCE   Kilimanjaro is the highest summit in Africa. A lone, snow capped peak rising dramatically from the surrounding equatorial plains, it is one of the world's greatest natural sights. This park plays a crucial role in protecting not only this magnificent environment, but also numerous mammals, many of them endangered.

The Great Mosque on Kilwa Kisiwani

KILWA KISIWANI AND SONGO MNARA RUINS

LOCATION   2 islands off the eastern coast of Africa; *Kilwa Kisiwani:* E 39° 46', S 09° 00'. *Songo Mnara:* E 39° 47', S 09° 07'.

DESCRIPTION   The ruins at Kilwa Kisiwani include the Great Mosque – 12th to 15th century AD, the Palace of Husuni Kubwa – 14th century AD, the Arab fort called the Gereza, Makutani the 'Palace of Great Walls' and several mosques. At Songo Mnara there is a palace, 5 mosques, a residential area and a cemetery.

SIGNIFICANCE   Kilwa Kisiwani and its dependant neighbour are the remains of the most important medieval city-state on the East African coast. They reached their zenith in the 13th and 14th centuries. These ruins reflect the successes of this maritime power that at one time controlled 1,600km (1,000mi) of coast. This power base declined in the 1500s as the Portuguese arrived but recovered 200 years later.

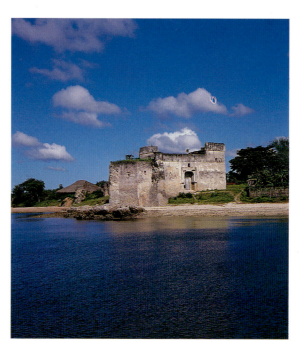

The Fort on Kilwa Kisiwani

TUNISIA

Tunisia, with an area of 164,000 sq km (63,300 sq mi), is the smallest of the three 'Maghreb' states – the other two being Algeria and Morocco. It is a country rich in cultural heritage, boasting a diverse and ancient lineage.

Phoenicians, Romans, Byzantines, Arabs, Ottoman Turks, French, Spanish, Maltese, Italians and Jews have all left their mark on this remarkable north African country.

The original inhabitants, the Berbers, were first influenced by the Phoenicians sometime during the 9th century BC. That great city of antiquity, Carthage, was founded around that time. Destroyed by a Rome enraged by the Punic Wars, its ruins now sit on the outskirts of Tunis.

Berbers now account for only 1% of the total population, mainly due to the great success of the Arab invasion which started around 670 AD.

A vessel of the Ottoman Empire for over three hundred years – although its leaders enjoyed a measure of local autonomy – it was a French protectorate from 1881 until 1956, when it became an independent republic. The two main languages today are still Arabic and French.

The World Heritage Convention was accepted in 1975; presently there are seven sites from Tunisia on the World Heritage List.

AMPHITHEATRE OF EL DJEM

LOCATION   Approximately 90km (56mi) south of Sousse, N 36° 00', E 11° 00'.

DESCRIPTION   This is a free-standing structure and is not, as was so often the case, built into or next to a hill. Its state of preservation is excellent and original, having survived the winds of time and avoided the restorers' hands. Seating capacity is around 35,000. The facade has 3 arched tiers in the Corinthian style. Inside, the podium, arena and underground galleries are virtually intact.

SIGNIFICANCE   This is without doubt one of the largest and best preserved of all Roman amphitheatres. It was here in 238 AD that Gordian was proclaimed emperor. After the decline of the Roman Empire, it fell into disuse until becoming a Byzantine fortress. This use was continued by the Muslim conquerors until well into the 18th century.

Carthage

Ichkeul National Park

Medina of Sousse

Medina of Tunis

Kerkwan

CARTHAGE

LOCATION   Several kilometres northeast of Tunis, N 36° 51′, E 10° 20′.

DESCRIPTION   This site comprises the Acropolis of Byrsa, the Punic ports, theatre, necropolises, circus, villas, baths and cisterns. The ruins follow the coastline on a north-south axis and are largely incomplete. Major excavations have been attempted but have not been overly successful. On the perimeter of the site the suburbs of Tunis have barely been halted from encroaching.

SIGNIFICANCE   The most distinguished site in Tunisia, due to its long history, Carthage was the great rival of ancient Rome. Until the catastrophic conclusion of the Punic Wars when the city was totally obliterated it was perhaps greater than Rome. Hannibal and his elephants gave Carthage a decisive edge in the great struggle, but this was squandered. The remains today are mainly from later periods, having been built following the Roman recolonisation of the area. Its historical and cultural importance was underlined when the Mayor of Rome declared in 1985 'Carthage must not be obliterated', a reference to the creed attributed to ancient Rome – 'Carthage must be obliterated'.

ICHKEUL NATIONAL PARK

LOCATION   In the governorate of Bizerta, N 37° 10′, E 09° 40′.

DESCRIPTION   The area of this park is 10,775ha (26,000ac), with a further buffer zone of 6,000ha (14,000ac). The dominant feature is the lake which is surrounded by extensive marshland. Apart from an isolated mountain, 811m (2,660ft) high, the landscape is mainly flat. This lake is the last remaining in a chain of lakes which once extended across northern Africa.

SIGNIFICANCE   The international importance of this lake and its associated marshes and waterways lies in its use as a stopover point for migrating birds. It is the surviving remnant of the ancient northern African lake-chain and therefore is of crucial significance. The beauty of the landscape, its ecological formations, the wealth of flora and fauna combine to make Ichkeul an ecological site, not only unique in Tunisia but in the whole of the Maghreb. It is an area untouched by agricultural disturbances which explains its continued survival.

MEDINA OF SOUSSE

LOCATION   East coast, 150km (93mi) southeast of Tunis, N 35° 49′, E 10° 39′.

DESCRIPTION   The town of Sousse sits on a hill overlooking the Mediterranean Sea. It is surrounded by a fortified wall with towers and crenellations. Shops operate out of indentations on the inside of the wall. There are

The Great Mosque, Kairouan

many interesting buildings; the kasbah or central fortification (citadel) is perched on the highest point within the walls and has been fully restored. The Kasrnern Ribat is a square fortress with a lofty tower and 7 bastions. An unusual building is the Kah wet-el-Kubba (Café of the Dome) which has a square base, a cylindrical body and is topped by a grooved dome. There is a large Great Mosque and a smaller mosque known as Bou Fata'ta.

SIGNIFICANCE   The site of Sousse goes back to ancient days when it was occupied as a Phoenician city, by the name of Hadrumetum. The fortifications of the present city were built in the 9th century AD. Pirates operated out of the town for many centuries and it has been the scene of many attacks, notably by the Venetians, the Knights of St. John and the French. The multitude of ethnic influences throughout the countries has left its distinctive mark on this unique old town.

MEDINA OF TUNIS

LOCATION   City of Tunis, northeastern Mediterranean coast, E 10° 20', N 36° 51'.

DESCRIPTION   This traditional complex covers an area of 270ha (651ac) and comprises the central 8th century Medina plus two 13th century suburbs. There are 700 historic monuments found in this area, including about

200 palaces and large residences and numerous mosques. The other notable features are the town gates, the souks (markets) and its unique urban plan.

SIGNIFICANCE   This complex stands on the site of an ancient town which was mentioned by Pliny the Elder. After the destruction of Carthage in the 8th century, this town was furnished with an arsenal, a port, canal and outer harbour. During the 12th century it became the capital of 'Aghlabid Afrigiyah' and soon came to be considered one of the greatest and wealthiest cities in the Islamic world. The tremendously rich heritage of those heady days is clearly evident today.

KAIROUAN

LOCATION   Around 130km (80mi) south of Tunis, N 35° 48', E 10° 10'.

DESCRIPTION   The city covers around 54ha (130ac) and is surrounded by 3.2km (2mi) of walls. There are several gates, notably the Corte de Tunis and the Bab Jalladine. More than 80 mosques and 50 mausoleums line the streets and squares inside. The Great Mosque of Sidi 'Oqba and the Mosque of the Three Doors are the most important buildings. There are also baths, souks (markets), the Aghlabites pools and the Sanctuary of Sidi Abid el Ghariani.

SIGNIFICANCE   Kairouan (Qairwan) is Tunisia's Holy City. Legend has it that 'Oqba went out into the desert in 671 AD in order to find the site which would become the centre of Islam in Africa. He struck his spear into the ground and proclaimed 'Here is your Qairwan (resting place)'. The town is also important architecturally, as its buildings are some of the earliest in the Islamic world. The Great Mosque was a model for many famous mosques that followed.

KERKWAN

LOCATION   Northeast coast, around 90km (56mi) east of Tunis, N 36° 35', E 10° 45'.

DESCRIPTION   These ruins of an ancient Punic town are relatively intact. They include the town walls, its residential quarters, a large temple, several palaces and an extensive sewage system. The necropolis lies 1km (0.62mi) northwest on a rocky hill. It is rectangular in plan, 100m (328ft) wide by 170m (558ft) long. There are more than 200 tombs, all different in layout and size, some with staircases, and many with painted decorations.

SIGNIFICANCE   These ruins are extensive and in excellent order. It is believed that the city was abandoned during the first Punic War, around 250 BC. The necropolis in particular, provides invaluable insight into the culture of this advanced civilisation.

Amphitheatre of El Djem

*I have spread my dreams under your feet;
Tread softly, because you tread on my dreams.*

WILLIAM BUTLER YEATS

Kairouan

⟨343⟩

Wetlands of the World

WETLANDS COVER about 6% of our planet's land surface. They range from the vast peatlands of Canada and the USSR, to the extensive tropical floodplains of Africa, Latin America and Asia, the estuarine and open coast mudflats and saltmarshes which are widespread in temperate regions, and the mangroves which replace them over much of the tropics. They include some of the largest and most spectacular of the world's natural ecosystems, notably the Pantanal which stretches across the borders of Bolivia, Paraguay and Brazil, and covers an area half the size of France, the Everglades, the world's largest freshwater marsh, the Sundarbans of India and Bangladesh, the world's largest mangrove system, and the inland deltas of the Okavango and Niger rivers of Africa.

Conservation interest first focused upon wetlands because of their role in supporting large populations of waterbirds and other species, and led to the development in 1971 of the Convention on Wetlands of International Importance Especially as Waterfowl Habitat, in Ramsar, Iran. The Ramsar and World Heritage Conventions now work together in conserving wetlands. Thirty two million ha are protected through the Ramsar Convention and twenty sites through World Heritage. Several sites are on both the Ramsar and World Heritage lists, notably Lake Ichkeul in Tunisia, Djoudj National Park in Senegal, the Banc d'Arguin in Mauritania, the Everglades in the USA, and Kakadu National Park in Australia.

In addition to their role in supporting wildlife, wetlands are today recognised to bring a wide range of benefits to people. Floodplain wetlands absorb floodwaters and regulate floods, while also helping to ensure a year round water supply in many arid regions. In addition, many freshwater wetlands, notably Papyrus swamp and reedbeds, absorb nutrients, retain sediment and so help to purify water supplies. Many coastal wetlands help buffer wind and wave action, providing protection from coastal storms. In addition to these ecosystem functions, many wetlands yield a range of products which can be harvested sustainably, including fish, fodder, timber, and agricultural crops.

In the face of demographic growth, extreme poverty, and changing administrative practices, many local people have been forced to overuse wetlands, leading to their degradation. Conservation measures must therefore include activities which can help local communities use wetland resources in sustainable fashion, thus bringing benefits to people and wildlife.

PATRICK DUGAN
Wetlands Program, IUCN

Nemrut Dag

TURKEY

Turkey, a bridge between Asia and Europe, is unique in that it covers the cultural mosaic of the many civilisations who have established settlements in Anatolia since 8000 BC.

The most precious possession of a nation is the collection of monuments which has developed during the course of its history. Every civilisation is honoured by the greatness of its scientists, philosophers and artists, and the importance and richness of their works and by transferring them to the next generation. However, there are no civilisations that can remain unaffected by other contemporary or previous civilisations. Thus as these scientific and cultural interactions between civilisations develop, new cultures emerge as the inheritors of their past heritage. Hence the nations of the world regard the old civilisations which occupied their land, not only as their national cultural possessions, but also as part of the world's heritage.

Anatolia, which has provided the homeland for many civilisations, has a unique place in history in that it hosted the oldest rural cultures in the Neolithic Age of 8000 to 6000 BC. Subsequent civilisations, the Hatties, Trojans, Hittites, Hurries, Urartians, Phrygians, Lydians, Karians, Lycians, Ionians, Greeks, Romans, Byzantines, Seljuks and Ottomans, are the main civilisations forming the cultural mosaic of Anatolia. Numerous unique works of art from these civilisations form their heritage to humanity.

One of the most sacred tasks of humanity is to preserve the values we accept as world heritage and to transfer them to future generations.

In the belief that the cultural values and riches we have are the common aspiration and wealth of humanity, I salute all cultures and peoples with love and respect.

MR NAMIL KEMAL ZEYBEK
Minister of Culture, Turkey

The paths are rough. The hillocks are covered with broom. The air is motionless. How far away are the birds and the springs! It can only be the end of the world ahead.
ARTHUR RIMBAUD

The Rock-hewn Churches of Cappadocia

THE SETTING FOR the rock-hewn churches of Cappadocia in Turkey is, literally, like nothing on earth. At its bleakest, it could be a moonscape. At its most fantastic, it could be a surrealist scene imagined by Salvador Dali.

Its origin was dramatic: a volcanic eruption millions of years ago that covered the terrain with lava. But its most bizarre features are due to a centuries-long process of erosion that has etched the volcanic rock and ash into steep-sided valleys, sometimes white, sometimes slashed with horizontal bars of different colours.

Here and there, where isolated layers or fragments of volcanic rock proved more resistant to erosion than the surrounding ash, nature has produced shapes stranger than any human sculpture. Singly and in groups, there rise from the valley floors rock cones, needles and what the local people call 'fairy chimneys', slim pillars topped by horizontal slabs that sit on them like hats.

Yet what is visible in the valleys of Göreme and Zelve is less strange than what is hidden: Byzantine churches with frescoes, flat ceilings, domes or vaulting, tunnelled into the cliff faces or hollowed out of rock cones by men who used the friable 'tuff' as material to reverse the normal sequence of architecture, taking away rather than adding on, carving out rather than building up.

Christianity came early to Cappadocia, long before the Emperor Constantine made Byzantium into 'New Rome' in 330 AD. For centuries it flourished, and Asia Minor abounded in Christian bishoprics. When Constantinople became Istanbul, the capital of the Ottoman Empire, in the fifteenth century, the most recent churches in the Göreme valley were already 300 years old.

The oldest churches probably date from the seventh century, but when the first Christian inhabitants arrived can only be guessed at. Possibly, they were hermits who hollowed their cells from the soft rocks. It is possible, too, that the mushroom shapes of the 'fairy chimneys' attracted the 'stylites', those early Christian polesquatters who spent their days on the top of pillars, to pray on their insecure summits.

However, the variety of styles in the rock-hewn churches indicates that they were constructed at different dates by different waves of migrants. Most of the churches apparently belong to the later Byzantine period, when the new faith of Constantine had become the old region, when the Church he made respectable had become in many instances a persecuted sect.

The wild regions of Cappadocia offered natural refuges for monks who wanted to live in peace in self-supporting communities. Where these developed, they attracted peasants to live around them, some in cave dwellings like those in Göreme, which riddle the cliffs like holes in some gigantic Gruyère cheese. Should armies come to their remote havens, monks and peasants had a second line of retreat – underground. The 'tuff' could be excavated downwards as well as laterally, and there are some twenty underground refuges in the Göreme area extending to seven or eight levels below the surface. Small entrances and narrow connecting passages which allow only one crouching invader to pass at a time have made those who used these pre-atomic age fall-out shelters secure from all except starvation through long siege.

In one of these underground villages is a Christian chapel with a stone altar and carved cross, but scholars cannot agree whether religious settlers created them or simply took over the refuges of earlier communities. Whatever the case, it takes no imaginative leap to see the church architects as not only motivated by the easily workable nature of the rock but also by the opportunity it gave to keep the mysteries of their religion away from hostile eyes. Perhaps they saw in the rock-hewn churches a link to the catacombs of Rome and the reputation of the Early Christians as 'gens lucifugera' – the people who flee the light.

They left behind a veritable museum of Byzantine styles. For example, in the Elmali or Apple church, one of the seven in Göreme and the Zelve valley selected for priority restoration work, two layers of decoration can be seen. The first, painted directly on to the rock, is made up of crosses and geometrical patterns and probably dates from the iconoclastic (literally 'image-breaking') period before about 850 AD when the representation of living forms was forbidden. The second, painted on to plaster, shows a Pantocrator, or Christ the Almighty, on the central cupola, with other frescoes depicting scenes from the life of Christ in the style of the eleventh century.

Cross-domed like the Elmali church is the eleventh-century Karanlik, or Dark church, which gets its name from the deep blue-grey of its frescoes, still well-preserved and illustrating the sophisticated style of Constantinople. In other churches of the valley, like the church of the Virgin Mary, the style is more provincial, showing the hand of local artists.

The barrel-vaulted El Nazar church is an example of a cruciform structure in which the main apse joins directly on to a central square without an intervening east cross-arm. Unlike the Dark church, which includes a refectory and a dormitory, and many of the others, it is not connected with a monastery but set apart in an isolated tent-shaped rock cone.

'Fairy Castles' at Cappadocia

Over the centuries, the Christians left their settlements and the churches were neglected until the 1920s and 1930s, when the writings of a French priest, Fr. Guillaume de Jerphanion, drew the attention of scholars and tourists. What had been religious communities became farming communities. Peasant families made their homes in the caves, many of them continuing to live there until recent years. In at least one case, this secularisation had an advantage: the frescoes of the Dovecote church in Cavusin were well preserved because the church was sealed up until 1964 so that pigeons, valued in the area for their guano, could be kept in it. But the Dovecote church, like the Carikli, or Sandal church of Go Greme, has been brutally exposed to the elements. In both cases the narthex, where once congregations stood in worship, has crumbled away and the modern tourist climbs a metal staircase to enter.

For the delicate rock which made the churches possible and the erosion which gave them their unique shapes are today the chief threats to their continued existence. Rain has soaked into the decorated surfaces, fading colours and flaking paintwork. More dangerously, it has seeped into cracks, then frozen and fissured the structures. Göreme is in a seismic zone and it was thanks to an earth-slip that the church of St John the Baptist was discovered as late as 1957. But tremors have destabilised more churches than they have revealed. Some churches have been totally destroyed, leaving only traces behind.

These threats explain why UNESCO has not only put the rock-hewn churches onto its list of monuments belonging to the cultural heritage of all mankind, but has launched an international appeal to save them for future generations. The perils to body or soul which drove the Christian communities of Cappadocia into these bleak valleys have long since faded. The men who conceived the churches, hewed them from the living rock and lovingly decorated them have been forgotten for centuries. But their faith and their artistry created something unique, that still hushes a group of modern visitors into silent wonder.

ANTONY BROCK, is a Paris-based British writer and journalist who specialises in educational and cultural topics.

Reprinted from the *Unesco Courier,* February 1991

Whatever befalls the earth befalls the sons of the earth. Man did not weave the web of life: he is merely a strand in it. Whatever he does to the web, he does to himself.
CHIEF SEATTLE

Istanbul, the Capital of Two Empires

ISTANBUL IS THE largest and most significant city in Turkey. Standing on two continents and situated at the mouth of the Bosphorus, it owes much of its beauty and glorious history to its topographical character. Throughout history it has controlled the sea traffic between the Black Sea and the Mediterranean and the land routes between Asia and Europe. As the capital of the Byzantine and Ottoman Empires it has been an urban centre for centuries, hosting different peoples and cultures. All these have led to its unique cultural heritage.

Although there are traces of settlements dating back to the end of the 4th millennium, archaeological evidence shows that the city itself goes back to the 7th century BC when it was colonized by the Greeks; its name Byzantium derived from its legendary founder, Byzas the Megarian. In 196 AD Byzantium fell to the Roman Emperor Septimus Severus who destroyed it. Soon enough he realized the strategic significance of the city and restored it in the manner of a Roman town, building a hippodrome, now the Sultanahmet Square, and a colonnaded road leading to the main gate in the walls. In 324 the city was taken by Constantine the Great, who decided to declare Byzantium the new capital of the Roman Empire, the *Nova Roma*, in 330 AD Constantine enlarged the city to five times its original size, completed the hippodrome and added the Forum Constantine midway along the colonnaded road where they stood a porphyry monument with a golden statue erected on top. He built several churches including the first Haghia Sophia and the great imperial palace overlooking the Marmara Sea. His successors followed the same path. Valens built the monumental aqueduct, one of the landmarks of the city, which served for centuries, including the years of Ottoman rule. In a short time Byzantium had grown into a metropolis of 14 districts over 7 hills and came to be known as Constantinopolis named after Constantine.

A new epoch began for the city when Justinian came to power in 527. The city was then reconstructed on an even grander scale making the city the largest capital of the Medieval period. The Church of Haghia Sophia, which crowned the glory of this medieval capital, was built on the ruins of the original basilical structure which had been built by Constantius, successor of Constantine. In 537 Justinian resurrected it appointing two renowned architects, Anthemius of Tralles and Isidorus of Miletus. The Haghia Sophia is a basilica with a dome of grandiose size buttressed by half domes and barrel vaults, a great achievement for its period. Although this church underwent several restorations during the Byzantine and Ottoman times, it still adorns the city as a symbol of traditional Roman monumentality and Christian spirituality.

Although in the following centuries of Byzantine reign the city went through states of unrest with assaults of Slavs, Russians, Arabs and Turks, the city was guarded by its walls. The Latin armies of the fourth Crusade in 1204 sacked Constantinople ruining the city. The last Byzantine rulers, the Paleologus family, recaptured the city in 1261 restoring the monuments and adding smaller churches and imperial residences. Among the late Byzantine monuments, the Monastery Church of Chora (Kariye) is noted for its mosaics and frescoes, which in style and iconographical content, rival the painted churches of the Early Renaissance.

By the end of the 14th century the Byzantine Empire had narrowed down to a small state around the city of Constantinople having lost most of his land in Anatolia and the Balkans to the Ottomans, who had resumed political dominance in the area. The Byzantine capital was totally surrounded by the Ottomans and subjected to their continued attacks. In 1451 Sultan Mehmed II built the fortress of Rumeli Hisar on the Bosphorus across the Anadolu Hisar built by Sultan Bayezid in 1394, cutting the city from the north and conquered the city in 1453. This victory earned him the title 'conqueror', 'Fathi' in Turkish. A new phase started for this imperial city when Mehmed II declared it the capital of the Ottoman Empire. The city came to be called 'Kostantiniyye' by the Turks and through the years its name was transformed to 'Stimbol', then to 'Istanbul'. Mehmed II had Turks and Christians brought from all parts of the empire to settle in Istanbul with Venetians and Genoese already living in the town. Conscious of both Islamic and Mediterranean heritage, the Sultan was equally tolerant to all his subjects regardless of belief or provenance. He was also a great patron of the arts. He converted the largest Byzantine church, the Haghia Sophia, into a mosque and on the site of the ruined church of the Holy Apostles, he built a complex of buildings in his name, the Fatih Kulliye.

In the following century the Ottoman Empire reached its furthest boundaries in three continents, and Istanbul lived through a golden age of prosperity and artistic production. It had also become the centre of the Islamic world, the seat of the caliphate, acquired by Selim I after his conquests of Mesopotamia and Egypt. His son, Suleyman the Magnificent reigned for 46 years marking the peak of Ottoman power that played a significant role in European history of the 16th century. Suleyman had inherited a sound administrative system and was conscious of his cultural heritage. He commissioned great many buildings in the capital giving the city its Ottoman skyline. It was during his reign (1520-1566)

The Blue Mosque, Istanbul

that Ottoman art and architecture achieved perfection in function and aesthetics. Sinan, the renowned architect of this period and one of the greatest figures in world architecture built several hundred buildings establishing the classical style in Ottoman architecture. Sinan's many works in Istanbul range from mosques to schools, bridges to waterworks marking Istanbul's architectural glory in the 16th century.

The classical expression stayed with Ottoman architects in the 17th century up until the end, when after continued loss of land in the Balkans, Ottoman history took a new course. Ottoman sultans of the 18th century, realizing that Ottoman supremacy was beginning to wane, established diplomatic and cultural relations with the European countries to acquire technical knowledge and European way of life. The new relations were influential in the cultural sphere. European travellers and artists frequented Istanbul and exchanges with Europeans brought a new style to the capital. The westernizing elite built houses on the Bosphorous for pleasure, so did the sultans. The 19th century sultans now preferred to live on the Bosphorus in the palaces of Dolmabahoe, Ciragan, Beylerbeyi or Yildiz instead of the Topkapi. These series of new palaces are in 19th century eclectic style of the neo-baroque the neo-classical built by Ottoman artists trained in Europe or invited European architects creating a new skyline in Istanbul.

In the 19th century with the reorganization of the administrative system and social structure, the city grew in the direction of the Galata region and the banks of the Bosphorus with new government buildings, schools, military barracks and apartment buildings. To these can be added buildings in the Turkish neo-classical style trying to revive traditional Ottoman architectural elements or the modernist buildings of the 20th century adding to the unique cultural heritage of this imperial city, which is no longer the capital of the country but is still the largest city in modern Turkey.

PROF. DR. GÜNSEL RENDA
Hacettepe University, Ankara

HATTUSHA

LOCATION   In the Province of Corum, district of Sungurlu, N 40° 01′, E 33° 39′.

DESCRIPTION   The ruins of the ancient city of Hattusha cover an area of 3sq km (1.2sq mi). They consist of several mounds, rocky peaks and plateaus which rise in a gentle slope approximately 300m (1,000ft) above the surrounding plain. A pair of gorges determine the natural boundaries of the site, which is split into an upper and lower city. A great wall 8km (5mi) long surrounds the whole site with several ruined towers. The individual

The Sphinx Gate, Hattusha

monuments within the city are in varying states of excavation but include a royal citadel (Büyük kale), the Sphinx gate, the New Castle and the Yellow Castle. Near the main area are several temple sites and the remains of the Hittite living quarters, plus a hieroglyphic inscription carved into a cliff-face detailing numerous exploits of the ancient kings and warriors. A tremendous series of rock reliefs is also to be seen at Yazilikuya nearby.

SIGNIFICANCE   This was the capital of the mighty Hittite Empire which ruled over a great part of Asia Minor and Syria between 2000 and 1200 BC. The 3 archives of clay tablets which form the main body of knowledge on the Hittites were found here. It is interesting to note that it has been thought that the Hittites spoke a language which was a precurser to the modern European languages.

HISTORIC AREAS OF ISTANBUL

LOCATION   Within the Province of Istanbul, N 45° 25', E 29° 00'.

DESCRIPTION   This historic area is 17.2sq km (7sq mi) of densely populated urban development, bounded by the Golden Horn to the north, the Bosphorus to the east, the Marmara Sea to the south and land walls to the west.

The following 4 areas have been particularly singled out for conservation; 1. archaeological park with the hippodrome, Agia Sophia (Byzantine Church), Agia Irene, numerous cisterns, various Byzantine remains and the Blue Mosque and Sokollu Mehmet Pasa complexes; 2. Süleymaniye conservation site with numerous small mosques and houses clustered around 2 major Ottoman religious complexes – the Sehzade and Süleymaniye Mosques. These are complete with Koran schools, kitchens, mausoleums, etc; 3. Zeyrek conservation site, another traditional area centred on the church of the monastery of Pantocrator, now known as Zeyrek Mosque; 4. Land walls conservation area which aims at maintaining the old fortified walls with 96 towers, 13 gates and 11 combined tower/gates. Near the walls and included in the conservation site are several religious complexes, a number of mosques and former churches, plus the mighty Kara Ahmet Pasa complex at Topkapi.

SIGNIFICANCE   Taken together, these complexes and sites chart an unbroken record of one of the greatest empires of the Christian and Muslim world. From St. Sophia, the greatest church in antiquity, through the city's role as Byzantium, then Constantinople, then as Istanbul, capital of all the middle and near east as well as most of eastern Europe, it is impossible to overestimate the importance of 'Old Stamboul'.

Hot Springs, Pamukkale

NEMRUT DAĞ

LOCATION   In the Province of Adiyaman, 65km (40mi) from Kähta, N 38° 00′, E 39° 00′.

DESCRIPTION   Nemrut Dağ is a mountain 2,150m (7,054ft) above sea level crowned by the tumulus (burial mound) of Antiochos I. The tumulus is 50m (164ft) high and 150m (492ft) in diameter. It is piled with fist-sized stones and surrounded on 3 sides by terraces, of which the eastern and western are symmetrical and adorned with colossal statues of kings and deities. The eastern terrace has 2 podiums with 5 statues of various deities flanked by double eagle and lion statues. A pyramidal stepped fire altar stands opposite the statues. The western terrace is similar but lacking the fire altar. A lion relief has astronomical symbols and is called the horoscope of Antiochos. The northern terrace has no statues and may have been a processional way while the tomb is believed to lie under the tumulus.

SIGNIFICANCE   Antiochos was the richest of the petty kings following the decline of the kingdoms which succeeded Alexander the Great. An inscription suggests that Antiochos intended the sanctuary for his own tomb but this has never been found. It is postulated that if it could be found it would contain fabulous wealth. The above ground statues similarly suggest this and are themselves of great religious and eclectic interest. The site itself, which commands vast vistas over a desolate, mountainous landscape, engenders an air of mystery which is unique.

GÖREME NATIONAL PARK AND THE ROCK SITES OF CAPPADOCIA

LOCATION   Nevsehir Province (Cappodocia) in Central Anatolia between the cities of Urgup and Avanos, N 38° 26′, E 34° 54′.

DESCRIPTION   The area is an erosion basin, and forms an open air museum. Due to severe weathering of the soft rock and soil, a large number of conical or dome shaped features have evolved, creating a fantastic landscape of so-called 'fairy chimneys', and these have been hollowed out to form churches, chapels and houses. There are 7 churches within the valley, dating from the 10th to 13th centuries. These religious structures are noted for their wall-paintings.

SIGNIFICANCE   In the dispute over representation of human form, particularly with regard to holy personages, that shook the Catholic Church during the 8th and 9th centuries, many monks retreated to Cappadocia to continue their artistic devotion, safe from iconoclasts.

Later, under the persecution of the invading Muslims many more men of religion took to finding a refuge in the rocks of Göreme. As time went by the various murals became increasingly sophisticated, until the expulsion of the monks in the Middle Ages. Geologically, the area is one of the most unusual on earth, being similar to places such as the Badlands of Dakota (United States), but having far more bizarre formations in a much smaller area.

HIERAPOLIS – PAMUKKALE

LOCATION   East of Denizli on the northern side of the valley of the Curuksu River, N 38° 00′, E 39° 00′.

DESCRIPTION   Pamukkale is a collection of terraces running down the foothills of the Cokelez Mountains. A series of hot thermal springs bubble up from the rock and flow down the terraces forming pools. The water from the springs is heavily laden with calcium carbonate and this has caused white stalactite configurations to form over the rims of the basins, suggesting a fanciful picture of melting pools. These white pools extend 2.5km (1.6mi) and are up to 500m (1,640ft) wide. Above the terraces, on a plateau, sits Hierapolis, the ruins of an ancient Roman spa town. It has a necropolis, baths, tombs and a theatre, all in a good state of preservation.

SIGNIFICANCE   One of the most striking visual experiences in Turkey, if not the world, Pamukkale has outstanding aesthetic value. The ruins of Hieropolis and its monuments give insight into a Roman spa town, more a holiday resort than a residential city. The hot waters which formed Pamukkale were the basis of the city's wealth.

XANTHOS – LETOON

LOCATION   Province of Mugla and Antalya, District of Fethiye and Kas, E 29° 16′, N 36° 22′.

DESCRIPTION   These ruins are of the ancient Lycian city of Xanthos and its sanctuary, Letoon, 3km (1.9mi) distant. The city is on a hill overlooking the ancient Xanthos River and has impressive remains of rock-cut tombs, temple and pillar tombs, stone mounted sarcophaguses, 7th century BC houses, a Roman theatre and early Christian and Byzantine churches. A bishop's palace remains unexcavated. At Letoon are several Greek temples and theatres, as well as many later Roman public buildings.

SIGNIFICANCE   The Lycian Kingdom controlled much of southern and southeastern Turkey and the Mediterranean until being conquered by Alexander the Great. It was at Xanthos, the capital, and in Letoon that royal decisions were made. The remains of the various monuments attest to the wealth, power and artistic skills of these early peoples.

Divrigi

GREAT MOSQUE AND HOSPITAL OF DIVRIGI

LOCATION   In the Sivas Province of Eastern Anatolia, N 39° 45′, E 37° 00′.

DESCRIPTION   This site is a large rectangular area which contains the mosque, hospital and some tombs. It is on a hillside where the castle of Divrigi was sited. The mosque has 5 aisles leading to the mihrab (niche indicating the direction of Mecca) and 25 multi-coloured vaults. The main dome is the outstanding characteristic of the mosque, with 16 supporting columns and some intricate ornamental details. The hospital has various unique plant-like and geometric stone decorations.

SIGNIFICANCE   The mosque dates from 1228 AD, the time of the first appearance of the Ottoman Turks. It is considered to be one of the finest examples of early Turkish architectural work. The decorative stone sculpturing of the northern portal arcade is particularly renowned.

The Roman theatre at Xanthos

UNITED KINGDOM

Britain has 14 World Heritage sites including one in a British dependency. Some sites, like the 'Giant's Causeway', a series of perfect hexagonal columns rising vertically out of the Irish Sea, are the product of geological activity, which in this case took place some 55 million years ago. Others, landscapes and buildings of breathtaking beauty and grandeur, are the result of natural features and resources harnessed to human needs.

Fourteen may seem a high number, but it is important to remember that they represent only a minute fraction of the British heritage. We also have 900 miles of unspoilt coastline in England and Wales alone, the Scottish coast and islands, open spaces of outstanding landscape beauty, a rich variety of natural habitats, and, from the peculiarly British tradition of country house building, a world-famous abundance of stately homes and gardens.

The World Heritage sites are valuable both as individual achievements and as symbols of particular periods or collective achievements. Thus Durham and Canterbury Cathedrals, Westminster, Bath and Fountains Abbey represent the finest periods of English ecclesiastical architecture, Ironbridge represents the beginning of the industrial revolution and a breakthrough in civil engineering, and the Houses of Parliament, another World Heritage site, symbolise a system of government whose influence has been felt throughout the world.

As objects of beauty, they have assisted our worship, kindled popular myths and legends, and inspired some of the greatest works of Turner and Constable, Shakespeare and Wordsworth, Jane Austen, Elgar and Vaughan Williams. Without the visible evidence of the land, stones and walls to which these works refer, or in which important historic events have taken place, the understanding of our culture and our history would be infinitely poorer.

Until the the twentieth century, the survival of these monuments in the face of Viking invasions, civil war, enemy bombardment, periods of rapid industrial development and profound demographic change, has been largely a matter of chance. Since the end of the last century, however, the UK has been more aware of the need for conservation and so more organised in its approach. This has been due to the efforts of private individuals like Octavia Hill, founder of the National Trust, to stop the disappearance of the natural and built heritage, and growing

Stonehenge

public concern. Voluntary bodies continue to play a key role in preserving open spaces and historic buildings today, through ownership and fundraising. The National Trust, the largest of these charities, owns 231,000 hectares of land, 840 km of coastline and 190 historic houses in England, Wales and Northern Ireland, and has over 2 million members.

At government level, conservation policies are incorporated in planning law and protect countryside, archaeological sites and buildings, according to a hierarchy of designations. The existence of a hierarchy of designations is particularly important in the case of some 20,000 archaeological sites covering a high proportion of land available for development. The designations provide a distinction between sites, like a river bed, which can be excavated prior to development, and others, like the stone circles of Stonehenge and Avebury, which must be preserved as well as recorded.

World Heritage site status enables us to take a wider, global, view of our monuments and refine our priorities. Such recognition has important consequences, bringing, as it does, responsibility and visitors. Property-owning bodies have learnt that the wider the recognition, the greater number of visitors, and the more onerous the burden of preser-

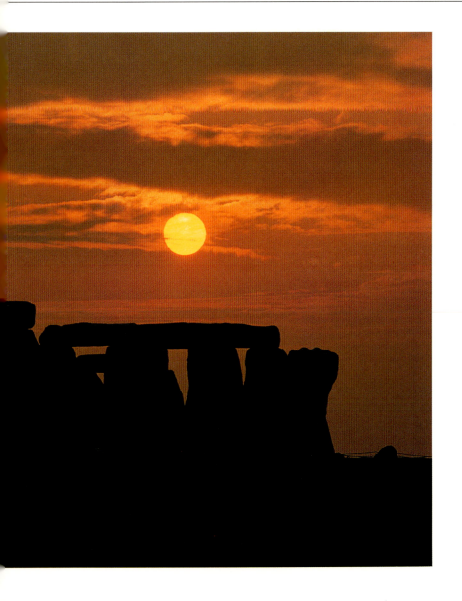

The Most Important Bequest

HERITAGE implies that there is something to be inherited; something of value to be received from a previous generation. If we are aiming to ensure that the generations that we expect to follow us can enjoy the beauties and wonders of this world, it might be more appropriate to be talking in terms of making them a 'bequest'. It is true that our generation is in the determined process of destroying our inheritance from previous generations, but the whole process of creating a 'World Heritage' at this time is so that we can bequeath it to our successors.

There is no way of creating a significant bequest of the kind we have in mind, except by caring for the global systems that make life possible on this fragile planet, and by protecting the intricate and inter-dependent web of plant and animal species. This is generally known as the conservation of nature and, in my estimation, it should be the first and most important item in our bequest to future generations. Without a healthy living matrix on the surface of the globe, human life, at least as we know it, will not be able to go on much longer. There may be any number of wonderful human cultural achievements in the arts and sciences that we would wish to include in our bequest, but they would be of no value if the quality of human existence itself were to be further degraded and its very survival put at risk.

The determination to make a bequest of a healthy planet is highly praiseworthy. We would all like future generations to enjoy the things, both natural and cultural, which we find beautiful or inspiring, so what is the problem? In the simplest possible terms, there are just too many people demanding too much space, too many resources and creating too much pollution and destruction of the natural environment. I realise that many people may find this statement to be offensive, and some may even argue that it is not true, but human population of this planet of fixed dimensions has grown from just over 300 million to the present total of 5,000 million, and it is still growing at over 2% a year. There have been some indications that this global rate may be slowing down, although not to the same extent in all parts of the world. Even so, it is estimated that numbers are unlikely to stabilise before the middle of the next century at between two and three times the present total; that is, between 10,000 and 15,000 million people. If the rate of increase does not slow down, simple mathematics predict an impossibly high world population by as soon as the year 2030. Considering the number of people who are already suffering from malnutrition, poverty, disease and unemployment, this prospect is seriously alarming.

vation. Without proper visitor management and reinforcement of the historic fabric, the effect of the tramp of thousands of pairs of feet on fragile and ancient sites is as devastating as neglect.

Amongst the more familiar pressures which lead to conflict with conservation in Britain are a high population density, economic development and a widespread desire to live in the countryside. The demand for more roads and houses, for example, the abandonment of agriculture in areas which have been farmed since the earliest recorded settlements, the exploitation of natural resources, and the desire for access to fragile landscapes and ancient buildings, have made the balancing of social, commercial and conservation interests difficult process.

Whilst it is necessary to accommodate change, it is also vital to preserve what is most precious in our environment for future generations. Within this changing environment, we welcome the World Heritage Convention as an instrument of protecting those sites whose integrity should never be breached.

LORD CHORLEY
Chairman, The National Trust for Places of Historic Interest or Natural Beauty

There can be no escaping the fact that if 5,000 million people have succeeded in creating the daunting environmental problems we are facing today, there is scant chance that two or three times that many people will be better able to solve those problems. The fact is that more people inevitably consume more resources and produce more waste, and the more prosperous they are the more they consume and the more waste they create individually. Less conspicuous consumption and better distribution can achieve so much, but there is not a hope that these measures alone can keep up with the rate of increase of the demand from the ever-growing population. Throwing a life-jacket to a drowning man may prevent him sinking under the waves, but you have to get him out of the water before you can save his life.

To suggest that the sheer size of the human population is a serious problem is one thing, to suggest remedies or solutions is quite a different matter. However, if there is a general refusal to acknowledge the existence of the problem; rather than making a handsome bequest, the chances are that we will be condemning future generations to life in an over-crowded and poverty-stricken society and within a degraded and crumbling natural environment.

The standard argument against the idea that population size is a problem says that there is lots of room and plenty of food to go round, and all it needs is a better distribution system. The trouble is that people cannot live by food alone, they need housing and clothing, productive land and machinery, clean water and clean air. All these things have to be provided by the natural environment and from the earth's limited mineral resources. The first is already over-burdened and declining, while the second cannot go on for ever.

Even if the Earth could support more people, there must be a limit somewhere. Every farmer knows that a field of a certain size and productivity can only support so many head of cattle before it becomes over-grazed and degraded and the cattle starve. The size of the Earth and its natural productivity are limited. The process of human 'over-grazing' started many years ago and we are now beginning to see the consequences. The natural forests and the wild fish stocks of the oceans are being exploited faster than they can re-generate; the pollution of the atmosphere has reached a stage when it is uncertain whether it can be reversed; deserts are increasing in size and new ones are being created; in some parts of the world the supply of fresh water is already far from adequate and the demand for land for human occupation is growing at an increasing rate. Something has to give way under this onslaught and it is becoming only too obvious that it is the natural environment and all its life support systems.

The point is that this natural environment includes

Canterbury Cathedral

all the natural beauties and wonders of this world. It includes the climate and the oceans, the huge variety of wild plants and animals and the natural wilderness in which they live. All the architectural and artistic wonders created by humanity could never hope to compensate for the further destruction of the natural world which our generation inherited. If we wish the next generation to enjoy a rich and varied 'World Heritage', we must start taking much more determined steps to halt the growth in the human population and the devaluation that it is causing to any bequest we may wish to make to the next generation.

H.R.H. THE DUKE OF EDINBURGH

The Tower of London

The Time Bridge Across the Next Century

THE TIME HAS COME to place in the public mind the position zoos have to play in the future. We cannot control the future, but our present actions will influence it and the more far sighted our actions the farther into the future will be their influences. Indeed, our actions will have a vital and wholly relevant effect on the options open to future generations, provided we make the right decisions.

I believe we should now be looking at the 22nd century. We should not be content with a 5 year, 10 year or 50 year scenario, instead we should be looking as far ahead into the future as we dare. The start of the 22nd century is about as far ahead in this context as is reasonable. It is only just over 100 years away, hardly double the lifetime of many people alive today. We should be telling people what we think the world is going to be like in the intervening, 21st century; telling them what zoos can do to offset the worst effects we foresee in that time and telling them how our actions now can influence the opportunities open to the people who will be making the decisions 100 years from now. I believe it would help to concentrate the public mind onto what we have to do if we adopt the theme for zoos of 'The time bridge across the 21st century'.

If we pre-empt the options open to our descendants by refusing to think ahead, our memories will be cursed and not blessed by those who will follow us.

Let me set out how I believe the scenario will change. For the next fifty to sixty years the human population of the world will continue to grow but, with more and more economic, moral and even political restraints, this growth will be gradually brought to a halt. For the sixty or so years following, there will be a steady decline in world population, as those already in existence age and die. After that there will be a dramatic fall in human numbers, reflecting the fall in the birth rate of sixty years earlier.

In the meantime, there will probably continue to be bloody and destructive local wars, and rebellions, as we have witnessed and are witnessing over the last half of the twentieth century. The resulting political turmoil will cause unpredictable collapses of local, and not so local, conservation efforts. We have already seen what a few short years of political anarchy did to the black rhinoceros population in Uganda: all 20,000 were wiped out. Similar disasters will happen again and again, we know not where.

The area of undisturbed land throughout the world will continue to be eroded, more so in some latitudes than others. At the same time there will be increased efforts to save what is left, but it is already becoming apparent that many areas of wild habitat are becoming too small to maintain long term viable populations of the larger and more specialised species on their own. Human encroachment interferes with traditional migration routes. Human mobility increases the amount of disturbance. Human technology increases the success rate of poaching and of unwarranted exploitation.

Not only do I see it as unlikely that there will be sufficient tracts of undisturbed environment to support all we would like to save by 2050, but I think we would be crazy to think that we can preserve the status quo by resisting human encroachment on a large scale. Instead we should be striving to obtain a sustainable level of land use in which the maximum amount of natural diversity compatible with the real political pressures can be obtained. To resist any change at all would be to place conservation into direct opposition to the aspirations of millions upon millions of desperately poor and hungry people.

What we have to do is to widen the conservation horizon so that human population pressure and the variety of natural life are seen by everybody as part and parcel of the same equation. We must encourage the preservation of as much representative environment as is politically feasible and we must get the message across that, though we are approaching the edge of an abyss, that abyss can be bridged. If we do not believe that, there really is little point in trying to do anything.

Zoos are an essential part of that bridging operation. The wildlife reserves that can be maintained over the intervening 100 years are also part of the same bridging operation. When the worst is over these two elements can be brought together again. Only then will our work come to its true fruition.

As the human population begins to recede in the 22nd century it will become possible and desirable once again to expand the areas of the wildlife reserves and for tracts of exploited land to be allowed to revert to natural habitat. The smaller and less specialised species will have survived in the wild (for it requires a smaller area to support a viable population of mice than to support one of antelopes). The larger and more specialised species will almost certainly have long since disappeared from the wild by the year 2100. Returning these latter species to the reconstituted natural areas will enable a new 'balance' of nature to be formed.

If we succeed we will be blessed and not cursed by our descendants in 2100. Our endangered species will still be around and the variety of natural life will be greater, more rewarding and more enjoyable than it might have been had we let apathy and indecision win.

DR MICHAEL R. BRAMBELL
Director, Chester Zoo, England

Remains of Fountains Abbey

'Temple of Piety', Studley Royal Park

Conway Castle, Gwynedd

The Edge of the World

THE MOST SCENICALLY spectacular property in the care of the National Trust for Scotland, the archipelago of St Kilda, situated in the North Atlantic 115 miles (185 kms) off the mainland of Scotland, was declared a World Heritage site by UNESCO in 1987.

It thus became the first site in Scotland and the first natural area in the UK to receive this accolade on account of its 'outstanding universal value for both its natural and its cultural heritage'.

Once described as 'the islands on the edge of the world', the St Kilda group is owned by NTS on behalf of the nation and is leased to the Nature Conservancy Council who have declared it a National Nature Reserve. It has also been designated as a National Scenic Area by the Secretary of State for Scotland on the advice of the Countryside Commission for Scotland.

The archipelago comprises the four islands of Hirta, Dun, Soay and Boreray and the sea stacs of Stac an Armin, Stac Lee and Levenish. The three larger islands are all over 370 metres (1230 ft) high and each has precipices which fall from that height to the sea. Stac Lee was described by Sir Julian Huxley, the first Director-General of UNESCO, as the 'most majestic sea rock in existence'.

St Kilda contains the most magnificent cliff scenery in Britain. The main island of Hirta rises smoothly and steeply from Village Bay to the hill of Conachair which falls away in a precipice of almost 430 metres (1430 ft).

The spectacular character of the great sea cliffs and stacs with their teeming sea-bird colonies, the many remains of past human settlement and the detailed record of the islands' natural and cultural history combine to impress all who venture to St Kilda.

The most outstanding wildlife feature of the St Kilda group is the massive sea-bird breeding population which forms one of the most important concentrations of sea-birds in the North Atlantic.

The largest colony of gannets in Europe breeds on Boreray and its stacs and there are large numbers of guillemots and kittiwakes. St Kilda was once the sole British locality for the fulmar although in the last century this species has found nesting sites all round the British coast. The most numerous bird is the puffin with a population which has stabilised at about 300,000 pairs from a prodigious level of 2–3 million pairs at one time. The St Kilda wren is regarded as a distinct sub-species.

Interesting mammals include a St Kilda species of the wood mouse and the feral Soay sheep descended from the most primitive domestic form in Europe.

The St Kilda archipelago is remarkable not only for its physical splendour and important birdlife but also for its history of human habitation. Despite its isolation and the severity of its climate, St Kilda had

Boreray Island, St. Kilda

been inhabited for more than 2000 years. The population was evacuated at their own request in 1930 after succumbing to an unequal struggle with the forces of nature and the influences of the modern world.

When St Kilda was bequeathed to NTS in 1957 by the 5th Marquess of Bute, the old village was in a ruinous state. A major objective became the preservation of the buildings and, by means of annual work parties of volunteers which began in 1958, several cottages have been restored together with the church and the schoolhouse and many of the island's cleits (food storage structures).

The history of St Kilda underlines the distinction which has to be made between sympathetic support for small communities and the destructive effects which can result from too much contact with a more vigorous culture.

LORD WEMYSS
President
National Trust for Scotland

CASTLES AND TOWN WALLS OF KING EDWARD IN GWYNEDD

LOCATION   Gwynedd, northwest Wales, N 53° 08′ to 53° 52′, W 03° 50′ to 04° 16′.

DESCRIPTION   There are 4 castles here. Beaumaris Castle is built on level ground near the harbour and is a concentric castle par excellence, being curtain-walled with towers and gates. A conspicuous feature of the walkways within the castle are the double-latrines. Caernarfon Castle is almost an island among 3 rivers, having a very long and irregular wall. Conway Castle on a rocky outcrop and protected by the Conway River has several identical towers, a prison, the King's Hall and Chamber. Many features date from the time of the English conquest of Wales. Harlech Castle sits on a rocky point washed below by the sea and has a ditch to the landward side. It is based on a central quadrangle with 4 square towers and the main buildings are largely ruined.

SIGNIFICANCE   The conquest of Wales by Edward I of England was a major step towards 'the United Kingdom' we know today. These castles were all built by Edward following his victories. They are the finest examples of 13th century military architecture in Europe.

CITY OF BATH

LOCATION   In Avon, N 51° 25, W 02° 20′.

DESCRIPTION   Bath is a city of 80,000 inhabitants situated on the River Avon. Its major buildings are divided into 3 architectural periods; Roman, medieval and Georgian. The remains of the Roman baths and temple cover an area 91 by 45m (299 by 148ft). A later medieval bath-house and abbey church are built on and beside the Roman ruins though little else of importance remains from this era. The architecture which dominates present-day Bath is from a much later period. It includes pump rooms, landscaped parks, neo-classical facades and monuments, Queen Square, the Circus and the Royal Crescent.

SIGNIFICANCE   There are 4,900 buildings listed for preservation, most built from the mid 18th century to the early 19th century when Bath was the favoured resort of the English aristocracy. The state of preservation is excellent and Bath is easily the most elegant and beautiful Georgian city in the United Kingdom.

BLENHEIM PALACE

LOCATION   Town of Woodstock, Oxfordshire, N 51° 50′, W 01° 20′.

DESCRIPTION   In a vast park, the palace is a romantic collection of turrets and pinnacles, grouped dramatically with a series of wings which derive from Palladio and Versailles. The main house has 4 square towers and

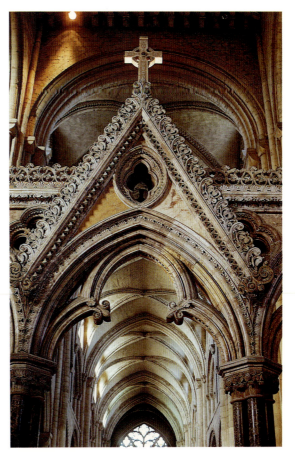

Durham Cathedral

concave quadrant arcades. A carving of the British lion savaging the French cock mounts a ringed Doric column proclaiming victory from all sides. The interior of the palace has a Great Hall and vaulted stone corridors. The west wing has saucer domes, miniature versions of the aisles of St. Paul's. The private apartments and the marble fireplace have carvings by Gibbons, while the library is decorated with numerous works by Hawksmoor and William Kent.

SIGNIFICANCE   Built as a national monument rather than a home, the palace was funded by Queen Anne and presented to John Churchill, Duke of Marlborough after the defeat of the French at Blenheim in 1704. Its outstanding visual aesthetics are complemented by its historical connotations with the various Dukes of Marlborough, and, perhaps its most famous resident, Sir Winston Churchill. He was born there in 1874, engaged there, and is buried nearby in Bladon parish church.

CANTERBURY CATHEDRAL, ST. AUGUSTINE'S ABBEY AND ST. MARTIN'S CHURCH

LOCATION   City of Canterbury, county of Kent, N 51° 17′, E 01° 05′.

DESCRIPTION   Strictly known as Christchurch Cathedral, this huge building occupies the northeast quarter of the ancient walled city and dates from 1100 AD, though much of it is no earlier than 14th century. There have been numerous additions and renovations

Hadrian's Wall

over the centuries. The cathedral is 157m (515ft) long with a tremendously high nave. It has 8 bays, side aisles and transepts. The site of the martyrdom of St. Thomas a Becket is marked by a modern stone altar. There are numerous tombs, statues and carvings. East of the Cathedral is St. Augustine's Abbey on a 12ha (29ac) site. It is largely in ruins but remnants of Saxon, Norman and medieval religious buildings can be seen. Various foundations and masonry remains are scattered about or else covered by playing fields. St. Martin's Church is east of the city with a western tower, nave and channel. Its complex patterns of masonry are evidence of a long history dating back to Roman times.

SIGNIFICANCE   Canterbury Cathedral is the seat of the Archbishop of Canterbury, head of the Anglican church, so it is a major centre of pilgrimage. Its enormous proportions are overwhelming from within and without, and the brilliance of the stained glass windows is dazzling. Architecturally it represents a blend of Romanesque, early and late Gothic styles. Both the Abbey and St. Martin's are important archaeological sites, revealing a rich and dynamic architectural history.

ST. KILDA

LOCATION   64km (40mi) west of North Uist, Outer Hebrides, Scotland, N 57° 49′, W 08° 34′.

DESCRIPTION   There are 4 main islands, Hirta, Dun, Soay and Boreray which cover 850ha (2040ac). There are also several sea-stacs (rocky outcrops) which are named Stac on Armin, Stac Lee and Levenish. All are known for their precipitous cliffs and thriving sea-bird colonies. These barren rocky islands have been occupied for over 2,000 years by various peoples including Iron-Age dwellers, Vikings and the Scottish Clans.

SIGNIFICANCE   Described as 'the most majestic sea rocks in existence' the unrivalled grandeur of the St. Kilda archipelago is legendary. The archaeological remains are testament to the ability of man to exist in an uncompromisingly hostile environment. The sea-bird colonies are the largest in Europe and include gannets, puffins, guillemots, razorbills and kittiwakes.

STONEHENGE, AVEBURY AND ASSOCIATED MEGALITHIC SITES

LOCATION   Wiltshire, N 51° 11′ to 51° 27′, W 01° 51′.

DESCRIPTION   Stonehenge is a circular arrangement of stones with lintels surrounded by an earthen bank and ditch. It measures 97.5m (320ft) in diameter. Originally built in 2100-2000 BC, the axis of symmetry of this circle of bluestone blocks is approximately aligned towards the rising sun at the summer solstice. Nearby are several monuments such as Robin Hood Ball, the Cursus, Woodhenge and several barrows. Avebury is larger than

Stonehenge, similar in layout but with fewer standing stones remaining. It had 2 avenues of upright stones and is believed to have been associated with various burial rites.

SIGNIFICANCE   Regarded by Henry of Huntingdon in 1130 AD as one of the wonders of Britain, Stonehenge is famous for its physical setting and mystical connotations. There is a legend that Merlin magically transported the stones from Ireland. This no doubt relates to the fact that there are at least 4 varieties of igneous rock used here that are foreign to the area. It remains a largely unexplained monument dating 4,000 years back into prehistoric times and hinting at levels of civilisation not yet chronicled. The attendant sites at Avebury are of similar unknown origin and of equal importance.

THE GIANT'S CAUSEWAY AND ITS COAST

LOCATION   Northern Ireland on the north coast of county Antrim, N 55° 15′, W 06° 20′.

DESCRIPTION   This is a spectacular line of coastal cliffs, exposing geological formations caused by severe and recurrent volcanic activity during the Tertiary Period. At the Giant's Causeway itself, a cross-section of horizontal columnar basalt lavas seems to form a pavement. At sea level the full extent of the basaltic jointing may be observed and clearly displays the succession of lava flows which formed the Northern Irish coast.

SIGNIFICANCE   The most magnificent example of such basaltic joining in the world, the Causeway and its coast are of international renown and Northern Ireland's premier tourist attraction. Due to its accessibility the area has led to a detailed scientific interpretation which has allowed a comprehensive understanding of Tertiary events in the entire North Atlantic region.

THE TOWER OF LONDON

LOCATION   London borough of tower hamlets, N 51° 32′, W 00° 05′.

DESCRIPTION   Covering 7.3ha (17.6ac), there are several towers, the most important being the White Tower. The Inner Ward is enclosed by a 12th century wall and contains 13 towers. The whole complex, built on Tower Hill, is surrounded by thick stone walls, has armouries and a hospital and is believed to have had up to 1,000 inhabitants.

SIGNIFICANCE   Construction of the tower began in 1066 under William the Conqueror. Many historically important events have occurred inside its walls. Sir Walter Raleigh was one of the many luminaries imprisoned here. Its significance lies in the combination of historical and architectural renown which has made the tower's reputation. It is also famous today as the vault for the Crown Jewels.

Blenheim Palace

Stone circle, Avebury

Roman baths, City of Bath

Westminster

Ironbridge Gorge Museum

IRONBRIDGE GORGE

LOCATION   220km (136.7mi) northwest of London in the district of Wrekin, N 52° 27′, W 02° 29′.

DESCRIPTION   The area along the Severn, including the 2 tributaries' valleys, Coalbrookdale and Hay Brook, is an area of early industrialisation and contains several features of historical interest. These include old furnaces, smelters, market squares, cottages and pathways which were once primitive railways. The old Ironbridge itself has been fully restored.

SIGNIFICANCE   In many ways the Ironbridge Gorge is one of the birthplaces of the Industrial Revolution. It was here that iron was first smelted with coke. Many writers and artists visited the area to marvel at the iron and steel works. In the late 18th century it was the most important industrial centre in the world.

WESTMINSTER (PALACE AND ABBEY) AND ST. MARGARET'S CHURCH

LOCATION   City of Westminster, London, N 51° 52′, W 00° 05′.

DESCRIPTION   Built in the Norman style by Edward the Confessor, and rebuilt by Edward III in the 13th century, Westminster Abbey is particularly associated with the coronation of Britain's monarchy. The palace stands between Westminster Abbey and the Thames River. Since the fire of 1834 the only medieval parts remaining are Westminster Hall, St. Stephen's Cloister and the Jewel Tower. The major buildings are the House of Lords, House of Commons and general administration buildings. The whole complex with the famous clock-tower of Big Ben covers 3.3ha (8ac) on a bed of concrete. There are over 1,100 rooms, 100 staircases, 3.2km (2mi) of corridors with more than 300 statues of various saints and sovereigns. Within the palace are 11 open courtyards, several galleries and chambers. St. Margaret's church stands on the north side of the abbey and is the official church to the House of Commons.

SIGNIFICANCE   Originally the king's residence, the palace has somewhat of a tortured history. It was severely damaged by fire in 1512, then in 1834 another fire destroyed most of it. It was rebuilt in 1840-1867 as it stands now, except for the Commons Chamber which was bombed in World War II. It is world renowned chiefly as a symbol of modern democratic government. The clock tower is famous for its 13 ton bell called 'Big Ben'. The abbey is one of the best known churches in the modern world, especially its 'Poets Corner' where many famous poets lie in state.

DURHAM (CATHEDRAL AND CASTLE)

LOCATION   Durham County, N 54° 47′, W 01° 35′.

DESCRIPTION   The Cathedral of Christ and the Blessed Virgin Mary is basically in the Norman style with some early English features and several other later extensions and additions. It is in fact more a complex, with several churches, chapels, tombs, monastic buildings and libraries. Durham Castle is designed around a central courtyard. It has a great hall, state rooms, numerous residential rooms, kitchens, cellars, libraries and many other rooms. Two of its main features are the Black Staircase and Tunstall's Gallery.

SIGNIFICANCE   This magnificent, rambling cathedral shows some of the earliest architectural features which are distinctively English in design, such as the ribbed vaulting of the choir aisles and the decorations of the internal pillars, which were unique for their day. Several sections, like the east end, are superb examples of late Norman work. The tomb of Bede, the 'father of English history' resides in this section. Another famous tomb is that of Saint Cuthbert. Durham Castle was built facing Scotland, the most likely direction of attack in the Middle Ages. It was the residence of the Bishop of Durham until 1837 – a position of immense power and prestige in the largely unprotected northern areas. It now forms part of the University of Durham.

HENDERSON ISLAND

LOCATION   Pitcairn Islands Group in the South Pacific Ocean, S 24° 22′, W 128° 20′.

DESCRIPTION   Henderson is the largest of the Pitcairn Group at 37sq km (15sq mi). It is uninhabited and a licence is required to visit. Composed of coral, it forms a classic ring-shaped atoll with a central lagoon. The surface is rugged with many deep trenches and jagged pinnacles. The central plateau is 33m (108ft) above sea level. Rainfall is 1,500mm (59in) per annum and the vegetation is mainly dense scrub up to 10m (33ft) high.

SIGNIFICANCE   One of the few pristine atolls remaining in the world, Henderson's ecological balance has barely been disturbed by man. Endemic species flourish here, with 10 flowering plants, 4 land birds and countless invertebrates unique to the island. In many ways Henderson is a living evolutionary laboratory, with all the dynamics of natural selection on display.

Giant's Causeway

HADRIAN'S WALL

LOCATION   Counties of Cumbria, Northumbria and Tyne and Wear, N 54° 54′ to 54° 59′, W 01° 35′ to 02° 55′.

DESCRIPTION   This listing comprises the actual wall built across the north of England and a series of Roman frontier works, road networks and surveillance posts. It originally stretched 185km (115mi) from Wallsend to Bowness. Construction is variously stone, turf and earth, and it originally had towers, forts and turrets. South of the wall was also a flat-bottomed ditch, the 'Vallum'.

SIGNIFICANCE   The wall was built on the orders of the Roman Emperor Hadrian in 122 AD with the purpose of defending the province from the northern tribes of Scotland. It is easily the best preserved complex of Roman ruins in Britain and the most extensive of any former Roman province.

STUDLEY ROYAL PARK AND THE RUINS OF FOUNTAINS ABBEY

LOCATION   North Yorkshire, in the valley of the River Skell.

DESCRIPTION   Built from 1716 to 1781, the park is one of the few complete 'Green Gardens' remaining in its original form. It includes various lakes, ponds and cascades as well as statues, towers, neo-classical temples, halls and monuments. Domestic buildings such as restaurants, lodges and stables are also found. Within the park's boundaries is the abbey and the church of St. Mary. Fountains Hall, a much earlier edifice (1161 AD) than the church, was built partly from the ruins of the abbey which is rather difficult to discern amid the lawns and gardens.

SIGNIFICANCE   The building of the park preserved, quite by accident, one of the oldest Cistercian abbeys in Britain. This throws light on the subsequent founding of the abbeys at Newminster, Kirkstall and Vaudey, and even one in Norway, under the patronage of the Fountains Abbey. The park itself is a beautifully preserved example of 18th century garden landscaping.

You brought it to my attention everything that was made in God; down through centuries of great writings and paintings. Everything lives in God; seen through architecture of great cathedrals down through the history of time; is and was in the beginning and evermore shall be.

VAN MORRISON

Henderson Island

'Bright Angel Trail', Grand Canyon National Park

USA

Not long ago I helped to celebrate the centennial of Yosemite National Park in California, and I was reminded that Yosemite is the place where the modern idea of wilderness preservation began. The park was first created in the 1860's as a state preserve; by the time Yosemite National Park was established in 1890, eighteen years after Yellowstone, Americans still did not agree on what preservation meant. But what a grand idea it was. It led to a whole network of national parks in the United States and helped spread the concept to more than 120 nations worldwide. Visionary, idealistic, and democratic, preservation has often been called the best idea America ever had.

Many of the parks spawned by John Muir and the other Yosemite pioneers can be found among the 337 World Heritage sites celebrated in this book. Whatever the reason they were set aside – scenic landscapes such as Yosemite's; an awesome array of rare plants and animals, such as Peru's Manu Biosphere Reserve; value as a laboratory for scientific study, such as the Great Barrier Reef Marine Park of Australia – the parks enrich us all by saving precious resources. They also rejuvenate the spirit, by providing islands of calm in a clamorous world.

These sanctuaries should be sacred places immune from crime, war, pollution, and heedless development. However, the pressures of the real world all too often intrude. No matter how big or how isolated or how protected, each of the world's natural areas, and each cultural site as well, is vulnerable in some way. I am convinced that the future of these places and indeed of the whole planet, depends on how well we learn the lessons of geography.

Our mission at the National Geographic Society is to explore the globe through geography's unique lens, and to invite others to look through that lens with us. An important part of the society's mission is to help people not only to understand and value the world's wilderness heritage, but also to appreciate how wilderness relates to everything around it. Only in acquiring a worldwide perspective, in grasping the connections that link us all, will we be able to manage our planet's environment and protect its natural and cultural wonders. Geography education *is* environmental education. Good stewardship will come only when people know that our every action has consequences that echo around the globe.

The problem of air pollution is a case in point. We

La Fortaleza, Puerto Rico

cannot just blame the summer crowds in Yosemite, with their campfires and their car fumes, for creating the haze that obscures the views. It is *city smog* that is drifting into the park, poisoning the trees and the streams and the animal life. The acid rain that is threatening the park's forests and streams is not just Yosemite's problem, it belongs to California, to the continent, and to the world.

The oil fires in Kuwait were literally worldwide fires, the long-reaching effects of which were measurable as far away as Hawaii. According to several estimates, the world's rain forests are disappearing at the rate of one football field's worth every second; with every one, untold numbers of possibly life-saving foods and medicines are lost forever. Environmental concerns have gone beyond saving a bird or a baboon to saving the planet.

When the National Geographic Society was founded in 1888, our first president noted: 'Because we know so little, we have formed this society for the increase and diffusion of geographic knowledge'. More than a century later, the need to learn and inform is more urgent that ever. Society magazines, books, television shows, and classroom materials reach millions of people.

Out in the mid-1980's a survey showed us that Americans were shockingly ignorant about geography, and the society decided to take more direct action. Today, a successful network of programs in nearly all of our states is restoring geography to the classroom, training thousands of teachers, and reaching out to millions of students. And we are using some of the newest technology to accomplish our goals. Kids Network allows youngsters across the country and around the world to share discoveries in science and geography using computers. They learn that environmental problems in the rain forests of Brazil will eventually impact farms in Kansas.

It is my belief that this knowledge fosters an environmental ethic, one that is desperately needed if future generations are to preserve not only the invaluable sites on the World Heritage list which are shown in this book, but also our entire planet.

GILBERT M. GROSVENOR
President, National Geographic Society

Entrance to Mammoth Caves

The First Twenty Years and What Lies Beyond

WHEN THE WORLD HERITAGE CONVENTION was first adopted in 1972, I and others who helped develop the World Heritage concept viewed it as a tremendous step forward in the international community's recognition of our shared responsibility to protect the global common. For the first time, there existed a legal and financial mechanism through which nations could work together to preserve and manage natural and cultural properties so unique and special that they should be considered part of the heritage not only of individual nations, but of all mankind. Today, nearly twenty years later, 115 nations are party to the World Heritage Convention, with 337 sites listed for special protection. As we enter the 1990s, it is my sincere hope that this program will continue to grow, and that more nations and areas will benefit.

But before I get ahead of myself, let me review some of the history of the World Heritage concept. In the autumn of 1965 when I was the new president of the Conservation Foundation, now merged with World Wildlife Fund, I had the privilege of serving as a member of the Committee on Natural Resources of the White House Conference on International Co-operation. The idea of a World Heritage Trust emerged in discussions between myself and the Committee Chairman, Dr. Joseph Fisher, then the distinguished president of Resources for the Future. The report of our committee recognised that;

> Certain scenic, historic, and natural resources are part of man's heritage, and their survival is a matter of concern to all.

and, after considerable elaboration of this theme, it was our recommendation:

> That there be established a Trust for the World Heritage that would be responsible to the [world] community for the stimulation of international co-operation efforts to identify, establish, develop and manage the world's superb natural and scenic areas and historic sites for the present and future benefit of the entire world citizenry.

So far as I recall, there was little or no official reaction at the time to this recommendation. Then, in April 1967, I gave an address on the subject of the World Heritage Trust at the International Congress on Nature and Man held in Amsterdam and sponsored, I believe, by the World Wildlife Fund. I pointed out that, 'the establishment of Yellowstone National Park in 1872 represented a national recognition that there are areas of the United States which are of such unique natural value that they must be preserved and managed for the benefit of all the people'. I argued that this principle had clear relevance on an international level, that there are certain areas of such universal interest that they belong to the heritage of the entire world.

After outlining some of the worldwide threats to the natural environment, I went on to emphasise 'that the same threats, the same problems, and much the same needs exist in connection with mankind's cultural heritage. In all parts of the world, major monuments to our past, to the glories of earlier civilisations are threatened by greed, over exploitation, ignorance or simply neglect. These, too, are part of the world's heritage. These, too, must be safeguarded'. In this connection, I called for 'the launching of an international co-operative effort that brings together in a unified program a common concern for both man's natural heritage and his cultural heritage. In so doing, we will be recognising that our civilisation, past and present, is inextricably linked to our physical environment. Indeed, the works of man are necessarily founded upon and moulded by the natural environment. Can we conceive of a Venice in isolation from the sea?'.

When I became the first chairman of the President's Council on Environmental Quality in 1970, I had the opportunity to give the World Heritage concept a very real push. Our Council had the responsibility of putting together President Nixon's environmental legislative program and for drafting his annual environmental message to Congress. As a result Nixon's 1971 Message on the Environment contained the following language:

> As the United States approaches the centennial celebration in 1972 of the establishment of Yellowstone National Park, it would be appropriate to mark this historic event by a new international initiative in the general field of parks. Yellowstone is the first national park to have been created in the modern world, and the national park concept has represented a major contribution to world culture. Similar systems have now been established throughout the world. The United Nations list over 1,200 parks in 93 nations.
>
> The national park concept is based upon the recognition that certain areas of natural, historical, or cultural significance have such unique and outstanding characteristics that they must be treated as belonging to the nation as a whole, as part of the nation's heritage.
>
> It would be fitting by 1972 for the nations of the world to agree to the principle that there are certain areas of such unique worldwide value that they should be treated as part of the heritage of all mankind and accorded special recognition as a part of a World Heritage Trust. Such an arrangement would impose no limitations on the sovereignty of those nations which choose to participate, but would extend special international recognition to the areas which qualify and would make available technical and other assistance where appropriate to assist in their protection and management. I believe that such an initiative can add a new dimension to international co-operation.

I am directing the Secretary of the Interior, in co-ordination with the Council on Environmental Quality, and under the foreign policy guidance of the Secretary of State, to develop initiatives for presentation in appropriate international forums to further the objective of a World Heritage Trust.

As a result of this initiative by President Nixon in 1971, both the International Union for Conservation of Nature (IUCN) and UNESCO developed draft conventions embodying the World Heritage concept. The IUCN draft included both natural and cultural sites as we had originally proposed, while the UNESCO draft was primarily oriented toward the conservation of cultural properties and sites. While the two draft conventions had some similarities, there were also significant differences.

Recognising the significant differences between the two drafts but desiring to avoid duplication and to expedite development of the World Heritage Trust, and believing that the desirable concept was a convention covering both the natural and cultural heritage, the United States proposed to UNESCO that the meeting of experts scheduled for April 1972, considered both of the draft conventions with a view to combining them into a single convention for a World Heritage Trust.

This suggestion was accepted and at the UNESCO meeting the two drafts were combined into a single convention. Key provisions of the convention where (and are): an equal and balanced treatment of both cultural and natural heritages; recognition that cultural sites and natural areas of outstanding universal value are part of the heritage of all mankind; undertakings by States to take national and international measures to preserve and protect that heritage and to pass it on to future generations; establishment of a World Heritage List to provide for such recognition and international assistance; and the creation of a World Heritage Fund from government and private sources.

As a result of the U.S. initiative, the final draft of the convention was then referred to the U.N. Conference on the Human Environment held in Stockholm that June where I was privileged to head the U.S. delegation. The U.S. had previously forwarded the World Heritage Trust as a proposed agenda item to the Preparatory Committee for the Conference. At the Conference the delegates in plenary session acknowledged that the draft convention, 'marks a significant step towards the protection, on an international scale, of the environment'. They voted overwhelmingly to invite governments to examine the draft convention, 'with a view to its adoption at the next General Conference of UNESCO'. This was accomplished in October-November of 1972 and the Convention was adopted.

Early the next year, the UNESCO newsletter *Nature and Resources* carried an article by me in which I outlined some of the technical aspects of the convention and then concluded:

> But what is more important that the technical details or even the actual working mechanism is the international acceptance of the concept that throughout the world there exist natural and cultural areas of such unique value that they are truly a part of the heritage not only of the individual nations but of all mankind. This is the real heart of the matter. This is the idea that challenges the spirit. It is the idea that gives eloquent expression through co-operative international action to the truth that the earth is indeed man's home and belongs to us all. This idea has been accepted and endorsed by most of the world's nations.
>
> The message is clear. The heritage trust is an idea whose time has come.

Since 1972, the World Heritage concept has blossomed into a vigorous, worldwide program. As I said at the outset, 115 nations are now party to the Convention, with 337 areas designated for protection on the World Heritage List. This list includes 17 areas in the United States. Yellowstone National Park – whose centenary in 1972 was marked by adoption of the Convention – was our first area to be included, joined later by the Grand Canyon, the Everglades, Independence Hall, the Mesa Verde, among others.

The 1990s and beyond present great possibilities for the World Heritage program, and it is my hope that the United States will take the lead in helping the program realise its potential. Unfortunately, this had not always been the case. While the United States has been active in nominating areas for World Heritage listing, it has often been less than forthcoming insofar as financial support is concerned. Starting toward the end of the Carter Administration and continuing in the Reagan Administration, the Federal budget as submitted to the Congress made no provision whatsoever for the World Heritage. In budgetary parlance, it was 'zeroed' despite regular support both from the Department of the Interior and from State. Congress in recent years has restored a modest level of funding – about $220,000 for the World Heritage Trust – and this past year more than doubled the amount to $450,000. Yet again funding for the trust has been zeroed out of the Federal budget for the coming fiscal year. This strikes me as an appalling state of affairs given the fact that the United States was the initiator of the Convention in the first place. I would like to note the support that the U.S. Committee for the World Heritage and its Secretary, Doug Williamson, have played in securing World Heritage appropriations in the past few years. These efforts will certainly continue.

So I hope that the future will bring only stronger efforts to realise the goals of the World Heritage Convention. Since its inception, the Convention has made a significant contribution to international co-

Chaco National Historical Park

To Save our Heritage is to Save the Earth

WE LIVE WITH THE LAND, the sea, and the sky. This home, our Earth, is the repository of our heritage we are now called upon to save.

Humankind's exploitation of the Earth's resources has yielded a burden of damage fast tampering with the planet's life-sustaining gifts.

In a wisp of time, the great herds of roaming beasts and the exotic creatures of nature's awesome genius, have been corralled into preserves, or placed on exhibition.

We have witnessed a rainfall of burning water, a shower of acid, corroding green to brown and converting lakes into dead pools. Entire landscapes of ancient forests, wetlands and tall grass prairies have disappeared. Deserts encroach on land stripped of vegetation. A spasm of species extinction is occurring within a blink of biological time as swathes of tropical rainforests vanish. Ultraviolet radiation streaming through a breach in the ozone shield may already be diminishing the phytoplankton base of the marine food chain. Coral reefs around the world are inexplicably dying. Evidence is mounting that global warming is already under way. The air in our cities is polluted. Hardly any of us live in a place clean of toxins contaminating some part of the land or water. Each year 100 million more of us lay claim to the resources being so treated.

We are altering the Earth's biological integrity. And we are doing so at an ever increasing rate of frenzy.

The admonition to care for the land is a common theme of our ethical inheritance. The American Indian and oriental wisdom express the idea as living as one, in harmony with the land. Our Judeo-Christian heritage speaks of stewardship, a holding in trust for those who are to follow.

Early in this century these concepts took political shape in the formation of the conservation movement. The impetus then was to preserve nature's most wondrous creations, to set aside from humankind's changing hand what was beautiful and wild.

Later as awareness grew of the scope of our collective effect upon the resources that maintain life, an evolution took place into the movement we now know as environmentalism.

The evolution has most recently gone beyond grasping the breadth of the challenges, to realising their urgency. Incremental steps to redress accretions of degradation are no longer sufficient. At issue is the immediate health of the planet and those who occupy it. In a few short decades the quest to preserve pieces at the margin has escalated into the imperative to forestall collapse.

operation in the protection of unique natural and cultural sites. It has led to strengthened recognition of the importance of such areas worldwide. It has significantly increased tourism to such areas. It has raised management standards and, most importantly, has provided technical training opportunities, particularly on a regional basis. World Heritage status has become an important bulwark against actions which threaten the integrity of listed areas and sites. The World Bank and other lending agencies now recognise World Heritage sites as being of central importance to natural area conservation. The Convention continues to be an active focus of international co-operation. Thus, the United States and the Soviet Union are presently developing a joint World Heritage proposal for the Land Bridge areas on either side of the Bering Strait.

Let me close simply by pointing out that the national park concept is a uniquely American contribution to world conservation and culture. It is one in which we can take great pride. The World Heritage Convention provides a vital international dimension to that contribution, and again we can be proud of the role of the United States in initiating that Convention and making the concept a reality. It deserves nothing less than our full support.

RUSSELL TRAIN
Chairman, World Wildlife Fund and the Conservation Foundation

The Statue of Liberty

Environmentalism may no longer be defined as an endeavour to protect aspects for the future. Today's environmentalism has become the necessity to preserve health, our own and the planet's, for survival in the present.

Environmentalism draws its inspiration from the ethical impulse to care for the land, to act with prudence in our use of the Earth's bounty. The indispensable corollary to this belief is that environmentalism begins with the individual. The life of environmentalism is wholly dependent on the choices individuals make, the actions they pursue to give meaning to their beliefs. The conviction that each one of us can make a difference is at the root of the environmental movement. Environmentalism is fundamentally a personal responsibility.

At the exact moment the individual might feel most daunted in face of enormous challenges, a tremendous opportunity presents itself to reorganise the vitality of our collective energies toward healing the damage to our planet.

This effort will require us to look past the old alliances based on fear and conflict toward the realisation of our interdependent common interests. Just as no one is truly safe as long as another is allowed to suffer injustice, so too, no part of our environment is truly healthy so long as we allow despoliation to occur elsewhere. Individuals must magnify their concern for the environment in new alliances that unite, rather than divide, the North and South, the East and West, the industrialised and the developing world. The engines of economic competitiveness must be retuned so that they generate sustainable growth and development instead of devouring our patrimony to the impoverishment of our children.

The task is huge. These are the aspirations of environmentalism: to educate and empower the individual, to reshape our understanding of global security and to forge the alliances that will create a sustainable future on an Earth at peace with itself.

This, environmentalists believe, is not just a vision, but a necessary choice for survival. On the success of our efforts rests whether environmental destruction will continue with unforeseen and possible tragic results, or if we will in fact preserve our heritage and save the Earth.

JAY D HAIR
President
The National Wildlife Federation, Washington, D.C.

Anazasi ruins, Mesa Verde National Park

Redwood National Park

The Time to Act is Now

ALMOST TEN YEARS AGO, I asked a group of students if they expected nuclear war in their lifetimes. Nearly every student raised a hand. When I asked the students if they believed there was much we could do to change that outcome, only two or three hands went up.

That day, I saw a verdict from a generation which, like my own, had never known a world without the threat of nuclear war. I realized that whatever else we do, we must somehow reverse that verdict and enable the next generation to face the future with hope.

Over the past decade, we have made great strides in addressing the fears of nuclear war. Around the world, people are choosing democracy, and communism is in retreat. Both superpowers appear to recognise the need for arms control as a matter of economic as well as physical survival.

But now, new clouds of a different sort are forming on the horizon. If you asked a group of schoolchildren what frightens them today, most of them would probably talk about the environment. This new challenge is in some ways more daunting than any clash between nations, or weapons, or ideologies. It is the most fundamental conflict of all, between humankind and nature.

We have entered into a brand new relationship with planet Earth. We are destroying forests at the rate of 1½ acres per second; we are poisoning our rivers, lakes, groundwater, and oceans; we are filling the atmosphere with gaseous wastes that are warming the Earth, and that threaten changes to the climate system in the next century as large as those which accompanied the ice ages during hundreds of thousands of years. An enormous hole has opened in the stratospheric ozone layer. Living species are dying at an unprecedented rate, one thousand times faster than at any time in the last 65 million years. We are changing, in some ways irrevocably, the world that sustains life as we know it. We are threatening its ability to provide that sustenance. Why don't we react to this crisis? Is it that hard to see?

When I was in elementary school, we had a map of the world in the front of the classroom. During a geography lesson, a classmate pointed to the outline of South America sticking out into the Atlantic Ocean and pointed to the outline of Africa indented on the other side of the South Atlantic and said, "Did they ever fit together?". The teacher said, "That's the most ridiculous thing I've ever heard. Of course not!". In fact, through the 1960s, the world's leading geologists confidently asserted that continental drift was nonsense because they had an assumption that continents are so big they obviously could not move. Their assumption was wrong.

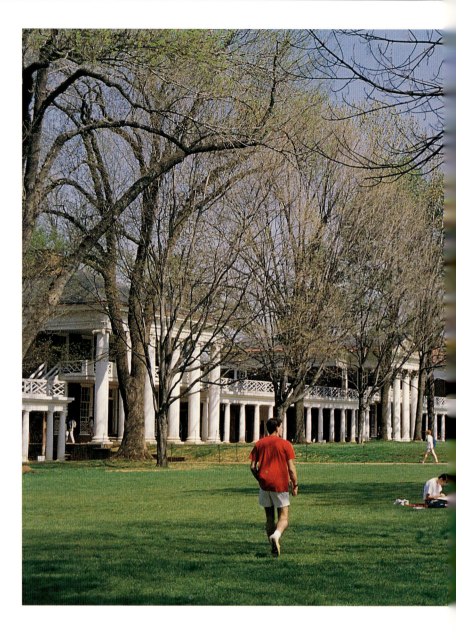

Today we have another assumption that must be overturned – namely that the Earth is so vast and nature is so powerful, human beings can't possibly cause irreparable damage. Our astronauts have taken pictures from space that show a stark contrast between the vastness of the Earth and the thinness of that fragile blue line around the outside of the Earth – the atmosphere – with a total volume small enough that the combined activities of our five billion people can now overwhelm and change its composition.

As one example, the air we breathe today has 600 percent more chlorine in each lungful than it did 40 years ago, or 40 million years ago. In the 1950s, consumers and manufacturers began using a new family of chemicals, chlorofluorocarbons. As those chemicals have been released over the years – by servicing air conditioners or manufacturing electronic equipment – they have delivered an enormously destructive payload of chlorine into the stratosphere. Recent scientific data stunningly reveals that the chlorine has eaten a hole not only in the ozone layer over Antarctica, but has danger-

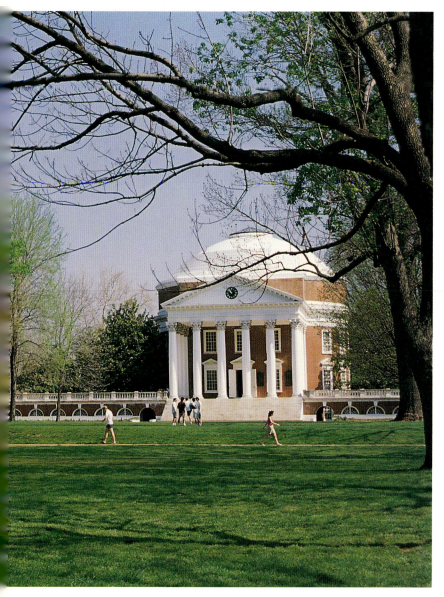

University of Virginia in Charlottesville

ously depleted ozone over densely populated areas in the United States, Europe, the Soviet Union, and Asia.

Clearly, the time to act is now. In the words of the environmental philosopher Ivan Illych, we need to stop running from "the shadow our future throws," and move quickly and decisively to confront the challenge we face. The solutions we seek will be found in a new faith in the future of life on Earth after our own; a faith in the future which justifies action in the present; a new moral courage to choose higher values in the conduct of human affairs; a new reverence for absolute principles that can serve as guiding stars for the future course of our species and our place within creation.

I congratulate the publishers of 'Masterworks of Man and Nature' for so vividly calling our attention to the richness of our world heritage. I sincerely hope that the images presented will inspire courage, vision, and commitment to action.

SENATOR AL GORE
Washington, D.C.

CAHOKIA MOUNDS SITE

LOCATION   Southwest corner of Illinois, N 39° 00′, W 89° 40′.

DESCRIPTION   This 1,091ha (2,630ac) site is the centre of a 324sq km (130sq mi) alluvial flood plain known as the 'American Bottom', which is below the confluence of the Missouri and Mississippi Rivers. This area includes alluvial terraces and low bluffs which were inhabited by large numbers of Pre-Columbian peoples. The town of Cahokia covered more than 120 mounds which partially define the extent of habitation. It was a complex of man-made hills, palisades and dwellings, remains of which are scattered. Several public buildings with clay floors and roof posts were built upon the numerous mounds. Structures, similar to Stonehenge in Britain, but made of wood, have been uncovered.

SIGNIFICANCE   Cahokia was one of the major concentrations of Pre-columbian peoples, with an agricultural and trading base exerting influence over more than 3 million sq km (1.2 million sq mi). Burial chambers, disclosing 6 separate types of internment, contained a wealth of grave goods from wide-spread areas. The size of the various mounds indicates an extraordinarily high level of labour organisation. Mond's Mound, which dominates the site, is the largest prehistoric earthen structure in the New World, being larger at the base than the great pyramids of Egypt, rising to over 33m (108ft) and covering more than 6ha (14.5ac).

At Cahokia, archaeologists have explored a series of outstanding structures which illustrate the astonishing extent of political and social organisation in these pre-Columbian civilisations.

EVERGLADES NATIONAL PARK

LOCATION   Tip of Florida Peninsula, Florida State, W 80° 20′ to 81° 30′, N 24° 50′ to 25° 55′.

DESCRIPTION   Everglades is a biological park of 567,017ha (1.36 million acres) dedicated to the preservation of a complex ecosystem. It is largely a shallow basin and it displays a remarkable interdependence between plant and animal life. Vast prairie-like expanses of dump saw-grass are edged by mangroves and long sandy beaches. Florida Bay covers 2,000sq km (800 sq mi) yet has an average depth of only 1.2-1.5m (4-5ft). The greatest depth is less than 3m (10ft).

SIGNIFICANCE   Everglades National Park contains an astonishing variety of endemic plant species as well as being a haven for 36 rare and endangered animal species. Being geographically at the meeting point of several climatic zones, plants as diverse as tropical palms and mangroves, temperate ash and oak, and even (in elevated places) cacti and yucca may be found. Today, Everglades National park is one of the greatest natural history and environmental education centres on our planet.

MONTICELLO AND THE UNIVERSITY OF VIRGINIA IN CHARLOTTESVILLE

LOCATION   State of Virginia, Monticello is outside Charlottesville, the University is within the town, N 38° 00', W 78° 20'.

DESCRIPTION   Monticello is on a hilltop within an estate of 400ha (964ac). It is a large house 35 by 29m (115 by 92ft) with a height of 14m (46ft). Construction is of red brick with white wooden trim, faced with Doric columns and having a large dome on the western facade. It served as Jefferson's 'essay in architecture'; he designed, built and remodelled it, and it reflected his studies of architecture over a 40 year period. The Jeffersonian precinct of the University is a U-shaped set of 10 buildings, each originally a separate school, terminating at the slightly elevated rotunda. Each building has classical elements drawn from various sources and styles, mainly Doric and Corinthian. These building complexes were conceived, designed and built from 1784-1809 (Monticello) and 1805-1824 (University).

SIGNIFICANCE   Thomas Jefferson's works as an architect are an integral part of his philosophical importance. His years in Paris, studying building styles and new movements such as the neo-classical based on various recent excavations (Pompei and others) influenced him greatly. As a statesman and diplomat and as an intellectual of great international standing he transferred his vision of the infant American democracy. His hopes for American idealism, such as universal freedom, self determination and self fulfilment based on classical Greek and Roman precepts, are embodied in these buildings.

PUERTO RICO

LOCATION   Puerto Rico, W 66° 06' to 66° 08', N 18° 27' to 18° 28'.

DESCRIPTION   There are 2 sites, both part of the fortifications which surround the city of San Juan. La Fortaleza is a fortress which, since the early 16th century, has evolved from a late medieval fortress into a 19th century palatial residence. It retains its function as residence and office of the Governor of Puerto Rico. The fortress is built around a central courtyard with a number of round towers along the thick stone walls. The remainder of the fortifications are at the entrance to San Juan Bay and include El Moro, a massive triangular structure, El Canuelo a smaller masonry fort on the principal channel leading into San Juan Bay, and Castillo de San Cristobel, a 17th century addition to the wall defences. All are administered as the San Juan Historical Site.

SIGNIFICANCE   These are the largest historic fortifications to be found in the entire Americas. Dating from 1530, the mixture of architectural styles epitomises the evolution of a medieval fort into a palatial residence, as well as providing a unique record of the many struggles between the dominant colonial powers in the area.

Independence Hall

INDEPENDENCE HALL

LOCATION   Philadelphia, Pennsylvania, N 39° 57', W 75° 09'.

DESCRIPTION   Independence Hall is a 2-storey red brick structure built from 1732 to the mid 1740s and added to in the 1750s. The bell tower steeple is built of wood and rests upon brick. It was erected in 1828 while the present arcades and wings were built in 1897-98. The steeple, with its oversized clock dials, the octagonal bell cupola, the carved urns and its corner pilasters with Corinthian capitals, are all features which have distinguished Independence Hall.

SIGNIFICANCE   Independence Hall has great historical significance. From 1753 when the first bell to 'proclaim liberty throughout the land' tolled, then in 1775 when the Second Continental Congress first met there, the hall has played a prominent part in United States history. Following the occupation of the city by British forces in 1777-78, the Congress continued to meet there, framing the Articles of Confederation. It was effectively the seat of Government of the United States with the various Congresses meeting there throughout the 1780s. From 1790 until the transfer of Government to Washington D.C. in 1799, Independence Hall was the scene of several sittings of both the United States Congress and the Supreme Court. Architecturally, it is a fine example of an American colonial building of Georgian influence.

Hawaii Volcanoes National Park

Wood storks, Everglades National Park

Yosemite National Park

Hurricane Ridge, Olympic National Park

CHACO NATIONAL HISTORICAL PARK

LOCATION   New Mexico State, N 36° 00', W 107° 00'.

DESCRIPTION   This park is in 4 detached areas totalling 13,749ha (33,149ac). The main area is the 16km (10mi) long Chaco Canyon, the 3 smaller areas are Kin Bineola, Kin Ya'a and Pueblo Pintado. These are all characterised by Anasazi and Pueblo Indian style rock and cliff dwellings upon the canyon mesa and butte heights. The numerous and extensive subterranean storage areas (kivas) imply a major economic centre, while over 300 of the recognised 2,800 archaeological sites have religious significance.

SIGNIFICANCE   Prior to the devastating 50 year drought thought to have occurred around 1140 AD, the Chacoans displayed an astonishing ingenuity to counter the extremely arid and hostile nature of their surroundings. The ruins here have provided an unequalled opportunity to study a prehistoric society interacting with a harsh environment.

GREAT SMOKY MOUNTAINS NATIONAL PARK

LOCATION   Along the north Carolina/Tennessee border, N 35° 26' to 35° 47', W 83° 45' to 84° 00'.

DESCRIPTION   This park comprises 209,000ha (503,899ac) of extremely rugged topography which rises from 260-2,025m (855-6,644ft) above sea level in a matter of a few kilometres (miles). There are 16 peaks over 1,800m (5,905ft). Several thousand hectares are totally roadless and rarely hiked. There are large tracts of virgin forest, offering unique vistas of truly primeval Pleistocene North America. Several unusual habitats such as grass and heath balds occur which are of exceptional ecological interest. Within the forests of red maple, hickory, beech and oaks are dozens of species of mammals, including approximately 20 types of rodent. In the multitude of pristine streams, the once common beavers are reappearing after a period of decline.

SIGNIFICANCE   Great Smoky Mountains National Park is remarkable for the beauty and tranquillity of its giant virgin forests. No less than 5 different species of tree reach their largest recorded height within the boundaries of this park. The undergrowth is also of interest – it has one of the richest collections of fungi, mosses, lichens and hepatics in the northern hemisphere. Many endemic and endangered species find their home here, including the peregrin falcon and the red-cockadel woodpecker. The blue smoky haze that covers this region gave the mountains their name.

HAWAII VOLCANOES NATIONAL PARK

LOCATION   2 sections on the southeast portion of the island of Hawaii, N 19° 11' to 19° 44', W 155° 01' to 155° 39'.

DESCRIPTION   97,950ha (242,034ac) in total, the park encompasses the 2 summits and surrounding flanks of the active volcanoes, Mauna Loa and Kilauea. These huge mountains rise directly from the Pacific Ocean floor, and are ringed by numerous recent lava flows which are still creating new land as they enter the sea. Within the caldera of Kilauea is a continuously molten pool of rock which is constantly active and often erupts into fountains hundreds of metres high.

SIGNIFICANCE   Since 1912 when the first observatory was established, these volcanoes have provided the best records and understanding of volcanic activity on earth. The constantly changing landscape due to the continuing lava flows also gives botanists an unequalled opportunity to study plant adaptation and development. The floral diversity of the park is limited, though interesting, as most plants are classified as rare. Fauna is largely limited to birds, owing to the hostile nature of the volcanic precincts to permanent habitation. Also within the park are numerous archaeological sites, bearing witness to the significance the volcanoes held for ancient peoples.

THE STATUE OF LIBERTY

LOCATION   Liberty island in the upper bay of New York Harbour, N 40° 40′, W 74° 00′.

DESCRIPTION   This statue is a hollow 46m (151ft) high figure of copper sheeting affixed to an iron structural frame. The sheets are riveted so that the female surface appears continuous. She is dressed in a Roman toga with an uplifted torch in her right hand. Cradled in her left hand is a tablet marked with the Roman date July 4, 1776 – The date of the United States Declaration of Independence. She is stepping forward from the shackles of slavery and a broken chain lies before her feet. The whole statue stands on a 27m (89ft) pedestal of granite and concrete which has massive concrete foundations set 6m (20ft) into the ground.

SIGNIFICANCE   After assisting in the American struggle against Britain in the War of Independence, France looked on as the American Civil War raged from 1861-65. Many French intellectuals saw a Northern victory as a precursor to the impending liberation of Europe from the scourge of religious and ethnic persecution. In this atmosphere, Edouard Laboulaye formed a Franco-American society and commissioned Frederic Burthold to create the statue. It was presented as a gift to the United States to celebrate the impending centenary of the United States Declaration of Independence. It was finally opened in 1886 and has since become a world famous symbol of freedom.

YELLOWSTONE NATIONAL PARK

LOCATION   Northwest corner of Wyoming and smaller, adjacent areas of Montana and Idaho, N 44° 08′ to 45° 07′, W 109° 10′ to 111° 10′.

DESCRIPTION   This park has 898,349 ha (2,165,919ac) of mostly volcanic plateau with 2 smaller areas of sedimentary rock. The plateau has been eroded by both the Yellowstone and Snake Rivers and has several spectacular canyons, waterfalls and gorges. Continuing volcanic activity causes hundreds of geysers and hot springs to erupt or flow while the abundance of water allows a rich diversity of flora and fauna.

SIGNIFICANCE   The central third of this, the oldest national park in the world, is the largest caldera (volcano crater) on earth, being 100 times greater than that of Krakatoa. The oldest rocks date back 2.7 billion years while the youngest are still being formed. Within this caldera are 27 fossilised forests. They are stunning to behold and quite unique in being largely intact, with several petrified trees standing upright. The spectacular concentration of over 10,000 geysers is one of the wonders of the world. Secluded watersheds and ecosystems provide the perfect environment for threatened species such as grizzly bears, mountain lions, bald eagles and even a remnant group of surviving wolves.

YOSEMITE NATIONAL PARK

LOCATION   Sierra Nevada, California, N 37° 30′ to 38° 11′, W 119° 12′ to 119° 53′.

DESCRIPTION   This park has 307,943ha (742,451ac) of rugged, granite overlain country displaying all the classic signs of glaciation. Large central valleys such as that of the Yosemite River are flanked by numerous hanging valleys which end abruptly in huge waterfalls. Domes, arches, moraines, sheer rock walls and glacial pavements attest to the effects of moving ice. A pair of large river systems drain the park from heights well above 2,000m (6,562ft), while more than 1,200km (746mi) of maintained trails lead hikers through the wilderness areas.

SIGNIFICANCE   The U-shaped valley of the Yosemite River is perhaps the best known on Earth. The occurrence of chaparral, conifer, meadow, red fir, sub-alpine and alpine vegetation systems within such close proximity to one another is also regarded as unique, while the multitude of glacial features is virtually unmatched. Its waterfalls, reaching single drop heights of nearly 500m (1,660ft) include the third highest on Earth and numerous others of outstanding scenic beauty. In the more heavily forested areas of the upper slopes are found the giant sequoia trees, the most massive living things on the planet. A number of other plants are believed to be endemic to this park.

GRAND CANYON NATIONAL PARK

LOCATION   Within the counties of Coconino and Mohave in the state of Arizona. W 111° 36′ to 113° 56′, N 35° 43′ to 36° 45′.

DESCRIPTION   The canyon was formed by the Colorado River cutting into and eroding the vast 2,500m (8,202ft) high plateau surrounding it. This has left the mightiest of natural monuments – a canyon 1.5km (0.9mi) deep and up to 30km (18.6mi) wide. From the canyon rim, remnant mountains up to 600m (1,968ft) high may be seen. The park covers 493,270ha (1,189,274ac).

SIGNIFICANCE   One of nature's finest masterworks, the deep and ongoing carvings of the Colorado River have exposed a geological record covering 2 billion years and have created, in the canyon walls, a museum stretching through 5 different life zones. The various rock strata display every known class of rock while ancient Mesozoic layers, now exposed, contain tracks of dinosaurs. More than 2,000 prehistoric ruins recorded by archaeologists, show the habitation of the canyon and rims by Cohonina people who farmed and gathered edible fruits here. The northern rim shows evidence of Anasazi or Pueblo Indian hunter habitation. The great importance of the cultural heritage of the Grand Canyon is that it represents a classic example of the adaptation of human societies to a severe environment.

Mammoth Terrace, Yellowstone National Park

Mond's Mound, Cahokia Mounds

OLYMPIC NATIONAL PARK

LOCATION   In the extreme northwest of Washington State, N 47° 29' to 48° 11', W 123° 07' to 124° 42'.

DESCRIPTION   The park is effectively an isolated peninsula of 362,849ha (874,829ac), surrounded on 3 sides by saltwater. Several major river systems drain from the Olympic Mountains, carrying large amounts of water and glacial silt to the sea. More than 60 glaciers continue to advance across the mountains, while the coast is edged by wilderness beach. Animal and sea life is varied, while the diversity of vegetation zones includes spruce, western hemlock, silver fir, moutina hemlock and subalpine fir.

SIGNIFICANCE   The most important feature of this park is the Olympic rainforest. This outstanding endemic habitat consists of colossal coniferous forest with extremely dense undergrowth. These areas contain one of the largest areas of living, standing biomass in the world. Numerous flora and fauna species are to be found which are unique to the area.

REDWOOD NATIONAL PARK

LOCATION   Along the Pacific Coast at the northern end of the State of California, N 41° 04' to 41° 49', W 123° 53' to 124° 10'.

DESCRIPTION   In this park there are approximately 42,000ha (101,262ac) of low coastal mountains, deeply dissected by streams and rivers. Abundant winter rain and frequent summer fog characterise the park, which is basically divided into 3 ecosystems. A narrow strip of redwood forest, diminishing in size as altitude increases, it is ringed by a marine/shore environment and an area of coastal shrubland to the north. There are various smaller and scattered areas of vegetation and occasional marshes or grasslands.

SIGNIFICANCE   The mighty redwood stands of the park include the 3 tallest trees on earth. The largest is 112.1m (468ft) and still growing. Nesting in these forest giants are several endangered bird species, while the numerous streams contain a multitude of fish such as steelhead salmon, candlefish and sea lamprey. Two rare

species of sturgeon are also found. Amongst the huge redwoods lived several Indian tribes who have left the remains of several sites dating back as far as 300 BC. These include semi-subterranean plank-houses, sweathouses, cemeteries, hearths and middens. These remains have yielded valuable insights into the customs and rituals of these early riverine forest dwelling societies.

MAMMOTH CAVE NATIONAL PARK

LOCATION   Kentucky, within the counties of Burren, Admonson and Hart, W 86° 00', N 37° 07'.

DESCRIPTION   Mammoth Cave National Park is noted for its karst topography. The underground drainage and cavern systems have over 320km (199mi) of interconnecting passageways and tunnels. It is believed another 480km of caverns remain unexplored. Within the major systems, below the mainly limestone Mammoth Cave Plateau, are several rivers and numerous chambers of tremendous size. Some passages are more than 30m (98ft) in height and extend up to 5km (3.1mi). Vertical shafts, called silos, can be found that are 13m (42.6ft) in diameter and 40m (131ft) high.

SIGNIFICANCE   This is the largest cave-system on earth, the known sections are approximately ten times as extensive as the next largest. The 200 species of fish and animals found in the caves include several rare and endangered species. Some, such as two types of 'blind fish' are found nowhere else. Of special concern is the Kentucky cave shrimp, found in only two pool systems within the caves. This shrimp, and the Indiana bat are two species which are on the verge of extinction and which rely on Mammoth Cave for their survival.

MESA VERDE NATIONAL PARK

LOCATION   Colorado, 50km (31mi) west of Durango, N 37° 15', W 108° 27'.

DESCRIPTION   Here we have 21,000ha (50,631ac) of semi-arid land dominated by Mesa Verde ('Green Table') a gently sloping tableland rising 460-530m (1,509-1,739ft) above the surrounding terrain. Topped by evergreen pinyon pine and juniper forests, the Mesa Verde is dissected by several cliff-edged side canyons containing numerous sandstone caves. Along these cliff tops and in these caves are many stone ruins of Anazasi Indian origin.

SIGNIFICANCE   Mesa Verde contains the most complete record of Anazasi Indian culture in existence. There are over 3,500 prehistoric sites and ruins, including ceremonial shrines, rock art, farms and residences which range from one roomed houses to enormous cave villages. Most sites are open to the public. The museum and staff provide comprehensive historical information to all visitors.

Think of your forefathers! Think of your posterity!

JOHN QUINCY ADAMS
(Speech at Plymouth)

Alfred Reagan Mill, Great Smoky Mountains National Park

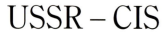

USSR – CIS

Formerly the USSR, the CIS (Commonwealth of Independent States) is presently the focus of world attention as events unfold and a new order takes shape. While the five World Heritage sites listed here were all nominated by the USSR, they will now be administered by the individual states.

A vast land with an area of 22,402,202 sq km (8,649,489 sq mi), the CIS occupies one seventh of the Earth's total land surface, crossing 11 time zones.

The commonwealth can be divided in terms of landscape and vegetation. The tundra is a treeless belt which follows the arctic coastline, where the permafrost penetrates as far as 1,000ft below ground, and where only the surface thaws during summer averages of 10°C (50°F). The treeline begins with the Taiga which, at 7 million sq km, occupies a third of the land. As the birch can tolerate extreme cold, it is the only deciduous tree which is found in great numbers east of the Urals, alongside coniferous forest, while in the west there are more deciduous trees, including oak, aspen, maple and lime. The steppes are an enormous expanse of cultivated grasslands which give way in the south-east to desert.

The CIS is laced with thousands of rivers, 10 of them over 2200 km (1400 mi) in length. But as more than half of the rivers flow into the Arctic Ocean they are frozen for much of the year. The CIS also possesses two inland seas, the Caspian Sea and the Aral Sea as well as the world's largest repository of fresh water, Lake Baikal, which at 1600 m (5315 ft), is also the deepest lake in the world. It has been estimated that it would take all the rivers of the world one year to fill the lake.

Greek colonies were established around the Crimea as long ago as the 7th century BC, and around the same time that barbarians such as the Huns and Avars swept across the country, Armenia and Georgia came under the influence of Christianity by way of the Byzantines. The eastern Slavs, who today we associate with "Russia", first appeared in

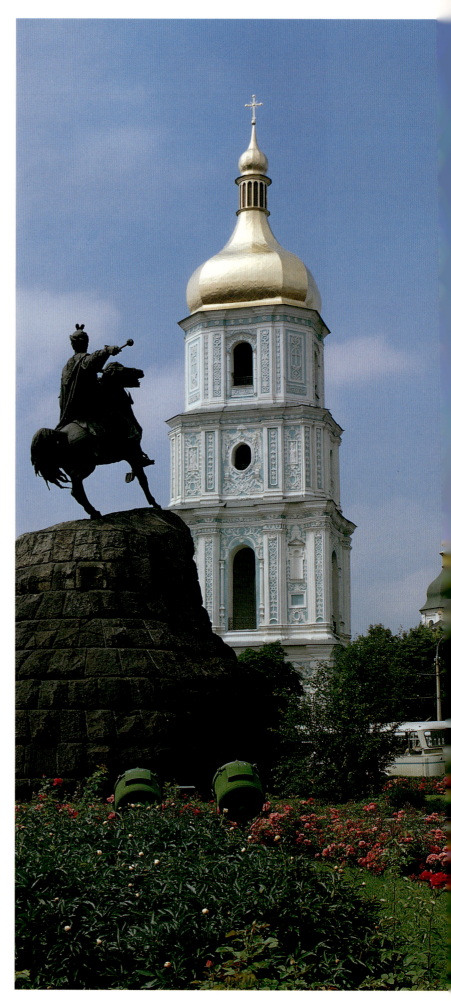

Saint Sophia Cathedral, Kiev

the 9th century AD. They were an agriculturally based people, with a strong tradition of militarism which quickly assimilated the Viking influence of the Varangians.

Today three cities, Kiev, Moscow and St Petersburg/Leningrad, which at one stage were all the capital city, are listed with the World Heritage which the USSR ratified in October 1988.

Kiev became the spiritual capital with the spread of Christianity in the 10th and 11th centuries. The wonderous monuments built during this period include the magnificent St Sophia, sister church to Agia Sophia in Constantinople. Kiev suffered terribly under the Mongol invasion of the 13th century, and never recovered its pre-eminence. It was passed on in the later half of the 15th century to Moscow which became the capital of a 'Greater Russia'. As well as being the seat of the Tzar, it was also considered to be the 'third Rome'. Among the magnificent religious edifices erected during this period is one of the most famous ensembles in the world: that of the 3 cathedrals of the Annunciation, the Archangel Michael and the Assumption, all built between 1467-509, and all dominated by the belfry of Ivan the Great, 82 m (273 ft) high, built of white stone and topped with a gilded cupola by Boris Godunov. Beside it is the heaviest bell in the world, the Emperor Bell, which weighs an astonishing 210,924 kgs (464,000 lbs). St Basil's and the Great Kremlin Palace are also impressive legacies from Moscow's golden period.

Peter the Great moved the capital to St Petersburgh in 1703 from where he tried to modernize the nation, instead alienating many with his autocratic ways and the demands he made on the peasantry. Today the magnificent old quarter is a legacy of his reign and those who followed him, particularly at the end of the 18th century. But the Empire was never able to introduce the kinds of liberal and democratic reforms which were being called for and was eventually toppled by the Bolshevik Revolution which began in what was then called Petrograd on November 7th 1917.

The Union of the Soviet Socialist Republics was formed in 1922-4, following a period of bloody civil war with Moscow again becoming the capital. Stalin quickly rose to power following Lenin's death in 1924 and forced Trotsky into exile in 1928.

Stalin instituted a dictatorship based on terror, and initiated the infamous forced collectivization of farming land, resulting in a disastrous famine which claimed millions of lives. His non-aggression pact with Hitler did not save the USSR from a brutal war which left tens of millions of Russians dead or dispossessed.

Following a decade of economic and political turmoil the CIS emerged at the end of 1991. Although the future may be uncertain, much of the treasures from its past are protected by the World Heritage Convention.

Itchan Kala

KIEV (SAINT SOPHIA AND KIÉVO-PECHERSK LAVRA)

LOCATION   Kiev, the Ukraine. N 50° 27', E 30° 29'.

DESCRIPTION   Located in the city of Kiev, this is a collection of historically important architectural sites dating from the 11th century to the 19th century. The area known as the 'Laure of Kiévo-Petchersk' includes two catacombs, a collection of religious monuments incorporating the College of Dormiton, the Trinity and the Saviour of Berestovo churches; ramparts, St Nicholas and the All Saints churches, a refectory and a 17th century convent and its walls and the Saint Sophia Cathedral. This Byzantine style cathedral was built in the 11th century and houses a variety of mosaics and frescoes. The pyramid style of the two galleries and the interior stairway make the cathedral one of the most majestic structures of its type.

SIGNIFICANCE   Kiévo-Petchersk was the birth place of Kiev's Christian movement and is linked to the development of Christianity in Russia. The architecture of the 'Laure' reflects the major stages in the historical development of the area. Apart from its religious significance, Kiévo-Petchersk was the cultural centre of the Ukraine. The first known Russian artist, Alipi, lived and worked in the Laure, as did the writer Nestor and the first Russian doctor Agapit. Since the Academy of Art was established in Kiev in the 17th century, the centre has attracted many people of different artistic backgrounds.

Khizi Pogost

KHIZI POGOST

LOCATION   Island of Khizi, Karelian Autonomous Soviet Socialist Republic, N 62° 04′, W 35° 13′.

DESCRIPTION   This is an ensemble of three buildings which are situated on the low, southern part of Khizi Island. They are: the Summer Church of the Transfiguration, the Winter Church of the Intercession and the Bell Tower. The entire ensemble is protected by a fence. In plan, they form the corners of a triangle. All are constructed of horizontally placed pine logs. The churches both have multi-domed roofs.

SIGNIFICANCE   This listing represents one of only five surviving such groupings which were typical of northern Russia in the Middle Ages and up to the 19th century. This particular ensemble is unique as both of its churches are multi-domed – a rare feature in Russian wooden architecture. The Church of the Transfiguration in particular, with its 22 cupolas, has no equal in the world of architecture. The state of preservation of these buildings is excellent and their originality has been unblemished.

ITCHAN KALA

LOCATION   The town of Khiva, Uzbekistan

DESCRIPTION   Itchan Kala is the historic centre of the modern town of Khiva. It is approximately 600m x 400m (2,000ft x 1,330ft) in size and is enclosed by defensive walls. There are four gates and several towers incorporated into these massive 6m (20ft) clay walls. Inside the walls are many buildings including mosques, palaces, madrasahs, mausoleums, bath houses, residences and shops.

SIGNIFICANCE   It is thought that this town evolved from the initial development of a caravanserai on the site in ancient times. It is known from the Arab chroniclers that Khiva was a great town in the 10th century with an important mosque. It was during the 18th and 19th centuries though, that the town flourished as a centre of Khorezmian culture. The original and excellent state of preservation of the numerous monuments and associated artworks found here provide an important living document of the history and cultural development of this area and of central Asia in general.

KREMLIN ENSEMBLE AND RED SQUARE, MOSCOW

LOCATION   Moscow, Russian Soviet Federative Socialist Republic, N 55° 45′, E 37° 37′.

DESCRIPTION   This enormous ensemble of monuments contains numerous significant buildings and includes a vast wealth of important artwork. Some of the more notable buildings are: The Grand Kremlin Palace, Armoury Palace, the Cathedral of St Basil, the Assumption Cathedral, the Annunciation Cathedral, the Arsenal,

St. Petersberg – Triumphal Arch

Saviour's Tower, Red Square

the Senate, the Bell Tower of Ivan the Great, the Church of Deposition and the Cathedral of Archangel Michael.

SIGNIFICANCE   The Kremlin's origins date back to the 11th century when Slavs began settling on Borovitsky Hill. Its present day form was not established until the 14th century when its role as a defence fortress began in earnest. Around that time, the Great Prince took it as his principal residence and it became known as The Kremlin. Today, The Kremlin and the adjoining Red Square are seen as masterpieces of their time and present a unique testament to the architectural genius of their creators.

Kremlin Ensemble and Red Square, Moscow

HISTORIC CENTRE OF LENINGRAD AND RELATED GROUPS OF MONUMENTS

LOCATION   The Russian Soviet Federative Socialist Republic, N 59° 57', E 30° 19'.

DESCRIPTION   This exceptionally broad listing comprises numerous monuments and some natural features. The historic centre includes several islands, the entire central city space and numerous outlying areas. The balance of the listing is divided into 34 separate sub-listings and includes highways, palaces, parks, villas, cemeteries, forts, hospitals and river embankments.

SIGNIFICANCE   St Petersburg, as Leningrad was known before the revolution, was one of the great cities of the 18th and 19th centuries. Its magnificence and splendour was world renowned. Peter the Great ordered a fort built on the site in 1703. A short 10 years later, St Petersburg was thriving as the great and illustrious capital of the Russian Empire. This remarkable history is exceptionally well preserved today in the form of this most important World Heritage site.

St. Petersberg

Let's Open the Doorways of Perception

IN FEBRUARY OF 1978, Boston was hit by one of the worst snowstorms in its history. Hurricane-force winds drove record amounts of snow into towering drifts that buried houses and paralysed roadways. Battered beaches disappeared in the night and shoreline houses were swept into the sea. More than one person died before it was over.

During the height of that storm, I was trying to walk across town and took shelter in a doorway to escape the storm's frozen blast for a few minutes. There were four other people already huddled in the doorway, stamping their feet and tightly gripping their collars, and I wedged myself between them with mumbled apologies. For a moment or two, we stood in silence, more than a little frightened by the terrible power of the storm, and then, as feeble streetlights winked on and the dim daylight surrendered to that titanic maelstrom, a most remarkable thing happened: we five strangers began to talk to each other.

Conversation is not, perhaps, a remarkable occurrence in most places, but in the rough, cold cities of the American northeast, a stranger talking to you is reason enough to back up against a wall and guard your wallet. But there, facing a fury that made any other fear seem trivial, we strangers found a bond between us, a common humanity, a danger shared. And on the basis of that common fear, that common frailty, we began our brief friendship. I never knew their names and I can't remember what we talked about; I can't even remember what the other people looked like, but lately I've been thinking a lot about that evening's shelter.

The year 1978 was notable not only for weather, but for the launching of the last of the original Landsat satellites. These Earth observation satellites opened an era of unprecedented understanding of our planet, and the information gathering, both from space and on the ground, through human researchers, has only gained momentum over the years since then. These mind-boggling amounts of data have greatly increased our understanding of weather, geology, biology, climate, and human development, but perhaps the greatest benefit conferred by our new knowledge is a new vision of the Earth as a single entity.

The notion has been around for a long time, of course. Whether in the minds of megalomaniacs trying to rule it, cartographers trying to map it or New Agers trying to visualise it, the idea of Earth as a single entity is not new. But the reality of that concept – the undeniable tangibility of our interconnectedness – that is quite new. It is also quite alarming. We can smell the smog over Alaska that comes from the industrial smokestacks in Eastern Europe; we can measure the DDT in Ant-

arctic penguins that comes from farmers' fields in Kansas; we can see from outer space the fires in Brazil that are destroying the last rain forests and threatening the biological integrity of the entire planet. Even without satellites, it's hard to ignore hurricanes and heatwaves or rising seas and failing crops.

We are beginning to understand that no one can exist in isolation anymore, and no one is safe from the effects of environmental damage. If the methane released from rice paddies in Asia raised the temperature of the global atmosphere and that in turn kills crops in Iowa, then the price of my food goes up, I can't afford that new Japanese car, and everybody loses.

On the other hand, if we all share the losses, then we all have a vested interest in finding the solutions to the problems. And not just in local terms. Our newfound knowledge makes it clear: what's good for Korea is good for Uruguay, and a healthy economy in Zambia ultimately means benefits for New South Wales. This kind of idea is relatively new for us humans; we're not used to thinking in global terms, and certainly not in terms of other people's welfare. Until now the world's countries have been acting like those strangers in northern cities, backing away from each other to protect our wallets. If we are to move to a more mutual way of living, our economic and political systems will need a major overhaul to accommodate it.

The overhaul undoubtedly will come, both in our systems and our sensibilities. The World Heritage program gives ample proof that we can do it, that it is, in fact, beginning to happen already. These sites are very much like that doorway in the storm – a common place for strangers to drop their strangeness. And if the storm raging in the world today is quieter and harder to see, it is also far greater and more dangerous than the snowstorm in Boston. My hope is that just as the shared danger of the snowstorm bred intimacy between strangers, the far greater danger of our global environmental threats will breed even more intimacy between nations.

MARK CHERRINGTON
Editor, Earthwatch

...a great many of Earth's children...quickly come to realise the reality of the world...a world where, if we continue to use up its natural resources, such as rain forests, future children may well inherit an uninhabitable planet.
MAIREAD MAGUIRE

YEMEN

Yemen occupies the south western coastal region of the Arabian peninsular. In common with many countries of the region, Yemen has an ancient lineage, but a relatively short history in its modern form. Founded in 1904, after a revolt against the Ottoman empire, Yemen achieved full independence in 1981.

After dividing into two countries – the Arab Republic of Yemen and the People's Democratic Republic of Yemen – unity was restored on the 19th May, 1990.

The bulk of the population comprises tribesmen known as Qabail, who belong to the original south Arabian or Qahtanic group. There is an ethnic religious aristocracy, who, it is said, are descended from Mohammed the Prophet. There are also many people of African descent.

There are two sites listed under the World Heritage Convention which was ratified in 1980.

OLD WALLED CITY OF SHIBAM

LOCATION   Seiyun District, N 16° 00′, E 48° 20′.

DESCRIPTION   There are approximately 500 tower houses, three government offices, five mosques and two palaces within the 6m (20ft) high walls of this old and still very active town.

SIGNIFICANCE   An important commerical centre thoughout its history, Shibam was established after the destruction of Shabwa around 300 AD. Floods damaged the new town several times up until 1535 AD, when it was almost totally destroyed. A dam was then constructed upstream and new walls were built. The oldest remaining building dates from 904 AD, otherwise the town dates mainly from that last great flood. The traditional way of life has been largely preserved.

You must teach your children that the ground beneath their feet is the ashes of our grandfathers. So that they will respect the land, tell your children that the earth is rich with the lives of our kin.

CHIEF SEATTLE

Sana'a

SANA'A

LOCATION   Governorate of the capital Sana'a, N 15° 22′, E 44° 11′.

DESCRIPTION   Sana'a is a fully contained medieval Arab city. Ancient mosques, souks (markets), houses and towers form an ensemble of rare beauty. There are 103 mosques, 14 caravanserais, 12 bathhouses (hammams) and various palaces. The Byzantine Christian cathedral and martyrium which was built on the personal instructions of the Emperor Justinian is one of the more notable buildings. The city presents an amazingly well preserved collection of winding streets filled with all the characteristic signs of a cultural and religious centre.

SIGNIFICANCE   Sana'a is considered to be one of the most ancient cities of the world, believed to have been founded by Shem, son of Noah. Due to its long history of foreign occupation by the Abyssinians, Persians, Byzantines and Muslims, Sana'a offers a tremendous variety of cultural and historical monuments, in a state of near-perfect preservation.

Shibam Valley

YUGOSLAVIA

Yugoslavia is in the middle of a civil war which will change the face of the Balkans forever. One of the many tragic consequences of this conflict is the irreparable damage which has been wrought upon several of the area's World Heritage sites, most notably to Old Dubrovnik. Such senseless destruction only serves to highlight the desperate need for international co-operation in preserving what remains of the world's dwindling heritage. Until the dust has settled it will not be possible to assess the scale of this damage and to know what remains of World Heritage in this former federation.

The history of this country is complex and diverse, reflecting the rich mosaic of cultures, landscapes, and wildlife which it comprises.

The original inhabitants of the Balkan peninsular were the Illyrians, followed by the Celts who arrived in the 4th century BC. The Romans arrived at the Adriatic coast in 229 BC, establishing a colony near Split. Just over 500 years later Emperor Diocletian retired to his Palace in Split, now one of the most impressive Roman monuments in Europe. It is also one of nine World Heritage sites inscribed on the list since this Yugoslavia ratified the World Heritage Convention in May 1985.

The middle of the 6th century saw a great migration of Slavic tribes, including Serbs, Croats and Slovens, into this region. After a brief period of independence in the 10th century, the Serbs re-established sovereignty in 1217. The World Heritage site of Stari Ras was the centre of their first independent state. The next 170 years was their 'Golden Age', until the Ottoman Turks came and ruled most of the region for some 500 years. Another site, the Monastery of Studenica, remained an important cultural and religious centre during the years of Ottoman domination.

The Turks never really established a strong foothold on the Adriatic coast, one of the reasons that the sites of Kotor, in Montenegro, and Old Dubrovnik, in Croatia, are so well preserved today. Both of these republics also have a natural World Heritage listing – Durmitor National Park in Montenegro and the National Park of the Plitvice Lakes in Croatia – reflecting the majestic beauty of this coastal region.

Two remaining sites complete Yugoslavia's World Heritage inventory. In Macedonia, there is Ohrid and its Lake, and Skocjan Caves are in the northern republic of Slovenija.

Split

Gateway to the Latin West

THE SEVENTH DECADE of the seventeenth century was an unhappy one for Europe. Throughout the 1660s waves of disasters and afflictions of all kinds swept the continent, from London to the shores of Asia Minor, from Sicily to Scandinavia. Wars and epidemics were rampant, and claimed hundreds of thousands of victims.

At this time one proud European city on the Adriatic enjoyed the blessings of peace and prosperity in such abundance that its citizens might have been forgiven for thinking that the kindly waters of their sea would protect them forever. This city, one of the most beautiful in seventeenth century Europe, had a banner which bore the inscription *Libertas* – freedom. Its name was Dubrovnik.

On 6 April 1667, the Wednesday of Holy Week, a cloudless day dawned over Dubrovnik. A calm, unruffled sea stretched beneath an azure sky. By 8 o'clock that morning the sky was still clear and the waves lapped gently against the city fortifications. A group of notables strolled outside the palace, waiting for the bell to summon them to the Great Council, which met at Eastertide to pardon convicted criminals. In the palace chapel a religious ceremony attended by the ruler and by Dubrovnik's highest dignitaries was drawing to a close. The bishop was intoning a prayer of gratitude for the peace and plenty that prevailed in the tiny republic and expressing his hope that they would long continue.

At that moment the earth began to tremble. Within a matter of seconds, amid a crescendo of noise, the entire city was transformed by an earthquake into a mass of rubble. Palaces, monuments, churches, fortifications – the pride of Dubrovnik – which had been lovingly and painstakingly created over the centuries, all collapsed like a house of cards.

The ruler of Dubrovnik, his retinue and the highest servants of State perished in the cataclysm along with three-quarters of the city's population. On the nearby island of Lopud, which was also hit by the earthquake no more than 400 of the 14,000 islanders survived.

Misfortunes never come singly. The earthquake was followed by a fire and a tidal wave. Then came an army of looters who for weeks on end pillaged the ruins and robbed the dead. The enemies of Dubrovnik, who until then had never dared to attack the mighty fortress, flocked by land and sea to the stricken and defenceless city.

Several times in its history Dubrovnik has risen from the ashes of disaster. Barely two centuries before the earthquake of 1667 the city had experienced and survived another terrible earthquake followed by an epidemic of plague which decimated the population. But neither natural catastrophes nor the vicissitudes of history could wipe this remarkable city from the map.

Many cities in the modern world pride themselves on their cosmopolitanism and boast that they provide a favourable setting for the intermingling of different cultures. Few can rival Dubrovnik as a cross-roads where the cultural heritage of the East and West have met and been mutually enriched. For Dubrovnik is remarkable not only for its vitality and its resilience in the face of ordeals, but as a gem which has been polished for centuries in the ebb and flow of East and West.

At the time of the great invasion of Dalmatia by the Avaro-Slavs, around 614 AD, the settlement of Epidauros (present day Cavtat) was sacked and razed to the ground. Tradition has it that the survivors of this massacre went on to found a new colony, Ragusium, two hours' march northwards along the rocky coast.

Close by this settlement, whose name is derived from a Latin word meaning escarpment, was the Slav forest colony of Dubrovnik (*Dubrova* in Serbo-Croat means 'woody'). The initial antagonism between the two populations slowly disappeared, and the two colonies merged into a single city. By the beginning of the 13th century 'Ragusium-Dubrovnik' had become a single community where different ethnic groups, cultures and religions developed a spirit of coexistence which still survives today.

In the course of its long history, Dubrovnik has transformed its handicaps into advantages: it has turned poverty into wealth, calmed the warlike, and reconciled different religions and opposing economic forces. All this it has achieved by obeying whenever possible an ancient local proverb according to which 'A bad quarrel is always better than a good war'.

Right from the start Dubrovnik's economic life was based on seafaring and trade. In the ninth century sailors plied eastwards as far as the Black Sea and northwards as far as England, whence they set out on even longer voyages in the Atlantic. By the beginning of the thirteenth century its fleet was so large that the tiny republic began to challenge Venice for mastery of the seas. Through a combination of diplomatic and maritime skills, Dubrovnik had become a great seaport by the 14th century.

Dubrovnik rapidly became the main trading centre of the Balkan Peninsula, and its operations extended as far as Italy and other Mediterranean countries. Nor was the shift of maritime trade from the Mediterranean to the Atlantic a major drawback to the city's economic fortunes; indeed it was in the sixteenth century and the first half of the seventeenth century that Dubrovnik achieved the very height of its prosperity.

To preserve its freedom, the city always had to pay a high price to the Venetians, the Byzantines,

the Turks and the Slav kingdoms in the north. The Serb kingdoms cast particularly covetous eyes on the tiny independent state, attracted by the wealth it had garnered from the four corners of the earth but above all because it was an incomparable outlet to the sea. And yet the sea receded before them like a mirage as they advanced, for all their efforts to wage open war against Dubrovnik ended in failure. Powerful protectors – Slav Tsars and Latin Kings alike – rushed to aid the republic whenever danger threatened.

After two perilous centuries, a ruler who understood the true importance of Dubrovnik came to the Serbian throne in the person of Tsar Dusan. An able statesman and a prodigious expansionist, Dusan decided to withdraw the sword of aggression and extend the hand of friendship. Like the other Slav rulers, indeed like all the Slavs, he was mesmerised by Dubrovnik. But paradoxically, for he was after all a Serb, he felt that the city should be treated as a precious relic. In 1346, shortly after his coronation as Tsar, he set out for Dubrovnik on a peace mission.

The meeting between Dusan and the patricians of Dubrovnik beneath the gilded beams of the Great Council Chamber marked a turning point in the history of the Serbian state and of the entire Slav world. It opened up a new channel of communication along which different traditions could flow and be exchanged. This fruitful alliance with Dubrovnik, a child of Western civilisation, would open for the Slavs a gateway to European culture.

Medieval chronicles recount how certain Serbian dignitaries persistently urged Dusan to attack and conquer Dubrovnik and how he categorically refused, preferring instead to confirm the city's centuries-old freedom and to shower lavish gifts on its churches and monasteries. Rather than trample on the banner of St. Vlaho, protector of the city, he would send young Slavs to Dubrovnik for their education. Contemporary writers report him as saying: 'I respect the Senate of Dubrovnik for its signal virtues. Through its latin erudition, its wealth and its trade, Dubrovnik is a fitting model for the edification and the prosperity of my reign; this fine city will be the trading centre of all the territories of my realm'.

In more recent centuries Dubrovnik also had to pay a high price for its freedom. When it came under Napoleon's domination in 1806, and two years later ceased to exist as a free republic, the city fathers fomented a plot without parallel in history.

As a gesture of protest and as a means of ensuring that no descendants of theirs should ever be subjected to foreign rule, the families of Dubrovnik vowed not to procreate until they were free once more. From that moment until the liberation of the city in 1815 no child was born to the nobility of Dubrovnik.

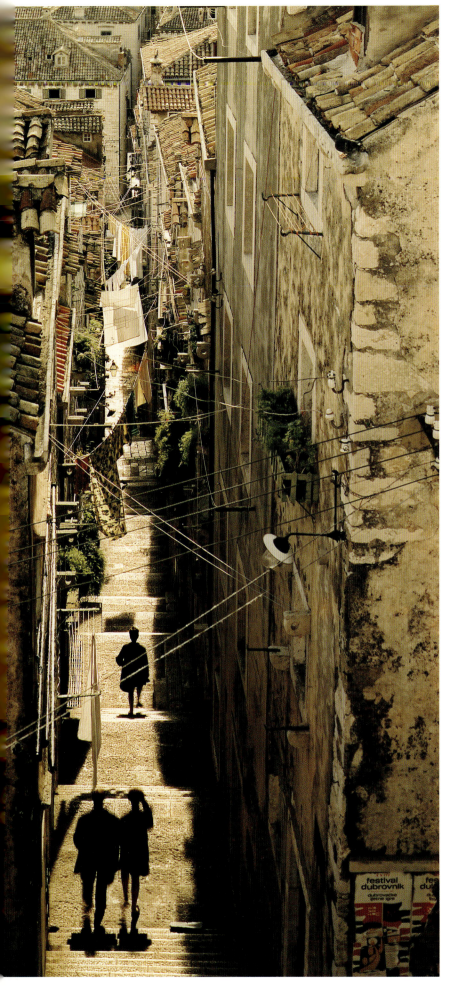

Dubrovnik (Old City)

In a long history stretching over twelve centuries, Dubrovnik has never spared any effort to preserve its freedom. This passion for independence may be partly due to the fact that the city's geographical position makes it a point at which world cultural trends and influences converge. But this is only part of the story. Dubrovnik has succeeded in resisting threats and dangers from East and West because of its links with what is today Croatia, a hinterland from which it has drawn linguistic and cultural sustenance. The Renaissance saw a great flowering of Croatian literature in Dubrovnik whose lasting achievements in poetry and the dramatic arts are just as important as the city's architectural masterpieces. By drawing life from the Croatian artistic genius, Dubrovnik brought Croatia into the great movement which was the Renaissance in the West.

Travellers of the past penned ecstatic descriptions of their first glimpse of Dubrovnik from the sea. 'An enchanting picture opens out before your eyes', wrote one of them. 'The islands are deployed like ships right as far as the port of Dubrovnik. Your boat glides over the calm sea and rounds the lighthouse; it is as if you were entering wonderland …'

Today the spell is still unbroken. The modern traveller is transported into the past as he approaches Dubrovnik's marble and granite monuments eternally caressed by the sun.

The city's long main street, the Stradun, runs along a valley which was formerly a marshy channel dividing the Latin settlement from the Slav colony. Seven hundred years ago the channel was filled in and became a thoroughfare along which Latins and Slavs would live together forever.

The people of Dubrovnik remain proud of their city and its cosmopolitan traditions. Walk along the Stradun today, especially in the summer months, and you will hear dozens of different languages being spoken. With its beautiful palaces, fountains and churches, Dubrovnik has remained faithful to its past. Each summer its music and drama festivals attract great performers from all over the world, further evidence that the cosmopolitan spirit still lives on. The Slavs – in our time the Yugoslavs – have preserved this gateway to the Mediterranean. This city on the shores of a sea which cradled more than one civilisation, continues to be a focus for the exchange of traditions. Here where the history of Europe began, it continues to be made and enriched.

VUK VUCO, Yugoslav poet and novelist, is also a critic specialising in the dramatic arts. His novel 'Les voleurs de Feu' (The Fire Robbers) has been published in France by Seuil Publishers, Paris. He is currently editor-in-chief of Danas, a magazine for Yugoslavs living in France.

Reprinted from the *Unesco Courier,* August/September 1978.

Saint Sophie Cathedral, Ohrid

Fresco detail, Monastery of Studenica

Kotor Bay

National Park of Durmitor

National Park of the Plitvice Lakes

KOTOR AND ITS GULF

LOCATION   In Montenegro, N 42° 30′, E 18° 13′.

DESCRIPTION   The town of Kotor sits on the innermost point of Kotor Gulf. It is a well preserved medieval town with its massive walls intact. Inside, there are 4 Roman Catholic churches, the Cathedral of St. Tripun, several palaces and numerous squares. The gulf is a submerged valley and is connected to the adjacent Gulf of Risan by a narrow strait. There are numerous grottos and springs in the area. The vegetation varies with the climate and topography, which changes from warm Mediterranean on the coast to subalpine in the surrounding mountains.

SIGNIFICANCE   Due to its brilliant strategic location, nestled under rugged mountains and at the end of a natural harbour, Kotor has been a coveted port for many centuries. Subsequently it has experienced long periods of prosperity, evident in the fine architecture that is so well preserved today. The entire area of the gulf has considerable biological significance due to the unique nature of the environment. Many prehistoric sites have been discovered, evidence of man's long appreciation of this area's natural hospitality.

STARI RAS AND SOPÓCANI.

LOCATION   In Serbia, E 43° 07′, N 20° 25′.

DESCRIPTION   This complex includes the Gradina Fortress, the lower town of Trgoviste, the Monastery of Djurdjevi Stupovi, St. George Church, the Monastery of Sopócani and St. Peter's Church.

SIGNIFICANCE   Stari Ras, as this complex is known, was the centre of the first independent Serbian state. St. Peter's Church, built in the 10th century on the site of a 6th century baptistery, is the oldest building. Sopócani has some valuable frescoes from the 13th century, particularly in the Holy Trinity Church which is attached to the monastery.

NATIONAL PARK OF THE PLITVICE LAKES

LOCATION   Croatia, N 44° 52′, E 15° 36′.

DESCRIPTION   The Korana River flows through this park which covers 350sq km (140sq mi) of spectacular forest, lakes and streams. More than 20 lakes and countless waterfalls, the highest 80m (262.4ft), cover this luxuriant landscape. The water has a high concentration of calcium carbonate which leaves many formations called travertine dams – naturally formed dams which grow around 1cm (0.4in) per year.

SIGNIFICANCE   This park contains a unique system of lakes and waterfalls, all part of the natural flow of the Korana River. The profuse growth of moss-like material over thousands of years has formed natural dams along the river's flow, creating a series of deep lakes, all connected with waterfalls. When in full flow, this system is one of the natural wonders of Europe. The wooded hills overlooking the water are a refuge for bears, wolves and many rare birds. This is one of Europe's last virgin forests.

NATIONAL PARK OF DURMITOR

LOCATION   Montenegro, N 42° 58′ to 43° 17′, E 18° 16′ to 19° 27′.

DESCRIPTION   This massive park can be divided into 3 sections. The first is the Basin of Mlinski with its enormous stands of pine forest, Lake Barno and the Black Lake. Second is the canyon of Tara River which is 59km (36.6mi) long and 850m (2,784ft) deep. Last is the basin of Lakes Škrč and Škrčka Jezera, along with the valley of the Sušica River.

SIGNIFICANCE   There are numerous important features to this fascinating and beautiful park. The peat bog which was discovered at an altitude of 1,450m (4,757ft), and is 5ha (12ac) in area, may well prove to be a rich source of fossils. The numerous stands of ancient pine trees that are found within the park are an invaluable treasure in modern Europe. Geologically, there are several interesting features, with the occurrence of rocks from the 3 major eras – Secondary, Tertiary and Quaternary, as well as abundant evidence of past glacial activity.

DUBROVNIK (OLD CITY)

LOCATION   Adriatic coast of Croatia, N 42° 38′, E 18° 06′.

DESCRIPTION   Covering 15.2ha (36.6ac), this listing includes all the buildings erected from the 12th to 16th centuries within the walls. The area is precisely defined by fortified walls, former moats and the steep coastline. The city was developed as a continuously evolving 'whole', with various documents showing the concern with controlling new building, based on the general city plan. A broad central square/main street, the 'Plazza', has all main north-south lines running perpendicular to it. Even following the great earthquake of 1667, the existing structural unity of the stone built city was maintained during its reconstruction. Major landmarks are the 'Castellum' which joins the rocky foundation of the city to the main coastline, the rector's palace, the cathedral and several fountains, public squares and public buildings.

SIGNIFICANCE   Due to the well preserved documents relating to various planning initiatives, Dubrovnik presents an almost intact record of medieval urban development both in conception and realisation. In many ways the city is the epitome of 'metropolitan' life, totally planned to fit its earlier role as a transport and economic hub. It exhibits both the characteristics of a political power base and an ecclesiastical seat. The town is permanently protected from any modern redevelopments.

SKOCJAN CAVES

LOCATION   In Slovenija, N 45° 39', E 14° 00'.

DESCRIPTION   Skocjan Caves are the beginning of a vast underground network which extends 40km (25mi) on to the springs of the Timaro River in the Gulf of Trieste. The protected zone covers 200ha (480ac) and includes the above ground canyon of the Reka River, with the spectacular natural bridge which spans it. The main caves are Mahorčič and Marinič with their underground lakes and waterfalls.

SIGNIFICANCE   These caves were inhabited in prehistoric times and were known in antiquity. Their unique and spectacular formations accord them a special place in the study of speleology. They also provide the habitat for several rare and endangered species of fauna, including 5 different bats and a salamander.

OHRID AND ITS LAKE

LOCATION   Southwest Macedonia, N 40° 54', E 20° 37'.

DESCRIPTION   The lake is 294sq km (118sq mi) in area and belongs to a large group of lakes in the Adriatic basin. It is situated 694m (2,277ft) above sea level and is fed by underground springs. There are numerous archaeological sites from the neolithic and Bronze Ages as well as from the Illyrian period scattered around the area. The medieval fortified city of Ohrid is on a hill overlooking the lake. Many churches and monasteries are preserved, St. Pantelejmon with the tomb of St. Clement, St. Naum and St. Sophie's Cathedral being the most important. Some Islamic monuments mark the 500 years of Turkish rule.

SIGNIFICANCE   Ohrid is one of the oldest Slavic cultural and religious centres in the Balkans. Clement, who was a 9th century follower of the 2 prominent Byzantine missionaries, Cyril and Methodist, founded an important education centre here. It was the capital of the first Macedonian Slav Empire of Samuilo, from 976 to 1014 AD. Its most precious treasure is the world renowned collection of Byzantine icons from the 11th to 14th centuries. This collection is the second most important in the world after the Tretiakov Gallery. The lake is also of great importance, both culturally and ecologically. Its archaeological sites are numerous and the lake itself supports several rare species of flora and fauna.

SPLIT (HISTORIC COMPLEX WITH DIOCLETIAN PALACE)

LOCATION   Adriatic Coast of Croatia, N 43° 30', E 16° 26'.

DESCRIPTION   The massive Palace of Diocletian, built from the late 3rd century to early 4th century AD,

Skocjan Caves

covered more than 30,000sq m (333,000sq ft). It is rectangular with peripheral towered walls and double gates. The remains of the imperial apartments to the south are built on a substructure supporting 50 vaulted rooms. There are temples and baths, the remains of porticos, servants' dwellings and the open entrance hall containing the Mausoleum of Diocletian. Within the well preserved Roman palace are several monuments and architectural complexes, dating from the Middle Ages to recent times. These include Romanesque monuments from the 12th and 13th centuries, Gothic palaces, medieval fortifications, baroque and Renaissance buildings. Outside the palace, the medieval town contains numerous churches such as those containing the sculptures of St. Anastasius and St. Arnir. Several baroque and Renaissance edifices can be found, though often having been substantially altered.

SIGNIFICANCE   Built specifically for Emperor Diocletian's retirement, this palace is one of the largest in Europe and the best preserved of all Roman monumental buildings. It is of inestimable value in the study and conservation of ancient structures. The town outside the old palace provides invaluable records of the series of rulers that followed the collapse of the Roman Empire.

Fresco detail, Monastery of Sopocani

MONASTERY OF STUDENICA

LOCATION   Serbia, N 43° 29′, E 20° 32′.

DESCRIPTION   This monastery is situated on a small plateau overlooking the Studenica River. The complex of buildings, made of stone and marble, is surrounded by a wall with several towers. The main monastic church is the Church of The Virgin with its later addition, the Exonarthex of King Radoslav. Other churches include those of St. Joachim and St. Anne, known as the Church of the King, remains of the churches of St. Nicolas, St. John, St. Georges and St. Demeter. The medieval refectory is furnished with 11 marble tables. Outside the walls is a series of small churches erected between the 13th and 16th centuries.

SIGNIFICANCE   The monastery was founded by Stefan Nemanja, who later became a monk. It was enlarged by his sons who imported the best Greek artists to decorate the Church of The Virgin with magnificent frescoes. The interior of the Church of the King is totally covered by mural paintings. The monastery has been the most important spiritual and cultural centre of the Serbian State, even during the Ottoman domination.

ZAIRE

Zaire is in the heart of tropical Africa. Wild and impossibly thick jungle, towering mountain peaks, gushing rivers, active volcanoes, abundant wildlife, forest villages and pygmies. This large country of 2,344,000 sq km (901,000 sq mi) is archetypal Africa.

When the Portuguese first arrived in 1482, they found a social structure of interacting small kingdoms whose economies were based on agriculture, fishing, trading, hunting and slavery. The most important of these kingdoms was called Kongo and it controlled the mouth of the Zaire river.

The Portuguese soon gained control and began sending slaves to Brazil. The interior of the country wasn't penetrated until the 19th century when Stanley made several expeditions. As the personal envoy of King Leopold of Belgium, Stanley claimed the entire area on the King's behalf, it became his personal empire and was known as the Congo Free State.

Henry Morton Stanley was a Welsh born African explorer. His discovery and development of this area was his most important work, although he was perhaps best known for his famous words 'Dr. Livingstone, I presume', when he relieved his famous colleague.

Eventually the territory was handed over to the Belgian government, who ruled as a colonial power until 1960, when independence was granted.

Zaire ratified the World Heritage Convention in September 1974 and now has four National Parks listed as World Heritage Sites.

Mountain gorilla, Kahuzi-Biega National Park

KAHUZI-BIEGA NATIONAL PARK

LOCATION   West of Lake Kivu, 50km (31mi) from the town of Bukavu, S 02° 10′ to 02° 51′, E 28° 40′ to 28° 50′.

DESCRIPTION   This national park takes its name from two extinct volcanoes, the Kahuzi and the Biega. It is a mountainous area with diverse types of vegetation, characterised mainly by mountain forests and large stands of bamboo. There are also alpine and sub-alpine meadows, marshlands, peat bogs and some rivers.

SIGNIFICANCE   The fundamental interest of the park lies in its mountain gorilla (gorilla beringei) population. There are several hundred individuals who live mainly in the zones situated between 2,100-2,400m (6,890-7,874ft). Their existence is related to the vast area of forests in the park which provide an ideal habitat for this species.

SALONGA NATIONAL PARK

LOCATION   In western territories of Monkoto, Bokungu, Lorilla Dekese and Oshwe, S 01° 00′ to 03° 30′, E 20° 00′ to 23° 00′.

DESCRIPTION   This massive park is in 2 sections which are separated by a populated zone. It covers 36,000sq km (14,400sq mi) of mainly equatorial rainforest. The climate is hot and humid and it provides the habitats for numerous flora and fauna, including many large mammals. There are many deep valleys and swift flowing rivers.

SIGNIFICANCE   This national park is the largest in Zaire and the second largest in the world. It was transformed into a national park in order to preserve a large part of the great equatorial forest which stretches across the centre of Africa. It is in virtually pristine condition, due mainly to its rugged terrain and thick, inaccessible forests. Innumerable species of flora and fauna live in these great forests, including many that would be extinct or endangered if this habitat was not protected.

VIRUNGA NATIONAL PARK

LOCATION   Close to the borders of Uganda and Rwanda, S 01° 00′, E 29° 30′.

DESCRIPTION   This park is a narrow strip of land, 300km (186mi) long and up to 50km (31mi) wide, a total of 8,000sq km (3,200sq mi) in area. It comprises a zone of extinct volcanoes as well as some that are still active. The landscape varies from lava plains to mountains to alluvial plains around Lake Amin and vast stretches of savanna. There is a great variation in altitude: 798m (2,618ft) in the equatorial forest ranging up to 5,119m (16,794ft) at the glaciers and perpetual snows of Ruwenzori. This has resulted in a similar degree of diversity of ecosystems, in turn responsible for a unique

Buffalo, Virunga National Park

and rich variety of flora and fauna. Many large mammals are found here, such as the mountain gorilla (gorilla beringei), chimpanzee, leopard, lion, elephant, kobus, waterbuck and antelope.

SIGNIFICANCE   First created in 1925 as a sanctuary for the endangered species of gorillas, it has been extended several times to its present boundaries. Its essential significance lies in the variety of species found in a relatively limited area. The population of hippopotami around Lake Amin and along the Semliki River is extremely dense and has the potential to outstrip the supply of natural food.

GARAMBA NATIONAL PARK

LOCATION   In the northeastern area of High Zaire, on the border with Sudan, E 28° 48′ to 30° 00′, N 03° 45′ to 04° 41′.

DESCRIPTION   This is an area of vast savanna, with pockets of forest and several large swamp depressions. The park is crossed by major rivers such as the Dungu, Aka and Garamba. It lies at an altitude varying between 700-900m (2,297-2,953ft), and its climate is characterised by a wet season and a dry season. The trees typical to the park are the Kigelia aethiopica and the Terminalia, both extremely fire resistant.

SIGNIFICANCE   This national park was created as a natural sanctuary to protect its remarkable fauna, particularly its big mammals. It is the habitat of the 4 largest mammals on earth; the elephant, hippopotamus, white rhinoceros and giraffe. The 2 last species were on the endangered list up until very recently. Their numbers are now slowly increasing, due mainly to the provision of this protected environment.

Garamba National Park

Hippos in mud, Virunga National Park

Poaching – Sabotage over Africa

POACHING is the term given to the illegal removal of a natural resource. It is usually thought of as the shooting of big game animals, but poaching can include the illegal harvesting of resources such as timber, small birds and fish. Most people associate poaching with the plains of Africa, and with good reason. Africa's large mammal species have been severely depleted through most of their historical ranges. Populations are now concentrated in relatively few protected areas. Some of the most important areas have been established as World Heritage sites. Among the most important World Heritage sites for large mammals in Africa are the Serengeti National Park and Selous Game Reserve in Tanzania, the Garamba National Park in Zaire, the Tai National Park in Cote d'Ivoire, and the Mana Pools National Park in Zimbabwe. However, although these are all World Heritage sites, all have been plagued with serious outbreaks of poaching.

In the Serengeti National Park for instance, the black rhino is now extinct. Commercial poaching for meat has almost wiped out buffaloes from the northern part of the park. In the Selous Game Reserve, there have been catastrophic declines in wildlife populations. Poaching for ivory has reduced elephant populations from some 110,000 animals in 1976, to 55,000 in 1986, to just 30,000 in 1989. During the period 1976-1986, some 98% of the black rhinos were removed, leaving only 100-200 animals. More surprisingly, most antelope species suffered major declines, including hartebeest, sable and greater kudu. These declines might have been the result of subsistence hunting by large numbers of elephant and rhino poachers operating in the reserve.

One of the most serious examples of poaching concerns the northern white rhino. In 1981, there were still some 700 animals in Sudan and Zaire. By 1983, only 12 remained, all in the Garamba National Park in Zaire.

From 1985 onwards, there has been severe poaching pressure on black rhinos in the Zambezi Valley of Zimbabwe, including the Mana Pools National Park. Here, anti-poaching activities have been more successful. Several hundred animals have been killed, but the overall population has remained stable. The cost of this anti-poaching operation has been enormous, both in terms of the millions of dollars spent, and also in the human lives lost (the anti-poaching operation has been described as warfare).

Poaching has been severe in the rainforest areas of Africa as well. Elephant populations are severely reduced, for instance, in the Tai National Park in Cote d'Ivoire. This area has also been suffering from a more insidious threat: commercialised timber poaching. This form of poaching results in habitat loss that threatens a whole array of species. As mentioned earlier, poaching is not restricted to the big and spectacular. In northern Tanzania, numbers of a small species of parrot, Fischer's lovebird, have been severely reduced through collecting for the pet trade. This has even taken place inside the Serengeti National Park.

Is poaching just a one way story? Can there be any successes? There are three reasons for having some degree of hope. First, some anti-poaching efforts have been successful. The Zimbabwe example was given above. A more spectacular one, which took place against all the odds, was in Garamba National Park. When the crisis of the northern white rhino broke, the World Heritage Committee acted swiftly and decisively, and funds were flowing within weeks. Poaching was brought back under control through the collaboration of a number of conservation organizations. The rhino population is now up to 27. Other species, including elephants, are also recovering their populations in Garamba. A second reason for optimism concerns the banning of the ivory trade. It seems clear that this has lead to greatly reduced poaching pressure on elephants, at least in eastern and southern Africa. It also seems that the reduction in elephant poaching is also correlated with reduced pressure on secondary species, such as some antelopes, buffalo and zebras (though not, of course, rhinos). Third, in some parts of southern Africa, some exciting new projects have involved local people in managing wildlife populations. Some of these, for instance in Zimbabwe, Namibia and South Africa, have shown early encouraging results. If the people derive benefits from the resources on their land, they have an incentive to conserve it and to combat poaching pressures. The local people know the lie of the land best, and are therefore in the best position to counter poachers. Many African countries still insist on centralised control, and policy and legal changes are often needed if local people are to manage wildlife.

The involvement of local people in the management of World Heritage sites in Africa is clearly a priority. The World Heritage Fund is, and could increasingly be, used to establish the necessary infrastructure to permit such locally managed programmes to succeed.

SIMON STUART
IUCN, Species Program Officer

---

*Fix your eyes on nature –
follow the path traced by her.*

JEAN-JACQUES ROUSSEAU

Victoria Falls (Mosi-Oa-Tunya)

ZAMBIA

Zambia is a landlocked Central African plateau country lying wholly within the tropics but with an excellent climate thanks to its altitude (1000m 3300ft), summer rainfall, sunshine and cool winter. The original population was a mixture of tribes: some, like the Ngoni, Bemba and Lunda, were fairly recent arrivals while others, like the Tonga and Ila, were more ancient inhabitants. The Zambezi river, after which the country is named, rises in the home of the Lozi people said to have originated from the Basuto nation in the South. Zambia, previously Northern Rhodesia, was never a cohesive land, and, like so many other African countries, owes its boundaries to an arbitrary distribution of land by the European colonial powers at the turn of the century.

Zambia's prehistory is as old as man himself as evidenced by several archaeological discoveries in both Central and East Africa. Apart from rock paintings, there is little record of recent history, so reliance must be placed on the early European travellers – the most famous though not the first being the missionary Dr. Livingstone, who travelled extensively in Central Africa between 1853 and 1872. He died in Chitambo's village in the Northern Province after suffering the most dreadful hardships and repeated bouts of malaria and dysentery. It was he who 'discovered' the great Musi-o-tunya Falls on the Zambezi, which he named Victoria Falls after his Queen. He approached the falls in dugout canoes on 16th November, 1855, accompanied by his friend the Makolol chief, Sekeletu. On reaching an island in the centre of the mile wide river, he was able to approach the brink of the falls. In his words, 'I believe that no one could perceive where the vast body of water went; it seemed to lose itself in the earth…At least I did not comprehend it until, creeping with care to the verge I peered down into a vast rent which had been made from bank to bank of the broad Zamberzi'. Few modern visitors approach the falls from this vantage point (now known as Livingstone Island), as there are safer and more spectacular panoramic views down stream. Even Livingstone did not appreciate the scale of the chasm, which he described as 36m (100ft) deep whereas, in fact, it is 124m (341ft).

A study of the geological features which led to the formation of such a remarkable natural waterfall on a major continental river reveals a whole series of similar hard basalt shelves over which the river has cascaded: this being the seventh location of the falls. It can only be a matter of conjecture as to how long the falls have taken to work back to their present position about two-thirds of the way through the basalt formations – certainly there has been little change in 140 years since Livingstone's first sighting. The original basaltic lava erupted some 150 million years ago, and this event has been followed by many changes in climate, earth movements, alluvial and windblown deposits – notably the thick deposit of the Kalahari sands – and shifting of the river course itself.

The modern and more adventurous visitor to the falls can take an inflatable raft from the base of the main falls downstream through numerous rapids, with the high gorge towering on either side, for several days until the river flows into the head-waters of Lake Kariba. The unique scenery with black basaltic cliffs and moonlike terrain, coupled with the excitement of 'white water' rafting is an experience unequalled on any other river. *Unfortunately, there are serious plans afoot to build a hydroelectric dam at Batoka Gorge which will, forever, flood most of the gorge and every rapid back upstream almost to the falls itself. If this takes place it will mean the destruction of a unique wilderness area which is an integral part of the falls, now a World Heritage site.*

Though the Victoria Falls is one of the most famous of Central Africa's natural features, the wildlife and wilderness areas are equally renowned. Zambia has 19 national parks covering 66,644 sq km (25,6000 sq mi) or about 9% of its land area. The Luangwa Valley has a reputation as one of the best African wildlife areas with a high density and variety of species and small but well run tourist lodges. In Livingstone's time the indigenous population was about one tenth of the present 8.5 million, so there was a natural balance between the wildlife population and man. The advent of early European ivory and sport hunters introduced a new factor, and, as firearms became more common there was a rapid and dangerous decline in the wildlife population. Poor economic circumstances in most African countries, shortage of foreign exchange and escalating ivory prices in the last 15 years have led to a disastrous reduction in the elephant population. The demand for rhino horn in the Middle and Far East has resulted in the very near extinction of this species. The tragedy is that much of the slaughter of these two species has been organised by foreigners who have benefited far more than the indigenous Zambian in this illegal trade. *In 1972 there were 100,000 elephants and several thousand rhinos in the Luangwa Valley. Today there are some 20,000 elephants and just a few dozen rhinos.*

As a result of the escalating demand for ivory and rhino horn in the early 1980s the Wildlife Conservation Society of Zambia recognised that if no action was taken, both species would be drastically reduced. Unfortunately world prices became so high that the anti-poaching operations set up by 'Save the Rhino Trust' to combat commercial poaching became unsustainable. Nevertheless, many elephants and a few rhinos owe their continued existence to this initiative and at least the operation spearheaded the drive which later, with the availability of more funds, proved a successful deterrent in limited areas where previously the poachers were in command.

The society now pursues a policy of creating public awareness, not only in wildlife conservation but also in the full spectrum of modern conservation which includes pollution, environmental degradation and resource management. In Zambia perhaps the most important aspects are tree cutting for agricultural purposes and domestic fuel, chemical and industrial pollution due to agricultural and mining activities and destruction of our wildlife population to the detriment of tourism and traditional protein supply for rural dwellers. Much of this work is carried out in co-operation with international bodies such as WWF, IUCN, AWF and the David Shepherd Conservation Foundation, all of whom support the society.

Wildlife Conservation Society of Zambia.

ZAMBIA AND ZIMBABWE
VICTORIA FALLS (MOSI-OA-TUNYA)

LOCATION   Southern Province of Zambia, Matabeland North Province of Zimbabwe, S 17° 56′, E 25° 55′.

DESCRIPTION   At 1,300km (808mi) from its source, the Zambezi River is interrupted by these falls which descend in several steps to a total of about 350m (1,148ft). The falls are 1,708m (5,604ft) wide and send a plume of spray 500m (1,640ft) up into the air which can be seen from 30km (18.6mi) away. After descending the falls, the water of the Zambezi swirls furiously in the 'Boiling Pot' before tortuously traversing the lower gorges, barely one-thirtieth the width of the upper river.

SIGNIFICANCE   When the Zambezi is in full flood, the falls are the largest curtain of water on earth. The whole area below and above the falls is of outstanding geological, geomorphological and hydrological interest. The flora and fauna of the nearby national park is rich in biological diversity. However it is from the enormous width and volume of falling water, that the falls attain their tremendous aesthetic value. The cultural history of the area extends back approximately 50,000 years with several stone artefacts having been uncovered. However, the various interactions between numerous tribes have left no clear or dominant ethnic characteristics. The main human significance lies in the wealth which accrued to the tribes controlling the rich wildlife resources in centuries past.

ZIMBABWE

The Government of Zimbabwe has committed itself to preserving its natural and historic sites. Zimbabwe has four sites inscribed on the World Heritage list:

Two are natural World Heritage properties and the Ministry of Environment and Tourism through the Department of National Parks and Wildlife Management is taking every possible effort to manage and enhance their natural values to the benefit of the Zimbabwean people and the international community in general. The other two are cultural properties and are administered by the National Museums and Monuments of Zimbabwe. They are maintained by custodian archaeologists with the special responsibility of preserving them.

Zimbabwe is proud to be associated with the World Heritage Convention and has acquired additional prestige for looking after the last viable herd of black rhinoceros in the Mana Pools National Park, Sapi and Chewore Safari Areas World Heritage site.

Despite intensified poaching activities the Government has resolved to protect the endangered wildlife species in this area at considerable cost both materially and in human life.

The Victoria Falls/Mosi-oa-Tunya World Heritage site forms the world's largest curtain of falling water with a mean maximum flow of more than 5000 litres (100 gallons) per minute. The waterfall is 1708 metres wide and descends about 100 metres.

Great Zimbabwe is the nation's most important cultural heritage, being an ancient town of some 10,000 inhabitants built nearly 1,000 years ago. At Great Zimbabwe indigenous stone masonry achieved a standard of excellence which remains unparalleled in Southern Africa. The Khami Ruins comprise an impressive set of terrace and freestanding dressed stone walls. Archaeological evidence suggests Iron Age occupation of the site.

Continued protection and preservation of Zimbabwe's World Heritage sites requires substantial funding. It is therefore desirable to increase public awareness of the convention in order to mobilise resources for the better protection of the sites. International assistance would therefore enhance Zimbabwe's efforts to preserve its monuments and sites.

DR H M MURERWA. M.P.
Minister of Environment and Tourism, Zimbabwe

Great Zimbabwe Ruins

The Ancient Secrets of Great Zimbabwe

DEEP IN THE HEART of southern Africa, away from the zones of influence of the Islamic and Christian powers, the basins of the Zambezi and Limpopo Rivers were for centuries the setting for a number of brilliant civilisations, the most famous of these being that of Great Zimbabwe. Thanks to painstaking research by archaeologists, linguists and anthropologists, the ancient city of Great Zimbabwe, with its cyclopean buildings, is gradually yielding up the secrets of its past.

Whatever the fundamental causes behind the rise of Great Zimbabwe, there is no doubt that it is a most impressive monument. The site is dominated by the acropolis, a long, granite hill covered with enormous boulders. Successive generations of occupants linked the boulders together with stone walls, making small enclosures and narrow passages. The westernmost enclosure is the largest, enclosed by a thick, free-standing stone wall. It contains a long sequence of later Iron Age occupation that provides the basis for subdividing Great Zimbabwe's history into at least three stages.

The most intensive occupation began in about the eleventh century; but no stone walls were built until the thirteenth century, when the small pole-and-mud huts of earlier times were replaced by more substantial mud houses. The stone retaining wall for the western enclosure was also built at that time, as more imports appear in the deposits. It was during the thirteenth or fourteenth century, also, that the first buildings were constructed in the valley below the acropolis.

The Great Enclosure with its massive free-standing walls was built progressively during the following century. The enclosing wall of the Great Enclosure has an average height of 7.3 metres (8.1 yards), is 5.5 metres (6.1 yards) thick at the base and between 1.3 metres (1.4 yards) and 3.6 metres (4 yards) at the top. A length of 52 metres (58 yards) is decorated with a chevron pattern. Inside is an unfinished enclosure wall which was evidently replaced by the present one and which helps to form a narrow defile between the two walls, leading to a skilfully constructed conical tower that dominated the Great Enclosure. The Great Enclosure itself was divided into a series of smaller enclosures, in which the foundations of substantial pole-and-mud houses are to be seen. It was presumably the dwelling place of the rulers of Great Zimbabwe, an impressive and politically highly significant structure.

Great Zimbabwe is a unique site only on account of its scale, for it is the largest of an estimated 150 ruins with between one and five enclosures, at least partially surrounded with free-standing walls and with mud-and-pole huts inside them, built near Zimbabwe and in Mashonaland. The regularly coursed masonry is in the Great Zimbabwe style. Those that have been excavated contain occasional gold objects, copper-wire bracelets, glass beads, and the fire pots and spindle whorls characteristic of the Great Zimbabwe culture. At the Ruanga and Chipadze ruins, cattle were important. five of the excavated ruins have produced dates that suggest they were all built and occupied between the beginning of the fourteenth and the end of the fifteenth centuries. Some have been dated as late as the sixteenth century.

All these ruins are small, having had but a minimal population. They were normally built near hills that were a plentiful source of stone. Too small to be viable economic units, they were probably built by external labour from surrounding villages that were able to support themselves by shifting agriculture on the savannah.

At Nhunguza ruins there was a single, very large hut, divided into three rooms. One of the rooms was large enough to hold a large number of people, a second contained a single seat, a third was a 'completely secluded room that must have contained objects of special value including...what must have been a monolith set in a grooved stone platform'. This unusual structure may well have been the location where a prominent religious authority held sway, an authority that was not only the reason for the building of the isolated enclosure, but also the human cement that held together the Great Zimbabwe State.

One has a sense of an extremely strong and unquestioned political and religious authority whose hold over the scattered rural populations was based on some form of unifying faith in the powers of the divine *Mwari* or some other religious catalyst that reached out to every family.

The borders of the Great Zimbabwe State are still ill-defined, although its heartland was in central Mashonaland. Some Great Zimbabwe-style ruins occur in what is now Matabeleland, where Great Zimbabwe people infiltrated Leopard's Kopje territory.

The influence of Great Zimbabwe and its tributary settlements were felt far outside the immediate, relatively limited boundaries of the State itself. The prosperity of Kilwa on the East African coast was closely tied to the fluctuations in the gold trade with Sofala. Already in the tenth century, the Arab geographer al-Mas'udi was writing of Kilwa and the gold trade. Four centuries later Ibn Battuta described Kilwa as one of the most beautiful cities in the world, a town whose prosperity depended on the southern gold trade.

Without question the wealth of the rulers of Great Zimbabwe waxed and waned with the fortunes of the coastal trade. Kilwa itself went through commercial

Great Zimbabwe Ruins

vicissitudes, reaching the height of its prosperity in the fifteenth century with the reconstruction of the famous Great Mosque and its elaborate domed and vaulted roof. But a century later Kilwa, the east African coast and Great Zimbabwe itself had all declined. By the time the Portuguese arrived at Sofala the coastal trade was but a shadow of its former self. For all its isolation, Great Zimbabwe's trading connections and the fold within its borders contributed not only to prosperity and economic growth on the east African coast, but also in much remoter lands as well.

In the fourteenth and fifteenth centuries, however, there was considerable trading activity in northern Mashonaland and the Zambezi valley, which is reflected in some remarkable archaeological discoveries. This region was settled during the Early Iron Age, which survived until the end of the first millennium. Between the twelfth and fourteenth centuries northern Mashonaland was occupied by the makers of Musengezi ware, subsistence farmers with minimal trading contacts, thought to be Shona speakers. Their culture is a far cry from the wealth of their southern neighbours at Great Zimbabwe, although more trade goods occur in later Musengezi settlements.

But the same is certainly not true of the extreme north-western corner of Mashonaland and the lower part of the middle Zambezi valley, where large settlements and the working and trading of copper assumed great importance. The Chedzurgwe site in the fertile Urungwe district covered over 24 hectares (58 acres) of fine grassland; abundant cattle and game bones testify to the importance of pastoralism and hunting. But copper and iron-working were of considerable significance, both ores being abundant nearby. Copper was made into standardised ingots of two fixed weights; wire bracelets made from copper and tin alloy were commonplace. Textiles were also in use, and extremely fine pottery was made, with a finish and delicacy of decoration on shallow bowls and beakers that is almost unparalleled elsewhere.

BRIAN FAGAN of the UK, is Professor of Anthropology at the University of California, Santa Barbara, USA. An anthropologist and archaeologist, he has published many studies on the Iron Age and Stone Age cultures in east and southern Africa.

Reprinted from the *Unesco Courier*, May 1984.

Mana Pools

GREAT ZIMBABWE RUINS

LOCATION   Masvingo Province, 29km (18mi) south of Masvingo, S 20° 17′, E 30° 56′.

DESCRIPTION   This monument consists of 2 sites, the hill ruins and the valley ruins. Both are groups of dry stone wall structures. The total area covers 722ha (1,741ac) and also includes many Iron Age artefacts. There is a museum on the site.

SIGNIFICANCE   These ruins date back to 1100 AD and are the focus of a unique culture. Known as the Zimbabwe Culture, this civilization flourished for 350 years until 1450 AD. It is thought that up to 10,000 people lived here. The adjoining article by Brian Fagan delves deeply into this ancient mysterious civilisation.

MANA POOLS, SAPI AND CHEWORE RESERVES

LOCATION   Within the Urungwe District, North Mashonaland Region, S 15° 36′ to 16° 24′, E 29° 08′ to 30° 20′.

DESCRIPTION   There is no permanent human habitation in this 6,766sq km (2,700sq mi) patch of the Zambezi Valley. The main geographical features are the Zambezi escarpment rising to 1,000m (3,281ft), the flat valley floor, traversed by the sandy Zambezi River, the heavily dissected Chewore Safari Area and the Mupata Gorge, 30km (18.6mi) long. The general course of the Zambezi is along a down-faulted trough, including the various valleys and gorges. Several rivers, mostly dry, lead into the Zambezi basin leaving large areas of alluvial deposits. The various grass and woodlands associated with the largely arid conditions are home to large herds of migratory grazing animals such as zebra, sable, buffalo and elephant and more than 380 bird species. Crocodiles are also found in abundance.

SIGNIFICANCE   Due to the characteristic flooding of the Zambezi and the resultant alluvial build up, the region is not home to large predatory animals. Thus, apart from man, the herds of herbivorous savanna animals are little threatened. As well, the broad open grasslands allow visitors to walk, rather than drive through the parks, as there is little chance of unexpected encounters with ferocious wild animals. The concentration of Nile crocodiles is one of the most important in Africa. Once the danger of over hunting is removed, the mid-Zambezi valley region will become one of the finest breeding areas for the larger mammals and reptiles on earth.

KHAMI RUINS

LOCATION   Matabeleland, S 20° 09′, E 25° 25′.

DESCRIPTION   These ruins comprise another series of dry stone walled structures. They extend over an area of 108ha (260ac) and sections follow the Khami River. Many artefacts such as beads, ironware, trading goods and golden objects have been unearthed.

SIGNIFICANCE   These ruins are thought to represent a later development of the culture which flourished at the Great Zimbabwe Monument. Carbon dating places their origin at the 15th century, flourishing until the 17th century.

A New Hope for the World's Heritage?

A NEW CONCEPT IN environmental policy has emerged in recent years under the rubric of 'global funding'. The idea is that funds should be raised internationally to enable individual states, mainly the poorer and poorest countries, to take actions which they could otherwise not afford. But the transfer of funds is in a sense outside the national budget, because it does not relate to domestic priorities. It is intended to cover items which benefit the global community at large, including future generations.

The items to be covered under this new type of resource transfer go well beyond the traditional notion of sites which are of global significance, and which therefore qualify under the World Heritage Convention. They include whole ecosystems, and in particular the vulnerable elements in those systems, the natural and historic heritage, as well as the atmosphere and the oceans. The best known example in the southern hemisphere is the ozone layer, and the need to eliminate those chemicals which are now known to have precipitated the graphic depletion which takes place over Antarctica each spring.

Using the laws of economics…

The justification for such funding can be derived very clearly from certain economic principles. If the full cost of an action to society or to future generations is not recovered through the price mechanism, this is described as an 'externality'. Most environmental issues can be explained in those terms – pollution of a river creates costs for the people downstream, the destruction of a rainforest leaves degraded land for future generations, toxic substances and other hazards can transfer costs to innocent members of society on a more or less random basis. Where health or the reproductive process of individuals is affected, or where actual deaths are caused, these 'externalities' are clearly very high and strong countermeasures, such as regulation and sometimes prohibition of chemical use are justified.

In many other cases, adjustment of the price mechanism will deal with the externality. The use of market-based mechanisms is favoured by the World Bank, not only because it is the preferred approach of many of our member countries, but also because it is the most efficient way to deal with environmental costs. Even the countries of Eastern Europe, as they move from the communist style of command economy, see the advantage in raising the cost of, say, energy so that pollution can be controlled at source. But they also recognise that environmental policy requires judgements to be made about the right mix between 'market forces' and 'command and control' techniques to handle major environmental threats in their countries (and across their borders).

International law can help too…

Returning to the global level, it has become more widely accepted that some controls are needed. These can be 'soft' controls, as reflected in the classification of a given site as part of the common heritage of mankind under the World Heritage Convention, or in the codes of conduct that manufacturers may adopt about the export to the Third World of hazardous chemicals.

Or they can be 'hard' controls, such as a ban on the use of certain substances and their withdrawal from production. Again, the schedule contained in the Montreal Protocol for the phasing-out of CFC's (chlorofluorocarbons) and other ozone-depleting substances is the most immediate illustration of this approach. In recent years, there has been a plethora of negotiations aimed at drawing up global contracts to deal with international environmental problems. Some have been reasonably successful, workable instruments of international law now exist of the financial and technical resources to put the principles into practice have also been provided.

Examples in this category are the London Dumping Convention (to control the release of harmful substances on the high seas), the Convention of the Transoundary Movement of Toxic and Hazardous Wastes (the 'Basel Convention'), the instruments covering radioactive substances and nuclear waste and a number of treaties which deal with river systems and international waters, such as the Barcelona Convention aimed at controlling the pollution of the Mediterranean Sea.

The legal process can however become extremely complicated when it is not exactly clear where the burden of responsibility for corrective action should lie, or how it should be distributed. Negotiations on such things as climate change, or on biodiversity of tropical forests will all encounter this central difficulty. The values which are embodied in the notion of 'the common heritage of mankind' tend to be the ones where the rationale for a global contract is hard to establish.

Developing countries certainly see these issues as low priority and they ask why they should be expected to adjust their national development priorities in order to accommodate the values of the wealthy countries. The more acerbic version of this response points out that industrial countries destroyed their forests, as did Australia and New Zealand, in the name of development, they polluted the atmosphere and they equated progress with high energy use, particularly in the form of transport fuels. Has the switch now been turned off? Is the party over?

It all costs money...

Whichever approach is adopted at the international level, the common factor is the need for some financial mechanism. It is not simply that some countries which are custodians of great biological diversity in global terms (the 'mega-diversity countries', such as Madagascar) are also extremely poor. The sense of urgency stems from an awareness of the global environmental crisis, and part of that crisis is the pressure of a rapidly growing population on the remaining natural resources of the planet. Even in the developed countries, where the pressure for more resources takes the form of increasing consumption (and waste) by a static but affluent population, the heritage items are under increasing pressure. The action needed to protect them is nowhere near cost-free.

In an earlier period, a few enthusiastic people could win protection for natural systems and historic sites mainly through the expenditure of time and energy. This is how the great national parks systems were developed. The enthusiasts did not win every battle, some dams and roading projects went ahead, more forests were cut over and burned...Indeed it is doubtful whether the conservationists could have turned each battle into a victory, even if they had enjoyed the fund-raising attributes of their modern counterparts. The ethic of development was too strong, the frontier was believed to be without limits and 'progress' was still seen as remoulding natural systems to meet human needs.

The most recent phase of the conservation battle is different. By the 1970s and 1980s it was clear that funds were the key. In some countries they were the way to win real political influence. Sometimes they were needed for science or for management of the areas in question; sometimes they could provide for the needs of local populations, and the idea of funding areas of improved land use around the protected area began to be implemented, thus bringing the term 'buffer zone' into the vocabulary of conservation strategy. New devices, such as the 'debt-for-nature' swap, were introduced to offset the burden of such expenditures on poor countries.

Whether a country is developed or developing, whether the government is theoretically (ie, politically) pro-environment or not, I know of no protected area manager who does not face extreme budgetary pressures. Costs are always increasing – and it is ironic that this is often a result of successful promotion by a tourist industry which appears to be supportive of the managers, but which does not pay for the additional services which are needed for high visitor usage (other than through indirect taxes which are often so often absorbed by other government priorities). More scientific study is always needed. The threatened indigenous species require astronomical expenditure to contain the threat of introduced predators – and so on.

First a trickle, then a...

In short, the need for money to be transferred if the world is to protect its remaining heritage, and if gross damage to global ecosystems is to be at least attenuated, is at issue. There are two important features of such transfers which distinguish them from previous flows of development aid or emergency relief (famine, hurricane, floods etc). One is that the benefits are by definition universal (even if, like the costs, they are difficult to quantify). This means that although there can be no compulsion, all developed countries should in equity contribute to such funds because their citizens will over time enjoy commensurate benefits. There should be no 'free riders'. Seen in this perspective, 'global funding' represents a form of international taxation and, like any other tax system, the rules will be very difficult to establish.

The second feature is that the investments to be made are essentially of a long term character, well beyond the normal framework for financial decision-making. This means that new criteria will have to be developed to test one possible form of investment against another, to assess priorities for action in diffuse areas such as the global atmosphere or oceans, and to apply the criteria of science to actions to preserve biodiversity. Many other issues, such as the transfer of appropriate technology, will assume greater importance as the volume of funding builds up.

Taking these two elements together, it is extremely hard to predict what the demand for global funding of this type might be in five or ten years' time. There will also be continuing debate about whether we know enough about the threats which the global community is likely to face. Some will use uncertainty to justify massive investments, others will argue that a 'do nothing' strategy is appropriate while we confine ourselves to further scientific study and monitoring. The consensus seems to be that in some areas (ozone, biodiversity...) we know enough to act immediately, where as in others (climate change, pollution of the oceans) we know enough to pursue those investments which make economic and technical sense, and which might at least serve to contain the threat. This is often described as a 'no regrets' policy.

At the global level, even this more restricted approach would suggest a rapid increase in the level of resources to be transferred in the next decade. Ecologists have dramatised the level of 'demand' by asserting that there is hope for the planet only if the massive expenditure on armaments and on the military (as well as on technology with primarily military applications) can be switched to the task of 'healing'. Estimates therefore start in the billions (of US dollars) and immediately it is apparent that there are practical limits because of 'absorptive capacity' and the lack of international experience with environmental funding of this magnitude.

Llama on stone wall, Machu Picchu, Peru

Blazing the trail…

These are some of the issues which will come into sharper relief over the first three years of the 1990's, which is the period during which the Global Environmental Facility (GEF) will operate as a pilot program. This Facility is administered by the World Bank, and operated in partnership with UNEP and UNDP – two organs of the United Nations with special ability to assist the international community in this first step towards a global funding mechanism. The total funds to be made available are somewhere between $1 billion and $1.5 billion; the purpose is to cover those costs which reflect 'global externalities' and thus assist developing countries to take actions which would otherwise be deferred (and from which they derive no short-term economic benefit).

It is worth noting that the GEF is supported financially by a number of developing countries (and also that it is not supported by all developed countries).

As a pilot venture in international co-operation, it will open up opportunities which ecologists and scientists have long been pressing for. It will also provide a test bench for the application of new techniques to deal with environmental problems at source. The key question to be answered is whether, even at this initial level of funding, the GEF can induce a change in the texture of development worldwide. If this is the case, the ball will quickly return to the court of the developed countries, who will have to decide what lessons they should derive from the experience of poorer countries. The net effect could be a completely new philosophy of managing (and funding) the world's heritage by the turn of the century.

KEN PIDDINGTON
Director
Environment Department, World Bank

CONVENTION CONCERNING THE PROTECTION OF THE WORLD CULTURAL AND NATURAL HERITAGE

The General Conference of the United Nations Educational, Scientific and Cultural Organization meeting in Paris from 17 October to 21 November 1972, at its seventeenth session.

Noting that the cultural heritage and the natural heritage are increasingly threatened with destruction not only by the traditional causes of decay, but also by changing social and economic conditions which aggravate the situation with even more formidable phenomena of damage or destruction,

Considering that deterioration or disappearance of any item of the cultural or natural heritage constitutes a harmful impoverishment of the heritage of all the nations of the world,

Considering that protection of this heritage at the national level often remains incomplete because of the scale of the resources which it requires and of the insufficient economic, scientific and technical resources of the country where the property to be protected is situated,

Recalling that the Constitution of the Organization provides that it will maintain, increase and diffuse knowledge, by assuring the conservation and protection of the world's heritage, and recommending to the nations concerned the necessary international conventions,

Considering that the existing international conventions, recommendations and resolutions concerning cultural and natural property demonstrate the importance, for all the peoples of the world, of safeguarding this unique and irreplaceable property, to whatever people it may belong,

Considering that parts of the cultural or natural heritage are of outstanding interest and therefore need to be preserved as part of the world heritage of mankind as a whole,

Considering that, in view of the magnitude and gravity of the new dangers threatening them, it is incumbent on the international community as a whole to participate in the protection of the cultural and natural heritage of outstanding universal value, by the granting of collective assistance which, although not taking the place of action by the State concerned, will serve as an effective complement thereto,

Considering that is essential for this purpose to adopt new provisions in the form of a convention establishing an effective system of collective protection of the cultural and natural heritage of outstanding universal value, organized on a permanent basis and in accordance with modern scientific methods,

Having decided, at its sixteenth session, that this question should be made the subject of an international convention,

Adopts this sixteenth day of November 1972 this Convention.

I. Definitions of the cultural and natural heritage

Article 1

For the purposes of this Convention, the following shall be considered as 'cultural heritage':

monuments, architectural works, works of monumental sculpture and painting, elements or structures of an archaeological nature, inscriptions, cave dwellings and combinations of features, which are of outstanding universal value from the point of view of history, art or science;

groups of buildings: groups of separate or connected buildings which, because of their architecture, their homogeneity or their place in the landscape, are of outstanding universal value from the point of view of history, art or science;

sites: works of man or the combined works of nature and of man, and areas including archaeological sites which are of outstanding universal value from the historical, aesthetic, ethnological or anthropological points of view.

Article 2

For the purposes of this Convention, the following shall be considered as 'natural heritage':

natural features consisting of physical and biological formations or groups of such formations, which are of outstanding universal vale from the aesthetic or scientific point of view;

geological and physiographical formations and precisely delineated areas which constitute the habitat of threatened species of animals and plants of outstanding universal value from the point of view of science or conservation;

natural sites or precisely delineated natural areas of outstanding universal value from the point of view of science, conservation or natural beauty.

Article 3

It is for each State Party to this Convention to identify and delineate the different properties situated on its territory mentioned in Articles 1 and 2 above.

II. National protection and international protection of the cultural and natural heritage

Article 4

Each State Party to this Convention recognizes that the duty of ensuring the identification, protection, conservation, preservation and transmission to future generations of the cultural and natural heritage referred to in Articles 1 and 2 and situated on its territory, belongs primarily to that State. It will do all it can to this end, to the utmost of its own resources and, where appropriate, with any international assistance and cooperation, in particular, financial, artistic, scientific and technical, which it may be able to obtain.

Article 5

To ensure that effective and active measures are taken for the protection, conservation and presentation of the cultural and natural heritage situated on its territory, each State Party to this Convention shall endeavour, in so far as possible, and as appropriate for each country:

(a) to adopt a general policy which aims to give the cultural and natural heritage a function in the life of the community and to integrate the protection of that heritage into comprehensive planning programmes;

(b) to set up within its territories, where such services do not exist, one or more services for the protection, conservation and presentation of the cultural and natural heritage with an appropriate staff and possessing the means to discharge their functions;

(c) to develop scientific and technical studies and research and to work out such operating methods as will make the State capable of counteracting the dangers that threaten its cultural or natural heritage;

(d) to take the appropriate legal, scientific, technical, administrative and financial measures necessary for the identification, protection, conservation, presentation and rehabilitation of this heritage; and

(e) to foster the establishment or development of national or regional centres for training in the protection, conservation and presentation of the cultural and natural heritage and to encourage scientific research in this field.

Article 6

1. Whilst fully respecting the sovereignty of the States on whose territory the cultural and natural heritage mentioned in Articles 1 and 2 is situated; and without prejudice to property rights provided by national legislation, the States Parties to this Convention recognize that such heritage constitutes a world heritage for whose protection it is the duty of the international community as a whole to co-operate.

2. The States Parties undertake, in accordance with the provisions of this Convention, to give their help in the identification, protection, conservation and preservation of the cultural and natural heritage referred to in paragraphs 2 and 4 of Article 11 if the States on whose territory it is situated so request.

3. Each State Party to this Convention undertakes not to take any deliberate measures which might damage directly or indirectly the cultural and natural heritage referred to in Articles 1 and 2 situated on the territory of other States Parties to this Convention.

Article 7

For the purpose of this Convention, international protection of the world cultural and natural heritage shall be understood to mean the establishment of a system of international co-operation and assistance designed to support States Parties to the Convention in their efforts to conserve and identify that heritage.

III. Intergovernmental Committee for the Protection of the World Cultural and Natural Heritage

Article 8

1. An Intergovernmental Committee for the Protection of the Cultural and Natural Heritage of Outstanding Universal Value, called 'the World Heritage Committee', is hereby established within the United Nations Educational, Scientific and Cultural Organization. It shall be composed of 15 States Parties to the Convention, elected by States Parties to the Convention meeting in general assembly during the ordinary session of

the General Conference of the United Nations Educational, Scientific and Cultural Organization. The number of States members of the Committee shall be increased to 21 as from the date of the ordinary session of the General Conference following the entry into force of this Convention for at least 40 States.

2. Election of members of the Committee shall ensure an equitable representation of the different regions and cultures of the world.

3. A representative of the International Centre for the Study of the Preservation and the Restoration of Cultural Property (Rome Centre), a representative of the International Council of Monuments and Sites (ICOMOS) and a representative of the International Union for Conservation of Nature and Natural Resources (IUCN), to whom may be added, at the request of States Parties to the Convention meeting in general assembly during the ordinary sessions of the General Conference of the United Nations Educational, Scientific and Cultural Organization, representatives of other intergovernmental or non-governmental organizations, with similar objectives, may attend the meetings of the Committee in an advisory capacity.

Article 9

1. The term of office of States members of the World Heritage Committee shall extend from the end of the ordinary session of the General Conference during which they are elected until the end of its third subsequent ordinary session.

2. The term of office of one-third of the members designated at the time of the first election shall, however, cease at the end of the first ordinary session of the General Conference following that at which they were elected; and the term of office of a further third of the members designated at the same time shall cease at the end of the second ordinary session of the General Conference following that at which they were elected. The names of these members shall be chosen by lot by the President of the General Conference of the United Nations Educational, Scientific and Cultural Organisation after the first election.

3. States members of the Committee shall choose as their representatives persons qualified in the field of the cultural or natural heritage.

Article 10

1. The World Heritage Committee shall adopt its Rules of Procedure.

2. The Committee may at any time invite public or private organizations or individuals to participate in its meetings for consultation on particular problems.

Article 11

1. Every State Party to this Convention shall, in so far as possible, submit to the World Heritage Committee an inventory of property forming part of the cultural and natural heritage, situated in its territory and suitable for inclusion in the list provided for in paragraph 2 of this Article. This inventory, which shall not be considered exhaustive, shall include documentation about the location of the property in question and its significance.

2. On the basis of the inventories submitted by States in accordance with paragraph 1, the Committee shall establish, keep up to date and publish, under the title of *World Heritage List*, a list of properties forming part of the cultural heritage and natural heritage, as defined in Articles 1 and 2 of this Convention, which it considers as having outstanding universal value in terms of such criteria as it shall have established. An updated list shall be distributed at least every two years.

3. The inclusion of a property in the *World Heritage List* requires the consent of the State concerned. The inclusion of a property situated in a territory, sovereignty or jurisdiction over which is claimed by more than one State shall in no way prejudice the rights of the parties to the dispute.

4. The Committee shall establish, keep up to date and publish, whenever circumstances shall so require, under the title of *List of World Heritage in Danger*, a list of the property appearing in the *World Heritage List* for the conservation of which major operations are necessary and for which assistance has been requested under this Convention. This list shall contain an estimate of the cost of such operations. The list may include only such property forming part of the cultural and natural heritage as is threatened by serious and specific dangers, such as the threat of disappearance caused by accelerated deterioration, large-scale public or private projects or rapid urban or tourist development projects; destruction caused by changes in the use or ownership of the land; major alterations due to unknown causes; abandonment for any reason whatsoever; the outbreak or the threat of an armed conflict; calamities and cataclysms; serious fires, earthquakes, landslides, volcanic eruptions; changes in water level, floods, and tidal waves. The Committee may at any time, in case of urgent need, make a new entry in the *List of World Heritage in Danger* and publicize such entry immediately.

5. The Committee shall define the criteria on the basis of which a property belonging to the cultural or natural heritage may be included in either of the lists mentioned in paragraphs 2 and 4 of this article.

6. Before refusing a request for inclusion in one of the two lists mentioned in paragraphs 2 and 4 of this article, the Committee shall consult the State Party in whose territory the cultural or natural property in question is situated.

7. The Committee shall, with the agreement of the States concerned, co-ordinate and encourage the studies and research needed for the drawing up of the lists referred to in paragraphs 2 and 4 of this article.

Article 12

The fact that a property belonging to the cultural or natural heritage has not been included in either of the two lists mentioned in paragraphs 2 and 4 of this Article 11 shall in no way be construed to mean that it does not have an outstanding universal value for purposes other than those resulting from inclusion in these lists.

Article 13

1. The World Heritage Committee shall receive and study requests for international assistance formulated by States Parties to this Convention with respect to property forming part of the cultural or natural heritage, situated in their territories, and included or potentially suitable for inclusion in the lists referred to in paragraphs 2 and 4 of this Article 11. The purpose of such requests may be to secure the protection, conservation, presentation or rehabilitation of such property.

2. Requests for international assistance under paragraph 1 of this article may also be concerned with identification of cultural or natural property defined in Articles 1 and 2, when preliminary investigations have shown that further inquiries would be justified.

3. The Committee shall decide on the action to be taken with regard to these requests, determine where appropriate the nature and extent of its assistance, and authorize the conclusion, on its behalf, of the necessary arrangements with the government concerned.

4. The Committee shall determine an order of priorities for its operations. It shall in so doing bear in mind the respective importance for the world cultural and natural heritage of the property requiring protection, the need to give international assistance to the property most representative of a natural environment or of the genius and the history of the peoples of the world, the urgency of the work to be done, the resources available to the States on whose territory the threatened property is situated and in particular the extent to which they are able to safeguard such property by their own means.

5. The Committee shall draw up, keep up to date and publicize a list of property for which international assistance has been granted.

6. The Committee shall decide on the use of the resources of the Fund established under Article 15 of this Convention. It shall seek ways of increasing these resources and shall take all useful steps to this end.

7. The Committee shall co-operate with international and national governmental and non-governmental organizations having objectives similar to those of this Convention. For the implementation of its programmes and projects, the Committee may call on such organizations, particularly the International Centre for the Study of the Preservation and the Restoration of Cultural Property (the Rome Centre), the International Council of Monuments and Sites (ICOMOS) and the International Union for Conservation of Nature and Natural Resources (IUCN), as well as on public and private bodies and individuals.

8. Decisions of the Committee shall be taken by a majority of two-thirds of its members present and voting. A majority of the members of the Committee shall constitute a quorum.

Article 14

1. The World Heritage Committee shall be assisted by a Secretariat appointed by the Director-General of the United Nations Educational, Scientific and Cultural Organization.

2. The Director-General of the United Nations Educational, Scientific and Cultural Organization, utilizing to the fullest extent possible the services of the International Centre for the Study of the Preservation and the Restoration of Cultural Property (the Rome Centre), the International Council of Monuments and Sites (ICOMOS) and the International Union for Conservation of Nature and Natural Resources (IUCN) in their respective areas of competence and capability, shall prepare the Committee's documentation and the agenda of its meetings and shall have the responsibility for the implementation of its decisions.

IV. Fund for the Protection of the World Cultural and Natural Heritage

Article 15

1. A Fund for the Protection of the World Cultural and Natural Heritage of Outstanding Universal Value, called 'the World Heritage Fund', is hereby established.

2. The Fund shall constitute a trust fund, in conformity with the provisions of the Financial Regulations of the United Nations Educational, Scientific and Cultural Organization.

3. The resources of the Fund shall consist of:

(a) compulsory and voluntary contributions made by the States Parties to this Convention,

(b) contributions, gifts or bequests which may be made by:

(i) other States;

(ii) the United Nations Educational, Scientific and Cultural Organization, other organizations of the United Nations system, particularly the United Nations Development Programme or other intergovernmental organizations;

(iii) public or private bodies or individuals;

(c) any interest due on the resources of the Fund;

(d) funds raised by collections and receipts from events organized for the benefit of the Fund; and

(e) all other resources authorized by the Fund's regulations, as drawn up by the World Heritage Committee.

4. Contributions to the Fund and other forms of assistance made available to the Committee may be used only for such purposes as the Committee shall define. The Committee may accept contributions to be used only for certain programme or project, provided that the Committee shall have decided on the implementation of such programme or project. No political conditions may be attached to contributions made to the Fund.

Article 16

1. Without prejudice to any supplementary voluntary contribution, the States Parties to this Convention undertake to pay regularly, every two years, to the World Heritage Fund, contributions, the amount of which, in the form of a uniform percentage applicable to all States, shall be determined by the General Assembly of States Parties to the Convention, meeting during the sessions of the General Conference of the United Nations Educational, Scientific and Cultural Organization. This decision of the General Assembly requires the majority of the States parties present and voting, which have not made the declaration referred to in paragraph 2 of this Article. In no case shall the compulsory contribution of States Parties to the Convention exceed 1% of the contribution to the Regular Budget of the United Nations Educational, Scientific and Cultural Organization.

2. However, each State referred to in Article 31 or in Article 32 of this Convention may declare, at the time of the deposit of its instruments of ratification, acceptance or accession, that it shall not be bound by the provisions of paragraph 1 of this Article.

3. A State Party to the Convention which has made the declaration referred to in paragraph 2 of this Article may at any time withdraw the said declaration by notifying the Director-General of the United Nations Educational, Scientific and Cultural Organization. However, the withdrawal of the declaration shall not take effect in regard to the compulsory contribution due by the State until the date of the subsequent General Assembly of States Parties to the Convention.

4. In order that the Committee may be able to plan its operations effectively, the contributions of States Parties to this Convention which have made the declaration referred to in paragraph 2 of this Article, shall be paid on a regular basis, at least every two years, and should not be less than the contributions which they should have paid if they had been bound by the provisions of paragraph 1 of this Article.

5. Any State Party to the Convention which is in arrears with the payment of its compulsory or voluntary contribution for the current year and the calendar year immediately preceding it shall not be eligible as a Member of the World Heritage Committee, although this provision shall not apply to the first election.

The terms of office of any such State which is already a member of the Committee shall terminate at the time of the elections provided for in Article 8, paragraph 1 of this Convention.

Article 17

The States Parties to this Convention shall consider or encourage the establishment of national, public and private foundations or associations whose purpose is to invite donations for the protection of the cultural and natural heritage as defined in Articles 1 and 2 of this Convention.

Article 18

The States Parties to this Convention shall give their assistance to international fund-raising campaigns organized for the World Heritage Fund under the auspices of the United Nations Educational, Scientific and Cultural Organization. They shall facilitate collections made by the bodies mentioned in paragraph 3 of Article 15 for this purpose.

V. Conditions and arrangements for international assistance

Article 19

Any State Party to this Convention may request international assistance for property forming part of the cultural or national heritage of outstanding universal value situated within its territory. It shall submit with its request such information and documentation provided for in Article 21 as it has in its possession and as will enable the Committee to come to a decision.

Article 20

Subject to the provisions of paragraph 2 of Article 13, sub-paragraph (c) of Article 22 and Article 23, international assistance provided for by this Convention may be granted only to property forming part of the cultural and natural heritage which the World Heritage Committee has decided, or may decide, to enter in one of the lists mentioned in paragraphs 2 and 4 of Article 11.

Article 21

1. The World Heritage Committee shall define the procedure by which requests to it for international assistance shall be considered and shall specify the content of the request, which should define the operation contemplated, the work that is necessary, the expected cost thereof, the degree of urgency and the reasons why the resources of the States requesting assistance do not allow it to meet all the expenses. Such requests must be supported by experts' reports whenever possible.

2. Requests based upon disasters or natural calamities should, by reasons of the urgent work which they may involve, be given immediate, priority consideration by the Committee, which should have a reserve fund at its disposal against such contingencies.

3. Before coming to a decision, the Committee shall carry out such studies and consultations as it deems necessary.

Article 22

Assistance granted by the World Heritage Committee may take the following forms:

(a) studies concerning the artistic, scientific and technical problems raised by the protection, conservation, presentation and rehabilitation of the cultural and natural heritage, as defined in paragraphs 2 and 4 of Article 11 of this Convention;

(b) provision of experts, technicians and skilled labour to ensure that the approved work is correctly carried out;

(c) training of staff and specialists at all levels in the field of identification, protection, conservation, presentation and rehabilitation of the cultural and natural heritage;

(d) supply of equipment which the State concerned does not possess or is not in a position to acquire;

(e) low-interest or interest-free loans which might be repayable on a long-term basis;

(f) the granting, in exceptional cases and for special reasons, of non-repayable subsidies.

Article 23

The World Heritage Committee may also provide international assistance to national or regional centres for the training of staff and specialists at all levels in the field of identification, protection, conservation, presentation and rehabilitation of the cultural and natural heritage.

Article 24

International assistance on a large scale shall be preceded by detailed scientific, economic and technical studies. These studies shall draw upon the most advanced techniques for the protection, conservation, presentation and rehabilitation of the natural and cultural heritage and shall be consistent with the objectives of this Convention. The studies shall also seek means of making rational use of the resources available in the State concerned.

Article 25

As a general rule, only part of the cost of work necessary shall be borne by the international community. The contribution of the State benefiting from international assistance shall constitute a substantial share of the resources devoted to each programme or project, unless its resources do not permit this.

Article 26

The World Heritage Committee and the recipient State shall define in the agreement they conclude the conditions in which a programme or project for which international assistance under the terms of this Convention is provided, shall be carried out. It shall be the responsibility of the State receiving such international assistance to continue to project, conserve and present the property so safeguarded, in observance of the conditions laid down by the agreement.

VI. Educational programmes

Article 27

1. The States Parties to this Convention shall endeavour by all appropriate means, and in particular by educational and information programmes, to strengthen appreciation and respect by their peoples of the cultural and natural heritage defined in Articles 1 and 2 of the Convention.

2. They shall undertake to keep the public broadly informed of the dangers threatening this heritage and of activities carried on in pursuances of this Convention.

Article 28

States Parties to this Convention which receive international assistance under the Convention shall take appropriate measures to make known the importance of the property for which assistance has been received and the role played by such assistance.

VII. Reports

Article 29

1. The States Parties to this Convention shall, in the reports which they submit to the General Conference of the United Nations Educational, Scientific and Cultural Organization on dates and in a manner to be determined by it, give information on the legislative and administrative provisions which they have adopted and other action which they have taken for the application of this Convention, together with details of the experience acquired in this field.

2. These reports shall be brought to the attention of the World Heritage Committee.

3. The Committee shall submit a report on its activities at each of the ordinary sessions of the General Conference of the United Nations Educational, Scientific and Cultural Organization.

VIII. Final clauses

Article 30

This Convention is drawn up in Arabic, English, French, Russian and Spanish, the five texts being equally authoritative.

Article 31

1. This Convention shall be subject to ratification or acceptance by States members of the United Nations Educational, Scientific and Cultural Organization in accordance with their respective constitutional procedures.

2. The instruments of ratification or acceptance shall be deposited with the Director-General of the United Nations Educational, Scientific and Cultural Organization.

Article 32

1. This Convention shall be open to accession by all States not members of the United Nations Educational, Scientific and Cultural Organization which are invited by the General Conference of the Organization to accede to it.

2. Accession shall be effected by the deposit of an instrument of accession with the Director-General of the United Nations Educational, Scientific and Cultural Organization.

Article 33

This Convention shall enter into force three months after the date of the deposit of the twentieth instrument of ratification, acceptance or accession, but only with respect to those States which have deposited their respective instruments of ratification, acceptance or accession on or before that date. It shall enter into force with respect to any other State three months after the deposit of its instrument of ratification, acceptance or accession.

Article 34

The following provisions shall apply to those State Parties to this Convention which have a federal or non-unitary constitutional system:

(a) with regard to the provisions of this Convention, the implementation of which comes under the legal jurisdiction of the federal or central legislative power, the obligations of the federal or central government shall be the same as for those States Parties which are not federal States;

(b) with regard to the provisions of this Convention, the implementation of which comes under the legal jurisdiction of individual constituent States, countries, provinces or cantons that are not obliged by the constitutional system of the federation to take legislative measures, the federal government shall inform the competent authorities of such States, countries, provinces or cantons of the said provisions, with its recommendation for their adoption.

Article 35

1. Each State Party to this Convention may denounce the Convention.

2. The denunciation shall be notified by an instrument in writing, deposited with the Director-General of the United Nations Educational, Scientific and Cultural Organization.

3. The denunciation shall take effect twelve months after the receipt of the instrument of denunciation. It shall not affect the financial obligations of the denouncing State until the date on which the withdrawal takes effect.

Article 36

The Director-General of the United Nations Educational, Scientific and Cultural Organization shall inform the States members of the Organization, the States not members of the Organization which are referred to in Article 32, as well as the United Nations, of the deposit of all the instruments of ratification, acceptance, or accession provided for in Articles 31 and 32, and of the denunciations provided for in Article 35.

Article 37

1. This Convention may be revised by the General Conference of the United Nations Educational, Scientific and Cultural Organization. Any such revision shall, however, bind only the States which shall become Parties to the revising convention.

2. If the General Conference should adopt a new convention revising this Convention in whole or in part, then, unless the new convention otherwise provides, this Convention shall cease to be open to ratification, acceptance or accession, as from the date on which the new revising convention enters into force.

Article 38

In conformity with Article 102 of the Charter of the United Nations, this Convention shall be registered with the Secretariat of the United Nations at the request of the Director-General of the United Nations Educational, Scientific and Cultural Organization.

Done in Paris, this twenty-third day of November 1972, in two authentic copies bearing the signature of the President of the seventeenth session of the General Conference and of the Director-General of the United Nations Educational, Scientific and Cultural Organization, and certified true copies of which shall be delivered to all the States referred to in Articles 31 and 32 as well as to the United Nations.

The foregoing is the authentic text of the Recommendation duly adopted by the General Conference of the United Nations Educational, Scientific and Cultural Organization during its seventeenth session, which was held in Paris and declared closed on the twenty-first day of November 1972.

In faith whereof we have appended our signatures this twenty-third day of November 1972.

The President of the General Conference

The Director-General

STATE PARTIES TO THE WORLD HERITAGE CONVENTION

STATE	DATE
Afghanistan, The Republic of	20-Mar-79
Albania, The Republic of	10-Jul-89
Algeria, The People's Democratic Republic of	24-Jun-74
Antigua and Barbuda	1-Jan-83
Argentina, The Republic of	23-Aug-78
Australia	22-Aug-74
Bahrain, The State of	28-May-91
Bangladesh, The People's Republic of	3-Aug-83
Belize	6-Nov-90
Benin, The Republic of	14-Jun-82
Bolivia, The Republic of	4-Oct-76
Brazil, The Federative Republic of	1-Sep-77
Bulgaria, The People's Republic of	7-Mar-74
Burkina Faso, The Popular Democratic Republic of	2-Apr-87
Burundi, The Republic of	19-May-82
Byelorussia, The Republic of	12-Oct-88
Cameroon	7-Dec-82
Cape Verde, The Republic of	24-Apr-88
Canada	23-Jul-76
Central African Republic	22-Dec-80
Chile, The Republic of	20-Feb-80
China, The People's Republic of	12-Dec-85
Colombia, The Republic of	24-May-83
Commonwealth of Independent States	see USSR
Congo, The People's Republic of	10-Dec-87
Costa Rica, The Republic of	23-Aug-77
Cote d'Ivoire, Republique de	9-Jan-81
Cuba, The Republic of	24-Mar-81
Cyprus	14-Aug-75
Czechoslovakia (The Czech and Slovak Federal Republic)	15-Nov-90
Denmark, The Kingdom of	25-Jul-79
Dominican Republic	12-Feb-85
Ecuador, The Republic of	16-Jun-75
Egypt, The Arab Republic of	7-Feb-74
El Salvador, The Republic of	8-Oct-91
Ethiopia, The People's Democratic Republic of	6-Jul-77
Fiji, The Republic of	21-Nov-90
Finland	4-Mar-87
France	27-Jun-75

Gabon	30-Dec-86
Gambia, The Republic of the	1-Jul-87
Germany, the Federal Republic of	23-Aug-76
Ghana, The Republic of	4-Jul-75
Greece	17-Jul-81
Guatemala	16-Jan-79
Guinea, The Republic of	18-Mar-79
Guyana, The Co-operative Republic of	20-Jun-77
Haiti	18-Jan-80
Holy See	7-Oct-82
Honduras, The Republic of	8-Jun-79
Hungary, The Republic of	15-Jul-85
India	14-Nov-77
Indonesia, The Republic of	6-Jul-89
Iran, The Islamic Republic of	26-Feb-75
Iraq, The Republic of	5-Mar-74
Ireland	16-Sep-91
Italy	23-Jun-78
Ivory Coast, The Republic of the	9-Jan-81
Jamaica	14-Jun-83
Jordan, The Hashemite Kingdom of	5-May-75
Kenya, The Republic of	5-Jun-91
Korea, The Republic of	14-Sep-88
Lao, People's Democratic Republic	20-Mar-87
Lebanon	3-Feb-83
Libyan Arab Jamahiriya	13-Oct-78
Luxembourg	28-Sep-83
Madagascar, The Democratic Republic of	19-Jul-83
Malawi, The Republic of	5-Jan-82
Malaysia	7-Dec-88
Maldives, The Republic of	22-May-86
Mali, The Republic of	5-Apr-77
Malta, The Republic of	14-Nov-78
Mauritania, The Islamic Republic of	2-Mar-81
Mexico	23-Feb-84
Monaco, The Pricipality of	7-Nov-78
Mongolian People's Republic	2-Feb-90
Morocco, The Kingdom of	28-Oct-75
Mozambique, The Republic of	27-Nov-82
Nepal, The Kingdom of	20-Jun-78
New Zealand	22-Nov-84
Nicaragua, The Republic of	17-Dec-79
Niger, The Republic of	23-Dec-84
Nigeria	23-Oct-74
Norway, The Kingdom of	12-May-77
Oman, the Sultanate of	6-Oct-81
Pakistan	23-Jul-76
Panama, The Republic of	3-Mar-78
Paraguay, The Republic of	28-Apr-88
Peru, The Republic of	24-Feb-82
Philippines	19-Sep-85
Poland, The Republic of	29-Jun-76
Portugal	30-Sep-80
Qatar, The State of	12-Sep-84
Romania	16-May-90
Saint Christopher and Nevis, The Federation of	10-Jul-86
Saudi Arabia, The Kindom of	7-Aug-78
Senegal, The Republic of	13-Feb-76
Seychelles, The Republic of	9-Apr-80
Spain	4-May-82
Spain	4-May-82
Sri Lanka, The Democratic Socialist Republic of	6-Jun-80
Sudan, The Republic of	6-Jun-74
Sweden	22-Jan-85
Switzerland	17-Sep-75

Syrian Arab Republic	13-Aug-75
Tanzania, United Republic of	2-Aug-77
Thailand, The Kingdom of	17-Sep-87
Tunisia, The Republic of	10-Mar-75
Turkey, The Republic of	16-Mar-83
Uganda, The Republic of	20-Nov-87
Ukraine, The Republic of	12-Oct-88
United Kingdom of Great Britain and Northern Ireland	29-May-84
United States of America	7-Dec-73
U.S.S.R. – Commonwealth of Independent States	12-Oct-88
Uruguay	9-Mar-89
Venezuela	30-Oct-90
Vietnam, The Socialist Republic of	19-Oct-87
Yemen, The Republic of	7-Oct-80
Yugoslavia	26-May-75
Zaire, The Republic of	23-Sep-74
Zambia, The Republic of	4-Jun-84
Zimbabwe, The Republic of	16-Aug-82

UNESCO's WORLD HERITAGE COMMITTEE

The World Heritage Convention is administered by the World Heritage Committee, comprising one representative from each of twenty-one states who are elected on a rotating basis from all the state parties to the convention. Representatives are elected for six year terms, with one third of them retiring every two years. The committee meets annually and has three primary responsibilities: selecting from a list of nominations by member states those properties which qualify for inclusion on the World Heritage List, informing the international community about these sites, and providing assistance for the preservation of these sites.

The World Heritage
UNESCO

This emblem symbolizes the interdependence of cultural and natural properties: the central square is a form created by man and the circle represents nature, the two being intimately linked. The emblem is round like the world, but at the same time it is a symbol of protection.

IUCN – THE WORLD CONSERVATION UNION

Founded in 1948, IUCN – The World Conservation Union – is a membership organisation comprising governments, non-government organisations (NGO's), research institutions and conservation agencies in 118 countries. The Union's objective is to promote the protection and sustainable utilisation of living resources.

The Union performs a function vital to the operation of the World Heritage Convention by assessing all natural sites which are nominated by signatory states for inclusion on the World Heritage List.

IUCN
The World Conservation Union

RECENT WORLD HERITAGE LISTINGS

The World Heritage List is updated annually. The 23 properties listed below were inscribed on the list in January, 1992, and so do not appear in the main text of this publication. They will be incorporated in the next edition. There are currently 80 states with 360 sites on the list.

AUSTRALIA

NAME   **Shark Bay.**

LOCATION   On the western-most point of the coast, Western Australia. S 24° 44′ to 27° 16′, E 112° 49′ to 114° 17′.

DESCRIPTION   This area covers 2,197,300ha (5,429,528ac) and constitutes a complete marine ecosystem. The listing comprises the entire 13,000sq km (5,000sq mi) of the shallow bay (including numerous islands), as well as a substantial area of the bordering mainland. The township of Denham, although within the boundaries, is specifically excluded from the listing.

SIGNIFICANCE   Shark Bay is truly a biological wonderland. The outstanding feature is the steep gradient in water salinity, which has created three distinct biotic zones. The marine flora shows a high species variation, and is dominated by seagrass beds which cover 4,000sq km (1,500sq mi). Especially notable are the ancient microbial life forms which are unique to the area and constitute a living fossil record. Five of Australia's 26 threatened mammal species are found within the area. More than 10,000 dugong reside here, around 12.5% of the world population, and humpback whales use the bay as a migratory staging post. Bird and fish life are rich, with more than 230 bird species and 323 fish species. Particularly renowned are the dolphins of the area, which regularly interact with humans at Monkey Mia. Many aboriginal midden sites have been discovered which indicate a history of human population dating back at least 22,000 years.

BOLIVIA

NAME   **Ville de Sucre.**

LOCATION   Oropeza Province. S 19° 12′, W 65° 12′ (approximately).

Monkey Mia, Shark Bay

DESCRIPTION Sucre is Bolivia's constitutional capital, that is, the seat of the Supreme Court. The city, with a population of around 100,000 sits in a fertile valley at an altitude of 2,590m (8,500ft). It was founded by the Spanish in 1538 on a Charcas Indian site (Chuquisaca) and was originally named La Plata. There are around 300 Spanish colonial buildings of significance remaining in the city today.

SIGNIFICANCE The historic centre of Sucre has an extremely rich heritage of well preserved Spanish colonial architecture which displays the blending of European styles with local traditions which was so distinctive to Latin America. Many of the religious buildings date back to the middle of the 16th century and bear testimony to the early development of the Spanish city. The town has a history of rebellion; its people revolted against Spain in 1809. Thirty years later it became Bolivia's first capital and was named Sucre after the first President, Antonio José de Sucre. A civil war followed attempts in 1898 to move the capital. A compromise was reached which resulted in the La Paz becoming the administrative capital, Sucre remaining the capital in both law and name.

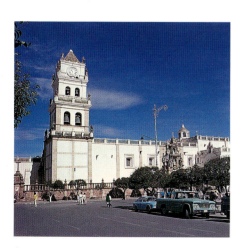

Sucre

BRAZIL

NAME **Serra de Capivara National Park.**

LOCATION State of Piaui. S 08° 25′ to 08° 55′, W42° 20′ to 42° 45′.

DESCRIPTION This park was established in 1979, after the systematic examination of more than 300 archaeological sites within the area was completed. The park borders two important geological formations: the Maranhao-Piaui basin and the Rio Sao Francisco depression. The main interest within the park is the series of shelters which have been hewn into the rock and the numerous rock-art paintings they contain.

SIGNIFICANCE This area preserves the oldest examples of rock-art on the South American continent. Some fragments have been dated back to 26,000BC. The oldest decipherable paintings date to 12,000BC. Most importantly, the paintings are providing an invaluable source of information on the religious and cultural practices of these early peoples. Four main cultural themes have been identified: dance, sexual practices, hunting rituals and rituals performed around trees. The dominant colour of the paintings is red. Several of the themes, such as the portrayal of human bodies heaped in pyramids, are so far incomprehensible.

FINLAND

NAME **Fortress of Suomenlinna.**

LOCATION Province of Uusimaa. N 60° 09′, E 24° 57′.

DESCRIPTION Suomenlinna is a bastion fortress, comprising a series of fortifications on 6 islands just off the coast of Helsinki. Construction of the walls is of granite, while the 190 buildings are brick. The area of the islands is 73ha (175ac). Four of the islands constitute a virtually enclosed fortress. In the middle there is a dockyard which was formed by blasting the seabed and damming between the islands. The adminis-

trative centre, the Great Courtyard of Susisaari, is also in the middle.

SIGNIFICANCE Work began on the construction of Sveaborg ('Swedish Fortress') in 1748, under orders from the Swedish Parliament. It was the largest construction project in Sweden in the 18th century, at the peak of activity the construction crew totalled more than 6,500. It was conceived to control entry into Helsinki and to provide a safe winter harbour. The name was changed to Suomenlinna ('Fortress of Finland') following Finland's independence in 1918. The unique conception and construction of this well preserved fortress provides a fascinating and invaluable study in military architecture.

NAME **Old Rauma.**

LOCATION Gulf of Botnia, Province of Turku et Pori. N 61° 07′, E 21° 30′ (approximately).

DESCRIPTION Rauma today is a modern city, but the old centre is intact and has been very well preserved even though it was decimated by fire in the early 17th century. The principal monuments of the old centre are the Franciscan Church and the City Hall.

SIGNIFICANCE Rauma is a remarkable example of an old Nordic timber city. It was originally built around a Franciscan monastery – the 15th century church which was attached to it still survives. It soon developed into an important harbour – now one of the oldest in Finland. The town is typical of the architecture of old northern European cities and it is without doubt one of the most beautiful and extensive examples that has survived.

FRANCE

NAME **Banks of the Seine in Paris.**

LOCATION Paris, Ile de France. N 48° 50′, E02° 21′.

DESCRIPTION The section of the Seine in this listing is based on the age-old distinction between Paris upstream and Paris downstream; upstream is the port and the centre of commercial river traffic, while downstream, the area encompassed by this listing, is the heart of aristocratic Paris. This area is bounded by Pont de Sully and Pont d'Iéna and includes Ile de la Cité and Ile Saint-Louis. There are numerous significant buildings and places along these banks, including: the Louvre Palace and Tuileries Gardens, Place Saint-Germaine-l'Auxerrois, Place de la Concorde, The Hôtel des Invalides, the Grand Palais and Petit Palais des Champs Elysées, Ecole Militaire, Champs-de-Mars, the Eiffel Tower, the Palais de Chaillot and the Trocadéro Gardens.

SIGNIFICANCE This world renowned riverside ensemble constitutes a remarkable example of urban architecture where the differing architectural styles of this great city's dynamic history are harmoniously and grandly displayed. The astounding density of masterpieces found in this area is not repeated anywhere around the world. Several of them were standard references for the spread of particular styles – such as Notre Dame which inspired countless Gothic constructions, or the Place de la Concorde and Invalides which

The Seine, Paris

both exerted considerable influence on the urban development of European capitals.

NAME **Notre Dame Cathedral, Palace of Tau and the former Abbey of Saint-Remi.**

LOCATION The town of Reims, region of Champagne Ardenne. N 49° 17′, E 04° 02′ (approximately).

DESCRIPTION This listing comprises three religious buildings in the old town of Reims. The predominantly Romanesque abbey dates back to the 11th century, when construction commenced on the site of St. Christopher's chapel. The cathedral of Notre Dame is classically Gothic in style, it replaced an older Carolingian church which was destroyed by fire in 1211. Construction was completed by the end of the 13th century. The archiepiscopal palace was built between 1498 and 1509.

SIGNIFICANCE Christianity was established in Reims by the middle of the 3rd century, when a bishropric was founded there. Several of the town's bishops were canonised, the most famous being St. Remigius (St. Remi). He annointed Clovis, the King of the Franks in Reims. Later kings desired to be annointed there with oil from the sacred phial which according to legend was sent from heaven by a dove for Clovis. This phial of oil was delivered from the abbey, where it was stored, to the cathedral, where the consecration took place. Later, a banquet was held in the palace, which was the episcopal see. So it may be seen that these buildings form an historical ensemble of considerable significance as they all played a role in the construction of the French sovereign. Architecturally they are also of considerable significance; Notre Dame is viewed as a masterpiece of Gothic art, while the abbey's perfect lines have exerted influence upon many subsequent churches, particularly in Germany.

GERMANY

NAME **Abbey and Altenmünster of Lorsch**

LOCATION The town of Lorsch, Hessen. N 49° 49′, E 08° 40′ (approximately).

DESCRIPTION This listing incorporates three principal elements: the site of the original monastery at Altenmünster (an island on the river), the monastery which was built on the riverbank to replace the earlier one, and the Carolingian gatehouse which is part of the later monastery. Within the largely intact walls of the later monastery, various buildings have been preserved: a nave of a Romanesque basilica, residential and administrative buildings, a tithe barn, and a bailiff's house and lodge. The gatehouse is well preserved and includes an impressive collection of wall murals and sculptures.

SIGNIFICANCE The first monastery was established around 764-765AD. The first Abbot was the Bishop of Metz who donated the relics of St Nazarius, which he had acquired from Rome. As its reputation grew, so did its population, resulting in plans for a new monastery which was duly built and consecrated in the presence of Charlemagne in 774. Improvements were made over the next century, culminating in it becoming, at the death of Louis II the German, the burial place for the Carolingian kings. This complex today represents a rare architectural and cultural document of the Carolingian era.

INDONESIA

NAME **Komodo National Park.**

LOCATION East Nusa Tenggara Province. S 08° 24′ to 08° 50′, E 119° 21′ to 119° 49′.

DESCRIPTION This rugged 219,322ha (526,372ac) park comprises a coastal section of western Flores, the islands of Komodo, Padar, Rinca and Gili Motong, as well as the surrounding waters of the Sape straights. All three islands are generally rocky, with the occasional sandy beach to be found in some of the sheltered bays. The section of coastal mainland is similar in topography, but with an abundance of freshwater, something lacking on the islands. There are extensive patches of coral reef as well as large areas of sea grass beds. The predominant land vegetation, covering 70% of the park, is open grass and woodland savanna. There are also cloud forests on the peaks, tropical forests along the valleys and mangrove forests in some of the sheltered bays. More than 70 species of birds have been recorded within the park. Mammals include primates, ungulates and a number of feral domestic species. The most famous inhabitant is the Komodo monitor, the world's largest lizard.

SIGNIFICANCE This dramatically beautiful park provides the only significant wild environment in the world for the Komodo monitor. The isolated and rugged nature of the park affords this magnificent and ancient lizard population of 5,700 the best chance of survival, as well as offering a rare glimpse of biological evolution at work. This area also has geological significance, being at the junction of the Asian and Australian tectonic plates.

NAME **Prambanan Temple Compound.**

LOCATION Central Java Province. S 07° 32′ to 08° 12′, E 110° 00′ to 110° 50′.

DESCRIPTION This compound is in fact an archaeological park, and includes the Loro Jonggrang Temple complex, the Sewu Temple complex and three temples which lie between. The Loro Jonggrang complex is Hindu (dedicated to Siva) and comprises three courtyards, adorned with hundreds of temples of various sizes. Many temples are in ruins, but restoration work is slowly reclaiming much of the complex's past glory. The Sewu complex is Buddhist and comprises one main temple and 240 minor temples over an area of 30,500sq m (329,000sq ft). There are four entrances, each guarded by giant statues. The three temples, Lumbung, Bubrah and Asu, which lie between the two complexes are in a state of ruin.

SIGNIFICANCE Loro Jonggrang, constructed during the first part of the 9th century, is the largest Siva ensemble in Indonesia. Its temples are extensively adorned with reliefs illustrating the life of the 3rd century Hindu hero Rama. The entire compound represents an outstanding example of Indonesian classical art, recalling an era when Central Javanese Culture was at is zenith.

NAME **Unjung Kulon National Park and Krakatau Nature Reserve.**

LOCATION West Java and Lampung. S 06° 45′, E 105° 20′.

DESCRIPTION This 76,119ha (182,685ac) park lies at the extreme south-western tip of Java, and comprises a section of the mainland as well as the Ujung Kulon peninsula and the islands of

Prambanan Temple Compound

Krakatau

Pulau Handeuleum, Pulau Panaitan and Pulau Peucang. Coastal features include coral islands and reefs to the north, and spectacular volcanic formations to the west. Vegetation encompasses lowland rainforest, palm forests, dense stands of bamboo, freshwater swamp forests, mangrove forests and grasslands. Krakatau Nature Reserve comprises the central island of Anak Krakatau, the peripheral islands of Rakata, Payang and Sertung and the surrounding coral reefs. Vegetation on this group varies from the early stages of biotic colonisation on the still active Setung to the extensive moss forests of Rakata. Fauna includes the Javan rhinoceros, several large carnivores, ungulates and primates. Around 300 species of birds have been recorded in the area, while the fish population is the richest in Indonesia.

SIGNIFICANCE   The Krakatau reserve presents the world's best known example of island vulcanism. The dramatic explosion of 1883 profoundly altered ecological processes in the area, today providing a remarkable opportunity to study biological colonisation and subsequent evolutionary processes on a tropical island. Ujung Kulon peninsula has the most extensive stand of lowland rainforest remaining on Java. There are several threatened species protected by this area, the most notable being the Javanese rhinoceros. This park provides this species with its only remaining viable natural refuge.

NAME   **Borobudur Temple Compound.**

LOCATION   Central Java Province. S 07° 07′, E 110° 10′.

DESCRIPTION   This compound comprises three temples: the main temple of Borobudur and two smaller ones to the east, Mendut and Pawon. The complex is built on several levels around a hill which forms a natural centre. The most striking visual feature of this ensemble is the main stupa of Borobudur which rises 35m (96ft) from the ground. Beneath the stupa, the base of the main temple is constructed in five square terraces. Above this are three circular platforms which are adorned by seventy-two smaller perforated stupas. Stairways provide access to the main stupa. Numerous reliefs decorate each of the temples, and there are many statues of Buddha in various sizes and positions. Construction is of stone and the masonry is to very high standard.

SIGNIFICANCE   Borobudur is one of the world's great Buddhist monuments. It was built around 800AD under orders from one of the Saliendra kings and represents the zenith of Indonesian Buddhist art. The complex was abandoned in the

Borobudur Temple Compound

11th century and was gradually consumed by the surrounding jungle. It was rediscovered in the 19th century and has undergone two major restoration programs.

MEXICO

NAME **The Historic Zone of Morelia.**

LOCATION The town of Morelia, State of Michoacan. N 21° 42′, W 101° 11′.

DESCRIPTION Despite the inevitable encroachment of modern urban development, Morelia has preserved its original structures very well. There are 249 historical monuments in total, most built from local pink stone. The layout of the old town is in the classical grid pattern that was commonly used in Spanish colonial towns. The most important buildings total 41, including 20 churches and a grand central cathedral.

SIGNIFICANCE In 1537 a Franciscan monastery was built near the Indian town of Guayangareo. The town was taken over by Spanish settlers and renamed Valladolid in 1541. The town became a bishop's see in 1580 and the College of St. Nicholas Obispo, an important institution of higher education, was transferred there. Economically and culturally, the town flourished throughout the 17th and 18th centuries. It was an important centre in the fight for Mexican independence early in the 19th century and was renamed Morelia in 1828 after the priest José Maria Morelos who was a principal figure in that struggle.

MOZAMBIQUE

NAME **Ihla de Mozambique.**

LOCATION Province of Nampula. S 15° 02′, E 40° 44′.

DESCRIPTION Ihla de Mozambique is a small urbanised island around 3km (1.9mi) long and averaging 300m (985ft) in width. It lies on a coral reef 4km (2.5mi) off the coast of the mainland. There are several monuments of importance: San Sebastian Fortress, San Paulo Palace and Chapel, San Domingos Convent, San Antonio Fortress, San Lourenco Fortress, the hospital church, the hospital and a mosque. Construction is mainly of ochre coloured limestone masonry, with white detailing and flat roofs. A smaller island, St. Laurent is also included in the listing.

SIGNIFICANCE Ihla de Mozambique was an Arab trading post from the early 10th century. The nature of society on the island changed dramatically after the arrival of the Portuguese explorer Vasco da Gama in 1498. It was established by the Portuguese as a station on the sea route to India and became the capital of Portuguese operations in Mozambique. The first fortress was built in 1508, construction of San Sebastian Fortress commenced 50 years later and was finished in 1620. San Paulo Palace, a Jesuit college, was established in 1610. Urban and commercial districts developed rapidly throughout the 17th and 18th centuries, resulting in the formation of a town council in 1761. At the

Historic centre of Lima

beginning of the 19th century, a new quarter was laid out in a grid pattern with a central square. Expansion continued until 1898, when the capital was transferred to the mainland. Today, the town and fortifications on Ihla de Mozambique, and the smaller island of St. Laurent, are beautifully preserved examples of a distinctive architectural style which blends local traditions, Portuguese influences, and to a lesser extent, Indian and Arab influences.

NIGER

NAME **The Strict Nature Reserve of Aïr and Ténéré.**

LOCATION Department of Agades. N 17° 12′ to 20° 30′, E 08° 06′ to 10° 57′.

DESCRIPTION This 77,360sq km (29,861sq mi) reserve includes the 12,805sq km (4,943sq mi) Sanctuary of Addax. The entire area lies within the Saharan region of Niger. It is arid, with an average rainfall of only 50mm (2in) per annum. There are two distinct zones, the extensive flat plain of the Ténéré desert, and the mountains of the Aïr which rise 2,000m (6,564ft) above it. Habitats are surprisingly diverse, including heavily wooded valleys and permanent rock pools in the mountains. Vegetation includes wild olives and figs, as well as the wild relatives of several important crops, such as millet and sorghum. There are significant populations of fauna, including 40 species of mammals, 165 birds, 18 reptiles and one amphibian. The mammals include several species of gazelles, Barbary sheep, monkeys, baboons, foxes and a small population of cheetah. Birds include the Nubian bustard and ostrich.

SIGNIFICANCE This reserve protects several species which are threatened with extinction, including three species of desert antelope – the addax, dama gazelle and slender-horned gazelle, and the last viable population of the West African race of the ostrich. Several animal populations, such as those of the olive baboon and patas monkey, have been isolated in the Aïr mountains for thousands of years and thus constitute a unique genetic heritage. The rare beauty of this environment is constantly undergoing change as the desert sands shift, endlessly eroding and modifying the many relict ecosystems that are of outstanding value to the world's hertiage.

PERU

NAME **Historic Centre of Lima.**

LOCATION Lima. N 12° 03′, W 77° 01′ (approximately).

DESCRIPTION Though separate, this listing is an extension to the Convent Ensemble of San Francisco listing. The historic centre of the town is located on the two banks of the Rio Rimac and includes numerous significant monuments: the University of San Marcos, Descalzos Monastery, Torre Tagle Palace, the Plaza de Armas, as well as the entire quarter between the Plaza de Armas and San Francisco monastery.

SIGNIFICANCE The old centre of Lima presents an outstanding example of the zenith of architectural and urban development in Spanish Peru. This exceptionally well preserved Spanish colonial town was of enormous economic, political and cultural importance to the growth of Latin America and so stands today as a tremendously valuable part of our heritage.

ROMANIA

NAME **Danube Delta Biosphere Reserve.**

LOCATION Tulcea Country. N 45° 00′, E 29° 00′ (approximate mid-point).

DESCRIPTION This 547,000ha (1,312,800ac) reserve is vast in European terms. It encompasses the delta of one of Europe's most important rivers, where it drains into the Black Sea, and includes numerous freshwater lakes and interconnecting channels, large areas of aquatic vegetation, floating islands of decaying organic matter and extensive marshlands. There are also several brackish lagoons, separated from the sea by sandbars. Areas of dry land support stands of forest, with oak, willow, poplar and alder predominating. More than 300 species of birds have been recorded, and it is an important breeding ground, with over 176 species regularly nesting. Fish numbers are also significant, more than 45 freshwater varieties are known. Otters, weasels and minks are also present.

SIGNIFICANCE This large alluvial delta is the second largest delta in Europe (the Volga is the largest) and provides a crucial wetland habitat for many migratory birds and other fauna. It contains the largest continuous marshland in Europe and the greatest stretch of reed beds in the world. The sheer scale and immense diversity of this wetland habitat is of critical value to the species it protects as well as to our body of human knowledge and understanding.

SPAIN

NAME **Monastery of Santa Maria de Poblet.**

LOCATION Cataluña. N 41° 30′, E 01° 00′ (approximately).

DESCRIPTION This complex comprises numerous structures and buildings from various eras. The focus centres around the large Cistecian abbey. North of this is a group of monastic buildings, including a cloister, fountain, chapter room, monks' dormitory, parlour, library, calefactory, refectory and kitchens. To the west are the lay brothers' buildings (which were later partially converted to a royal residence), while to the north is the infirmary. Within the complex, there is an inner wall 608m (1,968ft) in length which is 2m (7ft) thick with crenelated battlements, walkways, towers and a gateway.

SIGNIFICANCE Poblet has a fascinating history that is reflected in the diverse nature of its architectural forms. The blend of architectural styles is unusual in that the major functions of Cistercian monastery, military fortress and royal palace, residence and pantheon were all served within its boundaries. The monastery was founded in 1150 by the Cistercian monks of Fontfroide. It was fortified and transformed to serve these other functions during the 14th century by Peter IV the Ceremonious, King of Aragon. The entire complex is a unique artistic achievement and represents the zenith of the Cistercian style which endured throughout the 12th, 13th and 14th centuries.

SRI LANKA

NAME **The Golden Rock Temple of Dambulla.**

LOCATION District of Matale, Central Province. N 07° 59′, E 80° 38′.

DESCRIPTION This Buddhist cave-temple complex is found on a 25ha (60ac) area of Dambulla rock which rises 122m (400ft) above the surrounding plain. There are five caves and the remains of 80 rock shelters within the complex. The main cave temple is about 609m (2,000ft) in length and 33m (110ft) wide. The caves contain 157 statues of various sizes and over 1,951sq m (21,000sq ft) of painted surfaces. Remarkably, the complex is largely excavated – there being few natural caves or shelters.

SIGNIFICANCE This site has been in continuous use for over 22 centuries, since the time of its initial occupation by a Buddhist monastic establishment, just after the introduction of the religion to the island. It is the largest and best preserved cave-temple complex in Sri Lanka, and the second largest such complex in southern and south-eastern Asia. Of particular value is the art work found on the walls of the caves, notably

Drottningholm Palace

the exceptionally well preserved 18th century paintings from the Kandy school. Archaeological excavations in the area immediately surrounding the rock has revealed evidence of earlier occupation, dating back four millenia.

SWEDEN

NAME **Drottningholm Palace.**

LOCATION Queen's Island, Lake Malar, Province of Stockholm. N 58° 30', E 17° 00' (approximately).

DESCRIPTION The ensemble at Drottningholm includes the palace, a theatre, formal garden, English park, Chinese pavilion and a Gothic tower. Of particular interest are the perfectly preserved and functioning 18th century theatre and the Chinese pavilion which demonstrates the curious blend of French and Chinese styles that was typical of the period.

SIGNIFICANCE The first royal residence was built on the island at the end of the 16th century under Queen Catherine Jagellon. A century later Queen Hedvig-Eleonora ordered a new castle built, work that took almost a hundred years. During the middle of the 18th century, Crown Princess Lovisa-Ulrika had extensions, including a library and a portrait gallery, added. In 1766, when she was queen, she had the theatre built. The entire ensemble was sympathetically restored early this century and it now stands as a splendid example of an 18th century royal residence, typically influenced by the design of the Palace of Versailles.

THAILAND

NAME **Historic City of Ayutthaya.**

LOCATION Ayutthaya Province, N 14° 20', E 101° 33'.

DESCRIPTION The remains of this city, the second capital of Siam, are situated on an island at the junction of the Lopburi and Pasak rivers. The oval shaped city was once enclosed by 12km (7.5mi) of fortified walls, only segments of which remain. The ruins of the old royal palace are located at the centre of the island and at the heart of the present day historical park. To the north, is the largely intact palace of the crown prince which houses a museum. Numerous *wat* (monasteries and temples) are scattered throughout the city, some of these predate the establishment of Ayutthaya as the capital.

SIGNIFICANCE Ayutthaya was established as the capital of Siam, after the decline of the Sukothai kingdom, on March 4th, 1351 by King U-Thong and remained so until 1767 when it was razed by the Burmese. Throughout these four centuries of rule, the city experienced rich and varied relations with many countries, including neighbours such as Vietnam, Cambodia, Indonesia, Laos, Malaysia and Burma as well as Europe, China, Japan and Persia. This enormous depth of influence resulted in the development of extremely complex forms of art and architectural styles which are so distinctive of Thai culture today.

Sukothai

NAME **Sukhothai and Associated Towns.**

LOCATION Sukothai and Kamphaeng Provinces. N 16° 21' to 17° 26', E 99° 27' to 99° 48'.

DESCRIPTION There are three former cities in this listing, all now archaeological sites: Sukothai, Si Satchanalai and Kamphaeng Phet. All have walls and moats, special forested areas outside the walls which were for the use of Buddhist monks and numerous Buddhist temples constructed of brick. It is thought that the royal palaces that once graced the sites would have been constructed of timber and hence left no traces. The remains of kilns are found outside the walls of Sukothai and Si Satchanalai, once used to produce the famous Sangkalok ceramics. Sukothai shows the remains of an intricate system of canals, reservoirs and ponds which was typical of Khmer settlements before the rise of the Sukothai kingdom. The other two cities were built on rivers and adapted their layout to take advantage of the water flow.

SIGNIFICANCE During the 12th century, people from Yunnan in China settled in the northern parts of the Khmer state. They were known as *Thai*, meaning 'free men', and they quickly organised themselves into small communities. The first Siamese state, the kingdom of Sukothai, was formed after a Thai prince married a Khmer woman, rebelling against the controlling powers. This prince's second son, Rama the Strong, became a powerful sovereign, achieving numerous military victories and bringing with them much new territory. He invented the Thai alphabet, introduced strict Buddhist influence and organised a social order based on the vanquished Khmer neighbours. So the Sukothai culture was born and rapidly developed.

These three towns present a remarkable record of the emergence of the Siamese culture.

NAME **Thung Yai-Huai Kha Khaeng Wildlife Sanctuary.**

LOCATION Kanchanaburi, Tak and Uthai Thani Provinces, on the Burmese border. N 14° 56' to 15° 48', E 98° 27' to 99° 28'.

DESCRIPTION The neighbouring wildlife sanctuaries of Thung Yai and Huai Kha Khaeng together cover an area of 320,000ha (790,700ac). Both are generally hilly with many permanent and seasonal streams dissecting the landscape into small valleys and plains. A distinguishing feature of Thung Yai is the large central grassland plain from which it takes its name ('big field'). There are numerous small lakes, ponds and swamps, both permanent and seasonal, as well as many limestone sink holes. The many forests vary, with evergreen on the higher slopes and mixed deciduous and bamboo across the most of the lower areas. Almost 4,000 tribal people live within the area.

SIGNIFICANCE This is one of Thailand's least accessible and hence least disturbed forest areas. It supports numerous endemic species, as well as at least 28 rare or endangered species. More than one-third of Southeast Asia's mammal species are present, while the dry tropical forest which is typical here is the most complete in Southeast Asia. It is also an area at the crossroads of several biogeographic zones – it contains elements of each of the Sino-Himalayan, Sundaic, Indo-Burmese and Indo-Chinese zones. Its importance in preserving two large watersheds for the region cannot be overstated.

Ayutthaya

PHOTO CREDITS

Fred Salaff, FPG International; p. 282, Giraudon Paris; p. 282, S. Mutal, UNESCO Photo Library; p. 276, David Brownell, The Image Bank; pp. 278, 279, Westlight, Australian Picture Library; p. 280, Roger Drury; p. 277, Richard Bermannm, Photo Researchers Inc.; p. 280, A. LaBastille, WWF Photo Library; p. 282, S. Mutal, UNESCO Photo Library; pp. 286, 287, Bruno Barby, Magnum; p. 283, UNESCO Photo Library; p. 285, J. N. Hagar, Research Plus; p. 285, J. N. Hagar, Research Plus; p. 284, J. N. Hagar, Research Plus; p. 283, Bruno Barby, Magnum; p. 290, Donna Carroll, Research Plus; p. 291, Rob Atkins, The Image Bank; p. 293 John Bowen, Research Plus; pp. 288, 289, Australian Picture Library; p. 289, Buddy Mays, Research Plus; pp. 294, 295, Noboru Komine, Photo Researchers Inc.; p. 292, J. N. Hagar, Research Plus; p. 297, Jacques Versoru; p. 297, Michele Burgess, Research Plus; p. 296, Kindermann; pp. 298, 299, Buddy Mays, Research Plus; p. 299, Gilles Peress, Magnum; p. 302, Art Resource NY; p. 309, Gian Berto Vanni, Art Resource; p. 314, Juan A. Fernandez, INCAFO; pp. 300, 301, David Ball, Australian Picture Library; p. 311, Breval; p. 307, Scala; pp. 304, 305, Australian Picture Library; p. 306, Gian Berto Vanni, Scala/Art Resource NY; p. 311, Juan A. Fernandez, INCAFO; pp. 314, 315, Australian Picture Library; pp. 312, 313, Australian Picture Library; p. 302, Scala/Art Resource NY; p. 310, Candy Lopesino/Juan Hidalgo, INCAFO; p. 301, P. & G. Bowater, Australian Picture Library; p. 308, FPG International; p. 308, Gian Berto Vanni, Art Resource; p. 303, S. Vidler, Australian Picture Library; p. 322, Noboru Komine, Photo Researchers Inc.; pp. 320, 321, K. Reinhard, FPG International; pp. 316, 317, Koboru Komine, Photo Researchers Inc., p. 319, Luke Golobitsh; p. 318, M. Rautkari, WWF Photo Library; p. 314, Swiss National Tourist Office; p. 324, J.M. Reyero & A. Sacristan, INCAFO; p. 322, 323, Jess Lopatynski; p. 323, FPG International; pp. 326, 327, Brian Brake, Photo Researchers Inc.; p. 331, A. Larramendi, INCAFO; p. 331, A. Larramendi, INCAFO; p. 326, Noboru Komine, Photo Researchers Inc.; pp. 326, 327, DeGeorges, UNESCO Photo Library; p. 336, DASET, Australia; p. 338, Werner Forman/Art Resource NY; p. 338, Werner Forman/Art Resource NY; p. 332, Burt Glinn, Magnum; pp. 332, 333, p. Tevis, FPG International; pp. 334, 335, Dr. Claude Martin, WWF Photo Library; p. 336, Buddy Mays, Research Plus; p. 337, Buddy Mays, Research Plus; p. 340, Frédy Mercay, WWF Photo Library; p. 342, FPG International; p. 343, FPG International; p. 341 ICOMOS; p. 343 FPG International; p. 339, Gian Berto Vanni, Art Resource NY; p. 340, Gian Berto Vanni, Art Resource NY; p. 341, Gian Berto Vanni, Art Resource NY; p. 347, FPG International; p. 354, ICOMOS; p. 352, Susan Kuklin, Photo Researchers Inc.; p. 353, AM Picture Library; pp. 348, 349, AM Picture Library; pp. 350, 351, Australian Picture Library; pp. 344, 345, Charles Bowman, Australian Picture Library; p. 355, Gian Berto Vanni, Art Resource NY; p. 368, FPG International; p. 358, Bullaty Lomeo, The Image Bank; pp. 362, 363, Australian Picture Library; p. 369, Australian Picture Library; p. 365, Erich Hartmann, Magnum; pp. 366, 367, Australian Picture Library; pp. 373, Annette Parkes; pp. 364, 365, Ian Boyter; pp. 356, 357, David W. Hamilton, The Image Bank; p. 368, David W. Hamilton, The Image Bank; p.

361, Richard L. Hess, Research Plus; p. 361, Ed Vliek, Research Plus; p. 373, FPG International; p. 359, Bernard Van Berg, The Image Bank; pp. 370, 371, Australian Picture Library; p. 372, Richard L. Hess, Research Plus; pp. 378, 379, Buddy Mays, Research Plus; p. 392, M.G. Fernandez, INCAFO; p. 387, Helen Longest-Slaughter, Nature Images Inc.; pp. 376, 377, Tom Bynum; pp. 374, 375, Australian Picture Library; p. 393, Kenneth Layman, Photo Agora; p. 387, Australian Picture Library; p. 386, Michele Burgess, Research Plus; p. 381, Steve Vidler, Australian Picture Library; p. 389, Steve Satushek, The Image Bank; pp. 384, 385, Mary Ann Hemphill, Research Plus; p. 376, Michele Burgess, Research Plus; p. 382, 383, FPG International; pp. 390, 391, Australian Picture Library; p. 380, Marvin E. Newman, The Image Bank; p. 388, D. & J. Heaton, Australian Picture Library; pp. 396, 397, Bill Holden, Australian Picture Library; pp. 398, 399, Dominique Roger, UNESCO Photo Library; p. 395, INCAFO; p. 398, D. & J. Heaton, Australian Picture Library; pp. 398, 399, Steve Vidler, Australian Picture Library; p. 396, INCAFO; p. 395, 396, Bob & Ira Spring, FPG International; p. 401, Werner Forman/Art Resource NY; p. 400, Gerard Champlong, The Image Bank; pp. 404, 405, Scala; p. 407, Steve McCurry, Magnum; p. 406, Margot Granitsas; p. 408, Dr. Srecko Bozicevic; p. 408, Dr. Srecko Bozicevic; p. 406, Gian Berto Vanni, Art Resource NY; p. 410, Dr. Srecko Bozicevic; pp. 402, 403, FPG International; p. 411, Scala; p. 413, Jacques Vershuren; p. 411, INCAFO; p. 412, Jacques Verschuren; p. 413, Jacques Verschuren; pp. 414, 415, AM Picture Library; pp. 416, 417, Robert Aberman, Art Resource NY; p. 419, Robert Aberman, Art Resource NY; p. 420, Jim Tuten, FPG International; p. 423, The Image Bank; pp. 429, 430, 431, 432, 433, 434, 435, The Australian Picture Library.

ACKNOWLEDGEMENTS

The Publisher and Managing Editor gratefully acknowledge the invaluable assistance of the countless individuals and organisations who worked so tirelessly in the massive task of compiling and producing this book. We especially thank the many Consulate and Embassy staff who were all so enthusiastic in offering their assistance, and all of the following:

Abhinav Publications (India), Advisory Council on Historic Preservation (USA), Peter Ambrosy, An Taisce (The National Trust for Ireland), Mr. Bertalan Andrasfaly – the Hungarian Minister of Culture, Association Culturelle Franco-Australienne, Australian Council of Churches, Australian Department of Arts, Sport, the Environment and Territories, Australian National Parks and Wildlife Service – Jabiru NT, Nick Baker, Baltic Marine Environment Protection Commission, Frank Barnaby, Nigel Blackburn, Bolivian National Academy of Sciences, Gunnar Brusewitz, Bill Burford, Cairns Rainforest Unit, Cathy Carey, China Pictorial, Claretian Publications (Philippines), Les Clubs UNESCO, Columban Fathers Mission Awareness Philippines/Australia, Conservation International, Council of Europe, Cultural Survival Inc., Julie Curtis, Jean-Paul Delamotte, The East African Wildlife Society, Han Ebbeling, Egyptian

Antiquities Organisation, Endangered Wildlife Trust (South Aftica), Professor Feisal A. Esmael, European Council for Environmental Law, Faber and Faber Limited Publishers, The Faculty of Agricultural Science at Gembloux (Belgium), FAO, Freshwater Biological Laboratory at the University of Copenhagen, Gaia Books Limited, German Society of Mammalogists, Ivan P. Haskovec, Vaclav Havel, Marc Heberden, Mr. Nigel Hepper, Prof. Wolfe Herre, Howard University Press (USA), Bernie Huggins, ICOMOS Archives, Institute for European Environmental Policy, International Association of Fish and Wildlife Agencies (USA), International Chamber of Commerce, International Commission for the Protection of the Alps, International Council for Bird Preservation (UK), International PEN, Institute for Environmental Education (Netherlands), Japan Centre for Human Environmental Problems, Dr. Hussein R. Kazem, Kosei Publishing Company (Japan), Dr. Volker Kregel, The Landscape Institute (UK), D. Vaughan Lewis, Ronald Lockley, Mairead Maguire, A. F. Mark – Professor of Botany at the University of Otago in New Zealand, Ministry of the Environment in the Sultanate of Oman, National Parks Association of NSW Inc., National Park Foundation (USA), The National Society for the Conservation of Nature (France), National Trust for Historic Preservation (USA), New Caledonian Association for the Protection of Nature, Newtown Secretarial, Warren Nicholls, Nonesuch Expeditions Ltd. (UK), John Noonan, Norwegian Literature Abroad, NSW National Parks and Wildlife Service, Herbert Ochtman, Organisation of Eastern European States, Oxford University Press, Kevin Parker, The Poetry Society (UK), Polish Ecological Club, Rex Collings Ltd. (UK), Royal Dutch Society for Natural History, Serengeti Wildlife Research Institute, Professor Drasco Serman, Adrian Sever, Jim Sharp, Cui Sigan, Gerard Sournia, Spanish Society of Natural History, Marea Stenmark, David Suzuki, Peter Tsounis, Turkish Association for the Conservation of Nature and Natural Resources, UNESCO Archives Department, United Nations Environment Programme (UNEP), The Venezuelan Foundation for the Conservation of Biological Diversity, Wildlife Clubs of Kenya, Prof. Dr. Napoleon Wolanski, World Council of Churches, WWF India, WWF International, Zoological Museum at the University of Copenhagen, Zoological Society of Glasgow and West Scotland, Zed Books (UK), Zimbabwe National Commission for UNESCO, Karel van der Zwiep.

SPECIAL THANKS TO:
  UNESCO's World Heritage Secretariat
  IUCN – The World Conservation Union
  Mme Mireille Jardin, Division of Ecological Sciences, UNESCO
  Mr. Jay D. Hair, National Wildlife Federation (USA)
  Mr. Russell Train, World Wildlife Fund (USA)
  Mr. Byron Swift, IUCN – The World Conservation Foundation
  The UNESCO Courier
  The UNESCO Photo Library and Mme Michelle Spinelli

The sheer size and complexity of the project have no doubt caused some names to be omitted from these acknowledgements. We apologise if this is the case and invite such people to contact the publisher so that any oversights may be corrected in the next edition.

Glossary of Terms

acropolis Fortified part of ancient Greek city, it was usually built on an elevated position and housed the temple for the city's patron deity.

adobe Sun-dried brick.

agora Section of ancient Greek city set aside for public meetings and markets.

aisle One of the divisions to the side of a *basilica* parallel to he nave, but not as high.

alcove Recess in wall, usually arched.

Almohads 12th and 13th century *Berber* rulers based in Marrakesh, Morocco.

alter Flat-topped construction at one end of a church or temple where offerings are made to God and where Communion is held.

andesite A type of volcanic rock.

antechamber Secondary chamber, usually providing access to the primary chamber.

Apollo Ancient Greek god, the son of Zeus.

apse Large recess at one end of a church, often semicircular with a domed roof.

aqueduct A structure built for the transference of water; typically elevated and supported by a series of arches.

archiepiscopal Pertaining to an archbishop

architrave The lowest position of a *classical entablature.*

ashlar Trimmed, regular masonry with flat surfaces and square edges.

Asia Minor The Asian part of the modern state of Turkey.

Assyrians The inhabitants of Assyria, one of the two ancient Mesopotamian kingdoms (see *Babylonians*) during the 1st and 2nd millenniums BC. Assyria was to the north, corresponding to that area of modern day Iraq which is north of Baghdad.

Aztecs A major Indian group of the Americas, they inhabited what is now part of Mexico and rapidly developed a powerful and extensive empire. Their civilisation declined in the early 16th century with the arrival of the Spanish.

azure Sky blue.

Babylonians The inhabitants of Babylon, the nation which, along with *Assyria*, comprised the two ancient kingdoms of Mesopotamia. Babylonia was to the south, corresponding to that area of modern day Iraq which stretches between Baghdad and the Persian Gulf.

Bacchus Ancient Greek and Roman god of wine.

badlands Extensive area of highly eroded waste land.

balds Hills with no vegetation cover; 'grass bald' – grass cover only.

baptistery Originally a building where baptisms were held, now most often a part of a church used for that purpose.

baroque 17th century architectural style typified by dramatic lines and the free use of classical motifs.

basilica A large oblong building with a *nave,* an *apse* and *aisles,* originally a Roman law court, later adapted for use by Christians as a special type of church.

bas-relief See *relief.*

bastion That part of a fortification which projects out from the wall; designed so that the walls may be covered by defensive fire.

belfry A tower or part of a building which houses a bell.

Benedictines Order of monks founded in 529 AD by Saint Benedictine; founders of the herb flavoured brandy liqueur of the same name.

Berbers A broad grouping of Caucasoid peoples indigenous to northern Africa.

biota Animal and plant life found in a particular area.

boreal pertaining to the arctic, the north, or the north wind; from 'Boreas', the personification of the north wind in ancient Greek mythology.

Bretons Native inhabitants of Brittany, in the north of France.

Britons Native inhabitants of southern Britain before the Roman invasion.

bushmen A group of indigenous peoples from southern Africa.

buttress External structural support which is built against a wall.

byre Cow shed.

Byzantine empire The eastern Roman empire which was ruled from Constantinople over a period of 1100 years, from the 4th century to the 15th century AD.

caiman, cayman South American alligator.

cainozic (cenozoic) The third major era of Earth's geological history.

caldera Deep cavity on the summit of a volcano.

caliph Muslim civil and religious chief.

campanile Bell tower.

Canaanites The people who once inhabited Canaan, the ancient name for Palestine.

capital The upper part of a column.

Capital Ancient Roman temple to the god *Jupiter.*

caravanserai Public building in the middle east for the shelter of caravans and travellers; erected just outside town walls.

Carolingian Architectural style originating under Charlemagne around 800 AD.

Carthaginians People of Carthage, the north African city founded by the *Phoenicians* around 800 BC.

cartouche A tablet with an ornate frame.

Celts A broad grouping of western European peoples, including the *Gauls, Britons, Bretons, Irish, Gaels, Welsh* and *Manx.*

Chalukya The western and eastern Chalukyas were two ancient Indian dynasties.

chiaroscuro Patterns of light and shade.

Chimu South American Indians who inhabited Peru; conquered by the *Incas* in the mid 15th century AD.

choir That part of a church where the choir sits.

cist Box used to store sacred objects.

Cistercians An order of monks, also known as the White Monks.
Founded in the 12th century in Cîteaux, near Dijon in France.

citadel The main part of a city's fortifications.

classical Greek or Roman and their derivatives.

colonnade A row of columns.

conifer A tree which bears cone-like fruit.

corbel A horizontal support, projecting from a wall.

Corinthian One of the three *classical* architectural styles (see *Doric* and *Ionic*), featuring slender fluted columns with fillets, a high base and an ornate *capital.*

cornice The highest section of a *classical entablature.*

cosmogony Theory of the origin of the universe.

crampon Spiked plate affixed to boot to facilitate walking on ice or other slippery surfaces.

crenellations A series of merlons (section of solid wall) and *embrasures* (gaps for shooting through) in a defensive wall.

Creataceous A period of the *Mezosoic* Era.

cruciform Cross-shaped; particularly with respect to the floor plan of a *basilica* or church.

crusades A series of western European Christian expeditions instigated between the late 11th century and the mid 15th century to reclaim the Holy Land, including Jerusalem, from the Muslims.

cupola A small dome, forming part of a roof structure.

curassow Ground bird found in Latin America.

cycad A palm-like plant of the family Cycadaceae.

Dark Ages A term loosely applied to the period between the 5th and 10th centuries AD; refers to the lack of cultural advancement during those years.

deciduous A tree which renews its leaves every year.

didgeridoo Australian aboriginal musical instrument.

Doric First and least complicated of the three *classical* architectural styles (see *Corinthian* and *Ionic*); characterised by the absence of a base, short, sharply fluted columns and an unadorned *capital.*

duiker Bird; type of cormorant.

ecosystem A localised habitat of interacting organisms.

Elamites The peoples from Elam, the Biblical name for an area now forming the south western Iranian province of Khuzistan. The Elamite empire lasted from the third millennium BC until the rise of the *Persians* around 550 BC.

embrasure 1. The bevelling in a wall next to a door or window.
2. An opening in a fortification for a gun.

endemic Restricted to a given area; used to indicate the strictly local occurrence of flora or fauna.

entablature Applied to classical architecture, everything above the columns.

ewer Type of water jug.

fecundity Fertility.

flying buttress A *buttress* which is in the form of half arch and is positioned against that part of the external wall where an internal arch or vault is exerting outward lateral thrust.

fresco Painting which is applied to a wall while the plaster is still wet.

frieze That part of the *entablature* between the architrave and the cornice; often applied to the horizontal band of sculpture or painting found in this area.

funicular railway A cable-operated railway with counterbalanced ascended and descending cars.

gable The triangular end-part of a ridged roof (gable roof); called a *pediment* in classical architecture. Also, by extension, the triangular area over a doorway.

Gaels Gaelic speaking *Celts*.

Gauls Inhabitants of a large area, known by the Romans as Gaul, which covered what is now France and Belgium, with parts of northern Italy, Germany, Holland and Switzerland.

glacier Large, moving mass of ice formed by the accumulation of snow.

Gondwana The ancient name for a part of India which is now covered by the state of Madhya Pradesh.

Gondwanaland The name for the massive continent of ancient geological times which it is thought embraced Africa, India, Australia, New Zealand, Antarctica and South America.

Gothic An architectural style of medieval Europe characterised by the *flying buttress,* the *pointed arch* and the ribbed *vault*.

Hammam Arabic poet and satirist who lived between 641 and 728 AD; also known as Al-Farazdaq.

Hanseatic League Commercial and political confederation of northern German towns dating back to the 13th century.

Hellenism A term used to denote ancient Greek culture in all its phases; sometimes used more specifically for the latter phases.

Hermaphrodite Animal having characteristics of both sexes.

hieroglyphs Broadly, any system of writing utilising pictures.

hippodrome Ancient Greek and Roman arena for chariot races.

Hittites Ancient people who ruled over a large area of *Asia Minor* and Syria between 2000 and 1200 BC.

hummock Small hill, especially in marshland.

Huns Warlike, nomadic, Asian people who invaded Europe during the 4th and 5th centuries AD.

Hyksos Asiatic people who were the first to invade Egypt, during the 17th century BC.

hypogeum An underground chamber.

Iberia The peninsular which comprises Spain and Portugal.

ICOMOS International Council of Monuments and Sites.

icon A sacred painting, image, statue, etc; particular to the eastern Orthodox church.

Illyrians An ancient Greek name for the inhabitants of the Balkan coast of the Adriatic Sea.

Imam A title in the Muslim world with three senses:
1. the leader of all of Islam;
2. the leader of prayers in the mosque;
3. an honorary title conferred upon leading theologians.

Incas The people indigenous to that area now known as Peru, before the Spanish conquest.

incunabulum Early stages of development.

Indus Historically and geographically one of the great rivers of the world, the Indus rises in Tibet and drains into the Arabian sea. Along with the Tigris/Euphrates and the Nile, its valleys formed one of the main 'cradles of civilisation'.

Ionic One of the three *classical* orders of architectural style (see *Doric* and *Corinthian*), characterised by tall, slender columns with fluting, an elegantly moulded base and a capital with a spiral.

Isis The most well known of the ancient Egyptian goddesses, Isis was the daughter of Keb (earth) and Nut (sky) and was supreme in magic, cunning and knowledge.

isthmus Narrow strip of land which connects two larger land masses.

IUCN International Union for the Conservation of Nature and Natural Resources – The World Conservation Union.

Jupiter The chief Roman god, equivalent to the Greek's *Zeus*.

karst A region with a naturally formed system of underground drainage.

kasbah (casbah) The arab quarter of a northern African city, usually situated near the *citadel*.

Knights of St. John Strictly known as the Knights of the Order of the Hospital of Saint John of Jerusalem, this Order was founded in Jerusalem in 1099 AD after the victories of the first *crusade*.

Koran The sacred text of Islam; a collection of Muhammad's teachings.

Kurds Iranian speaking people who live mainly across an arc shaped area which extends from western Iran, through northern Iraq, the Armenian S.S.R. and across to eastern Turkey.

lacustrine Pertaining to a lake or lakes.

lahar Flow of volcanic mud.

loess plateau Plateau built up of a fine, light coloured dust deposited by the wind; extremely fertile.

loggia An open-sided gallery or arcade.

Macedonia A *Hellenistic* state that existed for a relatively brief period until 146 BC, until its most famous ruler, Alexander the Great, died and it became a Roman province.

Madrasah A large quadrangular building with an inner courtyard and a single doorway, peculiar to central Asia.

manatee Sea-cow.

Manichaean Describes the religion of Mani, a *Babylonian* prophet.

Manx The *Celtic* inhabitants of the Isle of Man.

martyrium Place of burial for martyrs or saints.

Mausoleum A richly adorned tomb, usually of a ruler.

Mayans A large grouping of American Indians indigenous to Central America.

medieval Used synonymously with *middle ages*.

megalithic Constructed with large stones.

Melanesian Members of dark-skinned race indigenous to the western Pacific islands.

Mesoamerica The name generally applied to that section of Central America which is considered to have constituted a cultural unity in pre-Columbian times; it includes central and southern Mexico, Guatemala, parts of Honduras, El Salvador and British Honduras.

Mesolithic The middle *Stone Age* period; from about 8000 to 2700 BC.

Mesopotamia Literally, 'the land between the rivers', those rivers being the Tigris and the Euphrates. The exect boundaries of this ancient land are open to interpretation, but Mesopotamia is generally considered to have encompassed *Babylonia* in the south and *Assyria* in the north.

Mesozoic The second major era of Earth's geological history.

midden Prehistoric refuse dump.

middle ages In a broad sense, the period between the 6th and 16th centuries AD.

minaret The turret connected to a mosque from which the *muezzin* calls at prayer hour.

Mogul The Arabic and Persian form of 'Mogul'; used, somewhat inaccurately, to describe the Indian dynasty founded in 1526 AD by Baber.

monastery The residence of a community of monks.

montane Pertaining to mountainous country.

Moors A group of Muslim people inhabiting north western Africa, of mixed Arab and *Berber* descent.

moraine Rocky debris deposited by glacial movement.

moufflon Wild mountain sheep.

mudejar 1. Moors who were converted to Christianity in medieval Spain;
2. The style of architecture developed by these people.

muezzin Person who proclaims the hour of prayer from a *minaret*.

Mughal See *Mogul*.

narthex Vestibule of an early Christian church.

nave The central space of a *basilica*; the body of a church.

necropolis An ancient cemetery.

neolithic The later period of the *Stone Age*

New World The western hemisphere; especially relating to Spanish colonial times in reference to the Americas.

Normans Scandinavian people who settled in *Gaul*, founded Normandy, then made colonies in the British Isles and Italy.

obsidian Dark volcanic glass-like rock.

oracle   In ancient times, a place of divine communication; often used to describe the person who effected the communications.

ossuary   Storage place for bones of the dead; often a cave where prehistoric bones are found.

Ottoman empire   A powerful empire, founded by Osman, which ruled from Constantinople for around 650 years, falling early in the 20th century.

palaeolithic   The earliest period of the *Stone Age*.

palaeozoic   The first major era of Earth's geological history.

Pali   Language used in Buddhist texts.

Pallavas   Ruling Indian dynasty, c.6th century AD.

pangolin   Type of ant eater; found in Asia and Africa.

pediment   See *gable*.

Persians   The inhabitants of Persia, the old name for Iran. The Persian or Iranian empire dates back to the beginning of the 1st millennium BC.

pelagic   Used to describe those fish which dwell in the upper layers of the open ocean.

Phoenicians   The inhabitants of Phoenicia, the ancient name for the coastal region stretching from modern day Syria down to Lebanon.

pilaster   A column with a rectangular cross section, usually attached to a wall as a decoration, serving no structural function.

plate tectonics   A theory which attempts to explain seismicity, volcanism and mountain building in terms of the motions of plates (rigid segments of the Earth's outer shell).

Pleistocene   One of the 7 epochs that constitute the *Cainozoic* era.

Pliny the Elder   Celebrated Roman author and historian who lived between 24 and 79 AD.

podocarps   A large family of conifers.

pointed arch   Arch formed by two curves meeting at an angle.

Polynesian   Indigenous inhabitants of Polynesia, a scattered group of islands in the eastern Pacific Ocean which includes New Zealand, Samoa and Hawaii, amongst others.

portal   Highly decorated doorway.

portico   *Colonnaded* porch at the entrance to a building.

pre-Columbian   Relating to the Americas; that time in history before the explorations of Christopher Columbus.

Proteaceae   A family of flowering plants which are usually found in arid country.

Punic   Of or pertaining to the *Carthaginians*.

rampart   Walkway on top of a defensive wall; also used to describe the fortifications themselves.

Ramsar Convention.   Convention on Wetlands of International Importance Especially as Waterfowl Habitat; initiated in Ramsar, Iran in 1971.

ravelin   Exterior part of fortifications.

refectory   Room in monasteries etc, used for meals.

relief   Carvings on a surface that are raised up against the background; high relief (*haut-relief*) is deeply cut, low relief (*bas-relief*) is more shallow.

Renaissance   Term used to describe the period at the end of the *middle ages*, when there was a remarkable revival in the arts under the influence of the ancient classics. The term also describes the art and architecture which emanated from this period.

rococo   An architectural style prevalent in 18th century Europe, characterised by flowing lines, arabesque ornamentation and ornate *stucco* work.

sacristry   The room in a church where the ceremonial devices are stored.

sanctuary   1. A holy place;
   2. Architecturally, that part of a church which contains the main alter.

Sangha   Early order of Buddhist monks.

sarcophagus   Coffin constructed of engraved stonework.

Sassanians   The ruling dynasty in the Persian empire from 211 to 651 AD.

savanna (savannah)   Landscape of grass plains with few trees in tropical and subtropical regions.

Saxons   Germanic people who inhabited what is now northern Germany around the 2nd century AD; they conquered parts of Britain during the 5th and 6th centuries.

scree   Unstable, rock-covered mountainside.

Semites   The name for those descended from Shem, the son of Noah (Genesis 10:21). These include the Jews, Arabs, *Phoenicians* and *Assyrians*.

Shamash   The semitic word for 'sun'; the *Semites'* sun-god. In the *Sumerian/Babylonian* religion, Shamash was the son of the moon-god Sin.

sherpa   Himalayan-dwelling people from Nepal and Tibet.

Siva   Along with Brahma and Vishnu, one of the three supreme Hindu gods.

slavs   Members of a broad grouping of central and eastern European peoples.

souk   A market place in Muslim countries.

stave   A curved piece of wood; in the case of a 'stave church', the staves are the tall posts which join the floor and roof beams.

stela (pl. -e)   Upright stone slab with inscription; usually a gravestone.

stucco   Plaster applied to walls with moulds as a form of decoration.

stupa   A round, usually domed, Buddhist building constructed of masonry, which is erected directly above a sacred relic.

sultan   Muslim ruler, especially relating to Turkish history.

Sumerians   Members of an advanced civilisation occupying *Babylonia* during the 3rd millennium BC; they developed the first written language.

Taoism   Religion based on the teachings of Lao-tse, a Chinese philosopher from around 500 BC.

tapir   A type of hoofed mammal.

Tartars (Tatars)   Indigenous inhabitants of a large area of central Asia, east of the Caspian Sea; predominantly Muslim.

tholos   Dome-shaped tomb.

Thracians   The inhabitants of Thrace, an area now occupied by northern Greece and Turkey. The original Thracians were a dark-skinned people who had been in the area since the *stone age*; later there came a marked *Celtic* influence. Their language was allied to Greek.

tipi (tepee)   Tent dwelling of some North American Indian tribes.

Toltecs   An American Indian tribe which inhabited central Mexico between the 10th and 12th centuries AD.

totem   An image of a natural object, usually an animal, which was commonly adopted amongst clans or individuals of northern American Indian tribes as an emblem representing kinship. A totem pole is a pole on which totems were hung or carved.

transept   Transverse section of a *cruciform* church, perpendicular to the *nave*.

tufa   Type of rock characteristically formed from sedimentation of mineral springs.

tundra   Treeless arctic landscape where the sub-soil is frozen.

UNESCO   United Nations Educational, Scientific and Cultural Organisation.

vault   A ceiling constructed of stone.

Venetians   Inhabitants of Venice.

vestibule   An *antechamber* situated next to the outer door of a building; the outer porch to a church.

Visigothic   A variation of the *Gothic* style of architecture.

Vision Quest   Spiritual ritual practised by some North American Indian tribes.

WWF   World Wide Fund for Nature; in Canada and the USA, World Wildlife Fund.

Zanatas (Zenatas)   An early Berber tribe of southern Morocco; the Beni Marin and Wattasi dynasties which reigned from 1213 to 1548, were Zanatas.

Zeus   The chief god of the ancient Greeks; the god of the weather and the sky.

ziggurat   Ancient *Mesopotamian* pyramidal temple.

zoomorphic   Pertaining to animal forms; commonly refers to religions which have their gods represented by animal forms.

As we approach the year 2000, we would do well to think back a thousand years to the Dark Ages. At that time, monks hand-copied ancient manuscripts to preserve knowledge. A millenium later, species and their genetic manuscripts — whole biological libraries and the ecosystems that sustain them — are disappearing every day. Like the ancient scribes, we cannot predict the ultimate value of what we are trying to save. We only know that, collectively, the threatened biological treasures of our planet are resources we cannot afford to lose.

PARKS IN PERIL, *Nature Conservancy*

INDEX

Late in June 1991, the International Chamber of Commerce (ICC) reported that almost half of the top 50 companies in the Fortune 500 list of the world's biggest industrial corporations had expressed support in writing for the Business Charter for Sustainable Development. The origins of the Charter go back nearly 20 years. Its core consists of 16 short principles for environmental management. The first emphasise the general priority that should be given to environmental considerations, while later points take up specific matters such as research, precautionary approach and emergency preparedness.

Many companies see the Charter as a major response to governmental and activist pressures for environmental 'codes of conduct'. The key question remains the diligence with which supporters follow up the Charter. The public listing of these supporters is seen as an encouragement to them to take this seriously, for the lists will certainly be scrutinised carefully by public authorities, environmental associations, their own workforce, as well as 'green' investor fund managers and the like.

NIGEL BLACKBURN
Director, International Chamber of Commerce

Reflecting the spirit of the ICC's Charter, the Publisher gratefully acknowledges the invaluable assistance and support received from the following organisations which made the production of this important publication possible:

Hitachi Data Systems Australia Pty Ltd
11-17 Khartoum Road
North Ryde, NSW 2113. Australia
Tel: 2-887 4455, Fax: 2-887 2624

Ingersoll-Rand Australia Ltd
80-110 Frankston Road
Dandenong, VIC 3175. Australia
Tel: 3-794 1611, Fax: 3-794 5105

Ambrosy & Fox, Solicitors
417 Malvern Road
South Yarra, VIC 3141. Australia
Tel: 3-827 4355, Fax: 3-826 0837

Holman Webb, Solicitors and Attorneys
14th Floor, 167 Macquarie Street
Sydney, NSW 2000. Australia
Tel: 2-221 1888, Fax: 2-221 6016

WORLD HERITAGE SITES

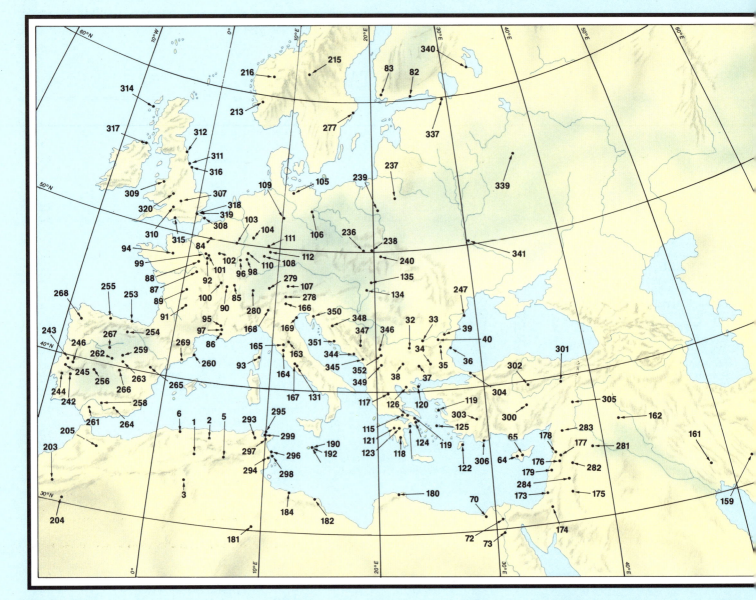